APPLIED CASE STUDIES IN MARKETING

'It is a fact that we teach more case studies from the Western world and few studies of our own success stories. I am happy to recommend *Applied Case Studies in Marketing* for it fills precisely that lacuna. This handsomely brought out book is neatly structured with colour-coded subheadings and boxes making the sections easy to identify. To make the book student and instructor friendly, Professor Shajahan has very thoughtfully included 'snapshots' wherein he summarizes the main ideas, capturing the essence of the text alongside. He has done this so that the reader can figure out at one glance the ideas that have been discussed and analysed. This useful feature will certainly facilitate the reader's preparation for examinations, presentations or corporate deliberations. The accompanying CD offers to the students and instructors a step-by-step guide on how to use the book, and at the same time highlights its salient features. Professor Shajahan narrates the case studies in a simple and lucid style and his judicious choice of sectors represents the emerging phase of the Indian economy.'

—PROFESSOR ASHOKE K DUTTA
Director, Indian Institute of Management Shillong

'*Applied Case Studies in Marketing* is a perfect example of how we can design curricula for a dynamic subject like marketing. I am happy to recommend this book to management students, scholars and teachers because it highlights the proactive nature of the discipline. Professor Shajahan has chosen his case studies with a focus on the emerging sectors of the Indian economy, while giving real time scenario-like narrations of the case studies and their subsequent analysis. This is going to add value to the current literature on marketing.'

—PROFESSOR OMKUMAR KRISHNAN
Institute of Management Technology Ghaziabad

'As a management professional, I have always felt that we are taught more about Western countries than about India. Most students know a great deal about markets abroad, consumer profiles, consumption patterns, brands and marketing best practices of foreign markets. The availability of organized information on India, however, is limited and the few good case studies available are written from a foreigner's perspective. While the theoretical frameworks and models might remain the same, it is important that students are able to relate the theory to a context they are familiar with. A market context where they would probably make their careers is more important for them. It is in this context that Professor Shajahan's effort is very commendable.'

—PROFESSOR ANANDAKUTTAN B UNNITHAN
Chairman, PG Programme, Indian Institute of Management Kozhikode

'*Applied Case Studies in Marketing* is a path-breaking volume, as it is time for us to celebrate Indian success stories. It is always a pleasure to teach concepts using Indian case studies and Professor Shajahan has brought out interesting Indian success stories like that of Jet Airways, Big Bazaar, Kingfisher, Hindustan Unilever Ltd., Shopper's Stop, Reliance Communications and Tata Teleservices.

'I congratulate Professor Shajahan for this timely and needed addition to the literature on Indian management. This is his sixteenth book. With each new venture, I find great improvement in his style of writing and the presentation of concepts and cases. I am sure that the students and faculty of marketing management will benefit a great deal from new addition.'

—PROFESSOR M J XAVIER
Director, Indian Institute of Management Ranchi

GO TO MARKET SERIES

Applied Multivariate Analysis: Concepts and Practices in the Indian Perspective

Managing Service Enterprises During Market Turbulence

Consumer Relationship Marketing: Global Best Practices and Cases

Marketing of Value Added Services During Market Turbulence

Organized Retailing Cases from the Indian Environment

Online and Mobile Marketing for New Age Indian Enterprises

Applied Case Studies in CRM

Post-Recession Market Dynamics of the Petroleum Industry in India

APPLIED CASE STUDIES IN MARKETING

S. SHAJAHAN

Dean (P and R), Indian Institute of Management, Shillong

PRIMUS BOOKS
An imprint of Ratna Sagar P. Ltd.
Virat Bhavan
Mukherjee Nagar Commercial Complex
Delhi 110 009

Offices at
CHENNAI KOLKATA LUCKNOW
AGRA AHMEDABAD BANGALORE COIMBATORE DEHRADUN GUWAHATI
HYDERABAD JAIPUR KANPUR KOCHI MADURAI MUMBAI PATNA RANCHI

First published 2011

ISBN 978-93-80607-11-5

Published by Primus Books

Laser typeset by Digigrafics
New Delhi 110 049

Printed at Shree Maitrey Printech Pvt Ltd, Noida

Contents

Detailed Contents

PART II APPLIED CASE STUDIES IN MARKETING

Preface

What you have to do and the way you have to do it is incredibly simple. Whether you are willing to do it is another matter.
— PETER F. DRUCKER

THE YEAR 2008 was pretty grim for the global economy and the stock markets. Even before the collapse of Lehman Brothers triggered the scariest recession in over half a century, the signs of the global economy hurtling towards disaster were all too apparent. The housing market in the US—and also in Europe—had begun to collapse. Unemployment was on the rise, with consumption displaying a decline. Defaults were rising and companies that had borrowed heavily and expanded rapidly were looking vulnerable. Stock markets the world over had started going downhill, though the pace of the fall accelerated only in the second half of 2008. It was only in April 2009, that economists, first in the US and Europe and then in India, began spotting the 'green shoots' of recovery. Though these were merely signs that the worst was possibly over as far as the economies were concerned, the stock markets reacted sharply and started rising far quicker than most experts thought was warranted.

The global economic crisis however, hastened the inevitable—China and India's march towards grabbing a larger share of the global GDP pie. By the close of 2009, India was set to overtake Africa and West Asia, while China's GDP was slated to be 50 per cent higher than the combined power of Latin America and the Caribbean Islands combined. According to the IMF World Economic Outlook in April 2009, US, the largest economy contributed 20 per cent of the global GDP as against its share of 24 per cent in 2000. The downfall of Western Europe is steeper: from 22.6 per cent in 2000 to 18.9 per cent in 2009. However, India improved its position marginally from 4 per cent to 5 per cent whereas China drastically jumped from 7.2 per cent to 12.1 per cent in 2009 then to 9.5 per cent in 2010.

A snapshot of the Indian economy in December 2009 is revealing. Several indicators could be used to gauge the health of the Indian economy. First, the hard, statistical measures, like the nonfood credit uptake figures, which indicated a rise, are a good guide. Stock markets also provided a good signal. Stock market indices have been on the rise for a while, with even the primary market rather buoyant. With the secondary market having touched a all time high of 21,421 in November 2010 investors and market analysts assumed valuations in the primary market would also be on fire. Most public offerings in mid-November 2010 were oversubscribed on the first day itself. The index of production figures are also a good pointer. The IIP growth rate for July and August 2009 combined is 8.8 per cent, compared to 3.8 per cent growth for July-August 2008.

Soft indicators assume similar importance. The surge in footfalls in malls and bazaars are a sure indicator that general consumers are once again beginning to feel good about spending. Retail giant Pantaloon recast its furniture business to a 'shop-in-shop' format and Shopper's Stop reinvented its home décor and furniture platform with Home Stop since the furniture format which began as a high margin business, turned out to be a low volume business. In the past, this format gave an 80 per cent margin to retailers—a figure now difficult to operate on. Auto sales also picked up sharply. Yet, the biggest indicator that sentiment had begun to change for the better came from the job market.

Most companies were beginning to recruit again in December 2009 after a year-long freeze. They were not just filling up slots left vacant as part of workforce rationalization, but were also hiring additional people in the expectation that new business would be coming in. This phenomena was witnessed across sectors—in retail, banking, information technology and manufacturing. Meanwhile, Human Resource consultancies also saw business go up.

Of all the criticisms levelled at higher education, one of the most significant is that business education no longer prepares students to become effective employees and leaders during market turbulence. In summarizing these criticisms, the American Assembly of Collegiate Schools of Business (AACSB) claims that business schools fail to provide the necessary tools (in problem-finding, problem-solving, communication, and people skills) and perspectives (viewing functional areas as part of a whole and an international/global outlook) that are essential for MBAs. Business school programmes have been attacked for focusing too much on quantitative and technical skills and too little on interpersonal and communication skills. Such an approach has created MBA graduates that are better suited for traditional hierarchical corporations than for the more fluid organizational forms that are emerging today. To make the educational challenge even more daunting, observers note that the rate of change in the marketplace is so rapid that uncertainty and chaos tend to rule. Universities have started to ask: what exactly is it that an MBA—or anybody else—will need to know or do, to be effective in business a decade from now. And, is it teachable?

For marketing education to remain viable, both the process and content of marketing curricula must be changed to match the needs of global businesses, especially during market turbulence. Innovative teaching techniques must be adopted to provide a grounding in the skills that are central to students' effectiveness in the organizations of the twenty-first century and beyond. And courses that address the new knowledge requirements must join or supplant traditional courses that limit the marketing mix to the '4Ps' (Product, Price, Promotion and Place) and view manufactured goods as the typical offering. An applied marketing course is a prime example of the new content that is needed in the marketing curriculum, for it introduces students to entirely new material as well as to different ways of viewing the traditional marketing content (as explained in the Annexure).

Again, there is a grave danger inherent in writing books on marketing management, and indeed in the whole idea of marketing as a course of study, that by analysing each aspect of it and trying to understand its mechanics, it is a challenging but thrilling job. We begin to believe that marketing is fact-finding, the analysis and the careful weighing of one alternative against another by following the standard literature. To study these processes may be an aid to successful marketing but marketing is about activity. It is doing, not merely thinking. To be successful at it, one must be creative as well as analytical, aggressive as well as meticulous.

Applied Case Studies in Marketing seeks to sharpen the marketing acumen of young MBAs to align their thought processes and those of the enterprise with customer expectations and thereby help a firm deliver the value these customers want. This has to be carried out consistently and continuously while yet representing the firm's marketing initiatives during a downfall. The book contains several real world marketing tools, methodologies and conceptual approaches for the company that wants to embark upon a customer-centric path and implement its glocal (global-local) marketing initiatives.

The ideas that have shaped the book had their inception in the two decades of experiences I acquired while undertaking and teaching marketing management in India and abroad. Most books in marketing management introduce unnecessary complexity by including an overwhelming volume of detail on far too many topics. Also, the standard set of prescribed books continue to analyse marketing in the global context without putting proper emphasis on the Indian market or global turbulences. Even fewer attempts have been made to understand the impact and use of information technology. I also discover that despite four decades of management education in India, few Indian books were available on the subject.

This book aims to provide a crisp, clear, easy-to-understand view of the methods, processes, tools and techniques used in product and services marketing. I have also tried to keep out unrelated material that comes in the way of a student's learning/understanding.

Features

Responding to rapid changes in technology and in the environment of marketing management in India, this book outlines current marketing concepts and practices. It contains eight chapters, six applied cases with detailed analysis, illustrations, exhibits, tables and fact sheets, photographs and emerging marketing concepts.

- The book focuses on marketing environmental analysis, STP marketing, relationship marketing and Internet-based marketing.
- It carries substantial coverage of IT-enabled marketing concepts, marketing campaigns, companies and packages in the current marketing environment. Coverage of technology issues/Internet applications are supplemented with company and service package literature. Chapters 7 and 8 discuss exclusively the application of technology in product and services marketing.
- This book also offers career assistance to both corporate executives and management and marketing students.

Live Features, Cases and Readings

The live features aspect of this book is a unique initiative developed out of the author's teaching and consultancy experience. It comes supported with visuals, insights, interpretations and illustrations from current marketing trends. Part II of the book discusses six case studies, which offer students more ideas and insight (and can lead to research topics) to help stimulate classroom discussion of real marketing industry issues. Again, the Annexure aims to provide the reader with an insight into pedagogical challenges while adopting applied marketing in a simulated academic environment. This book will help the reader acquire the skills and aptitude to become good marketing managers by providing case analysis/insights at the end of every live case.

Book CD, Web Link and Additional Resource Support

Today's business and corporate executives are faced with an ever-increasing bank of competitive intelligence and marketing information. Their search is look for an objective method of discovery as well as explanation. Existing Indian literature in the field still has a far way to go in supporting the basic needs of an executive. In this book, the author will attempt to share his nearly three-decade long consultancy in the business strategy/marketing arena with a view to mould the best talents from the Indian B-schools.

The enclosed CD contains presentations that are strongly grounded in IT-enabled marketing, making it easy to understand and accessible to the researcher as well as the professional. While focusing on SWOT, PEST, ANSOFF Matrix/GE Matrix, Five Forces Model and STP marketing, the author reduces the emphasis on basic marketing principles, choosing to focus instead on sectors and thereafter provide corporate insights. This exercise aims to bring out an application-oriented *Applied Case Studies in Marketing* textbook with a resource centre providing the reader with links to additional readings and sector-focused corporate PowerPoint presentations. Consequently, readers will be comfortable with both the literature as well as illustrations provided in the text. The CD accompanying the book contains four sections as listed below:

Section 1: Concept, Product and Sector Focus

(i) Familiarizing basic concepts and products

(a) Segmentation of products and services
(b) Positioning the products and services
(c) Product management
(d) Organized retailing (Sections 1, 2 and 3)
(e) Marketing mix of Nestlé India and Starbucks Coffee
(f) Branding strategies of P&G
(g) STP marketing of Heritage Red Wine, Coca Cola and ITC Bingo

(ii) Familiarizing important sectors: Sector focus

(a) Aviation and LCA
(b) Telecom
(c) PC Industry
(d) Retailing

Section 2: Corporate Insights

Familiarizing the reader with major companies in the following sectors:
(a) BFSI sector: HDFC, SBI and Citibank
(b) FMCG sector: HUL, Nestlé and Dabur
(c) PC Industry: DELL, Lenovo and HCL
(d) Aviation sector: SpiceJet and GoAir
(e) Telecom sector: Bharti Airtel and Vodafone
(f) Mobile phone sector: Nokia and Motorola
(g) Retail sector: PVR, Prestige and Pantaloon

Section 3: Suggested Readings

(a) Market Segmentation for Products and Services by S. Shajahan
(b) Overview of Product Management and Marketing Mix by S. Shajahan
(c) New Product Development by S. Shajahan
(d) The Lifecycle of a Product by S. Shajahan
(e) 'Winning the Indian Consumer', *The McKinsey Quarterly* 2005 Special Edition: Fulfilling India's Promise
(f) *Markathon*, vol. 2, issue 10, marketing magazine of IIM Shillong

Setion 4: Working Projects

Numerous projects are available to enable students and faculty to undertake STP marketing, environmental analysis, customer and competitor analysis described in the textbook. The projects have been handpicked to give an impetus to the creative thinking process of the readers.

(a) Undertaking business and footfall analysis of a retailer
(b) Undertaking a marketing project on a herbal deodorant
(c) Undertaking a marketing project on memory juice
(d) Undertaking a marketing project on flavoured water

Over three decades, my colleagues in both the academic and business worlds have provided me with valuable insights into marketing research through their writings, seminars, and conference discussions. Hence, this book presents an overview of updated, multifaceted, and the latest marketing techniques and strategies of leading firms in a glocal context. As faculty, I intend to provide the basics of marketing management in simple language. There exists a huge gap in the existing literature about applied product and services marketing. I hope this book will cater to the needs of students, scholars, tutors and executives in sharpening their business acumen and marketing skills, while they pursue a career in management and marketing. Further, I offer extended contact by providing supplementary notes, web-based assistance and practical advice on various marketing/corporate research issues emerging from time to time through: shaangrila@gmail.com/ drss@iimshillong.in.

Indian Institute of Management
Shillong

S. SHAJAHAN

Acknowledgements

This book could not have been written without considerable help and encouragement from the students of IIM Shillong, friends, colleagues, and professors. Although it is impossible to mention everyone who has had an influence upon the ideas in this book, I wish to acknowledge the support and guidance of Professor Ashoke K. Dutta, Director, IIM Shillong; Professor M.J. Xavier, Director, IIM Ranchi; Dr Shakeel Ahammed IAS, Secretary, Dept. of Education, Govt. of Meghalaya; F.P. Solo IPoS, Commissioner & Secretary, Dept. of Higher and Technical Education, Govt. of Nagaland; Athili Kathipri, Director, DTE, Govt. of Nagaland; K. Mitra, General Manager, EPIL, New Delhi; Viswanathan, SRM University, NCR campus, Ghaziabad; Samir S. Somaiya, Vice President, Somaiya Vidyavihar, Mumbai; Sakit Jain, Director, Sri Aurobindo Society, SAIFM, Puducherry; Joseph Manuel, Chief Knowledge Architect, First Discipline, Bangalore; Pratheep Philip, IPS, IGP, Social Justice, Chennai; Paul Srivastava, Becknell University, USA; Y.K. Bhushan, Senior Advisor, IBS Mumbai; Professor A.B. Unnithan, IIM Kozhikode; Professor Om Kumar Krishnan, IMT Ghaziabad; Shiladitya Sarkar, IL&FS Education & Technology Service Ltd., New Delhi; Jigyasa Laroiya, CEO, Occult, New Delhi; Reji Raman, Director, Centre for Research & Consultancy, Kochi; Piyali Roy Oberoi, Associate VP, Images Multimedia Group, Mumbai; Ambi M.G. Parameswaran, Executive Director & CEO, Draft FCB + Ulka, Mumbai; Professor (Dr) Suresh Ghai, Director, KJ Somaiya Institute of Management Studies & Research, Mumbai; Professors Issac Jacob, S.N.V. Siva Kumar and Monica, K.J. Somaiya Institute of Management Studies & Research, Mumbai; Professor Anagha Shukre, Institute of Management Studies, Ghaziabad; Professor Thomas Varghese, Saint Gits Institute of Management, Kottayam; Professor Asok Kumar Banerjee, Secretary, IIM-C Alumni Association & IISWBM, Kolkata; Akash Kumar, CMD, Benjamin Wright Infrastructure Ltd., New Delhi; A.K. Bharagava, MD, Apeejay Tea Ltd., Kolkata; Rajendra Chourse, Senior Vice President, DB Reality, Mumbai; Air Vice Marshal VM Khanna VSM and Wg. Cmdr. P.R. Prasad, EAC, Indian Air Force and PGP 2008-10 and 2009-11 batches of IIM Shillong.

My gratitude also goes to Saroj K. Datta, Executive Director, Jet Airways, Mumbai; Huang Zhigang, First Secretary, Department of Education, The Embassy of People's Republic of China in India; Wang Xinag Yun, Director, China National Tourist Office, New Delhi; Air Marshal V.K. Verma, Director, IGR Uran Academy, Rae Bereli; Bhupesh Joshi, Vice President, GMR-Delhi IGI Airport; Syed Nasim Ahmad Zaidi, IAS, Secretary, Ministry of Civil Aviation, Government of India; I.P. Rao, CEO, DIAL-GMR, New Delhi; Sanjay Aggarwal, CEO, Kingfisher Airlines; Kaushik Khona, CEO, GoAir; Aditya Ghosh, President, Indigo Airlines; and Raashid Syed, Professor, St. Kabir Institute of Management, Ahmedabad.

The bibliography at the end of the book is my acknowledgement of the various sources of study used in preparing this volume.

My thanks also goes to the management of ITC Ltd., Hindustan Coca-Cola Ltd., Pepsi India Ltd., Jet Airways Ltd., Kingfisher Airlines Ltd., HDFC Bank Ltd., SBI Ltd., Citibank, HUL, Nestlé, Dabur, DELL, Lenovo, HCL, SpiceJet, GoAir, Bharti Airtel, Vodafone, Nokia, Motorola, PVR, Prestige, Pantaloon and 75 other companies mentioned in the book.

I also wish to offer my sincere gratitude to Professor C.B. Bhattacharya, School of Management, Boston University; Professor Narakesari Narayandas, Harvard Business School; Professor Jagdish N. Sheth, Emory University; Professor Rajan Varadarajan, Texas A&M University, and Chairman, Special Interest Group of the American Marketing Association; Rediff.com, *The Economic Times*, *Business Standard*, *Financial Express* and in-flight magazines such as *Hi Blitz*, *Jet Wings*, *Spice Route*, *SimpliFly*, *Swagat* and the frequent flier/customer care/investor cells or divisions of major international and national airlines, telecom and handset manufactures for their print and cyber media support.

I request readers to send in their views to: drss@iimshillong.in, shaangrila@gmail.com or www.linkedin.com/in/drsshajahan09 for further improvements and suggestions.

Indian Institute of Management
Shillong

S. SHAJAHAN

PART I

Fundamental Concepts and Marketing Analysis

An Overview

Welcome to the World of New Age Marketing!

Marketing is different from the other functions of a company. Like every other part of a organization, marketing too needs to innovate, but its innovation occurs on a public platform. A good Chief Marketing Officer's game plan and tactical brilliance are on display everyday. In a style of operating similar to that of a cricket team, the infrastructure, brand history and tolerance for risktaking too are important elements in a marketer's success or failure.

The corporate life cycle of General Motors (GM), the global automobile giant founded in 1908 is startling. It sustained its leadership for nearly 100 years, but on 21 January 2009, GM surrendered the number one position to Toyota as the largest automaker. On 1 June 2009, after 101 years of business, it filed for bankruptcy protection at a court in New York. The product or the value proposition may be in decline (like General Motors), the infrastructure may not work or the brand may have no consumer interest or cache, yet to make consumers take notice, it is important to innovate. This will include taking more risk than just increasing marketing spending by 25 per cent. This is what GM has been doing in India through its subsidiary. The question of whether it will work for them, remains to be answered.

An analysis of the global economic scenario reveals that India is set to become a high-growth state. We are already in 2011 and the work programme of 2009-14 as chalked out in the ruling political party's manifesto should hopefully see no political constraints. The economy stands a good chance of notching up a double-digit GDP growth rate by 2014.

Keeping such circumstances in mind, Part I maps the speedy recovery of various Indian industries by portraying the early sales and quarterly performance of Indian corporates with a projection of its sustained performance. These are presented with adequate industry examples and illustrations through exhibits, tables, etc. I have also attempted to analyse the Indian market during the recession, changing emphases within marketing during market turbulence, while also explaining critical factors for undertaking successful marketing. I have also elaborated upon the fundamental concepts of marketing.

This section opens with an appropriate background on marketing during economic turbulence and then progresses to macro concepts like profiling of market and customers, market analysis for a new-age marketer, STP marketing, growth strategies during market turbulence besides micro concepts such as value chain analysis, product/services marketing mix and emerging concepts like web matrix, IT-enabled competition and competitive e-positioning.

CHAPTER 1 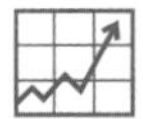 MARKETING IN TIMES OF ECONOMIC DOWNTURN AND RECOVERY

It is not the strongest of the species that survive, nor the most intelligent, but the ones most responsive to change.
— CHARLES DARWIN

The Backdrop

The 2009 economic recovery has brought a smile to everyone's lips, from consumers to businessmen to policymakers. But there is the occasional twinge of fear when the mind asks: Is this for real? Look at the stunning rebound in the industrial production index, a tenfold rise in growth rate from 1.1 per cent in April 2009 to 10.4 per cent in August 2009. Many experts believe that while the fiscal stimulus helped, the Reserve Bank of India's (RBI) reversal of tight money supply policy played a more important role in getting the economy back on track. That is why the market trusts the United Progressive Alliance (UPA) regime to continue for another term during the global economic crisis. The UPA government sets ambitious goals by aiming for inclusive growth. The finance ministry of the country believes that the first challenge is to get the economy back to the 9 per cent-plus growth rates in the medium term. Now, past 2009 and well into 2011 the market seems optimistic.

Recall the behaviour of the Indian stock exchanges in May 2009, on the eve of the formation of the new UPA government at the Centre. Investors became richer by a whopping ₹6,50,000 crore in one minute as the Bombay Stock Exchange (BSE) Sensex jumped a historic 2,111 points to touch the 14,000 level. The markets for sure were cheering the decisive win of the ruling UPA government! Investor wealth, measured in terms of the combined market capitalization of all the listed companies, increased by over ₹6,56,477 crore in a minute—in the first 30 seconds and then after the resumption of trading at 11.55 hours to ₹44,63,420.97 crore. The BSE Sensex zoomed 1,305.97 points to reach 13,479.39, hitting the upper circuit within seconds of opening of trade.

The excitement didn't end there. Analysis has revealed that the 30 companies that make up the Sensex and account for over 47 per cent of the total market capitalization saw their combined market valuations rise by over ₹3,16,000 lakh crore. Their combined market capitalization rose to ₹21,53,590.09 crore on 18 May 2009, from ₹18,36,841.33 crore at the end of trade three days ago. Reliance Industries was the major contributor to the increase in market capitalization and for the Sensex regaining the 14,000 level, along with other heavyweight stocks like BHEL and Bharti Airtel.

The Indian corporate score sheet looked promising even in the second quarter of 2009. Production and sales in key industries were rising healthily, profits were growing faster than sales indicating that cost cuts were at work more than revenue growth. Continued revival in consumer spending and government stimulus should rekindle revenue growth in 2010–11. The mood of optimism has come from robust growth, a healthy profit margin >>>

coupled with statistics such as 400 projects worth ₹1,30,000 crore commissioned in April-September 2009 and ₹3,00,000 crore investment likely between October 2009 and March 2010. A company like Maruti Suzuki has raised its market capitalization from ₹19,977 crore in 2008 (April-September period) to ₹33,730 crore in 2009 (April-September period) while global leaders like General Motors have gone into oblivion after 101 years of existence. However, rising inflation, fluctuating exchange rate, fiscal deficit and the uncertainty of global recovery are key risk factors. Domestic demand and consumption have been the backbone of India's economic resurgence with top eight cities accounting for almost 40 per cent of the total in 2010. However, there has been a tectonic shift in consumption patterns with smaller cities and towns emerging as the new power house with an estimated annual growth of 9 to 17 per cent during 2010–15 as estimated by Ernst & Young in August 2010.

Let us now analyse the Indian market during the recession and how fundamental marketing concepts will help it overcome this phase.

This Chapter Will

- *Map the speedy recovery of various Indian industries by tracking their early sales and quarterly performances and project their performance until 2025, with industry examples and illustrations.*
- *Analyse the Indian market during recession.*
- *Understand the changing emphases in marketing during slowdown and the factors critical for undertaking successful marketing during these times.*
- *Explain fundamental marketing concepts.*

1.1 Indian Market during Recession and Recovery

Crisil's Modified Credit Ratio (MCR) has increased to 0.88 for the first half of 2010-11, after dropping to a nine-year low of 0.86 in 2008–9.

In August 2010, though countries of southern Europe may be on their way to a collapse, yet it would be worse if they tightened their belts. Invariably the Indian rupee is getting strengthened every day as the Euro can buy less than ₹60 as against the standing rate of ₹30 a year ago. Indians however appear content in a complacent attitude and self regulation as RBI has raised repo rate to 5.75 per cent and reverse repo to 4.5 per cent in August 2010. The momentum in industrial production growth is moderating; in financial year 2010 it was 5.9 per cent growth as against 10.6 per cent growth in financial year 2011 during April-August period. The appreciation of capital goods is 29 per cent growth in financial year 2011 as against 3.4 per cent growth in financial year 2010. The consumer durable has touched 27 per cent growth in financial year 2011 as against 18.8 per cent in financial year 2010 during April-August of the corresponding years.

After facing tough times as a fallout of the global economic slowdown, Indian companies now have to bother less about credit quality due to the improvement in the business environment and easier access to funds. The credit quality of Indian firm is beginning to stabilize after going into a free fall for 2008–9, according to a study by the credit rating agency Crisil. Crisil's Modified Credit Ratio (MCR) has increased to 0.88 for the first half of 2010–11, after dropping to a nine-year low of 0.86 in 2008–9. Companies have easier access to funds as a result of the government's fiscal and monetary easing and positive stock market conditions. In addition, lower commodity prices have led to lower working capital needs. However, a recovery in credit quality would at best be gradual and might not necessarily be smooth.

The financial tsunami in the US which engulfed almost the entire world is expected to slow India's economic growth to about 5-7 per cent. It is not just the global financial markets; there's now a process of adjustment in the real economy as well. The US is India's major trading partner. India's export basket to the US covers a wide range of products and commodities such as software, gems and jewellery, auto and machine parts, apparels and pharmaceuticals, among others. According to experts, all these sectors will witness lower demand, but because of rupee depreciation, the prices of Indian products will still be competitive. It is a fact that the impact of US slowdown and financial market crisis on India will be less than that on more open or smaller economies.

MARKETING IN ACTION — **THE JAPANESE STORY**

Japan in mid-2009 reported an increase in factory output—the first in six months—raising hopes of an economic recovery. The world's second-largest economy, Japan had entered a severe slump in 2008 as consumers around the world stopped buying Japanese cars, hi-tech gadgets and other goods. However, analysts believe there are signs that the worst may be over for the Japanese. Factories boosted production by 1.6 per cent in March 2009 compared to February, after a plunge of around one-third in September 2008. After the increase in March, Japan has witnessed an increase for six continuous months with the latest being in August 2009 when the factory output increased by 1.8 per cent. Output is further expected to increase by 1.1 per cent in September and 2.2 per cent in October, according to various companies. Output is expected to rebound a further 4.3 per cent in April and 6.1 per cent in May, according to manufacturers. Analysts note that Japan's economy saw plenty of false dawns during its 'lost decade' of stagnation and deflation in the 1990s.

Source: Business Today, January 2010.

1.1.1 The Indian and Japanese Growths Compared

Both India and Japan witnessed an increase in production output from April to August 2009. In the case of Japan the industries instrumental have been steel, cars, electronics and flat panel TVs. The underlying reasons for this increase are the tax breaks and subsidies given for these products in Japan, the United States and China. It becomes evident that exports are a significant factor in the revival of the Japanese economy, along with the stimulus provided by the government.

A year after Lehman Brothers filed for bankruptcy—signalling the global financial system's descent into Great Depression II—the BSE Sensex rose to 18,144, after having hit a low of 8,160 points in early March 2009.

In case of the Indian recovery, the drivers have been domestic demand which was stimulated by low interest rates. Higher government spending is another factor in the recovery of the Indian economy. Unlike the Japanese economy, India is less reliant on exports. Various industries, especially car manufacturers are planning capital investments which will help in the long run in India, but in Japan declining demand and appreciation of the Yen have forced companies to adopt the wait and watch approach.

1.1.2 Nosedive and Recovery of the Indian Economy

Nearly two years later, in August 2010, Lehman Brothers, the 158-year-old Wall Street investment bank filed for bankruptcy—signalling the global

ECONOMY WATCH

SIGNS OF GROWTH: PAYMENTS BY DEBIT CARD RISE

Payments through debit cards rose over 40 per cent compared to 2008, touching ₹9,911 crore in the first half of 2009. Experts take this as an indication of a spurt in economic activities. With the global financial condition slowly stabilizing, there are signs of the domestic economy recovering and growing at a faster pace in the second half of 2009. The comparable figure in 2008 was ₹7,017 crore.

On the other hand, credit card transactions in the country slumped by more than 12 per cent in the first five months of 2009–10, to ₹24,427 crore as shoppers decided against using their credit cards amid the ongoing economic slowdown. The amount involved in such transactions till August 2008 was ₹27,834 crore but started declining towards the end of 2009, ending the financial year 2008–9 at ₹65,355 crore.

The credit card business has been on the decline since November 2008—a decline that indicates that people are averse to taking credit.

Analysts say it is surprising that the credit card payment is going down as retail credit disbursal has increased. However, some banks have reduced credit limits and this might have hampered business.

Source: Business World, December 2009.

financial system's descent into Great Depression II—the BSE Sensex rose to 18,144, after having hit a low of 8,160 points in early March 2009. Signs of stability were visible not only in the stock markets but also in the money and foreign exchange markets as prospects of faster economic growth improved in October 2010 and slowly touching the BSE sensex of 21,025 in December 2010. While the International Monetary Fund (IMF) predicted that the global economy will contract in 2011, there were signs of normalcy with Japan, Germany and France emerging from the recession.

However, things looked drastically different in September 2008. As Foreign Institutional Invertors (FIIs) withdrew $6.42 billion (around ₹33,000 crore) from the Indian stock markets between September 2008 and March 2009, the RBI sold $29 billion (₹1,49,706 crore) to check the rupee's free fall and pumped in over ₹6,00,000 crore primary liquidity into the system. In addition, the government stepped up spending and cut tax rates to spur demand. These measures seem to have had a positive effect. FIIs had invested over $10 billion (around ₹49,000 crore) into the stock markets as of November 2009. There are expectations of the rupee appreciating and call rates have eased to around 3 per cent. Banks do not have to access short-term funds at double-digit rates and investors do not have to worry about the fate of the debt funds that they invest in. The dilemma facing is the exit strategy, especially in the wake of the recent rise in commodity and food prices, which are stoking inflationary trends.

There is a genuine convergence in the forecasts of GDP growth for India in the recovery year 2009–10. Both for India and the rest of the world, the worst two quarters of GDP growth were the Lehman quarter (October-December 2008), and the follow-through first quarter of 2009. However, the Indian fiscal year runs from April to March; this means that the fiscal year 2009–10 will not contain either of these two worst quarters. Everyone accepts that the year 2008 was a mega-Black Swan event, and mega in two different ways. The swans were big, indeed the biggest in close to hundred years; and the black swans were many. There was the commodity price boom, and bust; there was the oil price extravaganza, and bust; there was the banking bust and the stock market nosediving.

The world economy can be affected in two distinct ways. The structure of the economy can change for the worse. While an alternative assumption is that 2008 will not have a permanent effect on future growth. In other words, one could reasonably argue that the potential trend of rate of growth is lowered. This seems to be the implicit assumption of many of the forecasters, led by the IMF. In other words, the structure of the world economy will remain intact, that the growth distribution, or the probability distribution of growth, will remain the same. Now, 2008 was an extreme event, a very unlikely event, but nevertheless, one from the same inherent structure. In due course, the world economy should get back to the same rate of growth that it was enjoying previously. If the alternative scenario does emerge in the long run, then there is a short run implication as well. It is that the recovery in the short run is likely to be V-shaped, i.e. since the decline was steep, the likelihood is that recovery will be equally sharp.

The world economy can be affected in two distinct ways. Either the structure of the economy can change for the worse or 2008 will not have a permanent effect on future growth.

Recent data favours the optimists. Indian GDP grew at a seasonally adjusted annualized rate (SAAR) of 8.5 per cent, April-June 2010. Industrial production growth over June, July and August in 2010 was proceeding at a healthy SAAR of 14 per cent. Adding up, a very likely possibility is that GDP growth in India for the first half of 2010 will be close to 8 per cent. For the full fiscal year 2010 it may well be higher, especially if the present trends continue.

There are two important signals to consider. First, GDP growth is reverting to its new trend growth of around 9 per cent per annum. The second signal pertains to inflation. For close to two decades now inflation in India is determined more by international inflation than any other factor. And the signal here is that world inflation, like growth, is also going to revert to pre-crisis levels. For India, that means inflation of around 4 per cent, plus/minus 1 per cent. Thanks to the crisis, real interest rates have come to less abnormal levels, and should make a downward trend over the next few years.

There are two important signals to consider. First, that GDP growth is reverting to its new trend of around 9 per cent per annum, and the second that pertains to inflation.

However, there are signs that monetary and fiscal easing and lower commodity prices are both temporary. Additionally, unlike in the late 1990s, Crisil sees no prospect of a sudden and sustained upturn in economic conditions to lift corporate performance. One can, therefore, rule out a sudden jump in MCR of the kind the Indian market saw in 1999-2000, when MCR rose to 0.92 from 0.61. In the first half of 2009–10, about 5.9 per cent of the average outstanding ratings were downgraded. This compares with a figure of 7.1 per cent in the immediately preceding six months.

1.1.3 Indian Corporates: A Report Card during Slowdown

According to *Business World* ranking (*BW* 500) of India's biggest companies Indian Oil Corporation was ranked first in 2009 while Reliance Industries stood second. SBI stood first in the subcategory of financial firms. The private sector giant ICICI Bank stood second with a net profit of ₹3,011.78 crore from a total income of ₹64,984.35 crore. The difference between the two banks obviously lies in the three-year shareholder returns. ICICI Bank offered a negative return of 41.11 per cent with a market cap of ₹37,048.98 crore as

According to Business World *ranking* (BW *500*) *of India's biggest companies, Indian Oil Corporation was ranked first in 2009, while Reliance Industries stood second. SBI came out tops in the subcategory of financial firms.*

compared to a positive return of 29.42 per cent from SBI with a market cap of ₹67,748 crore during 2009. In telecom sector, Reliance Communications with a market cap of ₹36,089.51 crore registered a net profit of ₹6,243.98 crore and Bharti Airtel with a market cap of ₹1,18,782.36 crore registered net profit of ₹7,757.24 crore with Return On Capital Employed of 21.57 per cent as against 10.16 per cent of Reliance Communications.

Business Today (BT *500) placed Reliance Industries as the top ranking company followed by Bharti Airtel in the second and Infosys in the third position.*

Business Today (*BT* 500) placed Reliance Industries as the top ranking company, followed by Bharti Airtel in the second and Infosys in the third position. *BT* observed that Reliance Industries gained ₹31,164 crore in their market cap while Reliance Communications lost ₹41,284 crore in 2009. The *BT* 500 Survey had Reliance Industries at a market cap of ₹3,61,460 crore and ONGC ₹2,27,570 crore in 2009. Bharti Airtel ranked first on the basis of topping the ten-year sales growth (CAGR—compound annual growth rate) of 139.44 per cent. However ONGC tops the list for registering an absolute profit of ₹16,126 crore over Reliance Industries' ₹15,637 crore.

Aviation firms are in the list of top loss-making companies. Kingfisher led with a loss of ₹1,363 crore and completing the list is Jet Airways with a loss of ₹402 crore.

The aviation firms are in the list of top loss-making companies. Kingfisher led the list with a loss of ₹1,363 crore and coming in last is Jet Airways registering a loss of ₹402 crore. The FMCG list is topped by ITC with a market cap of ₹79,390 crore in April-September 2009 with a sales figure of ₹23,827 crore and a net profit of ₹3,268 crore. Hindustan Unilever followed ITC closely and touched ₹22,500 crore turn over and net profit of ₹2,496 crore in 2008–9 with a market cap of ₹55,684 in April-September 2009. The third position was occupied by Nestlé India with a market cap of ₹18,794 crore, sales figures of ₹4,505 crore and net profit of ₹534 crore in 2008–9.

On the contrary look at Godrej's rediscovery of India. The company says they touch more customers than any other Indian company and not just wth soaps, locks and cupboards. The group is valued at ₹11,800 crore in 2010. Nearly 470 million Indians use a Godrej product each day. In Godrej's consumer products division, the company was able to register a sales of ₹2,041 crore with 47 per cent year-on-year growth in 2009.

In the food processing segment, Godrej touched a sole of ₹1,142 crore. Godrej properties (Godrej Agrovet) bagged ₹456 crore in 2009 with a growth rate of 53.2 per cent. Godrej Interio (Furniture Division) touched ₹1,200 crore followed by Godrej Appliances with ₹1,500 crore. The company's retail venture (Nature's Basket) pegged sales of ₹23,509 per sq. ft. (thrice the industry average) followed by Godrej's Hershey's products (confectionery and beverages) with ₹326 crore in 2009.

According to the Central Statistical Organization (CSO), Ministry of Statistics and Programme Implementation, the 2008–9 GDP, factor cost at constant (1999–2000) prices, was estimated to be ₹33,39,375 crore, showing a growth rate of 6.7 per cent over the Quick Estimates of GDP for the year 2007–8 at ₹31,29,717 crore. The sectors which experienced growth rates of 5 per cent or more were construction (7.2 per cent), trade, hotels, transport and communication (9 per cent), financing, insurance, real estate and business services (7.8 per cent), and community, social and personal services (13.1 per cent).

The Performance of Some Key Industries

FMCG

Recession had its effects on the FMCG sector worldwide, especially on the durable goods segment. But India may be an exception as both sale and prices are soaring. The FMCG sector is the fourth-largest sector in the Indian economy and registered a turnover of over US$30 billion in retail sales in the year 2009. In spite of the recent economic slowdown, the sector has shown a consistent growth pattern. The first quarter of 2010 saw a growth of 12 per cent in the sector with a predicted growth rate of 18-20 per cent for the second quarter. Based on 2009 trends, growth projections for the sector are clocked at around 10-12 per cent for the next decade. This would mean an industry size of US$43 billion (₹2,06,000 crore) by 2013 and US$74 billion (₹3,55,000 crore) by 2018. Recent policy initiatives of the government such as the GST (Goods and Services Tax) and opening up of FDI in retail can further accelerate this growth.

The FMCG sector is the fourth-largest sector in the Indian economy and registered a turnover of over US$30 billion in retail sales in 2009. In spite of the recent economic slowdown, the sector has shown a consistent growth pattern.

Budget 2009 provided several impetus to the sector in terms of regulatory environment and consumer spending:

- Introduction of GST
- Duty and service tax rate cut
- Change in FDI structure for the consumer market
- The Sixth Pay Commission

Guidelines issued by the Indian government in 2009 state that where an Indian company is 'owned and controlled' by resident Indian citizens any downstream investment by the company is not to be treated as FDI. In other words, an Indian promoter is now free to attract foreign capital make downstream investments. This policy bodes well for the retail sector of India and will definitely provide it an impetus. The new policy is in fact a milestone for the Indian retail sector. Though FDI in multi-brand retail is at present prohibited, it is possible that it may be allowed in the future.

The economic slowdown has affected every sector globally. And though FMCG in India is no exception, this sector and consumer durable sectors managed to post 10-20 per cent growth on the strength of strong demand from semi-urban and rural areas. The three consecutive stimulus packages announced after November 2008 gave a boost to consumer sentiments, while some softening of prices gave further fillip to the demand for consumer durables.

FMCG and consumer durable sectors managed to post 10-20 per cent growth on the strength of strong demand from semi-urban and rural areas.

Large scale promotional activities, stabilizing raw material prices, rural growth encouraged by several government schemes such as the National Rural Employment Generation Scheme (NREGS), generous farm loan-waivers and a growing middle class saw the FMCG sector clock volume growth of close to 17-18 per cent. Companies ploughed back savings from lower commodity prices into brand building, consumer discounts and promotions, coupled with improved distribution strategies.

However it would be unfair to say that the slowdown hasn't impacted the consumption pattern. The Indian middle class has curtailed consumption, and this is more than the percentage decline in real income levels. Spending on precautionary savings and on essentials went up at the cost of consumption spending. However, as a fall out of the recession the impact has been worsened due to the domino effect in BRIC nations, where consumer confidence has been higher. While rural consumers in India upgraded their consumption level, the urban consumers with fixed income levels downgraded theirs.

India in 2009 was the world's third-largest beverage consumer after US and China, accounting for approximately 10 per cent of the global beverage consumption. The Indian beverage industry is expected to grow by 17 per cent in 2011.

For instance, let us look at the beverage industry in India during the slowdown. The beverage industry covers a wide category of drinks ranging from carbonated drinks, alcohol, fruit juices to coffee and tea. In 2009, India was the world's third-largest beverage consumer after US and China, accounting for approximately 10 per cent of the global beverage consumption. The Indian beverage industry is expected to grow by 17 per cent in 2011.

Due to the tropical climate of the subcontinent, the market for non-alcoholic drinks is attractive and growing. The annual per capita consumption of packaged beverages in India is expected to reach 8.70 litres in 2012. India is also the world's biggest producer and consumer of milk; 65 per cent of milk and milk-based beverages are sold in the loose and unpackaged form. Milk consumption has increased by an annual average of 2.7 per cent since 2005. The carbonated soft drinks market is worth ₹5,520 crore; the packaged fruit drink market is around ₹1,200 crore and is growing at a rate of 18 to 20 per cent. The Union Budget 2009 withdrew 16 per cent excise duty on tea and coffee mixes, which have given a major boast to the tea and coffee industry during downturn.

Entertainment

The Indian entertainment sector too has been an ever-growing one. Offsetting recessionary dents, one can safely say that the growth in this sector has been satisfactory over the years. At present the entertainment sector is estimated to be more than ₹12,530 crore. At the organized level the industry contributes around 2.2 per cent to the services sector turnover. It caters largely to local customers—television, radio, even IPL cater largely to the Indian audience. The impact of recession in this sector has been felt to a lesser extent in South Asia than in the Western countries. Hence, the impact on people's spending is also less in India. This factor is highly beneficial for the entertainment industry.

The economic downturn brightened prospects for the gaming industry globally as people were expected to spend more hours at home due to job losses. The Indian animation, gaming and VFX industries have been the fastest growing industries in the Indian entertainment and media sector since 2005. This segment has seen a significant growth owing to high-end work outsourced from studios in the West and also because of increasing demand for animation snippets in Indian movies and television. The animation industry grew at 20 per cent in 2008 to reach ₹1,560 crore, up from ₹1,300 crore in 2007. On the other hand, the Indian gaming industry grew 47 per cent from 2007 to touch ₹400 crore in 2008, mainly due to the growth in the mobile segment. However, big cars (A_3-A_6 segments) Maruti Suzuki sustain robust volume by strong demand for the Swift DZIRE. In financial year 2011, 2,15,652 cars sold as against 1,54,451 units in 2009 till September 2009. Maruti Suzuki nods 30 per cent market share followed by Tata Motors (21.7 per cent), Honda (13.4 per cent) and Hyundai (9.7 per cent).

Automobiles

The recession did not affect the Indian automobile market much with the production of two-wheelers growing at a healthy rate. The country's largest motorcycle maker Hero Honda reported a 27 per cent year-on-year jump in revenues in September 2009 on the back of a 22 per cent rise in volume and lower excise duties. The launch of new top end models and efficient operations helped Hero Honda safeguard its market share (59 per cent) and enhance its operating profit margin to 18 per cent. 9.184 lakh motorcycles were sold in September 2010 as against 7.66 lakh units in September 2009 registering a growth of 17.7 per cent.

Out of the 400 BSE *500 companies studied by* The Economic Times *in November 2009, the second-quarter performance of 144 companies in manufacturing and services sectors were healthy in terms of sales and profit. Their aggregate profit increased 41.6 per cent.*

Out of the 400 *BSE* 500 companies studied by *The Economic Times* in November 2009, the second quarter performance of 144 companies in manufacturing and services sectors was healthy in terms of sales and profit. The aggregate profit of these companies increased to 41.6 per cent. Even after adjusting for extraordinary income, the rise is 40.5 per cent. These companies have reported a healthy 20 per cent rise in sales. Among the top performers, only 24 from manufacturing and services have done extremely well with a quarterly net profit growth of over 100 per cent from core operations. These firms, however, benefited from the stimulus package in the form of cut in excise duty and easing of liquidity through cut in interest costs. In general, sectors like diamonds and jewellery have reported a rise in profit and steel

ECONOMY WATCH — INDIA INC. BUCKS SLOWDOWN

Two of every five top companies in India generated better growth in revenues for the year ended March 2009 compared to 2007–8. Further, one in six companies accelerated profit growth, according to an Economic Times Intelligence Group (ETIG) study. The study, which looked at the financials of 1,050 companies, showed that as many as 400 firms reported higher net sales for 2009. Besides looking at firms that announced their annual results ended March 2009, the study also clubbed together accounts of the last four quarters of companies that follow a different financial calendar, to broaden the sample. The outperformers spanned diverse sectors such as information technology, automobiles, sugar, agricultural inputs, cement, FMCG and pharmaceuticals.

Some notable firms that reported better revenue growth despite the slowdown in the economy were Hero Honda, Coromandel Fertilisers, Axis Bank, MRF, Cipla, State Trading Corporation, UltraTech Cement and Infosys.

Besides revenue, firms also improved their earnings performance, despite facing cost pressures due to raw material prices as well as high interest rates. As many as 180 companies—one-sixth of the sample—actually reported better net profit growth compared to 2008. Firms that managed to accelerate profit growth included IT bellwether Infosys Technologies; the country's second-largest private bank HDFC; Coromandel Fertilisers, the second-largest phosphatic fertilizer producer in India; and the largest two-wheeler maker Hero Honda. Siemens, Shree Cement, United Phosphorus, Vardhman Textiles, Uflex, Cipla, Alstom and Nagarjuna Fertiliser were some other companies that managed to accelerate their profit growth or made a turnaround. A number of banks also came up with better results on the back of higher interest and treasury incomes. Around 60 companies came out of the red, 50 firms managed to prune losses and another 35 firms reported lower decline in profits. However the trend is slowly reversing in 2010.

Source: The Economic Times, May 2010.

companies have reported a decline in second quarter sales and profit in 2009. Automobiles, paints, cement and real estate sectors have posted 50 per cent growth in net profits. The six auto companies reported a combined net profit of ₹1,613 crore in the second quarter of 2009 as against ₹794 crore in the corresponding period in 2008. The average market cap of Maruti Suzuki went up from ₹19,977 crore in 2008 to ₹33,730 crore in 2009 with a sales figure of ₹24,195.60 crore and net profit of ₹1,143.60 crore in 2008–9 (see Table 1.1).

Table 1.1: Top performing companies in India during the first phase of market turbulence (2008–9)

Company	*Total income (₹crore)*	*Operating profit (₹crore)*	*Net profit (₹crore)*
Indian Oil Corporation	3,17,724.84	10,495.67	1,845.34
Reliance Industries	1,59,991.68	25,834.63	15,360.90
ONGC	1,15,887.18	42,471.13	19,195.09
State Bank of India	1,13,740.20	81,441.95	11,169.25
ICICI Bank	64,984.35	31,894.64	3,011.78
Tata Steel	1,48,787.01	18,968.05	8,883.82
Bharti Airtel	37,891.84	14,009.37	7,757.24
ITC	25,576.89	5,512.69	3,274.03
Maruti Suzuki India	24,195.60	2,388.30	1,143.60
Sources: Business Today, 15 November 2009 and *Business World*, 2 November 2009.			

There were 2,03,468 passenger cars sold in September 2010 as against 1,68,326 in September 2009 thereby registering a growth of 20.9 per cent. Maruti Suzuki sold 4,56,358 small cars (A_1-A_2 segment) till September 2010 as against 3,81,244 during September 2009; thereby registering a growth of 23.6 per cent. There were 9,15,836 small cars sold till September 2010 as against 7,41,447 units sold till September 2009, showing up a market growth of 23.5 per cent in financial year 2011. Maruti Suzuki holds 52.9 per cent market share in small car segment followed by Hyundai Motors (21.2 per cent) and Tata Motors (12 per cent).

1.1.4 What the Future Holds

To assess the likely evolution of India's consumer market, McKinsey Global Institute (MGI) assembled a proprietary database with twenty years of data linking macro-economic and demographic variables to the income and consumption behaviour of Indian households. MGI extensively used the Market Information Survey of Households (MISH) database (covering more than 3,00,000 households), created from income surveys conducted by India's National Council of Applied Economic Research (NCAER), as well as the Indian government's National Sample Survey Organisation (NSSO) household consumption database, created from consumer expenditure surveys across thousands of villages and urban blocks. MGI integrated the MISH and NSSO data, along with data from a variety of other sources, and then constructed an econometric model to forecast India's household income and spending from 2006 to 2025.

It is estimated that average real household disposable income will grow from ₹1,13,744 in 2005 to ₹3,18,896 by 2025, a CAGR of 5.3 per cent (see for instance Table 1.3). This is significantly more rapid than the 3.6 per cent annual growth of the past 20 years—and with the exception of China, much faster than the income growth in other major markets. For example, the average US real household income increased at a CAGR of 1.5 per cent over the past two decades; for Japan the figure was 0.25 per cent. All these economic data are impressive for a retail marketer who wants to start Indian operations.

MGI projects the market size to explode from $370 billion in 2005 to over $1,500 billion by 2025. The total household consumption will explode from ₹16,896 crore in 2005 to ₹69,503 crore (approx.) in 2025 (Figure 1.1).

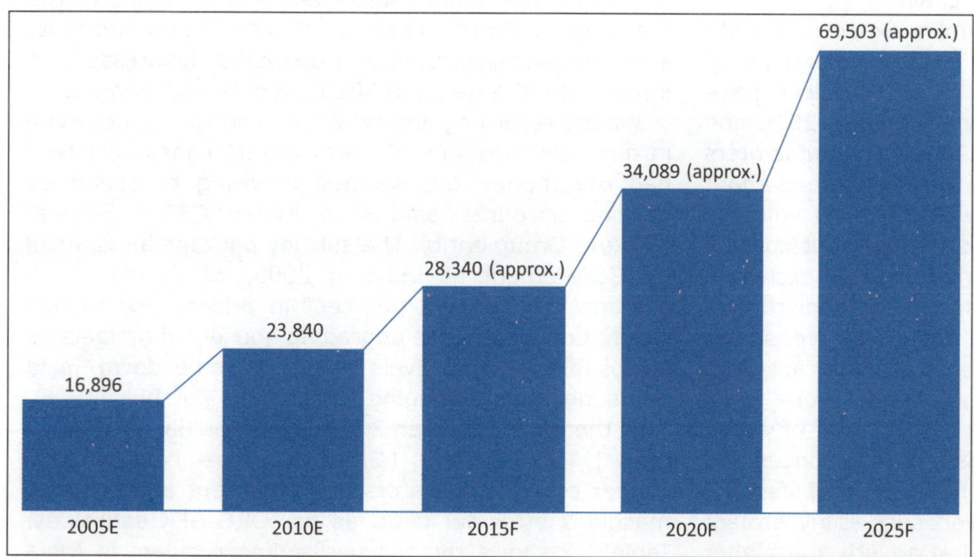

Figure 1.1: Total household consumption: projected market growth during 2005–25 (figures in ₹crore)

Source: MGI 2005.
Note: E—Estimate, F—Forecast.

MARKETING ANALYSIS — **CONSUMERS BACK IN BAZAARS**

Robust consumer spends on durables in urban and rural markets since January 2010 seems to defy the conventional logic about recessionary trends impacting discretionary purchases. Leading industry majors and retailers have reported an upbeat 20 per cent-plus growth in volumes for LCDs, laptops, ACs, refrigerators, washing machines and audio systems. The trend is all the more significant since these industries had cut down production in 2008. Industry officials say rural markets are more upbeat and insulated from the impact of the global meltdown and are throwing up good volumes.

'Given the projected GDP growth of 8-9 per cent it is hardly surprising that the demand for aspirational consumer products remains upbeat. I think there was a lot of hype about recession and job layoffs, which depressed consumer sentiment. While some businesses may have been impacted, there are new businesses that are simultaneously opening up. Consequently after sitting on the fence for a while consumers are now back to the showrooms', said Ajit Joshi, CEO of Tata Group-led Croma.

Table 1.2: Top performing retailers in India in 2008–9

Company	*Market cap (April-September 2009)*	*Sales (₹crore)*	*Net profit/loss (₹crore)*
Pantaloon Retail (India)	4,842	5,327	52
Trent	936	549	27
Shopper's Stop	624	1,409	–64

Sources: Business Today, 15 November 2009 and *Business World*, 2 November 2009.

Industry players say the trend indicates that the purchasing power of the average middle class Indian consumer is still strong. One school of thought is of the opinion that the trend is supported by the strong saving culture in India that is biased towards essential purchases. 'Most purchases are through cash, cheques and credit cards, with most financiers almost exiting the market, except for Bajaj Finance', said Nilesh Gupta of Vijay Sales, a durables retail chain.

Consumer durables manufacturers expect a growth of 12-15 per cent for consumer electronics and 15-20 per cent for home appliances in 2010. Prices have stayed firm across categories since January 2010 and officials rule out any drop this year. Leading manufacturers such as LG, Samsung and Onida were concerned about uncertain growth trends in late 2009 when volumes took a 20-30 per cent dip amidst rising input costs.

Currently, dealers are continuing to rely on exchange offers and freebies to woo consumers to showrooms. 'LCDs as aspirational purchases are driving consumer electronics sales, especially given the significant drop in prices in the last several months. Also, if one looks at the demographics, there are a vast number of young consumers who are taking up jobs, buying houses and purchasing durables which are a benchmark of lifestyle, Also, there are other demand drivers such as investment in rural economy, good agricultural growth and higher disposable incomes in the hands of consumers after the implementation of the recent Sixth Pay Commission,' said LG India Marketing Director V. Ramachandran.

Conventional trades in modern formats are recording robust volumes with a significant number being cash purchases. Modern formats like Croma, E-Zone and Next, among others, constitute roughly 10-15 per cent of the total industry sales. Soaring input costs in 2008 had made a dent in the profitability of most manufacturers who selectively hiked prices in an uncertain market. 'The challenge will continue to be to control operating costs and improve margins. But we do expect the pressure on input costs to ease up in 2010', said Ramachandran.

'We are recording around 25 per cent-plus sales even in our older formats. We also attract consumers who had the money but seemed unwilling to spend by offering discounts', said Manoj Kumar, CEO of E-Zone, a Future Group entity. The subsidy package announced by Government of India in 2009, which led to an average drop of 1-2 per cent in prices, also fuelled sales. 'Consumers are upgrading household gadgets as disposable income levels have not come down,' said Samsung India Managing Director, R. Zutshi.

In the calendar year 2009, sales for flat-screen TV grew by 18 per cent, LCDs by 124 per cent, ACs by 13 per cent, refrigerators by 7 per cent and washing machines by 8 per cent, as per ORG-GFK estimates. Table 1.2 shows the top performing retailers in India during 2008–9.

Source: Businss Standard, January 2010.

Let us look at MGI's projected scenario for all-India household distribution versus annual household disposable income by 2025 (Figure 1.2). MGI assumes that India's middle and lower classes will scale up in their social status, thereby transforming the tall, spiked income distribution of 1985 into a flatter curve.

Table 1.3: Small cities and big markets

Areas	*Split of population (%)*	*Estimated population*	*Estimated per capita urban expenditure (₹)*	*Estimated annual market growth (%) (2004–15)*
Metro	15	51,371,205	65,518	10
KUT	17	55,480,940	41,246	9
ROUI	68	2,31,300,828	29,126	17

Source: Ernst & Young Pvt Ltd., 2010.
Note: KUT—Key Urban Towns, ROUI—Rest of Urban India.

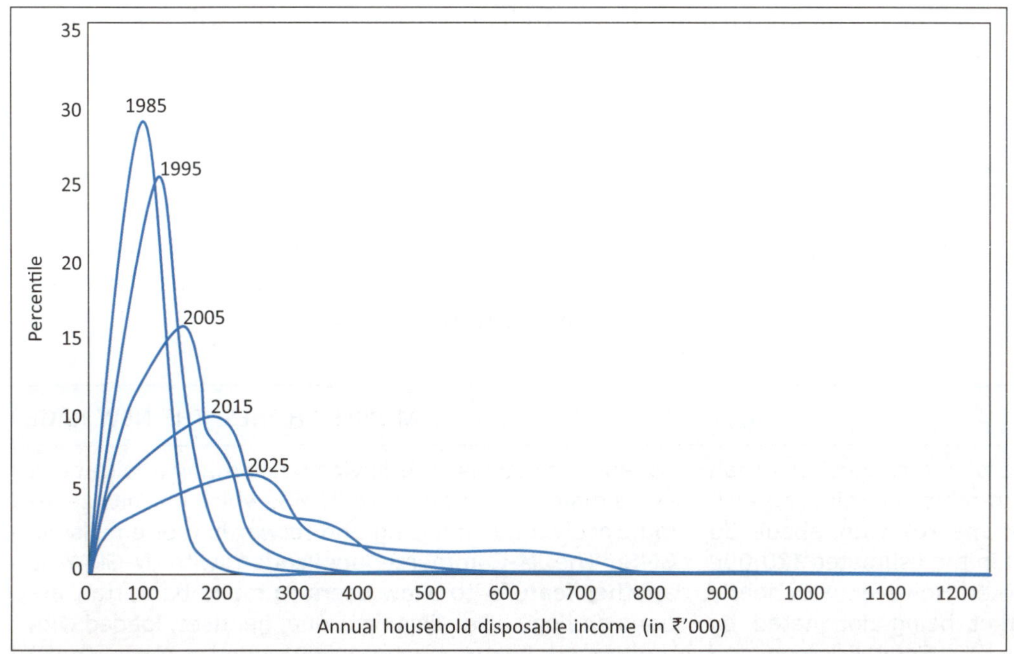

Figure 1.2: Annual household disposable income (in ₹'000) *v*. All India household distribution (1985–2025)

Source: MGI 2005.

As per MGI estimates, affluent India's share of national private consumption will increase from 7 per cent at present to 20 per cent in 2025, which helps to explain the recent rush into the Indian market of luxury brands such as Louis Vuitton and Jimmy Choo.

However, companies shouldn't underestimate the market made up by the country's affluent consumers: those earning more than ₹10,00,000 a year—$21,890 in 2000 dollar terms, or $1,17,650 in terms of purchasing power parity (PPP). Though they will remain a small portion of society: about 2 per cent of the population in 2025, up from 0.2 per cent today yet in absolute numbers, by 2025 India's wealthiest citizens will total 24 million, more than the current population of Australia. And by the same year, India's affluent class is slated to be larger than China's comparable segment, projected to be about 19 million people. As per MGI estimates, affluent India's share of national private consumption will increase from 7 per cent at present to 20 per cent in 2025—a statistic which helps explain the recent rush into the Indian market of luxury brands such as Louis Vuitton and Jimmy Choo.

Dependency ratio, which is defined as the percentage of non-working population (consisting of dependent children below the age of 15 years and adults aged above 64 years) to the people in the workforce, is a low 0.81 per cent. What is more, the population between the ages of 0 and 19 is a staggering 400 million—a considerable number waiting to join the workforce. Therefore, companies can afford to think of India as a market for FMCG luxury products like high-end cars, plasma TVs, for advanced healthcare instruments, and for software development tools and platforms. Not to be left behind, companies can even target rural India as a prime source of demand. Nearly 47 per cent of rural income now emanates from non-agricultural activities like trade and transport.

The 'global' Indians live mostly in the eight largest cities, and so are accessible to the large domestic and multinational companies. They have tastes similar to those of their counterparts in developed countries: branded goods, vacations abroad, the latest consumer electronics, high-end cars, ...

The upcoming changes in the Indian consumer market will create major opportunities and challenges for Indian and multinational businesses alike. For example, companies will need to attract and educate large numbers of new consumers, establish and retain brand loyalties as tastes will change with rising incomes, and introduce high-value products and services at sufficiently low prices to be and remain accessible to the emerging middle class. The quadrupling of the Indian market will present companies competing in India with a critical discontinuity to navigate—who the leaders of this changed market will be is yet to be decided.

MARKETING IN ACTION — MOBILE PHONES: THE NEW RAGE

Today, India has more mobile phone connections than landlines. There is a mad scramble for mindshare in the Indian telecom handset market with about 30 handset makers battling it out in the estimated ₹20,000 crore (annual) cell phone market. However, with nearly 85-90 per cent of this market being dominated by brands like Nokia, Samsung, LG, Sony Ericsson and Research in Motion (Blackberry), analysts say its a tough call for newer handset vendors. The mobile handset market crossed the 100 million unit mark in June 2009, recording a growth of 6.7 per cent, from 94.60 million units in the corresponding period in 2008, according to IDC India.

Nokia led the growth with a market share of 52.2 per cent, followed by Samsung with 17.4 per cent while LG stood third at 5.9 per cent in the 12-month period ended June 2010.

Emerging mobile handset vendors (around 26) managed a mere 6.5 per market share during the same period. Nevertheless, this was a marked improvement over the corresponding 12 months ending June 2009, when eleven emerging vendors shared the 1.2 per cent of overall shipments. IDC does not track the number of handsets brought on their person by passengers landing in the country or the 'grey market' handsets. 'We see the market getting further crowded, especially in the lower- and mid-market segments', opines Deepak Kumar, Associate VP, Research, IDC India. He, however, points out that simultaneously there is an evolution in the market as the rising competition is forcing vendors to offer newer, richer features at attractive price points. 'In other words, a combination of volume and value is at work', he says.

The new vendors, for instance, offer feature-rich (dual SIM card, QWERTY keyboard) and application-rich (IM-enabled) mobile handsets at attractive price points. They have also introduced entry-level models for the 'price sensitive' Indian consumer. Spice Mobile's multi-SIM functionality phones with prices starting at ₹2,000 is a case in point, not to forget the Micromax handset with a 30-day standby time targeted at niche consumers. Spice D-6666 offers the flexibility to choose between GSM+CDMA mode and GSM+GSM mode in a single phone, giving users the freedom to switch between connections. The device hosts many applications like a mailing solution, Email2SMS, which permits sending, receiving, composing and forwarding of emails via SMS. The M-Commerce application with N-GPAY is another feature 'to allow users to make bank transactions and pay bills'. This flexi-dual handset, loaded with multimedia features and value-added service (VAS) applications is currently available for ₹7,999.

'Indian consumers have moved towards multi-SIM and flexi-SIM phones to avail the cost benefits of operator bundled services. Spice Mobiles, that has an installed base of 6 million handsets is now positive of 1 million handset sales per month within the next 12 months,' says Kunal Ahuja, CEO of Spice Mobiles. Samsung's Marine handset too is priced below ₹10,000. Asim Warsi, GM (Marketing), Samsung India, says: 'Our entry level Guru series, which starts at around ₹1,500, has been a bestseller in volume terms followed by the Metro series that starts at about ₹5,000.' Samsung is also wooing the youth segment with handsets priced at ₹8,000-₹10,000 complete with features like social media applications and touch screen.

The fact that other major players, too, are not sitting easy makes it tougher for new players. They have introduced both high-end and low-end models; smartphones are their forte. The year 2009, for instance, saw the launch of high-end smartphones (such as Apple's iPhone 3G and the Blackbery Storm). IDG India estimates there were 7,00,000 smartphones in the country in 2009.

The big players have 'priority' centres, their own outlets and long-term tie-ups with distributors to promote their brand prominently on shelves. HTC India, for instance, introduced nearly 16 models of which over 90 per cent were touch screen ones. The company managed to sell close to 3,00,000 devices by end-2008. HTC policy is to bundles its phones with GSM players, and has successfully extended this telco-driven model to CDMA player Reliance Communications as well as to Idea Cellular.

In 2009, the company also launched India's first Android-powered phones (popularly known as Google phones). 'The Android-powered phone introduces a more natural way of reaching out to people and accessing information in a much easier and hassle-free manner. It has a fully customized user interface, called HTC Sense, which creates a distinct engaging experience,' says Ajay Sharma who heads HTC India. In keeping with its strategy, Airtel users of both models—HTC Magic and HTC Hero—across India get free data download of 100MB per month for six months. Market leader Nokia with a 40 per cent market share globally (and over 50 per cent in India) has also moved into services to counter falling handset prices and increased competition in the high-end mobile phone market, particularly from the likes of Apple's iPhone and Research In Motion (RIM's) Blackberry. Indian handset brands have taken on their MNC rivals. These desi brands source the handset from low cost producers in China, keep their prices 50 per cent below their rivals, double the profit margin of their dealers and focus on India-specific features and applications like dual SIM, Bollywood song download. They have invested heavily behind their brands, getting celebrity ambassdors and have caught the aspirational youngster in tier I and II cities first. During 2009–10, Nokia lost 11.8 per cent market share over 2008–9 and desi brands such as Micromax, Spice mobiles and Karbonn gained 4.1 per cent, 1.9 per cent and 3 per cent respectively during 2009–10.

With desire levels rising even in rural India, market dynamics of mobile phones are undergoing a major change. Consumers don't want Plain Jane handsets anymore. Neither do they want to flaunt fancy ones. What they desire is a basic phone with all the frills of a high-end handset. Hence, enter the mid-segment.

The data on mobile phones from the market research firm ORG reveals that sales of handsets ranging between ₹3,000 and ₹6,000 rose in 2010 as compared to 2008, while sales in the entry-level and premium segments took a hit. According to the same ORG data, the mid-segment of mobile phones saw a substantial increase of between 17 and 25 per cent over 2008.

The mid-segment is also known as the multimedia segment and as sales are fast picking up, mobile manufacturers too are readying to tap into it. Technology has made it easier for manufacturers to provide plenty of features in the mid-range handsets. Prices have also dropped considerably, provoking consumers to go for these comparatively slightly higher priced handsets. Consumers in the age group of 18-25 years have emerged as major buyers and they want to use their mobile phones for not only talking but also to listen to music and surf the web. Features like these are now available in this price range.

And here's why: Monochrome phones now contribute only 15 per cent to the total handset sales. About 85 per cent of all handsets sold in January 2010 were colour phones as compared to 83 per cent during the same period in 2008. And with more consumers preferring camera, FM, MP3 and video functionality on their phones, the market dynamics are also in a period of flux. For instance, the contribution of mobile phones costing less than ₹3,000 to the overall mobile sales dipped from 67 to 63 per cent in January 2010. The contribution of phones ranging between ₹6,000 and ₹15,000 also decreased to 11 per cent from 14 per cent.

In June 2009, after a successful pilot in Maharashtra, Nokia announced the commercial launch of Nokia Life Tools service in the state. It has a range of three primary services—agriculture, education and entertainment. In August 2009, Nokia announced the launch of its Music Store service in India, offering music lovers access to over three million international, Bollywood and regional soundtracks. 'Since the services and devices are integrated, we want our consumers to buy a Nokia solution,' notes Nokia India Director Marketing, Vineet Taneja.

'We do not talk about market share. But consider this. Around 80 per cent of all handsets are ₹4,000 and below. And most of our handsets are priced in the mid- and high-end bracket, which means, above ₹4,000. So are we talking about market share within this 20 per cent bracket?' asks Anil Sethi, President, Sony Ericsson India, adding: 'It's a meaningless discussion. We know the youth love our phones.'

Today, people are increasingly using their phones to do much more than just 'talk'. Consumers are definitely looking for more evolved features and enhanced experiences on their mobile phones. And with India all set to become the handset factory of the world with around 120 million mobile subscribers and still counting, manufacturers will definitely find out ways to provide enhanced experiences for consumers—even if that means treading the middle path.

Incidentally in May 2010, the country's largest mobile phone operator Bharti Airtel was looking at big-ticket acquisitions abroad in its quest to double its subscriber base. This comes on the heels of it becoming the third telecom company in the world to have more than 110 million customers on a single network, the other two being China Mobile and China Unicom.

Sources: The Economic Times, May 2010 and *Business Standard,* November 2009.

1.2 Indian Consumer Market in 2025

MGI estimated in 2010 that 80 per cent of consumption growth will come from rising income, while 16 per cent of the increase will be due to growth in the number of households.

In 2010 MGI estimated that 80 per cent of consumption growth will come from rising income, while 16 per cent of the increase will be due to growth in the number of households. Only 4 per cent will come from changes in India's household savings rate. As incomes grow, the class structure of consumption will change significantly as well. Consumption today is dominated by the deprived and aspiring income segments, which together make up 75 per cent of the spending. By 2025, however, the global segment will wield 20 per cent of the total spending and the new middle class will come to dominate, controlling 59 per cent of India's consumption power.

However, by 2025 the Indian consumer market will largely be an urban affair, with 68 per cent of consumption taking place in urban areas versus 32 per cent in rural areas. Over two-thirds of the future growth in the Indian market will be concentrated in urban areas despite the fact that even in 2025, urban areas will have only 37 per cent of the population.

Differences in income growth across urban and rural India are due to several factors, including variations in the type of economic activity, levels of educational attainment, and demographics (e.g. lower household size in urban areas). Urban India will not only drive India's growth but will also benefit from it disproportionately, compared to rural areas.

MARKETING IN ACTION

DURABLES MAKERS LAUNCH MODELS TO BEAT GLOOM

The ₹25,000-crore consumer durables industry, which grew 12 per cent in 2009, is following a rather contrarian approach to tackle the slowdown. Most leading manufacturers, such as LG, Samsung and Videocon are launching more models across categories to arouse consumer interest and, therefore, sales.

While Samsung Electronics had launched about 200 models across its entire range of products in 2008, it planned to launch 250 models in 2010. Similarly, Videocon, which launched 76 new models in 2008, planned to up that number to around 90 in 2010.

'Introduction of new products is an important part of our strategy for 2010,' says Samsung India Marketing Director (South-West Asia) Y.Y. Kim. 'It is important to keep consumer interest in the brand alive'. The South Korean durables manufacturer, which trades in consumer electronics, IT and telecom products, had revenues of $1.7 billion in 2008, growing by 30 per cent over 2007. It had a target of 27 per cent growth in 2009.

Similarly, LG Electronics India is also planning to launch 300 models in various categories, up from the 250 that the company had launched in 2008. The company had revenues of ₹10,730 crore in 2008 and planned to grow by 15 per cent in 2010, mainly on the strength of new launches.

Consumers postponing purchases owing to the economic slowdown has affected the consumer durables sector to some extent. However, marketers believe introducing new models and widening reach to tier II and tier III towns and to villages will augment sales. Agrees Haier Appliances India COO and Wholetime Director Pranay Dhabhai: 'We need to reach wider into the country and give consumers more options. In 2010, we would like to consolidate our market share in the areas in which we currently operate.' The company will launch about 38 models in various categories as against 25 launches in 2008. It notched up revenues of about ₹350 crore in 2008, a figure that it aimed to hike to about ₹550 crore by the end of 2010.

Says Videocon group Chairman Venugopal Dhoot: 'Introduction of newer products and models with better technology and features would help increase consumers' willingness to purchase.' In 2008, Videocon, which has interests in oil and gas apart from consumer durables,

Table 1.4: Best performing FMCG companies in 2008–9

Company	*Market cap (April-September 2009) (₹crore)*	*Sales (₹crore)*	*Profit (₹crore)*
ITC	79,390	23,827	3,268
HUL	55,684	22,500	2,496
Nestlé India	18,794	4,505	534
Dabur India	10,468	2,468	373
Godrej Consumer Products	4,834	1,176	162

Sources: Business Today, 15 November 2009 and *Business World,* 2 November 2009.

had revenues of about ₹10,000 crore. It planned to take it up to ₹11,000 crore in 2010.

Philips India, which launched 25 models in 2008, had also confirmed an increase in number in 2010. Says Philips India Chief Marketing Officer Vivek Sharma: 'Consumer durables still have low penetration in India and that helps our cause. We will focus on the health and well-being concept in 2010 and launch products.' Table 1.4 shows the top performing FMCG companies in India during 2008–9.

Sources: The Economic Times, May 2010 and *Business Standard*, November 2009.

1.3 Marketing in a Globalized World

Globalization brings together two important elements—size and number.

Globalization brings into play two important elements—size and number. Unless the size is reasonably large enough to open more outlets and expand product portfolios, it is very difficult to sustain in any market. General indications of performance include market leadership, percentage of a firm's sales to industry sales and product acceptance. Of course, to be most meaningful, these percentages should be computed separately for different geographical areas, product lines, and types of customers, provided suitable industry data are available.

The fact that Vodafone and Bharti Airtel Limited are competing in the same mobile phone service market space and for leadership position is ascertained on the bases of turnover and number of subscribers. *Business Standard* coming up with a circulation enhancing campaign by introducing the supplement *Spend* is a unique example of attracting youngsters aspiring for global careers and carrying the image and status of owning global brands.

1.3.1 Future Challenges for Marketers

The future, according to MGI, will see India continue on its recent path of strong growth. There are many reasons to believe that this assumption is realistic, most notably the scope for improved productivity in the economy. But India's performance depends strongly on continued long-term economic reforms that are needed to address serious deficiencies in the country's infrastructure and financial system. There's an urgent need to promote investment in human capital through better education and healthcare.

As we explained earlier, three-quarters of India's consumer market in 2025 doesn't exist today; a staggering ₹52,60,000 crore a year in future purchases will be up for grabs. Also, India's rapid upward mobility means that many of her households will be new consumers, enjoying significant discretionary consumption in the organized economy for the first time in their lives. So both incumbents and challengers alike are set to face hurdles.

1.3.2 Challenges for Existing Players

The incumbents, mostly domestic companies, will start with many advantages to their side: brands that enjoy existing relationships with customers, and an understanding of their needs, and recognition. The incumbents will also have established distribution channels—very important in a country of vast geography and limited infrastructure.

Yet, growing income and consumption will pressure incumbents from two directions. One, such companies will have to continue to adjust to the pace and magnitude of change, for as consumers rise through the income brackets, their tastes, aspirations, and brand loyalties will evolve along with their lifestyles. Two, India's growing consumption will also attract a host of challengers, and the ongoing economic reform will significantly intensify competition in many markets. New competition will come from multinationals entering the Indian market, as also from established Indian companies looking for expansion opportunities, and from new entrepreneurs. Indeed, if the country's policymakers create suitable conditions for India's entrepreneurs to succeed, major new companies could be built on the back of consumer growth.

With incomes growing, existing players need to understand how consumer aspirations change and find ways to meet the changing needs.

Many incumbents haven't prepared or aren't preparing enough for this discontinuity. Existing players will have to develop a deeper understanding of how consumer needs and aspirations will change as incomes grow and will also have to find ways of creating innovative products that meet those changing needs. In addition, they will have to think about how to introduce new consumers to their products, whether their brands are appropriate for those consumers, and what price and cost positions will help them compete most effectively for a share of the new middle class market. What's more, incumbents will have to keep a wary eye on the actions of their current competitors and on new market entrants. That's a full agenda, and companies that begin preparing today will no doubt be better positioned to benefit from the changes.

1.3.3 Challenges for New Players

For new players, the challenge will be to spot the gaps and opportunities that arise as India's income and class structures change. They might, for example, look for small markets or sectors with limited competition, or both. From another angle, they could also turn to other emerging economies to seek lessons on how tastes and needs will likely evolve in India, looking in particular for categories in which spending has shifted from local products and brands to international ones, following rising aspirations. Companies seeking to exploit these changes should consider what new needs will be unique to Indian tastes and to the Indian market as the middle class grows.

In India, as in many emerging markets, multinational companies will find themselves in tough spot between the desire of the country's consumers for a modern, middle class lifestyle and the realities of the limited budgets. In 2005 the average middle class family spent just over ₹3,00,000 annually (roughly $6,600)—a very modest sum in real terms, but in PPP terms equal to around $35,000. As one analyst noted, however, 'You can't put PPP dollars in the bank, only real dollars'.

Multinationals are required to innovate to deliver an aspirational, middle class lifestyle to families on an Indian budget. Companies that can develop new business models, design products with carefully targeted features, and create brands that appeal to the Indian upwardly mobile class will attract huge numbers of eager consumers. Desi mobile GSM handset Micromax sells from ₹2,000 to ₹5,000; Spice from ₹1,500 to ₹16,000; Karbonn from ₹1,800 to ₹6,000 and Lava from ₹1,400 to ₹6,000. Most of their sales are bunched in the ₹2,000 to ₹3,000 band. Low overheads and lean organizations ensure that not much gets added to the price. Look at the market potential of handset market in India; it grew from ₹80 lakh per month in 2008 to ₹1.10 crore in 2010. Even if a desi brand sells 50,000 units per month, it can touch ₹1 crore per month. Now, they are soon going to introduce 3G phones as low as ₹4,000 in 2011.

ECONOMY WATCH

CAR SALES AHEAD ON DISCOUNTS, DEPRECIATION GAINS

India's biggest car maker has sold a bigger share of more profitable cars and expects to do even better in 2010–11. The operating profit margin of Maruti Suzuki India Limited has increased to 11.9 per cent due to increased export demand for small cars from Europe and domestic demand from rural India in 2010. With rural spends less affected by the slowdown in the economy, Maruti was able to sell more cars, raising the sales volume in the home market by 20 per cent year-on-year. Compared to 12 per cent in 2008–9, analysts estimate that the rural market fetched the company 16 per cent of revenues in 2009. On the other hand, Maruti's business in the top ten cities of the county rose by 8 per cent in 2009. Seventy per cent of the company's sales come through financing schemes, compared to 66 per cent in June 2010. The volume of car sales is projected to grow by 12 to 13 per cent in 2011. Models like SX4, DZire and Ritz continue to remain popular choices from the Maruti stable.

Even in the peak of recession, January and February 2009 were respectable months for automobile sales. But it hit top gear in March. According to auto financiers, the auto market seems to have turned the corner in September 2010, managing to better 2009's tally.

Total car sales in September 2010 was estimated to be around 2,03,468 lakh units, up 20.9 per cent over September 2009. Auto financiers say the combined effect of discounts, dealer pushes as well as depreciation benefits helped sales. The stimulus package which cut excise duties and the excitement over the Nano launch also helped turn the sentiment around.

Maruti's sales grew 6 per cent and 19 per cent in the first two months of 2009, respectively. The revival in sales for the January-March quarter helped the company post its highest ever annual sales in its 25-year history, which increased 3.57 per cent to 7.92 lakh units in 2009 against 7.04 lakh units in 2008.

The turnaround though is restricted to cars and two-wheelers. Trucks, which have been badly hit, will take some time to make a turnaround. The crunch will ease but it will take more than a year for it to return to positive territory.

Maruti Suzuki registered rate of 83,107 small cars (A_1-A_2 segments) and 23.6 per cent growh in September 2010. The small car segments dominate the passenger car market with nearly 70 per cent of the total market. In September 2010, 1,61,010 small cars were sold as against 1,38,014 unis in September 2009, registering a growth of 16.7 per cent.

Utility vehicle (UV) market leader Mahindra & Mahindra (M&M) saw its domestic sales jump to 15,296 units in September 2010. M&M's total sales, including the Logan Sedan, increased 11.32 per cent from 23,128 units in March 2008. The domestic growth for the company is largely driven by UVs like Bolero, Scorpio and Xylo. The overall stimulus package, which included interest rate and excise rate cuts, helped M&M achieve this impressive growth amidst the global meltdown. The country's leading utility vehiclemaker created a record of sorts in April 2009, with three of its models taking pole positions in the domestic UV segment. In April 2009, sales of M&M's Xylo, Bolero and Scorpio models overtook Toyota's Innova and Tata Motors' Sumo and Safari models. Their combined market share stood at 65 per cent in March 2009 compared with 47 per cent in 2008. Over 6,000 units of the Bolero were sold in April 2009, with the newly-launched Xylo selling 3,509 units and the Scorpio doing 3,100 units. Against this, the Toyota Innova sold 2,834 units, while the Tata Sumo sold 1,642 units (including 174 units of the Grande) and the Safari sold 774 units in April 2009.

29,035 units of MUV sold in September 2010 registering a volume growth of 13.6 per cent. 1,55,915 units of MUV sold till September 2010 as against 1,28,751 units registered in September 2009; registering a growth of 21.1 per cent. Mahindra & Mahindra holds 52 per cent market followed by Toyota Kirloskar (21 per cent), Tata Motors (12.9 per cent) and General Motors (6.4 per cent) in MUV sigment.

Sources: The Economic Times, September 2010 and *Business Standard*, November 2009.

For the global players, India represents one of the largest consumer market opportunities of the next two decades. During the first millennium, merchants referred to India—with its dynamic, prosperous consumers—as the 'golden bird'. That bird is preparing to take flight again.

India's emergence as the world's fifth-largest consumer economy will signal significant benefits to the country and the world. Growth will pull millions of people out of poverty and into the world's middle class. With rising incomes, Indians will have the opportunity to realize the comforts and pleasures of the middle class the world over. In addition, rising domestic consumption will create further economic growth and employment as companies work to meet the new consumer demand.

For the world's businesses, India represents one of the largest consumer market opportunities of the next two decades. During the first millennium, merchants referred to India—with its dynamic, prosperous consumers—as the 'golden bird'. That bird is now preparing to take flight again.

The dynamics have changed. Companies in India are now focusing on customer-driven marketing practices, profitability and retail marketing in their chosen fields of operation. The commitment to innovation and customer-oriented business decision-making is only the first step in implementing the retail marketing concept. This commitment establishes the customer orientation culture, which is the foundation of the retail marketing strategy.

The next major shift is the focus towards profitability as against profits and sales volume. As we know, declining profitability is a red flag that the company's product offering is becoming less effective in delivering value and satisfying customer needs, relative to substitutes and competitive product offerings.

1.4 Changing Emphases in Marketing

In the new millennium, many companies in India are trying to focus on customer-driven marketing practices, retail marketing profitability, and market research.

As the part of the organization which interacts most directly and immediately with the customer, there is an obvious need for the retail marketer to investigate, analyse and respond to major environmental changes that are now taking place almost on a daily basis. If this is not done—or if it is done poorly—not only will opportunities be missed, but potential threats are also more likely to become actual threats, which will in turn be reflected in a decline in performance. Consequently, the retail marketer needs to develop a clear vision of the future and of the ways in which the business environment is most likely to develop. While doing so, it is essential that the retail marketer recognize how patterns of marketing thinking are changing and how the organization might best come to terms with areas of growing importance. In the new millennium, many companies in India are trying to focus on the following:

(a) **Customer-driven marketing practices:** The commitment to innovation and customer-oriented business decision-making is only the first step in implementing the marketing concept. This commitment establishes the culture of customer orientation, which is the foundation of the marketing concept.

(b) **Retail marketing:** Market segmentation, targeting and positioning (STP) constitute the three requirements to implement the focused retail marketing.

(c) **Profitability:** The next major shift in focus is towards profitability as against profits and sales volume. As we know, declining profitability is a signal that the company's product offering is becoming less effective, relative to substitutes and competitive product offerings, in delivering value and satisfying customer needs.

(d) **Market research:** A key part of customer orientation and integrated marketing is the use of market research to analyse customer needs and wants and to provide feedback to other parts of the business.

1.5 Factors for Undertaking Successful Marketing

MGI has identified eight technology-enabled trends set to shape businesses and the economy. These trends fall within three broad areas of business activity: managing relationships, managing capital and assets and leveraging information in new ways.

The business world always swings between the demand and supply of various products and services. Lifestyle changes create room for every marketer to operate in this dynamic world. No business firm today can claim to be placed comfortably; each has to continuously undergo restructuring and innovate new ways of doing business to retain profitability. Technology alone is rarely the key to unlocking economic value: companies create real wealth when they combine technology with new ways of doing business. MGI has identified eight technology-enabled trends that will help shape businesses and the economy in the coming years. These trends fall within three broad areas of business activity: managing relationships, managing capital and assets, and leveraging information in new ways. The following are some suggested tools for managing retail marketers in this millennium:

(a) **Distributing co-creation:** The Internet and related technologies give companies radical new ways to harvest the talents of innovators working outside corporate boundaries. Today, in the high-technology consumer product and automotive sectors, companies routinely involve customers, suppliers, small specialist businesses and independent contractors in the creation of new products. While outsiders offer insights that help shape product development, companies typically control the innovation process. Technology now allows companies to delegate substantial control to outsiders—the process of co-creation—by outsourcing innovation to business partners who work together sin networks. By distributing innovation through the value chain and, therefore, by eliminating bottlenecks that come with total control companies can reduce their costs and introduce new products into the market faster.

(b) **Using consumers as innovators:** Consumers also co-create with companies. The online encyclopedia Wikipedia, for instance, can be viewed as a service or product created by customers. But the differences in the way companies co-create with partners, on the one hand, and with customers, on the other, are so marked that the consumer aspects forms a separate trend. These differences include the nature and range of interactions, the economics of making them work, and the management challenges associated with them.

As the Internet has evolved—an evolution prompted in part by new Web 3.0 technologies—it has become a more widespread platform for interaction, communication, and activism. Increasingly consumers want to engage online with one another and with varied organizations. Companies can tap into this new mood of customer engagement for their economic benefit. Those that involve customers in design, testing, marketing (such as viral marketing which is word-of-mouth marketing generally through the Internet), and aftersales processes get better insights into customer needs and behaviour. Consequently they may be able to cut the cost of acquiring customers, engender greater loyalty, and speed up development cycles.

(c) **Tapping into talent:** Just as technology permits organizations to decentralize innovation through networks or customers, it also allows them to parcel out more work to specialists, free agents, and talent networks. As more and more sophisticated work takes place interactively online and new collaboration and communication tools emerge, companies can outsource increasingly specialized aspects of their work and still maintain organizational coherence.

(d) **Extracting added value from interactions:** The application of technology has reduced differences in the productivity of transformational (proactive, technology-savvy and customer-friendly) employees and transactional employees (those managing routine affairs of the company without much involvement) but huge inconsistencies still persist. For the transactional employees it is more about increasing their effectiveness, for instance, by getting them to focus on interactions that create value and ensuring that they have the right information and context than it is about improving their efficiency. Technology-enabled tools that promote tacit interactions,

ECONOMY WATCH — **ENTERTAINMENT BUSINESS TO GROW AT 12.5 PER CENT IN 2009–13**

The Indian media and entertainment industry was a ₹58,400-crore business in 2008, growing 15 per cent annually since 2006. But the growth projection for the industry for 2009–13 has been lowered to 12.5 per cent per annum from 18 per cent for 2008–12, says a joint study by the Federation of Indian Chambers of Commerce and Industry (FICCI) and KPMG. 'In many ways, the year 2008 was a testing time for the industry,' says the study. 'With the global economic slowdown affecting advertising spends, sectors like TV, print, radio and outdoor media that depend on advertising revenues were affected.'

The study lowered the projections for the advertising industry during the two periods under review from 18 to 12.4 per cent, adding that this segment had grown 20 per cent during 2004–7 and 17.1 per cent in 2006–8. Among other segments, the study says the print media business, estimated to be worth ₹17,260 crore, will grow at 9 per cent between 2009 and 2013, while the television industry, at present valued at ₹24,050 crore, will expand by 14.5 per cent.

The study bets high on gaming. Although it estimates this segment to be worth just ₹650 crore, it sees it growing at 33.3 per cent till 2013, while the ₹620-crore Internet business is seen growing at 27.9 per cent.

In the home video segment DVD and VCD sales increased by 30-40 per cent in April 2009 due to a combination of factors. First, there were no new films released in the theatres due to the stand-off between multiplex owners and producers. And with schools on vacation, people were spending a lot of time at home. It was not only the home video companies that had a windfall, but movie rental businesses like Seventymm and BigFlix.com also saw an increase in the average number of home video rentals per customer: a figure which doubled, going up from two to four films per month. 'People prefer spending less money and rent a DVD instead of going out to a theatre,' says K.N. Srikanth, CFO, Seventymm.

Another major player in the home video rental space, BigFlix.com, the home entertainment division of Reliance ADAG, saw an upswing both in the number of new subscribers and that of rentals. However, Kamal Gianchandani, COO, BigFlix.com, feels that the film producers' strike is not the only cause for the upsurge in sales. 'There was a 15-20 per cent increase in movie rentals in April 2009. But it is difficult to quantify how much of the upswing was due to the strike. This is usually a good period for the business because of the vacations,' he says.

The home video market is expected to grow at a compounded annual growth rate of 13.2 per cent from ₹8,630 crore in 2009 to ₹1,606 crore in 2013 as per the FICCI-KPMG report.

Source: The Economic Times, May 2009.

such as wikis, virtual team environments, and videoconferencing, may become no less ubiquitous than computers are now. As companies learn to use these tools, they will also develop managerial innovations—smarter and faster ways for individuals and teams to create value through interactions that will be difficult for rivals to replicate.

1.6 Fundamental Approaches to Marketing

1.6.1 Marketing: What and Why?

Philip Kotler, the marketing guru, observed that marketing is everywhere. Formally or informally, people and organizations engage in innumerable activities that could be called marketing. Good marketing is not an accident, but as a result of careful planning and execution. Marketing is both an art and a science—there is constant tension between the formulated aspect of marketing and the creative side. Skilful marketing is a never-ending pursuit.

Marketing is the only activity that guarantees or brings back money to the organization. It often expands even when a company's divisions and structures witness downsizing! In fact, financial success often depends on the marketing ability. Many firms have created the position of a Chief Marketing Officer (CMO) to put marketing on an equal footing with other functions like finance and operations. Marketing is tricky and making the right decisions is not always easy. To prepare to be marketers, you need to understand what marketing is, how it works, what is marketed, and who does the marketing!

Marketing is the only activity that guarantees or brings back money to the organization. It grows even when a company's divisions and structures witness downsizing!

1.6.2 Marketing Defined

Two fundamental beliefs form the basis for the concept of marketing. First, all company planning, policies and operations should be oriented towards the customer; second, a profitable sales volume should be the goal of a firm. In its fullest sense, it is that philosophy of business which states that the customers demand for satisfaction is the economic and social justification of a company's existence. Consequently, all company activities in production, engineering, and finance, as well as in marketing, must be devoted first to determining what the customers' wants are and then to satisfying those wants while still making a reasonable profit.

The marketing concept is based on two fundamental beliefs. First, all company planning, policies and operations should be oriented towards the customer; second, profitable sales volume should be the goal of a firm.

From a managerial point of view, marketing is the process of planning and executing the conception, pricing, promotion, and distribution of ideas, goods, and services to create exchanges that satisfy both individual and organizational goals. According to Kotler, 'Marketing management is the art and science of choosing target markets and getting, keeping, and growing customers through creating, delivering, and communicating superior customer value.'

The American Marketing Association (AMA) defines marketing as 'the process of planning and executing the conception, pricing, promotion and distribution of ideas, goods and services to create exchanges that satisfy individual and organizational goals.'

Peter Drucker, the world's leading writer in management, says:

> It is the customer who determines what a business is. It is the customer alone whose willingness to pay for a good or service converts economic resources into wealth, things into goods. What the business thinks it produces is not of first importance–especially not to the future of the business and to its success... What the customer thinks he is buying, what he considers value, is decisive—it determines what a business is, what it produces and whether it will prosper. And what the customer buys and considers value is never a product. It is always utility, that is, what a product or service does for him ... *Because its purpose is to create a customer, the business enterprise has two—and only these two—basic functions; marketing and innovation. Marketing and innovation produce results; all the rest are 'costs'.*

1.6.3 The Marketing Concept

Germane to marketing is the idea that organizations survive and prosper through fulfilling the needs and wants of customers—an important perspective commonly known as the marketing concept. The marketing concept is about matching a company's capabilities with the customers' wants. This matching process takes place in what is termed the marketing environment. An organization that adopts the marketing concept accepts the needs of potential customers as the basis for its operations. Businesses do not undertake marketing activities alone. They face threats from competitors, and have to deal with changes in the political, economic, social and technological environment. All these factors have to be taken into account as a business tries to match its capabilities with the needs and wants of its target customers. The success of the organization is dependent on satisfying customer needs.

Marketing *v.* Selling

The difference between marketing and selling is more than semantic. Selling focuses on the needs of the seller; marketing on the needs of the buyer.

The difference between marketing and selling is more than merely semantic. Selling focuses on the needs of the seller; marketing on the needs of the buyer. Selling is preoccupied with the seller's need to convert his product into cash; while marketing involves satisfying the needs of the customer by means of the product and the whole cluster of things associated with creating, delivering and finally consuming it.

Importantly, marketers are skilled at managing demand, seeking to influence the level, timing, and composition of demand. They are involved in marketing many types of entities: goods, services, events, experiences, persons, places, properties, organizations, information, and ideas. They also operate in four different marketplaces: consumer, business, global, and non-profit.

Businesses today face a number of challenges and opportunities including the effects of advances in technology, globalization, and deregulation. Their response involves a fundamental change in how they conduct marketing. We will now look at the evolution of modern marketing.

The Three Eras of Marketing

The Industrial Revolution of the nineteenth century brought about the production era, which continued till the late 1920s. Here the law 'supply creates its own demand' was applicable.

Although marketing as a concept emerged after the industrial revolution, the change in business in terms of adopting to the marketing concept was gradual. It took many years for businesses to realize that satisfying customers is the key for making sales and profits in the long run. Businesses have gone through different phases or stages of marketing over the years. These stages can be classified as the production, sales, and marketing eras.

(a) **Production era:** The Industrial Revolution of the nineteenth century brought about the production era, which continued till the late 1920s. In this scenario the law 'supply creates its own demand' was applicable. The market was a sellers' market as the demand for products was more than the supply. During this time companies focused primarily on manufacturing the product. Product features were deemed unimportant because it was felt that customers were concerned only with the availability of the product and not its features.

(b) **Sales era:** The sales era began in the late-1920s and lasted until the mid-1950s. The economic depression of the late 1920s proved that producing goods was not everything; companies also had to sell their goods. Businesses thus realized the need for product promotion and distribution. In this era marketers focused on selling the goods to the customers.

The sales era began in the late-1920s, lasting until the mid-1950s. Marketers of this era focused on selling goods to the customers.

(c) **Marketing era:** During the sales era companies ignored consumer wants and needs; they focused simply on their products. But by the end of the 1950s companies keenly felt the need to satisfy consumers' needs. So they identified the importance of consumer wants and expectations in the exchange process between the buyer and the seller. Thus began the period of customer orientation. During the marketing era, companies focused on marketing rather than on selling. They also embraced the concept of coordinated marketing management, which was directed towards the twin goals of customer orientation and profitability. Companies changed from product pushing to fulfilling customer needs according to their preferences.

During the marketing era, companies focused on marketing rather than on selling. They also embraced the concept of coordinated marketing management, which was directed towards the twin goals of customer orientation and profitability.

1.6.4 Societal Marketing Concept

The customer and the society are interrelated; therefore, whatever the company offers to the customer has a direct bearing on the society. Consequently, companies include societal interests in their marketing decisions. The societal marketing concept believes that apart from determining needs, wants and interests of the target market and providing quality products, organizations must also help maintain the society's well-being.

HUL: MARKETING WITH A HEART

The best example of societal marketing is Hindustan Unilever Ltd's voluntary engagement in social betterment. HUL supports *Asha Daan,* a home for handicapped children and AIDS victims in Mumbai. In Assam its Doom Dooma plantation runs *Ankur*, a centre for physically and mentally challenged children. In Bachua *taluka* of Gujurat, HUL has helped in the reconstruction of village Nani Chirai which was destroyed in the massive 2001 earthquake. The village has been renamed Yashodadham.

Source: www.hul.com

1.6.5 Total Market Orientation

The marketing concept holds that the key to achieving organizational goals consists of the company being more effective than its competitors in creating, delivering, and communicating superior customer value to its chosen target market. Reactive market orientation means understanding and meeting consumers' expressed needs. Proactive marketing orientation, on the other hand, is researching or predicting latent consumer needs through a 'probe-and-learn' process. Companies that practice both reactive and proactive marketing orientation successfully implement total market orientation.

1.6.6 Holistic Marketing

Holistic marketing recognizes that everything matters in marketing and that a broad, integrated perspective is often necessary.

Holistic marketing recognizes that everything matters in marketing and that a broad, integrated perspective is often necessary. The holistic marketing concept is based on the development, design, and implementation of marketing programmes, processes, and activities that recognize their breadth and interdependencies. The set of tasks necessary for successful marketing management include developing marketing strategies and plans, connecting with customers, building strong brands, shaping market offerings, delivering and communicating value, capturing marketing insights and performance, and creating successful, long-term growth.

According to Kotler, there are several important trends and forces elicit a new set of beliefs and practices on the part of business firms. He lists fourteen major shifts:

1. From 'marketing does the marketing' to 'everyone does the marketing'.
2. From organization by product units to organizing by customer segments.
3. From making everything to buying more goods and services from outside.
4. From using many suppliers to working with fewer suppliers in a 'partnership'.
5. From relying on old market positions to uncovering new ones.
6. From emphasizing on tangible assets to emphasizing on intangible assets.
7. From building brands through advertising to building brands through performance and integrated communications.
8. From attracting customers through stores and salespeople to making products available online.
9. From selling to everyone to trying to be the best firm in serving a well-defined target market.
10. From focusing on profitable transactions to focusing on customer lifetime value.
11. From focusing on gaining market share to focusing on building customer share.
12. From being local to being 'glocal'—both global and local.
13. From focusing on the financial scorecard to focusing on the marketing scorecard.
14. From focusing on shareholders to focusing on stakeholders.

1.7 Summary

- Creative leaders can use a broad spectrum of new, technology-enabled options to craft their strategies. These trends are best seen as emerging patterns that can be applied in a wide variety of businesses. Executives should reflect on which patterns can reshape their markets and industry—and on whether they have opportunities to catalyse change and shape the outcome rather than merely react to it.

- Along with the shift from rural to urban consumption, India will witness rapid growth of its middle class—households with disposable incomes from ₹2,00,000 to ₹10,00,000 a year. That class now comprises about 5 crore people, roughly 5 per cent of the population. By 2025 a continuing rise in personal incomes will spur a tenfold increase, expanding the middle class to about 58.3 crore people, or 41 per cent of the population. In twenty years the shape of the income pyramid will have become almost unrecognizable.
- The Indian middle class has already begun to evolve and by 2025 it will dominate the cities. By then about three-quarters of India's urbanites will be part of the middle class, compared with just over one-tenth today. The expansion will come in two phases, with the lower middle class peaking around 2020, just as the growth of the upper middle class accelerates. About 40 crore Indian city dwellers—about 10 crore people more than the current population of the United States—will belong to households with a comfortable standard of living. For many retail marketing companies, the sheer scale of the new urban Indian middle class will ensure that they pay significant attention to it.

CHAPTER 2  PROFILING MARKETS AND CUSTOMERS

Your most unhappy customers are your greatest source of learning. — BILL GATES

The Backdrop

The current macroeconomic environment in India is characterized by consolidation of economic growth after a sharp rebound, with a softening inflation trajectory and slower growth in money supply than RBI's indicative trajectory. GDP growth forecast was revised up to 8.5 per cent for financial year 2011 from 8 per cent in August 2010 and inflatiron projection for March 2011 to 60 per cent.

The Indian industry seems to have responded well to the fiscal and monetary measures initiated by the government. There are areas of the economy where the influence of government—or even the domestic consumers—is weak. For instance, exports saw negative growth in October 2009 and have not recovered yet, an indication that India's exports have been shrinking since October 2008. This is a reflection of a global slowdown in the export markets of India. Agriculture—still making up about one-fifth of the economy—also registered a negative growth in 2009–10. It is now understood that industrial revival is underway. The question is how to sustain it.

This Chapter Will

- *Describe the ways and means of understanding the market and customers during global financial meltdown.*
- *Explain the salient features of business-to-business (B2B) and business-to-consumer (B2C) markets.*
- *Describe the models of consumer behaviour, along with factors influencing consumer behaviour and illustrate how to use research to get into the consumer's mind.*
- *Explain the consumer adoption process, types of buyers and building relationships.*
- *Explain marketing strategy development.*
- *Develop a discussion agenda for marketers for the period 2010–15.*

2.1 Understanding the Market and Managing Recovery

People often confuse 'market' with 'marketing', using the terms interchangeably without understanding its implications. Economists describe market as a collection of buyers and sellers who transact over a particular product or product class. Marketers use the term 'market' to cover various groups of customers. They view sellers as constituting the industry and buyers as constituting the market. They talk about need markets, product markets, demographic markets, and geographic markets.

> Mohan Sawhney of Kellogg School of Management has proposed the concept of 'metamarkets' to describe a cluster of complementary products and services that are closely related in the minds of consumers but are spread across a diverse set of industries. An example is the automobile industry that consists of physical locations (car dealers) and market space locations (Internet locations) that consumers use in deciding what car to purchase.

The marketplace is physical; the marketspace is digital.

The marketplace is physical; the marketspace is digital. Marketing, on the other hand, is an all-embracing function that links business with customer needs and wants in order to get the right product to the right place at the right time.

However, no marketing is possible without an understanding of the market and the consumers' buying process. We will thus start by analysing the impact of slowdown on corporate India.

MARKETING IN ACTION — **HIGHLIGHTS OF THE ECONOMIC OUTLOOK 2010–11**

Dr. C. Rangarajan, Chairman, Economic Advisory Council to the Prime Minister released the document 'Economic Outlook 2010–11' at a Press Conference in New Delhi on 23 July 2010. The following are the highlights of the document:

1. Economy to grow at 8.5 per cent in 2010–11 and 9 per cent in 2011–12.
   - Agriculture grew at 0.2 per cent in 2009–10. Projected to grow at 4.5 per cent in 2010–11 and 4 per cent in 2011–12.
   - Industry grew at 9.3 per cent in 2009–10. Projected to grow at 9.7 per cent in 2010–11 and 10.3 per cent in 2011–12.
   - Services grew at 8.5 per cent in 2009–10. Projected to grow at 8.9 per cent in 2010–11 and 9.8 per cent in 2011–12.
2. Slow recovery in global economic and financial situation.
3. Rising domestic savings and investment to be chief engines of growth.
   - Investment rate is expected to be 37 per cent in 2010–11 and 38.4 per cent in 2011–12.
   - Domestic savings rate is expected to be over 34 per cent in 2010–11 and close to 36 per cent in 2011–12.
4. Current Account deficit estimated at 2.7 per cent of GDP in 2010–11 and 2.9 per cent of GDP in 2011–12.
   - Merchandise trade deficit projected to be $137.8 billion or 9 per cent of the GDP in 2010–11 and $160 billion or 9.3 per cent of GDP in 2011–12.
   - Invisibles trade surplus projected to be $96 billion or 6.3 per cent of the GDP in 2010–11 and $109.7 billion or 6.4 per cent in 2011–12.
5. Capital Flows can be readily absorbed by financing needs of the high growth of the Indian economy.
   - Against the level of $53.6 billion in 2009–10, the capital inflows projected to be $73 billion for 2010–11 and $91 billion for 2011–12.
   - Accretion to reserves was $13.4 billion in 2009–10. Projected to be $30.9 billion in 2010–11 and $39.8 billion in 2011–12.
6. Inflation rate projected at 6.5 per cent by March 2011 due to expected normal monsoon combined with the base effect.
   - The provisional headline inflation was above 10 per cent in June 2010.
   - Controlling high inflation rate is essential for sustainable growth in medium term.
   - Available food stocks must be released to have a dampening effect on prices.
7. Monetary Policy to complete the process of exit and operate with bias toward tightening.
   - Credit off take picked up. Strong growth rate in the first quarter of 2010–11.
   - Fund flow from capital market to commercial

sector quite strong. Bond issuance growth relatively higher than issuance of equity.
- Liquidity conditions are taut enough for monetary policy signals to be appropriately transmitted to the financial sector. A bias toward tightening is necessary.
- Exchange rate variations will remain within acceptable range.

8. Exit from the expansionary fiscal policy not only feasible but also necessary.
   - High buoyancy in direct and indirect tax collections. Telecom auctions and decontrol of the petroleum products prices to provide additional cushion.
   - Fiscal deficit outturn may be lower than the budgeted consolidated fiscal deficit of 8.4 per cent of GDP for 2010–11.
   - Revenue Deficit as a ratio of GDP expected to decline from 6.3 per cent in 2009–10 to 4.6 per cent in 2010–11.
   - Operationalization of Goods and Services Tax (GST) should be a priority.
   - Budgeted level of Fiscal Deficit and Revenue Deficit still beyond comfort zone.
   - Need to rationalize the food and fertilizer subsidies.
9. To sustain a growth rate of 9 per cent, focus is required on:
   - Containing inflation.
   - Improving farm productivity.
   - Closing the large physical infrastructure deficit, especially in the power sector.

Source: Business World, January 2010.

2.1.1 Indian Economy on Recovery Path?

Leading economic indicators like Nomura's Composite Leading Index (CLI), UBS' Lead Economic Indicator (LEI) and ABN Amro's Purchasing Managers' Index (PMI) indicate a pick-up in growth in the Indian economy soon.

Several leading economic indicators like Nomura's Composite Leading Index (CLI), UBS' Lead Economic Indicator (LEI) and ABN Amro's Purchasing Managers' Index (PMI) indicate a pick-up in growth in the Indian economy soon. These indicators, based on still-strong investment, an upward trend in hiring, improved freight movement at major ports and encouraging data from a number of key manufacturing segments, suggest that the downturn has bottomed out and that the economy is set to regain its vigour. Centre for Monitoring Indian Economy's (CMIE) capex database which tracks investment by companies, shows no significant slowdown in investment activity. The strong performance of sectors like auto, cement, steel and capital goods, along with improved port traffic corroborates the strong turnaround thesis suggested by the above-mentioned lead indicators.

Following three successive months of climb, UBS' LEI index for India in April 2009 stood at 2.10, after hitting a low of –2.08 in December 2008. LEI is a composite indicator of many variables, including government bond yields, M1 money supply, currency risk premium, foreign exchange reserves and stock market gains. UBS' economist Philip Wyatt expects the recovery in India to sustain because of low excess capacity, as well as low private sector indebtedness and non-performing loans. To quote: 'With this significant rebound in LEI, we are more confident of a turning point in industrial cycle by June 2009.' The April-June 2009 quarter witnessed an increase of 6.1 per cent in GDP over the previous year compared to 5.8 per cent the previous quarter. This indicates that the worst part of the economic crisis has passed.

Nomura's CLI, used to identify turning points in the growth rate cycle, rose in the first quarter of 2009 after four consecutive quarterly declines. Since the CLI indicates a turnaround in non-agricultural GDP growth rate with a two-quarter lead time, the pick-up in the first quarter of 2009 suggests a recovery in economic activity from June onwards.

ABN Amro's PMI—an indicator of manufacturing activity in the country based on a survey of 500 companies—improved from a low of 44 in December 2008 to 49.5 in March 2009. Though a reading below 50 indicates contraction; the fact that the PMI recovered to nearly 50 suggested that the contraction phase is over and manufacturing is now about to enter an expansion stage. The suggestion is that inventories have reduced, necessitating stepped up manufacturing activity. The automobiles sector proves the prediction right. Car sales in India have grown from 1,15,334 in December 2008 to 1,66,837 in March 2009. Two-wheeler sales were 4,61,302 in December 2008, and reached 6,54,017 in March 2009.

ABN Amro's PMI—an indicator of manufacturing activity in the country based on a survey of 500 companies—improved from a low of 44 in December 2008 to 49.5 in March 2009.

ECONOMY WATCH

IMPROVED CORPORATE RESULTS CHEERED FMCG FIRMS IN 2009

FMCG companies registered a modest growth in the July-September 2009 quarter on the back of rising consumer demand, which is expected to considerably reduce the impact of a disappointing monsoon on sales. Traditionally, summer and winter months make up 30-40 per cent of any FMCG company's overall sales. For instance, diversified conglomerate ITC posted a 26 per cent rise in net profit in the September 2009 quarter, helped by a strong performance in all its business operations, except hotels. Its FMCG (cigarettes and others) business reported a 14 per cent growth in revenue.

Godrej Consumer Products and Marico also reported robust earnings and sales in the July-September 2009 quarter based on higher volumes and lower raw material costs. A revival in the hair colours segment and acquisition of 49 per cent stake in Godrej Sara Lee gave Godrej Consumer Products a formidable FMCG portfolio to sustain growth. Godrej makes and sells several brands of soaps, hair care products and toiletries, but its flagship brands are Cinthol, and Godrej Expert Hair Dye. The price of palm oil, Godrej Consumer's primary raw material, had fallen sharply in the second half of 2008 and continued to fall. As a result, Godrej Consumer Products expanded its gross margins by 660 basis points after the second quarter of financial year 2009–10.

Marico's revenues increased due to volume growth in its flagship brands, Parachute hair oil and Saffola edible oil, mainly on account of price cuts and promotional offers. Prices of copra and safflower, the key inputs for Marico, came down by around 20 per cent in 2009.

Strong pricing power in the case of Parachute and continued traction in Saffola volumes are likely to boost volume growth. Analysts in fact expected strong double-digit sales growth in Marico's hair oil portfolio in 2009–10. Festive months are not so significant for FMCG companies as are summers and winters. For most FMCG companies, the bad monsoon in 2009 was a major concern but until November 2009 it had not impacted sales.

Analysts say rural India is giving a lot of reason to cheer even as urban consumers rationalize spending. While FMCG companies are seeing a volume growth of just 6-7 per cent in the metros, their growth in rural markets was over 20 per cent in 2009. Rural income levels are on the rise, according to a recent study by the Rural Marketing Association of India, driven largely by four years of continuous growth in agriculture. The government's rural development initiatives have further empowered consumers there, fuelling a fresh demand for FMCG products. Godrej Consumer, for instance, is focusing strongly on rural sales, which made up around 38 per cent of its turnover in 2009. The company intends to take this figure up to 50 per cent by 2009–10. Through its Project Dharti it covers close to 17,000 villages which will be extended to cover another 35,000 villages soon. This also means that the number of sub-stockists in rural areas would be more than doubled from the present 4,000, creating more employment opportunities.

During 2009, most FMCG companies had resorted to judicious price hikes to protect dwindling margins. However, as the economic slowdown takes its toll on consumer spending, even as inflation declines, FMCG companies are tweaking their pricing strategy to retain consumers and to safeguard their volume growth. Most commodity prices softened during the second half of 2009, which aided margin expansion for FMCG companies in year-on-year terms during the July-September 2009 quarter. Agri-commodity prices, particularly of those sourced domestically, are expected to remain firm. While wheat, barley, copra and safflower prices continue to remain benign, other commodities like sugar, tea, coffee and milk are expected to rise further in 2010, largely due to the poor monsoon.

Source: The Economic Times, December 2009.

CMIE's capex database of new and ongoing investments in India indicates that both the rate of new investment project announcements and the pace at which projects are being commissioned remain robust.

CMIE's capex database of new and ongoing investments in India indicates that both the rate of new investment project announcements and the pace at which projects are being commissioned continue to remain robust. The analysis suggests that the downward revision of projected growth rate for the fiscal year 2010 by the World Bank and the IMF are baseless. According to the database, the momentum in commissioning new projects will continue into the fiscal 2010. Over a 1,000 projects involving a total investment of ₹4,90,000 crore are on schedule and will be commissioned in 2010–11. Projects worth a record ₹7,90,000 crore have been announced in the quarter ended March 2010 itself, suggesting that corporates have not pared investments to the extent expected. Import data shows that even as overall imports have been slowing down, project import growth has remained robust.

Portfolio investment inflows have been fickle, but direct investment inflows have remained strong, prompting the official expectation that FDI inflows in 2010 would better the realized inflow of $3.30 billion in the calendar year 2008. This should put to rest fears of a slowdown 'as a result of weaker investment', as suggested by the IMF. It should also allay concerns over OECD's (Organization for Economic Cooperation and Development)

MARKETING IN ACTION

AUTO FIRMS ANTICIPATE SHARP RISE IN PROFIT

Domestic passenger car sales registered a healthy 34 per cent jump in October 2009 on continuing festive demand, while sale of commercial vehicles (CVs) soared 52 per cent, signalling that economic recovery was gaining ground. According to the Society of Indian Automobile Manufacturers (SIAM), domestic passenger car sales stood at 1,32,615 units in October 2009, the seventh consecutive month of growth compared with 99,052 units in October 2008. Motorcycle sales rose by 14.22 per cent from 5,35,642 units in October 2008 to 6,11,828 units in October 2009.

Carrying forward the upward march that began in July 2008, after an 11-month slump, sale of commercial vehicles in the country registered a robust 51.9 per cent growth in October 2009 at 42,562 units against 28,019 units in the previous year. In the passenger car segment, market leader Maruti Suzuki India's sales increased by 21.5 per cent to 63,365 units from 52,153 units in October 2008. Ritz, Swift, DZIRE, A-Star and Zen Estilo models accounted for the bulk of sales, while the demand for the M800, continued to slide down 5 per cent at 3,124 units in the reporting month. The country's second-largest car maker Hyundai Motor India registered 41.5 per cent growth at 28,301 units. Demand for models like Santro, i10 and i20 pushed overall sales of the company. Mahindra & Mahindra too witnessed a growth in demand for the Xylo, Scorpio and Bolero models, with its overall sales climbing 32 per cent in October 2009 to 18,410 units against 13,935 units in the same month in 2008. Tata Motors' sales went up to 17,557 units from 14,100 units in October 2008, a jump of 24.52 per cent; the Nano and Indica Vista sales playing a key role in the growth.

Premium Japanese car maker Honda Siel Cars India (HSCI) also posted a healthy growth in October 2009, selling 6,909 units, a growth of 347 per cent over 1,546 units sold in the same month in 2008. The new model of Honda City witnessed the highest demand in the period under study. Ford India's sales rose by an incredible 98 per cent in October 2009 to 3,458 units against 1,744 units during October 2008. This made October one of the best-selling months, with Ford India recording its highest sales in the past 25 months.

In the motorcycle segment, market leader Hero Honda's sales increased by 1.12 per cent to 3,32,476 units in October 2009 compared with 3,28,788 units in October 2008. Chennai-based TVS Motor also registered a growth of 2.18 per cent, reaching 45,220 units in October 2009 against 44,257 units in the same month in 2008. Honda Motorcycle & Scooter India (HMSI), however, saw its bike sales decline by 46.56 per cent to 17,932 units from 33,558 units in October 2008. This was largely due to labour issues hitting the company in August 2009.

The overall two-wheeler sales in October 2009 surged by 10.61 per cent to 7,50,229 units from 6,78,245 units in the same period in 2008. Total sales of vehicles across all categories increased by 15.62 per cent to 10,00,760 units in October 2009, as against 8,65,566 units in October 2008.

Source: Business Standard, December 2009.

warning of downside risk to India's growth trajectory. In his interim report on economic growth, India's chief statistician Pronab Sen exuded optimism: 'Keeping in mind the fact that a majority of the corporates have only deferred their investment plans and have not scrapped them altogether. If the global scenario improves, the growth rate in India will pick up at a fast pace.'

The second quarter of 2009 promised better prospects for the Indian manufacturing sector with six out of twelve sectors poised to witness positive growth. These six sectors are textiles, metal and products, machinery, cement, FMCG and miscellaneous industries. The Market Purchasing Managers' Index (PMI) for manufacturing in India stood at 55.3 in June 2009, which indicates expansion in this sector. The prices of manufactured items, which were firming up the last eight weeks since August 2009, after slipping continuously from August 2008 onwards, also hints at a revival in demand.

Let us look at the bases on which such a positive outlook is being forecast.

A. Core Sector Rebounds to Six-month High

The core sector growth is back on track. The index for the six core industries—crude oil, petroleum refinery products, coal, electricity, cement and finished carbon steel—turned in a growth of 2.9 per cent in March 2009 over March 2008. This has been the highest growth rate since September 2008, higher than the average of 2.7 per cent for 2008–9 as a whole. The biggest surprise in the core sector was electricity generation, which touched a 13-month high in March 2009.

The index for the six core industries—crude oil, petroleum refinery products, coal, electricity, cement and finished carbon steel—registered a growth of 2.9 per cent in March 2009 over March 2008.

Giving further strength to the government's assessment that the economy is beginning to respond to the booster shots administered by it, cement production surged 10.1 per cent in March 2009 while coal production grew by 5.2 per cent and showed a cumulative growth of 8.1 per cent for the fiscal 2009. Annual growth in finished carbon steel production contracted 2.6 per cent in March 2009, raising concerns.

ECONOMY WATCH — CAR BUYERS FACE LONGER WAITING PERIODS

The old days of waiting for cars returned in December 2009 with manufacturers reporting an unexpected surge in post-Diwali sales, forcing customers to wait a month to as much as four months for almost all models. Maruti Suzuki's newly launched hatchback Ritz reported a waiting period of over two months, while buyers had to wait for up to four months for the upper range of Honda City models. The average waiting period for the car is six to eight weeks. M&M's Xylo and Bolero (MUVs) and Scorpio (a sports utility vehicle) had average waiting periods of two to three weeks. Similarly, the Korean car brand Hyundai Motors too reported a sustained demand boom for its flagship models such as the i10 and i20 after Diwali. The boom in car sales was a result of the pent-up demand in the earlier quarters, attractive interest rates on vehicle loans offered by banks, discounts and other financial benefits offered by the manufacturers as well as a general fear of a rise in both automobile prices and lending rates in the coming months in 2009–10.

Dealers say the waiting period for diesel cars is 'going through the roof'. The Swift DZire diesel model has a waiting period of over three months. The same is true for the diesel models of the Swift and Ritz.

Better profits in 2009

Top automobile makers Tata Motors, Maruti Suzuki, M&M, Hero Honda, Bajaj Auto, Ashok Leyland and TVS Motors together expected around a sixfold rise in net profit (536 per cent year-on-year) in the third quarter ending December 2009. This was on the back of a low base as these companies had suffered a severe setback in the December 2008 quarter due to the global liquidity crunch and rise in interest costs. In the third quarter of

2008, M&M had reported a net profit of ₹1 crore while Tata Motors had recorded a net loss of ₹263 crore.

Historically, automobile companies generate around 26 per cent sales and 28 per cent profits in the third quarter. According to experts, the top seven auto makers were expected to show a robust 55 per cent rise in net sales in 2009. Except for Hero Honda, the net profit of the remaining six companies was expected to rise over 100 per cent each. However, the third quarter performance may not have been as good as that of the second quarter. Sales, expected to rise around 55 per cent over the December 2008 quarter, would have been lower by around 1 per cent over the sequential quarter.

However, the expected year-on-year growth in net profit (536 per cent) will be 12 per cent lower than the September 2009 quarter figure. Already, month-on-month sales of top auto makers are down 7.5 per cent (October 2009), mostly due to a 11.5 per cent decline in Hero Honda's month-on-month sales. Only cars, tractors and light commercial vehicles have posted a rise in month-on-month sales.

In the second quarter ended September 2009, the performance of automobile companies was driven by volumes and higher net realization due to lower excise duty. The recent increase in commodity prices could lead to some squeeze on margins. The things to watch out for are movement of commodity prices and roll-back of the excise duty cut. The benefits of lower commodity prices year-on-year and cost efficiencies had boosted companies' second quarter margins in 2009. Profit margins from core operations rose 728 basis points, largely due to savings in production costs and decline in prices of key raw materials. The cost of production as a percentage of sales declined from 93.9 per cent in 2008 to 86.64 per cent in the second quarter ended September 2009. Similarly, the cost of raw materials to sales declined from 75.06 per cent to 69.77 per cent.

Ashok Leyland expected a 59 per cent rise in net sales and a 363 per cent rise in net profit in the third quarter of 2009. The company anticipated sales to grow 65 per cent due to the low base effect. The company's Uttaranchal plant was to be operational in the fourth quarter and it expected an excise duty benefit of ₹60,000 per vehicle, which is 6 per cent of the average cost of the vehicle, says an auto analyst at Edelweiss Research.

Bajaj Auto expected to repeat its second quarter profit growth in the third quarter of 2009 on the back of a robust growth in volumes. The company hopes for an increase in input costs in the coming quarters, but increase in volumes from recent launches could partially offset this. The company expected to export 8,00,000 units.

Hero Honda expected to repeat its profit performance in the third quarter. However, increasing competition in the 100cc segment would be a threat to volumes. Maruti Suzuki's profit is likely rise sharply given the strong volume growth. The company sees good demand in the domestic market and is aiming to export 1,30,000 units by increasing sales outside Europe. The operating margin, however, is expected to be under pressure due to higher commodity prices and strengthening of the yen.

Tata Motors expects pressure from commodity and component prices. The company has effected a 2.5 per cent rise in commercial vehicle prices. M&M is expected to show a net profit of ₹612 crore, lower than the ₹703 crore earned in the second quarter of 2008. In the second quarter, higher operating margins were aided by lower input costs and lower exchange rate losses. Going ahead, high margins are not sustainable as input costs have started to rise. The management was treading warily on the outlook for the tractor business in the second half of 2009–10 due to drought.

Sources: *Business Standard*, 15 November 2009 and *The Economic Times*, May 2009.

B. Corporate India Showing Improved Performance

If the first and second quarter results of 2009 are any indication, the Indian corporate sector seems to be surviving the downturn. An analysis of the fourth quarter results of 2009 of 345 companies with a minimum market capitalization of ₹100 crore shows that net profits have not come down. The March-May 2009 quarter results show that companies have been able to arrest declining profits in comparison to the December quarter. Of the said companies, only 42 posted net losses during the fourth quarter of 2009.

The net profits were marginally negative at 0.17 per cent for the said companies compared to the quarter ending March 2008, while their December 2008 quarter net fell by around 10 per cent compared to the quarter ending December 2007. The net profits for the said companies have grown by around 15 per cent in the March 2009 quarter from the corresponding quarter in 2008. While the December 2008 quarter saw a dip in the net profits by almost 10 per cent on a quarter-on-quarter basis, it should be remembered that the companies have posted such results in the face of shrinking operating margins. The average operating margin has come down to 9 per cent in the fourth quarter of 2009 from 25 per cent in the corresponding quarter in 2008.

The results are clear signals of the economy looking upwards. Organizations such as Bank of Baroda, Reliance Communications, HDFC Bank, 3i Infotech, Axis Bank, Glaxo, Infosys Technologies and Hero Honda have increased their net profits by 30 per cent in the fourth quarter of 2009 as compared to 2008. Analysts point out that the positive results are mainly because the companies have rationalized their costs. For Bank of Baroda it has been a particularly spectacular quarter. The bank has posted a net profit growth of 172 per cent, amounting to ₹752 crore. Overall income growth and better cost control are to be given credit for Bank of Baroda's high profits. While the treasury income of the bank has increased by 131 per cent to ₹387 crore against ₹168 crore in the same quarter in 2008, profits from the sale of investments have gone up to ₹301 crore from ₹81 crore the previous year. Even the net interest margin has increased to 3.17 per cent from 2.72 per cent in the same period in 2008.

Organizations such as Bank of Baroda, Reliance Communications, HDFC Bank, 3i Infotech, Axis Bank, Glaxo, Infosys Technologies and Hero Honda have increased their net profits by 30 per cent in the fourth quarter of 2009 compared to 2008.

The Reliance Communications story is not different. The company's net profits have gone up by 122 per cent to ₹1,139 crore, bolstered by non-operational income to the tune of ₹894 crore in the fourth quarter of 2009 which included ₹157 crore of extraordinary income. However, if the consolidated figure of all its subsidiary companies are taken into account then the Q4 net was down 3 per cent to ₹1,454 crore. Infosys has been one of the few IT companies to put up an improved show. It has posted a net profit growth of more than 30 per cent, amounting to ₹1,569 crore.

According to Anup Bagchi, executive director of ICICI Securities, the results of these companies have on the whole been satisfactory and beyond the industry's expectations. A stable government undoubtedly promises further growth during the years 2009–11. The ripple effect of decrease in consumer demand has a significant impact on the B2B market. As consumption decreases, the spend of businesses decrease as well. A positive outlook with regard to all industries will have a positive effect on the B2B market.

2.2 Business-to-Business (B2B) Market

The business market consists of all organizations that acquire goods and services to further produce products or services to be sold, rented, or supplied to others. Demand in the business market is derived from demand in the consumer market and fluctuates with the business cycle. Nonetheless, the total demand for most business goods and services is generally price inelastic.

2.2.1 Business Market *v.* Consumer Market

Business markets have several characteristics that contrast sharply with those of consumer markets, such as close supplier-customer relationships; professional purchasing; several buying influences; multiple sales calls; derived and inelastic demand; geographically concentrated buyers and direct purchasing.

Business markets have characteristics that contrast sharply with those of consumer markets, such as a close supplier-customer relationship, professional purchasing, several buying influences, multiple sales calls, derived and inelastic demand, geographically concentrated buyers and direct purchases.

Business marketers need to be aware of the role of professional purchasers and their influencers, the need for multiple sales calls, and the importance of direct purchasing, reciprocity and leasing.

2.2.2 Buying Situations

The business buyer needs to take many decisions when making a purchase. The number of decisions depends on the buying situation—the complexity of the problem being solved, newness of the buying requirement, the number of people involved, and the time required.

Based on these, there are three types of buying situations: straight rebuy, modified rebuy, and new task.

Straight Rebuy: A purchase in which a customer buys the same goods in the same quantity on the same terms from the same supplier as the first buy.

Modified Rebuy: A buying situation in which an individual or organization buys goods that have been purchased previously but changes either the supplier or some other element of the previous order.

New Task: An organizational buying situation in which the organization has had no previous experience with the purchase of product of the kind required.

Purchasing agents are influential in straight rebuy and modified rebuy situations, where engineering personnel usually influence selection of product components and purchasing agents dominate in selecting suppliers.

TERMS TO KNOW

Here are a few business marketing terms that you should be familiar with:

Organizational buying is the decision-making process by which formal organizations establish the need for purchased products and services and identify, evaluate, and choose among alternative brands and suppliers.

The *buying centre* is the decision-making unit of a buying organization. It consists of initiators, users, influencers, deciders, approvers, buyers, and gatekeepers, who differ in their interests, authority, status, and persuasiveness. To influence these parties, marketers must be aware of the environmental, organizational, interpersonal, and individual factors.

Systems selling is a key industrial marketing strategy in bidding for large-scale industrial projects. Competition for these projects is fierce. The primary areas of competition include price, quality and reliability.

Systems buying is when a purchaser prefers to buy the total solution to a problem from one seller. This practice originated with the government.

The *institutional market* consists of schools, hospitals, nursing homes, prisons, and other institutions that provide goods and services to people in their care. Buyers for governmental organizations usually require to do a great deal of paperwork. They also favour open bidding and domestic companies.

Suppliers must be prepared to adapt their products and offers to the special needs and procedures found in institutional and government markets.

2.2.3 Business Marketers' Task

To effectively target their efforts, business marketers have to figure out:

- Who are the major decision participants?
- What decisions do they influence?
- What is their level of influence?
- What evaluation criteria do they use?

Small sellers concentrate on reaching the key buying influencers. Large sellers on the other hand, go for multilevel, in-depth selling to reach as many participants as possible. Business marketers must periodically review their assumptions about buying centre participants.

In defining target segments, different types of business customers can be identified, with corresponding marketing implications. Every organization has specific purchasing objectives, policies, procedures, organizational structures, and systems. Business buyers seek to obtain the highest benefit package in relation to the market offering's costs. A business buyer's incentive to purchase will be greater in proportion to the ratio of perceived benefits to costs. A marketer's task is to construct a profitable offering that delivers superior customer value to the target buyers.

Small sellers concentrate on reaching the key buying influencers. Large sellers go for multilevel, in-depth selling to reach as many participants as possible.

Marketers need to understand how business-purchasing departments work. Peter Kraljic, Director Emeritus, McKinsey, distinguished four product-related purchasing processes:

(i) Routine products—low value and cost and little risk
(ii) Leverage products—high value and cost but little risk
(iii) Strategic products—high value and cost and high risk
(iv) Bottleneck products—low value and cost but some risk.

Websites are organized around e-hubs: vertical hubs centered on industries and functional hubs. The buying decision process, mode of purchase and the type of product being purchased play an important role in the marketing initiatives taken by a company. With technology becoming an integral part of marketing, initiatives in technological means are of importance too.

2.2.4 Technological Initiatives in B2B Marketing

Technology has always been an important factor in determining the type of business being carried out. With advances in information technology, the way people do business has also changed to a great extent. The Internet has emerged as one of the busiest spaces which business people use to conduct their business activities. Companies use their websites for both purchasing and selling activities. An electronic marketplace allows buyers, sellers, independent third parties, and multi-firm consortiums to exchange information about prices and product offerings. It has been suggested that electronic markets will create benefits for both buyers and suppliers and it gives suppliers a greater reach and buyers the opportunity to obtain information about all available products.

An electronic marketplace allows buyers, sellers, independent third parties, and multi-firm consortiums to exchange information about prices and product offerings.

E-business and E-commerce

The concept of e-business emerged as a result of developments in Internet technology. The Internet is the largest network which companies use to carry out their activities more advantageously. E-business means the use of electronic means and platforms to conduct a company's business.

E-commerce is more specific than e-business. In addition to providing e-business services, e-commerce helps in making business transactions on the Internet more secure. With the development of e-commerce, the concept of e-marketing has also developed. This is a process by which companies inform potential and existing buyers about the services and products they offer globally.

E-commerce is more specific than e-business. In addition to providing e-business services, e-commerce helps make business transactions on the Internet more secure.

E-marketing

An electronic market is an inter-organizational information system through which multiple buyers and sellers interact to accomplish one or more of market-making activities such as identifying potential trading partners, selecting a specific partner and executing a transaction.

Electronic Data Interchange (EDI)

EDI is an inter-organizational system which transmits standard business documents electronically between trading partners. EDI allows firms to fundamentally change the way they do business, thus improving their overall performance and enhancing their competitive advantage.

While EDI provides economic benefits, it may be expensive to implement, especially when an organization does not achieve hardware or software compatibility. Security in particular becomes an issue, as EDI systems do not operate unilaterally. For example, organizations motivated to adopt EDI must either find similarly motivated trading partners or persuade and/or coerce their existing trading partners to adopt EDI. One key barrier to this is the lack of trading partner trust owing to a lack of open communication and information sharing. Scala and McGrath (1993) identified social and organizational issues that impact organizational culture, structure and levels of adoption of EDI. Ford was one of the earliest innovators of EDI network technology. It was adopted to streamline business processes and optimize supply chain management activities. Ford had two EDI systems and many application systems across its five branches, namely parts and accessories, original equipment, non-production, purchasing and Ford credit and finance. During the late 1980s, acceptance testing of EDI business transactions was carried out. Later Telstra developed the TradeLink software in 1988.

2.2.5 Building Relationships and Partnerships in the B2B Market

Business-to-business relations can be defined as commercial business between trading partners. B2B e-markets can be categorized into static/established and dynamic/discovered electronic markets. Enabling buyers to purchase from suppliers through electronic catalogues and auctions, allowing one to many transaction events for procuring or selling goods or services are examples of static/established markets.

Exchange matching supply and demand via real time, bid ask spot markets and e-Hub representing neutral Internet-based intermediaries providing extensive services and integrating into participants' systems are examples of dynamic/discovered markets.

Another categorization of B2B e-markets is dividing them into spot markets, open markets, private markets and information markets. Spot markets are markets where information is collected for each transaction to compare prices. Examples are financial services, raw materials and transportation services. Open markets are shops where you can buy standard commodities such as pens, diskettes and other office equipment. Private markets are markets where a few organizations conduct their purchases by inviting suppliers into the market. Information markets provide information on buyers and suppliers, but the actual transaction takes place outside these markets.

Four kinds of dynamic e-market models are emerging: procurement networks, service networks, supply networks and delivery networks. The expected benefits from electronic procurement markets include reduced transaction costs, negotiation of better agreements with suppliers, better utilization of frame agreements, and access to more suppliers. It has been suggested that companies expecting reduced transaction costs will be the most active users of electronic marketplaces. And reduced transaction costs will be of importance mainly to organizations with high procurement volumes.

Four kinds of dynamic e-market models are emerging: procurement networks, service networks, supply networks and delivery networks. The expected benefits from these markets include reduced transaction costs, negotiation of better agreements with suppliers, better utilization of frame agreements, and access to more suppliers.

To improve effectiveness and efficiency, business suppliers and customers constantly explore different ways to manage their relationships. Building trust between parties is often seen as an essential prerequisite for healthy, long-term relationships.

The relationship between advertising agencies and clients illustrates findings such as:

(a) In the relationship formation stage, one partner experiences substantial market growth.
(b) Information asymmetry between partners is such that a partnership would generate more profits than if the partner attempted to invade the other firm's area.
(c) At least one partner has high barriers to entry that would prevent the other partner from entering the business.
(d) Dependence asymmetry exists such that one partner is more able to control or influence the other's conduct.
(e) One partner benefits from economies of scale related to the relationship.

Vertical coordination can facilitate stronger customer-seller ties but it can, at the same time, increase the risk to the customer's and supplier's specific investments. Specific investments are expenditures tailored to a particular company and value chain partner.

Vertical coordination can facilitate stronger customer-seller ties but it can, at the same time, increase the risk to the customer's and supplier's specific investments.

They help firms increase profits and achieve positioning. They also entail considerable risk to both the customer and supplier. Specific investments are partially sunk. They lock-in the firms that make investments to a particular relationship. Sensitive cost and process information may also need to be exchanged. A buyer may be vulnerable to hold-up because of switching costs. A supplier may be more vulnerable to future hold-up contracts because of dedicated assets and/or expropriation of technology/knowledge. When buyers cannot easily monitor supplier performance, the supplier might shirk or cheat and not deliver the expected value. Opportunism can be thought of as 'some form of cheating or undersupply relative to an implicit or explicit contract'. Opportunism is a concern because firms must devote resources to control and monitor that otherwise could be allocated for more productive purposes.

2.3 Business-to-Consumer (B2C) Market

Organizational markets differ from consumer markets in a number of ways. The time spent in the purchase process by an individual customer is far less compared to the time taken for the purchase process in organizations. Organizational buyers are fewer compared to individual buyers, so it becomes easier for marketers to offer specialized marketing services to the former. Consumer markets are mostly segmented on the basis of geographic, demographic and psychographic factors. Industrial or organizational markets are usually segmented on the basis of factors such as operating variables, purchasing approaches, situational factors and personal characteristics.

The aim of marketing is to meet and satisfy the target customers' needs and wants better than competitors. Consumer behaviour is the study of how individuals, groups, and organizations select, buy, use, and dispose of goods, services, ideas, or experiences to satisfy their needs and wants. Gaining in-depth consumer understanding helps ensure that the right products are marketed to the right consumers in the right way.

ECONOMY WATCH — INDIA AND CHINA: TWO GROWTH MODELS

When the going gets tough the tough get going. A global recession is a good time to put this cliché to test, particularly in the context of the ability of economies such as China and India to ride out the impact of the recession and continue with policies that boost GDP growth.

Over the past few years, comparisons between the Chinese model of economic growth and the Indian model have been much debated in the media and economic forums. But given the current global economic scenario, it is pertinent to do a reality check and compare the prospects and challenges that these two economies face.

China which has been growing 10 per cent annually since 2003 has reached a speed bump. But the Chinese government is determined to sustain economic growth at a fairly rapid pace. With an economic stimulus package running to $585 billion, GDP growth rate was saintented at 8 per cent in 2009. As exports have nosedived the Chinese authorities have started focusing on boosting domestic demand by creating jobs, lowering distribution costs and improving product quality to keep the economy growing.

According to *The Economist*, since February 2009, China's 200 million rural households have become eligible for a government-financed discount on consumer goods. They will also be provided with subsidized cars in the near future.

Significantly, China's consumption growth is being fuelled by the younger generation of consumers that has cultivated Western patterns of consumption in the post-reforms age and has seen more prosperity than any other generation of the country. These consumers are big spenders on cosmetics, jewellery, fashion, transportation and communication. The UN estimates that the number of post-reform adults is expected to rise by 61 per cent during the period 2005–15, from 314 million to over 500 million. By 2015, these youngsters will form about 36 per cent of China's total population.

Unlike China, where exports and manufacturing have been the main engines of economic growth, India's growth has been stimulated by the rise of an educated middle class that has prospered in the services sector. The share of the services sector in the GDP has increased to 58 per cent and it is often said that the performance of this sector has become independent of the performance of other sectors of the economy. This argument will be put to the test during the slowdown in 2009–11.

Like China, India too has seen its middle class expand and boost economic growth. As the disposable income of this class grew, so did its propensity to spend on houses, financial services, holidays and consumer durables, leading to a cumulative growth of various sectors of the economy. Even in the last quarter of 2008, consumer spending and retail sales in China and India did not witness a significant decline.

Much of the prosperity in India has been starkly visible in the top 20 cities of the country. A look at the earnings structure across India's top 20 cities reveals that the average graduate earns ₹1.80 lakh per year compared to just ₹91,000 in rural areas. When translated into spending patterns, nearly 68 per cent of households in the top 20 cities have colour televisions compared to 47 per cent in other cities and 17 per cent in rural areas. Clearly then, if India expects its economy to grow at 7 per cent per annum, the government has to spend much more on infrastructure to bring the rest of India at par with the top 20 cities. India could take a leaf out of China's book: the Chinese government allocated over $480 billion to upgrade transportation infrastructure in the 2006–10 period.

On the flipside, among other challenges, India is a victim of low labour productivity and a growing job market. With nearly 14 million people being added to the labour market every year, creating jobs is the need of the hour. Labour productivity, defined as output per worker, according to the Asian Development Bank (ADB), declined from an average of 5.8 per cent in the financial year 1993 to 3.6 per cent from the financial year 1999 through 2004. Moreover, hardly any attention is being paid to the fact that rural India currently accounts for nearly 36 per cent of the organized manufacturing units, 38 per cent of its employees, 43 per cent of output and 41 per cent of net value added. Vocational training is a much-neglected area that has got little or no attention from the government or the private sector. Only 10 per cent of the educated young people in India are equipped with vocational skills.

India seeks to increase the amount of public investment in agriculture. But there are different opinions within the upper echelons of the government. Many are talking of the necessity of a second Green Revolution. However, they should not forget that the impact of the Green Revolution was felt in areas (Punjab, Haryana and Uttar Pradesh) which had already been developed by the British. On the other hand, a very different category of area are the eastern plains of Bihar, Orissa, Assam and West Bengal which are blessed with excellent alluvial soil, abundant rain, adequate ground and surface water, but progress is very slow due to several reasons including socio-political and economic factors.

The Indian government has, no doubt, taken some timely steps to aid the rural economy, including the institution of the NREGS that covers 596 rural districts and has benefited almost 3.60 million households so far as it guarantees one member of each family employment for at least 100 days a year. While this is indeed a step in the right direction, it is not enough to address the challenges that India faces.

Rural India still needs enormous amounts of money for research, infrastructure, electricity and roads to bring it at par with the urban areas. Indian agriculture research has lost its vision and focus. Current levels of productivity of most of the institutes comes from hardly 20 per cent of the researchers. Rural India needs able policymakers and administrators, not just an urban middle class but people who understand rural life and can organize the agriculture sector.

The one positive factor, both in China and India, is the growing awareness about the problem. This could be the beginning of change.

Source: The Economic Times, April 2010.

2.4 Consumer Behaviour

Consumer behaviour is the study of how individuals make decisions to spend their available resources (time, money and effort) on consumption-related items.

Buyer behaviour is an important tool in the hands of marketers to forecast the future buying pattern of customers and devise appropriate marketing strategies to create long-term customer relationships. A vital part of the marketing process is to understand why a customer or buyer makes a purchase. Without such an understanding, businesses find it hard to respond to customer needs and wants. Consumer behaviour is the study of how individuals make decisions to spend their available resources (time, money and effort) on consumption-related items. It includes the study of what they buy, why they buy, when they buy, how often do they buy and how often do they use the product. For example, consumer researchers want to know what types of toothpaste consumers buy (gel, regular, etc.); what brand (national, international and generic); why do they buy it (to prevent cavities, to remove stains and to brighten or whiten teeth); where do they buy it (supermarket, drugstore and convenience store); how often do they use it (when they wake up, after each meal, when they go to bed, or any combination thereof); and how often do they buy it (weekly, biweekly or monthly).

2.4.1 Models of Consumer Behaviour

An insight into psyche of the consumer helps us understand the processes that go behind their preference of certain goods and services over others.

MARKETING IN ACTION

NOKIA UNDERSTANDS INDIAN CUSTOMERS BETTER

More than a third of the 700-odd Nokia retail shops across the country are Wi-Fi enabled, allowing customers to surf the internet. These stores, which earlier used to have only one counter for sale of handsets and accessories, now have four zones—one each for music, gaming, email and navigation applications.

The salespersons at each counter will not only help customers choose a suitable handset, but will also assist them in choosing songs from the Nokia music store, download songs onto the customer's handset, if he/she wishes check email services, and choose from different games. These Nokia 'experience' outlets are, in fact, sending out a clear signal—that the $75 billion handset maker is now positioning itself as a services player too. There are many reasons for this key shift in the strategy of the world's largest handset maker with a 40 per cent market share globally (and over 60 per cent in India).

Nokia India's marketing director Vineet Taneja says: 'We have a very large installed base, which is a must for launching a successful services model. We started out by connecting people with calls and SMSs. Now the Internet, mobile and personal computer (desktop and notebook) talk to each other as devices converge. This prompted us to redefine our vision to keep in touch with consumers. Since the services and devices are integrated, we want our consumers to buy a Nokia solution.'

Analysts, of course, have another take. The move into services, they say, comes as Nokia is struggling with falling handset prices and increased competition in the high-end mobile phone market, particularly from the likes of Apple's iPhone and Research In Motion (RIM's) Blackberry. But Taneja insists 'this is an evolution and not a change of vision'. He adds that the journey towards services began around two-three years back with the launch of the N- and E-series phones where consumers were allowed to 'do new things with our devices'.

For instance, in December 2009, Nokia started offering its Global Positioning System (GPS) and navigation services with the Nokia 6110 Navigator bundled with pre-installed maps of eight cities. In April 2009, Nokia announced the availability of its gaming service, 'N-Gage' in India with additional games and an expanded online offering. Around this time, Nokia also unveiled the new addition to its E-series range, Nokia E75, with the Nokia Messaging Service which mobilizes email solutions on its devices.

Nokia has a subscription-driven model where payment is made through operators. 'We will soon introduce a per day and per month billing mechanism too,' says Taneja.

In June 2009, after a successful pilot in Maharashtra, Nokia announced the commercial launch of Nokia Life Tools Service. It has a range of three primary services: agriculture, education and entertainment. The Nokia Life Tools Agriculture Service, for instance, is available for ₹1-₹2 a day.

The Nokia Life Tools Education Service, available throughout India, offers English lessons at three levels: basic, intermediate and advanced. The Nokia Life Tools Entertainment Service includes astrology, news, jokes, cricket and ringtones, offered at existing market prices. All these services are delivered by SMS to ensure that the service works wherever a mobile phone works, without the hassles of additional settings or the need for General Packet Radio Service (GPRS) coverage. 'Having received a good response, we will launch full-fledged Nokia Life Tools Services from October,' says Taneja.

Towards the end of October 2009, Nokia announced the launch of its Music Store service in India. It offers music lovers access to over three million soundtracks across all genres. Nokia has tied up with leading international music labels such as Universal Music Group, Sony Music, EMI, Warner and major independent Indian record labels including T-Series, Yashraj Music, Saregama, BIG Music and Venus. The company has partnered with India's leading music body—Indian Music Industry (IMI), a consortium of over 150 music companies.

Given the low internet and credit-card penetration in the country, Nokia decided to introduce vouchers in its priority outlets for music. Besides this, explains Taneja, Nokia also bundles music with handsets—branded as 'Comes with Music', a one-year offering. Nokia also has free downloads with nearly 3,20,000 applications downloaded globally each month, with India being the most active market for downloads from its 'Try for Free' service, says Taneja.

Most of Nokia's services, except for the Nokia Music Store, are currently branded under the OVI (sub-brand) umbrella. 'All services will gradually be brought under the OVI fold,' says Taneja. OVI, in Finnish, means 'Door'. 'It's the door to your digital world,' Taneja explains. He adds that the 'advertising-based' business model for Nokia will take some time to pick up since it needs more active users (those who have used at least one Nokia service in the last six months in 2010).

Globally, Nokia is launching a financial management and payment service—Nokia Money—which will be rolled out in early 2010. It is promoting this service through its recent acquisition, Obopay, which has a presence in India and the US. And having sold over 20 million 3G-enabled handsets in India, Taneja is optimistic that 'once 3G services are rolled out, data connectivity will only get faster and Nokia services only better'.

Source: Business Standard, 10 January 2010.

Consumer behaviour not only helps companies plan market strategies, but also facilitates the process of new product development to cater to the needs of customers.

Traditionally, Indian consumers have a high degree of family orientation. As a result, values like nurturing and care have been preferred to ambition and achievement. So, brands with identities that support family values and exhibit strong emotions are more likely to be popular with Indian consumers.

India is home to over 1.17 billion people who represent a broad spectrum of cultures, traditions and ideologies. Indians thus belong to different market segments based on characteristics such as demographics, social status and income levels. Traditionally, Indian consumers have a high degree of family orientation. As a result values like nurture and care have been preferred to ambition and achievement. So brands with identities that support family values are more likely to be popular with Indian consumers. Many FMCG products have aimed at connecting with the cultural values of people. For instance, Cadbury India launched its Celebrations range as an expression of love and festivity for occasions like Raksha Bandhan. Nestlé's Nescafé Coffee emphasizes building relationships over coffee. We now look at popular models of consumer behaviour applied to the Indian context.

A. The Nicosia Model

The Nicosia model illustrates how a potential consumer responds to news of a new brand. The model's three-stage sequence begins with the consumer being made aware of the brand's existence and then traces the decision process through, from purchase to post-purchase evaluation and feedback. This sequence is assumed to begin with advertising, which makes the consumer aware of the brand's existence and of an unfilled want. The perception of the message is influenced by attributes of both the company and the consumer, and may lead to the development of an attitude towards the brand. The consumer is then assumed to search for alternative brands which are evaluated by means of other consumers, advertising messages, previous experiences with each company, and so on. This search process leads the consumer to either dismiss or purchase the product. The experience of purchase and consumption then has the effect of modifying the consumer's psychological state and acts as a feedback loop, leading either to a decision to repeat the purchase or not buy it again.

B. The Engel, Kollat and Blackwell (EKB) Model

The starting point for the EKB model is the consumer's perception of a want that must be satisfied. This stimulates the search for information internally (memory), externally (neighbours, colleagues, and friends) and from market sources (advertisements, trade literature, magazine reports). This search process identifies the various ways in which the want can be satisfied and leads to the consumer setting the criteria by which the alternatives can then be compared and evaluated. This leads in turn to the emergence of a set of attitudes and beliefs that ultimately determine choice. The outcome of this choice then feeds back to influence future behaviour.

C. The Howard and Sheth Model

Howard and Sheth's approach is broadly similar to those of Nicosia and Engel et al. in that it again attempts to coalesce a disparate set of variables. These are grouped under four main headings:

- **Inputs,** which stimulate the buying process. These include product-related factors (price, quality and distinctiveness), symbolic factors (images that stem from the mass media and sales people), and social factors (family, reference groups and social class influences).
- **Perceptual constructs**, which explain the consumer's cognitive activity in terms of information processing.
- **Learning constructs**, which represent the results of information processing.
- **Outputs,** which include not just the purchases but also the implications for perception and learning.

2.4.2 Factors Influencing Consumer Behaviour

People today have become far more empowered due to the widespread availability of information. This is causing a transformation in consumer preferences, much of which is powered by the evolving middle class. For instance, a vast majority of middle class women were housewives, so they preferred self-cooked meals that catered to the family's taste. With time, more women have begun to work, thus increasing the demand for packaged food. Some other changing consumer preferences are presented in Figure 2.1.

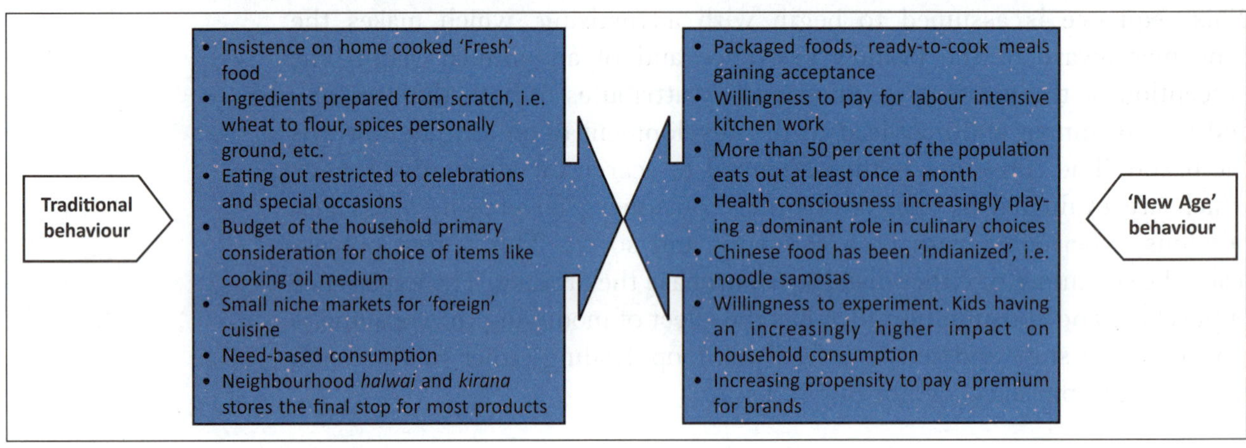

Figure 2.1: Changing consumer preferences

India's dramatic pace of urbanization is influencing lifestyle patterns and buying behaviour of consumers.

- Bulk purchases from supermarkets and hyperstores instead of frequent trips to the nearby shops: this is due to convenience, hygiene and an attractive ambience associated with the former. Consumers today are also more experimental and ready to take risks.
- A changing work culture leads to an increasing focus on ready to eat food instead of traditional cooking. ITC offers a range of such products under the 'Kitchens of India' label. Other packaged food products include Knorr and Maggi soups and MTR idli and upma mixes. Despite the presence of Indian brands, the ready to eat food segment is underdeveloped and has become the focus of foreign companies who are eyeing the growth opportunities presented by this market.

- There is a growing influence of Western culture on Indians, who have become more modernized and willing to experiment. A number of foreign brands have been successful in the FMCG sector in India due to this Westernization. For instance, many Indian women use L'Oreal and Maybelline products.
- Consumers today are also health conscious. They want to eat healthy and stay fit. Hence, a greater number of FMCG products position themselves as being healthy options. Maggi Atta Noodles, Sunfeast's Sachin Fit Kit Multigrain Biscuits, and Tropicana fruit juices are a few products that address this need.
- In India, celebrities, especially movie stars and cricketers, are frequently asked to endorse products and play a role in marketing communication. As the print and electronic media become all pervasive, the influence of celebrities has increased. They are closely followed and even their most mundane activities create headlines. They are watched and imitated. Consequently, roping in celebrities for advertising attracts a lot of consumer attention.
- Consumers like advertisements more if they feature their favourite celebrity. What the star says has a positive impact on the consumer's mind leading to positive vibes about the product. Also, these advertisements have a higher recall value amidst the advertisement clutter. For example, Lux soaps created headlines when they aired the advertisement featuring Bollywood hearthrob Shahrukh Khan along with four Bollywood beauties.

From the viewpoint of marketing strategy, the mix of cultural, social, personal and psychological factors which influence behaviour are largely non-controllable. Because of the influence they exert on patterns of buying, it is essential that we understand how they interact and influence purchase behaviour. In doing this, we should not lose sight of the differences that exist between customers and consumers, and the implications of these differences for strategy.

2.4.3 Customer and Consumer

A customer is the company, person or entity making a purchase from another person, company or entity. This customer may sell it to another person or use it for his own purpose. The term 'consumer' is typically taken to mean the final user, who as is evident from the above explanation is not necessarily the customer. For instance, in the case of foodstuffs such as breakfast cereals, the buyer (generally the housewife) acts on behalf of her family. For the marketing mix to be effective, it is quite obvious that the strategist understand not just what the customer wants (e.g. value for money) but also what the consumer wants (e.g. tastes, free fits and image).

The term 'consumer' is typically taken to mean the final user, who is not necessarily the customer.

2.4.4 Using Research to delve the Consumer's Mind

Customer analysis is designed to provide the strategist with a clear understanding of how and why people behave as they do. To help with this, two sets of techniques have been developed:

MARKETING IN ACTION — **DEMAND FOR HIGH-RESOLUTION PHONES ON THE RISE**

At a time when growth in the Indian cell phone market has flattened out, handset vendors are seeing a growing demand for mid- to high-end camera phones. As a result, mobile phone vendors are fine-tuning their business strategies by expanding their portfolio of high-megapixel phones at lower prices, rolling out various imaging solutions and tying up with partners in the photography ecosystem. According to marketing research firm ORG, the contribution of camera phones to overall handset sales in India increased from 34 per cent to 38 per cent over 2008. Of this, the market for handsets with one to two megapixel cameras grew from 48 to 58 per cent. The market for handsets with two megapixel cameras and upwards grew from 7 per cent to 10 per cent. At the same time, the contribution of phones with one megapixel and below has reduced from 45 per cent to 32 per cent, reflecting a shift towards high-resolution phones.

Industry sources added that the average selling price (ASP) of camera phones has dipped by 15-20 per cent over the last one year, thereby fuelling demand. According to Sunil Dutt, former country head, Samsung Telecom, there is a clear shift in consumer preference towards higher-resolution phones. In line with this, the focus will shift towards handsets with higher camera resolution and functionality akin to digital cameras. Samsung's portfolio of models with five and eight megapixel cameras will also grow. Samsung, the second-largest vendor of mobile phone handsets has over 30 camera phone models. It launched Pixon, India's first eight-megapixel phone with a touch screen. The phone has digital camera features like advanced shake reduction, blink detection, smile and face detection, and panoramic shot.

Nokia also rolled out its first eight megapixel handset N86 in June 2009 in India. The company also tied up with various players in the photography field and rolled out an array of imaging solutions. In fact, according to Nokia India the demand for models with higher camera resolution like 5800, N95 and N96 has been growing.

Motorola launched a five megapixel handset along with Kodak in early 2009 and has plans to launch more models. According to Faisal Siddiqui, country head (mobile devices), Motorola India, multimedia features including the camera, its megapixel, along with complete user experience in a mobile phone is now playing an important role in the consumer's final purchase decision.

Digital camera vendors, however, claim higher-resolution camera phones have not cannibalized their sales. Alok Bharadwaj, Canon India's senior VP, ascertained that company research indicates that consumers who buy digital cameras already possess good camera phones. Consumers still rely on digital cameras when they need to retain pictures for longer duration or for professional use.

Source: The Economic Times, September 2009.

IMPULSIVE BUYING

Impulsive buying is generally defined as a consumer's unplanned purchase. It forms an important part of buyer behaviour and accounts for as much as 62 per cent of supermarket sales and 80 per cent of all sales in certain product categories. As income levels increase, purchasing power shoots up and consequently impulse buying rises. A contributing factor is the pricing strategy of retail players and the number of festivals Indians celebrate all year through.

Consumer research deals with attitudes and opinions towards existing products and possible new ones.

Consumer research deals with attitudes and opinions towards existing products and possible new ones. The techniques used include simple structured interviews of large samples of consumers and lengthy discussions with small groups.

Market research observes what happens in the marketplace. The findings are then projected into estimates of total market size, trends, brand shares, and so on.

Market research observes what happens in the marketplace.

McDonald argues that companies should undertake detailed analyses to identify the full range of benefits they can offer to a customer as a prelude to identifying the range of benefits that customers actually want or will respond to. Benefits typically fall into four categories:

- **Standard benefits** which arise from the company and its products.
- **Double benefits** which bring a benefit to the customer and subsequently, through an improvement in the customer's product, to the end user.
- **Company benefits** which emerge as a result of the relationship that develops by virtue of having bought a particular product. A typical example would be worldwide service back-up.
- **Differential benefits** that distinguish a product from those offered by competitors.

Among others to have discussed the significance of benefits is Theodore Levitt who gives the illustration of drill bits. The customer, he suggests, does not buy a quarter-inch drill for its own sake, but for the quarter-inch holes it gives. The implication for the manufacturer is that he needs to define his business in terms of the means of making holes in materials. By limiting the definition to the manufacture of drills he is likely to fail to recognize the opportunity offered by, for example, industrial lasers which are capable of making holes more rapidly and accurately. Nevertheless, there are several influencing factors that have emerged from this research which merit consideration. These include:

- **The product's attributes** such as its price, performance, quality and styling.
- **The product's relative importance** to the consumer.
- **The consumer's perception** of each brand's image.
- **The consumer's utility function** for each of the attributes.

2.5 Consumer Adoption Process

How do potential customers learn about new products, try them, and adopt or reject them? Adoption is an individual's decision to become a regular user of a product. The consumer loyalty process follows the consumer adoption process and is the concern of every established producer.

The theory of innovation diffusion and consumer adoption *helps marketers identify early adopters.*

Years ago, new-product marketers used the *mass-market approach* to launch products. This approach had two main drawbacks: it called for heavy marketing expenditures, and involved many wasted exposures. These drawbacks led to a second approach, *heavy user target marketing*. This approach makes sense provided that heavy users are identifiable and are early adopters. However, even within the heavy user group, many heavy users are loyal to existing brands. New product marketers now aim at consumers who are early adopters. The theory of *innovation diffusion and consumer adoption* helps marketers identify early adopters.

2.5.1 Stages in the Adoption Process

An innovation is any product, service, or idea that is perceived by someone as new. The idea may have a long history, but it is an innovation to the person who sees it for the first time. Innovations take time to spread through the social system. Everett Rogers defines the innovation diffusion process as 'the spread of a new idea from its source of invention or creation to its ultimate users or adopters'.

The consumer-adoption process focuses on the mental process through which an individual passes from first hearing about an innovation to finally adopting it.

The consumer-adoption process focuses on the mental process through which an individual passes from first hearing about an innovation to finally adopting it. Adopters of new products have been observed to move through five stages:

(i) **Awareness:** The consumer becomes aware of the innovation but lacks information about it.
(ii) **Interest:** The consumer is stimulated to seek information about the innovation.
(iii) **Evaluation:** The consumer considers whether to try the innovation.
(iv) **Trial:** The consumer tries the innovation to improve his or her estimate of its value.
(v) **Adoption:** The consumer decides to make full and regular use of the innovation.

The new product marketer should facilitate movement through these stages. For instance, a portable electric dishwasher manufacturer might discover that many consumers are stuck in the interest stage; they do not buy because of uncertainty and the large investment cost. But these same consumers would be willing to use an electric dishwasher on a trial basis for a small monthly fee. The manufacturer could then consider offering a trial-use plan with an option to buy.

2.5.2 Factors Influencing the Adoption Process

Marketers recognize the following characteristics as influencing the adoption process:

- Individual readiness to try new products;
- The effect of personal influence;
- Differing rates of adoption; and
- Differences in organizations' readiness to try new products.

Readiness to try new products and personal influence: Everett Rogers defines innovativeness as 'the degree to which an individual is relatively earlier in adopting new ideas than the other members of his social system'. In each product area, there are pioneers and early adopters. Some people are the first to adopt new clothing fashions or new appliances; some doctors are the first to prescribe new medicines; and some farmers are the first to adopt new farming methods. After a slow start, an increasing number of people adopt the innovation, the number reaches a peak, and then it diminishes as fewer non-adopters remain.

Rogers sees five adopter groups differing in their value orientations:

(i) Innovators are venturesome; they are willing to try new ideas.
(ii) Early adopters are guided by respect; they are opinion leaders in their communities and adopt new ideas early but carefully.
(iii) The early majorities are deliberate; they adopt new ideas before the average person.
(iv) The late majorities are sceptical; they adopt an innovation only after majorities have tried it.

(v) Finally, laggards are tradition-bound. They are suspicious of change, mix with other tradition-bound people, and adopt the innovation only when it takes on a measure of tradition itself.

The classification suggests that an innovating firm should research the demographic, psychographic, and media characteristics of innovators and early adopters and direct communications specifically at them. According to Rogers, early adopters tend to be younger in age, have higher social status, and a more favourable financial position. They utilize a greater number of cosmopolitan information sources than do late adopters.

Personal influence refers to the effect one person has on another's attitude or purchase probability.

Personal influence: This refers to the effect one person has on another's attitude or purchase probability. Although personal influence is an important factor, its significance is greater in some situations and for some individuals than for others. It is more important in the evaluation stage of the adoption process than in the other stages. It has more influence on late adopters than early adopters. Also, it is more important in risky situations.

ECONOMY WATCH

JAPANESE MAJORS SLIP INTO THE RED IN 2009

Sony Corporation reported a loss of $1 billion Yen in 2008–9. Sony, which makes Bravia flat-panel TVs and Cyber-shot digital cameras is closing three plants in Japan to help turn its business around. It is also in the midst of cutting 16,000 jobs. The Japanese electronics and entertainment company was of the opinion that no quick recovery was in sight, projecting a ¥120 billion ($1.2 billion) loss for 2010.

Sony joins a string of other big Japanese corporations, including Toyota Motor Corporation and Hitachi that have announced huge losses and bleak outlooks. Hit by dropping sales and a strong yen, which erodes export income, Sony lost ¥165 billion in the January-March quarter, compared to a ¥29 billion profit for the same period in 2008. Sony's annual sales slid 12.9 per cent to ¥7.73 trillion. Sales fell in all key markets: down 20 per cent in the US, 17 per cent in Europe and 14 per cent in Japan. Its fiscal year 2009 loss was a reversal from the ¥369.40 billion profit it had in 2008.

Panasonic Corporation slumped deep into the red in 2008–9, joining the expanding club of big Japanese brands shell-shocked by their rapid descent from cash cows to money losers. The world's biggest plasma TV maker reported a ¥378.96 billion ($4 billion) loss for the fiscal year ended March 2009. This is its first loss in seven years since 2001 and the company expects to stay in the red in 2009–10. Business slumped across all segments amid lacklustre demand for everything from flatscreen TVs and digital cameras to home appliances and semiconductors. Sales were down 14.4 per cent to ¥7.77 trillion, and operating profits tumbled 86 per cent to ¥72.90 billion. For the January-March 2009 quarter, Panasonic booked a record net loss of ¥444.30 billion, compared with a profit of ¥61.60 billion in 2008. The results represent a swift reversal of fortunes for Panasonic, which in 2008 posted a record net profit of ¥281.90 billion. But it is only the latest among a score of bellwether brands in Japan releasing grim results as the world's second biggest economy gets battered by unprecedented slump in global demand.

Nissan Motor, Japan's third-largest automaker, reported a ¥33.70 billion ($2.40 billion) annual net loss in 2009—its first yearly loss in a decade. However the company expects 2010 to be better. This is the first time Nissan has reported an annual loss since Ghosn took charge a decade ago under an alliance with Renault SA of France, and wrested Nissan out of near bankruptcy. For the January-March 2009 quarter, Nissan lost ¥276.89 billion ($2.80 billion). Nissan's annual sales plunged 22 per cent to ¥8.437 trillion, but it was still better than its initial sales forecast. Worldwide, Nissan sold 3.40 million vehicles, down 9.5 per cent from 2008, as sales dropped in the US, Japan and Europe.

Toyota Motor Corporation, meanwhile, swung from a record profit to its worst annual loss since being founded in 1937.

Panasonic vowed to press ahead with drastic structural reforms to try to engineer a recovery. For the 12 months through March 2010, it forecasts a steeper than expected net loss of ¥195 billion on sales of ¥7 trillion. It predicts that operating profit will climb 3 per cent to ¥75 billion, though analysts say the projection looks overly optimistic. President Pumio Ohtsubo has said he wants to shut down unprofitable business lines, shift resources to those with growth potential and improve product quality. The firm is slashing capacity and aims to cut about 5 per cent of its 3,00,000-strong global workforce by next spring.

Source: The Economic Times, December 2009.

2.6 Types of Buyers

Dickinson, who studied buyer styles and their implications for marketing strategy, has identified seven types of buyers:

- **Loyal buyers** remain loyal to a source for considerable periods.
- **Opportunistic buyers** choose between sellers on the basis of who will best further their long-term interests.
- **Best buyers** concentrate on the best deal available at the time.
- **Creative buyers** tell the seller precisely what they want in terms of the product, service and price.
- **Advertising buyers** occasionally demand extra discounts.
- **Chisellers** constantly demand extra discounts.
- **Nuts and bolts buyers** select products on the basis of quality.

2.6.1 Stimulus-Response Model

The starting point to understand buyer behaviour is the stimulus-response model. Marketing and environmental stimuli enter the buyer's consciousness. The buyer's characteristics and decision process lead to certain purchase decisions. The marketer's task is to understand what happens in the buyer's consciousness between the arrival of outside stimuli and the buyer's purchase decision.

Multicultural marketing grew out of careful marketing research to reveal how different ethnic and demographic niches did not always respond favourably to mass-market advertising.

A consumer's buying behaviour is influenced by cultural, social, and personal factors. Cultural factors exert the broadest and deepest influence. Culture is the fundamental determinant of a person's wants and behaviours. Each culture consists of smaller subcultures that provide more specific identification and socialization for their members. Subcultures include nationality, religion, racial groups, and geographic region.

Multicultural marketing grew out of careful marketing research revealing how different ethnic and demographic niches did not always respond favourably to mass-market advertising. Virtually all human societies exhibit social stratification. This stratification sometimes takes the form of caste system where members of different castes are reared for specific roles and they cannot change their caste membership. More frequently, the stratification takes the form of social classes, relatively homogeneous and enduring divisions in society that are hierarchically ordered and whose members share similar values, interests, and behaviour.

Social classes have several characteristics:

(a) Those within a class tend to behave more alike than persons from two different social classes.

(b) Persons are perceived as occupying an inferior or superior position according to their social class.

(c) Social class is indicated by a cluster of variables (occupation, income, etc.) rather than by any single variable.

(d) Individuals can move up or down the social-class ladder.

(e) Social classes show distinct product and brand preferences in many areas.

(f) Social classes differ in media preferences. There are also language differences among them.

In addition to cultural factors, a consumer's behaviour is influenced by such social factors as reference groups, family, and social roles and statuses. A person's reference group consists of all the groups that have a direct (face-to-face) or indirect influence on his/her attitudes or behaviour. Groups with a direct influence on a person are called membership groups. Some memberships groups are primary, such as family, friends, neighbours, and co-workers with whom the person interacts fairly continuously and informally. Some membership groups are secondary groups such as religious and professional groups that tend to be more formal.

People are significantly influenced by their reference groups in at least three ways. One, they expose an individual to new behaviours and lifestyles, influencing attitudes and self-concepts (how one views oneself). Two, they create pressures for conformity that may affect actual product and brand choices. Three, people are also influenced by groups to which they do not belong: aspirational groups are those a person hopes to join. Dissociative groups are those whose values or behaviours an individual rejects. The buyer evaluates these elements together with the monetary cost to form the total customer cost.

Manufacturers of products where group influence is strong must determine how to reach and influence opinion leaders in these reference groups. An opinion leader is a person who through informal, product-related communication, offers advice or information about a specific product or product category. Marketers try to reach opinion leaders by identifying demographic and psychographic characteristics associated with opinion leadership, while also identifying the media preferred by the opinion leaders.

Buying roles and buying decisions constitute consumer decision-making behaviour. A customer can adopt various buying roles like initiator, influencer, decider, buyer, preparer, maintainer and disposer. A buyer's decisions are also influenced by personal characteristics. These include the buyer's age and stage in the life cycle; occupation and economic circumstances; personality and self-concept; and lifestyle and values. Each person has personality characteristics that influence his or her buying behaviour. Kotler has defined brand personality as the specific mix of human traits that may be attributed to a particular brand. Jennifer Aaker identified the following five traits:

Buying roles and buying decisions constitute consumer decision-making behaviour. A customer can adopt various buying roles like initiator, influencer, decider, buyer, preparer, maintainer and disposer.

- Sincerity (down-to-earth)
- Excitement (daring)
- Competence (reliable)
- Sophistication (upper class)
- Ruggedness (outdoorsy).

Consumers choose and use brands that have a brand personality consistent with their own self-concept. Although in some cases the match may be based on the consumer's ideal self-concept (how he would like to view himself), in certain cases they are influenced by others' self-concept (how he thinks others see him).

A lifestyle is a person's pattern of living as expressed in activities, interests and opinions. Lifestyle portrays the 'whole person' interacting with his or her environment. Marketers search for relationships between their products and lifestyle groups. Lifestyles are shaped partly by whether consumers are money-constrained or time-constrained. Consumers who lack time are prone to multitasking.

2.6.2 Consumer Decision Process

Core values go much deeper than behaviour or attitude and determine, at a basic level, people's choices and desires over the long-term.

Consumer decisions are also influenced by core values, the belief system that underlies a consumer's attitude and behaviour. Core values go much deeper than behaviour or attitude and determine, at a basic level, people's choices and desires over the long-term. The basic psychological processes play an important role in understanding how consumers actually make their buying decisions. It is imperative for marketers to understand every facet of consumer behaviour.

A. Problem Recognition

The buying process starts when a buyer recognizes a problem or need. The need can be triggered by internal or external stimuli. Marketers need to identify the circumstances that trigger a particular need so that they can develop marketing strategies that trigger consumer interest. The need can be internally generated like the sense of thirst or hunger or triggered through external stimuli like advertisements or people forming the consumer's reference groups. For example, a new car purchased by a neighbour could act as a stimulus.

B. Information Search

An aroused consumer will be inclined to search for more information. We can distinguish between two types of arousals. The milder state is called heightened attention where a person simply becomes more receptive to information about a certain product. The second level is active information search where a person looks for reading material or goes online to learn about the product. Of key interest to the marketer are the information sources to which the consumer will turn and the relative influence each will have on the subsequent purchase decision. These information sources fall into four groups: personal (family, friends); commercial (advertising, websites, salespeople); public (mass media, consumer organizations) and experiential (handling, examining, using the product).

Generally speaking, consumers receive most information from commercial sources. The most effective information, however, often comes from personal sources or public sources that are independent authorities. But it is important to mention here that the coming of the Internet has transformed information search. Most consumers are now hybrid consumers who use both online and offline means.

C. Evaluation of Alternatives

No single process is used by all consumers or by one consumer in all buying situations. The current models see the process as cognitively orientated. First, the consumer is trying to satisfy a need. Second, he/she is looking for certain benefits from the product solution. Third, the consumer sees each product as a bundle of attributes with varying abilities to deliver the benefits sought to satisfy his/her need. Evaluations often reflect beliefs and attitudes which are acquired through experience and learning. These in turn influence buying behaviour.

In the evaluation stage, the consumer forms preferences among the brands in the choice set. He/she may also form an intention to buy the most preferred brand. In executing a purchase intention, the consumer may make up to five sub-decisions such as choice of brand, dealer, quantity, timing and payment method. However, consumers don't always invest so much time and energy in evaluating brands. They often take 'mental shortcuts' that involve various simplifying choice heuristics.

In the *conjunctive heuristic method*, the consumer sets a minimum acceptable cut-off level for each attribute and chooses the first alternative that meets this minimum. In the *lexicographic heuristic method*, the consumer chooses the best brand on the basis of its perceived most important attribute. In the *elimination-by-aspects heuristic method*, the consumer compares brands on some select attributes and brands not meeting these attributes are eliminated.

Many products, however, entail little or low involvement on the part of the consumer and also the absence of significant brand differences. Marketers of such products use four techniques to try to convert a low-involvement product into one of higher involvement. They can link the product to some involving issue, to some involving personal situation, design advertising to trigger strong emotions related to personal values or ego defenses or add important features.

Some buying situations are characterized by low involvement but significant brand differences. Brand switching occurs not because of dissatisfaction but for the sake of variety. Mental accounting refers to the manner by which consumers code, categorize, and evaluate the financial outcomes of their choices. According to the American economist Richard Thaler, mental accounting is based on a set of key core principles such as 'consumers tend to segregate gains', 'consumers tend to integrate losses', 'consumers tend to integrate smaller losses with larger gains' and 'consumers tend to segregate small gains from large losses'. After the purchase, the consumer might experience dissonance and be alert to information that supports his/her decision. Marketing communication should supply beliefs and evaluations that reinforce the consumer's choice and help him/her feel good about the brand and the product he/she has bought. When a consumer senses a small loss, any communication to reinforce his decision will make the gains look more significant than the losses. The principle of mental accounting used in conjunction with marketing communication can help companies retain consumers. Marketers must therefore monitor post-purchase satisfaction, post-purchase actions, and post-purchase uses.

Depending on the extent to which his/her requirements are met, a customer may be classified as dissatisfied, satisfied or delighted.

Depending on the extent to which his/her requirements are met, a customer may be classified as dissatisfied, satisfied or delighted. A customer whose requirements are not adequately met, will be a dissatisfied customer. If his/her requirements are just met, he/she will be satisfied. If, however, his/her requirements have been exceeded, he/she will be delighted. Thus the dissatisfaction, satisfaction and delight of the customer depends on his/

her expectations and the performance of the product or service. If the expectations are high and the performance of the product or service is not up to the mark, dissatisfaction is the result. A dissatisfied customer will talk about his/her dissatisfaction to friends and they may prefer to go to the competition, along with the dissatisfied customer. A delighted customer on the other hand will also talk about his/her delight to friends and they too may become customers of the company. It becomes obvious that any organization that wants to succeed in a competitive business environment should try to convert dissatisfied customers into satisfied customers, and satisfied customers into delighted customers.

Customers will buy from the firm that offers the highest perceived value. This includes Customer Perceived Value, Total Customer Value and Total Customer Cost.

The premise here is that customers will buy from the firm that they see as offering the highest perceived value. *Customer perceived value* (CPV) is the difference between the prospective customer's evaluation of all the benefits and costs of an offering and the perceived alternatives. *Total customer value* is the perceived monetary value of the bundle of economic, functional, and psychological benefits customers expect from a given market offering. *Total customer cost* is the bundle of costs customers expect to incur in evaluating, obtaining, using, and disposing of the given market offering.

Whether the buyer is satisfied after his/her purchase depends on the offer's performance in relation to the buyer's expectations. In general, satisfaction is a person's feeling of pleasure or disappointment resulting from comparing a product's perceived performance (or outcome) in relation to his/her expectations. If the performance falls short of expectations, the customer is dissatisfied.

However, the link between customer satisfaction and customer loyalty is not proportional. Let us suppose that customer satisfaction is rated on a scale of one to five. At the lowest level of customer satisfaction (level one), customers are likely to abandon the company and even bad-mouth it. At levels two to four, customers are fairly satisfied but will still find it easy to switch when a better offer comes along. At level five, customer are likely to repurchase and even spread good word about the company. High satisfaction or delight creates an emotional bond with the brand or company, not just a rational preference. Xerox's senior management found out that its 'completely satisfied' customers were six times more likely to repurchase Xerox products over the following 18 months than its 'very satisfied' customers.

The profitability of customer promotions depends heavily on two data points—the response rate and cost of the offer.

The profitability of customer promotions depends heavily on two data points—the response rate and cost of the offer. This is true for 'hard' offers like discounts/upsells, and 'soft' offers like service upgrades. At any given time, some customers are more likely to respond than others. This likelihood to respond is influenced by the size (cost) of the offer made—the discount or the giveaway. A customer who did not respond to a 10 per cent discount might respond to a 20 per cent discount. Similarly, a customer who would have responded to a 10 per cent discount may be offered a 20 per cent discount, and he/she may take it.

In most markets, however, buyers differ enormously in terms of their buying dynamics. The task faced by the marketing strategist in coming to terms with these differences is consequently complex. In consumer markets, for example, not only do buyers typically differ in terms of their age, income, educational levels and geographical location, but more fundamentally in terms of their personality, lifestyles and expectations. In organizational and industrial markets, the differences are often exhibited in the goals being pursued, the criteria employed by those involved in the buying process, the formality of purchasing policies, and the constraints that exist in the form of delivery dates and expected performance levels.

The overwhelming need therefore is for regular assessments (and reassessments) of what customers really want, their current levels of satisfaction, and the scope that exists for developing new products and services that existing customers might buy.

2.7 Building Relationships and Moments of Truth

Jan Carlzon, president of the Scandinavian Airlines System (SAS), became a business legend thanks to the way he turned SAS from a heavy loss-making firm to a healthy profitable one in the mid-1980s. In his book, Carlzon (1987) says that each of SAS' 10 million customers came in contact with approximately five SAS employees for an average of 15 seconds each time. He referred to these contact as 'moments of truth', suggesting that for SAS these were 'created' 50 million times a year, 15 seconds at a time.

It is statistics such as these which indicate the scale of opportunity for managing and building relationships, or as Clutterbuck et al. (1993) define, these critical encounters are OTSUs (Opportunities To Screw Up).

Many researchers conclude that when a customer complains and feels that the complaint is handled properly, he or she comes away satisfied and is likely to be more loyal to that brand or supplier than a customer who has never experienced a problem.

The findings related to customer segment brand loyalty were as follows:

• Experienced no problem	87 per cent
• Satisfied complainant	91 per cent
• Dissatisfied complainant	41 per cent
• Non-complainant	59 per cent

Two key issues emerge here: first, dissatisfied customers should be encouraged to and assisted in lodging complaints, and second, the complaint must be resolved to the customer's complete satisfaction. Where customers remain dissatisfied, the implications are significant because not only will they fail to buy again, but they also tend not to keep quiet about their experience. Statistics surrounding this issue are quoted ubiquitously, but they all tell the same story. Mark Gerson, for example, states that a dissatisfied customer will tell ten people about his experience; approximately 13 per cent of dissatisfied customers will tell up to twenty people. Customers who are satisfied or have had their complaints satisfactorily resolved would tell between three and five people about their positive experience. The stark reality of these statistics is that three to four customers have to be satisfied for every one dissatisfied customer—a 4 : 1 ratio.

2.7.1 Service Quality Drives Satisfaction

In 2008, the American Management Association published an analysis of customer defections in the US. It was found that 13 per cent of defections were due to product performance, 12 per cent due to 'other reasons' and a massive 75 per cent due to shortcomings in customer service.

In 2008, the American Management Association published an analysis of customer defections in the US. It was found that 13 per cent of defections were due to product performance, 12 per cent were due to 'other reasons' and a massive 75 per cent due to shortcomings in customer service. Customers, even business customers, are placing increasing emphasis on the way they are treated. Today, the firms have to provide stellar service, going above the customers' expectations, leaving them with a 'wow' feeling, not an 'ok' feeling. The firms have to earn their confidence repeatedly, make them feel appreciated, and find some way to break through all the marketing clutter and the filters customers have invented to deal with all that clutter.

The good news is that customers, being human, make largely emotional decisions. While firms must create compelling, differentiating value for them, keeping them happy doesn't necessarily mean offering discounts or freebies. It can be as simple as a follow-up question, an acknowledgement of their continued business, or a smile from an employee who genuinely enjoys serving his/her customers. It can happen over the phone, in a few well-planned moments—if the firm build their customer interaction system to make it happen.

2.7.2 Lifetime Value of Customers

Lifetime value of customers is not a new concept. It has its roots in direct marketing (especially mail order), where long-term customer behaviour is the key to success, and calculating the difference between the cost of acquiring new customers and the benefits and costs of retaining existing customers is the norm. The concept is also widely used in consumer goods brand management, where the key calculation is how much to spend to prevent consumers from switching brands.

Using historical data of customers a firm already has, the lifetime value (LTV) can be calculated and then extrapolated, making adjustments where necessary. Some companies are uncomfortable about using past data as a

MARKETING IN ACTION — **DISHTV LAUNCHES LOW-COST SET-TOP BOXES**

Back in 2009 direct-to-home (DTH) market leader DishTV launched low-cost set-top boxes (STBs) and cheaper monthly subscription schemes to tap the 40 million non-cable and satellite television homes in India. In addition, the company also launched premium STBs for home theatre owners, apart from offering live TV on-the-go to car owners. DishTV has close to 50 lakh subscribers and was looking to add at least 20-25 lakh subscribers in 2009–10. According to the managing director Jawahar Goel, the company believes that the time is ripe for market segmentation and the firm is working on cheaper set-top boxes for 'Doordarshan homes'.

The company hopes to gain at least 10 lakh subscribers from this segment alone. There are an estimated 120-122 million television viewers, out of which 80 million subscribers are cable and satellite viewers. Most of the subscribers opting for DTH are cable and satellite TV viewers. In the past, DishTV had a tie-up with automaker Ford to offer live television by fitting an STB and dish antenna on its premium SUV. The company is working on a smaller antenna and STB that can be mounted on any vehicle. According to Salil Kapoor, COO of DishTV, STB will target consumers who are travelling long distance or driving in the city, but want to keep in touch with a sporting event or news. The smaller STBs will have limited channel capacity, but will ensure smooth signal.

Source: The Economic Times, December 2009.

predictor of future purchase behaviour. However, in many markets it has proved the most reliable method of forecasting.

There are two kinds of LTV measurements—absolute and relative. Absolute LTV is difficult to calculate, while relative LTV is easy to calculate and in many ways more powerful than the former. The most difficult part of calculating LTV is deciding what a 'lifetime' is. LTV is the value of the customer over the life cycle of the customer. LTV doesn't exist without a life cycle.

2.7.3 Calculating LTV and Customer Acquisition Cost

Let us assume that the average customer buys for two years, then stops for at least one year. Therefore, we define the LTV of a customer as two years. Over two years, the average customer makes 16 purchases. The LTV of the customer is thus

16 × ₹1.20 Profit per Unit = ₹19.20

The average customer brings three new customers to the firm. So, to break even, the maximum acquisition cost of a new customer should be:

4 × ₹19.20 = ₹76.80.

Customers who are more recent have higher potential value than customers who are less recent, for any given activity. Customers who made a purchase 15 days ago have higher potential value than customers who made a purchase 60 days ago. Customers who logged in last week are much more likely to revisit than customers who logged in 30 days ago, and so have higher potential value.

2.8 Marketing Strategy Development: Discussion Agenda in a Changing Market Scenario

How do we set strategies for marketing products and services of firms so they are in line with the changing needs and wants of the people? This is a difficult question to answer. However our theoretical frameworks and discussions throw some light on the issues and current practices of market leaders, which will help in formulating business strategies. The following are a few questions, answers to which will help managers formulate sound strategies for their firms:

A. Environmental Analysis

- What are the environmental threats, opportunities and trends?
- What major environmental scenarios can be conceived?
- What are the major strategic questions and information need areas?

B. Self-Analysis

- What is the company's current performance level?
- What has been the company's strategy?
- What are the company's assets and skills?
- What are the company's weaknesses?
- What are the characteristics of the company's organization—its structure, people, culture, and systems—that will affect strategy?
- What is the company's cost structure? Does a sustainable cost advantage exist or can it be developed?

- What is the company's existing business portfolio? What has been the level of investment in the various product markets?
- What are the company's strategic problems, constraints, and questions? What are the strengths and weaknesses relative to each strategic group of competitors?

C. Customer Analysis

- What are the major segments?
- What are their motivations and unmet needs?

D. Competitor Analysis

- Who are the existing and potential competitors?
- What strategic groups can be identified?
- What are their level of sales, share growth and profits?
- What are their strengths, weaknesses and strategies?

E. Market Analysis

- How attractive is the industry and its submarkets?
- What are the structures, entry and exit barriers, growth projections, and profitability prospects?
- What are the alternative distribution channels and their relative strengths?
- What industry trends are significant to strategy?
- What are the current and future key success factors?

F. Strategy Development

- What alternative growth directions should be considered?
- What should be the business mission?
- What investment level is most appropriate—withdrawal, milking, maintaining or growing?
- What alternative sustainable competitive advantages should be developed or supported?
- What skills or assets need to be developed or maintained?
- What are the alternative functional area strategies?
- What are the key strategic questions?
- What strategies best fit the strengths and objectives of the organization?

2.9 Summary

Changes are sweeping across countries; in India too such changes can be seen in customer care and strategic marketing. A look at the developments that have been taking place in the Indian environment after the 2009 budget speech provide enough evidence to this..

The government has permitted Navaratna and Mini Ratna PSUs to risk 30 per cent of their nearly ₹2,40,000 crore cash surplus in mutual fund investments. Godrej has roped in Hrithik Roshan to boost Cinthol sales and has increased promotional spends from 4 to 15 per cent in an attempt to capture the market from the leader Lux. Therefore, strategies of pure and hybrid players are still on and the battle is far from over.

CHAPTER 3  MARKET ANALYSIS FOR THE NEW AGE MARKETER

three

You have to live with your product, you have to know it through and through, you have to look at it, understand it, love it then, and only then, you can crystallize in one clear thought, one single theme, what must be conveyed about the product to the consumer.

— BILL BERNBACH

The Backdrop

Do people bathe less in a downturn? There is no research to indicate this, but people were definitely using less of Godrej No.1 and Cinthol towards the end of 2008. This was bad news for Godrej Consumer Products Limited (GCPL) as half of its turnover came from soap sales. Its profit after tax (PAT) dropped by 6 per cent in the third quarter of 2008–9 compared to the third quarter of 2007–8. But while the resources to fight back were limited, ideas were not. The company decided to focus on a few key brands—Godrej No.1, Cinthol and Godrej Expert in soaps and hair colours—and improve market share in 2009. GCPL's strategy was to double advertising and promotional spends and launch new variants. It also expanded to rural India and eventually rural sales of GCPL accounted for 42 per cent of total sales in 2009, up from 38 per cent in 2008.

GCPL's strategy is to capture the lower price points. Unlike Hindustan Unilever Limited (HUL), it does not resort to price cuts but focuses on the right size at the right price strategy. Its major brands were available in ₹5 packs in 2009, and this size already accounted for one-fifth of the revenues. The soaps business grew over 25 per cent; sales went up by 22 per cent and PAT by 78 per cent largely through its brands Godrej No.1, Cinthol and Fairglow. GCPL had a 10 per cent share in the ₹7,000-crore soap products market in 2009. In the ₹8,000 crore hair colour market the company grew at 20 per cent and was and remains a clear leader. The company is gaining market share, pruning costs, hiking advertising and promotion budget and building capabilities. The experience of GCPL shows Indian companies have already learned how to handle crisis during turbulent periods.

This Chapter Will

- *Seek to understand the ways and means of analysing the internal and external market and the opportunities and threats of doing business during a global financial meltdown.*
- *Use various tools like SWOT analysis and TOWS matrix, undertake internal analysis and value chain analysis across the business portfolio.*
- *Explain the missions and objectives of the firm and link them to the macro and micro environmental factors by elucidating Porter's approach to competitive structure analysis across sectors.*

Before implementing a strategy, a marketer should understand the internal and external environments and conduct a thorough SWOT analysis.

Before implementing a strategy, a marketer should have a clear understanding of the internal and external environments and conduct a thorough SWOT analysis. He/she should analyse the strengths and weaknesses of the firm and also assess the opportunities and threats in the environment. When the global recession started in September 2008, economists were sure that India, and most other newly industrialized countries (NICs) would escape lightly. And it soon became clear that the 'decoupling hypothesis', which had predicted that the NICs would farewell because of their high forex reserves and booming economies would prove to be right. Just look at the Indian automobile industry—a complete contrast to the global trend of shutting factories and dwindling demands.

MARKETING ANALYSIS

AGRIBUSINESS ITC'S PROFIT DRIVER, GROWS 128 PER CENT IN 2009

ITC, which was incorporated on 24 August 1910 under the name of Imperial Tobacco Company of India Limited, is one of India's premier private sector companies with diversified presence in various businesses such as cigarettes, hotels, paperboards and specialty papers, packaging, agribusiness, packaged foods and confectionery, information technology, branded apparel, greeting cards, safety matches and other FMCG products. It was a humble beginning for ITC when, during its initial days, it used to operate from a leased office on Radha Bazar Lane, Kolkata. On 24 August 1926, ITC purchased the plot of land at 37, Chowringhee Road (now renamed J.L. Nehru Road), Kolkata. Two years later the company's headquarter 'Virginia House' came up on that plot. Progressively the ownership of the company Indianized, and the name of the company was changed to I.T.C. Limited in 1974. The full stops in the company's name were removed on 18 September 2001 and the company was rechristened ITC Limited.

At present, ITC has a market capitalization of nearly US$15 billion and a turnover of over US$4.75 billion. It employs over 21,000 people at more than 60 locations across India. ITC has been rated by *Forbes* magazine as being among the World's Best Big Companies, Asia's 'Fab 50' and the World's Most Reputable Companies. *Business World* rated it among India's Most Respected Companies and *Business Today* included it among India's Most Valuable Companies. ITC believes that its aspiration to create enduring value for the nation provides the motive force to sustain growing shareholder value. The company practices this philosophy by not only driving each of its businesses towards international competitiveness but by also consciously contributing to enhancing the competitiveness of the larger value chain of which it is a part.

ITC's core corporate strategy has been to diversify which is aimed at creating multiple drivers of growth anchored on its time-tested core competencies:

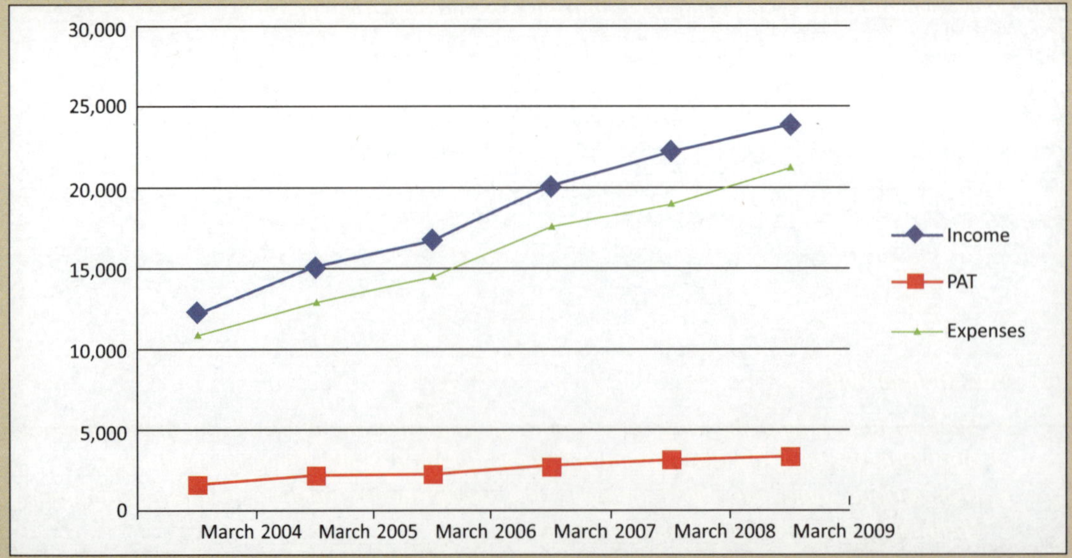

Figure 3.1: Year-on-year change in income, PAT and total expenses for ITC.
Source: http://www.itcportal.com

unmatched distribution reach, superior brand-building capabilities, effective supply chain management and acknowledged service skills in hoteliering. Over time, the strategic forays into new businesses are expected to garner a significant share of these emerging high-growth markets in India.

The cigarettes-to-hotels conglomerate recorded a 26 per cent increase in net profit to reach ₹1,009 crore in the quarter ended 30 September 2009, up from ₹802 crore in September 2008. This was the result of revenue growth in almost all its businesses except hotels. Its net income grew 18 per cent to ₹4,345 crore, up from ₹3,682 crore in the September 2008 quarter.

An analysis of the income statement (Figure 3.1) of ITC over the past six years (since March 2004) reveals that income has been steadily increasing at approximately 8 per cent every year, whereas PAT has remained more or less steady with a growth rate of less than 5 per cent. The expenses have been increasing, which is due to ITC spending heavily on diversification and penetration in the FMCG sector. The selling and distribution expenses have increased tremendously due to company's expanding portfolio.

Competition at the higher end of the Indian cigarette market is tipped to increase with the national rollout of Marlboro and Philip Morris. However, that should expand the market and in any case, ITC's volumes have been growing at 5-6 per cent. Neither the higher VAT nor the modest price hikes have impacted volumes negatively and the weak monsoon too hasn't hurt the business in 2009. That's one reason why the ITC stock has been re-rated, the other reason being losses for the non-cigarette FMCG business expected come down to around ₹400 crore in 2009, with the profitability of the biscuits and retailing businesses improving.

ITC's retail business has been restructured and that should pay off; already, with the economy recovering in 2009, store sales are picking up. Indeed, the better environment is helping the hotels business too, with both occupancy as well as Average Room Rates (ARR) improving though margins are expected to be under pressure for some more time. That apart, the rationalization of the agri-commodities business with focus on more profitable crops such as wheat and tobacco will help expand margins for this segment. In fact, the impact of some of the changes was seen in the June quarter of 2009 when ITC's operating profit margins rose 400 basis points to 33.60 per cent.

With the exception of the hotels segment, hit by the global economic slowdown, the company's cigarettes, FMCG, FMCG Others (includes retail, personal care, packaged foods, garments, education and stationery products), agribusiness, and paperboard and packaging divisions grew in net revenues by 21 per cent, 14 per cent, 19 per cent and 13 per cent, respectively in 2009. It is observed that profitability of ITC has improved on the back of better product mix, smarter sourcing of inputs and a series of targeted cost management actions. Investments in brand building in the personal care and branded foods businesses continue to impact the segment results of FMCG Others.

The company's cigarettes business continues to be its mainstay, growing by 24 per cent during the September 2009 quarter to ₹1,251 crore, amounting to 84 per cent of the total profits after interest but before exceptional items. In the September 2008 quarter, cigarettes accounted for 87 per cent of all profits.

Agribusiness was a major profit driver, growing 128 per cent to ₹174.10 crore, driven by the growth in leaf tobacco exports. ITC managed to pare its losses from the FMCG Others business to ₹85 crore during the September 2009 quarter, compared to a loss of ₹116.55 crore in the September 2008 quarter. Its profits from the composite FMCG business was ₹1,166 crore during the quarter, a growth of 31 per cent over ₹890 crore in the September 2008 quarter. Profits from hotels dropped 54 per cent to ₹31.56 crore, compared with the September 2008 quarter, while paperboard profits grew 52.34 per cent to ₹186.22 crore.

In the June 2009 quarter, ITC reported losses of around ₹100 crore for the non-cigarette FMCG business, the sixth consecutive quarter of losses. But ITC's personal care portfolio revenues, which were around ₹200-₹250 crore in 2008, are expected to grow to around ₹300-₹320 crore in 2009. Analysts believe the business should break even sometime in 2011–12, once it achieves scale.

In 2009, high ad spends are into the company's profits, though industry watchers say ITC has cornered 3.5 per cent of the soap market with both Vivel and Superia doing well. Poor brand loyalty in soaps, especially at the lower end, will however, remain a challenge for the company. Also, the high-end Fiama brand appears to be facing competition from Hindustan Unilever's Dove, which has gained market share.

The highlights of ITC's sterling set of numbers for the September 2009 quarter are the strong performance of the cigarettes and agribusinesses and smaller losses from the non-cigarette FMCG segment. ITC's operating profit margins rose by 620 basis points year-on-year in 2009, to just under 36 per cent, on revenues of ₹4,293 crore, up 14 per cent year-on-year. The strong profitability pushed up the operating profit of ITC by nearly 38 per cent to ₹1,537 crore. The management has indicated that non-cigarette FMCG losses would be brought down to ₹400 crore in 2009. It is significant to note that while ITC posted a loss of around ₹100 crore in each of the six consecutive quarters in 2008–9, the loss in the September 2009 quarter was ₹85 crore.

The company continues to enjoy a fair share of the branded, packaged foods space and that's evident from 13 per cent revenue growth during September 2009 quarter. Brands across various categories including staples, biscuits, confectionery and snack foods appear to be gaining salience. Moreover, the company's retailing venture is doing well after a restructuring exercise in early 2009, while the personal care portfolio is expected to clock revenues of ₹300-₹320 crore in 2009 and should break even in 2011-12.

Also, the focus on more profitable cash crops such as wheat and tobacco is clearly paying off; the September 2009 quarter saw the tobacco exports fetch good realizations.

Meanwhile, a sequential comparison of ITC's hotels segment with the June 2009 quarter suggests that occupancy and ARRs may be improving though it could be a while before they head back to levels seen before the global financial crisis broke out. In 2009, ITC is expected to post revenues in the region of ₹17,500 crore while net profits are expected to come in at around ₹3,800 crore, implying a growth in earnings of about 17-18 per cent over 2008-9.

Source: Business Standard, October 2009.

3.1 SWOT Analysis

The assessment of the internal and external environments is known as situational analysis or SWOT analysis. It helps a firm make maximum use of its existing assets and take adequate measures to correct the weaknesses.

3.1.1 Understanding Strengths and Weaknesses

Strengths and weaknesses are internal to the firm and can be largely controlled by the management. Opportunities and threats are factors external to the firm over which the marketer has little or no control. For this, PESTEL analysis would help.

Strengths and weaknesses are internal to the firm and can be largely controlled by the management. Points of attention during analysis include the financial performance of the firm and supplier relation. The financial resources, physical assets, management skills, sales force, merchandise, employee attitude towards the company are some of the factors examined to identify the strengths and weaknesses of a firm. While the strengths can be optimally utilized to achieve the firm's objectives, strategies can be developed to overcome weaknesses by employing an external consultant with an expertise in the weak area or by training the personnel or by studying similar cases in other firms.

While assessing the strengths, the marketer pays maximum attention to the financial performance of the firm. Aspects like costs incurred, profits, sales, assets, liabilities and net worth are regularly monitored by retail managers. Operational efficiency is certainly a factor that can give the marketer an advantage over competitors due to the lower operating expenses it incurs. Such marketers (like Walmart) often pass on a part of the savings in operating expenses to their customers, thereby attracting more customers.

The relationship with suppliers should also be given due consideration as it will have a significant impact on the operational expenses of a company. Collaborations with suppliers can help significantly in reducing operational expenses while not-so-cordial relationships can have detrimental effect on operational expenses.

3.1.2 Opportunities and Threats

Opportunities and threats are factors external to the firm over which the marketer has little or no control. For this PESTEL analysis would help. Every firm is part of a much bigger sphere, i.e. the business environment, social environment, natural environment, economic environment and political environment. Businesses therefore need to keep in mind the constraints and responsibilities imposed by the external environment before taking any decision. The knowledge of existing rules and regulations and upcoming trends in the legal, economic, social, and technological areas can help the marketer determine favourable changes that could be grabbed as opportunities as well as unfavourable changes that could pose a threat and need to be kept under check.

3.1.3 Piercy's Guidelines

In order to make better use of the SWOT framework, Piercy proposes the following five guidelines:

(i) Focus the SWOT on a particular issue or element, such as a specific product market, customer segment, competitor, or an individual element of the marketing mix.

(ii) Use the SWOT analysis as a mechanism to develop a shared vision for planning. This can be done by pooling ideas from a number of sources and achieving a team consensus about the future and on important issues.

(iii) Develop customer orientation by understanding that strengths and weaknesses are irrelevant unless they are recognized and valued by the customer. One of the ways in which this can be done is by applying McDonald's 'so what?' test. In this test the marketing strategist looks at each of the claimed benefits from the viewpoint of the consumer and asks 'well, so what?' to assess its true significance. By doing so, the marketing strategist is also likely to move away from the trap of making a series of so-called motherhood statements (a motherhood statement is warm, re-assuring and difficult to argue against).

(iv) Just as strengths and weaknesses must be viewed from the viewpoint of the customer, so should the analysis of opportunities and threats relate to the marketing environment relevant to the organization's point of focus. Anything else simply leads to a generalized—and largely pointless—set of comments.

(v) The final guideline is concerned with what N. Piercy refers to as structured strategy generation. Piercy suggests that during SWOT analysis, the strengths and weakness should be recognized by the customers while the opportunities and threats should be valid from company's perspective. This means, the firms should assess their internal resources and capabilities by following the Resource Based View (RBV); then priorities the actions/goals to be accomplished within a time frame.

Piercy suggests that during SWOT analysis, the strengths and weakness should be recognized by the customers while the opportunities and threats should be valid from company's perspective.

MARKETING ANALYSIS — INSIGHTS INTO NDTV

New Delhi Television Limited (NDTV) is India's largest news broadcasting company. The broadcasting industry in India is one of the fastest growing areas with a CAGR (Compounded Annual Growth Rate) of 29 per cent over the last five years. Its advertisement spending is expected to increase from the current 0.48 per cent of the GDP to 0.96 per cent of the GDP. The FDI cap in news channels has been increased to 26 per cent, which has increased the inflow of funds to this sector. NDTV is gradually moving up the media value chain with diversification into other media-related business, viz., media outsourcing, FM radio, and so on.

NDTV, founded in 1988, is India's largest private television production house. It was founded by its current Chairman and wholetime Director, Dr. Prannoy Roy, an eminent journalist. NDTV currently has more than 1,000 employees producing news from over twenty locations nationally and internationally. As of 2006, NDTV 24x7 held one of the largest market shares (31 per cent), among English news channels in the country. From a pure news-focused player, NDTV is metamorphosing into a diversified global media player and intends to consistently break new ground.

NDTV wants to stay focused on serious journalism and shun the growing tend towards tabloid news. It feels that credible journalism is what the viewers require and it wants to remain focused on that. However, it has a new venture called 'beyond news' which is a move towards the company's mission of becoming a 'total media' organization. This allows it to venture out of the news broadcasting business and move into entertainment, lifestyle and convergence businesses. However, NDTV wants to maintain credibility and impact in its news business. It wants to run successful campaigns. Leveraging its broadcasting and programming excellence, it has set up NDTV Convergence (digital media), NGEN (media process outsourcing) and NDTV Labs (media software and technology).

It has also introduced a slew of infotainment channels catering to the Indian viewer:

NDTV Good Times: A young and contemporary lifestyle channel programmed for those who want to 'live it up'.

NDTV Lumiere: This aims to bring the world's finest cinema to discerning film buffs.

NDTV Imagine: A clutter-breaking Hindi entertainment channel.

NDTV MetroNation: The country's first English language city-specific infotainment channel network.

Imagine Showbiz: An entertainment channel celebrating Bollywood.

NDTV Arabia: A comprehensive channel of information for the diaspora in the GEC and the Middle East.

Little wonder that NDTV is by far the country's highest rated news network (reaching 90.8 per cent of India's cable and satellite viewers) as well as its most respected media company (according to a survey by the *Business World* in 2007). The news experience is highlighted by www.ndtv.com, India's most visited news television website.

Let us look at a SWOT analysis of NDTV.

Strengths

- Leader in the news broadcasting space. At 31 per cent, NDTV enjoys the largest market share among English news channels in the country.
- The subscription for NDTV has been increasing in the DTH space.
- It has been generating revenue through consulting services for setting up new channels in countries like Malaysia and Indonesia. The company's footprint in the US, UK and Canada has been increasing. Its value has also been unlocked following increasing acceptance of DTH as a medium of distribution.
- It has made a foray into the FM radio industry in partnership with Astro Broadcast and Value Labs to tap the emerging opportunity in FM radio space.

Weaknesses

- The number of channels are increasing and there is intense competition to retain the primetime viewership.
- There is increased attrition rate; the channel has to depend on a few charismatic presenters.

Opportunities

- The DTH and CAS subscriptions are expected to grow by a CAGR of 29 per cent over the next five years. The current average monthly cable subscription collection from individual homes ₹130 though it is projected to increase to ₹250 by 2010. Larger base of TV households from lower SECs, new regulatory changes and delivery mechanisms (like CAS and DTH) will result in improved declarations.
- The advertisement spending is expected to increase from the current 0.48 per cent GDP to 0.96 per cent GDP. Growth in disposable incomes, urbanization, consumerism, and increased reach of the medium due to expanding delivery platforms and technology advancements will result in faster growth. Higher investment from sunrise sectors and continued support from traditional categories (FMCG, durables) is expected. Separate viewership measurement for upmarket audience is also on the cards.
- The FDI cap in news channels has been increased to 26 per cent. Indian channels/media groups are attracting foreign investment. Reuters, UK has taken equity stake in Times Global Broadcasting; Blackstone has invested $275 million in Eenadu while CNN-IBN is a partnership between Turner International and TV18.

Threats

- The Telecom Regulatory Authority of India's (TRAI) regulation prevents broadcasters from fixing the price based on market dynamics. The TRAI also has a lot of regulation on the content.
- There are still open issues with the regulation related to cross-media ownership. This prevents potential investors from long-term planning.
- The broadcasting channels loose a lot of revenue due to the under-declaration of subscribers by the cable operators.

3.1.4 Matching and Conversion Strategies

Strengths must be matched to opportunities, since a strength without a corresponding opportunity is of little strategic value. Strategies, though often difficult, are designed to change weaknesses into strengths and threats into opportunities. For example, let's assume that competitors are proving to be an increasing threat. However, by recognizing that a head-on battle is likely to prove expensive and counterproductive, the emphasis might shift to developing a strategic alliance which would provide both organizations greater combined strength and which, in turn, would allow both to capitalize on the growing opportunities.

Strengths must be matched to opportunities, since any strength without a corresponding opportunity is of little strategic value.

SWOT ANALYSIS FOR PROCTER & GAMBLE (P&G)

Strengths

- Diversification: Product diversification ranging from healthcare, home, men's toiletries, oral and baby care.
- Research and development: P&G invests 3-4 per cent of net outside sales in R&D. This amount easily exceeds that of their leading competitors. P&G India is looking at grabbing a chunk of parent P&G's global R&D spend of a staggering $1.67 billion.
- Innovation: In 2004–5, P&G was granted 27,000 patents globally. It has produced a number of new products like diapers, shampoo-cum-conditioners, toothpaste that prevents osteoporosis, and so on.
- High profitability: Procter & Gamble Hygiene and Health Care Limited announced a profit after tax of ₹51.48 crore for the first quarter ended 30 September 2009—up 4.71 per cent over the corresponding period a year ago.
- Strong brands: P&G has thirteen billion-dollar sales brands such as Always, Ariel, Bounty, Charmin, Crest, Downy/Lenor, Folgers, Iams, Pampers, Pantene, Pringle's and Tide. The total sales of these thirteen billion-dollar brands together would make a Fortune 100 company in itself.
- Leading market position: P&G is the world's largest consumer products company. It is the global leader in all its five broad business segments.

Weaknesses

- Absence of mass appeal: Most of P&G's products are priced at a premium. For instance, Whisper is priced much higher than its nearest competitor.
- Problem of quality control: In 2006, P&G was forced to suspend the sales of cosmetics in China owing to the presence of banned substances like chromium and neodymium.

Opportunities

- Developing markets: The consumer market in India is growing at a fast rate and the FMCG market is expected to reach US$33.40 billion in 2015.
- Rural markets: Rural India has a large consuming class with 41 per cent of India's middle class and 58 per cent of the total disposable income. This provides a huge opportunity for diversification.
- Growing bottled water market: Bottled water is a fast-growing segment in the world's food and beverage market owing to increasing health concerns. In May 2007, P&G launched PUR Flavor Options, a product that allows consumers to choose flavoured or unflavoured water from their home water filter. There's also a growing healthcare industry in the US.

Threats

- Increased competition: The Indian FMCG space has giants like HUL and ITC.
- Unorganized sector: Tide and Ariel are facing heat from local players like Ghadi detergent powder.
- Increasing price of raw materials: Currently the per capita spending on P&G products is less than a dollar per person a year in India. The company aspires to increase it to the level as in markets like Mexico. This could generate an incremental US$40 billion in annual sales. For P&G, the year 2010 would be the 'year of investments' as it hopes to increase market share in categories such as household products, beauty and grooming and healthcare products.
- With the launch of Rejoice, it has tried to explore newer areas with products catering to the mass segment.
- With population in the rural areas set to rise to 153 million households by 2010–11 and with higher saturation in the urban markets, future growth in the FMCG sector will come from increased rural and small town penetration. P&G must capitalize on this since HUL and ITC have already identified the opportunity and have initiated projects such as 'Project Shakti' and 'E-Choupal'.

Source: India Brand Equity Foundation, 2010.

3.1.5 Integration

As the marketing strategist goes through the process of identifying hidden strengths, matching strengths to opportunities, limiting weaknesses to the extent possible by forseeing the market conditions and competitions, the business models are set to be on the rolling.

3.2 TOWS Matrix

The limitations of SWOT that Piercy highlights have also been mentioned by Weihrich. His principal criticism of SWOT is that having conducted the analysis, managers frequently fail to come to terms with the strategic choices that the outcomes demand. In order to overcome this he argues for the TOWS matrix which, while making use of the same inputs (Threats, Opportunities, Weaknesses and Strengths), reorganizes them and integrates them more completely into the strategic planning process.

It is also often useful if, when planning and having made particular assumptions, the planner then prepares TOWS matrices for, say, three and five years with a view to identifying how the strategies, options and priorities may change. This way there is a greater likelihood that the planning team will come to terms with what the future truly demands.

MARKETING IN ACTION — **MARICO TESTS COOLING HAIR OIL SEGMENT**

FMCG major Marico entered the cooling hair oil segment in November 2009 by launching two products—Parachute Advanced Cooling Oil and Nihar Naturals Cooling Oil. The products have been test marketed in rural belts—Parachute in Andhra Pradesh and Nihar in Bihar and Jharkhand. Marico had entered the cooling oil segment earlier with Maha Thanda, but it did not go national. This move is seen as the company's attempt to gain a bigger piece of the overall hair oil segment in India, which is worth about ₹3,000 crore, of which Marico held a 21 per cent market share in 2009.

There are several regional players in the segment enjoying a huge presence in the rural markets. Emami's Navratna, for instance, is the biggest player in the cooling hair oil segment with a market share of around 70 per cent. The ₹300-crore brand, which has a prominent presence in Andhra Pradesh, seems to have left no stone unturned in its strategy to market Navratna. It has roped in Shahrukh Khan and Amitabh Bachchan as brand ambassadors at the national level and Telugu actor Mahesh Babu as the regional brand ambassador.

Marico's cooling oil will be differentiated on the fact that it will be coconut-based and will have cooling properties. Analysts say that although there are major hurdles for Marico's new brands, there are enough opportunities in this segment. The hair oil segment is difficult to break into and cooling hair oil is not a very aspirational product. Marico clearly seems to be riding on the success of its existing status in the market. Though cooling oil is more expensive, the price factor can be overcome with aggressive product promotion. Industry experts say Marico cannot afford to miss out on the ₹450-crore cooling hair oil market and could expect 20-30 per cent of its revenue from the segment. Even without the cooling oil variant, both Parachute and Nihar enjoy over 50 per cent market in the branded hair oil segment. Parachute coconut oil in rigid packs grew about 13 per cent sequentially in volume in the April-June 2009 quarter. During the period, its hair oils in rigid packs grew 9 per cent.

Source: Business Today, December 2009.

3.3 Internal Analysis

The resource-based view (RBV) consists of a well-developed set of concepts that helps us analyse how a firm's internal strengths and weaknesses affect its ability to compete. The following sections provide a description of this concept:

A. Assets

The factors of production in a firm may draw on customers with valuable goods and services called assets for carrying on their business activity. One should note that the RBV defines assets more broadly than accounting does. Assets may be tangible or intangible. Intangible assets are just as real as tangible resources, but they can't be touched or seen directly. For instance, Reliance Industries has the highest market capitalization in the country. Their asset includes the market cap along with RIL's human and non-human resources.

The factors of production in a firm may draw on customers with valuable goods and services are called assets.

B. Capabilities

RBV defines capabilities as the skills a firm needs to take full advantage of its assets. Without such capabilities assets are of little value. For example, General Motors once had more assets than any other car maker in the world, including the best and the biggest plants, the most advanced technology, the strongest brand name, the greatest market share, the largest workforce, and the most extensive distribution network. Japanese competitor firms started with a much smaller base of assets but they challenged General Motors' lead based on three different sets of capabilities. First, they became adept at lowering costs. Second, they went on to improve quality. Finally, they designed faster product-development processes. When they competed on these capabilities, they dramatically reduced GM's dominance in the industry. Today, Toyota is the number two car maker in the world, having pushed Ford pushed to third position. A new car comes out of a Toyota plant every six minutes! Economic downturn has taken a heavy toll on GM's prospects and the future of this giant seems bleak as its CEO has been asked by President Barack Obama to step down.

Capabilities are the skills a firm needs to be able to take full advantage of its assets.

C. Competencies

Although specialists argue about what constitutes competency, the word simply refers to the ability to perform. The concept of competence has long been recognized in the literature of strategic management. Scholars have and continue to refer to core competence, at one time called 'distinctive competencies', are the critical bundles of skills that an organization can draw on to distinguish itself from its competitors.

'Distinctive competencies' are the critical bundles of skills that an organization can draw on to distinguish itself from its competitors.

Central to the RBV is the notion that what a firm can do is fundamental to its success. However, we should not attach value to just any competence—a firm might develop a competence that is of little competitive value. For example, Amul says its butter taste is 'Taste of India'. In fact, an essential part of using the RBV is the ability to understand which resources, capabilities, and competence are valuable. While specific critical success factors vary from business to business, research has identified four aspects that determine the success factors crucial for any business. These are:

1. **Industry characteristic:** Critical success factors (CSFs) are often industry-specific. Success factors for supermarket chains would include product mix, inventory turnover, sales promotion, and pricing. In the airline industry, these would be fuel efficiency, load factor, and reservation system.

The CSF of a business include: industry characteristics, competitive position, general environment and organizational development.

Thus, no one set of CSFs applies to all industries. Observe at the banking and financial services industry (BFSI) and the automobile industry's fluctuating fortunes since the global meltdown in September 2008. The success factors which led them to become some of the most profitable organizations a few years earlier could not save them during the downturn.

DUBAI'S ULTIMATE MOTORS TO LAUNCH HYPER CARS IN INDIA

Super hyper cars, or ultra high-end exotic cars, which are designed to provide clean, safe and highly efficient performance, stormed Indian roads by December 2009. Dubai-based Ultimate Motors, one of the leading distributors of exotic and luxury sports cars in the world, launched three brands of Super Hyper Cars (SHCs)—Shelby, Zenvo and Arash.

The demand for luxury cars has been increasing in India and people are keen to have customized cars. US-based Shelby SuperCars' Ultimate Aero has been recorded as the world's fastest car with a speed of 413 km per hour (257 mph). It produces 1,183 horsepower thus making it the world's most powerful production car. It can reach from 0 to 60 mph in 2.78 seconds. Similarly, Denmark's Zenvo and UK-based Arash are also in the race to introduce their SHCs into the Indian market. Arash has a unique road car aerodynamics whereas the Zenvo comes with a full carbon body and steel chassis. All the three SHCs are priced in the range of ₹2.4-₹5.4 crore. SHCs are exotic cars whose performance is superior to that of contemporaries and have been defined specifically as expensive, fast and powerful cars with centrally located engines.

Initially, Ultimate Motors expects to sell three units of Shelby, two units of Zenvo and four cars of Arash by 2010.

Source: Auto World, January 2010.

2. **Competitive position:** This may vary with a firm's position relative to its competition. For example, in an industry dominated by one or two large competitors, the actions of the big players often produce new and significant problems that become CSFs for smaller firms. At one time, the smaller players in the personal computer industry believed it was critical for them to offer products compatible with Lenovo PCs. So, Lenovo's every move took on significance across the PC industry.

MARKETING IN ACTION — TATA TEA QUITS BEVERAGE BUSINESS RETAILING TO FOCUS ON BRANDED PRODUCTS

Tata Tea, the second-largest branded tea maker in the world, will exit the beverage retailing business, including Chai Unchai, as part of the group's strategy to focus on branded products. Another group company, Tata Coffee, which sold 34.3 per cent of its equity in the retail chain Barista to NRI investor C. Sivasankaran five years ago, has also dropped its plan to re-enter the business. Sangeeta Talwar, executive director, marketing, Tata Tea confirmed that Tata Coffee, a listed subsidiary of Tata Tea, would not pursue its plans in the cafe business.

As the cafe retail business in India is dominated by local players, the scope for new brands is limited. However, established brands like Lavazza and Cafe Coffee Day are expanding their business that will see 5,000 branded outlets across India in the next five years, up from the existing 1,200 outlets as of 2009. Since the margin from the cafe business is volatile, Tata Tea would be interested to cash in on its core competence, which is sale of branded products. The company, which unveiled Chai Unchai in Bengaluru in January 2008, was planning to add more outlets in the city in not just the existing movable kiosk format but also in the form of tea parlours, similar to urban coffee outlets. The company had about five Chai Unchai outlets in the city.

Tata Coffee was waiting for the non-compete contract it signed with Barista to expire before launching its cafe network.The largest coffee plantation company in Asia is also running its branded coffee powder retail business through Mr Bean Coffee Junction.

Tata Tea is going through a transformation and consolidation phase, focusing more on branded products and reducing exposure in commodities. The group markets beverages mainly under brands such as Tata Tea, Himalayan and Tata Coffee, in addition to acquired brands like Tetley, Good Earth and Eight O'clock Coffee. According to Sangeeta Talwar, the cold drink brand Tion, introduced in early 2009, has been a success in

Tamil Nadu, with 3 per cent market share in Chennai. The company plans to enter other south Indian states with the drink.

Though popularly called Tata Tea, the company is Tata Beverages for insiders and finding a new unified brand name is on the cards. The company is hunting for opportunities in the beverages segment across the world, says Tata Tea managing director Percy T. Siganporia. West Asia, South America, Africa and the US are the targeted geographies for fresh forays.

The company will soon begin operations in France and Australia. Tata Tea has ₹3,000 crore cash and cash equivalents on books and its gross debt stood at ₹2,500 crore in November 2009.

Source: Business Standard, January 2010.

3. **General environment**: Changes in any of the major aspects of the general environment (Political, Environmental, Social and Technological, or PEST) can affect the emergence of CSFs in the market. For instance, interest rate for bank deposits were made very lucrative in 2008 when the stock market was doing well; the State Bank of India in fact offered a rate of 10.5 per cent for deposits of over 1,000 days. However, it slashed the rate to 8 per cent for the same deposit period when the stock market hit rock bottom in mid-2009 and withdrawn the scheme in 2010.

MARKETING IN ACTION

GODREJ STRENGTHENS ROOTS IN VILLAGES WITH REGIONAL ADVERTISEMENTS

Most FMCG companies have a two-pronged strategy to tap rural markets. It comprises launching nano packs and scaling up rural distribution during market downturn and recovery. Godrej Consumer Products Limited (GCPL) is going a step further by adding a regional advertising component. According to Managing Director Dalip Sehgal, 'Our regional advertising and publicity (A&P) spends have increased between 50-60 per cent in the first half of FY 2010.' In 2009, the company spent 66 per cent of its total A&P spends on regional advertising. It spent 9 per cent of its total sales on A&P, which has more than doubled to ₹50.90 crore (second quarter of 2010) from ₹24.40 crore in second quarter of 2009. The company advertises on Doordarshan, local TV and radio channels, the local press and outdoor media. For its top performing brands, it spends most of the cut-out budget on regional advertising only.

For Godrej No.1 soap, the entire ad spends go in regional advertising. For Cinthol and Expert (powder hair dye), it is more than 50 per cent. The strategy bore fruit in 2009. Godrej No. 1 became the largest selling soap in north India in 2009, its annual sales exceeding ₹500 crore. It is also the country's third-largest soap brand. Simultaneously, Cinthol's market share increased from 2.5 per cent to 2.8 per cent, while Cinthol deodorant grew by 50 per cent in the second quarter of 2009.

Expert hair dye has a 26 per cent market share. To further promote sales, the company is running a campaign wherein local barber shops and salons are branded under the 'Expert' brand name. The strategy is to introduce the products to rural folks through barbers. The company has already engaged 50,000 barber shops and salons under this programme.

Price points are also important, so Godrej has been rolling out nano packs priced between ₹5 and ₹10. To increase its reach in the rural areas, the company in 2009 added 1,700 small towns and 5,000 new villages and aims to reach 8,000 towns (from 5,500 now) and 50,000 villages (from 15,000 now) by 2012.

Owing to the above efforts, GCPL's rural sales doubled in comparison with urban sales. Rural sales grew by 40 per cent, while urban sales grew at 20 per cent in the second quarter of 2009. The rural sector today contributes 42 per cent to Godrej's total sales and it expects to make this 50 per cent by 2012.

Source: The Economic Times, May 2010.

4. **Organizational development:** Internal developments may sometimes give rise to new CSFs. Firms have to address short-term issues before dealing with long-lasting issues. Thus, internal organizational considerations become temporary CSFs. For example, if several key executives of an investment banking firm quit to form a competing 'spin-off firm', rebuilding the executive group would become the first priority for the original organization.

CSF is both an advantage, because it allows managers to tailor the general concept to a particular situation, and a disadvantage, because of a lack of specific direction.

Obviously, there is a great deal of flexibility in identifying what constitutes CSFs. CSF is both an advantage, because it allows managers to tailor the general concept to a particular situation, and a disadvantage, because of a lack of specific direction. The value chain is a more directive framework that serves as a useful supplement to study the CSFs.

MARKETING IN ACTION — WOMAN POWER FUELS SCOOTY

An award-winning marketing scheme that trained women to ride two-wheelers helped TVS ramp up sales in 2009. The Mudra Group won the only Globe for India at the MAA Award Function in October 2009. The award recognizes the best of marketing programmes from around the globe. The award was won in the Best Activity Generating Brand Loyalty category. The MAA Award, overseen by 114 judges from 27 countries, was the fourth international recognition for Mudra in 2009 for its innovative campaign—Women on Wheels—for TVS Scooty. The campaign won medals at the PMM, the Abby's and the Grand Emvie as well.

Conceptualized and executed by the Mudra's trade marketing unit Multiplier, Women on Wheels was a simple programme that trained women to ride two-wheelers. As a part of this campaign, TVS set up driving schools called TVS Scooty Institute at its dealerships where girls above 16 years of age could take a week's training for just ₹350. Since women account for more than 70 per cent of Scooty sales, the campaign, positioned as empowerment of women, was a smart move. It helped TVS post a 24 per cent volume growth in Scooty sales against the overall industry growth of 18 per cent in 2009. The strategy—train and sell—was also in tune with a TVS-IMRB research study which found that any girl who learns to ride on a certain brand of bike would invariably like to buy the same brand, the training being a big influence on purchase decision. No wonder, Scooty accounted for 25-30 per cent of the total sales of TVS at around 3,00,000 two-wheelers in 2009. The company's Scooty portfolio includes Scooty Streak, Scooty Pep, Scooty Teenz and Teenz Electric.

The study also showed that while it is normal for men to lend their bikes to their male friends who want to learn how to ride, women face stiff resistance from even their family members. What makes it worse is that there aren't many formal two-wheeler training centres in the country. The findings prompted the company to set up the Scooty Institute. As most two-wheeler sales happen in tier II towns, TVS launched the institute in areas with a population of 1,00,000 to 5,00,000. The women undergoing training were in the age group of 18-25 years and who didn't want to depend on family members or the public transport system for commuting. In 2010–11, TVS is planning to scale up the programme to about 1,000 centres (from 80 now), using its extensive dealership and service network.

Under the programme, dealers approach girls' schools and colleges to offer training in riding two-wheelers. Residential areas and beauty salons are also targeted. Over 4,00,000 women have been contacted and more than 42,000 women trained in the last two years. 'In each centre, we want to increase the number of women being trained to 200 from the existing 60-70,' says S. Srinivas, general manager, marketing, TVS Motor Company. One in every five students bought a TVS brand within three months of the training.

While the Women on Wheels programme is doing fine, TVS has also been banking on aggressive above-the-line promotions using celebrities like Preity Zinta and Sania Mirza to endorse its products.

'It adds to Scooty's aspirational value,' says Harish Bijoor, CEO, Harish Bijoor Consults Inc. Bijoor says the product campaign reinforces the concept of women on the move. 'It is all about breaking the stereotype of the woman on the pillion and the man up front riding or driving,' he says. Styling, easy-to-use features and models available in 99 colours have all added to the aspirational value.

Analysts say TVS needs to step up these innovations as it is still far behind market leader Honda in the Scooty segment. According to SIAM data, Honda Motorcycle and Scooter India (HMSI) sold 52,552 units in September 2009 against TVS' 29,468 units. Hero Honda was in the third position with 17,299 units.

While HMSI, which has Activa, Dio and Aviator in its portfolio, doesn't advertise specifically for women, TVS may face tough competition from Hero Honda which is gaining ground fast with its 100cc, gearless scooter—Pleasure. Launched in January 2006, Pleasure is betting on cutting-edge technology. For instance, Pleasure comes equipped with the tuff-up tube, a technology which offers immediate remedy in case of a puncture by using an anti-puncture sealant gel. Hero Honda is also playing on the 'woman theme'. Apart from Priyanka Chopra as the brand ambassador, the company recently launched 'Just4her', the first exclusive showroom for women customers of Pleasure. There were more than 20 Just4her showrooms and workshops across the country in 2009, serviced exclusively by women staff. The company also introduced Lady Rider Club, an exclusive women's club which is a first in the automobile industry, TVS has tough competition indeed.

Source: The Economic Times, April 2010.

3.4 The Value Chain

This method of assessing strengths and weaknesses divides the business into a number of linked activities that may each produce value for the customer. Customer value is a function of factors that usually fall into one of three broad categories: those that differentiate the product, those that lower its costs, or those that allow the organization to respond to customer needs more quickly. The value chain framework helps analyse the contributions of individual activities in a business to the overall level of customer value the firm produces, and ultimately to its financial performance. If each part of the business produces value, the firm should be able to charge more and/or incur lower costs, either of which will lead to higher profit margin.

The value chain framework helps analyse the contributions of individual activities in a business to the overall level of customer value the firm produces, and ultimately to its financial performance.

MARKETING IN ACTION — **ECONOMY ON DIET, CAR MAKERS SHED WEIGHT**

With the economy on a diet, automakers are looking at ways to shed weight and make their products more fuel efficient without compromising on the safety quotient. Honda, Maruti Suzuki, Hyundai, Toyota and Tata Motors are all working overtime to reduce the body weight of their vehicles by turning to aluminium, high-tensile steel and plastic. The reduction in weight across car makers will be at least 5 per cent and in some cases as much as 12 per cent, say industry trackers. Efforts are also on to design smaller-capacity, fuel-efficient engines, said persons familiar with the development.

Weight can bring about the biggest gain in terms of overall carbon dioxide reduction, apart from enhancing the vehicle's performance and reducing fuel consumption. Some of the latest additions on Indian roads like the Suzuki A-Star, Ritz and the much-anticipated Tata Nano have all used lighter materials besides being powered by smaller-capacity, high-performance engines.

Consumers can experience these advancements in driving dynamics and engine response. Honda Siel's Jazz is produced on the same platform as the City but by reducing the weight, the makers have improved the efficiency of the vehicle without compromising on safety.

Industry trackers say that using lightweight materials will have a clear impact on the price of the car. Customers in urban areas want a sparry feel and a good driving experience. For them, price and fuel efficiency are not that critical. But for customers in the semi-urban and rural areas, pricing will be a key determinant. And with the industry reaching out to tier II towns and rural India to counter the demand slump in big cities, that's one factor automakers can't afford to overlook.

Source: The Economic Times, May 2009.

3.5 Missions and Objectives

The mission statement of a firm is the foundation of the whole planning process and hence should be precise and reflective of the firm's attitudes and philosophy. Moreover, the strategies in the subsequent planning stages should be consistent with the mission statement. A carefully-developed mission statement includes such details as the products and services to be offered, scope of business, target customers, growth plans, the kind of customer service to be provided, and the attributes for competitive advantage. For example, McDonald's mission statement, 'Quality, Service, Convenience and Value', emphasizes on delivering value to its customers by providing quality service and convenience. The company makes sure that every employee understands the spirit of the statement right from the day he/she joins the organization.

The mission statement of a firm is the foundation of the planning process and hence should be precise and reflective of the firm's attitudes and philosophy. It's objectives should be time-specific, measurable, attainable and indicative of business priorities.

The marketers, after conducting a situational analysis, should set objectives and specify long-term and short-term targets. A firm can set sales objectives that include overall growth in sales, stability in sales and profits, and achievement of a higher market share. Likewise, profit objectives can include the range of profits expected, the return on investment and operational efficiency. Objectives like achieving customer satisfaction, meeting the expectations of stockholders and enhancing the image of the store also have to be established.

To be effective, a good marketing system must be goal driven. The setting of marketing objectives is therefore a key step in the marketing process. In terms of its position within the overall planning process, objectives setting can be seen to follow on from the initial stage of analysis and, in particular, from the marketing audit. By setting marketing objectives, the planner is attempting to provide the organization with a sense of direction. In addition, objectives provide a basis for motivation as well as act as a benchmark against which performance and effectiveness can subsequently be measured. The setting of objectives is the prelude to the development of marketing strategies and detailed marketing plans.

The process of moving from the general to the specific should lead to a set of marketing objectives which are not just attainable within any budgetary constraints that may exist, but which are also compatible with the environmental conditions as well as the organizational strengths and weaknesses. It follows from this that the process of setting marketing objectives should form what is often referred to as an internally consistent and mutually reinforcing hierarchy. Objectives should be time-specific, measurable, attainable and indicative of the business priorities. If the objectives are specific and measurable, they motivate the employees to perform better. In contrast, objectives that are not attainable discourage/frustrate employees. However, objectives would not serve their purpose unless they are reviewed and evaluated periodically.

3.6 Macro- and Micro-Environmental Analysis

3.6.1 State of the Economy (National and Global)

During downturn, companies should use 'innovative strategies' to enhance market share. When the economic conditions leave little or no chance for sales growth, it is referred to as a 'stagnant economy'.

The economic situation of the country determines the purchases that consumers make and the amount of money that they are ready to spend. During downturn, 'innovative strategies' should be used by companies to enhance market share. In such times, rather than attempting to induce the customers to spend more, the marketers should make efforts to gain a larger share of the market using innovative strategies. They can also do so by venturing into new markets. Weak and uncompetitive marketers are pushed out of business when the economic conditions are challenging. When the economic conditions leave little or no chance for sales growth, it is referred to as a 'stagnant economy'.

Look at the financial condition of the world after the collapse of AIG, Lehman Brothers and with the takeover of Merryl Lynch by Amex. The turnaround strategy of the international financial market mechanism has yet to find its way to recovery. The result? The fall of the BSE index to below 8,000 points—a sharp decline of 65 per cent from its peak of 21,000 points, in a span of 10 months in 2009!

Now liquidity crisis is causing fears among corporates and investors the world over. The huge loss of investor wealth, created during years of unrealistic growth, is taking its toll globally. In the US alone, massive job cuts and closure of shops (600 Starbucks coffee shops shut within a week of the crisis) created panic among the public and in the international community, despite President Obama's announcemt of $3 trillion bailout package.

MARKETING ANALYSIS — RETURN OF CONSUMER FINANCE SCHEMES FOR FMCG DURABLES

The party is not over for consumer durables manufacturers, who recorded a 20-30 per cent growth during the festival period in 2009. They are anticipating the growth to continue thanks to the return of consumer-finance schemes. Till early 2008, the sale of financing-led consumer durables accounted for 15-20 per cent of the overall sales in the sector. However, this contribution fell to 8-10 per cent in the next 18 months after banks and finance companies drastically reduced lending. Following the credit crisis in banks in 2008, many top private sector lenders including ICICI Bank and Citibank scaled down or exited retail financing of small-ticket durables. That left the market to non-banking finance companies such as Bajaj Finance and Shriram Finance which, too, decided to go slow on such loans.

Analysts say many big players tend to avoid this business because of defaults, and retail outlets themselves provide loans for the products they sell. For instance, Future Group, which sells durables through its Big Bazaar hypermarkets and eZone electronics chain, offers a financing option to its consumers through its arm, Future Money. It is estimated that finance for consumer durables currently accounts for a meagre 2 per cent of banks' retail portfolio. However since November 2009 consumer-finance loans are back in the market and manufacturers are also busy reintroducing zero-finance schemes. Under such a scheme, the manufacturer bears the interest cost on the loan, while the processing fee for the application is either passed on to the consumer or shared between the dealer and the manufacturer. While the consumer benefits by buying on easy instalments, the company draws revenues on bulk sales.

In 2007 and 2008, around 10 per cent of the total units sold by Godrej & Boyce availed finance schemes. The figure was 5 per cent in October 2009. But on the back of these schemes, the appliance division of Godrej & Boyce anticipates a 20-30 per cent growth in sales volume in 2009–10. There was a lull during the festive season in 2008 as FMCG durable firms were hit by the slowdown but there's already a pick-up in consumer sentiments.

Analysts say it is difficult to retrieve money from defaulters of durables or smaller electronics items compared to car loan defaulter, a reason why many durables financing companies have exited the business. Citi, GE Money and ICICI did so at the end of 2008. However, Bajaj Finance has expanded in a big way since then. Samsung is running triple-zero finance offers for all products with Bajaj Finance. It has also tied up with Shriram Finance in the south. Finance-led sales is expected to have contributed around 7 per cent of consumer electronics sales of Samsung in 2009.

Samsung's tie-up with Bajaj Finance for a triple-zero finance scheme translates into zero initial payment, processing fee and interest. The offer is expected to help consumers upgrade to premium products easily. LG Electronics too introduced two zero per cent finance schemes, valid till November 2009. The schemes were valid on purchases above ₹5,000 and consumers could pay in 9-10 instalments. LG schemes are also in tie-up with Bajaj and Shriram.

Even Sony India has tied up with several banks to offer an interest-free equated monthly instalment (EMI) scheme for card purchases and the company says it is working well.

Source: Business Standard, January 2010.

3.6.2 Technological Development

Tele-marketing, e-marketing and credit card purchases are some examples of technological innovations.

Technological innovations have had a tremendous impact on the way businesses are run. Tele-marketing, e-marketing and credit card purchases are some of the examples of technological innovations. Transactions have become simpler and more convenient. Credit cards have efficiently replaced cash transactions. Customers can transfer money from their account directly into the retailer's through electronic funds transfer. Another development is electronic or catalogue retailing, which is high on convenience and also effective in attracting new customers.

MARKETING ANALYSIS — AUTO FIRMS INCREASE ONLINE SPENDS

Recession has made companies nimble. Auto companies, specifically, realized that when people are not buying as before, it is sane to put money where most potential buyers shop. So they have opted for plain banner ads, flash ads, and click-to-play videos.

Leading auto companies in the country including Maruti, General Motors, Volkswagen, Honda, Mahindra and Bajaj increased their online spends significantly in 2010. The reason is not hard to fathom. A report by J.D. Power and Associates declared that over a third of prospective vehicle customers in India are opting for the Internet to search for information on vehicles. The figure has risen from 21 per cent in 2007 to 34 per cent in 2009.

Vehicles are high-value items. With the urban upper middle and middle class population typically surfing the Internet, the shift to cyberspace is a lucrative option for auto companies. Maruti is a case in point. In 2009, it got an average of 3,500-4,000 test drive requests online every month and around 2,000 enquires for 'True Value', its used-car business. According to Shashank Srivastava, chief general manager (marketing), Maruti Suzuki, 'With our product range and profile moving towards younger audience, at Maruti Suzuki, we are focusing on this medium in a big way.' Maruti's focus on the Web can be gauged from its innovative initiatives like virtual test drives on the Web for Ritz and Swift Life, an online community portal for Swift owners. Its campaign for A-Star was extremely successful. Its initiative for the Ritz got it over 21 million impressions from Web users. Over 5.90 lakh unique visitors during the first month of Ritz's launch in 2009 helped build a strong brand positioning for the Ritz. Maruti was the first company to offer online booking as well as sales through the Internet for NRIs, which was started way back in 2006.

Another point in case is Tata Motors which used the Internet extensively for marketing the Nano. A section on the Nano website enabled users to design their own car. Nano communities established on Orkut and Facebook, prior to the car's launch in 2009, helped it gather the opinion and preferences of customers. It also launched a game and conducted regular contests on the website to keep customer interest alive. Tata Motors also introduced online booking for Nano in April 2009, allowing online payment. On the launch, the website received 5 million hits in a period of 24 hours. During the booking phase of Nano, the website received an average of 8 lakh hits per day. One could also buy Nano merchandise online.

The use of online marketing tools helped Tata Motors capture the preferences and feedback of the customers on a real-time basis as against the traditional media. As if on cue, other auto companies have revamped their websites. Websites which earlier used to look like information brochures now sport 3D views of automobiles and have online booking features.

Source: Business World, January 2010.

3.6.3 Product Life Cycle

In the mature and decline stages of the product life cycle, the main objective of the firm will be to extract maximum profit from the existing formats and markets by refining existing strategies (with no further investments).

In the mature and decline stages of the product life cycle, the main objective of the firms will be to extract as much profit as possible from the existing formats and markets by refining the existing strategies (without making any further investments). For example, in areas where Walmart reaches saturation, it closes down its smaller stores in the surrounding towns and opens regional 'superstores' that offer groceries, auto repair, and other services.

Marketers can also increase productivity by undertaking cost reduction, increasing merchandise turnover or prices and margins. Cost reduction can be achieved by implementing self-service schemes which will reduce labour requirements. Some other ways of reducing costs are reducing store hours, making better use of part-time helpers and cutting down on customer services.

Technology can also help reduce costs by providing information on individual contributions of each of the items in the merchandise towards the total profitability of the firm. The merchandise can thus be planned according to the merchandise movement, which will cut down inventory costs without compromising on availability. Using EDI with suppliers will also save costs by eliminating the need for paper-based transactions.

3.6.4 Brand Name

An important element of any marketing strategy is the role played by brand names. Brands are designed to enable customers to identify products or services that promise specific benefits. As such, they create a set of expectations in the minds of customers about the purpose, performance, quality and price of the product. This, in turn, allows the marketing strategist to build added value into the product and to differentiate it from the competitors. Because of this, well known brand names such as Rolex, Ray-Ban, Coca-Cola and Lacoste are of enormous strategic and financial value and are in many cases the result of years of investment in advertising. The significance of this in the case of Microsoft has been highlighted by the suggestion that the company's brand name is worth more than the GNP of many nations. It also helps to explain why pirating of brand names has developed so rapidly over the past decade.

Brands are designed to enable customers to identify products or services that promise specific benefits.

An organization can pursue various approaches in developing its brand strategy. Some of these are:

Corporate umbrella branding: This can either be used as a lead name such as Heinz, Kellogg's or Cadbury's, or as a supporting brand name such as P&G and HUL. In the case of Cadbury's, for example, the umbrella is used to cover a wide variety of chocolates and sweets including Cream Eggs, Dairy Milk, Milk Tray, Bournville, Celebrations, Fruit and Nut, Crackle and Roast Almond.

Corporate umbrella branding can either be used as a lead name such as Heinz, Kellogg's or Cadbury's, or as a supporting brand name such as P&G and HUL.

Family umbrella branding: These are used to cover a range of products in a variety of markets.

Range brand names: Range brand names are used for a range of products which have clearly identifiable links in a particular market. An example is the Park Avenue range of men's clothing and accessories by Raymond's.

Individual brand names: This is typically used to cover one type of product in one type of market, possibly with different combinations of size, flavour, service options or packaging formats. Examples of this include Lux soap in green, pink and white colour for oily, normal and dry skin with sample, regular and family packs in cake/solid or liquid form.

Individual brand names are typically used to cover one type of product in one type of market, possibly with different combinations of size, flavour, service options or packaging formats.

For many organizations, branding is a fundamental element of the product strategy and provides the basis for consumer franchise which, if managed effectively, allows for greater marketing flexibility and a higher degree of consumer loyalty. However, it needs to be recognized that branding involves a great deal more than simply putting a name on a package. Branding is about creating, maintaining and proactively developing perceived consumer value. It is only in this way that an organization can promise and deliver to the consumer superior value than that offered by competitors. It follows from this that any brand strategy is necessarily a long-term process, involving an investment in and commitment to the development of the brand over time.

Branding is about creating, maintaining and proactively developing perceived consumer value. The challenge for businesses is to create or retain differentiation of their respective product or service to prevent goods from being commoditized.

The challenge for businesses is to create or retain differentiation of their respective product or service so as to prevent such goods from being commoditized, thereby leading to destruction of value from the perspective of the stakeholders of such businesses. Traditionally, successful branding has served the purpose of creating and maintaining such differentiation to the benefit of the consumer, the retail channel, and the producer-owner of the branded product or service. However, the forces of change make the task that much more formidable (to serve a national, regional or global market, and yet ideally serve each market as if it has a 'single' consumer). Add to this the increasing media options, flurry of new product launches, and an economy that is not galloping and the challenge is very clear—brand building is getting tougher and the costs keep rising.

Established brands like Coca-Cola spend as much as 20 per cent of their revenue on marketing. Indian brands such as Raymond's and Titan spend up to 5-6 per cent of their annual revenue on marketing and brand building whereas Madura Garments has reportedly earmarked as much as 15 per cent of its current annual revenue for this purpose in 2010.

CSF in branding: Building a distinct business identity on the strength of the product and service combined with an unflinching orientation to customer needs.

Indian best practice examples include Jet Airways, Taj (Indian Hotels) and Oberoi Hotels, and more recently AirTel—each having built a distinct business identity on the strength of their product and service. Unflinching orientation to customer needs is the second key success factor. Proactive tracking of shifts in consumer behaviour, anticipating needs, and then reacting in 'real time' are essential to attract and retain customer loyalty—a key element of creating brand equity.

MADURA GARMENTS: A PIONEER MARKETER

Madura Garments began as a subsidiary of Madura Coats Limited (Madura Coats), in which Coats Viyella Plc., Europe's largest clothing supplier, held a majority stake. Coats Viyella owned internationally established brands such as Peter England, Louis Philippe, Van Heusen, Allen Solly and Byford, which were marketed in India by Madura Coats. The company was the pioneer in branded readymade men's wear in India.

The matrix given in Table 3.1 focuses on the product (what is sold) and to whom it is sold (the market). It highlights four alternatives open to the strategist:

Table 3.1: Ansoff's growth vector matrix

Market	*Product*	
	Current	*New*
Current	Market penetration	Product development
New	Market extension	Diversification

Source: Ansoff.

- Selling existing products to existing markets.
- Extending existing products to new markets.
- Developing new products for existing markets.
- Developing new products for new markets.

Although in practice, there are relative degrees of newness, both in terms of products and markets, and hence the number of strategies open to an organization is infinite, Ansoff's matrix is useful in that it provides a convenient and simple framework within which marketing objectives and strategies can be readily developed.

Ansoff's matrix is useful as it provides a convenient and simple framework within which marketing objectives and strategies can be readily developed.

CASE STUDY — A PEEK INTO TAJ HOTELS

The Indian Hotels Company Limited (IHCL) and its subsidiaries are collectively known as Taj Hotels Resorts and Palaces and are recognized as one of Asia's largest and finest hotel company. The IHCL consists of the Taj Group of Hotels (including Taj Exotica and Taj Safari), the Gateway Hotels, Ginger Hotels, Taj Air (a luxury private jet operation) and Taj Sats Air Catering Limited (the largest airline catering service in South Asia, a joint venture with Singapore Airport Terminal Services, a subsidiary of Singapore Airlines).

Taj Hotels Resorts and Palaces comprises more than 60 hotels in 45 locations across India with an additional 15 international hotels in Malaysia, United Kingdom, United States of America, Bhutan, Sri Lanka, Africa, the Middle East and Australia. Spanning the length and breadth of the country, gracing industrial towns and cities, beaches, hill stations, historical and pilgrim centres and wildlife destinations, each Taj Hotel offers luxurious service, warm hospitality, vantage locations, modern amenities and business facilities. The IHCL also comprises 17 Ginger hotels.

From a gross revenue of ₹873.24 crore in the period 2004–5, the company's gross revenue have increased more than twofold to ₹1,823.16 crore in 2007–8. IHCL operates in three value segments: luxury, premium and mid-market. These are given in Table 3.2.

Market penetration: Here the firm seeks to achieve growth with existing products in its current market segment by increasing its market share. Here IHCL can expand its Ginger and Gateway hotels network to different cities of India. It should target existing middle class customer in different cities.

Market development: Here the firm seeks growth by extending its existing products to new market segments. The IHCL has 60 hotels in India and 15 international hotels, so it is heavily dependent on Indian operations. It can increase its international operations by venturing into new countries.

Product development: Here companies develop new products to tap the existing market. IHCL has hotels targeting different customer segments. The Taj Group targets the higher class, luxury market; the Gateway Hotels target the mid-market and Ginger targets the economy class. The company should therefore not start a new product, i.e. a new chain of hotels, as that will lead to self-cannibalization.

Diversification: Here the firm grows by developing new products for new markets. IHCL can expand its business into other ancillary industries in the tourism and hospitality business, like providing package tours to customers. It can also venture into the travel business which will support its existing hotel business.

Table 3.2: The luxury, premium and mid-market offerings from IHCL

Company	*Key points*	*Value segments*	*Business description*
Taj	Present in world-renowned landmarks. Modern business hotels, idyllic beach resorts, authentic Rajput palaces and rustic safari lodges	Full-service luxury hotel	For high-end travellers seeking authentic experiences given that luxury is a way of life to which they are accustomed.
Taj Exotica	Resort and spa brand	Full-service luxury hotel	Known for the privacy and intimacy they provide. The hotels are clearly differentiated by their product philosophy and service design. They are centered around high-end accommodation and an environment that gives guests unrivalled comfort and privacy.
Taj Safari	Wildlife lodges	Full-service luxury hotels	Allows travellers to experience the unparalleled beauty of Indian jungles amidst luxurious surroundings. The only wildlife luxury lodge circuit based on the ecotourism model.

Company	*Key points*	*Value segments*	*Business description*
Premium Hotels	Contemporary and creative hospitality for the new generation with focus on technology	Premium full-service hotels and resorts	Provides new generation travellers a contemporary and creative hospitality experience that matches their work-hard play-hard lifestyles. Stylish interiors, innovative cuisine, hip bars, and a focus on technology set these properties apart.
The Gateway Hotels	Seven-zone hotels: Stay, Hangout, Meet, Work, Workout, Unwind, Explore	Mid-market full-service hotels and resorts	Hotels are designed keeping the modern nomad in mind. They believe in keeping things simple. The hotels are divided into seven zones: Stay, Hangout, Meet, Work, Workout, Unwind and Explore.
Ginger Hotels	Affordable hotels for the middle class	Economy hotels, self-service	Revolutionary concept in hospitality for the value segment. Intelligently designed facilities, consistency and affordability are hallmarks of this brand targeted at travellers who value simplicity and self-service.

Ansoff matrix		
Market	*Existing products*	*New products*
Existing	Market Penetration Expand Ginger and the Gateway Hotels	Product Development
New	Market Development Expand the International Chain of Taj Hotels	Diversification Venture into Travel and Tourism Business

BOX 3.1: QUALITATIVE ANALYSIS

Culture and leadership

- Sense of identity and affiliation a firm provides to its organizational members.
- Consistency in the cultures of subunits with each other and with the overall corporate culture.
- Ability of the culture to foster innovation, creativity and openness to new ideas.
- Capacity to adapt and evolve, consistent with the demands of changes in the environment and strategy.
- Executive, managerial and employee motivation (based on both monetary and non-monetary benefits).

Strength in the market

- The firm's advertising effectiveness.
- The product image and perceived quality.
- Brand awareness and the strength of the brand name.
- Consumer acceptance and trust of innovations from the company.

Legitimacy, reputation and image

- Effectiveness in coping with restrictive regulations (e.g. environmental, anti-trust, product liability laws).
- Relationship with consumer activist groups.
- Relationship with the media.
- Relationship with policymakers and government officials.
- Ability to obtain government grants and funding.
- Extent of trade-tariff protection.
- Relationship with public interest groups.

3.7 Standards of Comparison

The pros and cons of three common comparison standards for internal analysis include:

(i) Establish the dimensions of the marketing environment, the ways in which they may change and the probable impact of these changes upon the organization.

Any assessment of strengths and weaknesses is meaningless without an appropriate standard for comparison. This fundamental statement applies to both quantitative and qualitative assessments, regardless of whether you are analysing critical success factors, elements of the value chain or the core processes. Therefore, we consider the pros and cons of three common comparison standards for internal analysis. The first is designed to establish the various dimensions of the marketing environment, the ways in which they are likely to change and the probable impact of these changes upon the organization. The second stage is concerned with an assessment of the extent to which an organization's marketing systems are capable of dealing with the demands of the environment. The final stage involves a review of the individual component of the marketing mix along with its key competitors and customers.

(ii) Assessment of the extent to which an organization's marketing systems are capable of dealing with the demands of the environment.

(iii) Review of the individual component of the marketing mix along with its key competitors and customers.

The implications of new challenges during slowdown arising out of globalization and information technology, both individually and collectively, are significant and demand far more from an enterprise if it wants to survive the competition and sustain its growth momentum. This necessitates a strong need to understand the forces with which the enterprise is competing against and their capabilities. However, for mapping such forces, the marketing planner needs to focus not just upon the 'hard' factors (e.g. size, financial resources, production capability), but also upon the 'soft' elements (managerial cultures, commitment to particular markets, market offerings, the assumptions the management holds about itself and the market). Without this, it is almost inevitable that the marketing planner will fail to identify any competitive threats. Competitor analysis can be defined as a set of activities to examine the comparative position of competing enterprises within a given strategic sector. It seeks to provide an understanding of a firm's competitive advantages/disadvantages relative to its competitor's position and helps in generating insights into competitor's strategies—past, present and potential—and provide an informed basis for developing future strategies to sustain/establish advantages over competitors.

Competitor analysis can be defined as a set of activities to examine the comparative position of competing enterprises within a given strategic sector.

The new competitive environment demands a far more focused approach to strategic marketing based upon a greater understanding of the consumer. In short, this new environment is characterized by features such as generally higher levels of and an increasing intensity of competition (Airtel *v.* Vodafone, Linux *v.* Microsoft), new and more aggressive competitors who are emerging with ever greater frequency (Jet Airways *v.* Kingfisher), changing bases of competition as organizations search harder for competitive edge (Reliance Fresh), the geographic reaches of competition becoming wider (Pepsi *v.* Coke), niche attacks becoming more frequent (MTR *v.* ITC in the ready-to-eat foods category), increasing strategic alliances (becoming necessary, like Airtel, Vodafone, Reliance and Idea Cellular coming together for sharing transmission towers). The pace of innovation is speeding up (Nokia, Sony, MindTree Consulting in Bluetooth technology); stronger relationships and alliances with customers and distributors are becoming ever more frequent and necessary (e.g. booking air tickets at petrol pumps and post offices, apart from the Internet and travel agents); value added strategies are becoming more necessary (Country Club launched the Millennium Club life membership card with great success in 2007 by adding 300 network clubs and 52 own resorts in India and abroad).

Price competition is becoming ever more aggressive (Airtel, Reliance, BSNL, Vodafone all offer One India STD plan) and long-term differentiation is becoming more difficult to achieve. As a result, a number of enterprises are finding themselves stuck in the marketing wilderness with no obvious competitive advantage (Foodworld supermarkets and Big Bazaar retail outlets). 'Bad' competitors (i.e. those not adhering to the traditional and

Recent trends in the market include aggressive price competition, bad competitors becoming common, increasing strategic alliances, and an increasing pace of innovation.

unspoken rules of competitive behaviour within their industries) are becoming more common and difficult to cope with (Reliance Petroleum *v.* IOCL in petroleum retail pricing).

Table 3.3: Types of competition

Factors	*Pure monopoly*	*Avoided competition*	*Hyper competition*	*Perfect competition*
Product potfolio	Typically, one firm provides good or service that customers value	Typically, a small number of players	Typically, several players aggressively position against each others	Typically many players, more or less at parity with one another in terms of quality, cost, and/or speed
Segment	No segmentation, or very limited fragmentation, and no direct competition or rivals	Rivals work to segment market or otherwise position around each other while avoiding head-to-head competition	Emphasis is placed on either gaining an advantage, negating a competitor's advantage, or both	No one firm dominates the others
Profit orientation	Low level of competition allows abnormally high level of profits	Where rivals segments overlap, emphasis is placed on tacit collusion to limit price wars or other forms of severe competitions	Innovation is used to obsolete old goods and services in search of the latest improved means of providing customer value	With parity on quality and speed, competition often shifts to price and costs
Intensity of competitor	Little competitive pressure to provide higher level of customer value	Barriers to entry are used to limit threat of new entrants	Nature of competitive advantage is constantly being redefined	Absence of competitive advantage limits profitability
Market regulation	In free-market economies, government regulation is usually developed to limit monopolistic behaviour and encourage competition as a means of improving value available to consumers	Differentiation is used to limit treat of substitutes and reduce customers power	Market leadership continually changes hands or threatens to do so	Customer has many comparable options to choose between, but firms see limited profit potential and seek to avoid this form of competition
Power of suppliers/ customers	Very low	Vertical integration (or threat of it) is used to limit power of suppliers and customers	Abnormally high profits are intermittent as competitive advantages come and go	Very high
Status of competitor	Very high	To the extent competition is avoided, above-normal levels of profitability can be sustained.	Low	Very low

3.8 Porter's Approach to Competitive Structure Analysis

One of the major contributions in recent years to our understanding of the ways in which the competitive environment influences strategy has been provided by Porter. Porter's work is based on the idea that 'Competition in an industry is rooted in its underlying economics, and competitive forces that go well beyond the established combatants in a particular industry.'

The first determinant of a firm's profitability is the attractiveness of the industry in which it operates.

The first determinant of a firm's profitability is the attractiveness of the industry in which it operates. It is possible to see competition operating at four levels, such as competition among companies offering a similar product or service to the target market, utilizing a similar technology, and exhibiting similar degrees of vertical integration, e.g. Reebok, Adidas and Nike in sportswear and shoes. Competition consists of all companies operating in the same product or service category, e.g. malls like Garuda and Forum in Bengaluru, PVR and Inox in movie theatre, banks like HDFC, ICICI and SBI with their retail, corporate and investment banking services and insurance providers like HDFC Standard Life, SBI Life, ICICI Prudential and ICICI Lombard.

Competition can also consist of all companies manufacturing or supplying products that deliver the same service (Nokia, Motorola and Sony Ericsson in the GSM handset market). Competition can be among all companies for the same spending power (Visa and Master Card).

In most industries, the competitors can be usefully portrayed in terms of how intensely they compete with the business that is motivating the analysis. There are usually several very direct competitors, others that compete less intensely, and still others that compete indirectly but are still relevant. A knowledge of this pattern can lead to a deeper understanding of the market structure. The competitor group that competes most intensely may merit the most in-depth study, but other groups may still require analysis. The identification of the most competitive group will depend upon a few key variables and it may be strategically important to know the relative importance of these variables.

BOX 3.2: APPLYING FIVE FORCES THEORY TO TAJ HOTELS

Force 1: Competitive rivalry within the industry: High

- The competition within the industry is very intense.
- The competition in the 'luxury' segment is mainly on quality of service, value added services, and conveniences.
- The competition in 'budget' segment is mainly price based.
- The players who have a relatively larger reach in the market (like Sheraton, Taj Group) are giving tough competition to the new entrants.

Force 2: Bargaining power of suppliers: Medium to Low

- The bargaining power of suppliers (hoteliers) depends upon various factors like the income group the customers fall in, macro-economic factors like current trends in economy, protectionism, policies of the state, and so on.
- The players in the industry have to constantly enhance their value offerings in order to keep themselves above others in the race. The general bargaining power of suppliers, in that context, is low as customers have various options in all the segments of the hospitality industry, be it hotels, tourism, airlines, and so on.
- With the growth in customer base, especially the ones looking for luxury hotels, the demand for star hotels has also increased. Hence the bargaining power of suppliers in India, especially in the luxury segment, is pretty high. This trend is, though, reversing with the influx of foreign investment into the Indian sector.
- In the present times, due to global meltdown, the number of tourists has decreased tremendously worldwide. This has lead to disastrous business for most players, hence reducing the bargaining power further.

Force 3: Bargaining power of customers: Medium

- Bargaining power of customers, in general, is high. This is because of the intense competition among various players.
- In the Indian context, the customers' bargaining power is 'medium to low', especially in peak seasons. This is because there is a huge gap in the supply and demand. The scenario is slowly changing with the established foreign players entering the Indian market.
- In the low cost hotel segment, the market is relatively over-crowded and hence the choice for customers is high.

Force 4: Threat of new entrants: High to Medium

- Ease of entry for a new entrant depends on government policies as well as the capital intensiveness of the business.
- Foreign players are making rapid progress in India in competing with the few local companies. Several international majors like the Four Seasons, Shangri-La and Aman Resorts have entered the Indian market, besides the Carlson Group and the Marriott chain. This will increase the competition for the existing Indian hotel majors.
- As the hospitality industry is highly capital intensive, it is not easy for the less established players to enter new markets and beat the existing competition.
- The current trend is to enter new markets by converting existing hotel spaces into internationally recognized brands by means of strategic tie-ups, wherein the hotel space and brand names are traded, and profits shared by the two players.

Force 5: Threat of substitutes: Low

- Threat from substitutes in the hospitality industry is relatively very low, both in terms of substitute products and also in terms of existing competition.
- Brands like Taj, Hilton or Hyatt take a long time to be established. And there is no threat of substitutes for such big names.
- The industry is such that each major player is continuously striving to better its value offering. Hence they almost always offer more to customers than the normal industry standards. So, the threat from substitutes is virtually nil.

New rules of the game are: to tackle uncertainty by emphasizing a new set of basics, world class quality and service, enhanced responsiveness and continuous short-cycle innovation and improvement.

Dynamic enterprises device strategies to seize the opportunities and to fight the threats of environmental changes. The technological explosion, information revolution, emergence of well-developed international financial markets, cosmopolitan nature of consumers, growing democratization of nations, expanding world market, and so on tend to drive such enterprises multinational. New rules of the game include: tackling uncertainty by emphasizing a set of new basics, world class quality and service, enhanced responsiveness and continuous short-cycle innovation and improvement aimed at creating new markets.

Marketing strategies must not only identify direct competitors but indirect competitors as well.

Marketing strategies must not only identify direct competitors but indirect competitors as well who reflect the same general approach to the market, but also consider those who 'interact' with the company in each market, who possibly approach it from a different perspective, and who ultimately might pose either a direct or an indirect threat. As part of this, one need also to identify potential new entrants to the market and, where it appears necessary, develop contingency plans to neutralize their competitive effect.

Considerations in integrated marketing strategy are: planning procedures and opportunity analysis, defining productivity, performance measures, and scenario analysis.

It is vital for a marketer to view planning as an integrated and ongoing process, not as a fragmented and one-time-only concept. Considerations in integrated marketing strategy: planning procedures and opportunity analysis, defining productivity, performance measures, and scenario analysis. Planning can be optimized by following a series of coordinated activities such as senior executives outlining the retailers' overall direction and goals. This provides written guidelines for middle- and lower-level managers, who get input from internal and external sources. These managers are also encouraged to generate new ideas. Top-down (upper management) and bottom-up or horizontal (middle- and lower-level management) plans are combined.

Specific plans are enacted, including checkpoints and dates. Opportunities need to be systematically examined in terms of their impact on overall strategy, and not in an isolated manner. While evaluating new opportunities, marketers should develop sales opportunity grids which rate the promise of new and established goods, services, procedures, and/or store outlets across a variety of criteria. Opportunities are evaluated on the basis of the integrated strategies the marketer would follow if the opportunities were pursued. Just look at Cannon's analysis and its key elements given in Table 3.4.

Table 3.4: Cannon's analysis

Step	*Key elements*
1. Define the market	Develop Statement of purpose in terms of benefits Product scope Size, growth rate, maturity state, need for primary versus selective strategies Requirements for success Divergent definitions of the above by competitors Definition to be used by the company
2. Determine performance differentials	Evaluate industry performance and company differences Determine differences in products, applications, geography and distribution channels Determine differences by customer set
3. Determine differences in competitive programmes	Identify and evaluate individual companies for their Market development strategies Product development strategies Financing and administrative strategies and support
4. Profile the strategies of competitors	Profile each significant competitor and/or distinct types of competitive strategy Compare own and competitive strategies
5. Determine the strategic planning structure	When size and complexity are adequate Establish planning units or cells and designate prime and subordinate dimensions Make organizational assignments to product managers, industry managers and others

3.9 Summary

- It is an accepted fact that once the marketing strategy has been developed, it must be put into action, continuously evaluated, and necessary adjustments made. An important evaluation tool is the market audit, which may be defined as the systematic examination and evaluation of a firm's total marketing effort, or some specific aspect of it.
- The purpose of an audit is to determine what is being done, appraise how well the firm is performing, and recommend future actions. An audit should include an investigation of the marketer's objectives, strategy, implementation, and organization.
- Good auditing includes elements such as regularity, in-depth analysis, systematic amassing and analysis, and open-minded, unbiased perspective, There is a willingness to uncover weaknesses, as well as strengths to be exploited, Decision-makers are responsive to the recommendations.

CHAPTER 4  STP MARKETING

four

We don't ask consumers what they want. They don't even know. Instead we apply our brain power to find out what they need, and want, and make sure we're there, ready.

— Akio Morita, Sony Corporation

The Backdrop

The response to the current market turbulence may strengthen nationalization and cost cutting among financial service providers globally. It is a fact that the economy grows faster in good phases and slumps more sharply in downturns. Public debate during times of economic meltdown focuses on GDP growth rates but the readings are unreliable and change constantly, prompting statisticians to think of different ways of measuring an economy's products and services. In spite of the global slowdown, India continues to be a high-growth economy, and a significant portion of this growth is driven by private consumption. A case in point would be the Indian luxury market, though still at a nascent stage, continued to grow fast even during meltdown.

Getting a precise idea of the size of the Indian luxury market is difficult. The actual sale of luxury products in outlets within the country is not huge largely because rich Indians often go abroad to shop. However the number of High Networth Individuals (HNIs) is on the rise even though there has been a dip in the recent slowdown.

The Indian market, estimated to be around $2 billion in 2009, forms only 0.4 per cent of the global luxury market. But Mckinsey expects this market to grow at 25 per cent to reach $5 billion by 2015. As of 2008, the number of households that could afford luxury goods in India totalled 1.50 million, about 1,00,000 short of China, which has the fourth-largest population of wealthy customers in the world after US, Japan and UK. In India more than 40 per cent of the wealthy customers are located in Delhi and Mumbai. A Technopak report profiles these customers primarily as families whose annual disposable income is ₹8-₹9 lakh, who own a D- or E-segment car and mostly have a single income-earner, who is more often than not a male.

Selling to the super rich is an extremely challenging job because they tend to be particularly demanding. And while some of them get swayed by brand names, many others are truly discriminating. Then there are still others who equate luxury primarily with exclusivity, which means that anything easily available becomes that much less desirable.

This Chapter Will

- *Describe the ways and means of integrating demand management, resource management and network management. By aid of this integration process, companies can conduct their marketing activities on four platforms: market offerings, marketing activities, business architecture and operational excellence. Marketing offerings and business architecture are viewed as revenue drivers and the remaining two as cost drivers.*
- *Discuss segmentation, targeting and positioning company offerings during times of slowdown.*
- *Explain the fundamental concepts and approaches to STP (Segmentation, Targeting and Positioning) marketing, micro-profiling of target customers during market turbulence, adopting behavioural segmentation and identifying purchase decision influencers.*
- *Discuss retail service segments and target markets with various tools for positioning the message in the minds of customers.*

4.1 Fundamental Concepts and Approaches to Marketing

The old economy was built on the logic of managing manufacturing industries; the new economy is built on the logic of managing information and information industries. Today's market economy is a mix of both old and new economies. Markets are changing faster than marketing. Hence, marketing must be deconstructed, redefined and stretched to overcome recessionary pressures. Companies need to retain the skills and competencies that have worked in the past but they must also acquire new mindsets and new levels of competencies by recruiting fresh minds. Business needs to shift from focusing on product portfolios to focusing on competencies.

The downward spiral of companies accelerates when leading companies in the industry tend to get addicted to comparison programmes and 'be better' management strategies to improve their performances and bottom lines. Many 'good' competitors end up striving to be a little better than the others, all offering similar value to customers. The result is falling into the profit-killing tit-for-tat trap where competitors do not pursue significant differentiation and customers don't perceive any difference. When customers view no difference among various products/services, they can only see relative parity. And parity causes customers to select on the basis of price, which inevitably leads to lower profits.

Every marketer has to identify his target market, the needs and expectations of that market and subsequently meet those expectations with efficient service.

A marketer has to understand the nuances of marketing by understanding his customers. Every marketer has to primarily identify his target market, the needs and expectations of that market and subsequently meet those expectations with efficient service. There are certain principles that have to be followed by marketers for their businesses to be successful.

MARKETING ANALYSIS — INDIA'S FMCG SECTOR

Fast Moving Consumer Goods (FMCG) are popularly called consumer packaged goods (CPG). Items in this category include all consumables (other than groceries/ pulses) people buy at regular intervals. The most common in the list are toilet soaps, detergents, shampoos, toothpastes, shaving products, shoe polish, packaged foodstuff, household accessories and certain electronic goods. These items are meant for daily or frequent consumption and have a high rate of return.

A major portion of the household monthly budget is reserved for FMCG products. The volume of money circulated in the economy against FMCG products is very high, as the number of products consumers use is very high. Competition in the sector is highly intense, resulting in tight margins.

FMCG companies maintain a strong distribution network and spend a large portion of their budget on this. New entrants who wish to sell their products at the national level need to invest huge sums of money on promoting brands, though manufacturing can be outsourced. A recent phenomenon in the sector has been the entry of multinationals and cheaper imports—adding further pressure to a market already pressed by the presence of regional brands and local players, especially in the rural areas.

The liberalization of the Indian economy in 1991 changed the economic landscape. The lowering of trade barriers encouraged MNCs to invest in India to cash in on one billion Indians' needs. Rising standards of living in urban areas coupled with the purchasing power of rural India saw companies introduce everything from low-end detergents to high-end sanitary napkins. Sub-categories were created in products such as hair oils and skincare products, besides the introduction of many new product categories.

In the last decade the strategy of business players has been two-pronged—invest in expanding the distribution reach to enable market expansion and upgrade existing consumers to value-added premium products as well as increase usage of existing product ranges. The advent of cable TV and satellite channels has helped FMCG companies reach out to the Indian masses. But in this market only companies that continuously innovate on products, packaging and distribution channels to satisfy consumer needs survive.

The Indian FMCG sector with a market size of US$13.1 billion has the fourth-largest sector in the economy in 2009. It's characterized by a well-established distribution network and intense competition between the organized and the unorganized segments. The sector is expected to grow at 10 per cent over a five-year period. It has been estimated that the FMCG sector has jumped from ₹56,500 crore in 2005 to ₹92,100 crore in 2011. Haircare, household goods, male grooming and female hygiene products, and chocolates and confectionery categories are estimated to be the fastest growing segments. According to commodityonline.com, the Indian FMCG market is expected to treble from US$11.60 billion in 2003 to US$33.40 billion by 2015. There is untapped market potential in product categories like jams, toothpastes, skincare, hair washes, and so on, which have low per capita consumption.

With 12.2 per cent of the world's population living in the villages of India, the Indian rural FMCG market cannot be overlooked. Increased focus on the farm sector will boost rural income, hence providing better growth prospects to the FMCG companies. Better infrastructure facilities will improve their supply chain. The FMCG sector is also likely to benefit from growing demand in the market. Given the low per capita consumption of almost all the products in the country, FMCG players have immense possibilities for growth. And if they are able to change the mindset of the consumers, i.e. if they are able to change consumer preferences to branded products and offer new generation products, they would be able to generate higher growth. Also, increase in the urban population, along with increase in income levels and the availability of new categories would help the urban areas maintain their position in terms of consumption. At present, urban India accounts for 66 per cent of total FMCG consumption, with rural India accounting for the remaining 34 per cent. In urban areas, home and personal care products, including skincare, household care and hygiene, will grow at relatively attractive rates. Within the foods segment, it is estimated that processed foods, bakery products and dairy products are long-term growth categories in both rural and urban areas.

Source: Business Standard, January 2010.

4.1.1 Principles of Marketing

(i) Where marketers offer adequate and appropriate solutions to the shopping problems faced by customers. For instance, there might be customers who walk into a shop, make a quick buy and leave, while there may be others who may want to spend some time in the store. If the marketer were to treat both types of buyers in the same way, he might lose some potential customers.

(ii) The marketer is cautioned to treat customers with utmost respect. A customer who has not been treated well or has been ignored in a particular store is unlikely to visit again.

(iii) A marketer must relate with the sentiments of their customers. They should offer services that matches customer expectations and does not hurt their sentiments.

MARKETING IN ACTION **ALL PERK-ED UP**

In October 2009, Cadbury, the leader in the chocolate market with a 70 per cent market share, launched a new variant of its coated wafer brand Perk. The new glucose energy chocolate promises more for less. The new ₹5 Perk, at 21 gm. offers 50 per cent more. It is also available in single-serve 7.50 gm. packs priced at ₹2. This is part of the core strategy that Cadbury has been pursuing to widen the market. India's per capita chocolate consumption is just 54 gm. compared to the UK and US at 10.50 kg. and 10 kg. respectively. So as a market leader, Cadbury needs to innovate to increase consumption.

Cadbury is hoping the 'more for less' strategy help to increase consumption by at least 5 per cent in 2009. The small pack strategy is already paying off. Dairy Milk Shots, introduced in 2008 and costing ₹2 per packet, has already contributed 15 per cent to Dairy Milk sales.

It is important to mention that this is not the first time Cadbury has modified Perk. The brand was launched in 1995 in the chocolate wafer category as an anytime, anywhere snack. Around the same time, Nestle introduced Kitkat. But after a promising start, both brands fizzled out as consumers felt they were paying for chocolate biscuits rather than chocolate. Quick on the uptake, Cadbury relaunched Perk. It maintained the wafer quality, but changed its packaging to Cadbury's trademark purple to stress the fact that it was pure chocolate. However, that initiative too was short-lived.

In 2000, Nestle launched its brand Munch which has since been the leader in the wafer category. In terms of pricing, Perk has followed Munch's pricing of ₹2 and ₹5. In 2009, Nestle launched a bigger pack priced at ₹10. After competing with Perk, Munch has now set its sights on Dairy Milk.

Earlier in 2009, Cadbury came out with an advertisement for Dairy Milk that revolved around payday celebrations in the country. *Aaj pehli tarikh hai* (today is the first day of the month) was the premise of the ad. Soon enough, Munch came out with a campaign that announced *Khao bina tareekh dekhe* (eat without the need for looking at the date). Thus, Cadbury's salvo hasn't surprised anybody.

Perk Glucose Energy is also part of an insight the company gained following a study that suggested that consumers wanted a tasty recharge. Also, there's growing health awareness among consumers who have been shifting towards lighter chocolates, a category which is reportedly growing faster than pure chocolates. Cadbury needed a brand that connected to the youth and at the same time was powerful. The new Perk makes maximum sense in that context. On the brand building front, the company is spending about 10 per cent of its sales on its 360 degree campaign—Naya Perk—which will encompass TV, outdoor, tie-ups and sampling activities. The company expanded its market share by 5 per cent in 2009–10.

Source: The Economic Times, January 2010.

(iv) Marketers must realize that the customers' time is precious and should not be wasted.

(v) Products have to be priced honestly.

Abiding by these principles would help marketers handle their business effectively and successfully. The decisions a marketer has to take pertain to product assortment and procurement, and marketing and service mix, like price, place, promotion, store location and image.

4.2 Market Segmentation

Market segmentation is the process of breaking a market into smaller subgroups.

The process of breaking a market into smaller subgroups, market segmentation is not arbitrarily imposed but is derived from the recognition that the total market is often made up of submarkets (called segments). These segments are internally homogeneous, i.e. people in one segment are similar to each other in their attitudes about certain variables. Due to this intra-group similarity, people in the same segment are likely to have similar responses to a given marketing strategy. That is, they are likely to have similar feelings about a marketing mix comprising of a given product, sold at a given price, distributed in a certain way, and promoted in a certain manner. The requirements for successful segmentation are:

- Homogeneity within the segment.
- Heterogeneity between segments.
- Stability of segments.
- Segments are measurable and identifiable.
- Segments are accessible and actionable.
- Segments are large enough to be profitable.

By marketing products that appeal to customers at different stages of their life (life cycle), a business can retain customers who might otherwise switch to competing products and brands.

There are several important reasons why businesses should attempt to segment their markets carefully.

- **To enhance profits:** Customers have different disposable incomes, consequently their price sensitivities are different. By segmenting markets, businesses can raise average prices and subsequently enhance profits.

CASE STUDY — ENTERTAINMENT INDUSTRY SEGMENTATION

McKinsey's analysis of the consumption categories of the Indian population gives the indication that spending specifically on recreational activities has increased and will continue to rise in the future too (Table 4.1).

Table 4.1: Projected growth in spending on entertainment in India

Category	*2005 consumption billion, Indian rupees, 2000*	*2025 consumption billion, Indian rupees, 2000*	*Compound annual growth rate %*
Education and recreation	762	6,120	11
Books and education	711	5,844	11.1
Recreational goods	6	39	9.3
TV, video	22	161	10.5
Entertainment services	22	77	6.5

The above trend is inspiring for both the current players as well as the new entrants in the entertainment sector. In fact, the entertainment sector is emerging as a sector of immense potential and high growth.

The Indian entertainment industry caters largely to local customers (i.e. an Indian audience), be it television channels, radio channels, or even the Indian Premier League (IPL). The impact of the recession has been felt to a lesser extent in South Asia than in the Western countries. Hence, the impact on people's spending is also less in India. This factor has been highly beneficial for the entertainment industry.

Sector segmentation

Segmentation of the entertainment sector is important for an in-depth study and analysis. The segmentation becomes all the more important owing to the different industry practices, technologies, levels of competition and current state various segments. The entertainment sector is broadly segmented into four categories:

1. **Mass media:** This sector is the most prominent one with high returns and massive subscriptions. Since the sector caters to the needs of large sections of the society its products are mass customized. The break-up of the mass media sector into different subsectors is shown in Figure 4.1.

Figure 4.1: Subsectors in the mass media

2. **Live entertainment:** A country of numerous festivals, occasions to celebrate, artists and art lovers, the live entertainment sector increases its significance with art shows, music and dance concerts and theatre performances. The added opportunities of live shows, award functions and beauty pageants has provided an edge to this sector. Figure 4.2 shows the subsectors in the live entertainment segment.

Figure 4.2: Subsectors in the live entertainment segment

3. **Exhibition entertainment sector:** This includes theme parks, amusement parks, fairs and carnivals and zoos and wildlife sancutaries. Once dominant this sector was has become stagnant today. The large turnover of the mass media sector has wiped away this segment in terms of volumes.
4. **Electronic entertainment:** The latest and the most talked about segment, its advances are due to the rapid development of the Internet and mobile technology. The subsectors of this segment are shown in Figure 4.3.

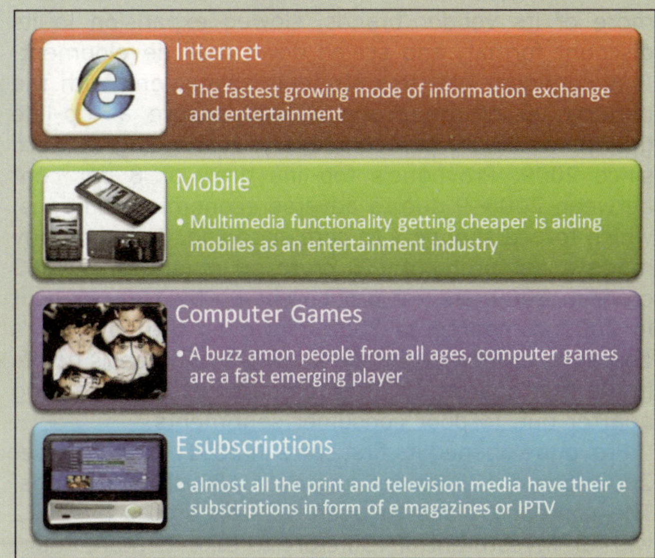

Figure 4.3: Subsectors in the electronic media segment

Through careful segmentation and targeting, businesses can often achieve competitive production as well as marketing costs and become the preferred choice of customers and distributors.

- **To better match customer needs:** Customer needs differ, so creating separate offers for each segment makes sense and provides customers with better solutions.
- **To retain more customers:** Customer circumstances change, for example they grow older, form families, change jobs or get promoted, or change their buying patterns. By marketing products that appeal to customers at different stages of their life (life cycle), a business can retain customers who might otherwise switch to competing products and brands.
- **To better opportunities for growth:** Market segmentation can build sales. For example, customers can be encouraged to 'trade-up' after being introduced to a particular product at an introductory lower price.
- **To target marketing communications:** Businesses need to deliver their marketing message to a relevant customer audience. If the target market is too broad, there is a strong risk that (i) key customers are missed, and (ii) the cost of communicating to customers becomes too high/unprofitable. By segmenting markets, the target customer can be reached more often and at lower costs.
- **Gain share of the market segment:** Unless a business has a leading share of a market, it is unlikely to maximize its profitability. Minor brands

suffer from lack of scale economies in production and marketing, pressures from distributors and limited space on shelves. Through careful segmentation and targeting, businesses can often achieve competitive production and marketing costs and become the preferred choice of customers and distributors. In other words, segmentation offers the opportunity for smaller firms to compete with bigger ones.

MARKETING IN ACTION — **PROVOGUE REWORKS BUSINESS PLANS, STRATEGIES TO BOOST REVENUES**

After a year of slow growth in 2008, apparel maker and retailer Provogue reworked its business strategy to boost revenues and prop up margins. Under the new strategy, it reduced the size of its stores, sold more of its vendor brands, slowed expansion in its discount format, and scaled down mall development. It is confident that this strategic shift, along with the perking up of the economy, will ensure a top-line growth of 25-30 per cent every year going forward since 2009. Provogue's top-line grew at 8 per cent between 2008–9 due to adverse economic conditions, which forced shoppers to curb spending. The company made a net profit of ₹70 crore on revenues of ₹363 crore in 2009. Its net profit went up by 180 per cent in 2009 compared to 2008. However, the company's operating profit margins went down by 500 basis points in the first quarter of 2009 compared to the preceding quarter due to poor consumer sentiments.

Provogue opened its first store in 2001; by November 2009 it had 126 stores and over 100 shop-in-shops. The company plans to open 50 new stores by 2012 with an investment of ₹35 crore to take its store count to 175. It would opt for smaller stores in the range of 800-2,000 sq. ft. to save on rents and costs. The company is very careful about expansion and wants to make every store profitable. It planned to open 20 Promart, its off-price shops, by mid-2010, but had opened only two stores by November 2009, high rents being the main reason.

In order to promote the Promart brand, Provogue is planning to rebrand it as a hip and high-value fashion brand. Though it started selling products at a discount in the Promart stores, the company realized that vendor products were fetching 60 per cent of the revenues and 50 per cent of the gross margins. Hence, it plans to sell 80 per cent of the merchandise at full price and the remaining 20 per cent at discount during 2010–11.

Prozone Liberty, the mall development arm of Provogue, has also scaled down its plans, given the slowdown in the retail sector. Originally, the company planned to build six malls, now it is going ahead with only three, in Jaipur, Indore and Aurangabad (as of 2009). The company is also exploring ways to use additional land in these sites for alternative uses such as residential development. Though it has reworked its plans in some segments, it is trying its hand in new areas such as foraying into West Asia and tying up with FMCG firms for distribution. It may be recalled that Provogue sells hair gels, body sprays and other accessories under its own brand name in its stores and select outlets of the department store Shopper's Stop.

Source: Business Today, December 2009.

4.2.1 Market Segmentation Strategies

Market segmentation refers to marketing efforts to group potential buyers by demographic characteristics, geographical region, lifestyle, usage pattern, and behavioural factors. Thus, submarkets are frequently established on the basis of income, age, sex, occupation, and complex behavioural dimensions. Product differentiation refers to the marketing efforts that distinguish a basically homogeneous product from competitors' products. A successful application of this strategy should result in an increased horizontal share of a generalized market. The methods used to accomplish this include altering the product's physical characteristics, branding, advertising, or packaging to stimulate the consumers' five senses. These promotional appeals can be especially successful in an affluent society.

Market segmentation strategy can aid in developing particular market segments in contrast to the strategy of product differentiation that distinguishes a particular product from among many similar products.

Market segmentation strategy can aid in developing particular market segments in contrast to the method of product differentiation that distinguishes a product among many similar products. Product differentiation and market segmentation are alternatively and complementarily used. A combined strategy approach is used for products such as colas, cigarettes, and soaps.

DEPTH SEGMENTATION AND BUYER PROFILE

When numerous variables are combined to give an in-depth understanding of a segment, it is referred to as depth segmentation. When enough information is combined to create a clear picture of a typical member of a segment, it is referred to as buyer profile. Multivariate statistical techniques commonly used in determining buyer profile are cluster factor and discriminant analysis.

FRESHNESS REDEFINED: LIMCA FOR EMOTIONAL REJUVENATION

Limca, the market leader in what is known as the 'cloudy lemon beverage segment', is redefining freshness—from driving away physical fatigue to emotional rejuvenation. The first batch of its out-of-home (OOH)-media campaign, *Doobo taazgi mein* (immerse yourself in freshness) in October 2009 plays on the emotional characteristics of freshness. The OOH communication initiative includes the actual use of water as 'mood-enhancers' in three-dimensional floating hoardings using acrylic designs. For instance, at bus stops, there will be hoardings with water-filled acrylic sheets and 3D Limca logos to give them a dimension of freshness. At malls, there will be aquarium-shaped glass boxes to simulate a wave-like effect. The vibrant interplay of light and colour with the soothing feel of water is the dominant theme.

Coca-Cola India marketing director Srinivas Murthy says the campaign, done by Ogilvy & Mather, in late 2009 is a 360-degree approach to freshness. So the OOH advertising would be in places where one usually waits for long hours and is thus stressed out. The television commercials show a young couple in a spectacular though pallid studio apartment, sitting jaded in a dreary afternoon. The girl sips Limca and experiences 'water-like freshness' and finds her surroundings gradually filling with water. This sparks of moments of playful romance between the couple. Together they swim around a floating piano and music notations, playing a sensual game around a bottle of Limca.

The commercials ask viewers to break away from the monotony of life and steal those blithe moments of bliss, fun and romance. Experts say brand Limca is mainly targeting the young, working population who long for freshness amid high-pressure jobs and a fast-paced life.

This is not the first time that Limca is undergoing brand repositioning. The brand's journey began in 1971 when it was marketed and promoted as a thirst quencher. In 2004, it rode on a physical freshness wave with the tagline *Mazaa taazgi ka*. Some analysts, however, feel that Coca-Cola has gone on the defensive with other players entering this segment. Coca-Cola's sudden aggressive advertising campaign for Limca could be because of the emergence of other players in the lemon beverage segment, including non-carbonated drinks. So experts regard this more as a reactive campaign than anything else.

Limca has a market share of over 60 per cent in the cloudy lemon segment, its closest competitors being Mirinda Lemon flavour and 7 Up Lemon of PepsiCo. The lemon beverage market, which is worth over ₹500 crore, has other non-carbonated players like PepsiCo's Nimbooz and Parle Agro's Lmn. In 2008 and 2009, the market saw few lemon brands but for Coca-Cola India and PepsiCo India, the clear lemon segment represented by Sprite and 7 Up. But this is the segment companies seem to have been focusing on during market recovery.

Source: The Economic Times, December 2009.

MARKETING ANALYSIS

In 2009 Provogue switched its brand ambassador from Saif Ali Khan to Hrithik Roshan. The brand needed the buzz as much for its new line as for ensuring its aggressive store expansion drive and meeting the expectations of curious consumers.

The brand has come a long way from 2000 when it was grappling with retail space constraints (a few multi-brand stores and one exclusive store). It now has 134 exclusive stores and is set to open 20 more by March 2010. This is apart from the brand's presence in 110 multi-brand outlets.

The company's sales grew by just 7 per cent in 2008–9 compared to 29 per cent in 2007–8. Operating profit in the first quarter of 2009 was down 500 basis points over 2008. The company has, however, been quick to correct its course by reducing the size of the new exclusive stores. From a 10,000 sq. ft. store space, it is now content with 800-2,000 sq. ft.

A tough 2009 has made apparel brands relook their positioning. Roshan's endorsement would have helped Provogue in the task. The change is in line with the company's strategy to avoid brand fatigue and Hrithik Roshan lends the brand contemporariness. In any case, a change was due in line with Provogue's strategy of roping in a new brand ambassador every third year. Analysts say it is a must for a lifestyle brand to keep rejuvenating itself. Provogue seems to have perfected the art by changing ambassadors from time to time, yet not in letting the brand ambassadors become larger than the brand itself. And with each new ambassador comes the possibility of trying out a new attitude. The company has changed its earlier tagline 'redefining fashion' in favour of 'be the change'.

Provogue wants to make the change more visible to its target consumer—the youth. And Roshan fits the bill as he is among the top ten popular celebrities in the country, according to a survey by Percept Talent Management in 2009. The 'attitude' is reflected in its new clothing lines as well. Provogue's factory in Daman has brought out an enhanced denim range and fashion formals with roll-up sleeves and small collar and cuffs, double pockets and contrast collars. Sameer Makani, managing director of Makani Creatives, the agency handling Provogue since the brand's inception ten years back, says 'If earlier the brand stood for being stylish and hot, now it is about having an attitude. So, in the campaigns, instead of putting the spotlight on the garment, we have tried to catch different attitudes that highlight the attributes the clothes will have.' Makani says that each letter in the word 'change' stands for a particular value—courage, hope, attitude, next, glory and edge. Each of the six different shots of Roshan will signify one of the six values, and there will be one consolidated shot of the actor.

Teaser ads gave way to hoardings and print ads that depict Roshan wearing this new attitude, in a ₹12-crore marketing campaign. The budget will be upped to ₹15 crore in 2010. The brand has also brought Narendra Kumar Ahmed, a renowned designer, on board to strengthen its women's wear range. Ahmed also finetuned the men's range in the festive seasons of 2009.

The focus on nurturing the brand has helped Provogue strengthen its position. The company operates in three segments: manufacture and trading of textile and related products, infrastructure, and other activities.

Source: Business Standard, March 2010.

4.2.2 The Ideal Approach to Segmenting Retail Markets

In deciding the range of products and services, marketers must keep in mind the requirements of the customers who constitute the target group.

The segmentation of the total market is based on several factors like the income level of the customer or the household, the age group of the consumers, their level of education, their level of sophistication, the size of the town or city of their residence, the climate of the place, and so on. In deciding the range of products and services, marketers keep in mind the requirements of the customers who constitute the target group. They need to develop products that meet the expectations of the target group and promote them in a manner that will appeal to the target audience. The ideal approach to retail segmentation of the market is shown in Box 4.1.

4.2.3 How to and Who Decides Target Segments

Research into choice criteria often begins with focus group interviews, in which customers from specific segments are brought together in small groups for a semi-structured discussion under the guidance of a professional. Insights from these discussions can then be used to construct formal survey instruments, which might be administered to scientifically selected samples by mail, telephone or other means. In short, the process of segmenting a retail market is a six-step approach comprised of identifying different needs, attitudes, behaviours and demographics across a variety of potential customers; identifying distinct segments of customers with similar purchase behaviours; creating a profile describing each segment; determining the size of each segment; selecting the target segments; and developing approaches for reaching the target customers.

Product/service retail firms that are developing strategies based on the use of technology recognize that customers can also be segmented according to their degree of competence and comfort in using technology-based delivery systems. An important marketing issue for any business is to accept that some market segments offer better opportunities than others do. Identifying who makes the decision to select a specific segment is also important. In some cases, its a single individual. In others, it may involve a decision-making unit of several participants. Consider a family trip to the movies. Each of the family members is likely to have a different opinion about which movie to see, how far to travel, whether to watch the movie in a conventional theatre or a multiplex.

Sometimes, the user is not always the decision-maker. In the case of choosing a hospital for a particular treatment, the decision-maker might be the end user (e.g., a patient) or more likely an intermediary (e.g., the doctor or even the insurance company). Take the case of Dr Manmohan Singh, the Prime Minister of the country in 2009 he opted for a private doctor in a government hospital to take care of his health!

After conducting a sufficient number of surveys, the marketer compiles the results to determine which markets make the most sense for his business. He must ensure that the market he chooses has easy access to company products and services, whether it is by visiting the company store or ordering

BOX 4.1: FLOW CHART FOR REACHING THE PRINCIPAL SEGMENT

(a) Research: Collect responses, research on needs, attitudes, behaviour and demographics.

↓

(b) Analysis: Identify distinct customer segments that appear similar.

↓

(c) Segment profiling: Define and describe segments based on demographics and other information useful for target marketing.

↓

(d) Segment sizing: Estimate the size of each segment by percentage of population and revenue potential.

↓

(e) Segment selection: Apply criteria and select most attractive segments.

↓

(f) Reaching the segments: Develop retail business and marketing strategies for reaching segments using various tools.

DEVELOPING CUSTOMER PROFILE

Just as a mission statement guides the operations of the company, a customer profile will guide the sales efforts. The following profile shows an overview of the target customers so that the manager and other employees are clear about whom the retail marketer is selling to.

MICRO-PROFILING OF TARGET CUSTOMERS

1. Ensure that the firm includes the following characteristics in the **demographic profile** of its target market:
   - Age
   - Gender
   - Profession
   - Education level
   - Household income level
   - Marital status
   - Geographic location
2. If target market is made up of **corporate customers,** include the following elements:
   - Company size
   - Location of headquarters
   - Types of products and services they provide
   - Annual revenue
   - Number, size and location of branches
   - Year founded
3. Analyse which of the following categories fit the **psychographic profile** of the firm's customers:
   - Conservative
   - Liberal
   - Orthodox
   - Environment-friendly
   - Socially conscious
   - Power-wielding
   - Fun-loving
   - Tech-savvy
   - Trend follower
   - Fashion-forward
   - Family-oriented

4. Also include the following **specific questions to know more** about individual customers:
   (a) How many family members are typically in your customers' households?
   (b) What hobbies and/or sports do your customers enjoy?
   (c) What types of entertainment do they like (movies, theatre, fashion shows, award nights/reality shows, cricket, etc.)?
   (d) What publications do they subscribe to?
   (e) How else do they enjoy their free time?
5. If the target market is made up of **corporate customers**, which of the following psychographic categories fit them?
   - Market leader
   - Innovative or cutting-edge
   - Liberal
   - Conservative
   - Environment-friendly
   - Employee-caring
   - Fast growing/adopting new ideas
   - Stable/set in their ways

   (a) What growth stage is the company in? (start-up, growth, maturity or decline)
   (b) What is the type of workforce they employ?
   (c) What is the company's work culture?
   (d) What is the management style?
   (e) What publications do they subscribe to?

by phone, fax, email or the firm's website. The market must not be inundated with other products and services that are indistinguishable from those of the firm. And the market must be willing to pay a price for the firm's products and services that allows the retail marketer a reasonable profit margin.

We will now discuss the various modes of product and service segmentation.

4.2.4 Geographic Segmentation

Geographic segmentation divides markets into different geographical units like country, state, district, taluka, *village, and so on.*

Geographic segmentation tries to divide markets into different geographical units like country, state, district, *taluka*, village, and so on. Geographic segmentation is an important process, particularly for multinational and global businesses and brands. Many such companies have regional and national marketing programmes which alter their products, advertising and promotion to meet the individual needs of geographic units.

4.2.5 Demographic Segmentation

Demographic segmentation demarcates the market into groups based on variables like age, gender, family size, income, occupation, education, religion, race and nationality.

It consists of dividing the market into groups based on variables such as age, gender, family size, income, occupation, education, religion, race and nationality. As one might expect, demographic segmentation variables are amongst the most popular bases for segmenting customer groups. This is partly because customer wants are closely linked to variables such as income and age. Also, for practical reasons, there is often much more data available to help with the demographic segmentation process. The main demographic segmentation variables are summarized below:

Age: Consumer needs and wants change with age although they may still wish to consume the same types of products. So marketers design, package and promote products differently to meet the wants of different age groups. Good examples include the marketing of toothpastes (contrast the branding of toothpastes for children and adults) and toys (with many age-based segments). Product examples are toys for children and jewellery for women.

Life cycle: The consumer stage in the life cycle is an important variable, particularly in markets such as leisure and tourism. For example, the promotional campaign of Country Club Holidays is more liberal (in terms of social norms and values) compared to its competitor Club Mahindra Holidays, which positions itself more as a family holiday provider.

Gender: Gender segmentation is widely used in consumer marketing. The best examples include clothing, hairdressing, magazines, toiletries and cosmetics. Product examples are scarves for women, ties for men, and so on.

Income: Income is another popular basis for segmentation, with many companies often targeting affluent consumers with luxury goods and convenience services. Good examples include Citibank, Thomas Cook, American Express and Elegant Resorts, an upmarket travel company. In contrast, several companies also focus on marketing products that appeal to consumers with relatively low incomes (even in the middle class). Examples include the Tata Nano, low-cost carriers like SpiceJet, Lifebouy soap, and so on.

Take the case of the toilet soap industry, which is highly fragmented in terms of category. There are more than 250 brands and their variants. In 2008, the penetration level of the industry was 96 per cent, its total value about ₹65,000 million, and total volume approximately 5.90 lakh tons. The market is segregated primarily on the basis of price. The premium segment players are Liril International, Pears, Dove, Cinthol and LTI (Laboratory Technologies Inc.), while the popular category includes Lux, Hamam, Margo, Lifebouy and Fairglow. The discount segment includes Nima Rose, Lifebuoy Active, Godrej No.1, Breeze, Nirma Beauty and the Carbolic group that includes Lifebouy, OK, and Nirma Bath.

MARKETING IN ACTION — **LIRIL WOOS THE FAMILY**

The Liril Girl had turned bathing into a fantasy. But HUL's premium soap is now pitching for family intimacy. Will the new campaign work?

Before she stopped bathing under a waterfall, Karen Lunel made sure that the Liril ad caught the nation's imagination. The ad with its famous jingle 'la-i-ra-li-ra' ran for 12 years beginning 1975 and single-handedly made Liril one of India's top-selling soaps with 14 per cent market share. The waterfall, the bikini and the jingle continued, though Lunel was replaced by an assortment of stars such as Preity Zinta and Deepika Padukone. But the new ads were seen to be merely an echo of the original film. So the 'Liril girls' took a final bow in July 2009 as the freshness soap's market share plummeted to 1.3 per cent.

Ad gurus say it was high time Liril did something different to survive. The waterfall and the bikini served their purpose at a time when women's liberation was taking wing. The Liril girls had then broken new grounds in the sense that they took bathing out of the bathroom and turned it into a fantasy. But with time that had become irrelevant. In the interim, HUL tried its luck by launching a few variants like Liril Orange, Icy mint, and so on which didn't quite pick up. According to Harish Bijoor, CEO, Harish Bijoor Consults Inc, 'Variants are essentially bells and whistles products. Most of the time they just add to the advertising zing but very little to top-line sales volume. Though they are necessary, they just come and go.'

Rebranding was the need of the hour to revive the old magic. Analysts felt that the 'emotional space' addressed by the Liril of the 1970s was no longer relevant to the consumers of today (urban women in the higher socio-economic class). So Liril became Liril 2000 and HUL launched a new campaign that stresses family intimacy and speaks about 2,000 sensitive points in the human body that the soap refreshes and rejuvenates. As part of the rebranding, the soap has a different packaging; the earlier tight-wrapped cover has been replaced by a box-type packing and the light green colour has given way to a darker shade and glossy finish. According to HUL the soap represents 'fundamental re-engineering with an improved product in a contemporary shape and has the signature Liril perfume'.

HUL also briefly moved the Liril account to McCann in 2007. It came back to Lowe Lintas in early 2009 and Lowe offered the 'relaunch' cure. Joseph George, executive director, Lowe Lintas, says, 'In the last decade, freshness has become generic to the personal wash category and lime and lemony fragrance is being used by any and all brands. The task therefore was to leverage Liril's premium heritage and find a new consumer benefit in skin cleansing to make the brand relevant to its audience once again.' Today, the premium end of the skin cleansing market is moving to skincare benefits. So, HUL looked at how it could re-interpret Liril's core equity of freshness in the context of skincare. The added benefit of soft skin (thanks to aloe vera) allowed it to offer a unique combination of fresh, clean and soft skin. In communication, this translated into 'Every part of the body becoming clean, fresh and touchably soft'.

The advertising has thus switched from celebrating 'individualistic pleasure' to 'family intimacy'. 'If the new proposition is relevant and compelling, people will accept it. Having said that, it is true that "freshness" is still at the core of the new proposition,' says George. The agency says the target audience remains the same. Liril was never targeted at the youth though the brand had youthful imagery. In order to broad-base the brand appeal, Liril is now talking to the family, experts observe.

The rebranding is being seen to address the loss of market share. Business Performance Services of KPMG observed that with time, the choices available to customers have increased. Liril had started losing market share, whereas other soaps like Lux and Lifebuoy had increased/maintained their shares consistently. HUL took the Liril girls out of its brand image in an attempt to improve the worsening scenario. Besides refreshing the brand, the repositioning makes sense from the portfolio management perspective, too.

Naimish Dave, director, OC&C Strategy Consultants, says, 'It will ensure an efficient deployment of HUL's brand portfolio in the personal wash segment. With Dove at the super premium end, Lifebuoy at mass-plus and Lux at mass price points, it is obviously a conscious decision to reposition Liril to target the premium soaps segment'. However, experts like Bijoor think Liril has now taken the safe route of building an intimate bond within marriage. But the new strategy of positioning the brand as being clean, fresh and intimate with the family can also be perceived by the market as boring and routine.

Source: Business Standard, January 2010.

Social class: Many marketers believe that consumers' 'perceived' social class influences their preference for cars, clothes, home furnishings, leisure activities and other products and services. There is a clear link here with income-based segmentation. Examples could include club memberships, philanthropic contributions, and so on.

Lifestyle: Marketers are increasingly interested in the effect of consumer lifestyles on demand. Unfortunately, there are many different lifestyle categorization systems, many of them designed by advertising and marketing agencies as a way of winning new marketing clients and campaigns.

Avocation: This could include products for fishing, golf, art work, knitting, and so on.

Special interests: Marketers could target pet lovers, science fiction readers, jazz music fans, and so on.

4.2.6 Behavioural Segmentation

Behavioural segmentation divides customers into groups based on the way they respond to, use or know a product.

Behavioural segmentation divides customers into groups based on the way they respond to, use or know of a product. Behavioural segments can group consumers in terms of:

Occasions: When a product is consumed or purchased. For example, cereals have traditionally been marketed as a breakfast-related product. Kellogg's has always encouraged consumers to eat breakfast cereals on the 'occasion' of getting up early in the day. More recently, they have tried to extend the consumption of cereals by promoting the product as an anytime snack food.

Usage: Some markets can be segmented into light, medium and heavy user groups. For instance, cosmetics users can be classified based on their usage. Those who use on a daily basis are heavy users, while others who use on special occasions as well as when going out on the weekends would be medium users. The light users would use only on rare occasions like weddings, parties, and so on.

Loyalty: Loyal consumers—those who buy one brand all or most of the time—are valuable customers. Many companies try to segment their markets into those where loyal customers can be found and retained compared with segments where customers rarely display any product loyalty.

MARKETING ANALYSIS

KRACKJACK TAKES ON 50-50, FIGHTS BACK TO REGAIN MARKET SHARE

Ek hi bite mein sweet bhi, salty bhi, says the television commercial of Parle Products' Krackjack. It's a direct potshot at market leader Britannia 50-50's *kabhi sweet, kabhi salty* proposition. The reason for the aggression is simple; Krackjack, the oldest brand in the ₹900-crore non-salt biscuits market, has lost out in a big way to the relative newcomer. According to the market research firm AC Nielsen, 50-50, launched in 1993, had 33 per cent value share of the non-salt biscuits segment in March 2009, while Krackjack (in the market since 1972) was far behind at 21 per cent. The other players in the segment include ITC's Sunfeast Sweet 'n' Salt and smaller regional players like Priya Gold, Anmol and Cremica.

The new campaign for Krackjack, introduced in November 2009, comes after a gap of two years. According to Pravin Kulkarni, general manager of Parle, the category growth has been stagnating at 3 to 4 per cent and as market leader, Parle decided to take the initiative to increase it. In its commercials, the brand reintroduced Krack and Jack, played by comedians Swapnil Shinde and Gaurav Gera. The characters were earlier played by Boman Irani and Vijay Patkar before the campaign was dropped. The idea this time is to use the 'sweet and salty' brand proposition as a metaphor. This duality is the essence of the brand, says Bhavin Panchamia, product manager of Parle. The company has tried to personify duality in terms of attitude, lifestyle and behaviour besides adding an element of fun. They have created the property of 'Pole Khol' basically to interact with the consumer in a better way and engage them with the brand.

In addition to the television commercials, the company has also changed its logo and product packaging, with a red and silver colour packet to highlight the contrasting qualities of sweet and salty taste brought into one biscuit. The new commercials have been conceptualized and created by the agency Thoughtshop. Vipin Dhyani, founder and creative director, Thoughtshop India, says the idea is to look contemporary. From the basic communication of sweet and salty taste, the product has moved a step ahead and communicated the core idea of duality by personalizing it. Krackjack has come up with three TV commercials titled 'Politician', 'Saas Bahu' and 'Romeo'.

Britannia 50-50, Krackjack's target competitor, has had a spectacular run after it launched its 50-50 campaign in 2008. The brand saw its growth rate decline two years ago, but the campaign as well as a new distribution strategy helped it to register a double-digit growth rate of 14 per cent in 2008. The growth mostly came from the semi-urban and rural pockets where regional and smaller players have a stronger hold. To penetrate these new markets, Britannia launched ₹5 packs and has since seen its sales increase tenfold. The ₹5 SKU of 50-50 accounted for 10 per cent of the total business in 2009 and the brand expects to maintain the 14 per cent growth rate for 50-50 in 2010 too.

Krackjack, which has over 60 per cent of its sales coming from the urban areas, is available at price points of ₹7, ₹10 and ₹20. The new communication from Krackjack is the result of a market survey conducted by the brand in the first half of 2009.

The new campaign gives the company a chance to extend the communication to other mediums like print and digital media and bring in new protagonists. However, some believe these moves may be a tad late as competition has already made a lot of headway, also gaining much ground. According to brand expert Harish Bijoor, in the period that Parle Products went inactive, players like Britannia, ITC Sunfeast went aggressive in advertising and garnering market share. Moreover, the entire snack food category is getting reinvented as players like PepsiCo (promoters of brands Aliva and Kurkure) are looking at the snack segment and are eating into the non-salt biscuits segment big time.

Source: Business World, April 2010.

Benefits sought: An important form of behavioural segmentation, this requires marketers to understand and find the main benefits customers look for in a product. An excellent example is the toothpaste market where research has found four main 'benefit segments': economic, medicinal, cosmetic and taste.

4.3 Purchase Decision Influencers

The FMCG industry is extremely competitive and consumers demand good price and quality. Increasingly disloyal to brands, consumers quickly choose those that make better offers.

With time there has been a paradigm shift in consumer tastes and preferences. There is a dire need for constant innovation to address changing customer needs such as 'increased utility' or 'health benefits'. Also, the modern retail format will slowly occupy a bigger share. This will lead to change in shopping behaviour and growth in the FMCG sector. The FMCG industry is extremely competitive and consumers demand good price and quality. They are also increasingly disloyal to brands, quickly choosing those that make better offers. The recent rise of private-label goods has led to increased competition within the FMCG industry. A focus on bringing high-volume products at lower prices to the market has pressurized all actors. Producers need to differentiate their products and quickly bring them to the market. This has spurred the rise of many more product variants and frequent replacement of products, in order to achieve the best positioning in the current market. Manufacturers must adapt and be able to produce products in smaller batch sizes to win the battle on the shelf. It is also necessary to have the freshest product. Additionally, the demand for FMCG can be very seasonal, which means manufacturers must have flexible production programmes. It also anticipates quick marketing of innovations in order to win customers. Hence marketers must isolate a specific segment of the market on which to focus. While doing this, they can consider more subtle influences on the purchase decision. Some of these are:

Preference for channel of distribution: Many prospects prefer to buy through a specific distributor or wholesaler. For individuals this may be due to subtle as well as economic reasons. For example, an individual prospect may immediately think of Big Bazaar or Reliance Fresh when considering a low priced offering like cereals, vegetables or fruits. A business, on the other hand, often prefers a single communication point for all purchases, since it results in lower purchase prices.

When selling to consumers or businesses, the more individuals or groups involved in the purchase decision, the more difficult the sale.

Number of decision-makers: When selling to consumers or businesses, the more individuals or groups involved in the purchase decision, the more difficult the sale. Marketing costs for selling bread can stay low because one person normally makes the purchase decision. Car purchases are more complex because the purchase decision often involves a family. Business sales to committees often require months to achieve a decision.

Financial strength of the prospect: Less affluent prospects may desire time payments versus a cash purchase and a Maruti Alto/Hyundai Santro instead of a Tata Safari.

Quantity/volume requirements: To cite a simple example, restaurants want large jars of pickles while individuals want small jars. Similarly, businesses use large amounts of electricity at predictable times unlike households which might use smaller amounts though at consistent, continuous times.

Ability to use the offering: Trying to sell to a prospect who lacks either the knowledge or the resources to benefit fully from the offering will result in a 'no sale' situation or an unhappy customer. The prospect should have knowledge and resources such as time, equipment, facilities, personnel and complementary products/services.

Commitment required: If the product demands customers' commitment in terms of time, resources or money, then the target should be prospects who 'really need' the offering rather than prospects who get some, but not a lot, of benefits.

Brand awareness/users: Examples are prospects who ask for mobile phones compatible with Microsoft operating systems (Windows mobile) to uplink data with the PC and the Internet. They may choose an Asus GSM handset instead of a Nokia in the Indian market!

Attitude towards a personality or enterprise: Reputation helps DHL get long distance parcel service, Michael Jordan causes Nike consumers to associate shoes with success in sport.

Attitude toward price versus value: Connoisseurs or collectors (of say stamps, coins, music, and so on) aren't price sensitive unlike purchasers of commodity items.

Experience with other products/services your enterprise has offered: Marketers are looking for reactions like 'I liked your first product so I'll try your second product too.'

After-sale support expectations: It is often beneficial to target prospects who have enough expertise that they will require a minimum of after-sale support.

Seller characteristics that can influence purchase decisions: Another form of influence is how the prospect perceives a marketer's offerings and/or enterprise. If marketers can determine the characteristics their prospects most value in the enterprise they purchase from, they can promote them to the prospect.

Unique employee skills and knowledge: Extensive experience with a specific market segment or field of scientific inquiry can be a powerful promotional tool. For example, if an enterprise could say, 'Our scientists know more about corn silk genetic structures than anyone in the world' they would have a strong sales statement.

Extensive experience with a specific market segment or field of scientific inquiry can be a powerful promotional tool.

Special relationships with distribution channels: Product or service accessibility is a critical factor in sales success. If an enterprise could say, 'Due to a unique relationship, the XYZ video stores give us more shelf space than any competitor' prospects will likely respond positively.

Customer service capabilities: Prospects like to know that they can depend on post-sale support from the product or service provider. State Bank of

India's statement, 'We have more ATMs and branches than any other bank in the country' has helped them secure retail and corporate banking business.

Unique product forms: Credible uniqueness such as, 'Our product is the only one that offers dynamic digi-whirling' appeals to the market. Tata Sky positioned itself against local cable TV operators with the message 'Cable TV with DVD picture and hi-fi sound quality, at your home anywhere in India.'

Manufacturing expertise: The market is always interested in purchasing from the 'best'. If Tata Motors can confidently state, 'We are the only enterprise that can offer a car under $3,000 price tag,' they have created an image of being the 'the most economical' and the best option for the middle-income householders. Toyota believes in 'quality with excellence' to drive its passenger car market globally.

Longevity: Reliability is important. LIC's 'We have been in business for 60 years, so you can count on us to be there when you need us' is a strong selling point for the organization.

4.4 Retail Service Segments

A retail service segment is composed of a group of current and potential retail customers who share common characteristics, needs, purchasing behaviours or consumption patterns. Effective segmentation should group buyers into segments in ways that result in as much similarity as possible on the relevant characteristics within each segment but dissimilarity on those same characteristics between different segments.

Two broad categories of variables are useful in describing the differences between segments. They are as follows:

User characteristics often vary. They reflect demographic characteristics, geographic location, and psychographics.

User characteristics: These vary from one person to another, reflecting demographic characteristics (age, income and education), geographic location, and psychographics (attitudes, values, lifestyles, and opinions of decision-makers). More recently, marketers have begun to speak of technographics—a term recently trademarked by technology consulting firm Forester Research that groups customers according to their willingness and ability to use the latest technology.

Usage behaviour relates to how a product is purchased, delivered, and used.

Usage behaviour: Another important segmentation variable are the specific benefits that individuals and corporate purchasers seek from a particular good or service. Usage behaviour relates to how a product is purchased, delivered, and used. Among such variables are when and where purchase and consumption take place, the quantities consumed (heavy users are always of particular interest to marketers), frequency and purpose of use, the occasions under which consumption takes place (sometimes referred to as occasion segmentation), sensitivity to such marketing variables as advertising, pricing, speed and other service features, and availability of alternative delivery systems. Finally, there are problem customers whose misbehaviour makes them undesirable. These customers misbehave with the frontline staff, complain unnecessarily and in an extremely rude manner.

In general, a service segment is composed of a group of buyers who share common characteristics, needs, etc. For instance, the Foodworld store in Bengaluru's Vijay Nagar area might target residents of the locality (geographic segmentation) who have monthly incomes of ₹25,000 and above (demographic segmentation), who value personal service from a knowledgeable staff, and are not highly price sensitive (both reflecting segmentation according to expressed attitudes and behavioural intentions).

Usage-level segmentation groups people into heavy, medium, light users or nonusers of the product.

Occasion segmentation means grouping people according to product use occasions. For example, airline passengers can be segmented into those flying for business, pleasure, or emergency reasons. Usage-level segmentation

MARKETING ANALYSIS — NESTLÉ INDIA

Nestlé India is a subsidiary of Nestle S.A. of Switzerland. With seven factories and a large number of co-packers, Nestlé India provides consumers with products of global standard and is committed to long-term sustainable growth and shareholder satisfaction. It ranks third among FMCG companies in India with a turnover of ₹4,505 crore and net profit of ₹534 crore (2008–9).

The company insists on honesty, integrity and fairness in all aspects of business and expects the same in its relationships. This has earned it the trust and respect of every strata of society that it comes into contact with and is acknowledged amongst India's 'Most Respected Companies' and amongst the 'Top Wealth Creators of India'.

Nestle's Milk Products and Nutrition business innovated extensively to strengthen its product portfolio and improve performance. The ambient dairy business saw good growth on two key brands, Nestle Everyday Dairy Whitener and Nestle Milkmaid Sweetened Condensed Milk. In addition, new opportunities were targeted with the launch of three health- and wellness-based propositions: (a) Nestle NIDO, a nutritious milk powder for growing children above the age of two years; (b) extension of the trusted Nestle Milkmaid brand into the healthy refreshment opportunity with Nestle Milkmaid Funshakes; and (c) Nestle Cerevita Multigrain Cereal, developed to address the expanding market for nutritious breakfast options.

The Fresh Dairy category had a good growth and further strengthened the image of the company as an innovator based on the launches of: (a) Nestle Fresh 'N' Natural Slim curd, a 98 per cent fat-free formulation; (b) Nestle Milkmaid Fruit Yoghurt which is 98 per cent fat-free and has real fruit; and (c) Nestle Nesvita, a 98 per cent fat-free, probiotic curd in plain and fruit varieties, which was developed based on Nestle's extensive experience with probiotics.

The business for Prepared Dishes and Cooking Aids too demonstrated rapid growth. The pioneering concept of 'Taste *bhi*, health *bhi*' was further strengthened as the business launched more health and wellness products. After the very successful launch of Maggi Vegetable Atta Noodles in 2008, the business leveraged its deep consumer insights, R&D strengths and knowledge of nutrition, health and wellness to roll out Maggi Rice Noodles, with the goodness of rice, and designed to provide 'balanced energy' as recommended by nutritionists. These were launched in three unique flavours suited to regional preferences.

The Chocolate and Confectionery business anticipated the needs of the emerging consumers and developed appropriate brands. The company is a leader in the light-wafer confectionery segment with Nestle Munch and Nestle Kitkat and in the white chocolayer segment with Nestle Milkybar. The company is also a leader in Eclairs and Fruit/Mint roll categories.

Well-targeted consumer advertising has made Nestle's brands more vibrant. A focus on consumer insights, innovation as well as improved distribution have contributed to good performances by the key brands. The efforts made to improve the distribution of chocolate and confectionary items are reflected in the company now being the leader in the distribution and availability of this category.

A detailed analysis of Nestlé India suggested the following:

- The company needs to focus on its infant foods product line. More innovation is required to increase the market share. Though the Milk Products and Nutrition business is reporting good sales volume, the maturity of the market requires additional promotion to sustain the growth rate. There is a risk of declining growth rate in this segment.
- Nestle India should continue new product launches in its Prepared Food segment, especially Maggi. Consumer research is essential to avoid failures like Maggi Dal Atta noodles. In the chocolates segment, Nestle needs to come up with more strong brands. Apart from Kitkat, it doesn't have any strong product, which makes the company vulnerable to competitors. Nestle needs a strong competitor for Cadbury's Dairy Milk.

Source: Investors' Report of Nestlé India Ltd., January 2010.

means grouping people into whether they are heavy, medium, light users or nonusers of the product. Lifestyle segmentation means grouping people by lifestyles, such as, 'furs and station wagon suburbanites' or 'shotgun and pick-up truck macho males'. Clearly, a market can be segmented in several ways. While segmenting the service marketer hopes to recognize a substantial unmet need that might represent a profitable market opportunity.

4.5 Target Market

Mass market marketers appeal to the largest market possible by selling products of interest to nearly all consumers.

Target markets are the market segments that a marketer wishes to serve. The first classification looks at the type of markets a firm intends to target.

(a) **Mass market:** Mass market marketers appeal to the largest market possible by selling products of interest to nearly all consumers. With such a large market from which to draw customers, the competition among these retail marketers is often fierce. HUL, with the support of the Indian Medical Associations (IMAs), targets Lifebuoy Carbolic soap at the rural masses as a solution for preventing epidemics breaking out due to lack of personal hygiene.

(b) **Specialty market:** Marketers categorized as servicing the specialty market are likely to target buyers looking for products with certain features that go beyond mass-marketed products, such as customers who require more advanced product options or a higher level of customer service. While not as large as the mass market, the target market serviced by specialty marketers can be sizeable. For instance, Café Coffee Day found out that some customers look for just a cup of coffee, some others want coffee but with strict preferences about coffee beans and brews; yet another group prefers to have snacks or even a meal with coffee. The younger customers prefer the 'dining and dating' approach in a typical club-like ambience. Accordingly the company came out with three variants of the original store format to lure specific target groups to its outlets.

Appealing to the exclusive market means winning discriminating customers who are often willing to pay a premium for features found in very few products and for highly personalized services.

(c) **Exclusive market:** Appealing to this market means appealing to the discriminatory customer who is often willing to pay a premium for features found in very few products and for highly personalized services. Since this target market is small, the number of retail marketers addressing it within a given geographic area may also be limited. A holiday company like Country Club Limited (CCL), Hyderabad, promoted the concept of private resorts and service apartments through time share and shared ownership among like-minded people.

4.6 Targeting

The procedure to evaluate the relevant characteristics and prospects to satisfy business objectives of potential market segments is called targeting the particular segment. While deciding to go for target marketing, a company can slice the market into finer homogeneous 'segments'. In fact, a marketer can distinguish various levels of market deconstruction—at the brand segment level, the niche level and the market cell level. Focusing on serving customers in a niche has several advantages for a marketer, including the opportunity to know each customer more personally, face far fewer competitors and earn high margins since customers are willing to pay more for convenience, assortment and quality. Marketing based on relationships, networks, and interaction recognizes that the marketing activity is embedded in the management of the networks of the selling organization, the market and society. It is directed to long-term, win-win relationships with individual customers, and value is jointly created by the parties involved.

While evaluating different market segments, the marketer must look at factors such as the segment's overall attractiveness and the company's objectives and resources. First, the firm must know whether a potential segment has the characteristics that make it attractive in terms of size, growth, profitability, scale economics and low risk. Second, the firm must consider whether investing in the segment makes sense in the long run amidst global uncertainties, given the firm's objectives and resources. In order to select the target market, the marketer can consider any of the following five patterns of target marketing:

(i) **Single segment concentration:** The company may select a single segment. Through concentrated marketing, it gains knowledge of the segment's needs and achieves a strong market presence. If the firm captures segment leadership, it can earn a high return on its investment. Johnson & Johnson's mid-1980 strategy was to concentrate on the baby-boom market and offer specialized products for babies globally. Food World concentrates on the middle-income housewife/families (monthly income of ₹15,000 to ₹25,000) for its retail outlet growth.

(ii) **Selective specialization:** The firm selects a number of segments, each objectively attractive and appropriate. There may be little or no synergy among the segments, but each segment promises to be a money-maker. Again, Johnson & Johnson's mid-1980 strategy was to target young mothers along with their newborn babies with an array of personal care products and toiletries. Mass marketers like Big Bazaar introduced foreign Stock Keeping Units (SKUs) for creating a separate brand identity for high-priced products within the discount store.

(iii) **Product specialization:** The firm specializes in making a certain product that sells to several segments. For example, Godrej safes and lockers were initially sold to nationalized banks and gradually penetrated government treasury and departments, MNC offices, commercial organizations, cooperatives societies, and so on. Through its lockers the company built a reputation in a specific product area. It floated a new company called Godrej Securities Limited (GSL) in 2008 with special instruments and integrated solutions for protecting the office from terrorist threat and theft. To cite another example, in 2009 Nilgiri's decided to withdraw all branded FMCG products from its retail outlets to sell its own products, under its own label, along with fresh vegetables and dairy products from its own farms. The firm has specialized in dairy products since 1953 and has loyal customers.

(iv) **Market specialization:** The firm concentrates on serving many needs of a particular customer group. Country Club's service apartments offer unique services of blending personal, professional and leisure needs of its customers by offering a whole range of services to its members. Similarly, a manpower rental agency can gain a good reputation for providing personnel for home care, office security, kitchen assistance, guest reception, laundry, cleaning, pet care, plumbing and electrical maintenance and then become a channel for further products that the customer group could use. Namdhari Fresh selling exotic, organic and export quality vegetables through its retail outlets is another example of market specialization.

(v) **Full market coverage:** The firm attempts to serve all customer groups with all products they might need. It's possible for large firms to undertake a full market coverage strategy, for example, Lenovo (computer market), Maruti Suzuki (automobile market) and Pepsi Cola (soft drinks market).

There are two broad ways in which large firms cover a whole market.

Undifferentiated marketing is the marketing counterpart of standardization and mass production in manufacturing. Here, market segment and differences are ignored and the firm goes after the whole market with one offer.

Undifferentiated marketing: It's the marketing counterpart of standardization and mass production in manufacturing. Here the market segment and differences are ignored and the firm goes after the whole market with one offer. It focuses on basic buyer needs rather than on differences among buyers. It designs products and marketing programmes that will appeal to the broadest number of buyers and relies on mass distribution and mass advertisement. Undifferentiated marketers aim to endow the product with a superior image in people's minds. The narrow product line keeps down R&D as well as production, inventory, transportation, marketing research, advertising and product management costs. Coca-Cola International is a typical example wherein the company offers the same cola to customer groups varying from 6-month-old to 60-year-old across 193 countries!

In differentiated marketing the firm operates in several market segments with a different programme for each segment.

Differentiated marketing: The firm operates in several market segments and has a different programme for each segment. For instance, Maruti Suzuki produces a car for every purse, purpose and personality. The price ranges from ₹2 lakh to ₹22 lakh under the same generic brand Maruti! Lenovo also offers many hardware and software packages for different segments in the personal desktop and laptop computer market. Though differentiated marketing creates more total sales than undifferentiated marketing, it increases the production, marketing and administrative costs of carrying out business.

While targeting a specific segment, the retail marketer should not take any undue advantage of vulnerable segments, like children. Though children have become potential influencers in the family decision-making process, ideally they should not be influenced by marketers to consume products that are not good for them. Thus the ethical value of the market should be maintained.

Further the retail company that is targeting more than one segment needs to examine the interrelationship between segments so that it can optimize its costs and performance. For instance, Giant Supermarket in Mumbai targets people who want to buy apparels, kitchenware, electronic goods, vegetables, liquor, groceries, and so on, thus targeting a super segment rather than an individual segment. While it's true that concentrating on a super segment pays, it is advisable to go one step at a time as it makes it difficult for competitors to know the direction in which the organization is moving. Ceat, the RPG-group tyre company decided to focus on two-wheelers to increase its sales volume rather than pursuing the traditional strategy of chasing four-wheelers.

It's the need of the hour that the marketers develop mutual cooperation and information sharing procedures among the segments they are targeting. This will enhance the effectiveness of the marketing programmes and enable marketers to offer better products with efficient service to the customers of each segment.

It's not usually realistic for a firm to appeal to all actual or potential buyers in a market, because customers are too numerous, too widely scattered, and too varied in their needs, behaviours, and consumption patterns. Different product/service firms also vary widely in their ability to serve different types of customers. So rather than attempting to compete in an entire market, each company needs to focus its efforts on those customers it can serve best. In marketing terms, focus means providing a relatively narrow product mix for a particular market segment—a group of buyers who share common characteristics, needs, purchasing behaviour or consumption patterns. This concept is at the heart of all successful service firms which have identified the strategically important elements in their operations and have concentrated their resources on them.

The extent of a company's focus can be described on two different dimensions—market focus and service focus. Market focus is the extent to which a firm serves few or many markets, whereas service focus describes the extent to which a firm offers few or many services. A *fully focused* organization provides a limited range of services to a narrow and specific market segment. A *market-focused* company concentrates on a narrow market segment but has a wide range of services for a fairly broad market. Finally, many service providers fall into the *unfocused* category because they try to serve broad markets and provide a wide range of services.

The extent of a company's focus can be described on two different dimensions—market focus and service focus. Market focus is the extent to which a firm serves few or many markets, whereas service focus describes the extent to which a firm offers few or many services.

Selective Focus

Marketers opting for selective focus can do so in the following ways:

Niches: Niches typically describe small sets of customers who have very narrowly defined needs or unique combinations of needs. Thus, a sports car market segment may be further refined into several buyer niches: a niche that wants very expensive, powerful racing-car type vehicles (such as Ferraris or Lamborghinis); a niche that wants less expensive, less racer-like cars but powerful ones nevertheless (such as Porsches); those who want more conventional looking cars with a sports-car like performance (such as BMWs); and a niche that wants a less expensive cars that look like sports cars but don't perform that way (such as Ford Mustangs).

Market cells: Companies may want to identify small groups of customers who share some characteristics that provide a market opportunity. Today many companies build databases containing information about their customers' demographics, past purchases, preferences and other characteristics. American Express and other credit card companies have tons of customer profile data, as do catalogue mail order firms, telephone companies, public utility companies, banks and insurance companies. These data warehouses are waiting to be analysed. Companies like IBM and Oracle offer a service called data mining, which uses high-powered analytical and statistical techniques to unearth interesting patterns and findings about customers. However, the majority of service businesses do not find such micro-segmentation worthwhile in their industries. Instead, they look to achieve economies of scale by marketing to all customers within a specific market segment and serving each in a similar fashion. The strategy of mass customization of a service with some individualized product elements to a large number of customers at relatively low price may be achieved by offering a standardized core product but tailoring supplementary service elements to fit the requirements of individual buyers.

4.7 Positioning

Positioning is the act of designing a retail company's offering and image so it occupies a distinctive place in the target market's mind.

Positioning is the act of designing a retail company's offering and image so it occupies a distinctive place in the target market's mind. After segmenting a market and targeting a consumer, the firm proceeds to position its product within that market. Positioning is all about 'perception'. As perceptions differ from person to person, so do the results of the positioning map. For instance, what one customer perceives as quality or value for money is different from other customers' perception of the same. However, there will be similarities. Products or services are mapped together with other products or services respectively on a positioning map. This allows them to be compared and contrasted in relation to each other—the main strength of this tool. Marketers decide on a competitive position which enables them to distinguish their products from the offerings of their competitors (hence the term positioning strategy).

The idea of positioning relates to the way consumers perceive and evaluate retail products and services. Specifically, it relates to the way in which consumers rank the features and attributes of a retail product/service against those of competing services.

The process of differentiation impacts the product's position in the consumer's mind. Different attributes of a product/service reflect different values which can be attached to that service in the consumer's perception.

Marketers use the positioning map to understand the position of other firms in the marketplace. The map is a two-variable one drawn on the basis of some selected attributes. For example, apparel retail marketers like Lifestyle, Wills Lifestyle, Westside, Park Avenue, Madura Garments and Benetton would differentiate the product attributes in their positioning map into fashion and assortment. For departmental stores, the same would be quality versus price.

The positioning map gives marketers a clear picture of the relative positioning of the firm with regard to its competitors.

The positioning map gives marketers a clear picture of the relative positioning of the firm with regard to its competitors, enabling them decide whether to reformulate the positioning strategy or improve the existing strategy.

MARKETING ANALYSIS | DABUR INDIA LIMITED

Dabur India Limited (DIL) is the fifth largest FMCG company operating in India with a turnover of more than ₹2,468 crore (2008–9) and a market cap of ₹10,468 crore (April-September 2009). With a legacy of 120 years built on attributes of quality and trust, Dabur has proven its expertise in the fields of health care, personal care, homecare and foods. It operates under three business categories, namely, the Consumer Care Division (CCD), Consumer Healthcare Division (CHD) and Dabur Foods Limited (DFL). (In July 2007, Dabur announced the de-merger of DFL with DIL).

When the Indian FMCG sector was struggling due to slow growth in the economy, Dabur decided to take numerous strategic initiatives, reorganize operations and improve its brand architecture. Beginning 2002, it decided to concentrate its marketing efforts on Dabur, Vatika, Anmol, Real and Hajmola brands—strengthen their brand equity, create differentiation and emerge as a pure FMCG player recognized as a herbal brand. This was decided on after a study by Accenture revealed that Dabur was mainly perceived as a herbal brand connected more with consumers over the age of 35 years.

With youth forming a major population of India, Dabur decided to revamp its brand identity. It got celebrities Amitabh Bachchan, Vivek Oberoi, Rani Mukherjee and Virender Sehwag to endorse its products. New packaging and advertising campaign saw the sales of Chyawanprash grow by 8.5 per cent in 2003–4. The year 2004–5 saw a whole new brand identity of Dabur. The old banyan tree was replaced by a new, younger and more contemporarily-rendered banyan tree.

Its leaves suggesting growth, energy and rejuvenation, twin colours reflecting the perfect combination of stability and freshness, the trunk representing three people raising their hands in joy, the broad trunk symbolizing stability, the multiple branches conveying growth, and warmth and energy displayed through the soft orange colour. 'Celebrating Life' was chosen as a new tag that summarized the essence of the brand.

It is clear that the Indian consumer class has become younger and more affluent. These consumers are much more conscious about lifestyle-related issues that affect their health and well-being. As a 'herbal specialist', Dabur was already focusing on regular therapeutic cures for health-related problems. It was only natural for the company to connect closely with the new set of Indian customers and extend its offerings across the larger and wider 'health and wellness' space. In pursuing 'Vision 2010', while the company continues to develop its traditional markets, which are primarily in tier II cities having a close affinity to ayurvedic products, it has recognized the imperative to devise products and propositions that appeal to the more affluent and younger Indian consumers. The company is in the process of re-orienting itself to meet this challenge. Thus, about 15 different brands and products have been relaunched in the last two years, coupled with completely revamped communication and packaging. Moreover, recognizing that customers are increasingly becoming more discerning about the products they buy, the company has made concerted efforts to promote the efficacy of its products through clinical studies. The idea is that the customer must be provided scientific proof to realize the effectiveness of Dabur's products.

Source: Investors' Report of Dabur India Ltd., January 2010.

4.7.1 Developing Value Proposition

No company can be good at everything. First, companies have limited funds and must decide where to concentrate them. Second, choosing to be good at one thing may reduce the possibility of being good at something else.

1. Choosing Broad Positioning

Professor Michael Porter in *Competitive Strategy* proposed three broad alternatives: a business unit could focus on being the product differentiator, the low-cost leader, or the niche player. He warned firms that if companies tried to be good in all three, but not superior in any way, they would lose out to firms superior in one way. In other words, the middle path is a trap.

Michael Porter in Competitive Strategy *proposed three broad alternatives: a business unit could focus on being the product differentiator, the low-cost leader, or the niche player.*

Firms normally don't have enough money to be good in all ways. In addition each positioning strategy calls for a different organizational culture and management system. However, critics point out that some firms have managed to be superior at both product differentiation and low cost. Procter & Gamble is not only a great marketing firm doing superior product differentiation, but it is also very lean in its manufacturing cost structure. Toyota not only produces the best quality automobiles but produces them at the lowest unit cost.

Subsequent to Porter, two consultants, Michael Treacy and Fred Wiersema, proposed an alternative three-way framework which they called value discipline. According to it, within its industry, a firm could be the product leader, the operationally excellent firm, or the customer-intimate firm. This framework is based on the notion that in every market, there are three types of customers. Some customers favour the firm that is advancing the technological frontier (product leadership), while another customer group does not need the latest products but wants highly reliable and dependable performance (operational excellence). A final customer group prefers the firm that is most responsive and flexible in meeting individual needs (customer intimacy). Operationally excellent companies like Reliance Industries, McDonald's or DHL operate highly efficient systems that are difficult to alter. In fact they operate like machines, and that is both their strength and their weakness. If they tried to be customer-intimate and made many changes to satisfy individual customers, they would not be able to perform at their promised level of efficiency. Treacy and Wiersema propose that a business should follow four rules for success:

(a) Become best at one of the three value disciplines.
(b) Achieve an adequate performance level in the other two disciplines.
(c) Keep improving one's superior position in the chosen discipline so as not to lose out to competitors.
(d) Keep becoming more adequate in the other two disciplines, since competitors keep raising customers' expectations about what is adequate.

2. Choosing a Specific Positioning

Services can be positioned in six different ways—by service attributes, user application, price/quality relationship, service class, service user, or competitor.

Companies need to go beyond broad positioning to express a more concrete benefit and reason to buy. Many companies advertise a single major benefit positioning, drawing from such possibilities as best quality, best performance, most reliable, most durable, safest, fastest, best value, most convenient, and so on.

Services can be positioned in six different ways—by service attributes, user application, price/quality relationship, service class, service user, or competitor. Price/quality relationship has been used by SpiceJet, which has positioned itself as a low-price, no frills airline in the leisure travel market. In hotels, the Taj has positioned itself at the high end of the price/quality relationship.

The steps in determining a positioning strategy are:

(i) Identify the extent of competition.
(ii) Assess consumer perceptions of each firm in the industry.

(iii) Determine the position of each firm.
(iv) Analyse consumer preferences.
(v) Make a position decision.
(vi) Develop a strategy to implement the new position or reinforce the current position.

We can distinguish five value positions:

(a) **More for more:** Some companies specialize in making the most upscale version of the product and charging a high price to cover their higher costs. Termed luxury goods, such products claim to be better in quality, craftsmanship, durability, performance and style. Examples include Mercedes automobiles, Mont Blanc writing instruments and Gucci apparel. The products are not only fine in themselves, but deliver prestige to the buyer. They become emblems of a higher lifestyle, a more exclusive status. Often the price far exceeds the actual increment of quality.

(b) **More for the same:** Companies have been able to attack a 'more for more' form by introducing a brand claiming comparable quality and performance but priced much lower. Toyota introduced the Lexus model with the 'more for the same' value positioning. It demonstrated the superior quality of Lexus in several ways: through raving reviews, through a widely distributed video showing the Mercedes and Lexus side by side.

Companies have been able to attack a 'more for more' form by introducing a brand claiming comparable quality and performance but priced much lower.

(c) **The same for less:** It seems that everyone is happy when they can buy a product or brand at less than the normal price. Everything—Arrow shirts, Ceat tyres, Akai TV sets—seems to be available at a lower price at some store or discount shop. Today shoppers are able to find good bargains on the Internet for goods ranging from cars, apparels, and jewellery to computers, books and other goods.

(d) **Less for much less:** Some people complain that manufacturers and service providers provide more than customers require and charge a higher price. One cannot tell a hotel, 'take out the TV set and charge me less', or order an airline to skip the insurance and charge less. About two decades ago, people bought video-cassette recorders (VCRs) that enabled them to play videotapes and record TV programmes, but most people didn't use it for the latter purpose. There would have been a market for cheaper VCRs offering fewer features. Therefore sellers had an opportunity to enter a market with a 'less for much less' offering. SpiceJet and GoAir, two low-cost air carriers, charge less by not serving food, not assigning seats, not using travel agents, and not transferring luggage to other carriers.

(e) **More for less:** Of course, the winning value positioning would be to offer prospects and customers 'more for less'. This is the attraction of highly successful stores like Walmart. When one walks into a Walmart outlet, one is greeted by friendly employees, sees an array of attractively laid-out, well-known branded goods, finds low prices and generous return policies, and leaves thinking of Walmart as a place where one can get more for less. In India, Big Bazaar and Vishal Mega Mart follow the same strategy.

4.8 Summary

- Generally, target segments should be selected not only on the basis of their sales and profit potential but also with reference to the firm's ability to match or exceed competing offerings directed at the same segment.
- In identifying a set of segments, the marketer has two choices. He can focus on one segment (single segment marketing), or two or more, each receiving a different and appropriate offering (multi-segment marketing).
- Positioning is very important for retail marketing as it involves careful tailoring of the retail product/service offering to the needs of target segments, which underpins marketing success. Additionally, positioning enables the organization to respond to the competitive environment positively, highlighting market opportunities and fulfilling specific marketing needs better than competitors.
- It is a fact that a country like India offers huge potential for many of the global services like insurance, retail and investment banking, logistics and so on.

CHAPTER 5  PRODUCT AND SERVICES MARKETING MIX

You don't build it for yourself. You know what people want and you build it for them.
— Walt Disney

The Backdrop

The global economic crisis has hastened the inevitable: China and India's march towards grabbing a larger share of the global GDP pie. By the end of 2010 India is set to overtake Africa and West Asia (has occurred) and China's GDP will be 50 per cent higher than the combined power of Latin America and the Caribbean Islands. However India's GDP as a percentage of the global GDP is only 5 per cent (as of 2010) as against US' GDP share of 20 per cent and Western Europe's figure of 18.9 per cent. The most remarkable improvement in GDP share has been that of China—from 7.2 per cent in 2000 to 12.1 per cent in 2009. India improved its share of GDP from 4 per cent in 2000 to 5 per cent in 2009.

There are several indicators one can use to gauge the prevailing health of the Indian economy. There are hard, statistical measures like non-food credit growth figures and IIP (Index of Industrial Production) numbers. The stock markets are also a good signal. Equally important are soft indicators like the surge in footfalls that one can see in malls and bazaars reflecting the confidence of consumers who are once again beginning to feel good about spending. Auto and FMCG sales have also picked up. But the biggest indicator that the sentiment is getting better comes from the job market. The available indicators suggest that good times have started (beginning October 2009) and hopefully will last a long time.

The most popular and fundamental marketing mix, known as the 4Ps framework with the variables Product, Place, Promotion and Price, originated from the study of manufacturing, from organizations engaged in the production and marketing of goods. It is therefore oriented to deal with goods marketing. It is a fact that modern marketing is a mix of ingredients. It blends various marketing activities in a manner that furthers the interests of a firm, including a service firm. The crux of any marketing strategy is to bring about the desired operations in the prevailing circumstances of a meltdown.

This Chapter Will

- *Explain the product concept.*
- *Discuss the special nature of marketing services.*

>>>

- *Highlight the importance of packaging and distribution in marketing.*
- *Explain the intricacies of pricing and the various pricing strategies.*
- *Discuss the different methods of product promotion, including advertising, personal selling, sales promotion, public relations.*
- *Underscore the need for integrated communication.*
- *Explain service promotion and how one should undertake it.*
- *Give an overview of the marketing challenges in the post-economic meltdown years.*

5.1 The Product Concept

5.1.1 Product Marketing

Marketing is the process of planning and executing the concept, pricing, promotion, and distribution of ideas, goods, and services to create exchanges that satisfy individual and organizational goals.

The term 'product' is widely used to refer to a market offering of any kind. In its broadest sense this may be anything from the physical to the abstract, like an idea or a moral issue. Generally, most products are made up of a combination of physical elements and services. They can be tangible, such as food in the food court of a mall, or they can be a 'pure' service, i.e. intangible in nature, like the mall ambience. The marketing of a product refers to an activity or activities that a marketer performs which results in the satisfaction of a need or want of a predetermined target customer. It is the offering of a firm in the form of activities that satisfy needs and wants.

Businesses today face a number of challenges and opportunities including globalization, deregulation, and advances in technology. They have responded by changing in a very fundamental way the process of marketing. From a managerial point of view, marketing is the process of planning and executing the concept, pricing, promotion, and distribution of ideas, goods, and services to create exchanges that satisfy individual and organizational goals.

The perception that marketers influence a consumer's purchasing decisions discounts a customer's freedom of choice and individual responsibility. With the coming of the Internet, consumers have greater freedom of choice and more evaluative criteria than ever before. They can and do make more informed decisions than previous generations. Marketers can rightly be accused of influencing wants, along with societal factors such as power, influence, peer pressure, and social status. These societal factors pre-exist marketing and would continue to exist even if there was no marketing effort expended.

CASE STUDY THE INDIAN BEVERAGE (FRUIT AND SOFT DRINKS) MARKET

The beverage industry covers a wide category of drinks ranging from carbonated drinks, alcohol, fruit juices to coffee and tea. India is the third highest beverage consumer in the world after US and China, accounting for approximately 10 per cent of the global beverage consumption. The Indian beverage industry grew by 17 per cent in 2010.

Non-alcoholic drinks

Given the tropical climate of India, the market for non-alcoholic drinks is attractive and growing. The annual per capita consumption of packaged beverages in India is expected to reach 8.7 litres in 2012.

Milk, tea and coffee

India is also the world's biggest producer and consumer of milk; 65 per cent of milk and milk-based beverages are sold in loose and unpackaged form. Milk consumption has increased by an annual average of 2.7 per cent since 2005. The Union Budget 2009 that withdrew 16 per cent excise duty on tea and coffee mixes and puffed rice has given a major impetus to the tea and coffee industry. India (1,002 million kg.) along with China (990 million kg.), Sri Lanka (318.7 million kg.) and Kenya (286 million kg.) accounts for about 75 to 80 per cent of the world's tea production.

Fruit juices

India is the second-largest market for fruits and vegetables in the world. The total production of fruits and vegetables is estimated to be around 148.5 million tons, out of which fruits account for only 48.5 million tons and the rest 100 million tons is accounted for by vegetables.

The fruit juice market has not been fully tapped owing to poor infrastructure, poor storage facilities, and a highly unorganized market chiefly constituted by roadside vendors. Consumers as of now prefer to buy juices from roadside vendors even if they are unhygienic. Increase in health consciousness among consumers, an increase in disposable incomes, and the emergence of a more sophisticated cocktail culture are expected to help this market grow rapidly. The branded fruit juice market (nectars, drinks and juices combined) in India is estimated to be worth ₹500 crore with the segment growing at about 30 per cent per annum.

Soft drinks

The non-alcoholic soft drink beverage market can be divided into fruit drinks and soft drinks. Soft drinks can be subdivided into two categories: carbonated and non-carbonated drinks. Carbonated drinks come in cola, lemon and orange flavours while mango-flavoured drinks come under the non-carbonated category. The soft drinks market till the early 1990s was in the hands of domestic brands like Thums up, Limca, Gold Spot, and so on. But with the economic reforms of 1991 and the entry of MNC players Pepsi and Coke, market domination has undergone a change.

The soft drinks market in India is worth about ₹8,500 crore. Coke and Pepsi are the dominant players with a combined market share of 95 per cent. While soft drinks were once considered products only for the affluent, 91 per cent of sales today are made to the lower, middle and upper middle classes. Soft drink sales are expected to grow at least 10 per cent per year through 2012. However, India has one of the lowest per capita consumption of colas in the world as it has traditionally been a country of tea and coffee drinkers. This also reflects an opportunity for growth for packaged cold drinks makers who have enormous potential in the country.

Product mix of Coke and Pepsi

Coca-Cola India reported 43 per cent growth in the second quarter of 2009 amounting to US$2 billion. The Indian carbonated soft drinks market is worth ₹5,520 crore; the packaged fruit drink market is around ₹1,200 crore and is growing at a rate of 28-30 per cent. Coca-Cola has its presence in the market through the availability of products like Thums Up, Coca-Cola, Sprite, Limca and Fanta. Coke has four of the top five brands in terms of market share, namely Thums Up, Sprite, Limca and Fanta.

Product mix of Coca-Cola

On the product front, the company seems to have overcome its near obsession with being everywhere with everything. Some discontinued brands of Coke in India are Gold Spot, Crush, Canada Dry, Sunfill, Rimzim, Portello and Shock.

Product mix of Pepsi Cola (in the beverage industry)

PepsiCo serves 86 per cent of the world's population and international sales account for 48 per cent of its revenue. The chunk of PepsiCo's revenues do not come from carbonated soft drinks. In fact, beverages account for less than 50 per cent of the total revenue; over 60 per cent of PepsiCo's beverage sales come from its key non-carbonated brands like Gatorade and Tropicana.

Consumer habits and practices

- Soft drinks are slotted under the impulse buying category. The market is impacted by brand loyalty, but the purchase decision is a low involvement decision. The attitude of impulse buying is changing to occasion-led buying and also to some extent of consumption through home refrigeration. With health consciousness in mind people have been avoiding non-alcoholic carbonated drinks and switching to fruit-based drinks. Consumers purchase soft drinks primarily to quench thirst. People on travel generally do not have access to hygienic water and often reach out for soft drinks or mineral water. This forms a large part of the sales. Brand consciousness plays a vital role in purchase decisions. The chill factor also affects purchase decision. This has made companies increase their retail distribution by offering coolers to retailers.

- Product differentiation is minimal as Coke and Pepsi are similar in taste. But brand loyalty is high in the case of children and youth. Consumers are sensitive to the expenditure whenever purchase of beverages is concerned. Therefore, the market is price sensitive.
- Due to the high cost of soft drinks, most consumers prefer beverages like tea, coffee or sherbet and squashes. The per capita consumption in India is one of the lowest in the world at five bottles per annum compared to approximately 800 bottles in the USA.

Sources: Hindustan Unilever Ltd., Coca-Cola India Ltd. and Pepsi India Ltd.

5.1.2 Total Product Concept

Levitt describes the Total Product Concept as consisting of a core or generic product surrounded by the expected and augmented product.

Most product and service businesses offer their customers a package involving delivery of not only the core product but also a variety of related services. Increasingly, these services are what differentiate successful firms from the relatively unsuccessful ones. Levitt describes this as the Total Product Concept which consists of a core, surrounded by two concentric circles. The core, or generic product, is defined as the basic skills and resources needed to play in the market. Levitt terms the inner band surrounding this core as the 'expected product', representing a customer's minimal expectations. It includes pricing, delivery, appearance of facilities and personnel, personality of service people, and so on. The third and the final circle is the 'augmented product' representing the value added to the offering above and beyond the minimal expectations.

The nature of a product is found to have considerable impact on product positioning. There are two classes of products—consumer goods and industrial goods—and this classification is useful in product positioning. The search for a competitive advantage—and an escape from price-based competition—often centres on the value-creating supplementary services that surround this core and add differentiation. Marketing managers should be aware of the importance of selecting the right mix of supplementary service elements—not more and not less than needed—and creating synergy by ensuring that they are internally consistent.

Customer research, evaluation of competitive offerings, and feedback from employees can all provide important inputs to the following aspects: (i) designing the right mix of supplementary service elements, (ii) establishing appropriate performance standards for each, and (iii) establishing supplementary prices as needed.

A company's greatest challenge for developing a 'be different' strategy is to be innovative while retaining its unique customer benefits and the customers' actual experience of the service itself.

Changing the typical operations-oriented retailing culture and 'beat the competition' mindset will help to embrace the power of internally developed innovation to derive profitable business growth. The greatest challenge for developing a 'be different' strategy is to be innovative while retaining both the unique customer benefits a company delivers, as well as how the customers actually experience the service itself. Experts encourage companies to focus on intangible actions in order to create a unique retail service experience—innovate the retail service process itself and how people in the organization add value to the experience.

Across service industries, customers care little about the tangible items that help deliver the promised experience; they care about the experience itself. It is the intangible actions that produce the experience and the tangible enablers are simply alluring mirages pretending to be valued by customers.

CITIBANK PRODUCTS PORTFOLIO

Citigroup is a diversified global financial services holding company, with over 200 million customer accounts in over 100 countries. Citibank, a subsidiary, is Citigroup's arm in commercial banking. Citibank's principal offerings include consumer finance, mortgage lending, retail banking, investment banking, commercial banking, cash management, trade finance, e-commerce products and services, and private banking products and services. Citigroup operates in North America, Latin America, Asia, Europe, the Middle East and Africa.

Citibank provides an array of banking, lending, insurance and investment services. The segment's distribution network includes 8,527 branches, approximately 20,000 ATMs, and 530 automated lending machines (ALMs), the Internet, telephone and direct mail, and independent representatives. The Global Consumer Group comprises the US consumer and international consumer businesses. The US Consumer Group is composed of four businesses: cards, retail distribution, consumer lending and commercial business. Operating in five geographies including Mexico, Latin America, EMEA, Japan, and Asia, the international consumer sub-segment is composed of three businesses: cards, consumer finance and retail banking. Global Transaction Services offer integrated cash management, trade, and securities and fund services to multinational corporations, financial institutions and public sector organizations around the world. With a network that spans more than 140 countries, Citi's Global Transaction Services supports over 65,000 clients. As of the fourth quarter of 2008, it held on average $292 billion in liability balances and $10.70 trillion in assets.

The Global Wealth Management (GWM) division comprises three brands: the Citi Private Bank, Smith Barney, and Citi Investment Research. The Citi Private Bank provides personalized wealth management services for High Net Worth clients in around 33 countries and territories. These services include investment management, investment finance and banking services. Smith Barney provides investment advice, financial planning and brokerage services to affluent individuals, companies, and non-profit organizations. Citi Investment Research covers more than 3,000 companies that represent 90 per cent of the market capitalization of the major global indices. It also provides macro and quantitative analysis of global markets and sector trends.

Alternative Investments (AI) manage capital on behalf of the Citigroup, as well as for third-party institutional and High Net Worth investors. AI is an integrated alternative investment platform that manages a range of products across five asset classes: private equity, hedge funds, real estate, structured products and managed futures.

NRI Indians have trusted Citibank NRI Business to manage their wealth for over two decades. Recognizing the needs of the NRIs, Citibank offers a number of products such as the Citibank Rupee Checking Account, international ATM and debit cards and an unparalleled service in draft delivery to beneficiaries in India. The business also provides wealth management for global Indians. The NRI Business provides an international suite of cutting edge products and services. The business has a presence across the globe with eight major regional hubs in the USA, Canada, UAE, UK, Australia, Kenya, Singapore, and Bahrain, and manages assets worth over US$6 billion for 2,00,000 customers. Citibank NRI Business has been present in the US since 1985 and today manages the banking and wealth management needs of over 1,20,000 clients in the country.

MAJOR PRODUCTS OF CITIBANK—LOANS AND CREDITS

Loans

Personal Loans
Home Loans
Loan against Shares
Ready Credit
Overdraft

Credit cards

Airline/Commute
Jet Airways Citibank Platinum Credit Card
Jet Airways Citibank Gold Credit Card
Jet Airways CitiBusiness Credit Card
Jet Airways Citibank Silver Credit Card
Delhi Metro Citibank Credit Card

Fuel/Auto

Indian Oil Citibank Gold Credit Card
Indian Oil Citibank Credit Card
Maruti Suzuki AutoCard

Shopping

Citibank Platinum Credit Card
First Citizen Citibank Credit Card
Citibank Cash Back Credit Card
Citibank Gold Credit Card
Citibank Silver Credit Card

Citibank Choice Credit Card
Reliance Gold Credit Card
Reliance Silver Credit Card

Telecom

Vodafone Citibank Credit Card

Lifestyle

Diners Club International Credit Card
Taj Epicure Diners Club Credit Card
Citibank Ultima Credit Card

Forex/Prepaid

Citibank World Money Credit Card

Special Interest

CRY Citibank Credit Card
WWF Citibank Credit Card
Citibank Woman's Credit Card
Citibank Woman's Visa Mini Credit Card

BANKING, INVESTMENTS AND INSURANCE

Banking

Citibank Savings Account
Suvidha Savings Account
Debit Card
Citigold
Foreign Exchange Services
Junior Account
Corporate Banking
Citibank Account for Expatriates

Citibusiness

Current Account
CitiBusiness Card
Loans
Personal Wealth Management

Investments

Mutual Funds
Demat
Deposits

Citibank insurance services

Life Insurance Solutions
Health Forever
Health Insurance
Travel Shield Gold

Travel insurance

Credit Shield Plus
Insurance on Citibank Credit Card
Insurance on Home Loan

SERVICES

Stay informed

Internet Banking
Access Bank Account Online
Credit Card and Banking Statement on email
Bill Pay
Online Bill Pay
CitiAlert
Get Account Statement on Mobile
Prepaid Mobile Recharge
Recharge Mobile Online

Services on credit cards

Loan on Citibank Credit Card
Electronic Clearance Services
Hassle-free Payment of Credit Card Dues

Credit Shield

Insurance on Citibank Credit Card
Good Health Policy

NRI banking home regions

USA and Canada
Middle East
Asia Pacific
UK and rest of Europe
Africa

Source: Citibank.

5.1.3 Product Development and Economic Cost

The economic cost of modifying a product arises from a change in the product's development expense, its unit cost, performance, and the development schedule.

The current economic downturn has added momentum to the flexible product development process. The economic cost of modifying a product arises from the impact of change on four factors: the product's development expense, its unit cost, its performance, and the development schedule. Changes in each of these factors can in turn be quantified and expressed in terms of cumulative profit impact. For example, suppose that a schedule change will raise product cost by 3 per cent and delay the schedule by two months. If a sensitivity analysis determines that the cost increases by ₹5,00,000 and the schedule is worth ₹7,50,000 per month, then this change has a total economic cost of ₹4 million. The higher the economic cost of modifying a product as a response to a given change, the lower a firm's development flexibility. A change in a development project should be made when the economic cost of making the change is less than its economic benefit. Thus a project can be considered flexible if the economic cost of change is low in relation to the change in the perturbing variable. Projects in which this economic cost is high can be viewed as inflexible.

Managers need to redefine the problem from improving forecasting to eliminating the need for accurate long-term forecasts.

Product complexity has dramatically increased in many projects. As products acquire more functions, the difficulty of forecasting requirements rises exponentially. Again the rate of change in most markets is also increasing, thereby reducing the effectiveness of traditional management approaches to forecasting the future. As a result, managers need to redefine the problem from one of improving forecasting to one of eliminating the need for accurate long-term forecasts. There are two important ways to reduce exposure to the consequences of forecasting errors. The most obvious is to shorten development cycles, since that will reduce the number of changes that will occur during development.

5.1.4 Target Costing

In fast-moving and 'turbulent' environments like the present, flexibility and the ability to accommodate evolving customer needs and technologies is of exceptional benefit. Such high flexibility can be attained by pursuing an efficient development strategy that can tolerate a higher risk of design alterations to make (late) product changes. This can lead to better solutions with respect to customer needs and technologies and avoid the need for product changes because design commitments can be made very late. Here the problem is not a lack of demand but lack of liquidity and resource crunch.

Imagine an environment wherein General Motors, Ford Motors and Chrysler are unable to open their factories due to lack of storage space as their own and their distributors' godowns are full with no fresh enquiries or sales. This happened in the last quarters of 2008. The top three auto giants approached the US Senate for a bailout plan to retain the 2,50,000 employees working with them.

Target costing manages a company's future profits by determining the life cycle cost at which it must produce a proposed product with a specified functionality and quality, if the product is to be profitable at its anticipated selling price, e.g. Tata's ₹1 lakh Nano car.

With the emergence of lean enterprises, economic downturn and global competition, companies face ever-increasing competition. To survive, they must become experts at developing products that deliver the quality and functionality that customers demand, while generating the desired profits. One way to ensure that products are sufficiently profitable when launched is to subject them to target costing. This technique manages a company's future profits by determining the life cycle cost at which a company must produce a proposed product with a specified functionality and quality, if the product is to be profitable at its anticipated selling price. Target costing makes cost an input in the product development process, not an outcome of it. By estimating the anticipated selling price of a proposed product and by subtracting the desired profit margin, a company can establish its target cost. The key is then to design the product so that it satisfies customers and can be manufactured at its target cost. A typical example is that of Tata's ₹1 lakh Nano car.

5.2 Transforming Services into Goods

Intense of competition, liquidity crunch, economic recession and customer expectations are increasing in nearly all service industries including retailing. Success in such a situation lies not only in providing excellent products but also in creating new approaches to customer service. Since the process and outcome of a service combine to create the consumer experience, both aspects must be addressed in new service development.

5.2.1 'Frozen Services'

'Frozen services' describes goods that allow customers to unlock the value through self-service, e.g e-books.

Technology allows the benefits of services that formerly had to be delivered by service personnel in a real-time environment to be captured in a physical product. Richard Norman has coined the term 'frozen services' to describe goods that allow customers to unlock the value through self-service. Many information-based services, for instance, can be captured in some form of storage medium for reuse at a later date. E-books are an established alternative to lectures in an educational setting. Live performances can be recorded and then relived on demand through the medium of CDs or audio and video clippings in the computer and mobile phone through Internet-based services and websites like YouTube.com. Expertise in almost any field can be captured in interactive computer software in the form of CD-ROMs or diskettes or even downloaded from the Internet.

5.2.2 Emerging New Services

Falling prices, greater affluence, and new easy-to-use technologies also allow individual and corporate users to replace service professionals in a variety of fields. Thus, washing machines and dryers have replaced laundry services for many types of clothes. As the wheel of progress turns, customers may continue to change the way in which they obtain the benefits they seek. The telephone created the need for answering services among busy people, many of whom solved this need first from services, then from manufactured goods, and most recently from services again. For instance, in customer service operations, CRM packages have automated answers to many of the frequently asked questions of customers over telephone and the Web.

Major service innovations are new core products (service characteristics and radical new processes) previously undefined.

We will now identify seven categories of new services, ranging from major product innovations to simple style changes. Major service innovations are new core products that have not been previously defined. These products usually include both new service characteristics and radical new processes. Major process innovations consist of using new processes to deliver existing core products in new ways with additional benefits. For example, Indira Gandhi National Open University (IGNOU) competes with other open universities in delivering undergraduate and postgraduate degree and diploma programmes in a non-traditional way. Its students get the benefit of a college degree but in half the time and at a much lower price than they would at other universities. TAPMI (T.A. Pai Management Institute) offers satellite-based classroom teaching wherein 24 centres across the country have only one teacher!

(i) **Product line extensions** are additions to current product lines by existing firms. The first company in the market to offer such a product may be seen as an innovator; the others are merely followers, often acting defensively. These new services may be targeted at existing customers to serve a broader array of needs or designed to attract new customers with different needs (or both). In India, Jet Airways is one of several major carriers to launch a separate low-cost operation (in its case, JetLite) designed to compete with discount carriers such as SpiceJet. The leading book retailing firm Landmark expanded to home furnishing, interior decoration and imported furniture SKUs along with modern office stationery items.

Product line extensions are additions to current product lines by existing firms.

MARKETING IN ACTION — **PUMA ON KIDSWEAR TRACK IN INDIA**

The year 2009 proved lucky for the German sports and lifestyle brand Puma's Indian operations. Despite being one of the first international players to have entered the country in the early 1990s, Puma came into its own only in 2006 when it took charge of its manufacturing and stepped up efforts to open exclusive stores. It launched its line of kidswear in October 2009. Kidswear, which has for long been in Puma's portfolio internationally, completes the range for the company in India. It is a take-off on their adult range of apparel, footwear and accessories, says Puma Sports India managing director Rajiv Mehta.

But Puma's presence in India did require corrections since the time it entered the market. While its tie-up with Carona fell through in 1998, its second foray in 2002 could not be sustained either. It had licensed Planet Sports to manufacture its apparel and accessories and distribute its footwear and eyewear. Analysts say that in both the instances, quality became the bone of contention.

In 2006, the brand finally took the plunge and set up a subsidiary, Puma Sports India which wielded more control over local manufacturing and imports. Puma managed to increase the number of its exclusive stores from 45 in April to 64 by September 2009. Its diversification in the ₹5,000-crore market that is growing at 15 per cent will be in partnership with Ginny and Jony, which knows the Indian kids market well. While Puma will keep production and imports under its control, the distribution will be through Ginny and Jony.

Puma's success in the kidswear segment will rest on its partner's pricing strategy. Kids outgrow their clothes and shoes fast, so pricing right is crucial. With the right prices, parents would come back to Puma brand to replenish their child's wardrobe, rather than be discouraged by prohibitive pricing. Puma's range will feature mid- to premium products, priced from ₹399 upwards.

Having been bitten twice, Puma is acting shy. The brand would watch the performance of its kidswear segment in 2010 before planning for the future. Puma has set itself a target of ₹40 crore in 2009–10. It has also kept a tight hold on how consumers experience the brand. Puma's exclusive stores might be run by franchisees, but it has placed strict guidelines for store executives who are Puma employees.

Source: Business Today, January 2010.

(ii) **Process line extensions** are less innovative than process innovations but offer more distinctive ways of delivering existing products, either with the intent of offering more convenience and a different experience for existing customers or to attract new customers who find the traditional approach unappealing. Most commonly, it involves adding a lower-contact distribution channel to an existing high-contact channel, such as creating telephone- or Internet-based e-tailing services for Foodworld or Fabmall.

Process line extensions involve adding a lower-contact distribution channel to an existing high-contact channel.

(iii) **Supplementary service innovations** take the form of adding new facilitating or enhancing service elements to an existing core service or of significantly improving existing supplementary services. The Foodworld outlets installed ATMs of major banks to facilitate cash transactions within its outlet in Spencer Plaza in Chennai. Computer

Supplementary service innovations adds new facilitating or enhancing service elements to an existing core service or significantly improves existing supplementary services.

kiosks installed at the entrance of stores will help customers find out the shelf of their SKUs and its quantity, thereby saving shopping time.

(iv) **Low-tech innovations** for an existing service can be as simple as adding parking at a retail site or agreeing to accept credit cards for payment.

(v) **Multiple improvements** may have the effect of creating what customers perceive as an altogether new experience, even though it is built around the same core. Theme restaurants like the Palazhi Houseboat in Alleppey is an ideal example of enhancing the core with new experiences.

(vi) **Service improvements** are the most common type of innovation. They involve modest changes in the visual merchandise of current SKUs, including improvements to either the core product or to existing supplementary imported SKUs, like Starbuck's Coffee, Australian oranges and wines, or apple juice from New Zealand.

MARKETING IN ACTION

ITC: GAINING FROM INNOVATION AND EXTENSION

The Indian FMCG market is no longer dominated by a few giants; small players are making a foray into the market and eating into the share of the big players. ITC is the largest FMCG company with a turnover of ₹23,500 crore in 2008–9. Borrowing recipes from the kitchens of its hotels, it has come with high-quality, unique flavours and launched a series of food products under the umbrella brand of Sunfeast. Similarly, the Essenza Di Wills brand of perfumes has come up with unique fragrances after extensive consumer research. ITC has also leveraged on its financial position to buy out Candico (Mint-o) and launch the Candyman range of candies for children. The launches of Superia, Vivel, Kitchens of India spices, Aashirwaad, and so on, clearly indicate the firm's desire to capture the FMCG market by carefully analysing consumer needs. For instance, Superia shampoo has been launched to cater to the lower strata and rural markets which have so far not been touched by the personal care segment.

Take a look at the product lines of ITC.

Division	*Category*	*Brands/commodities*
FMCG	Personal Care	Essenza Di Wills, Fiama Di Wills, Vivel Di Wills, Vivel UltraPro, Vivel, Superia
FMCG	Cigarettes	Insignia, India Kings, Classic, Gold Flake, Silk Cut, Navy Cut, Scissors, Capstan, Berkeley, Bristol, Flake
FMCG	Foods	Kitchens of India, Aashirvaad, Sunfeast, Bingo, Candyman
FMCG	Lifestyle retailing	John Players, Miss Players, Wills Lifestyle
FMCG	Stationery	Classmate, Paperkraft
FMCG	Matches	i-Kno, Aim, Aim Mega, Aim Metro
FMCG	Incense sticks	Mangaldeep, Expressions
Hotels		ITC Maurya, ITC Maratha, ITC Sonar, ITC Grand Central, ITC Windsor, ITC Royal Gardenia, ITC Kakatiya, ITC Mughal, Welcom and Fortune Hotels
Agri commodities		Soyameal, spices, rice, coffee, fruit puree, frozen fruit

Source: Investors' Report of ITC Ltd., January 2010.

(vii) **Style changes** represent the simplest type of innovation, typically involving no changes in either process or performance. However, they are often highly visible, create excitement, and may serve to motivate employees. Examples include overhauling store ambience, introducing new colour schemes, outfitting service employees in new uniforms, introducing a credit card with the name of the customer embossed on it, as Big Bazaar has done in India.

Style changes only enhance visibility, excitement, and employee motivation.

5.3 Packaging the Product

In the current market environment, the perceived value of a product depends to a large extent on its packaging, including the design and presentation of product information on the pack. Earlier, packaging was considered a major expense in marketing. For some toiletries, packaging costs actually exceeded the cost of contents. Today, however, it is fully recognized that packaging helps in branding and promoting brand loyalty. It also enables buyers to handle and carry their products with ease.

The perceived value of a product depends largely on its packaging, including the design and presentation of product information on the pack.

Figure 5.1: Colour and cheer: ITC's FMCG packaging
Source: Company's website.

Protection and presentation are the basic functions of packaging, especially for consumer goods.

Characteristics of good packaging include an attractive appearance, storage and display convenience, protection from damage or spoiling, and providing product description. Protection and presentation are the basic functions of packaging, especially for consumer goods. Modern marketing demands that the package must be convenient to handle and transport and be made strictly according to quality standards. Packages that are recognizable and have eye appeal serve to enhance the brand equity of the product.

Packaging decisions include the design and colour of the package and product line, which are not easy to devise. For example, all shaving creams come in tubes but different brands of shaving creams have different packaging; because of the high cost, some companies resort to refill packs. Again for fruit products like strawberries the consumer pack consists of specialized perforated polythene packets in a square box and a case (carton) consists of only 24 such boxes. Owing to its market demand and the customer's preference for fresh fruits, loading of such cartons is limited to only two tons per vehicle. The entire packaging allows for free flow of air around the strawberries and prevents them from being crushed during transportation and storage.

Attractive packaging colour helps to promote sales. Family packaging uses identical packages for all products or packages with some common features.

Colour is an important factor in determining customer acceptance or rejection of a product. The use of the right colours in packaging may help marketers reap huge advantage. A company must decide whether to develop a family resemblance in the packaging of its several products. Family packaging involves the use of identical packages for all products or the use of packages with some common features. An example for the same is Kellogg's which has the brand name on all its products, like cornflakes, wheat flakes, all-bran flakes, and so on. The sizes and the packaging are also consistent across all products.

5.4 Distribution

The route(s) followed by the products (or at least their ownership) as they travel to the ultimate customer by way of other organizations are called channels of distribution.

A producer has the choice of dealing directly with the consumers or passing his goods through other organizations, including wholesalers and/or retailers who are collectively referred to as resellers. The route(s) followed by the products (or at least their ownership) as they travel to the ultimate customer by way of these other organizations are usually termed channels of distribution.

There are several aspects to be considered when deciding on the distribution arrangement for any particular marketing operation. These include:

(a) the types of intermediaries to be used and the number of stages, e.g. retailers or retailers/wholesalers;
(b) the number of each type of intermediary to be used and the tasks and responsibilities to be carried out by the marketing organization and by the organizations forming the distribution chain.

It is customary to distinguish three levels of 'market exposure'.

(i) *Intensive distribution* is where efforts are made to get every possible suitable outlet to stock the product (batteries, ice cream).

(ii) *Exclusive distribution* is where the number of outlets is deliberately limited (high fashion goods). Some of the objectives that might lead to this approach are enhancing the 'image' of the product (and hence achieving higher mark-ups) and encouraging dealers to support the product more strongly and sell it more aggressively because it limits their competition and offers them high profit opportunities.

(iii) In between these extremes come varying degrees of *selective distribution*. Here the marketing organization seeks to find the optimum number of outlets that will on the one hand, give adequate coverage of the market but on the other will not lead to the expense of dealing with large numbers of outlets yielding only small sales volumes (domestic appliances, microcomputers, tyres and car batteries).

5.4.1 Physical Distribution

The logistics of a business consist of physically moving a product from the factory to the customer.

While deciding on the channels of distribution, one must also consider the business of physically moving a product from the factory to the customer—the logistics. The field of Physical Distribution Management (PDM) has been developed to deal with this part of the business in the most cost-effective manner.

Essentially, this deals with every aspect of getting goods from the end of the production line safely and economically to the user. It means approaching the whole business on a 'system' basis and not as a series of separate fragments. Some of the many elements making up the system are

MARKETING IN ACTION — **THE ITC WAY OF OPTIMIZING DISTRIBUTION COST**

The FMCG sector generally is a high-volume ball game where products have to essentially be available in the market at the time and at all given points of purchase. The supply of products takes place virtually on a daily basis in fixed quotas or otherwise to retailers as per their requisitions, the anticipation of demand and the performance of products in the recent past.

ITC's Value Network is common for all its SKUs. Yet it is important to analyse ITC's network as it has made a foray into new domains which has necessitated a restructuring of the value network.

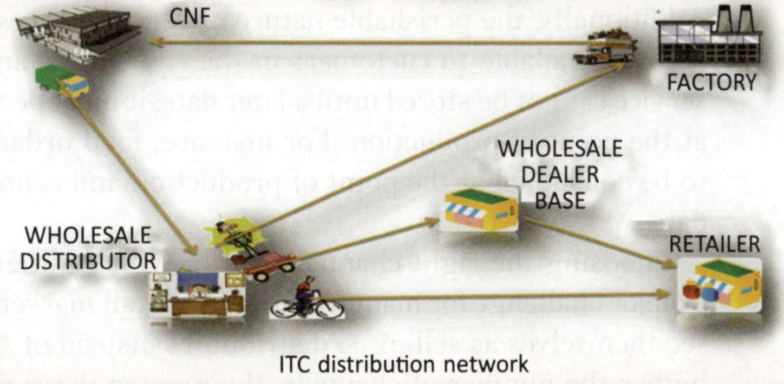

ITC distribution network

For FMCG alone ITC has more than 1,000 SKUs with a warehousing space of more than 3.50 million sq. ft. at more than 50 locations. Products are manufactured at 50 plants with more than 650 trucks moving them everyday. There is direct distribution from factories to distributors.

The company has a very strong distribution network through its cigarette segment. It has made full use of it to enter the saturated FMCG foods and personal care market, where it created high visibility for its products by leveraging its relationship with distributors. For the agricultural products the suppliers include local farmers and small-scale manufacturers. ITC has maintained a strong value network, which has helped it grow in the competitive market.

ITC uses the first-in first-out (FIFO) method to reduce wastage of goods due to expiry. It also moves the goods from low sales areas to high sales ones besides collecting all the expired goods four times a year.

Source: Investors' Report, January 2010.

transportation, warehousing (including location decisions), stock control, packing and materials handling, and order processing. The costs of each of these cannot be viewed in isolation, nor can their efficiency in terms of ultimate satisfaction to the customer. For example, looking purely at warehousing, it might appear that money could be saved by reducing the number of area depots from fifteen to twelve. However, some customers would then be farther from a delivery point and transport costs could well rise to an extent greater than the savings achieved by cutting out some depots. Reducing stock levels would save interest on the capital tied up (or enable it to be employed more profitably elsewhere), but it would also increase the risk of being out of stock (unless other steps, also with costs attached, are taken to offset the risks), with the consequent chance of delays in delivery and ultimately loss of business through poor service to customers.

To make a decision between centralized stocks as against regional storage depots, one would have to balance the savings on building or renting of depots coupled with double-handling and transport (factory to depot, depot to customer) against the cost of longer journeys (factory direct to customer) with half-empty vehicles and probably the need for a more expensive vehicle fleet. Similarly, using expensive forms of transport (such as airfreight to overseas markets) may enable urgent delivery requests to be met at a lower total cost than holding stock at numerous points around the world and thus attempting to cut transport costs.

5.4.2 Service Distribution

The 'place' element of the marketing mix for a service enterprise is concerned with accessibility and availability.

The 'place' element of the marketing mix for a service enterprise is concerned chiefly with two main issues: accessibility and availability. The inseparable nature of services means that the services must be accessible to customers and potential customers in order for exchange to take place. Accessibility must be a component of the actual retail service offering for it to have value. Additionally, the perishable nature of retail services means it is essential for it to be available to customers in the right place and at the right time. The service cannot be stored until a later date; it must be available for consumption at the point of production. For instance, food ordered in a restaurant needs to be consumed at the point of production and cannot be stored until a later date.

Choosing the right channels and convincing them to work as partners is a major challenge for manufacture-cum-retail marketers.

Choosing the right channels and convincing them to work as partners is a major challenge for manufacture-cum-retail marketers. Too many companies see themselves as selling *to* distributors instead of selling *through* them. The higher the number of channels, the greater the company's market coverage and rate of growth of its sales. But problems like product or service quality may emerge as market coverage is always gained at the expense of market control. This is what happened to Starbuck's Coffee. As the number of franchisee outlets expanded, customers failed to recognize the company's core product—the Starbuck experience—and many of them even questioned the existence of such a product!

5.5 The Price

Customers tend to buy within a certain price bracket and perceive price as a signal of quality.

In economic terms, price reflects the level of demand, but in practice it is a far more complex matter. Buyers have subjective views on what is an appropriate price; there is normally a range of prices for a given product which they find acceptable. To put it simply, buyers tend to shop within a certain price bracket. Price is also a signal of quality to the buyer.

From the seller's point of view, cost is only one element in fixing the price. Cost is in any case not simple to arrive at because cost per unit normally varies with output, which is itself is influenced by the price. Break-even analysis enables cost per unit to be calculated at various levels of demand on different price assumptions. Companies may be profit-maximizers but are more likely to see their objectives in terms of reaching an acceptable profit target, when they regard as 'satisfiers'.

Competitors' pricing policies may influence the pricing strategy between the two extremes of skim-the-cream and penetration pricing. A company's price structure will take account of wholesale and retail profit margins. In addition, or as an alternative, it may include quantity discounts. In some situations a differential pricing policy may be adopted. Prices may be adjusted on different occasions and the impact of this on consumers, distributors and competitors will need to be accurately predicted.

Marketing is essentially concerned with adding maximum value to a product or service to make it attractive and desirable to customers while keeping costs at a maximum. Value can be added in the following ways:

(a) converting raw materials into components or finished goods (steel-making, car manufacture),
(b) by breaking the bulk products and packing or processing them (wholesaling, takeaway meals),
(c) by transporting goods from one place to another (importing tropical fruits) and by making goods available at a more convenient time (canned or frozen foods).

5.5.1 Pricing and Marketing

The three basic pricing options available to the marketer are discount, at-the-market and upscale. Pricing of merchandise should get the product accepted in the market; maintain market share as competition increases and earn profits.

A marketer must set prices in a manner that achieves profitability for the company and also satisfies customers while adapting to a variety of constraints. Pricing has a direct relationship with marketing objectives and interacts with other marketing mix elements. Objectives can be in terms of sales, profit, and return on investment. A marketer has three basic pricing options. These options are:

- Discount (e.g. off-price retailers and discount department stores),
- At-the-market (e.g. traditional department stores and drugstores), and
- Upscale (upscale department stores and specialty stores).

The key to successful retail marketing lies in providing good value, in the consumer's perception, for the particular price orientation chosen.

Pricing of merchandise should accomplish three objectives: get the product accepted in the market; maintain market share as competition increases; and earn profits. Price offers potential customers important cues about the firm's overall image. When developing a marketing approach to pricing, firms must establish prices that are compatible with what the target customers expect and what they are willing to pay for it.

5.5.2 Product Mix Pricing Methods

A significant part of setting appropriate prices is tracking competitors' prices regularly; however, what the competition is charging is just one variable in the pricing mix. While setting prices, companies should try to match competitors' prices or even beat them. But setting appropriate prices is very difficult, since the demand pattern and market segments vary significantly from product to product. There are different methods of product mix pricing described as follows:

MARKETING ANALYSIS — **BINGO: MORE FOR LESS**

ITC is adding more spice to Bingo. The packaged snacks brand, which had a 13 per cent market share in November 2009, has added 50 per cent more content to all its packs. The spicier part of the new strategy is that the company has not increased prices in the western region—its biggest market. The move is aimed at maximizing revenues by driving high sales volumes in the high potential western India market. Chitranjan Dar, chief executive, Foods Division, ITC, says schemes and promotions are part of the marketing mix that are deployed at various times through the year during market recovery. The objective obviously is to build a greater brand franchise through enhanced consumer experience and encourage repeat use and trials.

Similar offers are being made across different regions of the country, though the quantum of offer varies. Analysts believe the move has paid off as Bingo has attracted a sizeable number of new consumers. The strategy has, however, taken everyone by surprise as the prices of Bingo's inputs—corn, oil, soya, potato and foodgrains—have increased sharply since October 2009.

However, ITC's procurement and manufacturing synergies across divisions have helped it to reduce costs for Bingo as well. Its e-choupal model for direct procurement is also well known, under which ITC partners with over 1,00,000 farmers for spices and wheat procurement. This kind of rural pedigree is hard to beat.

Experts say that Bingo's move may have been prompted by the fierce competition in the snack foods space. For example, PepsiCo has started giving 20 per cent extra content with its flagship brand Lays while Parle Products has started offering 50 per cent extra on Musst Chips and Stix. The Business Performance Services of KPMG observed that the snack foods market in the late half of 2009 was heating up in India with the ongoing war between the three big players (Pepsico, ITC and Parle). ITC and Parle Products are expected to garner bigger market share in 2010 with extremely aggressive marketing and advertisement plans. The snack food market in India is estimated to be worth $3 billion with a branded snack market at $1.34 billion and is growing at 15-20 per cent yearly. The unorganized sector, worth $1.56 billion, is also growing at 7-8 per cent. According to analysts, ITC is eating into the market share of PepsiCo's Lays, which leads the pack in 2009. While Lays has a market share of around 48 per cent, Parle's Musst Chips and Musst Stix have a combined 5-7 per cent market share.

Bingo has tough competition from Parle with the launch of its health snack Monaco Smart chips. Parle is now eyeing a 25 per cent market share through an aggressive marketing and distribution strategy. According to Mayank Shah, group product manager at Parle Products, the company has witnessed good demand for Parle snacks. It has increased the volume of Musst in the west, east and north of India and is in the process of replicating it in the south. But Parle and Frito Lay can hardly afford to underestimate Bingo. ITC has several other surprises up its sleeve, which are set for completion by 2010. Analysts say Bingo, which is already worth ₹400 crore, has the ability to shake the market.

Since variety is the core of a snacks brand, ITC asked the chefs at its hotels to suggest 16 flavours to retain consumer interest. The result is flavours like *chatkia nimbu achar* and *tandoori paneer tikka* flavoured potato chips, chilli and tomato flavoured snacks inspired by Gujarati *khakras*.

The second part of the variety came through irreverent and fun campaigns in 2009. Consumers were asked to design ads for Bingo using the angular shape of the chips as the central theme. Marketers call this 'crowd sourcing', which serves two purposes—it engages the end consumer and the campaign is done at the lowest possible cost. Bingo also ensured that it reached its audience through every possible medium. It first created a website (www.bingeonbingo.com) with offers, online games, downloads and even mobile games. The site was advertised through banners on websites such as Yahoo!, Rediff and Sify.

Analysts believe the Bingo story is also about well-leveraged distribution. ITC, for example, distributed more than 4,00,000 large racks to display the brand at all points of sale. The racks created a huge impact. The importance of Bingo is evident from the fact that potato-based snacks are the largest product segment (85 per cent share) in the Indian snacks market, followed by snack nuts, chickpeas and other pulse-based savoury.

Source: Business Standard, January 2010.

(a) **Product line pricing:** When marketers offer more than one product item in a product line, they usually set the price for the entire product line instead of setting prices for individual products. In such a pricing, the sale of one product in the product line may affect others, so marketers consider the interrelationship between different items when setting prices. They usually offer products that will increase the sale of the other products as well. Retail marketers can adopt different price points within a product line so that customers perceive the quality of these products on the basis of the price points. Retailers do the same in most FMCG products. Most retailers sell numerous products in the same product line. For instance, in detergents the premium products are Ariel and Surf Excel while Wheel, 501 and Nirma are the cheaper alternatives.

In product line pricing marketers set the price for the entire product line instead of individual products.

(b) **Optional feature pricing:** This pricing is done for the accessories that come along with a product. For example, during the purchase of a car, accessories such as seat covers, floor mats, metal guards, air conditioner, music system, and so on, do not form a part of the standard features and are therefore priced separately. Maruti has priced the base model of Alto below ₹3 lakh, the optional features being priced separately.

Optional feature pricing is done for accessories that come with a product.

(c) **Captive product pricing:** Here, manufacturers price the ancillary products or spare parts relatively higher to overcome the low profits earned on the basic product. Gillette follows this strategy for its Mach III blades. The original razor comes at an attractive price, but the blades that have to be used along with the razor are priced higher. Hewlett-Packard adopts the same strategy for its printers and cartridges. Though the cost of an HP Inkjet printer is around ₹3,000, the cost of the cartridges (black and colour) is around ₹2,400. Incidentally, this strategy sometimes paves the way for duplicate and pirated products to enter the market.

In captive product pricing manufacturers price ancillary products or spare parts relatively higher to overcome the low profits earned on the basic product.

(d) **Two-part pricing:** This type of pricing is normally followed in services in which a company charges a fixed price for an initial service and subsequent charges for over and above the minimum service consumed. For example, Tata Indicom charges a fixed price for its CDMA phone service that allows subscribers a certain number of calls based on the amount they pay; any calls made beyond that limit are charged extra. Landline telephone service providers also follow the two-part pricing strategy.

Two-part pricing is followed in services when a company charges a fixed price for an initial service and subsequent charges for over and above the minimum service consumed.

(e) **By-product pricing:** This is a process of setting prices for by-products obtained from the original product. The pricing of diesel, kerosene and other petroleum by-products like crude oil is done in a way to sustain the competitive pressure in the original product.

Leader pricing involves selling a product (leader) at a substantially low price to generate customer traffic and increase the sale of complementary products in the stable.

(f) **Leader pricing:** Leader pricing involves selling a product (leader) at a substantially low price to generate customer traffic and increase the sale of complementary products in the stable. Usually, retailers regard these low-priced products that are often sold below cost as loss leaders. But leader pricing need not always involve pricing loss leaders below the cost price. Products selected for leader pricing should be those that are frequently bought by target customers. Many retailers select items like onions, tomatoes or potatoes as price leaders to attract customers.

In product bundling pricing the manufacturer provides a set of related products at a price.

(g) **Product bundling pricing:** Product bundling pricing is a procedure where the manufacturer provides a set of related products at a price. In this strategy, marketers anticipate customer needs and accordingly bundle either accessories or other related products with the main product. For example, most PC manufacturers bundle free software (anti-virus, office suits, etc.) with the PC. Similarly, computer magazines like *Chip*, *Computers Today*, *PC Quest* and *DataQuest* bundle a CD of free software. Microsoft bundles the word processor, spreadsheet, database and Web design tools in a package called Microsoft Office.

Multiple-unit pricing occurs when the price of each unit in a package is less than the price of each unit if it were bought individually.

(h) **Multiple-unit pricing:** Multiple-unit pricing occurs when the price of each unit in a package is less than the price of each unit if it were bought individually. Customers who buy in bulk benefit from such offers. General merchandise and apparel retailers commonly use this strategy. For example, Pantaloon offers three shirts as a bundle for a certain price (say ₹1,000), which would be less than three such shirts bought separately (say ₹399 × 3). Multiple-unit pricing increases the volume of sales as well as the profit. Specifically, it is also useful to clear out goods, especially end-of-season merchandise.

5.5.3 Price Discrimination

The price of a product in a monopoly is likely to be higher than in a competitive market and the quantity sold less, generating monopoly profits for the seller. These profits can be increased if the market is segmented with different prices set for different segments (referred to as price discrimination). Obviously, those segments willing and able to pay more are charged higher prices and those whose demand is price elastic are charged less. The price discriminator might need to create rate fences that will prevent members of a higher price segment from purchasing at the prices available to members of a lower price segment. This behaviour is rational on the part of the monopolist, but is often seen by authorities as an abuse of monopoly position, whether or not the monopoly itself is sanctioned.

Normally, when the price of a product goes up, the demand for it comes down and vice versa. The factors affecting price sensitivity are as follows:

Unique value effect: When a product is a new innovation and offers unique value proposition to customers, it is less price sensitive.

Substitute awareness effect: When customers lack knowledge about the substitutes available for a product, they tend to be less price sensitive.

Difficulty in comparison: Customers are less price sensitive when it becomes difficult for them to compare a product with its substitutes in terms of features, quality, and so on.

Total expenditure effect: When the expenditure on a product is very little compared to the overall income of the customer, it is less price sensitive.

End-benefit effect: Customers are less price sensitive when the cost incurred on the product is too little compared to the total cost of the end product.

Shared cost effect: When the cost of the product is partly borne by another party, customers are less price sensitive.

Sunk investment effect: Customers are less price sensitive when the products are purchased as an extension of products purchased in the past.

Price quality effect: When the product is considered to be of high quality or to be an exclusive product, buyers are not price sensitive.

Inventory effect: Buyers are less sensitive to price changes of products which they cannot store.

Technological solutions like the Internet which allow price comparisons have made customers increasingly price sensitive. Therefore, marketers have to work harder to differentiate their products from those of competitors. For instance, Virgin Mobile, an American telecommunications company, differentiated its services from those of its competitors across the globe by offering value-added services at the lowest price.

Technological solutions like the Internet which allow price comparisons have made customers increasingly price sensitive.

Normally, price changes made by a company influence a competitor's product pricing. Competitors may react to a price change in three ways: they can maintain status quo (not react in any way to the price change); set the price equal to that of the competitor company; or attack the price change by setting its price lower than that of the competitor company.

The selection of the pricing policy is vital, since it is the single-most important factor on which the existence of the organization depends. Price selection is dependent on the internal and external environment. The internal environment includes the personnel, technology, patents, and so on. The external environment encompasses political, economic, social, technological, environmental and legal environment in which an organization operates.

The selection of the pricing policy is vital and dependent on the internal and external environment.

5.5.4 Implementing Pricing Strategies

The implementation of a pricing strategy involves a variety of separate but interrelated decisions. Some common pricing strategies are:

- *Customary pricing* exists when a retail marketer sets prices and tries to maintain them over an extended period of time.
- Under the *one-price policy*, a marketer charges the same price from all customers who seek to purchase an item under similar conditions.
- In contrast, *flexible pricing* allows consumers to bargain over the selling price. Those who are good at bargaining obtain lower prices than those who are not. This pricing is used by many jewellery stores, auto dealers, online auctioneers and consumer electronics stores.
- *Contingency pricing* is a special form of flexible pricing wherein the firm is not paid until after the service is performed and the payment is contingent on the service being satisfactory. This method is employed in the media industry. TV commercial slots are purchased based on an

In contingency pricing the firm is not paid until after the service is performed. The payment is contingent on the service being satisfactory.

expected TRP rating. Any deviation will accordingly lead to an increase or decrease in payment.

Instead of stocking merchandise at different price levels, retail marketers usually employ price lining and sell merchandise at a limited range of price points, each price point representing a distinct level of quality. Price lining or product line pricing is a method that primarily uses price to create separation between different models. For instance, a marketer may sell a base model, an upgraded model and a deluxe model each at a different price. So, price floors and ceilings are first set, then a limited number of prices (price points) are established within the range. A price lining offers many benefits including reducing customer confusion. It also aids in the selection of suppliers, in negotiations with suppliers, in reducing inventory investment and increasing turnover.

Markdown policy during downturn has to be timed properly. It can be an early or late or staggered markdown policy.

Markdown timing must be planned during a downturn. An early markdown policy offers merchandise at reduced prices when the demand is fairly active. Lower markdowns help to clear out merchandise, free selling space for new merchandise, and improve cash flow. A late markdown policy provides the retail marketer with every opportunity to sell the merchandise at the original price. Under the staggered markdown policy, prices are marked down gradually through the selling season. It helps in maintaining the demand through the downturn and generating revenue.

5.5.5 Consumer Rights

Consumer rights are provisions which ensure that the consumer is protected from harm when dealing with a provider of a service or a distributor of a product.

Consumer rights are provisions which ensure that the consumer is protected from harm when dealing with a provider of a service or a distributor of a product. People's dependence on the market for goods and services and the scope for profit in mass production and sales gives manufacturers and dealers plenty of opportunity to exploit consumers. Without a set of guidelines or rules it is very likely that the goods and services provided will not match the amount paid. With developing technology more questionable practices are coming to light, like genetically modified food and the use of dangerous chemicals in manufacturing. Consumer rights protect consumers from these malpractices. These rights are necessary not just for consumer protection but also for the enforcement of trading standards laws, which are designed to create fair competition and to protect consumers in areas as diverse as pricing, special offers, weights and measures and age-related sales.

MARKETING IN ACTION — **ITC'S PRICING STRATEGIES**

The pricing of a product is determined by the consumer segment targeted by the firm. Since competitors already exist in each segment, ITC can opt a pricing strategy across the categories as listed below:

Personal care

ITC launched Fiama Di Wills in September 2007, in competition to Sunsilk and priced products similarly. In order to cater to the lower end of the shampoo market, ITC recently launched the Superia range of soaps and shampoos, priced much lower than Fiama Di Wills. Placed in middle segment is another soap brand, Vivel, priced at ₹16 for a 75 gm. cake, which makes it a direct competitor for brands like Lux and Godrej No.1.

Foods

In this segment, ITC came up with the Kitchens of India spices and Aashirvaad flour. There are a lot of local players in the spices segment; hence ITC's pricing had to be close to the prices offered by the other local players. The pricing was done at par with competitors like Shakti Bhog and MDH. In the sweet candy segment, Mint-o and Candyman are both priced at par with competitors Polo and Alpenleibe, respectively.

Lifestyle retailing

Here it is crucial for ITC to price its products appropriately as it caters to the premium segment. Consumers are willing to pay extra for the name and quality of the brand, hence the prices are generally above ₹2,000 for all products. Consumers looking for John Players apparels are more concerned about the quality and variety offered than the price. Price is a secondary factor in the decision-making in this product line, hence ITC has more liberty of pricing here. The competition is from brands like Van Heusen, Allen Solly, and Adidas.

Stationery

In the Classmate and Paperkraft range of notebooks, ITC has made a strategic move by pricing them higher than the price of locally made notebooks. The prices are generally ₹2 to ₹3 higher than the local products. However, the colourful covers and trivia at the end of each book have attracted consumers, mainly schoolchildren. Also, ITC has leveraged its strong distribution network here to make its products widely available and visible in the market. Its direct competition is with another similar player, Navneet, which too offers highly colourful notebooks.

Incense sticks and matchsticks

With these product lines ITC has forayed into the traditional cottage industries' market. With great packaging and a strong distribution network, the high-priced incense sticks are attracting consumers. The Aim Matchsticks on the other hand are priced at ₹0.50 per box of 50 matches, similar to competitors like HomeLite and SmileLite.

Agribusiness

The ITC agribusiness division aims to be the one-stop-shop for all agri-products. A unique rural digital infrastructure network coupled with an indepth understanding of agricultural practices and intensive research has helped ITC build a competitive and efficient supply chain that creates and delivers immense value across the agricultural value chain. One of the largest exporters of agri-products from the country, ITC sources the finest of Indian feed ingredients, foodgrains, edible nuts, marine products, processed fruits, coffee and spices. The prices in this line are decided by international and national demand and supply patterns.

Cigarettes

ITC's flagship product line is cigarettes. At present it has a monopoly in the market and hence a greater degree of freedom in setting the price. An example was seen when it drove out competition from Capstan by selling filtered cigarettes (Navy Cut) at a low price (₹20 for 10 cigarettes). Capstan was without a filter, hence consumers started shifting to Navy Cut, slowly drying out the former's market. ITC was able to sell filtered cigarettes at such low prices only because of its financial muscle power. Currently ITC enjoys a monopoly in the market, being the sole manufacturer of cigarettes and hence price is much higher than the cost of production. Enjoying a high profit margin in the cigarette segment enables ITC to experiment in newer market segments in other product lines.

In fact pricing in the cigarette segment is extremely crucial for the company to generate sufficient revenue to make a foray into other segments and limit its dependence on cigarettes.

Apart from pricing, ITC offers numerous incentives and gifts to retail shop owners to boost sales and establish better relations with its distribution channels. It is this value network that ITC has created over a period of time that has helped it acquire a commendable position in the cigarette market besides allowing it to enter into other segments. Therefore, apart from pricing the products as such, the benefits offered to the distributors have also helped ITC.

Source: Investors' Report of ITC Ltd., January 2010.

5.6 Promotion

People need to be aware of the existence of a product if they have to buy it. Similarly, they must be persuaded that Product A is worth testing against Product B, which they perhaps already use, and that Product A has some distinctive features. Marketing promotion involves any communication by a firm to inform, persuade, and/or remind the target market about any aspect of the firm through advertising, public relations, personal selling and sales promotion.

Marketing promotion involves any communication by a firm to inform, persuade, and/or remind the target market about any aspect of the firm through advertising, public relations, personal selling and sales promotion.

Promotion consists of four components. Though each of these components is an individual function, a good promotional strategy integrates all these components, depending on the retailer's overall strategy. Box 5.1 details the various tools used in marketing promotion.

5.6.1 Marketing Communication

Marketing communication has evolved from the time when the firm alone communicated with the consumers. Today, consumers too can communicate or approach organizations. One way of doing this is through toll-free numbers, which retailers provide for customer complaints and queries.

Marketing Budget

The marketing budget should be divided so that the marginal value of an extra dollar will be the same in all the components of the mix.

The effectiveness of the various elements of marketing mix with respect to problems or opportunities should be the factor that determines what share each component receives of the total marketing budget. Conceptually, the budget should be divided so that the marginal value of an extra dollar will be the same in all components of the mix; the budget should favour areas that will produce the greatest incremental sales volume. In evaluating the advertising budget, therefore, it is important to keep in mind that incremental amounts of money put into advertising must be more useful than the same amounts put into distribution or product refinement, or even reduced prices.

BOX 5.1: TOOLS USED IN MARKETING PROMOTION

Advertising	*Sales promotion*	*Public relations*	*Sales force*	*Direct marketing*
Print and broadcast ads	Contests, games, sweep-stakes, lotteries	Press kits Speeches	Sales presentations Sales meetings	Catalogue Mailings
Packing-outer	Premiums and gifts	Seminars	Incentive programmes	Telemarketing
Packing inserts	Sampling	Annual reports	Samples	Electronic shopping
Motion pictures Brochures and Booklets	Fairs and trade shows Exhibits Demonstrations	Charitable denotations Sponsorships Publications	Fair and trade shows	TV shopping Fax mail Email
Posters and leaflets	Coupons	Community relations		Voice mail
Directories	Rebates	Lobbying		
Reprints of ads	Low-interest financing	Identity media		
Billboards	Entertainment	Company magazine		
Displays signs	Trade-in allowances	Events		
Point-of-purchase	Continuity/loyalty programmes			
Displays signs				
Audiovisual material				
Symbols and logos				
Videotapes				

Retail Marketing

At a time when consumers want more information and when retailers have reduced staffing levels, retail marketing performs a vital service and augments cost-reduction efforts. It is one of the few mass advertising media that can convey the same strategic message in differing languages to varying audiences in the same village, city or region. Point-of-purchase (P-O-P) signage and in-store media educate and draw the attention of the consumers towards a product's availability and attributes. Today's P-O-P displays are easily assembled, maintained and, at the same time, more powerful in entertaining and informing in the retail environment.

Unlike many businesses, retail marketers usually do not take their merchandise to the marketplace. Their sales depend on the customers' initiatives like visiting their store or placing an order through telephone or mail. The retailers thus have to motivate the customers to visit their stores. A customer would visit a particular store only when he knows about its presence, location and the merchandise it offers. The customer would also like to have information on the prices, modes of payment (like cash and credit cards), availability of various services (like free home delivery of the goods), store timings, and so on. Retailers generate sales by making its target customers aware of the merchandise they offer through promotional activities. There are four channels through which a firm communicates with its target customers: advertising, sales promotion, public relations, and personal selling. I will discuss the role of promotion programmes, planning marketing communication programmes, allocating promotion budget, implementing advertising, sales promotion and publicity programmes and evaluating the effectiveness of advertising.

The four channels through which a firm communicates with its target customers are: advertising, sales promotion, public relations, and personal selling.

A. Advertising

Advertising has both forward and backward linkages in the process of need satisfaction. The explicit function of advertising is to make the potential audience aware of the existence of a product, service or idea which would help customers fulfil their felt needs and spell out the differential benefits in a competitive situation. The Institute of Practitioners in Advertising (IPA), the body which represents advertising agencies, defines advertising as: 'The means of providing the most persuasive possible selling message to the right prospects at the lowest possible cost.' Kotler and Armstrong provide a different definition: 'Advertising is any paid form of non-personal presentation and promotion of ideas, goods and services through mass media such as newspapers, magazines, television or radio by an identified sponsor.'

Advertising should make the potential audience aware of the existence of a product, service or idea which would help customers fulfil their felt needs.

The thirteen types of structures identified by them are given below:

(i) **Storyline:** This is a commercial that tells a story. It is a clear, step-by-step unfolding of a message with a definite beginning, middle and end.

(ii) **Problem-solution:** It presents the viewer with a problem and the sponsor's product as the solution to that problem. Problem-solution is

Problem-solution is the most widely used and generally accepted example of a TV commercial.

MARKETING ANALYSIS

CELEBRITY ENDORSEMENT MARKET BACK ON TRACK

After a lull of eight months when virtually no new endorsement deal of any significant value was signed, the ₹400-₹450 crore celebrity endorsement business seems back on the recovery path since October 2009. Celebrity management firms like Globosports and World Sports Group (WSG) say the celebrity endorsement market is estimated to clock a healthy growth in the next few years. While there is no organized agency to track the deal size of endorsements, the market size is expected to grow 15 to 17 per cent in 2009. Endorsements by film stars, estimated at around ₹150 crore and growing at 25 per cent, have displaced those by sports personalities to gain the top slot. According to Globosports, a sports and celebrity management firm that manages the commercial interests of Sania Mirza, Lara Dutta, Saif Ali Khan, among others, cricketers have seen a slow growth of 10-12 per cent largely due to India's poor run at important tournaments like the World Cup T20 and the ICC Champions Trophy in early 2009.

In September 2009, some of the big brand endorsement deals that were announced included Hrithik Roshan's deal with Reliance Communications estimated to be worth ₹5-₹7 crore (for one year) and Gautam Gambhir's with MRG through its new agent, the World Sports Group.

According to sources in the business, categories like telecommunications, food and beverages, sports apparel and personal care emerged as the top spenders on celebrities in 2009. It is estimated that the top four categories would together be spending over one-fourth of the overall celebrity endorsement business. This is because the endorsement fees charged by celebrities have gone up, especially in these categories. Industry sources say overall, there are over 50 cricketers who endorse an array of brands, from sports apparels to food and drinks. However, only half-a-dozen like Mohinder Singh Dhoni, Sachin Tendulkar, Yuvraj Singh, Rohit Sharma, Gautam Gambhir and Virender Sehwag command a bulk of the endorsement pie.

Cricketers control almost 80 per cent of the sports celebrity endorsement business. In recent times, this market has been pretty stagnant but the things are looking up now. The World Sports Group is a Singapore-based sports marketing company and is also the co-telecast rights holder for the Indian Premier League (IPL). It has recently signed cricketer Gautam Gambhir and looks after the brand endorsement deals for Sachin Tendulkar. But other sports stars are not as lucky. Despite an Olympic medal, ace shooter Abhinav Bindra has not got any big endorsement deals apart from Samsung and a few others. Same is the case with another Olympic medalist and world's top boxer in his weight category Vijender Singh. Before his multi-crore contract with Percept for the Indian version of the TV boxing show 'The Contender', Vijender was not getting more than ₹40 lakh per endorsement. Same is the case with Saina Nehwal, the country's leading badminton player who commands a much lower endorsement fee compared to any cricketer.

But what is pushing the growth in this business? Veteran ad filmmaker Prahlad Kakkar says, 'The value charged by celebrities like Dhoni and others along with the entry of youngsters is pushing the business. Dravid and Ganguly are out of this race but there are always new faces that keep coming up.' Sources say Aamir Khan received a meager ₹15-₹17 lakh for his brand endorsement deal with Pepsi in the early 1990s. Currently, he charges around ₹8 crore per endorsement for just one year. Dhoni charges around ₹5 crore per endorsement currently, up from ₹25-₹30 lakh when he started a few years ago.

Source: Business World, January 2010.

the most widely used and generally accepted example of a TV commercial.

(iii) **Chronology:** This delivers the message through a series of related scenes, each one growing out of the one before. Facts and events are presented sequentially as they occurred.

(iv) **Special effects:** This has no strong structural pattern but it strives for and often achieves memorability though the use of some striking device, for example, an unusual musical sound or pictorial technique.

(v) **Testimonial:** Also called word-of-mouth advertising, it uses well known figures or an unknown 'man on the street' to provide product testimonials.

(vi) **Satire:** A commercial that uses sophisticated wit to point out human foibles, generally produced in an exaggerated style. Parodies on James Bond movies, Bonnie and Clyde, and the like are good examples.

CASE STUDY | TELECOM ADVERTISING IN INDIA

The major telecom operators use Above the Level promotion schemes like advertising on TV and print media, as well as Below the Level promotion schemes.

Airtel: Airtel has a variety of TV advertisements as well as print ones. It has used celebrities like Shahrukh Khan, Sachin Tendulkar and more recently R. Madhavan and Vidya Balan as its brand ambassadors. Airtel has always focused on the mass market rather than the

niche. And since people identify with celebrities and emulate them, endorsements have worked for the company.

Recently, Airtel has resorted to sentimentality to connect with the people. On 1 November 2009 Airtel sponsored the half-marathon at Delhi where 30,000 people participated and many more came to view. This move is expected help increase brand recall and gain respect. Airtel has been a sponsor of several other events.

Vodafone: Vodafone's advertisements have always been exceptional. Their ads have great emotional appeal and brand recall. Their 'Wherever you go our network follows' campaign reflected their position as having a good network.

During the 2009 IPL tournament, it launched the Zoo Zoo campaign which has redefined the mascot advertising concept. It portrayed 15 different ads corresponding to 15 different value-added services provided by Vodafone. Needless to say it was a big hit.

The print ads of Vodafone are equally appealing.

Reliance: After launching the simply Reliance tariff plan, the company came up with a new advertisement

with celebrity Hrithik Roshan. Customers are often left confused with the wide variety of tariff plans available. This advertisement gives them a relief from the headache of choosing from the plans, providing the cheapest tariff rates.

Sources: Bharati Airtel Ltd. and Vodafone Investors' Report, January 2010.

(vii) Spokesperson: This is the use of an on-camera announcer who 'talks'. The talk may be hard-sell or a more personal, intimate sell.

(viii) Demonstration: This uses some physical apparatus to demonstrate a product's effectiveness. Analgesic, watch, and tyre commercials employ this approach heavily.

(ix) Suspense: This has a structure similar to storyline or problem-solution, but the build up of curiosity and suspense to the final resolution gives it a heightened sense of drama.

(x) Slice-of-life: A variation of the problem-solution structure, it begins with a person at the point of or just before the discovery of an answer to a problem. This approach is heavily used by detergent manufacturers.

Analogy offers an extraneous example and then attempts to relate it to the product message.

(xi) **Analogy:** It offers an extraneous example and then attempts to relate it to the product message. In other words, instead of delivering a message simply and directly, an analogy uses one example to explain another by comparison or implication: 'like vitamins tone up your body, our product tones up your car's engine'.

(xii) **Fantasy:** Fantasy uses caricatures or special effects to create a fantasy surrounding the product and its use: for instance, washing machine that becomes a 10-feet tall giant to fight dirt!

(xiii) **Personality:** This is a technical variation of the spokesperson or announcer-on-camera kind of straight-sell structure. It relies on an actor/actress/sportsperson rather than an announcer to deliver the message. The actor plays a character who talks about the product, reacts to its use, or demonstrates its use directly to the camera.

Stages of an Advertising Campaign

An advertising objective is a specific communication task to be achieved with a specific target audience during a specified period of time.

Advertising is a purposeful communication designed to achieve specific objectives. The focus of advertising must be on the audience most likely to buy the product or service. It must reach the target audience identified for such communication. The resource allocation for advertising, as for other marketing inputs, is expected to have the effect of value imputation which may be measured in order to estimate the cost-benefit ratio.

The measurement of payoff or returns on advertising is complicated, owing to problems in identifying measurable parameters and taking into account the influence of a large number of environmental factors which contribute in varying degrees to the total impact of advertising. There are five main stages in a well-managed advertising campaign:

Stage 1: Set the advertising objectives

An advertising objective is a specific communication task to be achieved with a specific target audience during a specified period of time. Advertising objectives fall into three main categories:

(a) To inform, e.g. tell customers about a new product.
(b) To persuade, e.g. encourage customers to switch to a new brand.
(c) To remind, e.g. remind buyers where to find the product.

Stage 2: Set the advertising budget

Marketers should remember that the role of advertising is to create demand for a product. The amount spent on advertising should be relevant to the potential sales impact of the campaign. This in turn will reflect the characteristics of the product being advertised. For example, new products tend to need a larger advertising budget to build awareness and to encourage consumers to make a trial of the product. A product that is highly differentiated may also need more advertising to help set it apart from the competition.

Setting the advertising budget is not easy—how can a business predict the right amount to spend? Which parts of the advertising campaign will work best and which will have a relatively little effect? Businesses often use the rule of thumb as a guide to set budgets.

Stage 3: Determine the key advertising message

A successful advertising message is meaningful, distinctive, and believable.

Spending a lot on advertising does not guarantee success. Research suggests that the clarity of the advertising message is often more important than the amount spent. The advertising message must be carefully targeted to make an impact on the target customer audience. A successful advertising message should have the following characteristics:

(a) **Meaningful:** Customers should find the message relevant, e.g. the ad by Vodafone made it clear that their network extends everywhere customers want it to reach.

(b) **Distinctive:** The ad must capture the customer's attention, like the Hoodibaba ad by Baja Auto. The photography and sound effects generated much interest.

(c) **Believable:** This is a difficult task, since researchers suggest that most consumers doubt the truth of advertising in general.

Stage 4: Decide which advertising media to use

The key factors in choosing the right media include reach, frequency, media impact and campaign timing.

There are a variety of advertising media from which to choose. A campaign may use one or more of the media alternatives. The key factors in choosing the right media include:

(a) **Reach:** What proportion of the target customers will be exposed to the advertising?

(b) **Frequency:** How many times will the target customers be exposed to the advertising message?

(c) **Media impact:** Where should the target customer see the message for it to have most impact? For example, does an advertisement promoting holidays for elderly people have more impact on television (if so, when and which channels) or in a national newspaper or perhaps a magazine focused on this segment of the population?

Another key decision is the timing of the campaign. Some products are suited to seasonal campaigns on television (e.g. Diwali or Christmas hampers) whereas for other products, a regular advertising campaign throughout the year in media such as newspapers and niche magazines (e.g. a resort holiday in a hill station) may be more appropriate.

Stage 5: Evaluate the results of the advertising campaign

The evaluation of an advertising campaign should focus on two key areas:

Communication effect: Is the intended message being communicated effectively and to the intended audience? For example, it is important for the company to make a note of the effects of its communication efforts. Airtel saw a huge increase in sales after the release of its ad featuring A.R. Rehman.

Sales effect: Has the campaign generated the intended sales growth? This is much more difficult to measure than the communication effect.

B. Personal Selling

Personal selling is oral communication with potential customers with the intention of making a sale.

This consists of oral communication with potential customers with the intention of making a sale. Personal selling may focus initially on developing a relationship with the potential buyer, but will always end with an attempt to 'close the sale'. One of the oldest forms of promotion, it involves the use of a sales force to support a push strategy (encouraging intermediaries to buy the product) or a pull strategy (where the role of the sales force may be limited to supporting retailers and providing after-sales service).

The level of personal selling used by a firm depends on the image it wants to convey, the types of products sold, the level of self-service, interest in long-term customer relationships, as well as expectations of the customers.

Among the goals of personal selling are persuading customers to make a purchase, stimulating purchases of impulse items or products related to the customers' basic purchases, completing transactions, providing feedback, providing adequate levels of customer service, improving and maintaining customer satisfaction and creating awareness for items marketed through the Web, mail, and telemarketing.

Effective personal selling requires sales force promotion the tools for which are bonus, sales force contests, sales meetings and sales conventions and conferences.

Personal selling is highly essential in marketing. To make this form of selling effective, sales force promotion is essential. The tools of sales force promotion are bonus, sales force contests, sales meetings and sales conventions and conferences.

A bonus is usually offered to salesmen who sell in excess of the quota assigned to them. Similarly, sales force contests are arranged to encourage salesmen to try harder, and increase the efforts and enthuse the sales force. Sales conventions and conferences are arranged for the purpose of educating and inspiring the sales force.

Kotler describes six main activities of a sales force:

(a) *Prospecting:* Trying to find new customers.
(b) *Communicating:* With existing and potential customers about the product range.
(c) *Selling:* Contact with the customer, answering questions and trying to close the sale.
(d) *Servicing:* Providing support and service to the customer in the period up to delivery and also post-sale.
(e) *Information gathering:* Obtaining information about the market to provide feedback for the marketing planning process.
(f) *Allocating:* In times of product shortage, the sales force may have the power to decide how available stocks are allocated.

There are, in fact, a number of jobs that frequently only the sales personnel can do, even when the marketing task has been thoroughly and carefully carried through and a product that matches a need has been developed. One important reason for this is that very few purchases are made on purely objective criteria. Certainly a product will need to do the task expected of it satisfactorily, but with most consumer products and numerous industrial products that is virtually taken for granted. So the customer chooses from a whole range of products, any one of which will do the job. Other factors then come into the picture. Thus, visual design, colour and 'appearance' of the product generally have great importance, even with industrial products. The role of the sales force therefore includes the following:

(i) *To understand:* The formidable task of understanding the customers' subjective (psychological) needs and demonstrate how the given product will satisfy them becomes the responsibility of the sales team. In some cases (such as life insurance) customers may initially have only a vague idea what their requirements are, and the salesperson will have to help them articulate their needs.

(ii) *To negotiate:* Very often there is a gap between the price being asked for a product and what the customer is willing to pay. The easy way to close the gap is to cut the price, but that move will also cut down profit. The salesperson can solve the problem in another way—enhancing the value of the product by demonstrating its particular benefits to the customer and showing how paying a higher price will bring additional value. In some cases (such as cars and certain industrial equipment), the negotiation will frequently necessitate agreeing on a 'trade in' price for the customer's present model.

(iii) *Two-way communication:* The company needs to communicate information to its customers. Often the salesperson is the most effective channel (letters, leaflets and other written communications may never be read, partly because they are likely to be couched in general terms rather than speaking specifically about the customer's particular situation). The company also needs feedback from its customers—what pleases them and what annoys them about the service being provided, what are their future plans and what opportunities for profitable sales will these offer?

After several years of study, David Meyer and Herbert M. Greenberg came up with two vital qualities—(a) empathy, or the ability to feel as the customer does, and (b) ego drive, a strong personal need to make the sale (not simply for monetary rewards) for a salesman to succeed in his ventures.

ADVERTISING *V.* PERSONAL SELLING

In many situations the ability to communicate effectively will be important, and in others strong creative qualities will be necessary in order to identify ways in which potential customers can benefit from the products available. Occasionally the tough-skinned, 'foot-in-the-door', rather brash type of selling may be called for (perhaps what comes to mind as 'typical' salesmanship). This approach however is increasingly rare as the level of sophistication of both products and customers is on the rise.

Unlike advertisements, there is an inbuilt element of flexibility in personal selling, because the salesperson can judge a customer's response to the message as the contact takes place and modify the message accordingly.

Personal selling can be used to get far more information across than an advertisement can do, and is used widely in industrial sales where complex specifications and technical details need to be discussed. It is also widely used in the financial services sector for similar reasons, in that both the customer and the seller need to ask many questions and provide substantial amounts of information for the right service offering to be specified.

Personal selling has other advantages in that it can be aimed at specific target markets and prospects and also provide more direct feedback than other promotional methods.

C. Sales Promotion

Sales promotions are activities that shape buying patterns, attract new audiences or increase sales. It is a grab-bag of a word that encompasses everything that falls outside advertising, publicity and direct marketing, although these might be used as part of a firm's sales promotion campaign.

More than any other element of the promotional mix, sales promotion is about action. It is about stimulating customers to buy a product. It is not designed to be informative—a role which advertising is far better suited to.

Sales promotions are activities that shape buying patterns, attract new audiences or increase sales. These include advertising campaigns, increased PR activity, free sample campaigns, free gift offers or trading stamps, arranging demonstrations or exhibitions and holding competitions.

Sales promotions are designed to boost the sale of a product or service. Commonly referred to as 'below the line' promotions, they consist of paid communication activities other than advertising, public relations and personal selling, that stimulate consumer purchases and dealer effectiveness. Sales promotions may include advertising campaigns, increased PR activity, free sample campaigns, offering free gifts or trading stamps, arranging demonstrations or exhibitions, holding competitions, temporary price reductions, door-to-door selling, telemarketing, personal letters, frequent shopper programmes, referral gifts, and other limited-time selling efforts outside of the ordinary promotion routine. The goals of sales promotion are to increase short-run sales volume, to maintain customer loyalty, to emphasize novelty and to complement other promotion tools.

A firm may create a sales promotion campaign to launch a new product, counter a competitor's strategy, increase sales, etc.

Sales promotion can be directed at the ultimate consumer (a pull strategy encouraging purchase) or at the distribution channel (a push strategy encouraging the channels to stock the product). Examples of the former include coupons, sampling, premiums, sweepstakes, low-cost financing deals, and rebates. Sales promotion aimed at the distribution channels is known as 'selling into the trade' and may take the form of slotting allowances, specifically for featuring the product in retail advertising, display and merchandising allowances, and so on.

A firm may create a sales promotion campaign to:

(a) *Stimulate trial purchase:* This is usually done when a firm wants to attract new customers. A reduced price or a rebate may induce trial purchases.
(b) *Encourage repeat purchase:* In-package coupons valid for the next purchase are examples of promotions aimed at encouraging repeat purchases.
(c) *Encourage larger purchase:* Price reductions, two for the price of one, a discount on the second purchase are aimed at encouraging larger purchases.
(d) *Introduce a new brand/product:* A sales promotion may be undertaken to attract attention to a new product/brand or service that has been launched by the firm and to induce trial purchase.
(e) *Counter competitor's strategy:* If a firm comes to know through market intelligence that a competitor is launching a new product or brand, it may want to counter that by introducing a sales promotion campaign.

A.H.R. Delans defines sales promotion as steps taken to obtain or increase sales. Often this term refers especially to selling efforts that are designed to supplement personal selling and advertising and by coordination helps them to become more effective.

Typical Sales Promotion Tasks

Sales promotion tasks include a wide range of activities which are used in diverse situations. Some of the most common ones are:

(i) Encouraging dealers to stock: Most retail dealers feel they already have far too many different products, and every new addition means dropping an old item or having more capital locked up in stock. So they need considerable persuasion to take in a new line. They must be convinced it will be profitable for them and, therefore, must be convinced that customers will buy it in reasonable volume. Sales promotion activities can be used both to convince the dealers and also to provide direct cash incentives to them.

(ii) **Encouraging customers to sample:** With some products like food items and confectionery, it is crucial that customers try or sample the new product—they are most certainly already buying an alternative that they find reasonably satisfactory. They must be given an incentive to try something new. A special price offer, a 'two for one', or even an exciting display may tempt them sufficiently to make the test.

(iii) **'Locking in' existing customers:** Some sales promotion techniques such as 'three for the price of two', are used by companies to encourage customers to stay loyal rather than switch brands. Other devices used for this purpose include 'collectables' such as coupons, which can be exchanged for goods from a catalogue.

(iv) **Combating competition:** A competitive situation, such as a new competing product, may call for an intensive short-term promotion of an existing product to ensure that present customers are not wooed away, and that, if possible, some new ones are gained to fill any gaps in the ranks.

(v) **Improving distribution:** This is a situation similar to (i). An existing product may have 'patchy' distribution, and sales promotion techniques can be used to fill in the gaps and gain extra dealers in poorly represented areas.

(vi) **Adding excitement:** A well-established product may suffer from familiarity. Since most people are well aware of it, it can become boring. Sales promotions liven it up again and revive interest in it.

DIFFERENCE BETWEEN ADVERTISING AND SALES PROMOTION

We drew a distinction between advertising and sales promotion in terms of the media used. Some of the other distinctions are as follows:

(i) **Sales promotion is often tactical:** To a large extent advertising is used strategically, i.e. it is part of the continuing 'attack' on competitors, often with long-term objectives. Creating a brand-image, generating a flow of enquiries, influencing a whole new market favourably towards a product all call for carefully planned advertising (usually in conjunction with other forms of promotion) spread over a long period. Even when short-term results are expected, as in direct sales advertising, the campaign will usually need to be frequently repeated so that the advertising is continuous. Sales promotion, on the other hand, is more often tactical, i.e. designed to achieve a short-term and limited objective, possibly in a limited area or through certain outlets. For example, an introductory price cut or premium offer may be made, coupled with special dealer discounts in order to encourage dealers to stock the product and customers to sample the same. The promotion could continue for a few weeks or till stocks last. However, this tactical aspect must be kept in prespective because continuous use of sales promotion does have long-term effects.

(ii) **Sales promotion is normally concentrated at point of sale:** In general, advertising involves the marketing company speaking directly to the customer. Sales promotion usually takes place in close association with dealers who stock the product. Often the promotion takes place 'at the point of sale', i.e. at the place where the customer buys the product. The customer may get free mugs with a pack of coffee or may be asked to fill a form at the check-out desk for a free holiday offer. Some sales promotion activities take place on the street (for example, 'personality promotions' where authors do autograph sessions in select bookstores) or on a door-to-door basis (as with some forms of sampling), but even then there is usually a strong tie-in with local dealers.

Methods of Sales Promotion

The main consumer sales promotional techniques available are summarized below:

Price promotion offers either a discount on the normal selling price of a product, or more of the product at the normal price.

(i) **Price promotions:** Price promotion is also commonly known as 'price discounting'. This offers either a discount on the normal selling price of a product, or more of the product at the normal price. Increased sales gained from price promotions are at the expense of a loss in profit, so they must be used with care. A producer must also guard against the possible negative effects of discounting on a brand's reputation, e.g. price discounts offered by companies as an end-of-season sale or festival sale.

Coupon promotions maximize the redemption rate.

(ii) **Coupons:** Coupons are another, very versatile way of offering a discount. Consider the following examples of the use of coupons: on a pack to encourage repeat purchase, coupons sent out with newspapers which can be redeemed at retail outlets, a cut-out coupon as part of an advertisement and on the back of bill receipts. The key objective with a coupon promotion is to maximize the redemption rate—this is the proportion of customers actually using the coupon. One drawback with coupons is that they may simply encourage customers to buy what they would have bought anyway. Another problem occurs when retailers do not hold sufficient stocks of the promoted product, causing customer disappointment. Use of coupon promotions is, therefore, often best for new products or perhaps to encourage the sale of existing products that are slowing down. For example, Pantaloon offers a green card for people who shop above a certain limit. This card gets customers special discounts, free passes to shows, and so on.

In the 'gift with purchase' scheme the customer gets something in addition to the main purchase.

(iii) **Gift with purchase:** The 'gift with purchase' scheme is also known as premium promotion, in that the customer gets something in addition to the main purchase. It is widely used for subscription-based products (like magazines), consumer luxuries (like perfumes), and so on. Everyday examples are newspapers and magazines giving gifts to people who subscribe for a period of time.

(iv) **Competitions and prizes:** This is another popular promotion tool with many variants, most competition and prize promotions are subject to legal restrictions. Lucky draws, for instance, are common in the Indian market.

(v) **Money refunds:** Here a customer receives a money refund after submitting a proof of purchase to the manufacturer. These schemes are often viewed with some suspicion by customers, particularly if the method of obtaining the refund looks unusual or onerous.

(vi) **Frequent user/loyalty incentives:** Repeat purchases may be stimulated by frequent user incentives. Perhaps the best examples are the many frequent flyer or user schemes offered by airlines and car hire companies.

(vii) **Point-of-sale displays:** Research into customer buying behaviour in retail stores suggests that a significant proportion of purchases results from promotions that customers see in the store. Attractive, informative and well-positioned point-of-sale displays are, therefore, an important part of the retail sales promotional activity. For instance, Maggi and Cadbury's have special stalls installed for their products in supermarkets.

Additionally, promotions are also used by manufacturers to 'discriminate' between different segments of consumers—for example, only those consumers who have the time to cut the coupons will use them and obtain a lower price, while those consumers who are pressed for time won't use the coupons (and will end up paying a higher price). Finally, retailers use promotions to clear their inventory of slow-moving, out-of-season, or shelf-unstable products (products such as fresh produce that will spoil if they are not sold quickly). Retailers thus run their own promotions aimed at consumers, such as price cuts, displays, frequent shopper programmes, and so on.

Manufacturers use promotions to 'discriminate' between different segments of consumers and clear their inventory of slow-moving, out-of-season, or shelf-unstable products.

Sales promotion techniques are used to give a short-term 'lift' to a product, in order to achieve a tactical objective—such as getting retailers to stock, getting customers to sample, or attempting to raise sales off a plateau. This contrasts with the long-term advertising objective of building brand recognition or creating right associations with the product in a consumer's mind.

Often a product much advertised over a long period reaches the point where there is nothing novel to be said about it. A competition or giveaway reintroduces the desired novelty and excitement. Often the purpose of sales promotion is to relieve the boredom of a well-established product.

D. Public Relations

The Institute of Public Relations defines it as the planned and sustained effort to establish and maintain goodwill and mutual understanding between an organization and its publics. A business may have many 'publics' with which it needs to maintain good relations and build goodwill. The role of public relations is to identify the relevant publics and to influence the opinions of those publics by reinforcing favourable opinions, transforming neutral opinions into positive ones and changing or neutralizing hostile opinions.

Public Relations is defined as the planned and sustained effort to establish and maintain goodwill and mutual understanding between an organization and its publics.

I. *Public Relations Techniques*

There are many techniques available to influence public opinion, some of which are more appropriate in certain circumstances than others.

Consumer communication includes customer press releases, trade press releases, promotional videos, consumer exhibitions, competitions and prizes, product launch events, celebrity endorsements and websites. *Business communication* in turn consists of corporate identity design, company and product videos, direct mailings, websites and trade exhibitions. *Internal/employee communication* tools include in-house newsletters and magazines, intranet, notice boards, employee conferences and email.

External corporate communication comprises company literature (brochures, videos, etc.), community involvement programmes, trade, local, national and international media relations. And *financial communication* tools include financial media relations, annual reports and accounts, meetings with stock market analysts and fund managers, shareholder meetings (including the annual general meeting).

II. *Media Relations*

Media relations is the process and technique of providing information to the press (print, radio and television).

It is the process and technique of providing information to the press (print, radio and television).

Public relations thus constitutes the wide activity of communicating with the many groups of people who constitute on organization's public, as well as its suppliers, customers and other 'trading' contacts. A company that maintains a good relationship will find it easier to launch new ventures, besides having a firmer base from which to deal with difficulties.

Communicating effectively with all stakeholders may call for the use of films, house journals, advertising and many other media, as well as the use of press relations activity. The subjects on which communication takes place will also be very broad, so public relations in this full sense is far more than just an aspect of marketing activity. Products which are no longer new may, of course, find it more difficult to be featured in this way. Then we have to look for: (a) application stories: new ways in which a product is being used or new problems that it is solving; (b) orders and expansions: large overseas contracts, new factories providing employment; (c) visiting royalty or dignitary seen using the products, and (d) sponsorship.

Like all forms of promotion, PR must be conducted on a planned, systematic basis. The following seven-step sequence is a useful approach:

(a) State the problem or aim (launch a new product, inform or motivate the sales force, encourage a favourable attitude amongst potential customers).
(b) Do the research to establish the situation.
(c) Identify the public (who do we need to talk to and what do we need to say to them).
(d) Choose the appropriate media (from TV to newsletters, conferences, films, and so on, depending on the objective and the public concerned).
(e) Monitor the effects to make sure the message is being received and understood in the way intended.
(f) Look to the future. PR never ends; it is always part of a continually changing situation.
(g) Maintain financial checks at all stages to ensure the operation is cost-effective.

A company that has a good relationship with its public will find it easier to launch new ventures and will have a firmer base from which to deal with difficulties.

It is actually difficult to measure whether the key messages have been communicated to the target public. In any event, this would be an expensive exercise since it would involve a large amount of regular research. Instead, the measures of effectiveness concentrate on the process of public relations, and include monitoring the amount of media coverage obtained (press cutting agencies play a role in keeping businesses informed of this), measuring attendance at meetings and conferences and measuring the number of enquiries or orders received in response to specific public relations efforts.

5.7 Integrated Communication

It is important that the ingredients used in the marketing and promotional mix, whatever they are, make a coherent whole. Each activity and piece of promotional material (advertisement, leaflet, display stand) must be part of a well-conceived plan. Often the term 'integrated campaign' is used to describe this carefully worked out scheme in which all the individual pieces fit together and support each other. If this is not done, a conflicting effect can result, with poor response from customers who may be confused rather than motivated by the varying messages they receive. An integrated campaign, on the other hand, can have a synergistic effect. Outstanding examples are Esso's classic 'a tiger in your tank', Coca-Cola's 'the real thing' and 'Intel Inside' which drew benefit from the same message being stated in various languages but in the same well-recognized format all over the world.

As consumers increasingly begin to be addressed by the same marketer in a variety of different ways—through image-building advertising, public relations, direct marketing, sales promotions, point-of-sale material, collateral material (brochures and catalogues), and sales force calls—there is the obvious need to ensure consistency regarding positioning, message, and tone across these different media. Ideally, these different communications would all begin from the same vision of what the consumer is supposed to be hearing from the marketer so that they all operate seamlessly, reaching the consumer with one voice. This implies that the different marketing communications elements need to be created in a tightly coordinated manner by the different agencies and organizations (the PR firm, direct response agency, sales promotion firm, ad agency, client company).

Different communications begin from the same vision of what the consumer is supposed to hear from the marketer so that they operate seamlessly, reaching the consumer with one voice.

5.7.1 Advertising *v.* Public Relations

There is no 'best' way of communicating with customers. To debate about whether advertising is 'better' than public relations or personal selling is meaningless. Each method has its pros and cons, and depending on the circumstances, one may be more cost-effective than the other. Every marketing situation calls for its own special marketing mix and its own unique promotional mix. This mix is arrived at by considering what has to be communicated to which groups of people and then selecting the most cost-effective media to carry that particular message. As a general rule, personal selling is favoured as an element in the marketing mix when dealing with a few people buying a product of high unit cost; advertising comes strongly into its own with low-cost items sold to a mass market. But there are many other factors and many other promotional methods, each with its own strengths and weaknesses. Normally a range of methods will be used, and it then becomes important that they are carefully planned to operate in support of each other in an integrated campaign. Valid generalizations are few, but Table 5.1 can be used as a rough guide to rate some of the main methods of communicating with customers.

Every marketing situation calls for its own special marketing and promotional mix which is arrived at by considering what has to be communicated to which groups of people and then selecting the most cost-effective media to carry that particular message.

A marketer's consumer communication needs to raise brand awareness, create or change brand preference and image, and get sales trial or repurchase.

Table 5.1: Methods of communication

Marketing tools	*Believable*	*2-way*	*Fast*	*Cheap*	*Controllable*	*Action*
Word-of-mouth	✓	×	×	✓	×	✓
Personal selling	×	✓	×	×	✓	✓
Seminars	✓	✓	×	×	✓	✓
Advertising	×	×	✓	✓	✓	×
Sales promotion	×	×	✓	✓	✓	✓
Public relations	✓	×	×	✓	×	×

Notes: 1. In the table, a cross means 'No rather than Yes' a tick 'Yes rather than No'. The judgements are subjective ones and simply illustrate the kinds of assessment that have to be made – based on facts if they are available or judgement if they are not. 2. The criteria used are the following: **Believable.** Do the receivers of the message tend to regard the source as believable? **2-way.** Is there good communication back to the company. **Fast.** Does the message travel quickly from source to destination? **Cheap.** Is the cost per message received relatively cheap? **Controllable.** How much control does the company have over the message as received and **Action.** Is the message very likely to produce immediate action? 3. Seminars, in this context, are meetings to which prospective customers are invited to hear a technical presentation of new products or techniques. 'Hard sell' is kept minimum.

A marketer's consumer communication needs to raise brand awareness, create or change brand preference and image, and get sales trial or repurchase.

And it has to do all of the above at the same time. Improving image without getting a sales result is not good enough, nor is getting short-term sales (e.g. via sales promotion) at the expense of the brand's long-term image. Thus, it is argued that all marketing communication materials, particularly ads, should attempt to simultaneously achieve targeted communication goals (e.g. raising attitudes or building image) and lead to some behavioural action (e.g. trial or repurchase). To communicate successfully, a marketer should carefully plan his overall promotion strategy.

CASE STUDY

PROMOTION: THE ITC AND PEPSI WAY

ITC

A category-wise overview at the way ITC is promoting its products is revealing.

Cigarettes: ITC's promotional strategy is to create visibility in the marketspace. Since competition is minimal, the thrust here has been on keeping the distributors and retailers happy. Consumers in this segment exhibit strong brand loyalty, so it is imperative to have good relations with the distributors. The latter can serve as information collection centres for the company. Thus promotion is entirely through the distribution channel. An example of strong channel relationship and promotion strategy can be seen through the continuous increase in profits for the company even after a government ban on smoking in public places, and a law on putting a warning logo on all packets.

Non-cigarette FMCG segment: The company has adopted the usual strategy of promotion through advertising, celebrity branding and packaging. It leverages its strong distribution network and financial muscle power to introduce new products into the market. Backed with advertising, publicity and retail shop owners' support, the company has stormed into the FMCG sector. It has roped in Deepika Padukone (Fiama Di Wills), Amrita Rao (Vivel), Hrithik Roshan (John Players), among others, to attract customers.

ITC's ads for Bingo have been widely appreciated and have helped create awareness about the product. With good advertising the snack brand has quickly grabbed market share despite competing against well-established players like Frito Lays, Uncle Chips and Kurkure.

ITC's Point-of-Purchase Promotion through Special Product Shelves

More important than the standard promotion strategies through sales persons, retail shop owners and advertising is the implicit promise which the company makes to its consumers. ITC itself has evolved as a brand encompassing all the sub-brands it produces. Consumers are assured of quality when purchasing an ITC product and this is more important for any firm than a well-made television advertisement or a sales-driven strategy.

ITC has made continuous attempts to identify the latent needs of the consumers and create a niche for itself in the saturated FMCG segment.

The community social responsibility (CSR) initiatives taken by the company have earned it worldwide acclaim and have created a positive image in the market. The e-Choupal initiative is one of the examples of many CSR steps taken by ITC. It has helped the company immensely in brand building and creating value in the mind of the consumer.

PEPSICO

Providing the customers with convenient, easy-to-use, and innovative products is Pepsico's top priority. The company uses the following methods to achieve this:

Sales promotion: Use of incentives and gimmicks, e.g. competitions, prizes.

Sponsorship: Includes products sold under licence that promotes the brand.

Publicity: Advertisements in local papers or special promotional materials. Due to the cola wars, promotion and advertising have always been integral parts of marketing for both Pepsi and Coke. The popularity of its products has increased due to advertisements, especially due to endorsements from cricket players and Bollywood personalities.

Pepsi kicked off a rural campaign, spread over two months in November and December 2009. Decorated Pepsi vans would roll out into market and consumers buying a drink from these vans got to play a game and win prizes like t-shirts, autographed posters and calendars.

Advertising is being carried out through numerous channels. The channels used include newspapers, consumer magazines, television, direct mail, radio, business publications, and outdoor advertising. Pepsi also sponsors sports events and other mega events. Some of the popular advertisement campaigns in India are:

1990–1: *Yehi hai right choice Baby Aaha*.

1996–7: 'Pepsi: There's nothing official about it'.

1999-2006: *Yeh dil maange more.*

2007–present: *Yeh hai youngistaan meri jaan.*

Famous faces: celebrity endorsements have worked well for Pepsi

Slice, the fruit drink brand from the Pepsi stable, was launched in India in 1994 mainly because Indians are known to be very fond of mangoes. Initially it was launched just as a mango drink, but later a number of variants were introduced and Slice was used as an umbrella brand for all fruit juices. This cost Pepsi dearly and affected the Slice brand in the long run. Slice has chosen to target the younger generation as a whole rather than targeting kids. It has roped in the Bollywood diva Katrina Kaif as brand ambassador. It launched the first Aamsutra campaign during the summer of 2000 and the second in the summer of 2009.

The soft drink Mirinda is available in several fruit varieties including orange, grapefruit, apple, strawberry, raspberry, pineapple, banana, and lemon. In India the orange flavour is the most popular and Mirinda is the market leader in this segment, with a market share of 60 per cent. Asin was chosen as the brand ambassador for Mirinda in the southern market, exemplifying the brand values of mischief and vivaciousness. Mirinda recently conducted a promotional campaign to consolidate its position as market leader in Tamil Nadu. A new translucent packaging was also introduced.

Mountain Dew was launched in India in 2003. It is one of a kind product as the rival Coca-Cola has no concurrent product to take on Mountain Dew. In the international market the drink comes in many flavours but only the core product is being offered in India. Mountain Dew chose a bright green and red packaging because soft drinks are impulse buys and flashy, eye-catching colours help grab consumer attention. Since Mountain Dew targets the young 'adventurous' consumers, it associates itself with events like terrain racing, stunt biking, video games, and so on. In fact it has a contract with Microsoft X-Box 360 for its promotion through their games, but not in India since the Indian market is considered to be immature for this type of promotion.

On its launch in India in 2003, Mountain Dew positioned itself as an 'energy and exhilaration' drink. In 2009, its logo was changed from 'Mountain Dew' to 'Mtn Dew', though once again not in India since the product is still in the growth stage. In October 2008 Pepsi spent $1.20 billion on global brand revamp.

7Up was introduced as a lemon-flavoured, non-caffeinated soft drink though flavours like cherry, orange and raspberry were later added. However, in India only the lemon flavour is available. Recently 7Up launched a new variant called Nimbooz.

7Up was launched in India in 1992 along with its mascot Fido Dido. All the promotion strategies were based around this mascot. However this mascot could not connect with the Indian masses. In 2008, Bollywood star Mallika Sherawat was signed on as the brand ambassador.

Its positioning too underwent a change, from a cold drink to a 'lemony thirst quencher'.

Sources: Investors' Report of ITC Ltd. and PepsiCo India Ltd., January 2010.

5.8 Service Promotion

The key communication elements for service businesses are corporate design and word-of-mouth advertising.

Service promotion consists of messages designed to stimulate awareness of, interest in, and purchase of a firm's various products and services. Companies use advertising, sales promotion, salespeople and public relations to disseminate messages designed to attract attention and interest.

A key communications element for service businesses is corporate design, which refers to the consistent use of distinctive colours, symbols, letterings, and layout on such tangible elements as signages, retail store-fronts, vehicles, uniforms, and stationery to provide a unifying and recognizable theme linking all the firm's operations. Word-of-mouth advertising is another highly credible form of communication. It urges service advertisers to seek continuity over time through the use of recognizable symbols, spokespersons, slogans, trademarks and music.

Further, service delivery sites (such as hotels, hospitals and banks) often stand in prominent locations offering exposure to a broad audience. Memorable architecture and attractive signage can convey a variety of messages, from the overall image to highlighting a particular competitive advantage. When a business operates out of a retail storefront, as with restaurants or airline ticket offices, window displays can be used to promote specific services. The different communication elements that we have described are potentially powerful tools and may be expensive to employ. A key task for service marketers is to select the most appropriate mix of communication elements and within each selected item, specify the media vehicles to convey the desired messages efficiently and effectively to the target audience.

Well-planned and well-executed promotions represent an important tactical weapon to service marketers in their search for profitability and a competitive advantage.

Efficiency is essential if the marketer is to avoid needless waste of money. Well-planned and well-executed promotions represent an important tactical weapon to service marketers in their search for profitability and competitive advantage. Reduced demand outside peak periods poses a serious problem for service industries with high fixed costs, such as hotels. One strategy is to avoid lowering the list price too much and instead run promotions (which may have significant monetary value) in an attempt to stimulate demand without using price directly as a weapon; once demand picks up the number of promotions can be reduced or eliminated.

A carefully executed campaign should help the company to ensure that the target audience receives the message correctly within the available time and budget.

5.9 Additional Services Marketing Mix

The characteristics of the service process design and implementation which should be considered include the customer co-producing the service, difficulty in the visualization of the service, intangibility and perishability.

The peculiar characteristics of services make it very difficult for managers to market it by adopting the 4P framework. They find that customers are looking for evidence of the intangibles and also observing the process as the points of production and consumption are the same. Hence they recommended adding additional 3Ps in the form of process, physical evidence and people who operate the system. A proper understanding of the additional 3P framework will help marketers follow the traditional marketing mix variable.

5.9.1 The Process

The study of process—the way things are done and the steps taken to achieve the desired results—has been given considerable attention over the years in the areas of manufacturing, engineering and computer programming. The principles by which service delivery processes can be designed, implemented and monitored are really no different from those mentioned relating to the fields of manufacturing, computing, and so on. There are certain specific characteristics of the service process design and implementation, however, which should be considered. These characteristics include the customer co-producing the service, difficulty in visualization of the service, intangibility, perishability, and so on.

5.9.2 Physical Evidence

The physical setting of an exchange may be described in terms of 'atmospherics', including visual, olfactory and tactile perceptions.

An important factor that influences consumer satisfaction over a service exchange is the physical setting within which it occurs. While the physical setting may have an effect on the exchange of goods and services, it is suggested that the setting's symbolic value will have greater impact upon the evaluation of a service. This again is largely due to the relative absence of tangible product characteristics with which to assess the exchange of a service.

Kotler suggests that the physical setting of an exchange may be described in terms of 'atmospherics', including visual, olfactory and tactile perceptions. Noting that the physical environment has the potential to influence one's impression of the service, such characteristics as the colour or brightness of the surroundings, the volume and pitch of the sounds employed, the scents and freshness of the air, and the temperature prevailing at the time of exchange may all help to shape a consumer's feelings concerning a service rendered. In addition, the use of space and the style of furnishing, as well as the presence or absence of other 'cues' may provide the consumer with tangible indications of the service.

The service environment (or servicescape) consists of four dimensions: the physical facility, location, ambient conditions and interpersonal conditions.

The service environment (or servicescape) consists of four dimensions: the physical facility, the location, ambient conditions and interpersonal conditions. The physical facility includes the exteriors and interiors, consisting of the décor, furnishings and equipment. In addition to the physical elements, the servicescape includes the intangible elements or ambient conditions of the service environment such as temperature of the room and odours and noises present. The last component of the servicescape is the interpersonal conditions between customers and service personnel.

CASE STUDY — **MARKETING MIX OF SINGAPORE AIRLINES**

Singapore Airlines Limited (SAL) is the national airline of Singapore. Its operating hub is at Singapore Changi Airport and has a strong presence in South-East Asia, East Asia and South Asia. Singapore Airlines is the parent airline company of the Singapore Airlines Group of Companies. The airline is a subsidiary of the Singapore government's investment and holding company Temasek Holdings, which owns 54 per cent of the voting stock. Singapore Airlines, along with its subsidiaries, is engaged in passenger and cargo air transportation, air charters, airport terminal services, engineering services, training of pilots, and tour wholesaling and related activities.

A three decade-old airline like SAL has earned a lot

of brand equity amongst customers by way of its excellent service. Singapore Airlines is the first airline in the world to operate the A380, the world's largest passenger aircraft, which has won accolades from customers and commentators the world over. Singapore Airlines achieved a profit attributable to equity holders of $2,049 million for the financial year 2007–8. It recorded revenues of S$15,972.50 million (approximately $10,831 million) during the financial year ended March 2008, an increase of 10.2 per cent over 2007. The operating profit of the group was S$2,124.50 million (approximately $1,441 million) during the financial year 2008, an increase of 61.6 per cent over 2007. The net profit was S$2,049 million (approximately $1,389.40 million), a decrease of 3.8 per cent over 2007. The group primarily operates in East Asia. It is headquartered in Singapore and employs 30,088 people as on 31 March 2008. As suggested by Bernard Booms and Mary Bitner, SAL possess 7Ps, instead of the conventional 4Ps.

Product

This is the most basic and important part of the marketing mix. For an airline company, the flying experience is the basic service it provides. SAL provides ontime, smooth flying experience to its customers, and is especially popular in the long-haul segment. Some features which differentiate SAL here are that it is the first to incorporate new aircrafts into its fleet. It also has one of the youngest fleets. Its in-flight entertainment system is among the best in the industry which helps improve the customer flying experience.

Price

Singapore Airlines ranks among the world's best airlines with exceptional amenities and service but its prices are often cheaper than competition (although on some non-stop routes where they are the only ones flying the fares are slightly higher).

Place

Accessibility of services is the key differentiator here. SAL claims that 97 per cent of its tickets are booked online.

Promotion

SAL uses conventional advertising channels like television, print and Internet for its promotional strategy.

People

All the people who are directly or indirectly involved in the consumption/usage of service are an important part of the marketing mix. Knowledge partners, employees, management and consumers add significant value to the total service offering. The staff of SAL is well trained in offering world-class services.

Process

This involves the procedure, mechanisms and flow of activities by which services are consumed. SAL is fully automated in its operations, ticketing and baggage handling.

Physical evidence

This deals with the delivery and communication of the service to the customers. For an airline company, this would include the behaviour of the staff right from booking until the final see-off. The hospitality and service offered by the cabin crew are crucial service differentiators and have contributed to building the SAL brand.

Source: Investors' Report of Singapore Airlines Ltd., January 2010.

The servicescape can also affect employee attitudes and motivation levels. Individuals who work in a comfortable physical environment tend to have a better attitude towards work than employees who work in an undesirable physical environment. If employees are proud of the way a service facility looks they will take better care of it and will be motivated to be more productive for the company.

5.9.3 People

Customer satisfaction and perceptions of quality are often influenced by the actions of the service personnel.

The inseparable nature of services means that the human element forms an intrinsic part of the service package. People make the difference in service marketing. A Gallup survey of 6,000 consumers in the US found that 'people', the seventh P of the marketing mix, are by far the most important determinants of customer brand loyalty. Customer contact employees in the service industry serve in a boundary-spanning role or a role linking an organization or business with its environment through interaction between members of the organization and members of the environment.

Customer perceptions of quality are very often influenced by the actions of the service personnel. Levels of satisfaction or dissatisfaction depend on the way in which personnel deal with the specific needs and requirements of customers; steps taken by the service personnel in the event that some aspect of the service goes wrong; and by service which goes beyond the customer's expectations, usually by the personal actions of an individual employee. Empowering customer-contact employees has resulted in many service-related problems being solved quickly.

Internal marketing is treating a firm's employees with the same importance as external customers.

Internal marketing is nothing but treating a firm's employees with the same importance as the external customers, through proactive programmes and planning to bring about the desired organizational objectives by ensuring both employee and customer satisfaction. Internal marketing should also cover issues which are traditionally linked with other areas in an organization, such as human resources management.

Customer service is the critical element which internal marketing influences, whatever business or industry the organization operates in, and customer service is one of the most crucial aspects of an organization's competitive advantage.

Internal marketing is attracting increasing attention and growing recognition as an implementation tool for adoption by all organizations. The most advanced systems for developing marketing plans and strategies are worthless if the plan fails at the implementation stage.

To achieve both good service and the impression of being caring, companies must have employees who are focused on serving customers.

Many firms operate in more than one market, and these markets can be very different indeed. Even segments within the same market can have individual and distinctive characteristics. This means that most firms will have external marketing plans which will be continuously monitored and fine-tuned to suit changing market conditions, whilst the internal market may be changing either more slowly or at a greater speed. To achieve both good service and the impression of being caring, companies must have employees who are focused on serving customers. Strong customer service must be created, nurtured, and properly managed. Service firms today are critically examining their job descriptions to determine whether these descriptions coincide with the goals of the company. Creating a customer service atmosphere requires proper recruitment.

CASE STUDY — MARKETING STRATEGY OF HEAD & SHOULDERS

HEAD & SHOULDERS

Head & Shoulders is the world's leading anti-dandruff shampoo from Procter and Gamble Inc. It made its debut in India in 1997, vying for a share of the highly competitive Indian shampoo market estimated to be worth ₹1,800 crore.

When the brand was launched in India, the anti-dandruff market was in its nascent stage and dominated by Clinic All Clear. The high profile launch of Head & Shoulders fuelled the growth of this specialty market. Now anti-dandruff segment constitutes around 15 per cent of the total shampoo market.

STP STRATEGY

Segmentation

- Mainly used in urban and semi-urban markets.

- Also done on the basis of age groups.
- Different varieties for different hair like black hair/ shiny hair, and so on.

Target customer

- Men and women conscious of their hair and dandruff problems associated with it.

Positioning

- Extended positioning from anti-dandruff to 'soft hair + dandruff removing' proposition.
- It was able to differentiate itself from other shampoo brands by the introduction of a new formula called ZPT (zinc pyrithine) which has anti-fungal properties.

5Ps OF HEAD & SHOULDERS

Product

Product depth analysis of Head and Shoulders

- Head & Shoulders smooth and silky: Makes hair smoother and silkier.
- Head & Shoulders refreshing menthol: Removes scalp itch and provides a cool sensation.
- Head & Shoulders clean and balanced: Provides the right balance of cleaning and conditioning.
- Head & Shoulders silky black: Formula with Black Sesame and Walnut Extract nourishes hair and scalp to make black hair look silky.
- Head & Shoulders naturally clean: For cleaning up oil, dirt and grime on the scalp. H&S Naturally Clean transforms unhealthy, sticky hair into healthy, dandruff-free and naturally clean hair. Currently sold only in south and east India.
- Head & Shoulders nourishing Aloe Vera for dandruff-free, beautifully growing hair.

Packaging

- The product uses white and royal blue combinations as its base packaging which creates a positive impression in the minds of the consumer.
- The bottles are sleek, stylish and compact.
- Different colours for different varieties help consumers to recognize the brands easily.

PRODUCT MAP

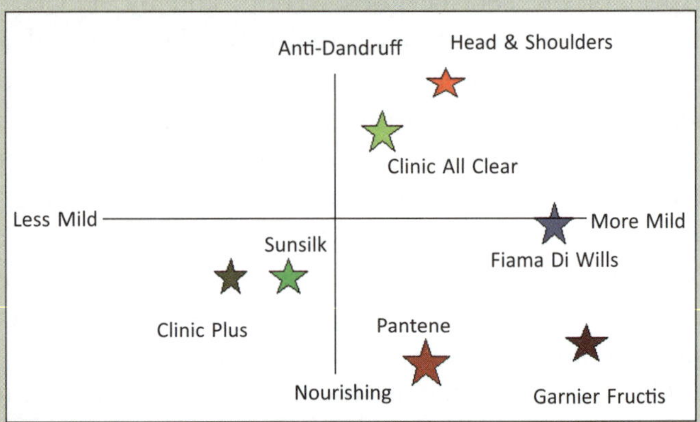

Pricing

Head & Shoulders is available in three different pack sizes—200 ml, 100 ml and 7.50 ml sachets with the 200 ml priced at ₹139 and the sachet at ₹3.

Place

The distribution of Head & Shoulders follows the conventional route of marketing; from distributor to the wholesaler to the retailer to the consumer.

Promotion

It roped in Bollywood actress Kareena Kapoor as its brand ambassador. The promotion campaigns emphasize on beautiful, long and healthy hair. It extensively uses attractive banners and hoardings for communicating the values of the brand.

Source: Investors' Report of Procter & Gamble, January 2010.

5.10 Post-economic Meltdown: 2009–11

The financial crisis in the US began spreading to the European and Asian economies in September 2008. The BSE Index came down to 8,752 points in October 2008 from the peak level of 21,000 points (in January 2008), then slowly revived and touched the 15,000 mark in June 2009. The global financial crisis has affected the liquidity of most business operations. Today's chief marketing officers (CMOs) confront a painful reality: their traditional marketing model is being challenged and they can foresee a day when it will no longer work. Companies all over the world have to look for quick cash inflows through promotions. So the case in point is effectiveness of ads in the traditional and electronic media.

The main media used for advertising are newspapers and magazines, television, radio, cinema, posters, hoardings and direct mail. Advertisements may also be put up on bus shelters, buses, road dividers, kiosks, balloons, and so on. The media vehicle chosen by a firm largely depends on the reach of that particular medium among the target audience. For example, a Food Bazaar or a Big Bazaar may advertise on a bus in a city, but a store like Beautiful Boulevard may advertise in an upmarket magazine.

The declining effectiveness of mass advertising is only the visible sign of distress. Marketers also face proliferation of media and distribution channels, declining trust in advertising, multitasking by consumers and digital technologies that give users more control over their media time. These trends are simultaneously fragmenting both audiences and the channels needed to reach them. The danger for marketers is that the change will render the time-honoured way of getting messages to consumers through TV commercials less effective at best and a waste of time and money at the worst. Among marketers, there's much frustration and little agreement about what to do next. Some are reaching for marketing-mix models that use sophisticated econometric methods to tease out the different effects of marketing mix on business results. But the historical data that fuels such techniques may prove an unreliable guide to future returns.

The effectiveness of mass advertising is on the decline due to proliferation of media and distribution channels, falling trust in advertising, multitasking by consumers and digital technologies that give users more control over their media time.

Marketers need a more rigorous approach to a fragmenting world—one that jettisons mentalities and behaviours from the advertising's golden age and treats marketing not as 'spend' but as the investment it really is. In other words, it will be necessary to boost marketing's return on investment (ROI). By adhering to the same investment principles that other functions follow, a CMO can improve the alignment between marketing and financial objectives, capitalize on a brand's most distinctive elements with greater success, target the consumer and media vehicles more precisely and yield the largest and fastest payoffs, manage risk more carefully, and track returns more closely. In short, a thoughtful and systematic application of investment fundamentals to marketing can help CMOs respond to the complex challenges they face.

5.10.1 The ROI Challenge

Today's ROI challenge has its roots in the halcyon days of mass advertising—the 1960s and 1970s. During these years marketers wrote the rules that still inspire many marketing investments or as some tellingly say, marketing spend. When network television was the king, marketers and advertising agencies rightly focused on the massive audiences that tuned into the most popular shows. The emphasis was on 'mass messaging': developing powerful advertisements that would imprint themselves on the minds of consumers. Many marketers based their TV spending on 'share of voice', which meant making sure that the advertising budget of a brand was in line with its market share, the spending of competitors, and the company's growth expectations. Plans for other media expenditures received less attention.

The golden-age marketers often relied on tools such as day-after recall (a metric tracking how well consumers remembered advertisements) and compared the results with internal benchmarks to assess the effectiveness of advertising copy. As it became clear that recall wasn't the best measure of creative effectiveness, companies developed more elaborate testing

The golden-age marketers often relied on tools such as day-after recall, the audience response system (ARS).

regimens such as the audience response system (ARS), a technique to determine the persuasive impact of new messages as compared with those of competitors. Meanwhile, more precise reach and frequency assessments made media-spending decisions better informed.

While the model worked well for consumer product companies such as Coca-Cola, Colgate-Palmolive, Procter & Gamble, and Hindustan Unilever, it wasn't perfect. Share-of-voice thinking and up-front media buys created considerable inertia about spending. What's more, the runaway success of TV-driven brand building meant that many marketers never really had to justify their budgets or develop metrics that made sense to businesspeople elsewhere in the organization. Indeed, the absence of consensus on how to define much less measure returns on marketing investments sometimes put the credibility of marketers at risk.

Nonetheless, in a world of largely captive audiences, effective messaging, plenty of growth, consistent consumer behaviour, and well-understood competition, the approaches perfected during the golden age worked very efficiently. They established priorities, managed risk, and measured the impact of spending on consumer attitudes. Indeed, the model worked so well for its pioneers that during the 1980s and 1990s, companies in industries such as pharmaceuticals, retailing and telecommunications began recruiting marketers from packaged-goods leaders and adopted their techniques.

5.10.2 Changing Market Scenario

Fragmenting media and changing consumer behaviour are forcing modern days marketers to interact with consumers in novel ways by focusing more on new media and mastering an environment where messages will have to 'pull' customers.

Fragmenting media and changing consumer behaviour are exposing the traditional model's limits. In India, the handful of TV channels has proliferated into more than 600 broadcast and cable TV channels. Consumers are increasingly selective about what they watch and the advertising messages they trust. Many researchers suggest that 65 per cent of viewers feel they are 'constantly bombarded with too much advertising', 69 per cent are 'interested in products and services that would help skip or block marketing', and 54 per cent 'avoid buying products that overwhelm with advertising and marketing'.

By 2010, MGI estimates that television advertising could be only 35 per cent as effective as it was in 1990. Although the impact of recent trends on B2B marketing is harder to measure, it is likely to be as similarly dramatic as marketing vehicles (such as sponsorship events and trade magazines) become less effective. And while television in some form will remain a formidable medium for many years to come, marketers of all stripes will also have to interact with consumers in novel ways by focusing more on new media (such as the Web and viral marketing) and mastering an environment where messages will have to 'pull' customers.

Setting goals, developing messages, and measuring results have thus become more difficult. Marketing expenditures come in an ever-expanding variety of forms, each with different target segments, payback horizons, and metrics for success. These differences make it harder to follow the old rules of thumb of budgeting, of focusing messages on building mass awareness or loyalty, of optimizing spending across a portfolio of brands, and identifying the segments most responsive to different marketing initiatives. As consumers become increasingly difficult and costly to reach, it becomes still harder to track the way they use media. At the same time, many marketers have observed a declining level of discipline in the way the potential impact of advertising is tested and its actual impact reviewed. Some think that in today's fragmented environment it has become more difficult to measure the impact of marketing programmes on jaded consumers. Others suggest that marketing units are too busy delivering messages across proliferating media channels to conduct campaign post-mortems. Jim Stengel, P&G's global marketing officer, observed that, 'Today's marketing model is broken. We're applying antiquated thinking and work systems to a new world of possibilities.'

5.10.3 Marketers' Response to the Change

Its time for marketers to be consistent in applying investment fundamentals such as clarifying the objectives of investments, finding and exploiting points of economic leverage, managing risk, and tracking returns that have long been well-established elsewhere in companies. Such principles of investment management, applied to the marketing function can create a coherent overview of a company's entire marketing outlay at a time of splintering audiences and media.

Following these principles will also help marketers make specific interventions at the points of economic leverage where ROI are highest, thereby mitigating the dilutive effect of a fragmenting environment. Smart marketers won't apply the principles blindly. Translating them to the marketing function calls for a subtle sense of the marketer's art.

5.10.4 Clarify Investment Objectives

Good financial advisers start by asking clients about their investment horizons, growth expectations and appetite for risk. Marketing investments should start with similar questions. Answering these questions helps align the goals of marketers with those of the company as a whole—essential if marketing is to be reconnected to the broader business objectives. If, for example, a company needs growth in contiguous businesses to meet its overall objectives, marketing must help more people accept the brand and expand its relevance to a broader set of products. IBM has shown the way by extending its brand through a consistent association with e-business.

The principles of investment management, applied to the marketing function can create a coherent overview of a company's entire marketing outlay at a time of splintering audiences and media. Optimization of investments can be done by distinguishing between 'maintenance' and 'growth' objectives for different segments and media channels.

To address the increasingly acute problem of optimizing a number of investments, each with different time horizons and measures of success, across brands and media channels, it's also vital to distinguish between 'maintenance' and 'growth' objectives for different segments and media channels. By maintenance, we mean the minimum spending required for a competitive presence in the marketplace. Although differentiating between these two types of investments can be tricky, the discipline involved in attempting to do so typically promotes a valuable internal dialogue that helps CMOs impose economic discipline. Over time, savvy marketers get better at categorizing investments, identifying the right maintenance levels for different categories, and allocating growth dollars to the products that they will yield the highest returns.

5.10.5 Find and Exploit Economic Leverage

For CEOs, the key to economic leverage is allocating capital to the businesses generating the highest returns. For marketers, economic leverage comes from aligning messages and spending with a brand's most compelling elements. By doing this, marketers target their message more precisely to the consumers using vehicles that provide the biggest and fastest payoffs. Finding and exploiting economic leverage helps marketers know how much it is worth to increase brand awareness as compared with brand loyalty, and which segments are most profitable and most responsive to marketing programmes at which stages of the consumer decision funnel.

The heart of this activity is the identification of brand drivers: the critical factors that influence a brand's image and consumer loyalty and that, if improved, increase revenues and profits. In an image-driven business, such as beer targeted at young men, the brand driver could be, 'This brand is irreverent' or 'I like to drink this brand when I am with friends.' In a more transactional business such as retailing, it could be, 'I get good service' or 'I found what I wanted'.

Brand drivers can be an integrated metric to determine whether a brand's media and message are effective and in line with the company's strategy.

Most marketers understand their brand's drivers, but few of them use these drivers rigorously enough to manage multimedia programmes, or assess the influence of particular drivers on specific customer segments at various points across the consumer decision funnel. Fortunately, proven analytic techniques such as structured equation and pathway modelling can help marketers assess the historical outcome of specific programmes to enhance brand drivers over time. In fact, brand drivers can be an integrated metric for determining whether a brand's media and message are effective and in line with the company's strategy.

5.10.6 Manage Investment Risk

Its difficult to boost returns in retail markets without assuming additional risks. But for most businesses, selectively reducing risk is a critical element to improve the ROI. A savvy strategist, for example, minimizes risk by staging them. Marketers whose risks were smaller when the media environment was more stable must now use similar tactics to keep risks in line. Even in a fragmenting world, marketers must push to ensure that they spend 75 to 80 per cent of their money on proven messages (such as advertising copy qualified by research) that are placed in proven media vehicles and supported by proven rupee levels (at or just above the threshold levels needed to influence customers). In these proven programmes, marketers should seek to regain the testing and validation discipline that many of them once had. The remaining 20 to 25 per cent of spending should finance well-structured experiments.

The best way to diagnose a retail marketing organization's ROI discipline is to assess the extent and quality of the media and messaging tests in progress at any given time.

One of the best ways to diagnose a retail marketing organization's ROI discipline is to assess the extent and quality of the media and messaging tests in progress at any given time. Some will be simple, such as testing higher levels of expenditure on new media for a proven message, reducing the frequency of mailings to see if the response rates change, and testing a new advertising message in a particular region. Others, such as a simultaneous test of a new message and new media for a growing segment of profitable customers, are bigger departures from the routine. Retail marketers who skimp on experimentation may be overtaken by changing media patterns or forced to assume large risks by rolling the dice on unproven programmes when markets shift.

The recent success of upstart brands such as Red Bull in building consumer awareness through trade promotions, sponsorships, and word-of-mouth demonstrates the power of alternative approaches. Yet fruitful as they can be, shifting the bulk of an established marketing plan to them is probably too risky.

5.10.7 Track Investment Returns

The idea that to boost ROI it is necessary to measure it carefully might appear simplistic, but this approach can be a major departure for companies that take a narrow view of their spending or measuring success. Recording all expenditures and ensuring that marketers direct the right messages to the right consumers can make a big difference.

Although marketers could formerly evaluate just the rupees in their marketing budgets, its now vital to consider all of the marketing plan's expenditures, including, at a minimum, all sponsorships, major media, and sales collaterals. Many companies should also integrate sales promotion activities and store-level spending (particularly retailers, banks, and consumer telecom companies). The act of recording total expenditures and of ensuring that marketers direct the right messages to the right consumers can make a big difference. For example, the realization by a leading European mobile services provider that it had unintentionally been focusing too much on its existing customers led to changes in the budget process.

Making expenditures transparent is a necessary but insufficient step. While all marketers track their progress, few measure it end-to-end by following the trail all the way from the effect of spending on a brand's drivers to the influence of those drivers on consumer loyalty and the influence of loyalty on revenues and margins and, finally, to the question of whether any increase in profits justifies the spending. Only with an end-to-end view can marketers understand not only the current returns on marketing programmes but also, and equally important, why they did or didn't work and the information needed to improve future returns.

Most CMOs are prepared now to begin pulling the levers that will improve their returns. They should start by integrating the existing research and data sets (such as test results, segmentations, consumer decision funnels, and spending analyses). This can become the basis of a unified approach to boosting ROI through the steps discussed below:

Step 1: Build transparency by identifying (and including in marketing plans) all the critical buckets of consumer communications spending, even if they are not in the marketing function's domain.

Step 2: Isolate the most important drivers across brands and track the drivers' impact across segments and media channels.

New technologies, new modelling approaches and changes in mindsets and behaviour as derived from the golden age need to be recognized. Unless an organization's mindset and behaviour evolves, efforts to improve marketing's ROI will not succeed.

As marketers dive into the issue of ROI, they also will recognize opportunities for selective investments in new tools, capabilities and relationships. Exciting developments lie on the horizon. New technologies are beginning to track and link the detailed elements of consumers' media exposure with their actual purchasing behaviour. New modelling approaches are creating more integrated 'what-if' simulators by combining econometric tools with analyses of brand drivers revealed by consumer research. Third parties such as ad agencies, research providers and media companies, which must also struggle with the changing environment, may be willing to collaborate in new ways.

Beyond tools and techniques, marketers need to change the mindsets and behaviours derived from the golden age. The requisite transformation represents a major challenge for most marketing organizations, agencies and media partners. One company, for instance, had to make a series of changes to its processes, culture, and people to reinforce and embed ROI thinking in its day-to-day marketing approach. Some changes were symbolic, such as using a hard-nosed analysis of returns to dump a 'sacred-cow' sponsorship the CEO favoured. Others involved formal training for marketers on the goals they should target and the tools and processes they should use. The company's business planning processes, performance assessments, and team structures had to change as well. Unless an organization's mindset and behaviour evolves, efforts to improve marketing's ROI will not succeed.

Marketers aiming for strong returns should start seeing themselves as investment managers of their marketing budgets. That may be more difficult and time consuming than relying solely on old rules of thumb or new analytic approaches, but it is the only answer in today's marketing environment.

5.11 Summary

- A good marketing promotion mix effectively combines the components of advertising, sales promotion, public relations and personal selling.
- The communication methods of a marketer can be classified as impersonal or personal, and paid or unpaid, on the basis of the functions of the promotional programme—informing, persuading, and reminding. Thus, there are four types of communications: paid impersonal, paid personal, unpaid impersonal and unpaid personal.
- Advertising can be used to build a long term image for a product. It can be done by using any form of media like television, radio, or print. The major advantage is its ability to reach a large audience at a very low cost.
- Sales promotion is a form of attracting the consumers by offering them benefits in the form of incentives or by adding value to the product. Examples are coupons, discounts, rebates, samples, and so on.
- Publicity is a non-paid form of communication about the firm's market offering, like news articles in papers or reports on television or radio. Public relations helps to create a positive opinion about the firm in the market. The company can develop its public relations with several members of groups such as suppliers, customers, employees, shareholders, and so on. It produces positive results in the long run.

- Personal selling involves selling a product or service directly to the consumer by explaining or demonstrating its features to him/her. It is highly specific with regard to its target audience and helps to get immediate feedback from customers. Its disadvantage is the high cost involved in employing salespersons. In direct marketing, the retail marketer communicates directly with the customers through mail or telemarketing or marketing through the Internet. Its advantage is that it is highly cost effective and gives maximum mileage. The response can be easily measured, so success or failure can be known without too much effort.
- Every day, more and more businesses are looking at service and support globalization as an opportunity to improve customer satisfaction, operational productivity and efficiency. A successful identity system, combined with a planned image management system, will assist the service organization in managing change and remaining flexible in its response to changing market conditions, competition and innovation. Implementing a corporate identity system is also a useful way of changing a company's image by providing a catalyst for the initiation of internal and external reforms vital to successful marketing and the creation of highly efficient and flexible service organizational structures.

CHAPTER 6 

GROWTH STRATEGIES DURING DOWNTURN AND RECOVERY

We embarked on consciously building Virgin into a brand which stood for quality, value, fun and a sense of challenge. We also developed these ideas in the belief that our first priority should be the people who work for the companies, then the customers, then the shareholders. Because if the staff are motivated then the customers will be happy, and the shareholders will then benefit through the company's success. — RICHARD BRANSON

The Backdrop

Is the slowdown finally over? In the second half of 2010 all large cap stocks were riding a high price equity ratio. Even the mid-cap shares were expensive and IPOs were oversubscribed a couple of times on the very first day. Hiring employees had restarted, though most of it can be classified as replacement hiring and not job creation. Across the board, in manufacturing and in services, there seemed to be cause for cheer. The Big Three IT firms of the country had bagged orders worth billions of dollars from new clients. And IIP numbers had been on the rise with substantial improvements and car sales were robust.

Despite these positive indications, there are worries that if the world economy doesn't recover as quickly as the Indian economy seems to be doing, the momentum cannot be sustained. Let us look at growth strategies companies can adopt during turbulent times.

This Chapter Will

- *Discuss the framework for growth strategies, the various models of portfolio analysis, and alternative growth strategies during downturn.*
- *Discuss the pattern of growth—life cycle analysis for new products, listing the common characteristics of market life cycle stages.*
- *Discuss the framework for devising best growth strategies during downturn including growth in existing product markets, increasing usage in existing product markets and product development for the existing market.*
- *Discuss the finding synergy in various corporate growth strategies.*

6.1 Framework for Growth Strategies

The impact of the recession was not the same across all economic sectors. For example the two-wheeler and the cruiser bike segments witnessed tremendous growth.

The impact of the recession was not been the same across all economic sectors. Look at the Indian two-wheeler industry, estimated to be the second-largest market for consumption and production of two-wheelers in the world. The Indian two-wheeler makers produce about 7.5 million vehicles annually, and the sector is said to be growing at a CAGR of approximately 12 per cent. It is also a sector that is relatively insulated from the global crisis due to a booming domestic market. It holds a relatively large, untapped potential due to a large and as yet virgin rural market.

However, customer tastes are changing and the two-wheeler industry has had to adapt in order to survive. The change is glaringly seen in the fast-expanding electric scooter market that reflects the increasing climate awareness in the country. Electric bikes are expected to expand sales in the two-wheeler market, some even predicting a 200 per cent expansion in the two-wheeler market.

Another major growth area is that of niche segments like cruiser bikes. The Indian cruiser market is estimated to be bigger than what was previously projected and is anticipated to grow fast with the impact of the recession behind. Many global majors are also interested in shifting their manufacturing and back-end to the Indian market to lower costs.

In business it is not enough to be simply profitable; companies must sustain their growth.

In business it is not enough to be simply profitable; companies must also grow. In fact, if they don't grow, they won't be profitable for long. Staying with the same customers, products, and markets is a recipe for disaster. Investors want to see a growing top line; employees want opportunities to advance; and distributors want to serve a growing company. Growth is energizing. The maxim 'If you stand still, you get shot' is very true for business.

Companies often excuse their lack of growth by saying that they are in a mature market. In truth, there's no such thing as a mature market. What companies need are mature executives to find ways to grow. Table 6.1 shows the strategies companies can adopt to grow and the pitfalls of each strategy.

Table 6.1: Steps taken by the companies

S.No.	*Steps taken to grow*	*Problems*
1	Cost/Price cutting	Matched and neutralized
2	Aggressive price increase	Difficult to pass on during sluggish economic times
3	International expansion	Most international markets are highly competitive or protected
4	Acquisition	Expensive
5	New products	Number of new product winners are few

Take the case of plastic money. Only 12 per cent of the total market uses credit cards even though many more have the capability to use them. What companies fail to realize is that their markets are rarely penetrated. HDFC Bank recognized this and created the Silver Card, Gold Card, Titanium Card, Platinum Card and the Platinum Plus Card in the Visa and Mastercard categories. In order to grow, a company can make segment moves as shown in Table 6.2.

Table 6.2: Growth by segment moves

S.No.	*Segment moves*	*Example*
1	Move into adjacent segment	Nike—Athletics—Basketball—Tennis
2	Do a finer segmentation	Nike—Basketball shoes—Aggressive player, high jumping player
3	Enter new segments	Nike moved into selling clothing tied to various sports
4	Resegment the whole market	Reebok resegmented the market by introducing stylish shoes for the leisure market that could be worn everyday without a sport in mind

Another growth approach is to redefine the market in which the company operates. Jack Welch once said, 'Redefine your market to one in which your current share is not more than 10 per cent.' For example, Coca-Cola had 35 per cent share of the soft drink market but it had only 3 per cent share in the beverage market and needed to grow. This thought should serve as an inspiration for companies to grow. Generally, growth strategies can be summarized under four heads:

Growth strategies include market penetration, product and market development and diversification.

(a) **Market penetration:** Sell more of the current products to the current customers. This means encouraging customers to consume more per occasion or consume on more occasions.

(b) **Product development:** Sell additional products to the current customers. Identify other products that the current customers might need.

(c) **Market development:** Sell more of the current products to new customers. Introduce current products into new geographical areas or into new market segments.

ECONOMY WATCH — THE INDIAN TWO-WHEELER INDUSTRY

The Indian two-wheeler market can be divided into three categories. The motorcycle segment is the largest and comprises about 77 per cent of the entire sales of the auto manufacturers.[1] There are about five major players in this segment and new global majors are expected to enter the market soon with higher-end. For example Harley-Davidson entered the Indian market in 2009, catering to the upwardly mobile Indian consumer.

Mopeds are a small part of the two-wheeler mix at present at about 5 per cent of the entire market. But the annual growth rate of this segment is the highest among all the two-wheeler segments and has been pegged at 24.7 per cent[2] albeit on a smaller base. The announcement of the entry of Mahindra and Mahindra into this mix is expected to increase the competition. Mahindra and Mahindra bought out Kinetic Motors and has forayed into this lucrative segment.

The scooter market is the second-largest in the two-wheeler industry and comprises about 13 per cent of the entire market. This represents a massive fall for the scooter market that dominated the two-wheeler category in the mid-1990s. Scooters however grew at a rate of 13.7 per cent in 2008–9 and with the entry of new players like Piaggio, it is hoped that the fortunes of the scooter market will undergo a revival.

The rural market in India is as yet largely untapped by the two-wheeler manufacturers as compared to the urban market which is expected to reach maturity sometime in the near future. The number of two-wheelers per thousand is about 211 in the rural markets whereas it is about 644 per thousand in the urban markets.[3] Thus rural India has the potential to be a major growth area for the Indian domestic market. All the two-wheeler manufacturers in India are planning to take advantage of this factor and it is expected that the rural market will continue to grow for many years to come, thus providing the auto majors with a growing market to offset the expected decline in the urban markets that are expected to mature about six to seven years since 2010. One important factor to keep in mind while considering the rural market in India is that it is largely agriculture based and the monsoons play a very large part in determining the sales.

Notes: [1]SIAM (Society of Indian Automobile Manufacturers). All percentages include sales of three-wheelers also; [2]SIAM; [3]Credit Analysis and Ratings (CARE) Research.

Source: The Economic Times, January 2010.

(d) **Diversification:** Sell new products to new customers. Acquire or build new businesses that cater to new markets.

6.2 Models of Portfolio Analysis

6.2.1 BCG Growth-Share Matrix

Undoubtedly the best known approach to portfolio analysis, the Boston Consulting Group's (BCG) Growth-Share Matrix involves Strategic Business Units (SBUs) being plotted on a matrix according to the rate of market growth and the SBUs' market share relative to that of the largest competitor. In using these dimensions as the bases for evaluating the product portfolio, the BCG forces the management to give explicit consideration both to the future potential of the market (i.e. the annual growth rate) and to the SBUs' competitive position. Having plotted the position of the SBUs, the health of the portfolio can be seen fairly readily. A balanced portfolio typically tables certain characteristics, including a mixture of cash cows and stars. In contrast, an unbalanced and potentially dangerous portfolio would have too many dogs or question marks and too few stars and cash cows; the likely consequence of this is that insufficient cash will be generated on a day-to-day basis to fund or support the development of other SBUs. Let us look at the fourfold categorization of the BCG Growth-Share Matrix.

BCG Growth-Share Matrix involves Strategic Business Units (SBUs) being plotted on a matrix according to the rate of market growth and the SBUs' market share relative to that of the largest competitor.

A. Dogs (Low Share, Low Growth)

Dogs are those businesses that have a weak market share in a low-growth market. Typically they generate either a low profit or return a loss. The decision faced by the company is whether to hold on to the dog for strategic reasons (e.g. in the expectation that the market will grow, or because the product provides an obstacle, albeit a minor one, to a competitor). Dog businesses frequently take up more management time than justified and there is often a case for phasing out (shooting) the product.

Dogs have a weak market share in a low-growth market and generate either a low profit or return a loss.

B. Question Marks (Low Share, High Growth)

Question marks are businesses operating in high growth markets but with a low relative market share. They generally require considerable sums of cash since the firm needs to invest in plant, equipment and manpower to keep up with market developments. These cash requirements are, in turn, increased significantly if the company wants to improve its competitive position. These businesses are called question mark because the management has to decide whether to continue investing in the SBU or withdraw from the market.

Question marks are businesses operating in high growth markets but with a low relative market share and generally require considerable sums of cash.

C. Stars (High Share, High Growth)

Stars are products which have moved to the position of leadership in a high-growth market. Their cash needs are often high with the cash being spent to maintain market growth and keep competitors at bay. As stars also generate large amounts of cash, on balance there is unlikely to be any positive or negative cash flow until such time as the state of market growth declines.

Stars are products which have moved to the position of leadership in a high-growth market. But they have high cash needs in order to maintain leadership position.

At this stage, provided the share has been maintained the product should become a cash cow.

D. Cash Cows (High Share, Low Growth)

When the rate of market growth begins to fall, stars typically become the company's cash cows and generate considerable sums of money.

Hero Honda is the leading two-wheeler manufacturer in the world.

When the rate of market growth begins to fall, stars typically become the company's cash cows. These products generate considerable sums of cash for the organization, but because of the lower rate of growth, use relatively little cash. Economies of scale are often considerable here and profit margins high.

Two further groups of SBUs have been identified by H.C. Barksdale and C.E. Harris. These are war-horses (high market share and negative growth) and dodos (low share, negative growth). Figure 6.1 shows the BCG matrix of Hero Honda. Hero Honda began as a joint venture between India's Hero group and Japan's Honda company in 1984. They both own 26 per cent of the company shares each. Today, Hero Honda is the leading two-wheeler manufacturer in the world. It has introduced new-generation motorcycles that focus on fuel thrift and low emission. It has held onto the position of 'largest two-wheeler company of the world' for eight consecutive years since 1995. The company has shown continuous growth over the years and was one of the few companies to enjoy a flat sales curve even during recession. Hero Honda has crossed the ten million units milestone over a span of 19 years and has added an additional 5 million in another five years since 2009. As the economy treads the path of recovery, it is hopeful to successfully continue its stint. According to Brijmohan Lall Munjal, chairman, Hero Honda Motors, the company has pioneered India's two-wheeler industry and steered it through difficult times; now it is Hero Honda's responsibility to set the pace again.

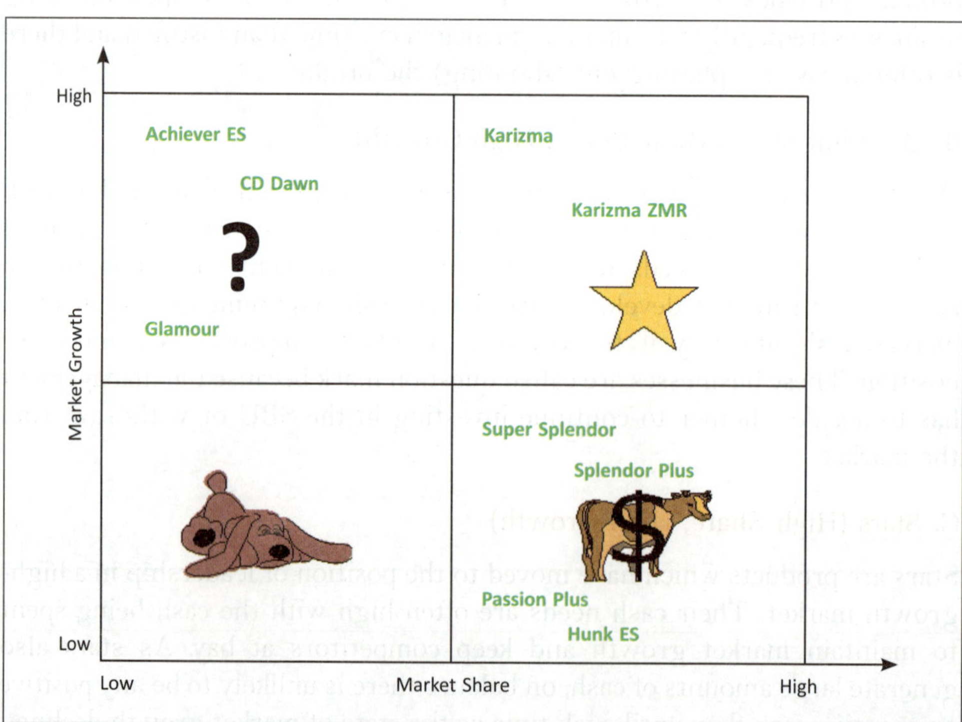

Figure 6.1: BCG matrix of Hero Honda

CASE STUDY — BCG MATRIX OF TAJ HOTELS

The Indian Hotels Company Limited (IHCL) consists of 60 Taj and Gateway hotels in India, 15 international Taj hotels and 17 Ginger hotels in India. The Taj hotels are high-end luxury hotels and generate the maximum revenue for the company. The Gateway hotels focus on the upper middle class and the Ginger hotels are economy hotels aimed at the middle class.

For IHCL, the Taj hotels are stars as they have high market share. But the investment in this segment is also high. However, the company should continue investing since the Taj Group has the potential to turn into a cash cow. In this stage the growth rate is low but the business generates revenues and captures a large market share.

The Ginger and Gateway hotels are in the 'Question Mark' section of the BCG matrix. Their growth rates are high but market shares are low. The Indian middle class is growing at a steady rate which will help both these hotels to grow in the future. So the company should focus on opening more Ginger hotels across tier I, II and III cities so as to increase market share. The company can fund the Ginger and Gateway hotels from its existing businesses operations.

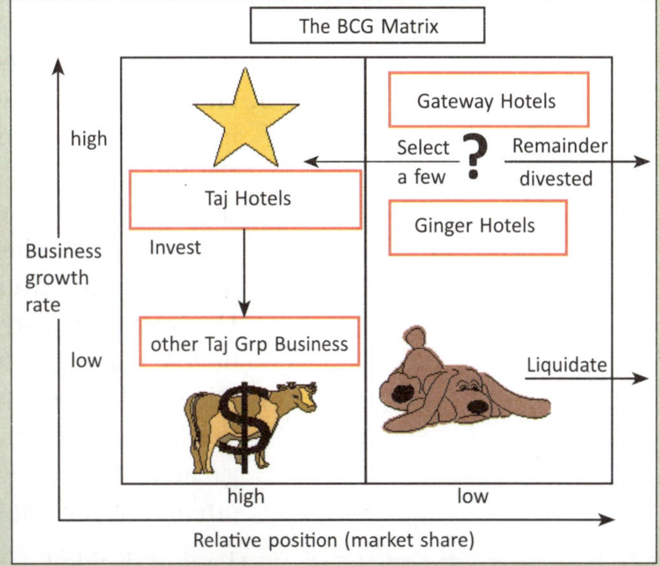

Source: Investors' Report of Indian Hotels Company Ltd., January 2010.

CASE STUDY — BCG MATRIX OF NESTLÉ

The BCG matrix for Nestlé India identifies the products which have a strong potential to grow and those products whose market share is dwindling. Nestle's strength has always been its prepared food products and chocolates business. The products in this category, especially Maggi and Kitkat, have been star performers. Maggi with its new launches like Atta noodles and Cuppa Mania has tremendous potential to grow.

Nestlé is a strong player in the beverage market and is continuing its good show. It has also been trying some innovative ideas like creating an 'out-of-home' segment. Nestle consumption zones, cafe outlets and vending machines in offices, colleges and other locations that experiences footfalls is proving to be a good strategy.

In the chocolates segment Nestlé enjoys high market growth but relatively low market share. Kitkat is reporting good sales volume in 2010. The company is also a leader in the Eclairs and fruit/mint roll categories. Well-targeted consumer advertising is required to make these brands more vibrant. In the coming years, Nestlé needs to focus on consumer insights, innovation, renovation as well as improved distribution for a good performance on the key brands.

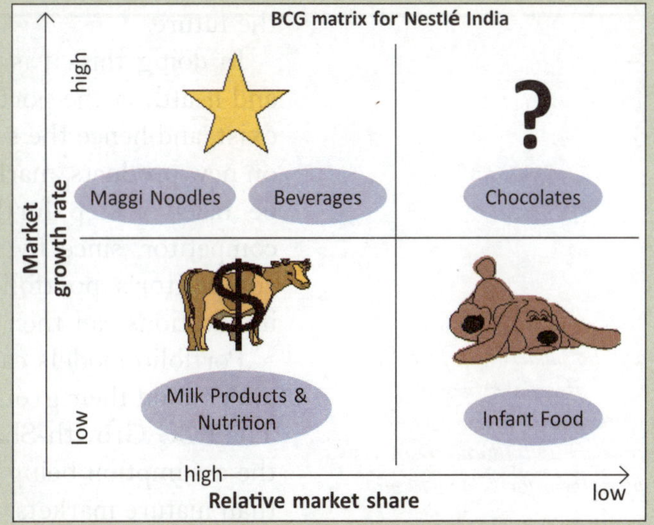

Source: Investors' Report of Nestlé India Ltd., January 2010.

Having identified the nature of the portfolio, planners needs to consider the objectives, strategy and budget for each SBU. In essence, four major strategies can be pursued:

Strategy suitability includes: Build—question marks, Hold—cash cows, Harvest—weak cash cows, divest—dogs and question marks.

1. **Build:** The primary objective of a building strategy is to increase the SBU's market share in order to strengthen its position. In doing this,

short-term earnings and profits are deliberately forsaken in the expectation that long-term returns will be far greater. It is a strategy best suited to question marks so that they become stars.

2. **Hold:** The primary objective in this case is to maintain the current share. It is typically used for cash cows to ensure they continue to generate the maximum amounts of cash.
3. **Harvest:** By following a harvesting strategy the management tries to increase short-term cash flows as far as possible, even at the expense of the SBU's longer term future. It is a strategy best suited to cash cows that are weak or which are in a market with a seemingly limited future. It is also used when the organization is in need of cash and is willing to mortgage the future of the product in the interest of short-term needs. Harvesting is also used for question marks when where there appear to be few real opportunities to turn them into stars, and for dogs.
4. **Divest:** The essential objective here is to rid the organization of SBUs that act as a drain on profits or to realize resources that can be used to greater effect elsewhere in the business. It is a strategy which again is often used for question marks and dogs.

BCG Matrix is used to analyse how SBUs have developed and how they are likely to develop in the near future.

Having decided which of these four broad approaches to follow, the strategist needs to give consideration to the way in which each SBU is likely to change its position within the matrix over time. SBUs typically have a life cycle which begins with their appearance as question marks and their progression through the stages of star, cash cow, and finally dog. It is essential therefore that the BCG matrix is used not simply to obtain a snapshot of the portfolio as it stands currently, but rather that it is used to see how SBUs have developed so far and how they are likely to develop in the future.

In doing this, it is possible to gain an impression of the probable shape and health of the portfolio in several years' time, any gaps that are likely to exist, and hence the sort of strategic action that is needed to make decisions on new products, marketing support, and product deletion. This process can be taken a step further if similar charts are developed for each major competitor, since by doing this the strategist gains an insight into each competitor's portfolio strengths, weaknesses, and potential gaps. The implications can then be fed back into the organization's own strategy.

Portfolio models help firms that operate diverse businesses, to understand their group of businesses and allocate resources among them for a long-term.

Portfolio models can help firms that are operating diverse businesses, to understand their group of businesses and to allocate resources among them. The BCG Growth-Share Matrix rates markets on the basis of their growth, the assumption being that growth markets are more attractive investments than mature markets. Market position, indicated by relative market share, is also crucial to an experience curve-based strategy. The resulting matrix has four quadrants that define an SBU as star, cash cow, dog, or problem child. The baseline strategy is to use cash generated by cash cows, selected dogs and problem children to fund embryonic businesses, promising problem children, and any stars requiring investment in excess of their own cash flow.

Limitations of the BCG Matrix

BCG matrix limitations include a focus on cash flow, sensitivity to market and product definitions and an inability to predict market attractiveness.

Among the model's limitations are the fact that the experience curve is not always relevant or easy to work with and the growth dimension is inadequate to reflect market attractiveness. Other limitations include measurement of market share, which is extremely difficult.

The sensitivity to the product and market definitions is another drawback. As the definition of the market changes so does the market share. For example, Pepsi's market can be considered either as carbonated drinks or as beverages. Choosing either one definition will lead to a different market share. The BCG matrix has also been criticized for focusing on cash flow and for the difficulty of implementing implied strategies.

We have to opt for better versions of the portfolio model to understand the above changes in the market.

ECONOMY WATCH — ECONOMIC AND TECHNOLOGICAL ANALYSES OF THE TWO-WHEELER INDUSTRY

It is a fact that the global economic recession of 2008–9 has adversely affected businesses worldwide. Some of the factors that have affected the two-wheeler industry are as follows:

- **Recovering economy:** The economy appears to be recovering and this has translated into higher sales for the industry during 2010–11.
- **Low monsoon:** A low monsoon in most parts of the country has affected rural consumers adversely and might decrease automobile sales in the second half of 2009 but compensated in 2010.
- **Sixth Pay Commission:** Payment of the Sixth Pay Commission arrears to government servants has increased their spending power thus increased the sale of automobiles in 2009.
- **Exchange rates:** The dollar has been falling steadily, thus making dollar realizations less valuable for automobile manufacturers during meltdown.
- **Emerging economies:** The emerging economies are one of the biggest sources of future growth for automobile manufacturers.
- **Raw material prices:** The prices of raw materials like steel tend to be cyclical and are a major source of concern for the industry.
- Further, the **technological revolution** has put more power in the hands of the consumers. Thus it is very important to analyse the technological aspects of the auto environment.
- **DTSI:** This has been one of the most important innovations in the last decade giving Bajaj Auto an edge in the market.
- **Electric bikes:** The advent of electric bikes in a large number is expected to be a game changer in the auto industry.
- **Chinese engines:** The availability of inexpensive Chinese engines can also be a factor in the near future.
- **Better servicing:** Better use of technology has also helped in better servicing of the products.
- **Smaller PLC:** The product life cycle has decreased drastically with the advent of newer technologies.
- **Emission norms:** Indian emission norms are becoming tighter and more in tune with global norms. The Indian two-wheeler industry has been subjected to specific Indian norms which according to SIAM are one of the most stringent in the world. One result of the Kyoto Protocol has been the phasing out of two-stroke engines and tighter emission norms.

Source: SIAM, January 2010.

6.2.2 Industry Attractiveness-Business Position Matrix

The BCG portfolio model is deliberately simplistic in that it focuses on cash flow and uses only two variables, growth and share. General Electric planners, reacting to the limitations of the BCG model, developed the industry attractiveness-business position matrix, drawing upon portfolio approaches used by the consulting firm McKinsey. The structure of the matrix is shown in Box 6.1.

BOX 6.1: BUSINESS POSITION MATRIX STRUCTURE

The industry attractiveness-business position matrix is richer and therefore potentially more valid but also more ambiguous and less reliable. Both industry attractiveness and business position assessments are made on the basis of as many factors as appear relevant in a given context such as size, growth, share by segment, customer loyalty, margins, distribution, technology skills, patents and marketing.

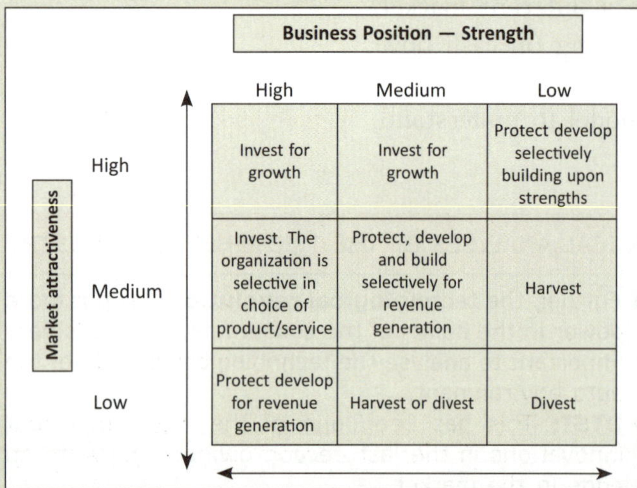

The Directional Policy Matrix (DPM) is similar in structure. It is associated with a more quantitative approach toward determining the position of an SBU in the matrix. A numerical value is generated for each SBU reflecting its position in the matrix. The numerical value reflects the SBU's competitive capability and its market position.

The DPM also offers more specific baseline strategy recommendations and is associated with a proposal to add environmental-risk assessment as a third dimension to the portfolio models. Both are more suitable for use with groups of businesses within SBUs, or divisions.

A study of the Fortune 1,000 companies revealed that over a third of them use portfolio analysis to some extent. The keys to successful application were the definitions of SBUs, the use of a portfolio matrix, the de-emphasis on labels such as dog or cash cow, and the use of the framework to assign growth and financial objectives.

A useful exercise is to attempt to predict whether the firm under study's position or the attractiveness of the industry will change assuming the current strategy is followed. In the Indian scenario, one can see how Reliance Retail is cornering competition and pocketing market share by splitting the company into 34 new entities. RIL understood the fact that the country's 6 million rich population shops worth US$ 28.36 billion every year. More than 80 per cent of the 12 million retail outlets in India are small family businesses that use only household labour. India has the highest retail densities in the world at 6 per cent (912 million shops for nearly 209 million households). That modern retail has entered India can be seen in the sprawling shopping centres, multistoried malls and huge complexes offering shopping, entertainment and food all under one roof. Reliance Industries Limited (RIL) took the right step of investing ₹25,000 crore over a period of five years to tap this market. But public protests, especially from traders (*kirana* stores) made the company think a different route.

Now Reliance Retail is splitting into 34 companies for anchoring more in retailing and overcoming the public protest of traders. Some of the important verticals that the company is looking at hiving off into separate profit centres in the initial phase include the hypermarket Reliance Mart, health and wellness chain Reliance Wellness, consumer durables format Reliance Digital, lifestyle chain Reliance Trends and the footwear chain Reliance Footwear. The company's food and grocery chain Reliance Fresh has already been hived off into a separate company called Ranger Farm (formed in December 2007).

Similarly, take the case of Harley-Davidson's foray into India. Harley-Davidson is an American motorcycle manufacturing company that started its operations in 1903 in Milwaukee, Wisconsin. It specializes in selling heavyweight motorbikes which are known to be a delight on highways. Harley-Davidson bikes is rolling out in India from its base in Gurgaon. Despite stiff import tariffs imposed by the government, the company is planning to launch its products and has started to finalize dealers in Mumbai, Delhi, Bengaluru and Hyderabad. The bikes are priced from ₹4 lakh to ₹14 lakh. The company for now plans to import the bikes and accessories. It is certainly worth waiting to see how this giant performs in India.

BOX 6.2: HARLEY-DAVIDSON AND GE MATRIX

If Harley-Davidson applies the GE matrix, it should invest selectively for growth in new markets like India and China. While entering new markets, it should be kept in mind that tastes and preference of customers change as borders are crossed. Furthermore, in a market like India where cultural diversity is among the highest, more cautious investments should be made. However, given the market size of India and China, it is recommended that Harley enter these markets, especially since the heavyweight motorcycle segment is mostly free (in India, Harley's only possible competition is from Enfield).

Harley-Davidson needs to delve into new markets to increase its customer base. The US market no doubt gives a huge brand loyalty to Harley, but it is saturated, given the fact that 42 per cent of the sales of Harley are repurchases by existing customers. The company is also targeting markets like Europe, which is one of the biggest motorbike markets in the world along with emerging markets like India and China.

6.3 Pattern of Growth: Life Cycle Analysis for New Products

The existence of imitative products/services and the emphasis of management on such products cannot be ignored. This may be due to the recognized marketing gap hitherto unfilled by existing producers, or product deficiencies or identified consumer dissatisfaction with available products in the market. The super-cautious attitude of management towards innovation, which may be due to fear and high cost of product failures may also be a reason for increased emphasis on imitative new products. Just like a human being passes through different stages of the life cycle, a product in the market should also pass through different stages from introduction to decline and possible abandonment.

The concept of product life cycle indiscriminately applies both to innovative and imitative products. The noted stages of a product's life cycle include introduction, growth, maturity and saturation, decline and possible abandonment.

The noted stages of a product's life cycle include introduction, growth, maturity and saturation, decline and possible abandonment.

BOX 6.3: ALTERNATIVE STRATEGIES

1. **Invest to hold**: Attempt to stop erosion in position by investing enough to compensate for environmental and competitive forces.
2. **Invest to penetrate**: Aggressively attempt to move the position up, even at the cost of earnings.
3. **Invest to rebuild**: Attempt to regain a previously held position that has been lost by a milking strategy which, for whatever reason, is no longer appropriate.
4. **Selective investment**: Attempt to strengthen position in some segments and let position weaken in other segments.
5. **Low investment**: Attempt to harvest the business, drawing cash out and cutting investment to a minimum.
6. **Divestiture:** Sell or liquidate the business.

ECONOMY WATCH — **OVERVIEW OF THE SCOOTER MARKET**

The Indian two-wheeler industry was traditionally a scooter market. However, in the 1990s it witnessed a gradual migration towards motorcycles. The Indian motorcycle market is growing at a faster rate compared to the scooter market. In 2007, out of every 100 two-wheelers sold in the country only 12 were scooters. That number went up to 16 in 2008 and 20 in 2010. There's more: the scooter market grew in double digits in 2008, outperforming the two-wheeler market as a whole which grew 2.6 per cent in the same period. The golden days of the early 1980s, when scooters had 64 per cent market share, are still far away. But the revival signals are strong.

The market leader in the scooter segment is Honda Motorcycle and Scooter India Private Limited (HMSI), the wholly-owned Indian subsidiary of Honda Motor Company Limited, Japan. The Honda entered the Indian market with the launch of the Honda Activa, a 100 cc scooter. HMSI followed need-based segmentation, based on the fact that people found conventional scooters too big and difficult to handle but the mopeds too small. Activa filled that gap perfectly. The target consumers for Activa were families and working women.

Activa's competitors were TVS, Hero Honda and Mahindra Kinetic. But Activa positioned and differentiated itself with its easy handling, better ride quality and excellent engine. Honda moved away from convention by adopting a new strategy of segmentation—creating a segment within two existing segments. In 2008, Honda launched the 125cc Stunner CBF intended for not the conventional 125cc segment but between the 125cc and 150cc segment.

Honda is going to exit from the geared scooter segment in India by 2010. It has already phased out its 150cc Eterno as the company plans to focus on the gearless segment. HMSI is looking at 18 per cent growth in two-wheeler sales in 2010–11.

Mahindra and Mahindra's foray into the two-wheeler segment began with ₹110 crore plus 20 per cent stake in Kinetic Motor Company Limited (KMCL) in July 2008. It was a strategic move for M&M to associate itself with a company with a rich legacy in the two-wheeler segment. For Mahindra, two-wheelers are an additional touch-point for consumers' association with its products and services in a nascent stage of the 'personal transport solutions' value chain. This will give an opportunity for M&M to gain visibility in every household, given the company's dominant presence in the rural and semi-urban segments. Moreover, the focus on more inclusive growth and improvement in rural transport infrastructure will only expand the demand trail and increase two-wheeler incursion into semi-urban and rural areas as well.

Its stringent quality checks will exemplify the company's high standards. The company's technological partners in this segment are Italy-based Engines Engineering and Taiwan's Sanyang Industry Company Limited (SYM). These associations along with Mahindra's strong in-house R&D team have resulted in a perfect blend of style and power in the company's products.

Mahindra's strategy is to market a range of scooters, value-engineered motorcycles and high-end motorcycles. In keeping with this strategy, the company introduced the Flyte as its first two-wheeler offering across all markets in India in April 2009. In September 2009 it launched two other products, Mahindra Rodeo and Mahindra Duro. Rodeo has been projected as a power scooter targeted at the young urban male youth. The feature-packed scooter has a distinctly macho demeanor. It offers the comfort and convenience of a scooter coupled with the thrill and power of a motorcycle. The Duro has the largest fuel tank in the scooter segment, the widest wheelbase for better stability and a generous storage space. This ergonomically designed scooter incorporates a wider seat and better legroom for maximum comfort and good ground clearance to help the rider tackle rough roads.

The three scooters of M&M are priced in the same range as the Hero Honda Pleasure and TVS Scooty Pep, which are 5 to 6 per cent cheaper than market leader Honda Activa, even though they have an engine that is 12 to 18 per cent larger. These are also 8 to 12 per cent cheaper than Suzuki Access. The pricing strategy (low inaugural prices) seems to be similar to the strategy Mahindra adopted for the Scorpio, the point being that prices can be ramped up once the brand is well known in the marketplace.

SNAPSHOT OF SCOOTER MARKET

1. Activa		• First scooter model released by HMSI. • Marketed as a family vehicle. • Recommended for its practical and conservative styling, ease of use, better ride quality and excellent 102 cc engine.
2. Dio		• Stylish version of the Honda Activa, having almost the same technical specifications. • Engine is slightly more powerful. The Dio is targeted at young people. Honda calls it India's first 'motoscooter'.

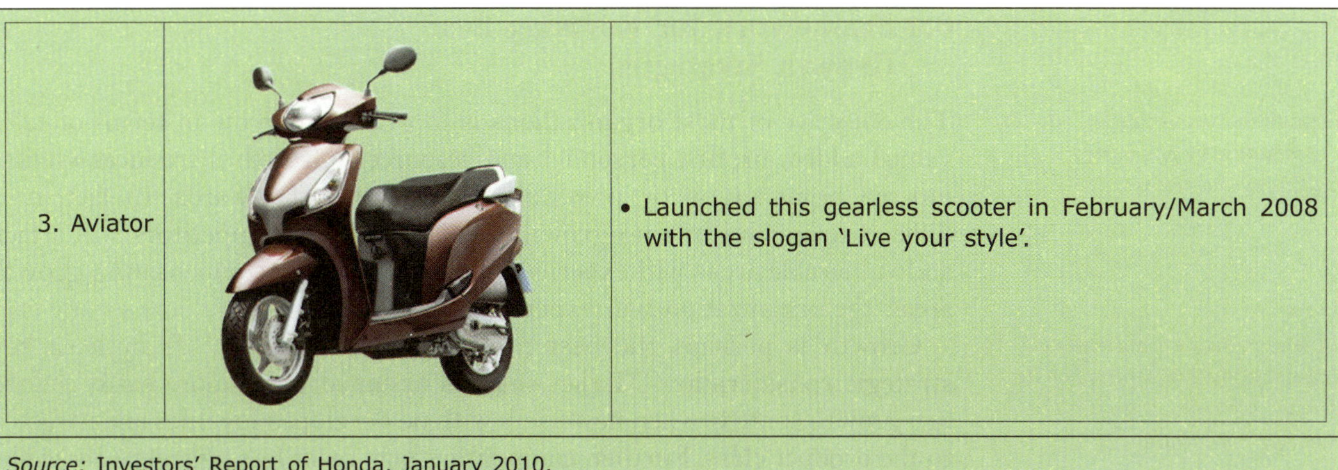

3. Aviator		• Launched this gearless scooter in February/March 2008 with the slogan 'Live your style'.

Source: Investors' Report of Honda, January 2010.

Table 6.3: Common characteristics of market life cycle stages

	Life cycle stage			
Characteristics	*Introduction*	*Growth*	*Maturity*	*Decline*
Overall market growth	Building rapidly but on a small base	Faster than GDP	Equal or less than GDP	Decreasing
Product technology	High level of major product innovation, dominant designs not yet established	Dominant design emerges, emphasis placed on product variety	Small incremental innovations, many based on cost savings *v.* performance improvement	Little or no charges in product
Production technology	Emphasis placed on flexibility, process not fixed until dominant design emerges	As dominant design emerges, production process can become more specialised	Emphasis on efficiency, most likely stage for automation	Little or no charges in process
Pricing patterns	Prices are high but volatile	Prices decline rapidly as costs fall and competition rises	Prices decline slowly as productivity	Prices low, but stable
Promotional efforts	Target innovators and try to build awareness of product	Build brand awareness	Tailor promotion to a variety of market segments	Limit market, largely depend on inertia to maintain viable level of sales
Entry and exit	A few pioneers begin to explore the market	Many firms scramble to enter what appears to be a promising market	As market is saturated, growth slows an shakeout begins	A few survivors remain to serve the market
Nature of competition	Limited, focus is often inward, looking toward product rather than toward competitors	Growth may mask success of competitors	Competitive rivalry peaks as competitors try to survive the shakeout	As shakeout is completed survivors seek to de-escalate competition
Capital investment requirement	Substantial, needed to support initial creation of business and/or product	Peak period, needed to fund growth	Reinvestment as needed to maintain viability	Minimal, may in fact 'disinvest' by selling off assets
Profitability and cash flow	Unprofitable, substantial negative cash flow	Profitable, but cash flow may still be negative	Profits declining, but larger investment level may mean cash flow is strong	Profits are low, cash flow is small (either negative or positive)

6.4 Framework for Revising Best Growth Strategies

Growth introduces vitality into an organization by providing challenges and rewards.

The objective of most organizations is to grow—to grow in terms of sales valued added, profits, personnel and resources. Growth introduces vitality into an organization by providing challenges and rewards. In fact, it is difficult to survive in a no-growth scenario because competitors will attack and vulnerable areas will experience decline. With no compensating growth areas, the organization will experience losses.

In terms of market share growth is perhaps the best measure of the product life cycle, hence is a key strategic consideration.

Growth is perhaps the best measure of the product life cycle, a key strategic consideration. Market share is assumed to be more easily gained in a growth context when new users with no developed loyalties are attracted to the product class. Further, competitors may react less aggressively to the loss of new customers than to the loss of their base of existing customers. Share gain is important in part because of its link to the experience curve. A market position in a growth market will be worth more in the future as the market grows, assuming the position can be retained. It is normally easier to retain market share than to gain it.

ECONOMY WATCH — MARUTI SUZUKI INDIA RETAINS OMNI AND MARUTI 800

Engineers at Maruti Suzuki India Ltd. (MSIL), the country's biggest car maker by volume, can upgrade the engine that powers Maruti 800 to comply with the Bharat Stage (BS) IV emission norms set to kick in by April 2010. In April 2009, MSIL had issued a statement declaring that the M800 would be phased out from 11 cities by 2010 and the entire country by 2015-16 due to its inability to upgrade the engine owing to cost factors. According to I.V. Rao, managing executive officer (engineering), MSIL, the company can do some after-treatment on the engine of the M800 which will help it take on the BS IV norm. The decision of phasing out the car lies completely with the MSIL marketing team. If they find it unviable, they will have to stop its (M800's) production.

Additionally, another MSIL dark horse—the Omni—was also set to be phased out around the same time in 2010. However, the spurt is demand for the vehicle, which is classified as a multipurpose vehicle (MPV), has prompted the company to roll back its decision. Both the Omni and the M800 share the same 796cc, petrol-fired, 3-cylinder MPFI engine, with two valves per cylinder. However, the M800 is calibrated for extra power at 37 bhp, while the Omni delivers peak power of 35 bhp. According to company officials, the Omni will continue to remain under production even as its engine gets fine-tuned to adhere to the new emission regulations.

It is noted here that a large chunk of M800 sales come from the rural and semi-rural markets, where the car figures as the 'first buy' in many families. The cost of ownership of the M800 and Omni are the lowest in India and around the world. Due to its low cost of running and the easy availability of spare parts at affordable prices, both cars continue to give Maruti respectable numbers every month, although there has been a huge decline in late 2008. The M800 sells about 2,500-3,000 units every month, while the Omni sold about 5,000 units in mid-2009. Launched in 1983, the M800 has sold over 2.7 million units and was the highest selling car for MSIL until recently when the Alto took the lead.

Source: The Economic Times, May 2009.

In a growth market, demand often exceeds supply; excess demand will support premium prices and profit levels.

In a growth market, demand often exceeds supply; excess demand will support premium prices and profit levels. By aggressively entering into a growth market and establishing a sustainable competitive advantage, a firm can discourage competitors from entering the same market.

CASE STUDY

GROWTH STRATEGY OF HERO HONDA

Look at Hero Honda's strategy in the Indian market. As mentioned earlier, Hero Honda was an early entrant in the four-stroke two-wheeler segment and hence gained the first mover advantage. Honda has been known for its technological excellence in the automobile sector and this has translated into the development of technologically-sound, environment-conscious, fuel-efficient and high quality two-wheelers.

Hero Honda is predominant in the motorcycle segment of two-wheelers with presence in scooters through Hero Honda Pleasure. Its market segmentation is based on price, age group and engine capacity. Traditionally the two-wheeler market has been segmented into Economy/ entry Segment (100cc), Executive Segment (125-135cc) and Premium Segment (150cc and above). Hero Honda has motorcycles in all the three segments. Though the entry segment has been shrinking, the market share of Hero Honda (35 per cent) in this segment has only grown, indicating that sales of all manufacturers in this segment has reduced. In the Executive Segment, which is the largest segment in the motorcycle industry, Hero Honda continues to maintain a stronghold with its share growing to 50 per cent. In the Premier Segment, the share of Hero Honda increased by 8 per cent in 2008 and accounts for close to 24 per cent of the segment in 2009.

Hero Honda launched new Splendor+ and Hunk in 2009. Splendor+ has been priced at ₹40,000 whereas Hunk is tagged with a price of ₹56,676 (in 2009). The Splendor is targeted at office goers who want a bike with good mileage and minimum maintenance. Passion is targeted at the younger generation that has an eye on fuel efficiency. Hunk is targeted at youngsters who are looking for a bike with a macho image. Karizma is targeted at the elite group who are ready to spend extra. Pleasure is Hero Honda's only scooter targeted at the working women.

Each of Hero Honda's products is positioned strategically to meet the needs of the target group. Initially, the company's famous tagline 'Fill it, shut it, forget it' tried to attract those who gave importance to fuel economy. The recent tag lines position the bikes differently. The punch line of Karizma is 'Always game', CBZ Extreme is 'Thinking is such a waste of time' and Hunk is positioned to emphasize its macho looks. The Pleasure has been rightly positioned for the urban Indian women with the catchy tagline 'Why should boys have all the fun?'

The expansive dealer network of Hero Honda is clearly one of its biggest assets. The company is known for its reliable after-sales service. Its bikes are regarded as the most fuel efficient (good mileage) and their resale value is high compared to that of competitors. The reason for this is the easy availability of spares and authorized mechanics. The implementation of mySAP CRM and mySAP SRM has improved order execution efficiency and responsiveness and thus enhanced the company's competitive edge.

Hero Honda has always been aggressive in advertising and often associates itself with sporting events. It has gained a lot of visibility by sponsoring the Delhi Daredevils team though the initial expenditure did cause a dent in the first quarter of 2010 profit margin. It sponsored the India Australia 2009 cricket series and also hosted the 2009 edition of the Indian Open Golf at the DLF Golf Club, Gurgaon. It is the title sponsor of the reality show MTV Roadies, which is all set for its fifth edition in 2010. The show served as a perfect platform to project the Hero Honda Karizma and associate it with masculinity and power. Earlier, in 2005, it was the title sponsor of the music reality show *Sa Re Ga Ma Pa*.

The company's 'Fill it, shut it, forget it' advertising campaign went a long way in emphasizing the great mileage that these bikes provide. The *Dhak dhak go* and *Desh ki dhadkan* campaigns, on its 25th anniversary, were a huge success which helped reinforce the fact that the world's largest two-wheeler manufacturer was India's pride. It has roped in Hrithik Roshan as its brand ambassador; earlier represented by Sourav Ganguly.

The company spends ₹130-₹140 crore on advertising and wants to make rural India its focus. However, Hero Honda's rural sales have ridden more on word-of-mouth publicity than advertising. Research has showed that the company's target age group is between 18 and 35 years of age and their four primary interests are cricket, adventure, music and movies. Hero Honda responded to the findings and roped in brand ambassadors from cricket and Bollywood.

Hero Honda recognizes that customer satisfaction is among its top priorities. It launched a unique CRM programme called Hero Honda Passport by which every rupee spent by a member translates into reward points. In an attempt to increase customer satisfaction, the company in July 2001 increased its warranty period to two years. The company website has an exclusive customer care section which gives details and tips about identifying genuine parts of Hero Honda. It has a separate section on service and maintenance and another one for rider education, which provides tips for maintenance and achieving fuel economy.

Hero Honda in the process of introducing a low-cost motorcycle by 2010–11. In 2009, the cheapest model of Hero Honda was priced around ₹31,000. It is planning to introduce a model in the price range of ₹25,000. With the entry of brands like Harley-Davidson into the Indian two-wheeler market, Hero Honda is bound to face tough competition in the coming years. However, the company receives its technology power from Honda's strengthened R&D plant in India and in Japan. With technical collaboration agreement between Hero and Honda renewed until 2014, the company is likely to continue its past growth, since the leading edge Honda technology has been vital in the success of the company in the Indian market.

Source: Investors' Report of Hero Honda, January 2010.

CASE STUDY — DABUR'S VISION 2010

Dabur has maintained its leadership position in the FMCG market in India and delivered consistent results. Although the economy has been growing rapidly over the last five years, all has not been well for the FMCG industry. There were several complex challenges facing the sector. On the revenue side, there were periods of industry-wide slump in demand. For example, 2003–4 saw both the shampoo and toothpaste segments recording negative growth, and others growing at low single-digits. Since then, while the demand conditions have improved, there have been many new entrants in terms of companies and products across several categories, making competition extremely intense.

On the distribution side, it has been a tough task for all FMCG players to reach out to consumers deep in India's heartland—the upcountry rural space that now represents new demand opportunities in the country. There has also been the all-important task of continuously providing value propositions for consumers who have been exhibiting rapid changes in preferences and tastes. On the inputs front there has been regular pressure in the form spiralling costs of several key raw materials, mainly primary goods and petroleum and petroleum-based products. Thus, there have been several external pressures to dampen top-line and profit growth for FMCG companies in India.

In 2010, Dabur has remained resilient and has leveraged opportunities to deliver superior results over the last five years. In doing so, the company has steadily transformed itself to remain ahead of the changing times.

From 2002 to 2006, Dabur has recorded a compound annual growth rate of 18 per cent in net revenues, and even more satisfactorily, a compounded growth rate of 33 per cent in profit after tax. After the successful implementation of the four-year business plan from 2002 to 2006, Dabur has launched another plan for 2010. The main objectives of the Vision 2010 plan are:

- Doubling of the sales figure of 2006 (₹1,757 crore). (This has already shot up to ₹2,080 crore in 2007 and ₹2,468 crore in 2008.)
- Focusing on expansion, acquisition and innovation. Although Dabur's international business has done well—growing by almost 29 per cent to ₹292 crore in 2006–7, plans are to increase it by leaps and bounds.
- Growth will be achieved in international business, homecare, healthcare and foods.
- Southern markets will remain the focus area to increase its revenue share to 15 per cent.

The first phase saw DIL implementing a fourfold strategy whose key elements were:

- Emphasis on driving higher growth by drawing on its core strength of being India's most well-recognized herbal specialist company.
- Focusing on five key brands—Dabur, Vatika, Anmol, Hajmola and Real—and backing these up by new and innovative product launches, stronger advertising and higher marketing spends.
- Substantially streamlining and strengthening the distribution network.
- Undertaking organizational changes to drive efficiencies and synergies across all its FMCG brands.

The aim was to transform an Ayurvedic products company into a rapidly growing, modern FMCG player rooted in the herbal tradition—one that would embody all the characteristics of a FMCG company while creating a niche for itself with a herbal-based product portfolio. There was thus a clear focus on positioning Dabur as one of the FMCG leaders in India.

Today, as the company is poised to move into its next phase of business opportunities and challenges, it is useful to step back and reiterate the key elements of Dabur's long-term growth story. It consists of two building blocks: strategic impetus and execution thrust. On the strategic front, there were two distinct phases: the first one between 2003–4 and 2005–6, while the second one commenced in April 2006 with clear milestones until 2010.

All of this was backed up by excellence in execution. Six of the company's brands record sales of over ₹100 crore each. Dabur has a portfolio of over 350 products that are sold through a distribution network which reaches out to over 2.50 million retail outlets. And the company has been rated as one of the three most-respected FMCG companies in India (*Business World*, March 2007).

The first phase of the journey has been successfully completed. As targets were met, an organization-wide transformation began to take place. In the course of this makeover, the experience and skills that the company developed in marketing and brand management, sales and distribution, manufacturing and purchase, supply-chain and finance put it in a position to take on far greater challenges.

In April 2006, Dabur embarked on its next strategic phase and unveiled 'Vision 2010'. The focus of this initiative is to continue the rapid growth in revenue and profits leveraging three key strategic drivers—expansion, acquisition and innovation. In this roadmap, while Dabur will continue to be positioned as a herbal specialist leveraging its knowledge and credentials, it will also widen its business canvass by extending its products and organization capabilities to service the entire 'health and wellness' space. Vision 2010 is designed to address the changing macroeconomic trends in India.

As India grows, there are some distinct transformations happening within the Indian consumer class. Much of India's growth has come from higher levels of consumption expenditure. Between 2003–4 and 2007–8, private consumption expenditure increased at a CAGR of 6.9 per cent. The growth in private consumption raised real per capita private consumption by 23 per cent in a space of four years—from ₹13,918 per annum in 2003–4 to ₹17,145 per annum in 2007–8.

With the growth in per capita consumption, many areas in the vast Indian upcountry, which were hitherto non-viable markets due to relatively low purchasing power, have started becoming important demand centres. Dabur's DARE initiative has a special focus to tap such rural markets.

Simultaneously, there has been a disproportionate growth in consumption spends among the higher income groups. According to the National Sample Survey Organisation (NSSO), the top 20 per cent accounts for 45 per cent of the consumer market in India. Their significantly greater spends have opened up new opportunities at the higher end of the FMCG market—a segment that focuses on quality, global trends and the finer elements of life. This is a fast growing and an increasingly profitable market. It also has positive spillover by creating a demonstration effect on the middle income groups, thus raising their aspirations as well.

There is a steady shift in structure of our population towards younger ages. According to the Census of India, the proportion of population in the age group of 15-19 years has increased from 10.1 per cent in 2001 to 10.7 per cent in 2006. Similarly, the 20-24 year age-group's share has increased from 8.9 per cent in 2001 to 9.3 per cent in 2006. While these changes are not dramatic in percentage terms, they mean a lot in actual head count terms.

Given these macro-level developments, it is clear that the Indian consumer class has become younger and more affluent. They are much more conscious about their lifestyle, health and well-being. As a 'herbal specialist', Dabur was already focusing on regular therapeutic cures to health-related issues. It is only natural for the company to connect closely with the new set of Indian customers and extend its offerings across the larger and wider 'health and wellness' space. In pursuing Vision 2010, while the company continues to develop its traditional markets, which are primarily in second tier cities having a close affinity to Ayurvedic products, it has recognized the imperative to devise products and propositions that appeal to a more affluent and younger Indian consumer. The company is in the process of re-orienting itself to meet this challenge. Thus, about 15 different brands and products have been relaunched in the last two years, coupled with completely revamped communication and packaging. Moreover, recognizing that customers are increasingly becoming more discerning, the company has made concerted efforts to promote the efficacy of its products through clinical studies. The idea is that the customer must be provided scientific proof to realize the effectiveness of Dabur's products.

EXPANSION STARTEGY

Entering new categories

- **Skincare:** New Ayurvedic skincare range under a new brand to be launched.
- **OTC healthcare:** Leveraging Ayurveda knowledge for developing OTC portfolio.
- **Fruit drinks:** Entry into the fast-growing fruit drinks category leveraging the real franchise.
- **Home care:** Expansion of air fresheners, insect repellants and hard surface cleaners.

Targeting inorganic opportunities

- **Market entry:** Acquisitions critical for entry into new markets and building scale in existing categories.
- **Synergies:** Should be synergistic and make a good strategic fit.
- **Geographies:** Domestic and global opportunities.

Strong innovation programme

- **Contribution:** New products to contribute 5-6 per cent of revenues.
- **Focus categories:** New product activations lined up in all categories.
- **Renovation:** Packaging renovations to keep older products salient.

Expanding across geographies

- **Overseas markets:** 19 per cent of overall company sales target to sustain higher growth rates.
- **South India:** Increased contribution from 6 per cent to 10 per cent; targeting 15 per cent of domestic revenues.

Considering how Dabur sailed through its previous plans, this vision seems possible. Time and again, the company has made decisions that have led to its present position. However, if it could adopt a more aggressive approach, it can rise to unprecedented levels.

Source: Investors' Report of Dabur India Ltd., January 2010.

6.5 Growth in Existing Product Markets

Growth can be achieved in existing product markets by increasing share through capture of sales held by competitors or increasing product usage among existing customers.

Existing product markets are often attractive growth avenues. The firm is established with a base upon which to build and momentum that can be exploited. Further, the firm is experienced and knowledgeable so that resources, especially human resources, are already in place. Growth can be achieved in existing product markets by increasing share through capture of sales held by competitors. Alternatively, product usage among existing customers can be increased.

6.5.1 Increasing Market Share

Strategic Competitive Advantage (SCA) can be achieved by offering products involving enhanced customer value or by overcoming or neutralizing a competitor's SCA.

Perhaps the most obvious way to grow is to improve market share. A share gain can be based upon tactical actions such as advertising, trade allowances, promotions, or price reductions. The problem is that share gain by such means can be difficult to maintain. A preferred approach is to generate a more permanent share gain by creating a Strategic Competitive Advantage (SCA) involving enhanced customer value or by overcoming or neutralizing a competitor's SCA. Thus, the need is to create or enhance one's own assets and skills and neutralize those of competitors.

6.5.2 Increasing Product Usage

Attempts to increase market share will very likely affect competitors directly and therefore precipitate competitor response. The alternative of attempting to increase usage among current customers is usually less threatening to competitors.

6.5.3 Increasing Frequency of Use

A product can change its image from an occasional to a frequent use product by a repositioning campaign. Asking why customers do not use the product or service more often can lead to approaches for making product use easier. Incentives such as low price can increase consumption frequency. Sometimes there are good reasons why a customer is inhibited from using a product more frequently. If such reasons can be addressed, usage may increase. For example, some people might believe that frequent shampooing might not be healthy. A mild shampoo product that is designed to be gentle enough for daily use might alleviate the worry and stimulate increased usage.

Table 6.4: Increasing usage in existing product markets

Approach	*Strategy*
Frequency of use/consumption	Reminder communication Position for frequent use Position for regular use Make the use easier or more convenient Provide incentives Reduce undesirable consequences of frequent use
Level of use/consumption	Reminder communication Provide incentives Influence norms Reduce undesirable consequences of increased use level Develop positive associations with use occasions
New applications for existing products	Use at different occasions Use at different locations Different functions

6.5.4 Increasing the Quantity Used

The marketer can make conscious efforts to affect the usage level norms of the people with apt promotions and advertising.

A fastfood restaurant like McDonald's, for example, might attempt to increase the number of items purchased during lunch by bundling items and providing them at discounts. The marketer can make conscious efforts to affect the usage level norms. For example, the size of a 'normal' serving in a pub might be changed by creating a large glass or container and getting it accepted while serving the draught beer (unfermented beer whose product life is only 24 hours). The perceived undesirable consequences of heavy consumption of such a product might be addressed by initiating such modification with free food.

Take the case of Maggi. The global FMCG major Nestlé SA's Indian subsidiary Nestlé India launched Maggi in five flavours—Masala, Chicken, Capsicum, Sweet and Sour, and Lasagna. Maggi had to fight hard in the early 1980s to be accepted by Indian consumers with their hard-to-change eating habits. In the initial years, Nestlé's promotional activities for Maggi included schemes offering gifts (such as toys and utensils) in return for empty noodle packs. Its advertisements with the taglines 'Mummy *bhookh lagi* (Mom, I'm hungry)', '*Bas do minit* (Only two minutes)' and 'Fast to cook, good to eat', became part of Indian advertising folklore. Maggi's popularity was also attributed to its 'extremely high appeal' to children. The brand successfully used the kids' 'pester power' to get mothers to buy Maggi. Soon, mothers got used to the convenience offered by the product and children got used to its taste. Interestingly, Maggi gradually began to be consumed by people across age segments, even though it was always positioned as a children's product. As a result, Maggi's annual growth reportedly touched 15 per cent during its initial years.

6.5.5 New Applications for Existing Products

Finding new applications is particularly important for a declining industry in need of revitalization or when a new, unfamiliar technology is involved and a market needs to be created.

New applications are often uncovered by asking when and where the usage is occurring. Can new times or places be introduced? Fruit juice flavours have been introduced in the blended tea market, and coffee drinks like cardamom coffee are part of the business strategy to move from the highly competitive breakfast-only beverage business to a more specialized business of drinks positioned for times other than breakfast. Finding new applications is particularly important for a declining industry in need of revitalization or when a new, unfamiliar technology is involved and a market needs to be created.

Intel, the first company to market microprocessors, conducted a massive education campaign for its new product. It distributed booklets with descriptions of actual applications and conducted hundreds of seminars presenting the marketing potential of the technology as well as the technical details. In 2010 the Intel Centrino Core 2 Duo Processor is a hallmark of reliability.

The identification of new application areas demands creativity and an in-depth understanding of the customers and the market. One approach is to survey customers directly or through the salesforce to determine the nature of the applications. The output could be a long list of applications. Consider business computers, for example, which may involve several general categories of application and numerous specific applications. The real payoff, however, is to the firm that can provide applications not currently in general use.

6.6 Synergy

Initial growth lies in a company's existing products and existing markets. After the initial growth it will turn to growth directions that imply a movement beyond the existing product market. This usually involves some measure of risk. It also often involves the potential of introducing synergy. It is important to understand synergy because it can be the key to a successful move into new product markets.

Synergy during market turbulence means that two SBUs (product + market strategy) operating together will be superior to the same two SBUs operating independently. This can give a sustainable SCA.

Synergy means that the whole is more than the sum of its parts. In this context, it means that two SBUs (product + market strategy) operating together will be superior to the same two SBUs operating independently. In terms of products, positive synergy means offering a set of products will generate a higher return over time than would be possible if each of the products operated autonomously. Similarly, in terms of markets, operating a set of markets within a business will be superior to operating them autonomously. As a result of synergy, the combined SBUs will either have increased revenues, decreased operating costs, or reduced investment.

Synergy can provide an SCA that is truly sustainable because it is based upon characteristics of a firm which are probably unique. A competitor might have to duplicate the entire organization in order to capture the assets or skills that are involved.

Look at the interesting case of Coca-Cola India's (CCI) rural India penetration strategy. As you are aware, CCI re-entered India in 1993 through a strategic alliance with Parle Exports. The alliance gave CCI ownership of five popular brands of Parle (Thums Up, Limca, Maaza, Citra and Gold Spot) with a market share of around 60 per cent and a well-established network of 56 bottlers. In 2000, CCI faced stagnant sales in its cola brands and volumes in urban areas were not growing. In order to expand sales, the company decided to diversify into the bottled water and powdered soft drink segments in association with Kinley and Sunfill brands, respectively. Kinley was launched in 2000, while Sunfill was launched the following year.

However, poor rural infrastructure and consumption habits in the countryside that were very different from those of the urban people were two major obstacles CCI had to overcome to crack the rural market. People in rural areas preferred traditional cold beverages such as *lassi* and lemon juice. Also, erratic power supply meant that most grocers in rural areas did not stock cold drinks. Further, the price of the beverage was a major factor for the rural consumer. CCI's rural marketing strategy was based on three *A*s—Availability, Affordability and Acceptability. The first 'A' emphasized on the availability of the product to the customer; the second focused on product pricing, and the third on convincing the customer to buy the product.

CCI's rural marketing strategy was based on three As—Availability, Affordability and Acceptability. This synergy of well-thought out strategies, plans and marketing mix elements took the company forward even during the downturn.

Under the hub-and-spoke distribution system, stock was transported from the bottling plants to the hubs and then from the hubs, the stock was transported to the spokes which were situated in small towns. These spokes fed the retailers catering to the demand in the rural areas. CCI not only changed its distribution model, but also the type of vehicles used for transportation. The company used large trucks for transporting stock from the bottling plants to the hubs and medium commercial vehicles transported the stock from the hubs to the spokes. For transporting stock from the spokes to the village retailers the company utilized autorickshaws and cycles.

A survey conducted by CCI revealed that 300 ml bottles were not popular with rural and semi-urban residents; often two persons shared a 300 ml bottle. It was also found that the price of ₹10 per bottle was considered too high by the rural consumers. For these reasons, CCI decided to make some changes in the size of its bottles and pricing to win over the rural consumers. Hence, it launched 200 ml bottles (*Chota* Coke) priced at ₹5. CCI announced that it would push the 200 ml bottles more in the rural areas as this market was very price-sensitive. It was widely felt that the 200 ml bottles priced at ₹5 would increase the rate of consumption in rural India. Reports put the annual per capita consumption of bottled beverages in the rural areas at one bottle as compared to six bottles in urban areas in 2002. In 2001, CCI announced its maiden profits. To sustain its growth CCI continued focusing on the rural market in the early 2000s, given the flat sales in the urban areas. The CCI case presents a synergy of well-thought out strategies, plans and marketing mix elements that took the company forward even during downturn.

6.7 Product Development for Existing Markets

Product development includes addition of product features, expansion of the product line, development of new-generation technologies, and development of new products for the existing market.

Product development can occur at a variety of levels, so it is helpful to distinguish between the different types. Product development can include addition of product features, expansion of the product line, development of new-generation technologies, and development of new products for the existing market.

6.7.1 Product Feature Addition

Examples of product feature addition could be a car company adding a transmission or sunroof option such a strategy helps in market penetration and enhances sales.

An automobile firm could add a transmission or sunroof option that will improve its penetration in the market in which it is competing. For confectionary firms, the creation of novel packages can act as the key to sales. Look at Samsung LCD TV Bordeaux, whose tagline says 'Even when you turn it off, it will continue to turn you on'. Samsung assures many wonders when any of its offerings—Mosell Blaque, Bordeaux Art, Sonoma Trenz and HD Plasma—comes to the living room. Customers are led to

MARKETING IN ACTION — **THE MAKING OF THE PEOPLE'S CAR**

Tata Motors on 23 March 2009 launched Nano, the world's cheapest car, in a move that could dramatically change the auto market in the world's second most populous nation. Nano definitely script a new beginning in Indian auto sector. India's car penetration level is extremely poor—9 people out of 1,000 own a car. Nano might just dent that a bit.

With over four million Tata vehicles plying in India, Tata Motors is the country's market leader in commercial vehicles and among the top three in passenger vehicles, with revenues of US$ 8.8 billion in 2007–8. It is also the world's fourth-largest truck manufacturer and the second-largest bus manufacturer.

Tata Motors chairman Ratan Tata has said his inspiration for the affordable car was the common sight of a family of four riding on a motorbike; the Nano despite its size and cost can seat four people. Nano's launch will enhance India's position as a highly cost-competitive manufacturing hub for small cars and will encourage continued emphasis on product development in the low-cost car category by manufacturers across the world, with India as the focal point.

The basic model of Nano comes with a price tag of $2,168 (the air-conditioned version costs $3,392), though the first lot of randomly chosen 1,00,000 consumers will get car at the promised price of ₹1 lakh ($1,961).

The product is available in three variants. The Nano Standard (BS II and BS III) is the standard version that comes in three colour options, single-tone seats and fold-down rear seat. Tata Nano CX (BS II and BS III) is equipped with heating and air-conditioning, two-tone seats, parcel shelf, booster-assisted brakes and fold-down rear seat with nap rest. This variant is available in five colour options. Tata Nano LX (BS III) encompasses all the features of the CX. It has complete fabric seats, central locking, front power windows, body coloured exteriors in three premium shades, fog lamps, electronic trip meter, cup-holder in the front console, mobile charger point, and rear spoiler. Many of these features are presently not available in the entry-level small cars in the country.

Let us look at some more features of this cheapest car. The wheels are made of pressed steel, which is less expensive than alloy. Positioning the engine in the rear has also helped keep costs down. The engine was built in-house by Tata Motors, whose engineers worked with Germany's Krug to reduce capital and variable costs, such as paint and the number of tools used to make the parts.

Tata says the ₹1 lakh price tag would only be available for a limited period in 2009. Prices of motorcycles range from ₹30,000 to ₹12 lakh. Tata has said the Nano aims to give people the chance to shift from owning a bike to owning a car. Tata Motors claims the Nano's safety performance exceeds the current Indian regulatory requirements. It has an all-sheet metal body and safety features include crumple zones, intrusion-resistant doors, seat belts, strong seats and anchorages. The Nano's tubeless tyres, apart from reducing friction, provide better balance and stability. Tata Motors says the Nano's tailpipe emission performance exceeds regulatory requirements. It has a lower pollution level than two-wheelers being manufactured in India today. The Nano Europa has a carbon dioxide emission of less than 100 gm per km. Environmentalists, however, worry that India's roads and infrastructure will struggle to cope with a surge in car ownership.

To help finance Nano purchases, Tata has entered into a partnership with India's largest nationalized bank, State Bank of India and its seven subsidiaries. Their 1,350 branches in 850 cities will be the hub of the Nano's financing and marketing plan. The State Bank alliance is crucial to Tata's plans to popularize the Nano. The automaker is targeting lower- and middle-income buyers in urban and small-town India, and by teaming up with State Bank, the company hopes to ensure that loan facilities are available in even the remotest Indian villages. Prospective buyers have to pay $6 (₹300) for a booking form and then make an initial payment of $60 (₹2,999), with the rest coming in as bank loan.

The Tata Nano has drawn over 2.03 lakh fully paid bookings amounting to nearly ₹2,500 crore—an encouraging response. The Nano website recorded an unprecedented 3 crore (30 million) hits from the date of launch of the car (23 March 2009) to the closure of the booking period (25 April 2009), amounting to nearly 1 million hits a day. About 14 lakh people walked into Tata Motors' showrooms, Croma and Westside stores across the country to catch a glimpse of the car. A total of 6.10 lakh forms were purchased from the booking centres; 70 per cent of the 2.03 lakh bookings received were financed, while 30 per cent of the applicants booked in cash by paying fully. About 4,000 cash bookings were made online through tatanano.com, a first for the auto industry in India. Among the three variants of the car, 20 per cent bookings are for the Nano Standard, 30 per cent for the Nano CX and the remaining 50 per cent for the top-end Nano LX.

As per the data collected by KPMG from the Society of Indian Automobile Manufacturers (SIAM) and CRISIL, until the landmark year of 1998-9 when a bevy of auto companies entered the small car segment, Maruti 800, the first and only A1 small car model, held a 58 per cent market share. Later with the introduction of a range of A2 compact car models—larger than A1 and a good ₹2-₹5 lakh more expensive—the share of Maruti 800 fell to 5.8 per cent, to be replaced in popularity by A2 cars whose share increased to 72 per cent by the end of 2008. The A2 models created a metro-based upwardly mobile market segment.

But the Nano, actually an A0 car, moves further down the pyramid where the market is also wider. By bringing down the cost of ownership to less than three times that of a two-wheeler, it captures the aspirational but cost-sensitive market in tier II and III towns. However, at ₹1,001.26 crore, Tata Motors posted a 50 per cent decline in net profit for the year ended 31 March 2009, compared with ₹2,028.92 crore for the previous year.

Source: The Economic Times, March and May 2009.

believe they will discover new dimensions of beauty and that that was what they had wanted all along. In the price range of ₹57,000 to ₹4.50 lakh, Samsung was clearly targeting the global, affluent Indians and the youth in particular.

6.7.2 Product Line Expansion

A second type of product development activity aimed at existing markets is to expand or broaden the product line. The marketing and distribution effort and perhaps even much of the manufacturing will be common to the product line extension. A paint firm like Asian Paints may want to add wood stains like teak wood to its line of paints.

6.7.3 Developing New Generation Technologies

Growth can be obtained in the existing market by creating new technology products. For example Blackberry software for mobile Internet technology.

Growth can be obtained in the existing market by creating new technology products. Such products can obsolete existing ones, thus providing a source of sales. The computer industry has long had sales fuelled by new generation equipment. However, new generation products can be created in frequently purchased consumer products as well. Blackberry software for mobile

Internet technology (connecting internet and mobile phone) is an invention and high-end GSM sets are sold with this GPRS facility.

6.7.4 New Products for Existing Markets

Products that are not line extensions but are very different even though they share customers with existing products can enhance growth by taking advantage of distribution synergy.

A classic growth pattern is exploiting a marketing or distribution strength by adding compatible products, products that are not line extensions but are very different even though they share customers with existing products. Synergy is usually obtained at least in part by the commonality in distribution, marketing, brand name recognition and image. Nokia E series says 'Nothing in life should stop you especially when you have Nokia *E61i* device.' With Web browsing, email, high-resolution screen, camera, and high voice quality conference calls, it is the ultimate tool to tame your opportunities. Its catch phrase 'Work together and Smarter' is catching on among aspiring or evolving global Indians, especially when they realize the value of time and money in the twenty-first century (source: www.nokia.co.in).

6.7.5 Market Development Using Existing Products

Market development often involves the virtual duplication of a business operation, perhaps with minor adaptive changes. Market expansion can use the same expertise and technology and sometimes even the same plant and operations facility. Thus, the potential for synergy is large.

6.8 Market Expansion

Market expansion can be geographical or an expansion into different market segments.

Of the two basic approaches to market expansion, the first, and most obvious, is geographical expansion. The second is expansion into different market segments.

6.8.1 Expanding into New Market Segments

Segmentation variables include usage pattern, mode of distribution channels, price and attribute preference.

A firm can also grow by reaching into new market segments. There are of course a variety of ways to define segments and therefore growth directions:

1. **Usage:** The non-user can be an attractive target. An audio electronics firm could target those not owning audio systems.
2. **Distribution channel:** A firm can reach new segments by opening up a second or third channel of distribution. A retail sporting goods store could market to schools via a direct salesforce. A direct marketer such as Avon could introduce its products under another brand name in department stores.
3. **Price:** A line extension could be coupled with an effort to reach a segment defined by its preference on the price-quality dimension. For example, a premium designer clothing firm could introduce a lower priced line for price-sensitive customers.
4. **Attribute preference:** A firm that has focused on frequency of response in its instrumentation at the sacrifice of accuracy might extend its line to include more accurate equipment to serve the segment that demands more accuracy. Take the case high-definition LCD TV market in India.

CASE STUDY

GROWTH STRATEGY OF BAJAJ AUTO LIMITED

Bajaj Auto Limited, the Bajaj group's flagship company, is ranked as the world's fourth-largest two- and three-wheeler manufacturer. Bajaj Auto began its operations as an importing agent for Vespa scooters of Piaggio in 1948. Today it enjoys 27 per cent of the two-wheeler market, manufactures two- and three-wheeled vehicles which include scooters, motorcycles, passenger carriers and goods carriers. The company segments motorcycles into three segments based on consumer categories and approximate price points:

Entry segment: 100 cc motorcycles in the price band of ₹35,000. This segment caters to the middle-class, office-going people as it gives high mileage and good value for money. Bajaj targets this market through its model Platina and has captured around 34 per cent of this segment in India (2008–9).

Executive segment: 100cc-135cc motorcycles priced between ₹40,000 and ₹50,000. Bajaj is catering to this segment through its brands XCD and Discover.

Performance segment: These sleek, high-performance bikes are for people who love riding for the sheer thrill of it and do not mind spending on their dream machine. In this segment the value from sales is higher than the volume achieved. The price is in excess of ₹50,000. Bajaj targets this segment through its flagship brands like Pulsar and Avenger with a market share of more than 47 per cent.

The company is trying to get a hold in the executive segment and has time and again introduced different variants of models to boost sales in. It faces tough competition from Hero Honda Splendor and Passion and introduced the XCD 125 and its upgraded version to generate sufficient sales. Bajaj Discover has been positioned as a fuel-efficient motorcycle. It promises to be as frugal as any executive bike (or more so), perform like heavier bikes but appear a little easy for the average height/size Indian (unlike Pulsar which can be a little intimidating for some bikers). Bajaj is banking on this brand to increase price elasticity and brand loyalty and ensure customers are not just being driven by low prices.

In the premium segment Bajaj faces tough competition from Yamaha FZ-16 and Suzuki GS150R, yet it has a market share of 50 per cent. The company unveiled its model of Pulsar in the 150cc range to take on the competition in December 2009. In order to compete better with bikes which give the same acceleration and a slightly higher top speed, Bajaj improved the initial acceleration. This is because one cannot go above the 100-105 kmph on city roads, so it is the initial pick up which brings about the difference in experience. Secondly the new Pulsar is priced slightly lower to attract customers.

Pulsar, a highly successful brand from the very beginning, has been banked upon to its utmost potential. Bajaj has come out with as many as four variants of motorcycles under the umbrella brand of Pulsar, making the image bigger and better in the minds of consumers. The unveiling of Pulsar 200 was a strategic move to ensure line filling in the performance bike segment so that buyers have enough choice within the Pulsar brand, enabling Bajaj to retain them. Looking to the future, as the performance two-wheeler buyer matures, and as competition in the 150cc-plus engine size category hots up, Bajaj would perhaps want to make the Pulsar 200 its primary offering in the segment.

Kristal has been positioned as a macho brand. It is targeting a new segment—college going girls who want good speed, comfort and fuel economy, helping them save their pocket money. Costing around ₹35,200 with DTS-i and ExhausTEC technology the scooterette gives good value for money to the female riders and has

Product	*Price*	*Positioning*	
Bajaj Avenger 200cc DTS-i	₹66,515	Low-rise cruising bike with a smart, sporty look and enhanced fuel economy	
Discover DTS-Si 100cc	₹40,000	Bike with muscular look and persona	
Bajaj Discover 135 DTS-i	₹45,943	Latest offering with several similar features to Pulsar 150cc plus better performance	

Product	Price	Positioning	
Bajaj Platina 100cc	₹33,210	Visual appeal and outstanding mileage	
Bajaj Platina 125 DTS-Si	₹39,000	Most fuel-efficient bike with DTS-Si technology	
Pulsar 150 DTS-i	₹58,482	Excellent aerodynamic shape, branding itself the 'male bike' with best ride quality	
Pulsar 200 DTS-i	₹67,755	Tubeless tyres, both rear and front, with powerful engine for the cruising experience	
Bajaj Pulsar 180 DTS-i	₹59,720	Upgraded version resembling the Pulsar 200cc with better power	
Bajaj Pulsar 220 DTS-i	₹70,000	The fastest Indian bike, ideal for those who love to zoom	
Bajaj XCD 125	₹38,511	A bestseller with a handsome look	
Bajaj XCD 135	₹43,000	Reliable bike with macho look and breeze-like ride	
Kawasaki Ninja 250R	₹69,580	Best-looking bike in the 250cc segment with improved features	
Kristal	₹35,200	Targeted at a new segment of college going girls who want good speed, comfort and fuel economy	

helped Bajaj enhance its product mix.

Bajaj's R&D team has pioneered various new technologies, including the DTS-i (Digital Twin Spark Ignition) and the DTS-Fi (Digital Twin Spark Fuel Ignition). Bajaj is also a pioneer in product innovation, having introduced technologies such as ExhausTEC (Exhaust Torque Expansion Chamber), LED tail lamps, LCD display, SNS, spare parts (tubeless tyres, rear disc brakes), and black colour scheme.

Scooters have been able to maintain the growth momentum, witnessing a double-digit positive growth of 14.68 per cent. In order to tap the young males, Bajaj will launch Bajaj Blade, an ungeared 125cc scooter equipped with the company's patented DTS-i technology. Such line stretching will definitely help Bajaj increase its consumer base and enable it to tap a different market segment altogether.

Bajaj Auto will also increase focus on the rural market as growth of the motorcycle industry in the urban market is almost flat. Products like the 100 cc Discover DTS-Si could well attract the attention of buyers in rural areas.

The company's thrust will be on providing finance schemes to customers in the rural areas, both via in-house financing, viz. Baja Auto Finance Limited, as well as making finance available through other financing sources. The rural markets are expected to help two-wheeler companies maintain their growth momentum of 7 to 8 per cent CAGR in terms of volumes over the next five years since 2009.

Source: Investors' Report of Bajaj Auto Ltd., January 2010.

LG came up with Pearl Black, a new launch in 2008 which assured dynamic contrast ratio with very high precision (10,000 : 1) and 5 ms. response time, thereby aligning visual and sound with elegance. (Most HDTV brands lack sound and picture clarity when the screen size is increased.)

6.8.2 Evaluating Market Expansion Alternatives

Although the synergy can potentially be high, several considerations are involved in market expansion. First, is the business operating well in its initial market? There is no point in exporting failure or even mediocrity. Second, in what ways does the new market differ from the existing one? Special attention should be given to the key success factors, the intensity or nature of competition, the distribution channels, and customer habits and attitudes. Third, to the extent that conditions differ, is there a convincing plan in place to adapt the business to the differing conditions.

6.8.3 Benefits of Market Expansion

Backward integration gives access to supply and forward integration to demand. Vertical integration is significantly probable in markets with highly specialized products and services in terms of location, technology or knowledge.

1. **Access to supply:** In some contexts a key success factor is access to raw materials or some other input factor. Backward integration can reduce the availability risk.
2. **Access to demand:** Similarly, forward integration could be motivated by a concern about product outlets.
3. **Idiosyncratic products and services:** Whenever only one buyer and one seller exist for highly specialized products and services, there will be an incentive to consider vertical integration. Three types of specializations can be identified:
   (i) *Locational:* Transportation or thermal economics can dictate that two parts of a production process should be geographically close. A steel firm needs to have its blast furnace and rolling mill located together. To save transportation costs a can-making plant may be located near a brewery.
   (ii) *Technological:* A petroleum plant may be designed to use high-grade inputs that are available only from a few sources. If the raw material source is jeopardized, the plant may become economically unviable. The plant could therefore be designed to accept a variety of grades of petroleum. Obtaining such flexibility would, however, require substantially more investment.
   (iii) *Knowledge based:* A supplier may acquire specialized knowledge and thus become the only practical source for an input factor. For example, a law firm or an engineering contractor might become so familiar with the involved product, service and client that for all practical purposes no competing suppliers exits, although at the outset of the relationship there may have been several able competitors. Vertical integration will prevent suppliers from making abnormal profits and perhaps further enhance the degree of knowledge transfer between the two firms.

4. **Control of supply or demand:** It can become necessary to integrate vertically in order to gain sufficient control over the product or service to maintain the integrity of a differentiation strategy. A firm may want to integrate forward in order to create a brand name or to guarantee that its marketing and service programme is administered competently.
5. **Enter a profitable business area:** A vertical integration decision can simply be motivated by an attractive profit potential. Thus, a chain of retail stores may simply be an attractive business investment, and the fact that they now are an outlet for the firm's product may be a relatively minor consideration.
6. **Enhancing technological innovation:** Vertically integrated firms may have an advantage in achieving technological innovation. First, technical information is more readily shared between business units if they are in the same firm. Thus, the R&D effort of an in-house supplier organization can be more focused. Second, because the scale is larger, the potential is greater for innovation and that can impact upon several stages of the production process, producing larger returns. Third, vertical integration

MARKETING IN ACTION

INDIA'S TOAST TO GRAIN ALCOHOL, FINALLY

A lot of money is suddenly flowing into grain alcohol that is used worldwide as a base for whiskey, gin and vodka. Companies are setting up breweries that can distil alcohol from rice, wheat and maize. India can now make 200 million litres of grain alcohol a year, and that's just the beginning. In the year 2011, that figure will be significantly higher. Why the scramble for grain alcohol only now when it has been around for decades? Seagram, for instance, has been using grain since 1994 for all its alcohols made in India. Many others also have licences.

The answer is simple. There is finally money in it. Look at it from the brewers' point of view. Alcohol companies were using mainly molasses, a sticky dark brown residue left behind when sugar is made from cane juice. When cane supply reduced in 2009, molasses became scarce too. So breweries had to pay a hand and an arm for their chief raw material. It was enough to sober up anyone. So companies did the smart thing by casting around for an alternative, which was grain.

It was a no-brainer actually. Alcohol can be made by fermenting anything containing sugar. Molasses contains sucrose but grains contain starch (maize is 64 per cent starch) and starch has glucose. Since this extra starch-to-glucose step increases the cost of grain alcohol, and molasses was affordable and ample, companies didn't bother with grain alcohol. Now, with molasses at ₹7,000 per ton, maize-based alcohol is almost 25 per cent cheaper.

There are other advantages too. Grain prices are steadier because supply is bounteous. That means fewer headaches of coping with the volatility in molasses prices. Grains yield a good amount of alcohol. One ton of wheat gives 375 litres of alcohol, while one ton of rice gives 400 litres. That beats 225 litres from one ton of molasses.

Grain alcohol factories are relatively cheaper to put up. Radico set up India's first grain alcohol plant in 2007 at Rampur in Uttar Pradesh, which uses rice, wheat and millets to make alcohol. It now has two more plants in Maharashtra. This makes Radico India's top grain alcohol producer. Best of all, grain alcohol wins hands down on taste. Radico's grain alcohol will go straight into its premium whiskey.

World over the best whiskey brands are grain based because of the special flavour grains impart. Now Indian consumers can get the same taste in local brands too. In other words, for liquor companies grain alcohol scores on all counts: cost, profit margins, and consumer choice. Chances are that the liquor industry will pay better than food companies or the Food Corporation of India because its margins are heftier.

This potential to improve farm incomes is also motivating states to offer sops to alcohol makers. Maharashtra, for instance, wants to help coarse grain farmers in backward Marathwada and Vidarbha regions by giving a ₹10 per litre discount on excise duty to grain alcohol companies in that region. The discount will bridge the cost gap between grain and molasses. Punjab and Haryana view it as a way to encourage food processing.

Everyone is betting grain will get more out of alcohol than alcohol will get out of grain.

Source: The Economic Times, December 2009.

can facilitate the implementation of new processes or the introduction of new products.

7. **Operating costs:** Vertical integration can create potential operating costs that can outweigh the operating economies. The complexity and related planning and coordination will strain the management system. Besides, there is no guarantee that the associated costs will not exceed the transaction costs between the two firms. The two integrated operations are unlikely to match exactly with respect to capacity appropriate for efficient operation. As a result, one or the other will probably have excess capacity that will elevate costs. Without the discipline of outside price competition, there may be less incentive for cost control. After all, the supplying operation is assured of its customer. A transfer price simulating a market price is usually used to cover intra-firm transactions. The danger is that faulty information or organization pressure can cause this transfer price to be either too high or too low. In either case, suboptimal decisions can easily be stimulated.

Vertical integration can be motivated by an attractive profit potential or achieving technological innovation.

Risks associated with vertical integration are increased operation cost, reduction in operational efficiency and additional commitment.

8. **Management of a different business:** A move towards vertical integration often involves adding an operation that requires organizational assets and skills that differ markedly from the firm's other business areas. As a result, the firm may not be suited to run the integrated operation effectively and competitively.
9. **The risk of increasing commitment to business:** If the business becomes weak, the additional investment and commitment created by integration will inhibit consideration of an exit alternative. Further, if one operation becomes dependent upon the other, it may be awkward to try to exit from one.

6.9 Diversification

Diversification is the art of entering product markets different from those in which the firm is currently engaged. It is helpful to divide diversification into 'related' and 'unrelated'. A related diversification is one in which the two involved businesses have meaningful commonalties, which provide the potential to generate economies of scale or synergies based upon the exchange of skills or resources. In a related diversification the resulting combined business should be able to achieve improved ROI because of increased revenues, decreased costs, or reduced investment, which are attributable to the commonalties.

Diversification is the art of entering product markets different from those in which the firm is currently engaged. It can be 'related' or 'unrelated'.

An important issue in any diversification decision is whether in fact there is a real and meaningful area of commonality that will affect the ultimate ROI. If such a meaningful commonality is lacking, the diversification may still be justifiable, but the rationale will need to be different.

6.10 Summary

- Once a product passes through the growth or market acceptance stage in the PLC, it enters the maturity stage followed by saturation. The saturation stage is characterized by increase in sales but at a low rate and company alters the stagnation in sales by investing more on promotions.

- The maturity stage in a product's life cycle is characterized by increasing sales and profit, but the rate of increase is less than that in the growth stage. This reduced growth rate is due to competition in the market.
- One should not forget that innovative products face competition from new and improved imitative market entrants from time to time, whereas imitative products have to contend with already existing products.
- When the question of guarding against the phenomena of maturity and saturation stages arises, a clear forecast of the setting-in of these phases is required. Otherwise designing effective marketing strategies to prevent the early setting-in of maturity and saturation is not possible. If a product's sales are close to the break-even level, losses become inevitable, especially in the saturation stage.

CHAPTER 7  TECHNOLOGICAL REVOLUTIONS IN MARKETING

Knowledge is a process of piling up facts; wisdom lies in their simplification.

— ALEXANDER GRAHAM BELL

The Backdrop

We are well aware of how and in what ways information technology has made an impact on the lifestyle of people and changed the world as a whole. With the emergence of new technology in each dimension of IT, life has taken new turns. Modern IT systems rely on numerous aspects, namely, people, networks and hardware. With the computer becoming an increasingly integral part of modern living—involved in the most mundane jobs (online banking) to miraculous breakthroughs (DNA decoding)—our quality of life has significantly improved.

Today everything is integrated. Earlier people listened to music on their music system, used TVs, cameras, video players, for their separate functions. Now people use their PCs to watch TV, download music on their iPods and to store pictures. The next challenge for PC makers would be to integrate these systems further to enhance and increase sales.

With the IT sector having penetrated deep into the social and economic life of every individual it has also changed the way we approach problems and deal with them. Finally, with the global recession easing, the IT industry since November 2009 has been experiencing positive developments, after 20 months of gloom.

Having conquered the world, India's IT majors are now eyeing home territory. The industry (comprising of IT services, BPO, software products, engineering services and hardware) registered a CAGR of 18.57 per cent during 2000–4 and 24.83 per cent during 2005–9. In 2008, the market crossed ₹1 lakh crore, growing further to ₹1,16,784 crore in 2009. While the Indian companies were looking Westwards, MNCs believe that the next billion-dollar companies in IT could come out of India in 2011. The slowdown syndrome adds to challenges facing the IT companies, having to make the best offers at optimal costs with a lean organizational structure. Also, IT-enabled marketing has become an integral part of many corporates and SMEs.

How does technology impact marketing? Marketing is the management process responsible for identifying, anticipating and satisfying customer requirements profitably. The marketing concept is based on two fundamental beliefs: first, all company planning, policies, and operations should be oriented towards the customer; second, profitable sales volume should be the goal of a firm. In its fullest sense, the marketing concept is a philosophy of business which states that the customers' want for satisfaction is the economic and social justification of a company's existence. Now technology is identified as cost optimizer and cutting edge technology will help companies to tide over financial stresses and liquidity crises by increasing the customer base.

This Chapter Will

- *Explain the ways and means of integrating technology while making business more customer-centric, especially during market turbulence.*
- *Explain the various tools for undertaking web-based marketing, with detailed coverage of Internet and product marketing, marketing through mobile phones, emerging marketing technologies and managing information technology during downturn.*

7.1 Internet and Product Marketing

Almost three-fourths of India's English-speaking population is PC literate, but only 55 per cent of it has experienced the Internet. Thus, there exists potential for Internet converts amongst existing PC users. After scaling the outer limit of growth amongst the English speakers, the next challenge would be to reach out to the non-English speaking population. IMRB and the Internet and Mobile Association of India (IAMAl) estimate that as of August 2010 there were 68 million 'ever' users (who have used the Internet at any point in time) in India including one million in rural India. Thus, the World Wide Web is reaching out to the less affluent sections of society too. And it is not just the smaller towns which are contributing to the Internet revolution; it is also being driven by the less affluent sections of society, the lower socio-economic classes (SECs). The move has taken the combined effort of Internet stakeholders to reduce the initial inertia and promote this interaction. First, the mass media has helped create an awareness for the Internet, especially as a tool for empowerment. Second, PCs and Internet connections have become more affordable, making it easier for many more people to own a PC and use the Internet.

On the applications side, several one-time applications like examination results and ticketing, which are non-communication oriented, have encouraged the less affluent to be on the Internet. As corporate digital divide programmes and national e-governance initiatives bear fruit, usage amongst lower SECs should witness a phenomenal increase in the coming years.

E-business is the use of electronic means and platforms to conduct a company's business.

E-business is the use of electronic means and platforms to conduct a company's business. The advent of the Internet has greatly increased the ability of companies to conduct their business faster, and more accurately, over a wider range of time and space, at reduced cost, and with the ability to customize and personalize offerings for customers. Countless companies have set up websites to inform and promote their products and services. They have created intranets to facilitate communication among employees and to facilitate downloading and uploading of information to and from the company's website. Companies have also set up extranets with major suppliers and distributors to facilitate information exchange, order placement, transaction completion, and bill payment. Bill Gates of Microsoft claims that Microsoft is almost entirely run electronically; there is hardly any paper floating in the company because everything is on the computer screen. Look at social media as a great marketing tool. Facebook started in 2004 by Mark Zukerberg has 500 million users globally in 2010. If Facebook were a country, it would be the third-largest country in the world.

7.1.1 Internet: The New Mass Media

As user engagement grows, the Internet is set to grow faster than other media. In India the Internet can be viewed as a funnel. At the top is the universe of urban population; at 243 million it offers tremendous scope for Internet growth in urban India. Every tenth individual in urban India has accessed the Net. However, access to the Net is a function of many variables, chief amongst them being a basic level of familiarity with English and with the most common access device, the PC.

The Internet 'ever' user base has doubled since 2004. The number of PC literates is growing steadily, up by 270 per cent since 2000! The growth of 'ever' users and 'active' users (who have used the Internet once in the last one month) has been even more impressive, with 540 and 950 per cent growth, respectively, since 2000. 'Ever' users as a proportion of PC literates

The trend of 'active' users as a proportion of 'ever' users has grown from 40 per cent in 2000 to the current proportion of 66 per cent.

CASE STUDY — **ITC'S E-CHOUPAL INITIATIVE**

ITC's biggest CSR initiative so far has been the 'e-Choupal'. It was launched in June 2000 with the aim of helping four million farmers grow a range of foodstuffs—soybean, coffee, wheat, rice, pulses and shrimps—in around 40,000 villages through 6,500 kiosks across ten states (Madhya Pradesh, Haryana, Uttaranchal, Karnataka, Andhra Pradesh, Uttar Pradesh, Rajasthan, Maharashtra, Kerala and Tamil Nadu).

ITC's International Business Division is one of India's largest exporters of agricultural commodities. It has deployed e-Choupal as the supply chain to deliver value to its customers around the world. The model has been crafted to handle the hindrances posed by the unique features of Indian agriculture, characterized by fragmented farms, weak infrastructure and the involvement of numerous intermediaries, among others.

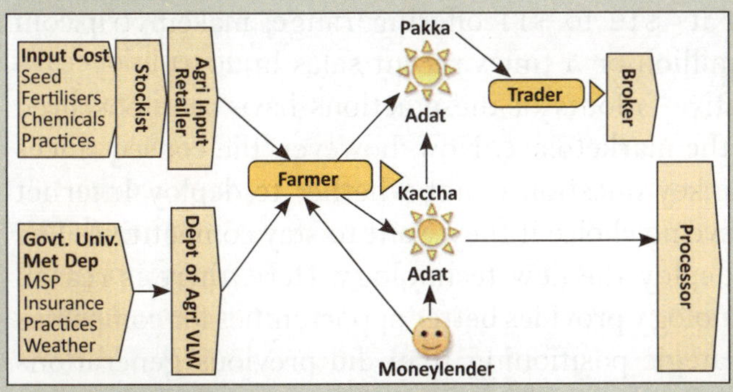

Value chain: from the farmer to the factory gate

Farmers can now be better informed about the local weather, the upcoming scientific farming practices and market prices through e-Choupal. The facility is available in Hindi as well as in languages like Marathi, Kannada and Telugu. With around 1,000 hubs across the country spread across many states, it called for a massive human resources initiative to ensure that the personnel receive the best of training on par with international standards. And direct contact was the best way to ensure effectiveness of training than through computer-based training modules.

Initiatives after e-Choupal's success

Choupal Saagar: This is a storage facility and a unique rural hypermarket that offers multiple services

under one roof. Twenty-four active Choupal Saagars are spread across Madhya Pradesh, Maharashtra and Uttar Pradesh. ITC is looking to scale up the initiative by establishing a chain of 100 Choupal Saagars.

Choupal Fresh: This is ITC's fresh food wholesale and retail initiative. The company has established a cold chain for ensuring availability of fresh products in the market, besides directly sourcing farm fresh produce from the farmers. Six Choupal Fresh stores are currently functional, all located in Hyderabad.

Source: Investors' Report of ITC Ltd., January 2010.

has been constant over the years at about 30 per cent, except in 2008 when it grew to 54 per cent. Thus, every second PC user in India has now experienced the Internet at some point in time. This has created a critical mass for rapid growth.

The trend of 'active' users as a proportion of 'ever' users has grown from 40 per cent in 2000 to the current proportion of 66 per cent. This is a clear indication that people are not using the Internet on a trial basis but continue to actively make use of it. Internet trials are increasing in the small towns and non-metro cities as more users log on and gain confidence becoming part of the global community. From 27 per cent in 2001, the non-metros and small towns now account for 39 per cent of all Internet users. The growth in smaller towns is driven by better access and increasing awareness, as mass media and word of mouth promote the Net. The top eight metros which have been the traditional early adaptors continue to be the biggest contributors to India's Internet population. However, their proportion has come down significantly since 2001 and should drop even more in the coming years as more small city users log on.

7.1.2 Internet Doesn't Change Everything

Caught in the general fervour, people have assumed that the Internet changes everything, rendering the old rules about companies and competition obsolete. Though a natural reaction, it is a dangerous one.

The Internet is an extremely potent technology, so it is no surprise that it has received so much attention from entrepreneurs, executives, investors, and business observers. Caught in the general fervour, many have assumed that the Internet changes everything, rendering all the old rules about companies and competition obsolete. Though a natural reaction, it is a dangerous one. It has led many companies, dot.coms and incumbents alike to make bad decisions—decisions that have eroded the attractiveness of their industries and undermined their own competitive advantages. Some companies, for example, have used the Internet technology to shift the basis of competition away from quality, features, and service toward price, making it hard for anyone in the industry to profit. Others have forfeited important proprietary advantages by rushing into misguided partnerships and outsourcing relationships. Websites like makemytrip.com have commoditized the airlines industry, making it easier for consumers to compare prices and choose the cheapest. The company www.makemytrip.com commands half of web travel agency booking in India, where an arising middle class is increasingly on the go. The company, established in 2000 initially had its roots in selling travel to expatriate Indians. Revenue reached $83.6 million in 2009 and at the top of its $12 to $14 offering range, makemytrip.com would be valued at $478 million or 5 times recent sales in 2010.

Until recently, the negative fallouts of these actions have been obscured by distorted signals from the marketplace. Now, however, the consequences are becoming evident. The key question is not whether to deploy Internet technology—companies have no choice if they want to stay competitive. The question is about how to deploy the new technology. Here, there is reason for optimism. Internet technology provides better opportunities for companies to establish distinctive strategic positioning than did previous generations of information technology. Gaining such a competitive advantage does not require a radically new approach to business. It requires building on the proven principles of effective strategy. The Internet per se will rarely provide a competitive advantage. The companies that succeed in the long-term will be those that use the Web as a complement to traditional ways of competing, not those that set their Web initiative apart from their established operations.

This is particularly good news for established companies which are often in the best position to combine the Internet and traditional approaches in ways that buttress existing advantages. But dot.coms can also be winners, if they understand the trade-offs between the Internet and traditional approaches and then fashion distinctive strategies. Far from making strategy less important, as some have argued, the Internet has actually made strategy more essential than ever. It is hard to come to any firm conclusion about the impact of the Internet on business by looking at corporate results, but two broad conclusions can be drawn. First, many businesses active on the Web are artificial businesses. Competing by artificial means and propped up by capital that until recently had been readily available. Second, in periods of transition as in 2001, it often appears as if there are new rules of competition. The creation of true economic value once again becomes the final arbiter of business success.

Economic value for a company is nothing more than the gap between price and cost, and it is reliably measured by sustained profitability.

Economic value for a company is nothing more than the gap between price and cost, and it is reliably measured by sustained profitability. Generating revenue, reducing expenses, or simply doing something useful by deploying Internet technology cannot be considered as sufficient evidence that value has been created. Nor is a company's current stock price necessarily an indicator of economic value. Shareholder value too is a reliable measure of economic value only over the long run. In thinking about economic value, it is useful to draw a distinction between the uses of the Internet (such as operating digital marketplaces, selling toys, or trading securities) and Web technologies (such as site-customization tools or real-time communication services) that can be deployed across several uses.

Many have pointed to the success of technology providers as adequate evidence of the Internet's economic value. This is, however, a faulty line of reasoning. It is the uses of the Web that ultimately creates economic value. Technology providers can prosper for a time irrespective of whether the uses of the Internet are profitable. In periods of heavy experimentation, even sellers of flawed technologies can thrive. But unless the uses generate sustainable revenue or savings in excess of their cost of deployment, the opportunity for technology providers will begin to shrivel as companies realize that further investment is economically unsound. So then how can the Web be used to create economic value?

Answers to that question require us to look beyond the immediate market signals to the two fundamental factors that determine profitability: industry structure, which determines the profitability of the average competitor; and sustainable competitive advantage, which allows a company to outperform the average competitor. These two underlying drivers of profitability are universal; they transcend technology and type of business. At the same time, they vary widely by industry and by company. The broad, supra-industry classifications so common in Internet parlance, such as business-to-consumer

(B2C) and business-to-business (B2B) prove meaningless with respect to profitability. Potential profitability can be understood only by looking at individual industries and individual companies.

7.2 New Business Practices

The internet and the web have changed the operational and strategic dynamics of many businesses.

Changes in technology and economy elicit a new set of beliefs and practices on the part of business firms. The internet has changed the operational and strategic dynamics of many businesses. As an electronic medium, the Web facilitates interactive selling approaches such as auctioning and market-making (like ebay). It also facilitates personalized marketing whereby information and product offerings can be tailored to individual customer preferences. It allows customers to easily gather, retrieve, and analyse product information. Ultimately, the web provides the ideal vehicle for delivering online analytical tools directly to customers. Yet even the most commercial websites are not making use of such customer decision support systems.

ECONOMY WATCH — **ADVERTISEMENT SPEND ON SOCIAL MEDIA SET TO GROW BY 44 PER CENT**

Social media sites have enjoyed a steep surge in popularity, but have failed to attract advertisers at the same pace. In 2008–9, only 13 per cent of the total internet ad spend went into social media initiatives, says a recent study of the top 500 marketers in India ('Digital Media Outlook 2009', report by Webchutney). However, things are looking up for this sector. The report predicts that in 2009–10, ad spend on digital media by the top 500 marketers is likely to grow 44 per cent, from the current ₹278 crore to around ₹400 crore. One sector which will contribute most to the rise in ad spends on social media is the fast moving consumer goods (FMCG) sector. FMCG brands are increasingly logging on to Net advertising since their target audience uses social media, notes the report.

Examples of online advertising in the FMCG sector abound. For instance, Coca-Cola India in August 2009 launched its campaign for Sprite first on the Internet. Pepsi, ITC and Colgate-Palmolive are some other FMCG brands that have begun using online advertising in a big way.

The Webchutney report pegs current online spend of the FMCG category at around ₹16 crore, and adds that the spend is expected to increase to almost ₹72 crore in 2009–10. In India, Facebook tops social media spends, followed by Orkut and LinkedIn, but all earn revenue less than ₹10 crore. Neville Taraporewalla, Head, Microsoft Advertising, Microsoft India, admits, 'Search is far ahead of social media. Social media is used differently (brands go on social media for word-of-mouth factor).' Apart from MSN, Microsoft owns Bing, Widows Live Planet and Facebook. It is a fact that not many brands are comfortable with social media because of the user generated content (UGC) element. Brands fear that they will have to put up with uncontrolled and inappropriate content from consumers. They also point out that regular ads designed for display media don't work well on social media. The latter needs advertisements that engage and involve the users, those that have games, forwards or other social activities built in. There are very few agencies which create such ads.

Google is optimistic though. Parminder Singh, Business Head, Google India, says, 'With the growing popularity of social networks, many advertisers are showing great interest in tapping the audience on these platforms. But the context and objectives of the campaigns on social networks is different from campaigns on other media platforms, so it's not a fair comparison.' It may be mentioned that Google owns Gmail, Orkut and YouTube. Also, take a look at Five Popular Indian brands in Facebooks. They are Vodafone ZooZoo (609,169 fans), Fastrack (301,680 fans), Cafe Coffee Day (160,225 fans), Tata Docomo (156,888 fans) and Kingfisher (101,828 fans) as on 7 July 2010.

Social media is more popular with businesses targeting the youth like apparel, accessories, electronics and automobile manufacturers. Regular advertisers like travel, hospitality and banking/financial services companies in India are not placing too many bets on social media yet. However, retail and consumer products firms are beginning to take the plunge on social media.

Source: Business Standard, January and July 2010.

Table 7.1: Traditional *v.* Web Marketing

Traditional marketing	*Web marketing*
Bound by geography and location	The Web market is borderless
Marketing costs are relatively high	Web marketing rates are relatively low
Lead times for implementation are substantial	Lead times are virtually non-existent
Limited interactivity exists, if at all	Web marketing is based on high level of interactivity
Getting customer feedback is a painstakingly slow process	Customer feedback is immediate
Tracking the effectiveness of the marketing efforts is relatively difficult	Effectiveness can be easily monitored
Marketing efforts are restricted by time and space	On the Internet, marketing can be carried out 24 hours a day, 365 days a year
Traditional marketing is static	Web advertising is dynamic and multimedia supported
Traditional advertising does not invoke immediate action	Web advertising, requires the user to take immediate action like clicking on the banner ad and then going to the site to learn more about the company
Advertisements are passively received	The user has a high attention level while he is on the Net. Thus advertisements get noticed, remembered, and acted upon
Advertisements are ubiquitous	The content may be a bit more specific. For instance, while searching for travel sites, ads related to travel agencies are displayed
Advertising does not target a focused audience	Advertisements are very focused. PC software can be displayed to PC users, while MAC users are not shown those ads

MARKETING ANALYSIS

ENTREPRENEURS USE FACEBOOK AS A MARKETING TOOL

Entrepreneurs have increasingly realized the role of social media in expanding their consumer base during market recovery. A growing number of businesses are making Facebook an indispensable part of hanging out their shingles. Small businesses are using it to find new customers, build online communities of fans and dig into gold mines of demographic information. And with 500 million people on Facebook, and still growing, that's increasingly where the audience is for a lot of products and services. For most businesses, Facebook Pages (distinct from individual profiles and Facebook groups) are the best place to start. Pages allow businesses to collect 'fans' the way celebrities, sports teams, musicians and politicians do. There are currently 2 million Facebook Pages and they collect more than 40 million fans every day, according to the site.

Businesses can easily create a Web presence with Facebook, even if they don't have their own website. Businesses can claim a vanity address so that their Facebook address reflects the business name, like www.facebook.com/Starbucks. Facebook pages can link to the company's website or direct sales to e-commerce sites like Amazon. Facebook offers an array of tools and networks, and it's easy to wander down its many paths. It is believed that small business firms ask friends and family to become fans of their Pages so that they display a respectable crowd of supporters when they debut. Pages can grow organically by word of mouth—the average Facebook user has 130 friends on the site—or by advertising and promotion. One can enliven a Page with photos, comments and useful information. As entrepreneurs grow more comfortable, they can add videos or business applications. Starbucks with 9,382,743 fans and Coca-Cola with 6,829,105 fans (as on 7 July 2010) top the list of most popular brands on Facebook.

Experts advise patience with social media. People are not going to flock to the site overnight. Technology is about network effect; it takes time for connections to be built.

Source: Business Standard, January 2010.

Web marketing and e-business are both irreplaceable parts of the cyber world. They may be new concepts right now but they will be the most essential part of business in the near future. In fact, the future we are talking about is already here! And to survive in this cut-throat competition, the sooner an organization enters cyberspace, the better.

Table 7.1 compares Traditional and Web marketing to highlight the importance of the latter in today's world.

7.3 Virtual Marketing

Successful Internet marketers will base their models and value propositions on a deep understanding of customer needs and not on products.

Today's online marketing professionals must have the basic skill set of offline marketing professionals but they must react more quickly and manage more information and channels in order to stay one step ahead of competition. The skill set has not changed tremendously, but the tools need to be applied with more vigour and sometimes with greater speed. Successful Internet marketers will base their models and value propositions on a deep understanding of customer needs—not on products.

The proliferation of the Internet user base in India is already leading to significant growth in Web advertising and electronic commerce. Businesses are devoting larger portions of their marketing budgets to Web advertising. An ever-increasing user base whose understanding of the Web is at par with the users of any advanced nation holds tremendous promise for e-commerce activities.

A look at the profile of Indian web users is revelatory. They are young (70 per cent in the 15-30 age group), affluent (over 60 per cent with monthly household income of over ₹10,000), from upper SEC (A : B = 2 : 1 *v.* 0.50 : 1 for all), with time for the Net (64 per cent spend about 30 minutes everyday) and who surf during prime TV time (7.30-11 p.m. = 41 per cent).

The Internet universe can be divided into six exclusive and exhaustive segments based on specific demographics. In India users between the ages of 18-35 years are the biggest segment accounting for 50 per cent of all Internet users. This has been aided by the traditional focus of Internet content providers on youth-centric applications. Like their peers in other countries, the Indian youth are also inclined to adopt technology faster and show the way to the other segments. Overall the proportion of different segments has been stable over the last couple of years; however as Internet penetration increases, the 'at home' segment, like non-working women and children, would grow in proportion in the next few years. Anticipating this growth, many content providers have come up with games and stories targeting school children, while also planning women-specific content.

MARKETING IN ACTION — **NESTLÉ: GAMING ITS WAY TO PROFIT**

Nestlé is trying to promote four of its children's food brands with the aid of online games. The company, with the help of the internet entertainment agency, the Ayzenberg Group, is developing online games for kids based on popular games available on leading children's gaming sites. The company is also trying to target parents with the site verybest.com. The site contains links to other Nestlé sites developed for kids.

Nestlé has developed specific games for specific brands. For instance, a game called 'Chocolate Mountain Challenge' has been developed for its popular chocolate drink Nesquik. For still younger children, the company has developed a site that focuses on sing-along games using popular rhymes. For older kids, there are sites that have more skilled games and contests.

MARKETING IN ACTION **AUTO COMPANIES TAKE THE DIGITAL PATH TO TAP TECH-SAVVY CUSTOMERS**

After the rural market rejuvenated car sales, auto companies are now building on digital marketing activities to gain access to a new set of tech-savvy customers. The strategy is to generate business through consumer interface over the Internet and mobile phone.

Maruti claims over a lakh of cars it sold in 2008 originated from digital marketing initiatives. Tata Motors in early 2009 saw 4,000 customers booking the Nano over the Internet. Other automakers are also witnessing a similar response on their digital platforms. Honda's third-generation flagship car, the Honda City regained its leadership position in the midsize car segment in the first month of its launch in November 2008 on the back of strong digital interface with customers. Volkswagen too is using the Internet and the mobile phone to tap the 2.50-lakh customers in India owning cars over ₹10 lakh, for its Jetta and Passat premium sedans.

Leading passenger carmaker Maruti Suzuki India first tasted online success with its small car A-Star, which generated huge interest over the Net with more than 2.50 lakh hits. 'We sold around 4,000 A-Stars based on customers' interface on the Internet. So we doubled the online marketing activity for the new hatchback Ritz with a microsite launched a week ahead of the launch (of the car) and offering various exclusive options to loggers. Around 17-18 per cent of our sales are now estimated to originate from digital marketing, up from mere 2-3 per cent in 2005,' said MSI Chief General Manager (Marketing) Shashank Srivastava.

Other carmakers are also actively tapping the interactive social networking sites and blogs. Honda launched a new programme in July 2009 to track sales originating from the Net.

'Our cars are primarily targeted at rich and younger customers who are Net savvy and take keen interest in blogs and different web activities. Digital marketing helps us build a strong brand,' Honda Siel Cars Vice-President (Sales and Marketing) Jnaneshwar Sen said. He added that preliminary estimates suggest that the Internet is responsible for 5 per cent of Honda's total sales in India.

Earlier, Tata Motors' website dedicated to the Nano got over 30 million hits from the date of launch of the car to the closure of booking. 'It's easier to reach professionals like doctors, engineers and chartered accountants and other target audience with a strong influence on purchase decision,' said Amardeep Bajpai of Webisdom, an Internet marketing solution company.

Source: The Economic Times, December 2009.

7.3.1 Virtual Marketing in the Retail Sector

The most modern retail format is online retail marketing where new technologies have driven the development of this model of grocery retail marketing. The supply chain function has come into its own, with awareness, people, and the technology to move materials improving at decreasing cost. It is now possible to supply almost anything across the world. Technologies like Bluetooth, Customer Relationship Management (CRM), Supply Chain Management (SCM), Enterprise Resource Planning (ERP) and concepts like outsourcing and co-optation have made this possible.

In India too, the success or failure of online grocery retailing will depend on the sophistication and reliability of technology. Many have painted a bright picture for Internet growth in India. However, there are costs involved. While there may be no rental, lease or taxation costs, you need substantial investments to set up a website, install software for data capture, records and an interactive system for customer dialogue. The costs are sometimes underestimated, leading to losses. An analysis by the Helsinki Institute of Technology revealed the differences between the profit margins of an online retailer (Streamline in the US) and that of a typical supermarket. The net profit for the online grocer was higher by virtue of saving costs on every part of the supply chain—from store to stocking to overheads. In spite of this, many online grocers have failed.

In India, two distinct models of online grocers exist: the channel model and the intermediary model.

In India, two distinct models of online grocers exist: the channel model and the intermediary model. The role of the e-grocer is different in the two models. In the former, there is a need for a brand name, incentives in terms of price cuts and discounts which are clearly more advantageous than the physical format. However, the supply chain—the last mile connectivity—has to be very efficient and reliable. It also involves a lot of money, time and effort.

That is probably why more enterprises are moving towards the intermediary or hybrid model of retailing. For starters, the need for a large, expensive front end is obviated. That alone increases return by that much amount. Second, synergy with an existing physical store can be obtained. For example, Fabmart used the 'pick off the shelf' model in a tie-up with Mumbai's Balaji supermarket. The order generated by the website is transmitted to Fabmart; Balaji keeps the order ready to be picked up by Fabmart's third party logistics and delivered to the customer. (Fabmart, however, discontinued this system towards the close of 2002 citing high costs.) Others purchase each time the order is received, i.e. the just-in-time approach, while some have their own stores.

The various technological features bring down the costs of running an online grocery store vis-à-vis brick and mortar stores. Research the worldover shows that an average online store keeps one-third the SKUs of a physical store. This alone keeps purchase, storage and handling charges low. Second, online stores help in better information gathering, storage and recall. And finally for standardized, national and low-involvement brands where the touch and feel aspect is not critical, online stores could hold an advantage. For one, these goods are easily available and have the same meaning for all concerned parties, thereby reducing the possibility of wrong orders and confusion. In an online store, these can be put up for sale without even holding stock. Amazon.com is an example in which the return of books was 1-2 per cent in comparison to a traditional bookshop with returns in the range of 25 per cent.

With these gains, the cost of food, staples and groceries should fall. Pro-Net retailers attack the cost of supply chain in traditional selling, but it is pertinent to note that there are plenty of hidden charges in online retail marketing. As media reports and research over the past five years show, online grocery shopping has its own supply chain whose costs are actually passed onto the customers. Another supply chain issue is the number of times delivery is done. Often it has been observed that the grocery is delivered in parts even though the order is placed in one go. And each time a delivery charge is added. These are the hidden costs. It is thus clear that even in India's fledgling online grocery markets, there is a need for scaling up the volume and margin.

7.3.2 Broadband to Aid Retailing

User intimacy with the Internet will grow as interaction through multiple platforms and access points becomes common. The gap between PC owners and Internet subscribers is reducing. This growth in Internet adoption can be attributed to faster and cheaper access options driven by broadband technology.

ECONOMY WATCH	INDIA 118TH IN BROADBAND CONNECTIVITY

'There is lack of user experience. Internet content in India is not available in regional languages. Moreover with the economic slowdown, there is a lack of push for online game clubs,' said Manufacturers Association for Information Technology (MAIT) Executive Director Vinnie Mehta. 'While TV offers localized content and entertainment Internet does not,' said Desi Valli, COO of Net4, India's second largest ISP. 'Once IP telephony and IPTV kick in fully, we might see an increase in the number of subscribers,' he added. According to a JuxtConsult survey, only 13 per cent Internet users in India prefer to read content in English.

'Globally, countries having high internet penetration have the government behind them as the major investor,' said David Belson, Director of market Intelligence in Massachusetts-based Akarnai Technologies, a US-based Internet services platform provider. According to a global survey by Akamat, India ranked 118 in broadband penetration, with 0.0901 broadband IPs (Internet Protocol addresses) per capita in the last quarter of 2008. Another survey by World Economic Forum and INSEAD, released in April 2009, ranked India at 60th position in terms of Internet access in schools. It ranked India 68th in terms of monthly broadband subscription charge as a percentage of monthly GDP per capita.

A broadband connection is available at about ₹250 per month, much lower than the average ARPU from a prepaid mobile subscriber in India in 2010. The issue of unbundling of the local loop of BSNL to promote more competition in broadband penetration in rural areas is still on the table, even after the Telecom Regulatory Authority of India's (TRAI's) repeated recommendations. TRAI's recommendations to open unrestricted IP telephony have also found resistance from mobile operators. There have been many suggestions like tax sops on money spent on broadband subscription for citizens but none have been implemented so far.

Meanwhile, the ₹25,000 crore in the Universal Service Obligation (USO) fund, which can be used for subsidizing rural Internet, is also lying idle.

Source: The Economic Times, January 2010.

Broadband is the new face of Internet connectivity and Indian households are fast adopting it as it gets cheaper and more widely available. Though dial-up connections continue to dominate the market due to sheer historical build up, it is estimated that broadband connections will overtake dial-ups by 2020. This growth in broadband has been driven by telecom companies pushing into smaller towns and cable operators offering last mile solutions. As bandwidth constraints are removed and last mile connectivity issues resolved, broadband growth will see a sharp upturn. The fall in bandwidth prices will also augur well for growth, particularly as small and medium businesses and cyber cafes will now find it more affordable to get broadband connectivity.

Though dial-up connections continue to dominate the market due to sheer historical build up, it is estimated that broadband connections will overtake dial-ups by 2020.

Growing broadband adoption in India is reflected in the increasing importance of home as an access point, but the upswing is limited because the lower SECs still largely access the Internet from cyber cafes. Increasing Internet access from home is a healthy sign for the industry as it will lead to higher user intimacy with this media. Users will interact in the privacy and comfort of their homes without being constrained by external factors. Amongst the other points of access, cyber cafes still continue to be the most popular. They have served an important function, often being the first point of initiation.

7.3.3 Ten Cs for Internet Marketers

The new tools provided by the digital media, changing consumer lifestyles, the integration of technology and emergence of multiple channels increases the complexity of business. According to Richard Gay, Alan Charlesworth and Rita Esen, the Ten Cs provide a useful framework for marketers to assess the scope of the modern digital market, from both an internal and external perspective. The ten Cs are:

The customer is anyway the king but the Internet further empowers the customer through tools like search engines, price comparison sites, an expectation of real time and multi-channel offerings and makes him more demanding.

(i) **Customer:** The customer should be the central focus of any marketing-driven organization and marketing activities must be designed to achieve high levels of customer satisfaction. From satisfaction comes loyalty and from loyalty comes improved profitability through up-selling, cross-selling, referrals and acquisitions. The customer is anyway the king but the Internet further empowers the customer through tools like search engines, price comparison sites, an expectation of real time and multi-channel offerings and makes him more demanding. The Web, coupled with emerging software technologies enables more precise segmentation, targeting and analysis of customers. This facilitates the implementation of personalized offerings, but due to the power shift from sellers to buyers, these offers should be extended to customers after seeking their permission. This will go a long way in building trust and loyalty, rather than indulging in what is referred to as interruption marketing, such as the dreaded pop-ups. The interactive nature of the Internet also allows faster customer feedback and updating of content.

(ii) **Corporate culture:** As with any business seeking commercial success, shared vision and commitment are priorities. An Internet-based operation is no different though it has other issues to consider such as risk, appropriate IT architecture, front and back office systems and partnerships. Alternatively, the organization may already have an entrepreneurial culture and positive attitude towards the adoption of new technology networks such as the use of EDI. The exponential growth in technological improvements requires constant and expensive investment in new services and features.

(iii) **Convenience:** The Internet and other digital media have enabled greater freedom, flexibility and convenience. The ability to shop at the will and convenience of the customer signals a shift in power away from retailers towards consumers—a shift which marketers have to address. Digital technologies provide mobile convenience to consumers and businesses alike, including Wi-Fi, personal digital assistants (PDAs) and of course mobile phones with their expanding range of interactive tools and services. Businesses and consumers want instant access and connectivity. From a B2B perspective, the Internet and related technologies provide convenience by streamlining ordering, invoicing, fulfilment and payment processes that produce significant cost reductions and help maintain competitiveness through improved supplier and distributor relations. Instant updating of prices, e-catalogues and other Web-based promotional communications create more real-time efficiencies.

(iv) **Competition:** The Internet has brought greater transparency, especially in terms of price, promotions, PR and new product and organizational developments. Price comparison sites such as rediff.com give consumers more knowledge, obviating the need for sales staff to carry out this laborious task. But on the flipside, the same information is also available to competitors.

(v) **Communication:** Communication models consider the interactions and outcomes between the sender and the receiver based on the one-to-many model associated with mass media. The death of mass media, the emergence of the paperless office and growth in one-to-one interactions were forecasted years ago. However, traditional creative marketing skills like headline and copywriting have found a new home online. News, PR and online sales promotions come more quickly and more frequently via newsletters and email marketing campaigns requiring a more succinct style in a world of sound bites and time-starved receivers. Style, tone and an attractive offer or reason to buy, or read on, remain essential elements of successful communication. Receivers were formerly passive. Now they actively seek out sites which appeal and deliver either by search engines, viral marketing or bookmarks. With online communities, the communications dialogue is more two-way than with traditional 'push' communications, and if handled carefully, can be utilized to improve loyalty.

(vi) **Consistency:** Consistency is needed across all communications and all channels to ensure that the brand experience is satisfying, especially if the organization is operating in both the virtual and physical worlds. A brand reflects a company's personality and positioning, but it also reflects something of the customer's self-image. Customers rely on brands for a reassurance of quality but anecdotal evidence suggests that online consumers are mirroring their own offline behaviour and gravitating toward brands and sites they trust and enjoy, rather than being guided purely by price.

A brand reflects a company's personality and positioning, but it also reflects something of the customer's self-image.

(vii) **Creative content:** If the Web has to motivate people to return time and again, then the site content has to be informative, topical, stimulating and of course relevant to the needs of the target market(s). Organizations depend heavily upon Content Management Systems (CMS) to provide real-time information from multiple sources. Further, 'site stickiness' works on the basis that the more time a customer spends online at a firm's site, the more likely he is to spend on its offerings. This is an important aspect in the brand building and retention process. At another level, site content can also play an important role in online customer service and marketing research.

(viii) **Customization:** The Internet provides customized benefits to both buyers and sellers. The term 'mass customization' is used to refer to more personalized, tailored communications as database systems redefine market niches with greater precision. Customization also comes from the ability of the consumer to order more bespoke products unique to them, such as a PC with a specific processor speed, style of monitor, peripherals and printer. This places demands across a range of functions but if it provides a competitive advantage then it is wise to adapt systems to cope with the demand.

The term 'mass customization' is used to refer to more personalized, tailored communications as database systems redefine market niches with greater precision.

(ix) **Coordination:** Marketers have long argued that marketing is a coordinating function. For effective operation of an e-business, real-time dissemination of information from customer to shopping cart to order despatch is required. This in turn demands a scalable IT infrastructure supported by organizational competence across all supporting functions.

(x) **Control:** As another mode of direct marketing, the Internet has the ability to test events and activities. Response and measurement provide marketers with the statistical and financial accountability to further champion the electronic cause within an organization. The Internet, through e-CRM also provides real-time control down to the individual account level that improves profitability resulting from enhanced customer relationship handling.

All economic indicators suggest that the Internet growth is now steady rather than explosive, as buyers and sellers understand its potential after the early dot.com hype.

In short, the Internet as a commercial entity has come a long way in a short time, though its technical development stretches over five decades. Much attention has been given to the economic efficiency generated by the Internet. After the bursts of wild enthusiasm and optimism, the Internet revolution has completed a phase of experimentation, learning and maturity as marketers begin to realize the potential benefits of the technology and how they can use it.

In the new millennium, cost reduction has increased in importance as a critical business driver in the increasingly competitive global market. All economic indicators suggest that the Internet growth is now steady rather than explosive, as buyers and sellers understand its potential after the early dot.com hype. The Internet's scope has also received global governmental appreciation besides other agencies that see not only the economic and competitive benefits but also the wider social impact of this medium.

7.4 Web Marketing

Marketing on the Web is taken as the process of using the Internet to market one's company, its products and services.

Web marketing is marketing on the Web, unlike traditional marketing which takes place in the real world. Marketing on the Web is taken as the process of using the Internet to market a company, its products and services. The very first requirement for Web marketing is the presence of a company website that competes with other company websites to promote its products and services. The well known successes of companies such as Dell Computers emphasize the importance of the Web as a medium for marketing and selling customized products. The Web not only enables customers to give their input and make specific choices from among a set of products and attributes, but also provides an infrastructure for data communication that enables custom-configured online orders to be efficiently fed into production. Assisted by other IT-enabled production and planning processes, manufacturers can effectively mass customize and market products to meet individual customer needs.

Web-enabled customization also extends to the service industry, where increasingly personalized marketing efforts such as Charles Schwab's 'My Schwab' (www.schwab.com) provide a front end for the customized-selling of services. In many ways, an e-commerce strategy is an important enabler of a product customization strategy.

To encourage repeat visits, companies need to pay attention to context and content factors. Visitors will judge a site's performance on its ease-of-use and its physical attractiveness. Ease-of-use breaks down into three attributes: (i) the website downloads quickly, (ii) the first page is easy to understand, and (iii) the visitor finds it easy to navigate to other pages that also open quickly.

A site's physical attractiveness is determined by the following factors: (i) the individual pages are easy on the eye and yet crammed with content, (ii) the typefaces and font sizes are very readable, and (iii) the site makes good use of colour (and sound).

Context factors facilitate repeat visits, but they do not necessarily ensure that this happens. Returning to a site depends on the content, which must be interesting, useful, and continuously changing.

Certain types of content function well to attract first-time visitors and bring them back again. These include: (i) in-depth information with links to related sites, (ii) changing news of interest to visitors, (iii) free offers that are changed frequently, (iv) contests and sweepstakes, (v) humour, and (vi) games.

Web marketing is conducted through interactive online computer systems which link consumers with sellers electronically.

If traditional marketing is about creating exchanges that simultaneously satisfy the firm and the customer, Web marketing is the process of using online activities to build and maintain customer relationships to facilitate exchange of ideas, products and services that satisfy the goals of both parties.

MARKETING IN ACTION — **NEO RETAIL HEALTH PORTAL TARGETS ₹100 CRORE SALES**

Neo Retail Limited, which floated the specialty webstore, www.healthshoppe.com, for health, beauty, fitness and wellness products, in July 2009 plans to attract some three lakh customers by March 2011. The company also expects to clock ₹100 crore revenue by then, despite the economic slowdown and fall in consumer sentiments. The webstore has a partnership with 100 brands and sells 4,000 SKUs. These include reputed brands like GNC, Sundown, Nature's Gate, +H2O, Baidyanath, Durex, Schwabe, Times Wellness, Dr. Morepen, 11 Morrison, Will Medicare, Scortis and Rite Bite. Neo Retail plans to tie up with another 300 brands and expand its offering to 25,000 SKUs by January 2011.

Neo Retail founder and CEO Deepak Saraf said the penetration of affordable broadband connectivity along with a rising number of credit card transactions on the Internet will be a prime sales trigger for his online venture. 'Moreover, we will offer attractive deals which consumers will not get in a store. This is an internationally time-tested business model,' he said.

Bennett, Coleman & Company Limited (BCCL) has invested in Neo Retail. 'The partnership with BCCL will accelerate our growth process manifold and will give us a huge competitive advantage,' said Saraf.

This apart, Neo Retail plans to set up touch screen kiosks in hospitals, clinics, gyms, health centres, doctor chambers, spas and airports. 'Such kiosks will act as another point of sale. We are currently finalizing the rollout plan across the nation,' he said.

The webstore has a partnership with ICICI Bank's Internet payment gateway to process online transactions. 'We offer a safe, secure and convenient way to search and buy products. Going forward, we also plan to set up a call centre where consumers can buy products. This will help us to target people who are not Internet savvy,' Saraf said.

Source: The Economic Times, May 2009.

7.4.1 Characteristics of Web Marketing

(a) Process: Like traditional marketing programmes, an Internet marketing programme also involves a process. The process has several stages; it includes setting corporate and business-unit strategies, framing the market opportunity, formulating the marketing strategy, designing the customer experience and designing the marketing programme. These stages must be coordinated and be internally consistent. While the process can be described in a simple linear fashion, the marketing strategist often has to loop back and forth during the formative stages.

Successful marketing programmes move target customers through three stages of relationship building: awareness, exploration and commitment.

(b) **Building and maintaining customer relationships:** The goal of marketing is to build and create lasting customer relationships. Hence, the focal point shifts from finding customers to nurturing a sufficient number of committed, loyal customers. Successful marketing programmes move target customers through three stages of relationship building: awareness, exploration and commitment. It is important to stress that the goal of web marketing is not simply to build relationships with online customers. Rather, the goal is to build offline as well as online relationships. The Web marketing programme may well be part of a broader campaign to satisfy customers who use both online and offline services, which can be devised under two phases as described below:

Phase 1: Setting Corporate and Business-Unit Strategies

Corporate strategy addresses the interrelationship between the various business units in a firm, including decisions about which units should be kept, sold or augmented. Business-unit strategy focuses on how a particular unit in the company attacks the market to gain a competitive advantage.

Phase 2: Framing the Market Opportunity

Stage two entails the analysis of market opportunities and an initial first pass of the business concept, that is, collecting sufficient online and offline data to assess the opportunities. This can be done in four stages: seeding the opportunity, specifying unmet or undeserved customer needs, identifying the target segment, declaring the company's resource-based opportunity for advantage, assessing opportunity attractiveness and making the final go/no-go decision. The final go/no-go choice is often a corporate or business-unit decision in which marketing plays a critical role by assessing the opportunity.

Web marketing strategy is based upon corporate, business-unit and overall marketing strategies of the firm. The marketing strategy goals, resources and sequencing of actions must be tightly aligned with the retail business-unit strategy. Finally, the overall marketing strategy comprises both offline and online marketing activities.

7.4.2 Stages of Web Marketing Strategy

Firms must understand the type of customer experience that needs to be delivered to meet the retail market opportunity. Hence the importance of designing the customer experience. The experience should correlate with the firm's positioning and marketing strategy. Thus, the design of the customer experience constitutes a bridge between high-level marketing strategy and retail marketing programme tactics.

When customers have basic information, knowledge or attitude about a firm or its offerings but have not initiated any communications with the firm, they are in the awareness stage.

(i) *Awareness:* When customers have basic information, knowledge or attitude about a firm or its offerings but have not initiated any communications with the firm, they are in the awareness stage. Consumers become aware of firms through a variety of sources, including word-of-mouth, traditional marketing such as television advertising and online marketing programmes such as banner ads. Awareness is the first step in a potentially deeper relationship with a firm.

(ii) *Exploration:* In the exploration stage, the customer (and firm) begin to communicate and initiate actions that enable an evaluation of whether or not to pursue a deeper relationship. This stage is also likely to include some trial on the part of the customer. Exploration is analogous to sampling songs, or test driving a car. In the online world, this exploration may take the form of frequent site visits, some e-commerce retail exchanges and possibly even the return of merchandise. It may include phone call follow-ups on delivery times or emails about product inventory. The exploration stage may take only a few visits or perhaps years to unfold.

Exploration is analogous to sampling songs, going on a first date or test driving a car.

(iii) *Commitment:* In this context, commitment involves a sense of obligation or responsibility for a product or a firm. When customers commit to a website, their repeated, enduring attitudes and behaviours reflect loyalty. Commitment is a state of mind as well as a pattern of behaviour.

Commitment involves feeling a sense of obligation or responsibility for a product or a firm.

(iv) *Dissolution:* Not all customers are equally valuable to the firm. In an industrial marketing context, managers often refer to the 80/20 rule of profitability. That is, 20 per cent of customers provide 80 per cent of the profit. By implication, therefore, a large number of customers are unprofitable or incur the company high costs to serve. Firms should segment their most valuable and less valuable customers. The most valuable customers may be identified on the basis of profit, revenue, and/or strategic significance.

7.4.3 The Web Marketing Mix

The 4Ps of marketing—product, price, promotion and place/distribution are part of the Web mix too. Online marketing, however, has two additional elements: community and branding. Community is the level of interaction that unfolds between users. A firm can encourage community formation and nurture community development. However, community is intrinsically about user-to-user connections.

Branding is a critical component of building long-term relationships on the Web. Thus, rather than view branding as a sub-component of the product, it is developed here as a moderating variable upon the product levers, pricing, communication, community and distribution.

(i) *Product*: The product is the service or physical good that a firm offers for sale. A wide range of product forms are being offered on the Internet, including physical goods (e.g. clothing), information-intensive products (e.g. online edition of *The Wall Street Journal*) and services (e.g. online grocers). Frequently, the offerings are a combination of all three forms. In the course of building customer relationships, a firm can use a variety of product levers to cement enduring customer relationships. Product packaging is often used to build customer awareness; while upgrades and complimentary services enable customers to explore a deeper connection; and customized offerings strengthen commitment. The key point is that specific product levers can be used to encourage a stronger connection with a brand. Retail price is critical because it influences the perceived customer value (the complete product offering minus cost is often termed customer value). Traditional levers include such potential choices, such as tiered loyalty programmes, volume discounts, subscription models and targeted price promotions. The Web has created an entirely new category of pricing tools for new-economy firms to use, including dynamic pricing strategies.

Marketing communication can encourage exploration, commitment and also dissolution.

(ii) *Communication*: Marketing communication can encourage exploration, commitment and also dissolution. Viral marketing (where one user informs another user about a site through emails) often leads to exploration of a firm's offerings by new customers. Permission marketing (where customers opt to receive communications from a firm) is intended to encourage commitment to the firm. Both offline and online communication levers can encourage customers to build a stronger bond with the firm and ideally should be integrated in every marketing programme.

Community is defined as a set of interwoven relationships built upon shared interests, which satisfy members' needs otherwise unattainable individually.

(iii) *Community*: Community is defined as a set of interwoven relationships built upon shared interests, which satisfy members' needs which are otherwise individually unattainable. A unique aspect of the Web is the speed with which communities can be formed. Of equal importance is the impact that these communities can have on the firm. A critical question confronting Web marketers is how communities should be leveraged to forge deep customer relationships. Communities can be leveraged to build awareness (e.g. user-to-user communication to make customers aware of a product promotion), encourage exploration (e.g. user groups discussing which automotive options to purchase or not purchase), and commitment (e.g. bonds between users lead to deepening involvement with the site).

(iv) *Distribution*: The Internet is a completely new form of commerce, a revolution in how customers and firms interact. It is also a distribution channel for a firm's products. With respect to its role as a distribution channel, the Web has the power to shift customers to a new channel or to use this channel in combination with other channels (e.g. search the Web and then purchase at a retail store). Distribution levers include the number of intermediaries (both online and offline), the breadth of channel coverage, and messaging from the channel. Broad levels of distribution impact both customer awareness and the potential for further customer exploration of the firm and its offerings.

(v) *Branding*: Internet brands have proven difficult to build, perhaps because of the lack of a physical presence and direct human contact which makes virtual business less tangible to customers than traditional business. Despite huge outlays on advertising, product discounts and purchasing incentives, most dot.com brands have not touched the power or draw of established brands, achieving only a modest impact on loyalty and barriers to entry.

However, branding plays two roles in marketing strategy. First, branding is an outcome of a firm's marketing activities. Marketing programmes affect how consumers perceive the brand, and hence its value. Second, branding is a part of every marketing strategy. That is, each marketing activity is enhanced if the brand is strong or suppressed if the brand is weak. Branding levers work in concert with other marketing levers to produce positive results for the firm.

The first concept in branding is individual-level marketing exchange. In addition to high levels of interactivity, customers expect to have a personal experience with the firm. Broadcast approaches send the same message to all members of the target audience. But the Web enables the firm to engage in customer-specific actions—in fact broadcast to an audience of one. Equally important, the customer too can control the degree of customization by setting the level of customization as desired. Hence, the extent of individualization can be controlled both by the firm and the customer.

The first concept in branding is individual-level marketing exchange. In addition to high levels of interactivity, customers expect to have a personal experience with the firm.

Interactivity is the extent to which a two-way communication flow occurs between a firm and its customers. The Web enables a level of customer dialogue that has not previously been experienced in the history of business. Certainly customers could have conversations with retail store clerks, sales representatives, or managers; however, it is not possible at the scale that the Web affords. Hence, the fundamental shift is one from broadcast media such as television, radio and newspapers to one that encourages debate, exchange of ideas and dialogue.

Pricing can be both interactive and individualized—indeed, that is the essence of dynamic pricing. And market communication can be both interactive and individualized, which is the purpose of real-time customer service on the Web. Furthermore, products and services can be designed in real-time by the customer, to maximize both interactivity and customization. This level of customer dialogue has revolutionized the impact of the Internet on marketing.

7.4.4 Crafting the Customer Interface

The Web has shifted the locus of exchange from the marketplace (i.e. face-to-face interaction) to the marketspace (screen-to-face interaction). The key difference is that the nature of the exchange relationship is now mediated by a technology interface. This interface can be a desktop PC, sub-notebook, personal digital assistant, mobile phone, wireless applications protocol (WAP) device or any other Internet-enabled appliance. As this shift from people-mediated to technology-mediated interface unfolds, it is important to consider the types of interface design considerations that confront managements and one must seek ways and means to find answers for questions like: what is the look-and-feel or context of the site? Should the site include commerce activities? How important are communities in the business model?

7.4.5 Evaluating the Marketing Programme

This final stage involves the evaluation of the overall Web marketing programme. This demands a balanced focus on both customer and financial metrics.

7.4.6 Customer Advocacy and Insight

An insatiable curiosity for customers and marketplaces is a necessity for today's marketing professionals. This appetite is behind an individual's desire to transform customer data from disparate sources into meaningful and actionable insights, which in turn become a platform for advocacy. Since the Web enables a much higher degree of interaction with customers, designing and promoting these around customers' needs to progressively gain deeper insights are critical components of creating positive customer experiences. A true customer advocate will look to provide demonstrable added value to each customer interaction to form the basis for a meaningful relationship. As both customer behaviour and enabling technologies simultaneously evolve, an indepth understanding of customer needs should serve as the guidepost that drive marketing decisions.

7.5 Integration

Today's marketing professionals need to have an integrated or holistic view of the customer and the enterprise in order to create a uniquely advantaged strategic plan.

As discussed earlier, the Internet represents both a new channel and a new communications medium. Today's marketing professionals need to have an integrated or holistic view of the customer and the enterprise in order to create a uniquely advantaged strategic plan. In today's multi-channel environment, a consistent message and experience must be maintained across customer touch points in order to create a consistent brand image. Beyond strategy, a marketing manager must fundamentally understand how to integrate these new tools into the overall marketing mix. Managers who are able to integrate their marketing plan are more likely to capitalize on the synergies between marketing elements and thus derive greater effectiveness.

Look at the advantages of Web-based marketing efforts for reaching a larger customer base.

7.5.1 Advantages of Web-based Marketing

Using the Web marketing can become a global effort and enterprise, enabling marketers to reach potential customers the worldover. Web marketing allows customers to shop online at their convenience from their home or workplace. It also allows firms to provide customers with video clips and statistics, thereby giving the former ample scope to compare a firm's products and services with those of its competitors. Web-based marketing enables direct interaction between the marketer and the customers, enabling both to enjoy a close relationship with one another.

It offers immense opportunities to marketers to expand their businesses on a global scale. Companies that have traditionally catered to small markets are today competing with multinationals by expanding their business online and reaching prospective customers across the globe. On the other hand, online advertising enables marketers to reach maximum customers at minimum cost.

Maintaining Web stores does not have traditional costs associated with the maintenance of a conventional store. For instance, costs related to real state, shelf space, interiors, and insurance premiums are almost absent in online marketing. Web marketing allows marketers to count the exact number of customers visiting the site, thus allowing them to devise promotional strategies accordingly.

There are, however, certain challenges that online marketers have to face. With an increasing number of marketers going online, there are about 17 lakh commercial websites competing with each other to attract buyers. This brings a significant increase in marketing costs, since the cost of acquiring an online customer surpasses the average lifetime value of that customer. The lifetime value of online customer is low because information is readily available and the cost of switching sides is lower on the Web. Strategies for advertising on the Internet have to be innovative. Banner ads are often used to advertise products and services. However, their effectiveness is constantly being questioned.

With an increasing number of marketers going online, there are about 17 lakh commercial websites competing with each other to attract buyers to their websites.

Apart from innovative strategies, marketers have to focus on marketing their products and services by entering into strategic collaborations with other sites through which they can enhance their chances of reaching potential customers. Online marketers could also advertise their offerings through conventional media such as print, radio and television.

CASE STUDY

TECHNOLOGY INTEGRATION IN THE ENTERTAINMENT INDUSTRY

Technology has been one of the key drivers of the entertainment industry, often altering the industry's existing products, cost structure and distribution. Empirical evidence suggests that though technological innovations create disruptive changes in the entertainment industry, they add value to its products. Technological breakthroughs in the areas of sound, visual effects and animation have been significantly beneficial to content creation. These breakthroughs offer audiences a hi-tech content viewing and listening experience. Leading global broadcasting companies are forced to put development and use of new technologies at the centre of their core strategies because of the growing adoption of digital television.

For a content distributor, the future lies in making specialized offerings, such as high-resolution pictures, high-speed Internet access, online games and information, pay-per-view electronic commerce services and voice telephony. New technologies, such as satellite radio, are characterized by their ability to reach out to larger audiences than ever before, reducing the cost per contact. While these technologies typically require high initial capital expenditure, the same may be off set by incremental volume gains through increased reach. It is this trade-off that needs to be evaluated before an investment is made in any new technology.

If one were to look at emerging trends in technology and their impact on entertainment consumption, the most significant are seen in the areas of media distribution, though some may be regarded as product innovations.

The increasing penetration of technology is a major force shaping the entertainment landscape today. It will completely revolutionize content delivery as well as the viewership experience. Once these technological changes attain a critical mass, they can have a shattering effect on the existing industry equilibrium. Due to the imminent impact of these and other technologies, successful media and entertainment companies will be those that are prepared for the disruptive effects on their business models and the industry structure.

UTV New Media Ltd., the digital arm of UTV, launched India's first exclusive music video channel UTV@play on Mobile TV. This service provided Indian music lovers with India's first exclusive mobile channel where users could access their favourite videos and music at just the click of a button. It also offered a vast catalogue of music videos not only from Bollywood but also from other language films.

Television

Digital distribution platforms such as direct-to-home (DTH) and Mobile TV are also transforming the industry. And Mobile TV, where content streams in on mobile handsets, currently at an introductory stage, is poised to grow with 3G.

DTH

Direct-to-Home (DTH) is a wireless digital audio/video service delivered to a consumer through satellite. DTH transmission is received directly on the consumer's TV set through a small dish antenna unlike with a regular cable connection. The encrypted transmission is decoded by a set-top box (STB).

Year	*Market growth rate (subscribers/month)*
2005	42,000 (first private player, Dish TV)
2006–7	1,70,000 (entry of Tata Sky and Sun Direct)
2007–8	5,00,000 (entry of Big TV and Digital TV)

- 10 million DTH subscribers by the end of 2008.
- 57 million DTH subscribers projected by 2015.

A DTH connection offers immense opportunity to both broadcasters and viewers as it does not involve the local cable operator and puts the broadcaster directly in touch with the consumer. Besides transmitting numerous channels over a single platform, the technology allows the broadcaster to introduce a large number of interactive applications in the television market, like broadband Internet connection, gaming, and video-on-demand. A user can scan up to 700 channels. Doordarshan Direct Plus, Dish TV, Tata Sky, Sun Direct, Big TV and Airtel Digital TV are some of the DTH service providers in India.

Mobile TV

Mobile TV is a technology that allows people to view regular live television content on their mobile phones or other mobile devices. This is possible through traditional cable or pay TV subscriptions.

Mobile TV stands for live TV transmitted through digital broadcasting technologies, for example DVB-H (digital video broadcasting-handheld) and DMB (digital multimedia broadcasting). The broadcast network for Mobile TV is different from cellular networks, but 3G is not a precondition for Mobile TV. In India, Nokia has already launched DVB-H-enabled devices N92 and N77 for ₹21,000 and ₹22,500.

The auction of spectrum for Mobile TV services has been recommended by TRAI. Operators with a cellular mobile telephone service licence or unified access service licence would not require any other licence to offer Mobile TV services on their own network. A new class of Mobile TV operators has also been suggested by TRAI. However, the suggestions still need to be accepted by the government.

As early experiments in 2009 appear to be promising, Star Mobile Entertainment has joined hands with Sony Ericsson to put forward pre-loaded PLUS application in handsets falling in the Walkman and Cyber-shot ranges. For this service, users can access over 200 videos for ₹30 a month. Similarly, MTV, the music channel, has tied up with Vodafone to launch a series of animated music videos. Channels like NDTV, CNBC and Cartoon Network have connections with BSNL.

Reliance charges ₹3 per minute for Mobile TV service, expensive when compared with a 99-paise call. However, Idea Cellular promises a basic streaming service comprising 20 channels for ₹150 a month. Some operators are experimenting with daily pricing to encourage sampling and make people comfortable with the idea of Mobile TV.

3G Technology

Third Generation (3G) technology is mainly seen as a facilitator for Mobile TV revolution with high speed data transfer. 3G technology is a convergence of various 2G telecommunication systems. The technology is intended for Smartphones, or multimedia cellphones. The term '3G' refers to the next generation of wireless communications technology, the 'first generation' having been analogue cellular and the 'second generation' (2G and 2.5G) being today's existing GSM/GPRS networks. Video broadcasting and other e-commerce services such as stock transactions and e-learning will be possible much faster. It offers 3 Mbps speed for downloading, which is very high compared to that of 2G technology. 3G provides for Internet surfing, downloading, email attachment downloading, audio-video conferencing, fax services and other broadband applications. The major advance in 3G systems is moving from speech and low-rate data transmission to medium- and high-speed data for video (TV) transmission and Internet browsing.

3G mobile systems will increase the data transfer rate by 200 times. They will also improve audio quality, marking a total change in telephone usage from exclusively voice to predominantly data services.

Internet Protocol Television (IPTV)

Internet Protocol Television (IPTV) is a system through which digital television service is delivered using the architecture and networking methods of the Internet Protocol Suite over a packet-switched network infrastructure, e.g. the Internet and broadband Internet access networks, instead of being delivered through traditional radio frequency broadcast, satellite signal, and cable television (CATV) formats.

IPTV services may be classified into three main groups: live television, time-shifted programming, and content (or video) on demand. It is distinguished from general Internet or Web-based multimedia services by its ongoing standardization process (e.g. ETSI) and preferential deployment scenarios in subscriber-based telecommunications networks with high-speed access channels into end-user premises via set-top boxes or other customer-premises equipment. BSNL, MTNL, Reliance and Bharti Airtel are a few IPTV service providers.

The scope of advertisement for Indian companies has been on the increase everyday with the invention of new technologies and channels.

A major factor that contributes to the growth of online business is word of mouth. Online marketers should, therefore, take special care to make their presence known on the Net and improve sales through word of mouth. Active public relations will also help the company secure higher sales.

7.6 Affiliate Marketing

The Internet is the perfect medium for direct marketers, because it enables immediate and trackable interactions with customers. Experienced direct marketers well-versed in efficient customer acquisition, brand building, database marketing, fulfilment, and customer service are uniquely positioned to take on the challenges and exploit the benefits that e-commerce presents. Direct marketers also realize that the Web is different from other media, for both marketing and selling. The chaotic and dispersed nature of the Web sometimes makes it seem to be an indirect medium. The first major challenge in moving to the Web is getting customers to visit one's site. Since the marketer cannot send his site to them like a catalogue, he has to market the site to their front door, so to speak.

It is in this context that affiliate marketing is gaining popularity as an advertising tool. An affiliate marketer is someone who actively promotes the products or services of one or more businesses, and receives commissions on sales generated through his/her referrals. When it comes to the Web, Amazon.com started the ball rolling on affiliate marketing. In July 1996, it launched its 'associates' programme that now accounts for over 4,50,000 sites in its network in December 2010.

An affiliate marketer is someone who actively promotes the products or services of one or more businesses, and receives commissions on sales generated through his/her referrals.

Within a short time, affiliate marketing has become a significant force in how commerce on the Web occurs. The concept behind it remains simple. It allows customers to buy targeted traffic to the company site. The affiliates are paid to divert traffic from their websites by means of advertising and promotions. It is an economical means of ensuring advertising expenditure since it is spent only on 'targeted' recipients. The firm only pays when a customer (or potential customer) takes the trouble of visiting their site.

EMERGING VEHICLES OF INTERNET MEDIA

Blogs (short for weblogs) are online journals or diaries hosted on a website.

Online games include games played on dedicated game consoles that can be networked. It also includes 'massively multiplayer' games which involve thousands of people who interact simultaneously through personal avatars in online worlds that exist independently of any single player's activity.

Podcasts are audio or video recordings—a multimedia form of a blog or other content. Podcasts are often distributed through aggregators such as iTunes.

Social networks allow members of specific sites to learn about another members' skills, talents, knowledge, or preferences. Commercial examples include Facebook and MySpace. Some companies use such systems internally to help identify experts.

Virtual worlds such as Second Life are highly social, three-dimensional online environments shaped by users who interact with and receive instant feedback from other users through the use of avatars.

Web services are software systems that make it easier for different systems to communicate with each other automatically to pass information or conduct transactions. A retailer and supplier, for example, might use Web services to communicate over the Internet and automatically update each other's inventory systems.

Widgets are programmes that allow user desktops to access Web-based content.

Wikis, such as Wikipedia, are systems for collaborative publishing. They allow many authors to contribute to an online document or discussion.

7.7 Web-based Advertising

As the Internet gained popularity with the average person, marketers began to explore if this medium was lucrative to advertise on.

The growth of the Internet as a provider of standard global access to systems and networks all over the world is an area of huge interest currently, and will very soon become a major consideration for the marketing departments of most Indian organizations. As the Internet gained popularity with the average person, marketers began to explore if this medium was lucrative to advertise on. They realized the medium gave them more than what the previous mediums could offer. It provided consumers with interactivity. They could now interact with their product and build their own experience with it. Marketers believed that this form of brand conditioning would enhance the consumer's brand experience.

We will now look at the principal modes of online advertising.

Banner ads: Banner ads are rectangular boxes of a size pre-specified by the IAB that appear on websites communicating the marketer's message. These ads generally provide a link to another website where the marketer provides further information about his product or service. The effectiveness of the banner is calculated using click-through (clicking the banner and progressing to the linked page) or total exposure (the number of people visit the page the banner is appearing on and are likely to be exposed to the ad). AdRelevance, a US-based research firm, reported that 54 per cent of all ad impressions were branding ads (ads that promote brand positioning, awareness, and benefits). Among these, ads generating awareness accounted for a third of total impressions, followed by positioning ads (20 per cent) and ads promoting a brand benefit (1 per cent).

MARKET WATCH — **HOW COMPANIES ARE MARKETING ONLINE: A MCKINSEY GLOBAL SURVEY**

McKinsey Global Institute (MGI) surveyed 410 marketing executives from public and private companies around the world, representing industries such as business services, energy, retail, technology, and telecommunications. MGI asked respondents about the frequency and effectiveness with which they applied Web-based, digital techniques to five core marketing functions: sales, service, advertising, product development, and pricing. They also enquired about future plans for digital marketing, including where respondents anticipated spending more money in the future. Data was weighted by the GDP of constituent countries to adjust for differences in response rates.

Throughout the brief history of the Internet, expectations have run high for it to 'change everything'. The McKinsey survey showed that things are starting to change in marketing. Companies are moving online across the spectrum of marketing activities, from building awareness to after-sales service, and they see online tools as important and effective components of their marketing strategies. However, the executives also indicated they were making less frequent use of digital tools—from familiar ones such as email and informational websites to new possibilities such as wikis and virtual worlds—than their importance would suggest. Lack of capabilities in companies and their marketing agencies is a critical reason, respondents said, along with the often-cited concerns such as the absence of meaningful metrics.

Companies use the Web to reach customers throughout the decision-making process. In 2010 respondents expect a majority of their customers to discover new products or services online and a third to purchase goods there. A majority of the respondents also expect their companies to be getting 10 per cent or more of their sales from online channels—twice as many companies have hit that mark today. These expectations appear to be driving plans for future spending, at least in some areas.

In addition to established online tools such as email, information-rich websites, and display advertising, survey respondents displayed keen interest in the interactive and collaborative technologies collectively known as Web 2.0 for advertising, product development, and customer service. Web 2.0 technologies which rely on user collaboration include Web services, peer-to-peer networking, blogs, podcasts, and online social networks.

Web-based sales and services were early uses of the Internet for marketing. Respondents said that some approaches—providing service information on websites, interacting with customers via email, and executing transactions on company websites—are widely used. Most companies focus on their own websites for both sales and services, but some are experimenting much further afield: 15 per cent of respondents in the high-tech industry, for example, said they were experimenting with selling in virtual worlds.

Companies using digital tools frequently across the marketing spectrum were more likely than others to be using more complex tools for online services; 42 per cent offered 'click to call' and more than a quarter offered text chats with service personnel, compared with 18 per cent of other companies in each case.

The flexibility and degree of personalization the Web offers would seem to make pricing another natural area for companies to move online. Nonetheless, companies have been slower to act here than in any other facet of marketing, and most don't think online tools are particularly important to pricing. More than a quarter said they were not at all important. Spending on digital advertising seems set to increase significantly. Today a third of the companies that advertise online are already spending more than 10 per cent of their advertising budgets there. Three years from now, twice as many respondents said they will be spending at least that much online, and 11 per cent said they would be spending the majority of their budgets online.

Just over a third of the survey respondents were frequent users of digital advertising tools ranging from emails to blogs. The share of online spending currently allocated to each vehicle is roughly aligned with usage. Companies that are frequent users of online marketing tools for the full range of marketing activities also make use of the complete range of online advertising vehicles more actively. They are more likely to use each vehicle than companies that are less active online, and they are particularly likely to be making more use of video ads, branded sponsorships, blogs, and social networking.

The majority of respondents said they found online vehicles more efficient than traditional media. Interestingly, search advertisements—considered to be the most efficient—ranked only third in usage. However, respondents also said that they were likely to increase their spending on search and on video ads over the next three years, while display ads and email were among the least likely vehicles to gain spending.

Marketers said that online tools helped them meet their goals throughout the customer decision-making process, sometimes in ways that contravened the conventional wisdom about how these tools are best used. Search advertisements, for example, were developed to generate direct response, but the survey respondents said that the ads are almost equally useful in brand building.

It is also clear that companies are experimenting: respondents described such a wide variety of objectives for some vehicles that many companies still seem to be deciding which digital marketing techniques are most effective for what purposes. Collaborative tools such as blogs, wikis, and social networks are being used in advertising, product development, and customer service. At the simplest level, for instance, 22 per cent of the respondents said that their companies hosted user forums for customers to help one another. Further, 31 per cent of all the survey respondents were using collaborative product-development tools such as initiating discussions in blogs to test ideas, involving customers in the use of collaborative design tools, and testing how well products sell in virtual worlds. Frequent users of digital tools for all marketing purposes are much likelier than others to exploit these collaborative product development tools.

According to the marketing executives surveyed by MGI, by 2010 the Web will play a role in the first two stages of the consumer decision-making process—product awareness and information gathering—for a sizeable majority of all consumers, though with notable variations among industries. The expectation that most consumers will seek out new products online may be a factor in the plans of companies to increase spending significantly on digital advertising tools they see as most useful in building brands.

Again, some companies, particularly the most frequent users of the full range of online marketing tools, have already begun to integrate their online and offline marketing efforts. Most, however, have not: only 42 per cent ran integrated campaigns, and 32 per cent used online tools to influence offline sales. As online tools and techniques take on a larger role in marketing strategies, these numbers will likely grow, increasing the possibility of reaching a sizeable number of online customers through successful efforts that could reap benefits offline as well. A smaller proportion of customers, respondents expect, will use the Web to execute transactions or access services. Even so, 53 per cent of all respondents expected that their companies would be making more than 10 per cent of total sales through online channels three years from now, more than twice as many who do so today.

Source: 'How Businesses are Using Web 2.0: A McKinsey Global Survey', *The McKinsey Quarterly,* Web exclusive, March 2007.

Web banner and panel ads: These are small rectangular graphic images that usually have a call to action (like 'click here'). These banners are placed on high-traffic websites like Yahoo!, AOL, ebay, and so on, so as to get an opportunity to increase traffic to one's website. They can be placed at the top, bottom, middle of a page, or anywhere you like them to be. Needless to say banner ads works best when the advertised brand is closely associated with the information available on that site.

Slipstream ads: Firms like General Motors focus on 'slipstream' ads, which are highly targeted spots that run in live audio or video streams, augmented by click-through facilities.

The real goal of any ad is to incite a potential customer to seek out more information.

7.8 Understanding Mobile Marketing

Mobile marketing is the use of the mobile medium as a communications and entertainment channel between a brand and an end-user. This is the only personal channel enabling spontaneous, direct, interactive and/or targeted communication, any time/any place. Mobile marketing can be used on all mobile devices including PDAs and laptops. Communications include short messaging service (SMS), multimedia messaging service (MMS) that combines text with simple graphics and sound, wireless application protocol (WAP), mobile internet and WAP-push services, and full multimedia third generation (3G) services.

Mobile marketing is highly personalized, interactive, and has an immediate impact. When used in cross-media promotions, mobile marketing has been proven to generate significant increase in sales.

Mobile marketing is highly personalized, interactive, and has an immediate impact. When used in cross-media promotions, mobile marketing has been proven to generate significant increase in sales. This form of marketing is fast becoming a more open, universal and integrated aspect of the wider multimedia environment. Mobile phones now support complex applications which were traditionally found only on PCs. Operators are extending their high-speed data networks, making it quick and easy to download and access these applications. The billing model is opening up to include more traditional systems, allowing companies to choose their own billing methods and integrating them more easily in the systems they already have in place.

From music and photographic images in the consumer field to CRM or ERP solutions in the corporate world, companies offering all kinds of products and services are starting to take advantage of mobility.

There are several types of companies that operate in the wireless world, and the number is growing as the industry expands. These companies are important parts of the overall structure, and all of them generate revenue from it. They range from the behemoth network operators down to the ringtone and content aggregators. As the mobile industry has now turned from a specialized technology market to a mass consumer market, practically any company can enter the wireless world. The question that needs to be asked is how can a company best profit from the range of services on offer?

7.8.1 Players in the Wireless World

Phone users: These are the end-users who use all the services, whether they are aware of it or not. They are the 'grassroots' of the wireless world.

Network operators: Network operators are the overlords of the wireless world; without them there would be no network. The main network operators in the world are Vodafone, Orange, T-Mobile, Hutchison Telecom and NTT DoCoMo, and Bharti Airtel in India. Network operators route messages, bill phone users and collect revenue from them. There is some crossover with fixed landline operators in some countries, but generally they remain separate entities.

Access providers: These are gateways for companies and mobile networks. They offer companies a window to the wireless network and let them take advantage of the technologies on offer (GPRS, SMS, WAP, etc.). An access provider manages commercial and technological relationships with network operators and guarantees quality ('always-on') service.

An access provider manages commercial and technological relationships with network operators and guarantees quality ('always-on') service.

Platform providers: Platform providers are similar to access providers, except that they go one step further to provide a software-based platform to enable the launch of a mobile-based service. They handle the whole process, from user experience through to network billing and customer support. Given this they need to work closely with and have an in-depth knowledge of the other service providers in the wireless world.

Content and application developers: With the advent of rich media browsing on mobile phones, content developers have become an essential part of the wireless world—and an important revenue stream both for themselves and for the rest of the industry. Sprite Interactive is one of the top content providers in the UK, and this company, like numerous other content providers, produces topical and entertaining content for mobiles, either to certain specifications or as part of their own inhouse catalogue. Examples of mobile content include news streams, ringtones, logos, Java games, videos, and Java applications.

Content aggregators and publishers: These are the companies that sell the content developed by content and application developers directly to phone users. There can be some crossover between content aggregators and content developers, but generally the two areas remain separate. Content aggregators usually advertise products in magazines and newspapers, from their own Web portal and on the television.

Corporate companies: This group includes companies that have an interest in the wireless world as a means of communicating with customers, employees and suppliers and generating revenue.

Marketing and media agencies: These agencies are involved strictly as consultants, advising companies on how best to penetrate the wireless world.

Mobile consultants: There is usually some crossover here with access or platform providers. Mobile consultants advise companies on how best to define and implement their wireless strategy.

Mobile Virtual Network Operator (MVNO): MVNOs are mobile operators who don't own spectrum or network infrastructure. Instead, they have business arrangements with traditional mobile operators to buy minutes of use (MOU) for sale to their own customers. They are similar to resellers of telecom services such as long distance, local exchange and mobile network services. MVNOs are similar, but they usually add value to the resale of mobile services, such as brand appeal and distribution channels. An example of MVNO is Virgin Mobile, which provide SMS facilities for as little as 3 paise per text in 2010.

Successful MVNOs are those that have positioned their operations so that customers do not distinguish any significant difference in service or network performance, yet offer some special affinity to their customers.

Successful MVNOs are those that have positioned their operations so that customers do not distinguish any significant difference in service or network performance, yet offer some special affinity to their customers. Well-diversified independent MVNOs offer a product mix that traditional mobile operators cannot match; for example, supermarket MVNOs could offer a package of shopping rewards and benefits.

MVNOs have full control over the SIM card, branding, marketing, billing and customer care operations. SMS messages are generally no more than 140-60 characters in length, and contain no images or graphics. When a message is sent it is received by a Short Message Service Centre (SMSC), which must then get it to the appropriate mobile device. To do this, the SMSC sends an SMS request to the home location register (HLR) to find the roaming customer. Once the HLR receives the request, it will respond to the SMSC with the subscriber's status: (1) inactive or active; and (2) where the subscriber is roaming. If the response is 'inactive', then the SMSC will hold on to the message for a period of time. When the subscriber accesses his or her device, the HLR sends an SMS notification to the SMSC, and the SMSC will then attempt delivery. The SMSC transfers the message, in a short message delivery point-to-point format, to the serving system.

After this the system pages the device and, if it responds, the message gets delivered. The SMSC receives verification that the message has been received by the end-user, then categorizes the message as 'sent' and will not attempt to send it again.

An SMS message is made up of two parts. The first is the header, which is the message protocol information and includes the sender's address, type of coding and message validity. The second consists of the data, which is the body of the message with the information to be transmitted. An SMS can be interpreted with three types of encoding: 7-bit, which is the code for the Latin alphabet; 8-bit, which is the code for data; and 16-bit, which is used for Greek and Arabic alphabets (the number of characters for 16-bit is limited to 70).

There are two types of SMS transmissions: Mobile Originated (MO) and Mobile Terminated (MT). MO messages are messages sent from a mobile phone; these can be sent to another mobile, a computer or a landline. MT messages are messages sent by the network to a mobile phone. To enable the identification of corporate servers by the networks, specific numbers can be used; these are called shortcodes.

There are several organizations worldwide that provide guidance on the use of SMS for marketing. Two such organizations are the Mobile Marketing Association (MMA) and the Institute of Practitioners in Advertising (IPA), both of which are made up of credible people from strong marketing backgrounds. Although both have drafted guidelines, the IPA has launched new guidelines for mobile marketing campaigns. These guidelines have been created by the IPA's Digital Marketing Group, which is dedicated to raising the digital standard of the industry, to help ensure that IPA members utilize the best practices, are aware of regulatory requirements and avoid inadvertently 'spamming' when executing their own SMS campaigns or working with mobile marketing agencies and mobile network service providers. The option to 'unsubscribe' from receiving SMS messages is also covered in this guideline.

The **Multimedia Messaging Service (MMS)** adds images, text, audio clips and, ultimately, video clips to SMS. Although SMS and MMS are both messaging technologies there is a dramatic difference between the two as far as content goes, with the average size of an MMS message being much larger than that of an SMS message.

At the heart of MMS technology is the Synchronized Multimedia Integration Language (SMIL) application, which allows for the creation and transmission of 'presentations' over a mobile phone. These presentations take the form of miniature slide shows, much like a scaled-down version of PowerPoint. SMIL lets the user define what each slide contains, the timing for each slide, and the order in which the slides should appear. SMIL data is not supported by certain handsets, but without the SMIL code MMS data is displayed as successive content that the user must scroll through.

i-mode: i-mode is NTT DoCoMo's mobile internet access system popular in Japan. The 'i' in 'i-mode' stands for information. The i-mode is in fact a multibillion-dollar ecosystem and is part of Japan's social and economic infrastructure. Approximately 30 per cent of Japan's population uses i-mode about ten times or more a day. The system allows them to send emails, book train tickets and to perform other Internet-style activities. i-mode started in Europe (Netherlands, Germany, Belgium, France, Spain, Greece and Italy) in April 2002, and then expanded to Taiwan and Australia.

The year 2010 has witnessed a large amount of crossover in the industry between different types of players. A number of content developers run sites to sell their content, and so can also be defined as content aggregators. Many of the platform and access providers are also aggregators. Every company needs others to best profit from the wireless world. The 3G networks provide high-speed, high-bandwidth support to bandwidth-hungry applications such as full motion videos, video calling and full Internet access. With 3G you can watch music videos, chat with your friends via video calling, send video messages and even watch mobile TV. 3G roll-out has so far been slow in India, but one expects to see 3G-enabled applications and content becoming widespread across mobile networks and service providers.

As the market reaches maturity, the business models that underpin the mobile market are also changing. Look at the changes: voice has become a commodity; SMS is universal and of low added value; voice ARPU (average revenue per user) is falling and SMS ARPU is reaching an upper limit. Operators are seeking new revenue sources and looking at value-added services, particularly via mobile browsing, to help ARPU up scale.

As the market reaches maturity, the business models that underpin the mobile market are also changing. Look at the changes: voice has become a commodity; SMS is universal and of low added value; voice ARPU (average revenue per user) is falling and SMS ARPU is reaching an upper limit.

With voice becoming a commodity, new types of voice offers are arising in some of the more advanced markets, such as all-inclusive schemes where customers pay a fixed monthly fee, no matter how many minutes you call.

Table 7.2: Mobile operator revenue models

Mobile data revenue model	*Description*	*Examples*
Session-based charging	Per minute charges, per session charges	Linking to multilayer games, Wi-Fi 802.11b connectivity
Volume-based charging	Per kilobyte charges	Download tunes, downloading music, uploading digital photographs
Per message (SMS and MMS)	10 cents per minute, 2 cents per minute with certain packaged deals	Carriers make money from selling airtime
Flat rate per content type	Pay for what you use	No monthly fees, flat rate charging per minute; Mobile One Asia charges 20 cents during peak hours, 10 cents during off-peak hours, and 5 cents after 9 p.m. and on weekends
Flat rate per content type	'All-you-can-eat' models	SMS messaging, corporate and personal email, instant messaging
Mobile Internet access and basic content subscription services	Portal service (limited number of kilobytes allowed)	America Online; NTT DoCoMo (successful i-mode service charges users a $2.50 monthly fee, plus 25 cents per data packet where one packet is equivalent to 128 bytes of data); Palm.net basic plan (30 messages, 20 stock quotes, 10 sports scores, 10 traffic reports, 10 weather reports)
Mobile Internet access with unlimited or premium content subscription services	Advanced portal services (unlimited kilobytes included in monthly fee)	America Online; Vetizon Express Service; Palm.net Unlimited Volume Plan; Earthlink OmniSky pricing plan offering Internet service to wireless handheld computer users for a fee per month, credit for free calls/products in return for watching ads, Vindigo—text-based ads on palm
Advertising-based models and Revenue-sharing models	Credit for free calls/products in return for watching ads. The mobile operator receives a piece of whatever business is generated from a mobile surfer who clicks through a link to a partner site.	Vindigo—text-based ads on palm Under NTT DoCoMo's i-mode model, 91 per cent business is generated from a mobile surfer, in contrast, the best-case revenue sharing scenario in Europe is a 50/50 arrangement between operators and developers.

In countries where the penetration rate has not reached the same level of maturity, there is strong competition among operators to gain new users (often prepaid users who spend less than contract users and hence lower ARPU).

Today, companies are focusing on wireless solutions that can deliver faster ROI and increased productivity. Mobile phones can help increase productivity in a number of ways, with a growing range of options for mobile voice and data transmission. Analysts agree that despite the economic downshift, mobile wireless technology spending will continue to increase over the next five years since 2010.

Instead of employing mobile wireless technologies to deliver services to customers, many companies are focusing on wireless solutions that can deliver cost reductions through productivity enhancements, which can confer powerful competitive advantages. In particular, firms are investigating wireless solutions that enable employee collaboration, enhance communication and data access between the field and the office, and streamline key business processes.

7.9 Emerging Technologies

Technology alone is rarely the key to unlocking economic value: companies create real wealth when they combine technology with new ways of doing business. MGI has identified eight technology-enabled trends that will help shape business and economy in the coming years. These trends fall within three broad areas of business activity: managing relationships, managing capital and assets, and leveraging information in new ways.

(a) **Distributing co-creation:** The Internet and related technologies give companies radical new ways to harvest the talents of innovators working outside corporate boundaries. Today, in the high technology consumer product and automotive sectors, companies routinely involve customers, suppliers, small specialist businesses, and independent contractors in the creation of new products. Outsiders offer insights that help shape product development, but companies typically control the innovation process. Technology now allows companies to delegate substantial control to outsiders—co-creation—by outsourcing innovation to business partners that work together in networks. By distributing innovation through the value chain, companies reduce their costs and usher new products into the market faster by eliminating bottlenecks that come with total control.

By distributing innovation through the value chain, companies reduce their costs and usher new products into the market faster by eliminating bottlenecks that come with total control.

Information goods such as software and editorial content are ripe for this kind of decentralized innovation. The Linux operating system, for example, was developed over the Internet by a network of specialists. But companies can also create physical goods in this way. Loncin, a leading Chinese motorcycle manufacturer, sets broad specifications for products and then lets its suppliers work with one another to design the components, making sure everything fits together, and thereby reduce costs. In the past, Loncin did not make extensive use of information technology to manage the supplier community—an approach reflecting business realities in China and in this specific industrial market. Recent advances in open standards-based computing (for example, computer-aided design programmes that work well with other kinds of software) are making it easier to co-create physical goods for more complex value chains in competitive markets.

If this approach to innovation becomes broadly accepted, the impact on companies and industries could be substantial. MGD estimates, for instance, that in the US economy alone roughly 12 per cent of all labour activity could be transformed by more distributed and networked forms of innovation—from reducing the amount of legal and administrative activity that intellectual property involves, to restructuring or eliminating some traditional R&D work.

Companies pursuing this trend, however, will have less control over innovation and the intellectual property rights that go with it. They will also have to compete for the attention and time of the best and most capable contributors.

Companies that involve customers in design, testing, marketing (such as viral marketing), and after-sales process get better insights into customer needs and behaviour and may be able to cut the cost of acquiring customers, engender greater loyalty, and speed up development cycles.

(b) **Using consumers as innovators:** Consumers also co-create with companies. The online encyclopedia Wikipedia, for instance, could be viewed as a service or product created by its customers. The differences between the way companies co-create with partners, on the one hand, and with customers, on the other, are so marked that the consumer aspect is really a separate trend. These differences include the nature and range of interactions, the economics of making them work, and the management challenges associated with them. As the Internet has evolved—an evolution prompted in part by new Web 3.0 technologies—it has become a more widespread platform for interaction, communication and activism. Consumers increasingly want to engage online with one another and with organizations. Companies can tap this new mode of customer engagement for their economic benefit.

OhmyNews, for instance, is a popular South Korean online newspaper written by upwards of 60,000 contributing 'citizen reporters'. It has quickly become one of South Korea's most influential media outlets, with around 7,00,000 site visits a day. Another company that goes out of its way to engage customers is the online clothing store Threadless. It asks people to submit designs for T-shirts. Each week, hundreds of participants propose ideas and the community at large votes for its favourites. The top four to six designs are printed on shirts and sold in store; the winners receive a combination of cash prize and store credit. In September 2007 Threadless opened its first physical retail operation in Chicago.

Companies that involve customers in design, testing, marketing (such as viral marketing), and after-sales process get better insights into customer needs and behaviour and may be able to cut the cost of acquiring customers, engender greater loyalty, and eventually speed up development cycles.

But a company open to allowing customers to help it innovate must ensure that it isn't unduly influenced by information gleaned from a vocal minority. It must also be wary of focusing on the immediate rather than longer-range needs of customers and of raising and then failing to meet their expectations.

(c) **Tapping into a world of talent:** As more and more sophisticated work takes place interactively and new collaboration and communications tools emerge, companies can outsource increasingly specialized aspects of their work and still maintain organizational coherence. As much as technology permits them to decentralize innovation through networks or customers, it also allows them to parcel out more work to specialists, free agents, and talent networks.

Software and Internet technologies are making it easier and more affordable for companies to integrate and manage the work of an expanding number of outsiders.

Talent for a range of activities—from finance to marketing and IT to operations—can be found anywhere. The choices are diverse. The best person for a task may be a free agent in India or an employee of a small company in Italy rather than someone who works for a global business services provider.

Software and Internet technologies are making it easier and more affordable for companies to integrate and manage the work of an expanding number of outsiders. This development opens up many contracting options for managers of corporate functions.

The implications of shifting more work to freelancers are interesting. For one thing, new talent deployment models could emerge. TopCoder, a company that has created a network of software developers, may represent one such model. TopCoder gives organizations that want to develop software access to its talent pool. Customers explain the kind of software they want and offer prizes to the developers who do the best job—an approach that costs less than employing experienced engineers. Furthermore, changes in the nature of labour relationships could lead to new pricing models that would shift payment schemes from time and materials to compensation for results.

This trend should gather steam in sectors such as software, healthcare, professional services, and real estate, where companies can easily segment work into discrete tasks for independent contractors and then re-aggregate it.

As companies move in this direction, they will need to understand the value of their human capital more fully and manage different classes of contributors accordingly. They will also have to build capabilities to globally engage talent or contract with talent aggregators that specialize in providing such services. A competitive advantage will naturally shift to companies that can master the art of breaking down and recomposing tasks.

(d) **Extracting more value from interactions:** Companies have been automating or offshoring an increasing proportion of their production and manufacturing (transformational) activities, as also their clerical or simple rule-based (transactional) activities. As a result, a growing proportion of the labour force in developed economies primarily engages in work that involves negotiations and conversations, knowledge, judgement, and ad hoc collaboration—tacit interactions, as we call them. By 2015 MGI expects employment in jobs involving such interactions to account for about 44 per cent of the total US employment, up from 40 per cent today. Europe and Japan will experience similar changes in the composition of their workforce.

The application of technology has reduced differences among the productivity of transformational and transactional employees, but huge inconsistencies persist in the productivity of high-value tacit ones. Improving this is more about increasing the employees' effectiveness, for instance, by getting them to focus on interactions that create value and ensure that they have the right information and context. It may not necessarily be about efficiency. Technology tools that promote tacit interactions, such as wikis, virtual team environments and videoconferencing may become no less ubiquitous than computers are now. As companies learn to use these tools, they will develop managerial innovations—smarter and faster ways for individuals and teams to create value through interactions—that will be difficult for their rivals to replicate. Companies in sectors such as healthcare and banking are already moving down this road.

As companies improve the productivity of these workers, it will be necessary to couple investments in technologies with the right combination of incentives and organizational values to drive their adoption and use by employees. There is still substantial room to automate transactional activities, and the payoff can typically be realized much more quickly and measured far more clearly than the payoff from investments, to make tacit work more effective. Creating the business case for investing in interactions will be challenging but critical for managers.

(e) **Expanding the frontiers of automation:** Companies, governments, and other organizations have put in place systems to automate tasks and processes: forecasting and supply chain technologies; systems for ERP, CRM and HR, product and customer databases, and websites. Now these systems are becoming interconnected through common standards to exchange data and represent business processes in bits and bytes. What's more, this information can be combined in new ways to automate an increasing array of broader activities, from inventory management to customer service.

During the late 1990s FedEx and UPS linked data flowing through their internal tracking systems to the Internet—no trivial task at the time—to let customers track packages from the websites with no human intervention required on the part of either company. By leveraging and linking systems to automate processes for answering customer enquiries, both companies dramatically reduced their costs while increasing customer satisfaction and loyalty. More recently, Carrefour, Metro, Walmart and other large retailers have adopted (and asked suppliers to adopt) digital-tagging technologies such as radio frequency identification (RFID) and have integrated them with other supply chain systems in order to further automate the supply chain and inventory management.

The rate of adoption disappoints the advocates of these technologies, but as the price of digital tags falls they could very well reduce the costs of managing distribution and increase revenues by helping companies to manage supply more effectively.

Companies still have substantial headroom to automate many repetitive tasks that aren't yet mediated by computers, particularly in sectors and regions where IT marches at a slower pace.

Companies still have substantial headroom to automate many repetitive tasks that aren't yet mediated by computers, particularly in sectors and regions where IT marches at a slower pace. Interlinking these 'islands of automation' would give managers and customers the ability to do new things. That said, automation is a good investment only if it lowers costs and also helps users get what they want more quickly and easily, not if it leads to unpleasant experiences. The trick is to strike the balance between raising margins and making customers happy.

Technology helps companies utilize their fixed assets more efficiently by disaggregating monolithic systems into reusable components, measuring and metering the use of each, and billing for that use in ever-smaller increments cost effectively.

(f) **Unbundling production from delivery:** Technology helps companies utilize their fixed assets more efficiently by disaggregating monolithic systems into reusable components, measuring and metering the use of each, and billing for that use in ever-smaller increments in a cost effective manner.

Information and communication technologies handle the tracking and metering critical to the new models and make it possible to have effective allocation and capacity-planning systems. Amazon.com, for example, has expanded its business model to let other retailers use its logistics and distribution services. It also gives independent software developers opportunities to buy processing power on its IT infrastructure so that they don't have to buy their own. Mobile virtual-network operators, another example of this trend, provide wireless services without investing in a network infrastructure. At the most basic level of unbundled production, companies responding to an MGI survey on Web trends said they were investing in Web services and related technologies. Although the applications vary, many use these technologies to offer other companies—suppliers, customers, and other ecosystem participants—access to parts of their IT architectures through standard protocols.

Unbundling works in the physical world too. Today one can buy fractional time on a jet, in a high-end sports car, or even for a designer handbag. Unbundling is attractive from the supply side because it lets asset-intensive businesses like factories, warehouses, truck fleets, office buildings, data centres, and networks, to raise their utilization rates and therefore their returns on invested capital. On the demand side, unbundling offers access to resources and assets that might otherwise require a large fixed investment or a significant scale to achieve competitive marginal costs. For companies and entrepreneurs seeking capacity (or variable additional capacity), unbundling makes it possible to gain access to assets quickly, to scale up businesses and yet keep the assets on the balance sheets light, and to use attractive consumption and contracting models that are easier on the income statements.

Companies that make their assets available for internal and external use will need to manage conflicts if demand exceeds supply. A competitive advantage through scale may be hard to maintain when many players, large and small, have equal access to resources at low marginal costs. The best example is 'cloud' computing.

(g) **Putting more science into management:** Just as the Internet and productivity tools extend the reach of and provide leverage to desk-based workers, technology helps managers exploit ever-greater amounts of data to make smarter decisions and develop the insights that create competitive advantages and new business models. From 'ideagoras' (ebay-like marketplaces for ideas) to predictive markets to performance-management approaches, ubiquitous standards-based technologies promote aggregation, processing, and decision-making based on the use of growing pools of rich data.

Leading players are exploiting this information explosion with a diverse set of management techniques. Google fosters innovation through an internal market: employees submit ideas and other employees decide if the ideas are worth pursuing or if they would be willing to work on it full-time. Intel integrates a 'prediction market' with regular short-term forecasting processes to build more accurate and less volatile estimates of demand. The cement manufacturer Cemex optimizes loads and routes by combining complex analytics with a wireless tracking and communications network for its trucks.

The amount of information and a manager's ability to use it have increased explosively, not only for internal processes but also for the engagement of customers. The more a company knows about them, the better it is able to create offerings they want, target them with messages

The amount of information and a manager's ability to use it have increased explosively, not only for internal to processes but also engage customers.

that get a response, and to extract the value that an offering gives them. The holy grail of deep customer insight—more granular segmentation, low cost experimentation, and mass customization—becomes increasingly accessible through technological innovations in data collection and processing and in manufacturing.

Examples range across a wide spectrum of industries. Amazon.com stands at the forefront of advanced customer segmentation. Its recommendation engine correlates the purchase histories of each individual customer with those of others who made similar purchases to come up with suggestions for things that the customer might buy. Although the jury is still out on the true value of recommendation engines, the techniques seem to be paying off. CleverSet, a pure-play recommendation-engine provider, claims that the 75 online retailers using the engine are averaging a 22 per cent increase in revenue per visitor. Meanwhile, toll road operators in USA are beginning to segment drivers and charge them differential prices based on static conditions (such as time of day) and dynamic factors (traffic).

Technology is also dramatically bringing down the costs of experimentation and giving creative leaders opportunities to think like scientists by constructing and analysing alternatives. The financial-services concern Capital One conducts hundreds of experiments daily to determine the appropriate mix of products it should direct to specific customer profiles. Similarly, Harrah's casinos mine customer data to target promotions and provide exemplary customer service.

Given the vast resources going into storing and processing information today, its hard to believe that we are only at an early stage in this trend. The quality and quantity of information available to any business is set to grow explosively as the costs of monitoring and managing processes fall. Analytics is the science which analyses the data and supports decision-makers with the right type of insight into their customers.

Leaders should get ahead of this trend to ensure that information makes organizations more rather than less effective. Information is power. Broadening access and increasing transparency will inevitably influence organizational politics and power structures. However, environments that celebrate making choices on a factual basis must watch out for analysis paralysis.

The Internet has brought greater transparency to many markets, from airline tickets to stocks, but many other sectors need similar illumination. Real estate is one of them.

(h) **Making business from information:** Accumulated pools of data captured in a number of systems within large organizations or pulled together from many points of origin on the Web are the raw material for new information-based business opportunities. Frequent contributors to what economists call market imperfections include information asymmetries and the frequent inability of decision-makers to get all the relevant data about new market opportunities, potential acquisitions, pricing differences among suppliers, and other business situations. These imperfections often allow middlemen and players with more and better information to extract higher rents by aggregating and creating businesses around it. The Internet has brought greater transparency to many markets, from airline tickets to stocks, but many other sectors need similar rejuvenation. Real estate is one of them. In a sector where agencies have thrived by keeping buyers and sellers partly in the dark, new sites have popped up to shine 'a light up into the dark reaches of the supply curve', as Rich Barton, the founder of Zillow (a portal for real estate information), puts it. Barton, the former leader of the e-travel site Expedia, has been down this road before. Sanjay Bickchandani, the founder of www.naukri.com also set up www.99Acres.com for real estate buying and selling in India.

The aggregation of data through the digitization of processes and activities may create by-products, or 'exhaust data' that companies can exploit for profit. A retailer with digital cameras to prevent shoplifting, for example, could also analyse the shopping patterns and traffic flows of customers through his stores and use these insights to improve shop layout or the placement of promotional displays. He might also sell the data to vendors so that they could use real observation of consumer behaviour to reshape their merchandizing approaches.

Another kind of information business plays a pure aggregation and visualization role: scouring the Web to assemble data on particular topics. Many business-to-consumer shopping sites and business-to-business product directories operate in this fashion. But that sword can cut both ways; today's aggregators, for instance, may themselves be aggregated tomorrow. Companies relying on information-based market imperfections need to assess the impact of the new transparency levels that are continually opening up in today's information economy.

7.10 Managing Information Technology during Market Turbulence and Recovery

During market turbulence, economies around the world look for ways to trim spending and improve the bottom line. Although information technology often represents a small fraction of the corporate cost base, senior executives inevitably turn their attention to IT budgets for substantial contributions. Yet in some instances, IT investments deliver more value to a company's top and bottom lines by creating new efficiencies than any other savings gained from traditional IT cost cutting.

IT has come a long way over the past decade. Budgets grew rapidly during the dot.com boom and the run-up to Y2K, then declined drastically when the bubble burst. Over the following years, Chief Information Officers (CIOs) working with business unit leaders, improved the performance of IT departments by streamlining application portfolios, reducing infrastructure costs, improving governance, consolidating vendors, and outsourcing many activities.

Much has changed across the business landscape as well. Technology now meshes tightly with operations in ways that weren't possible a decade ago. The apparel maker Li & Fung, for instance, uses IT to manage supply chains with a network of over 7,500 different suppliers. At the same time, e-business, once a buzzword, now forms a part of the corporate status quo. IT capabilities have fostered new sales channels, defined new customer segments, and even helped create new business models. These factors make reductions in IT spending more complicated than ever. Simplistic cuts, applied across the board, may endanger critical business priorities from sales support to customer service. That potent message should resonate even among corporate officers anxious to find quick savings. CIOs, of course, should continue to make their operations more efficient and to reduce costs, especially in areas that show signs of bloat. Discipline tends to slip during a lengthy upturn in spending, such as the one that has occurred in recent years. Reducing pockets of unproductive expenditure will bring savings that help meet corporate cost targets.

Still, except in the most dire circumstances, turning off technology investments during a downturn is counterproductive. When business picks up, one may lack critical capabilities. Besides, many technology investments can improve profitability in the short to medium term. When business and IT executives jointly take an end-to-end look at business processes, the resulting investments can have up to ten times the impact of traditional IT cost reduction efforts. The trick is to scan for opportunities—such as improving customer experience, reducing revenue leakage, and improving operating leverage.

7.10.1 Creating an Impact with Technology

Such an effort begins with a survey of operations to look for areas likely to produce near-term revenue and efficiency gains. In its work across a variety of industries, MGI has identified a number of ways technology investments can have a substantial impact:

(i) *Manage sales and pricing:* Develop insights into customer segments and improve pricing discipline so as to increase revenues without increasing prices.

(ii) *Optimize sourcing and production:* Rethink supply chains and logistics to improve the scheduling of deliveries and inventory management.

(iii) *Enhance support processes:* Improve the management and use of field forces (such as installers and field technicians) and customer support centres.

(iv) *Optimize overhead and performance management:* Sharpen awareness of risk exposure and improve decision-making and performance-management processes.

7.10.2 Developing New Insights

Few companies have successfully capitalized on the explosion of data in recent years. Often this information, residing in separate IT systems or spread across different business units, has never been mined for insights that could add value. Small teams of business and IT staffers can find opportunities by combining a detailed understanding of business processes with straightforward analyses of consolidated data sets. When such teams use the data to compare best practices across regions or to identify under- and over-served customers, for example, they can identify areas of revenue leakage.

7.10.3 Optimizing Processes

As IT becomes tightly integrated with processes, breaks in workflow often get built into systems and diminish productivity. Shining a light on these areas with an integrated view of operations and technology may well locate the problems, which often involve outdated processes, manual steps, redundancies, and bottlenecks. An 80/20 approach can highlight a modest number of activities that, when corrected, deliver a disproportionate amount of value.

At times, new systems may be needed, but most often modest enhancements or targeted work-arounds suffice. An addition error check in a credit application, for instance, can reduce the need to rework incorrectly entered data. Adjustments to workflow processes may also promote greater adherence to corporate sales-discounting and bidding policies. Applied in high-opportunity areas, these two levers can not only make a short-term contribution to earnings but also build a foundation for future performance.

At times, new systems may be needed, but most often modest enhancements or targeted work-arounds suffice. An addition error check in a credit application, for instance, can reduce the need to rework incorrectly entered data.

7.10.4 Revenue and Pricing Discipline

Maximizing revenues is always important, but even more so during a downturn, particularly when revenues can be increased without raising prices. For many companies, especially those with complex pricing in business-to-business transactions, poor pricing discipline is endemic. Since most pricing regimes depend on IT systems for the process and the workflow, these systems can play a central role by capturing lost revenues. So CRM technologies are going to make an impact on the bottom lines of many companies during market turbulence.

For many companies, especially those with complex pricing in business-to-business transactions, poor pricing discipline is endemic.

MARKETING IN ACTION — **MICROSOFT OFFICE REMAINS MOST UNDERUTILIZED**

Microsoft Office, the most popular product from the world's largest software firm, remains one of the most underutilized products. Using Office efficiently could save an hour for an average business user who spends about four hours a day working on it, says an expert. Most consumers use up to 20 per cent of the features, with some using as low as 5 per cent, says MaxOffice Founder and CEO Nitin Paranjpe. He should know; he makes a living out of teaching people how to utilize Office better to save time and improve productivity.

'The value of Office lies in efficiency improvement and no one realizes that. It's not seen as a business investment by most organizations,' says Paranjpe. Productivity doesn't only mean a reduction in time taken to perform a task, he adds. It could also mean analysing data in a better way. For instance, most people using Excel sheets often struggle managing multiple worksheets. They don't use inbuilt features such as consolidating information using multiple sheets. Some are effective in reducing risk to businesses. For instance, Microsoft Excel comes with features to identify and correct errors in a dynamic worksheet where numbers are being added.

Paranjpe says ignorance is particularly unhealthy in the current downturn. 'With retrenchment taking place at many organizations and budgets being slashed, the same or more work is being demanded from fewer resources. In that scenario, efficiency assumes greater importance,' he says. MaxOffice has worked with firms in the banking, telecom and manufacturing sectors. Some of these firms have used the training to reduce time spent on critical functions to 4-5 hours from as much as 24 hours. Most users, he says, don't look up the Help section in Office ever. There is also an updated section online that they could visit. For instance, many users don't realize that Word 2007 identifies contextual mistakes (such as using 'no' instead of 'know'), just as older versions recognize errors in spelling and grammar. Also, there are not too many users with Office 2003 who have downloaded the Microsoft Office Compatibility Pack to read, edit and save documents created in Word 2007.

Windows security centre, called Windows Action Center, encompasses both security and maintenance of the computer. Windows 7 will include Internet Explorer 8 and Windows Media Player 12.

At Tech.Ed, Microsoft demonstrated Windows 7 on some old machines (at least a few were three years old). This was to allay fears that people will have to buy new hardware to run Windows 7. The software firm will also release stripped-down versions of Windows 7 for Net books and smaller, Internet-centric devices.

Windows 7 is the most publicly available version of Microsoft Windows released in 2010, a series of operating systems produced by Microsoft for use on personal computers, including home and business desktops, laptops, netbooks, tablet PCs, and media center PCs. Windows 7 was released to manufacturing on 22 July 2009, and had general retail availability on 22 October 2009, less than three years after the release of its predecessor, Windows Vista. Windows 7's server counterpart, Windows Server 2008 R2, was released at the same time.

Unlike its predecessor, which introduced a large number of new features, Windows 7 was a more focused, incremental upgrade to the Windows line, with the goal of being fully compatible with applications and hardware with which Windows Vista is already compatible. Presentations given by Microsoft in 2008 focused on multi-touch support, a redesigned Windows Shell with a new taskbar, referred to as the Superbar, a home networking system called HomeGroup, and performance improvements. Some applications that have been included with prior releases of Microsoft Windows, including Windows Calendar, Windows Mail, Windows Movie Maker, and Windows Photo Gallery, which are not included in Windows 7. Most are instead offered separately as part of the free Windows Live Essentials suite.

Windows 7 includes a number of new features, such as advances in touch and handwriting recognition, support for virtual hard disks, improved performance on multi-core processors, improved boot performance, DirectAccess, and kernel improvements. Windows 7 adds support for systems using multiple heterogeneous graphics cards from different vendors (Heterogeneous Multi-adapter), a new version of Windows Media Centre, a gadget for Windows Media Centre, improved media features, the XPS Essentials Pack and Windows PowerShell being included, and a redesigned calculator with multiline capabilities including Programmer and Statistics modes along with unit conversion.

Many new items have been added to the Control Panel, including Clear Type Text Tuner, Display Colour Calibration Wizard, Gadgets, Recovery, Troubleshooting, Workspaces Centre, Location and Other Sensors, Credential Manager, Biometric Devices, System Icons, and Display. Windows Security Centre has been renamed Windows Action Centre (Windows Health Centre and Windows Solution Centre in earlier builds), which encompasses both security and maintenance of the computer

In only eight hours, pre-orders of Windows 7 at Amazon.co.uk surpassed the demand Windows Vista had in its first 17 weeks. It became the highest-grossing pre-order in Amazon's history, surpassing sales of the previous record holder, the seventh Harry Potter book. After the launch, 64-bit versions of Windows 7 Professional and Ultimate editions sold out in Japan. Two weeks after its release, it was announced that its market share had surpassed that of Snow Leopard, released two months previously as the most recent update to Apple's Mac OS X operating system. According to Net Applications, Windows 7 reached a 4 per cent market share in less than three weeks. In comparison, it took Windows Vista seven months to reach the same mark. Nearly 3,000 Indian corporates changed over to Windows 7 in November 2009—a welcome sign indeed.

Source: The Economic Times, December 2009.

7.11 Summary

- Technology is evolving day by day. Firms that can make disparate technologies work for consumers will have a new role as market makers. With system integration, different technologies need to be made compatible with each other. The future will be dominated by players who sense this opportunity and are able to capitalize on it. Companies need to maintain a proper vision while maintaining their customer base to innovate and adapt to the market so as to maximize value to the different stakeholders.
- Creative leaders can use a broad spectrum of new technology-enabled options to craft their strategies. These trends are best seen as emerging patterns that can be applied in a wide variety of businesses. Executives should reflect on which patterns to use to reshape their markets and industries, and on whether they have the opportunities to catalyze change and shape the outcome rather than merely react to it.
- Like a creative leader, good marketing also requires that a firm gives its customers rational reasons for their emotional buying decision. There is an e-formula for success: depending on the business, offer frequent special

promotions to customers by mail, telephone or in person. Everyone wants to feel appreciated and personally acknowledged. By offering customers specially priced deals or the first choice, the company engages them through mutual dialogue.

- At the same time, its crucial to enhance customer perceptions about Unique Selling Propositions, preferably through IT-enabled techniques. The rapid growth of Web-based online marketing can be attributed to many factors.
- Goods, services and ideas can move across continents efficiently at the click of a mouse. As the penetration of the Web has increased significantly, marketers are using Web-based advertising and marketing techniques to increase their reach at the global level. This can be attributed to the increased usage of online services by people and significant importance being given to e-commerce by the government.
- A firm has to design its business processes effectively in order to succeed in e-business. It can employ various methods of online business and Web-based marketing to expand its business.

CHAPTER 8  CUSTOMER RELATIONSHIP MARKETING DURING MARKET TURBULENCE

Ultimately, strong branding is not just a promise to our customers, to our partners, to our shareholders and to our communities; it is also a promise to ourselves . . . in that sense, it is about using a brand as a beacon, as a compass, for determining the right actions, for staying the course, for evolving a culture, for inspiring a company to reach its full potential. — Carly Fiorina, CEO, Hewlett-Packard

The Backdrop

Bogged down by the recession in the first half of 2009, insurance firms are still struggling to expand their retail business, in particular with low customer conversion and high operating costs. New business generated, which grew by almost 50 per cent over three years since 2005, increased by only 4 per cent in 2009. SBI Life had the best return per employee (₹30.58 lakh per employee), private players like ICICI Prudential (₹8.64 lakh per employee), Birla Sunlife (₹8.51 lakh per employee), Bajaj Alliance (₹6.82 lakh per employee) and HDFC Standard Life (₹5.60 lakh per employee) lagging far behind. In terms of ratio of operating expenses to gross written premium too, SBI Life stood first with 8 per cent in 2009. That the company was able to slice down the ratio from 20 per cent in 2005 to 8 per cent in 2009 was a remarkable achievement, especially when private players like Reliance Life and Max New York Life had the highest operating expenses.

SBI Life displayed maximum efficiency with the highest new premium collection in 2009. Look at the figures during 2008–9. SBI Life secured ₹2,156 crore with productivity per unit manager of ₹115.60 lakh and that of agents standing at ₹3.12 lakh. They secured ₹34,245 crore in 2008–9 with productivity per unit manager at ₹123.68 lakh and that of agents at ₹2.28 lakh. The comparative figures for ICICI Prudential (₹21.33 lakh for unit managers and ₹1.10 lakh for agents), HDFC Standard Life (₹18.54 lakh for unit managers and ₹1 lakh for agents) and Bajaj Alliance (₹21.17 lakh for unit managers and ₹0.99 lakh for agents) were unimpressive.

It is observed that insurers backed by banks generate more premiums per agent. This is due to best CRM practices followed by the banks. So companies grow with customers and not with sales or profit during market turbulences, because 20 per cent of best customers generate 80 per cent of the profit. These companies invariably treat their customers as their most valuable asset and monopolize the market with truly valuable and meaningful offerings. It is the customers' willingness to pay for a good or service that converts economic resources into wealth, things into goods. And what customers buy and consider of value is never a product. It is always utility, that is, what a product or service does for the customer.

This Chapter Will

- *Understand the ways and means of creating and sustaining long-term relationship with customers during global financial meltdown.*
- *Explain the different types of Customer Relationship Management (CRM) practices and programmes.*
- *Understand the shift from Make and Buy to Sense and Respond (SR) business model.*
- *Explain technologicalship marketing, customer technologicalship and managing downturn.*
- *Appreciate the significance of internal marketing, learning organization, building and sustaining relationship in marketing and response measurement.*
- *Differentiate between transaction marketing, relationship marketing and technologicalship marketing.*

8.1 Shift from 'Make and Buy' to 'Sense and Respond' Business Models

Today's businesses face fierce and aggressive competition in both the domestic and the global market. This diverse and uncertain environment has forced organizations to restructure themselves in order to ensure survival and growth. The restructuring efforts have included, among others, the emergence of a 'new paradigm' commonly referred to as relationship marketing. Establishing personal relationships and sustaining interactions and social exchanges are the core elements of relationship marketing.

Establishing personal relationships and sustaining interactions and social exchanges with partners and customers are the core elements of relationship marketing. Technology is a key enabler in this.

Technology has made the world a smaller, faster place that penalizes slow moving and 'stable' institutions. Companies that can quickly get ideas and information through their organizations for discussion and action will gain distinct competitive advantages over others. It is a known fact that success is the result of the symbiosis of technology and marketing. Many companies believe that blending technology with customer requirements is an important success element in establishing and developing customer relationships.

The rapid and radical changes in today's marketing environment have resulted in an emphasis on relationship marketing, i.e. the importance of building and keeping a close relationship with partner companies, customers, and other business parties. The importance of IT in creating and enhancing business relationships should be stressed here. While technology has a prominent role in organization theory, its absence in marketing theory is conspicuous. Marketing thought is shifting from an emphasis on transactions and acquisitions to relationships and customer retention. Meanwhile, IT is changing the role of the customer and the patterns of market communication, relations, and interactions. There is a pressing need to understand the sources and implications of these evolving forms of linkages: how will IT and interactivity transform markets? Today IT is the most important factor in creating, developing and tightening relationships.

8.2 Building and Sustaining Relationships in Marketing

The new trend in marketing is not about 'products and services' but about 'value'. Successful value creation requires, first and foremost, understanding what really constitutes customer value and second, understanding how

Relationship marketing is not about 'products and services' but about 'value'.

business subsequently aligns its resources to deliver that value to its chosen value segment. This marketing concept requires specific resource commitments, most of which do not pay off in the short term. Budgeting for these investments puts the marketing function in direct conflict with other management functions. It is therefore necessary to develop market-driven organizations and strategies.

8.2.1 Need for Relationship Marketing

Relationship marketing helps in channelizing resources towards understanding customer needs and delivering them the right products and services.

Many organizations pay scant attention to which customer needs it should focus on. A key part of customer orientation is the use of market research, which itself is an uncertain aspect as customers are not rational in their needs. The 4Ps are also losing credibility as they are more production than customer-oriented and are flawed in their definition. As a consequence, most of the resources are directed toward less significant issues, over-explaining what we already know, and toward supporting and legitimizing the status quo. What we need is a creative process to look at the market, understand potential customer needs and wants, consider the basic capabilities of the firm, conceive potential product offerings based on the present and potential capabilities, design and develop such products, and eventually deliver them with the full bundle of supporting services to a clearly defined target market.

MARKETING IN ACTION — **INITIATIVES OF ITC IN BUILDING CRM**

ITC believes big brands develop the foundation for a lasting consumer relationship and provide a competitive edge to business. The lifestyle retailing business of ITC has been carefully nurturing relationships with consumers by seeking to understand their preferences and needs and crafting superior products that deliver value beyond their expectations. ITC has worked towards building lasting consumer relationships by its marketing programmes.

ITC Infotech, ITC's global IT services company has also launched a suite of mobility solutions in partnership with Singapore-based NewsPage. This solution is designed to address the various CRM, direct store delivery (DSD) and route accounting processes across the consumer goods and life sciences segments. Another initiative by ITC Infotech is the end-to-end field salesforce automation solution powered by NewsPage EXPRESS, an enterprise class mobility framework which caters to the specific needs of the demanding sales scenario. This solution is responsible to manage and automate the activities of distributors, sales and trade marketing representatives, including inventory receipt, route planning, sales projection, pre-sales and van sales, amongst others.

ITC's partnership with NewsPage has helped it bring in the latter's domain knowledge and industry-ready mobility applications, which has enabled companies in engaging, transacting and servicing their customers while 'on-the-go'. This mobility solution has offered demonstrable benefits to customers in terms of streamlining their operations and improving sales force efficiency and productivity. The mobility solution was aimed to develop better customer relationship management, better management of the sales team, monitor performance at all times and provide faster and up to date access to customer information.

Source: Business World, March 2010.

8.2.2 Value-oriented Strategy

A marketer must understand and properly apply the concepts of 'value' and 'relationship' from the perspective of the customer and other channel members, as well as from the point of view of marketing itself. The goal is to have customers believe that the firm offers value for money and to have both customers and channel members alike doing business with that company.

Some firms reward their customers so as to entice them to continue with their loyalties. This is especially true in the Indian context for destination retailers and FMCG companies. Destination retailers are popular retailers (catalogue, store, or website) from whom customers, attracted by the ambience, price, and/or variety, will make a special effort to buy.

Sellers undertake a series of activities and processes to provide a given level of value to the consumer. Consumers then perceive the value offered by sellers, based on the perceived benefits received versus the prices paid. Perceived value varies by type of customer. From the perspective of the manufacturer, wholesaler, and retailer, value is a series of activities and processes—value chain—that provides a given level of value to the consumer. From the customer's perspective, value is the perception of all the benefits obtained out of the overall purchase.

Consumers then perceive the value offered by sellers, based on the perceived benefits received versus the prices paid and it varies by type of customer.

A value chain in marketing represents the total bundle of benefits offered to consumers through a channel of distribution. For a retailer, it comprises many elements such as store location and parking, retailer ambience, the level of customer service, the products/brands carried, product quality, the retailer's in-stock position, shipping/logistics, prices and the retailer's image. Some elements of a retail value chain are visible to shoppers. They include store windows, store hours, in-store personnel, and computerized point-of-sale equipment. Elements which are not visible include credit processing, store maintenance, company warehouses, and merchandising decisions.

A value chain in marketing represents the total bundle of benefits offered to consumers through a channel of distribution.

Value Orientation in Retail Marketing

There are three complementary components to a value-oriented retail strategy. An expected retail strategy represents the minimum value chain elements a given customer segment expects from a given type of retailer. An augmented retail strategy encompasses the extra elements in a value chain that differentiate one retailer from another. The elements of an augmented value chain are: valet parking, free delivery, personal shopper service, exclusive brands, superior sales people, and loyalty programmes. A potential retail strategy comprises value chain elements not yet perfected by a competing firm in the retailer industry category.

Components of value-oriented retail strategy: expected, augmented and the potential retail strategy. The nature of a given value delivery system must be related to target market expectations.

Value Orientation and Channel Partners

Members of a distribution channel (manufacturers, wholesalers, and retailers) jointly represent a value delivery system comprising all the parties that develop, produce, deliver, sell and service particular goods and services. This has ramifications for retailers: each channel member is dependent on the other; so every value delivery activity must be enumerated and responsibility assigned for it. Small retailers may have to use suppliers outside the normal channel to get the products they want and gain adequate supplier support. The system is only as good as its weakest link.

The nature of a given value delivery system must be related to target market expectations. Channel member costs and functions are influenced by each party's role. Value delivery systems are more complex than ever due to the vast product assortment of superstores, the many forms of retailing, and the use of multiple distribution channels by some manufacturers.

Value Orientation in Non-Retail Marketing

Non-store retailing requires a different system unlike store retailing. Due to conflicting goals, some channel members are adversarial. But it is when they forge positive relationships that members of a value delivery system can better serve each other and the final consumer.

In the category management approach, channel members collaborate to maximize performance by offering assortments and prices that better meet consumer needs.

One relationship-oriented practice that some manufacturers and retailers are trying to use is *category management.* With this approach, channel members collaborate to maximize performance by offering assortments and prices that better meet consumer needs. It is based on the following principles:

(a) Rather than just buy goods and services, retailers listen more and better to customers and stock what they want.
(b) Profitability improves because inventory follows demand closer.
(c) By being better focused, each department can deliver more to shoppers.
(d) Retail buyers are assigned more responsibilities and accountability.
(e) Retailers and their suppliers must share data and must increase computerization.
(f) Retailers and their suppliers must plan together for the best assortments.

8.3 Emergence of Relationship Marketing

The marketing management paradigm has dominated marketing thought, research and practice since it was introduced almost 50 years ago. Today, this paradigm is beginning to lose its position as new approaches emerge in marketing research. The globalization of business and the evolving recognition of the importance of customer retention, market economies and customer relationship economics, among other trends, reinforce the change in mainstream marketing. Relationship building and management, or what has been labelled Relationship Marketing, is a leading new approach to marketing, which has also entered marketing literature.

Relationship marketing is a practice that encompasses all marketing activities directed toward establishing, developing, and maintaining successful customer relationships.

Generally, customers think about products and companies in relation to other products and companies. What really matters is how existing and potential customers think about a company in relation to its competitors. Customers set up a hierarchy of values, wants, and needs based on empirical data, opinions, word-of-mouth references, and previous experiences with products and services. They use that information to make purchasing decisions. Market leadership can catch a consumer's attention and can be an important factor in the purchase decision. The catch, however, is that there is more than one leader in almost every market segment today. Most often several companies share the top position, one being the technical leader, another the market leader, another the pricing leader, and still another the challenging upstart. Multiple positioning opportunities exist within every industry. A distinct market position is attainable even in a crowded marketplace. In short, relationship marketing is a practice that encompasses all marketing activities directed toward establishing, developing, and maintaining successful customer relationships. The focus of relationship marketing is on developing long-term relationships and improving corporate performance through ensuring customer loyalty and customer retention. Hence, conducting more effective Internet marketing entails integrating email and postal databases. With a centralized, multi-source database, e-marketers can personally communicate and exchange information with individual consumers.

The concept of relationship marketing emerged within the fields of service and industrial marketing. The phenomenon described by this concept is strongly supported by ongoing trends in modern business. Grönroos defines relationship marketing as: 'Marketing to establish, maintain, and enhance relationships with customers and other partners, at a profit, so that the objectives of the parties involved are met. This is achieved by a mutual exchange and fulfilment of promises.' Such relationships are usually but not necessarily long-term. Establishing a relationship, for example with a customer, can be divided into two parts: *to attract* the customer and *to build* a relationship with that customer so that the economic goals of that relationship are achieved.

Establishing a relationship consists of two parts: attracting a customer and building a relationship.

An integral element of the relationship marketing approach is the *promise concept* which has been strongly emphasized by Henrik Calonius. According to Calonius the responsibilities of marketing include making promises and thus persuading customers as passive counterparts in the marketplace to act in a given way. A firm that is preoccupied with making promises may attract new customers and initially build relationships. However, if the promises are not kept, the evolving relationship cannot be maintained and enhanced. Fulfilling promises that have been made is equally important to achieve customer satisfaction, retain customer base, and ensure long-term profitability.

An integral element of the relationship marketing approach is the promise concept which includes making promises and thus persuading customers as passive counterparts in the marketplace to act in a given way.

8.3.1 Relationship Marketing and IT

Its obvious that face-to-face interaction between customers and representatives of suppliers allows for a closer relationship between the two. Although the service itself remains important, people and social processes add value. Interactions may include negotiations and sharing insights in both directions. This type of relationship has long existed in many local environments ranging from co-operative banks to hospitals, where the buyer and seller know and trust each other.

Relationship marketing depends on the flow of information about the customer and the company, to and from the customer. The continuing advance of IT makes it easier to record customer information, match customers to already recorded information, and attune the company offers to customer needs. For large companies, information systems become the organizational memory of all recorded contacts. The problem of access to the manufacturer/marketer is removed for customers willing to do so through IT. This opportunity to improve 'information-driven' relationship marketing is already delivering results for innovative companies that have experienced the connection and taken action. In future, relationship marketing can well be a constant agenda item for IT management, driven by business strategies premised on information-driven relationship marketing. IT

Relationship marketing depends on the flow of information about the customer and the company, to and from the customer. The continuing advance of IT and growth of Internet are major enablers in CRM.

redevelopment can become a major cost area that should be balanced carefully with the benefits. The growth of the Internet as a provider of standard global access to systems and networks the worldover is at present an area of huge interest, and will very soon become a major consideration for the marketing departments of most Indian organizations marketing to consumers and businesses.

Managing the customer as an asset is critical to a firm's CRM success. Marketers must take IT more seriously and must be aware of the new developments in technology and their possible effects.

Managing the customer as an asset is more critical to a firm's success than ever before as it helps in taking better decisions than when the focus is only limited to product and brand considerations. Changes in market conditions, driven by advances in information systems, communications and production, will help companies that understand and manage the value of each individual customer overtake competitors and then displace mass marketers. To keep in step with the present trend, managers need to create a business model that uses technology for strategic purposes—adding value for customers and committing the organization more deeply to both increasing productivity and having a positive impact on the bottom line. Thus, the successful implementation of relationship marketing practices—the need of the hour—requires a strategic approach which encompasses developing customer-centric processes, selecting and implementing technology solutions, employee empowerment, customer information and knowledge generation capabilities to differentiate the firm's offerings and the ability to learn from best practices.

The impact of technology on marketing relationships is one of the most serious challenges. IT is much broader than advertising, data collection, selling products/services, direct mailing, or public relations. It has as profound an effect on the way firms market products and services as the airplane, car, and television have had on other aspects of our lives. Marketing scholars, managers, and marketers must therefore take IT more seriously.

They must be aware of the new developments in technology and their possible effects, because technology influences communication and coordination processes with alliances and other collaborators within a network.

8.4 Response Measurement: Tracing a Customer's Behaviour

Online marketing helps companies to know about their customers and interact with them directly.

The rate of technological change in the marketing environment affects relationship marketing success in a big way. Thus, the relationship between the rate of effective IT use and relationship effectiveness is directly proportional. Marketing on the Internet marries the needs of consumers with the ever-evolving cyber technology. The result: companies go electronic to communicate with their customers, create awareness of their products and, perhaps, make a profit. Also, online marketing is self-selective. Companies know that customers who visit their sites are interested in knowing more

Campaign management is defined as the process of designing, executing, and measuring marketing campaigns through the use of applications that:

- Select and segment customers.
- Track the contacts made with customers.
- Measure the results of those contacts.
- Model those results to more efficiently target customers in the future.

about the product. Not only does this help identify the highest-potential consumers, it permits a depth of sale that no other medium can provide. It reaches consumers in literally every part of the world. Another benefit of online marketing is that it is interactive. It enables companies to engage consumers in away that no other medium can. One-to-one marketing is online's unique capability.

The major objective of CRM is to refine an organization's insights into its customer base.

One of the major objectives of customer relationship management is to continually refine an organization's insights into its customer base. These insights drive how an organization communicates with customers, so that each contact is more intelligent and meaningful than the previous. Often, necessary data is not in place to draw meaningful conclusions from previous customer experiences. To move towards information-based, data-driven business decisions, organizations must have processes and tools in place to complete all four components of campaign management.

CASE STUDY — PVR CINEMAS

The economic boom in India has empowered consumers leaving them with more disposable income than a decade earlier. The demand for entertainment is growing as consumers have started demanding premium services to satiate their needs. Not surprisingly, the entertainment industry is one of the fastest growing segments in India. According to PricewaterhouseCoopers, the size of this industry is $5 billion and is growing at a compounded annual growth rate of 20 per cent. It is estimated to cross $10 billion by 2010. Technological advances have opened various distribution channels such as broadband Internet, mobile entertainment and satellite television.

Traditionally, the film industry has provided staple entertainment to Indians and PVR has been responsible for redefining cinema viewing in India. It has made a trip to the movies a family outing by adding facilities like food joints, shopping, and games in its multiplexes, keeping in view the needs and interests of its target audience—families, youth and kids.

The company has made watching movies an exciting experience for the customer. PVR multiplexes are mostly located in malls simply because mall developers use multiplexes to increase footfall. Multiplex owners reap further benefits from the arrangement as these malls are located in prime areas and attracted huge crowds.

PVR multiplexes have for the first time in India provided a comfortable stadium-like seating which allows customers to watch movies without the viewers in the front row obstructing their view. PVR has also installed digital sound systems, better air conditioning, carpeting, and plush interiors. It has introduced luxury cinema halls under the sub-brand, Cinema Europa.

Cinema Europa theatres are luxurious cinema halls with reclining seats, double armrests, ample leg room to provide a relaxed cinema experience and business class treatment. The Europa theatre is complemented by the Europa Lounge, an island bar and restaurant furnished with plush leather seats and special lighting reflecting contemporary ambience. Customers are served cocktails and can enjoy music played by an inhouse DJ.

PVR has also ushered in the concept of ultra-premium cinemas with PVR Gold Class, a hall with 32 reclining seats providing a lavish cinema viewing experience with personalized service. The audience is served meals and snacks at their seats while they enjoy their movies.

PVR doesn't limit itself to the cinema exhibition business. It has entered areas which offer it synergies in the business of entertainment by venturing into film distribution, franchising, film production and managing multiplexes. These ventures are expected to strengthen PVR in its existing exhibition business. The urban population in India in the age group 15-34 years is the most frequent movie going segment in the country. This segment is expected to grow from 107 million in 2001 to 138 million by 2011. Though these figures are impressive, the impending competition has the potential to spoil the party for PVR. PVR's long-term vision is to remain India's most premium and most preferred retail entertainment company. To achieve this vision, the company continues to provide the highest exhibition standards at its cinemas besides increasing the number of cinemas under operation on a pan-India basis. It further looks to bringing allied retail entertainment concepts to India to complement and complete the entertainment experience for consumers.

Customer relationship management in PVR

Technology has been a key enabler at PVR right from its inception. At present, all PVR cinemas are connected to each other by Business Intelligence applications at the backend. It has not only automated all data but also enabled centralized control, which among other things helps monitor the functioning of its network of halls.

With the introduction of online booking, which constituted 23 per cent of PVR's ticket sales in 2009, and increased competition, there was an ever-pressing need to be more customer driven. The need for automation was felt to minimize manual interface and address customer complaints faster. The other factors that pressed PVR to go further with technology was speedy reaction to customer mails, increased advanced online bookings, and customer feedback, which are often hushed up at the theatre manager level.

PVR also wants to check if there is a pattern in the customer feedback. They want to know what company initiatives are being received well. All these factors prompted PVR to go live with its CRM programme in April 2007. It zeroed in on Microsoft's application, while an IT team internally handled the project. The company has also made the bookings at the box office automated, and launched RFID. PVR's website wears a fresh look and it has planned several online initiatives like collaborating with networking sites Facebook and Orkut.

PVR's CAGR (revenues) between 2003 and 2008 was 37 per cent. The total income was ₹2,447 million and ₹1,718.60 million in 2008 and 2007, respectively; 17.97 million movie goers visited PVR multiplexes in 2007–8, compared to 14.73 million in 2006–7. The average occupancy during 2008 was 39.9 per cent compared to 42.7 per cent in 2007. For the year ended March 2008, despite a drop in occupancy, the footfalls from comparable properties grew by 4 per cent.

Source: Investors' Report of PVR Cinema, January 2010.

Table 8.1 displays the types of relationship marketing programmes that are prevalent among different types of customers. Obviously, marketing practitioners in search of new ideas develop many variations and combinations of these programmes to build closer and mutually beneficial relationships with their customers.

Table 8.1: Types of relationship marketing programmes

Programme type	*Customer type*		
	Individual consumers	*Distributors/resellers*	*Institutional buyers (Business to Business)*
Continuity marketing	Loyalty programmes	Continuous replenishment and ECR programmes	Special supply arrangements (e.g. JIT, MRP)
Individual marketing	Data warehousing and data mining	Customer business development	Key account management
Co-marketing/partnering	Co-branding	Co-operative marketing	Joint marketing and co-development

8.4.1 Continuity Marketing

The basic aim of continuity marketing is to retain customers and increase loyalty through long-term special services.

Given the growing concern for retaining customers as well as the emerging knowledge about customer retention economics, many companies have developed continuity marketing programmes that are aimed at both retaining customers and increasing their loyalty. For consumers in mass markets, these programmes usually constitute membership and loyalty card programmes in which consumers are rewarded for becoming a member and for displaying loyalty to the marketer. These rewards may range from privileged services to points for upgrades, discounts, and cross-purchased items.

For distributor customers, continuity marketing programmes take the form of continuous replenishment programmes ranging from JIT inventory management to efficient consumer response initiatives that include electronic order processing and ERP. In B2B markets, these may be in the form of preferred customer programmes or special sourcing arrangements, including single sourcing, dual sourcing, network sourcing, and JIT sourcing arrangements. The basic aim of continuity marketing is to retain customers and increase loyalty through long-term special services that have the potential to increase mutual value as partners learn about each other.

8.4.2 Ladder of Customer Loyalty

The relationship with a customer goes through a number of states—a sort of ladder of customer loyalty. A 'prospect' is defined as a potential customer who has no direct relationship with a prospective supplier. However, a prospect will have some expectations and perceptions of the supplier that are based on knowledge acquired in the marketplace. The relationship can progress to the point that the prospect becomes a 'customer' who is defined narrowly as someone who has had one direct encounter with the organization. A 'client' is defined as a customer who has had repeated transactions with the supplier, but is neutral or negative toward the supplier. This is contrasted with a 'supporter', who has positive commitment to the relationship, and an 'advocate', who actively promotes the company through word-of-mouth marketing. The final step on the ladder is 'partnership', where both the customer and the supplier are linked through mutually beneficial exchanges—for example, information exchanges of customer sales that speed up order and delivery time while also giving the supplier better knowledge of customer requirements.

'Prospect' is defined as a potential customer who has no direct relationship with a prospective supplier.

'Client' is defined as a customer who has had repeated transactions with the supplier, but is neutral or negative toward the supplier.

'Supporter', is one who has a positive commitment to the relationship.

An 'Advocate' actively promotes the company through word-of-mouth marketing.

'Partnership', is where both the customer and the supplier are linked through mutually beneficial exchanges.

The ladder of loyalty is a useful tool to enhance awareness of customer segmentation opportunities; for example, the emphasis on different elements of the marketing mix may vary for customers at different rungs of the ladder. In addition, not all customers are suited to the higher rungs of the ladder; customers with low profit potential are not necessarily suitable candidates for the investment that may be needed to take them to the level of advocates or partners.

Loyalty built through customer retention can prove to be advantageous as the profit earned from each individual customer grows as the customer stays with the company. In addition, the benefits of customer retention compound over time. Even a tiny change in customer retention can cascade through the business system and result in enormous long-term profit and growth.

Ladder of loyalty is a useful tool to enhance awareness of customer segmentation opportunities.

In many business situations customers' degree of loyalty varies. They can be hardcore loyal, loyal and soft loyal. This degree depends upon the feeling customers have about the rewards they get for their loyalty. This has two implications. First, loyalty approaches should seek to differentiate the relationship and service package provided to loyal customers, and second, they should use ways of giving 'special recognition' at the point of customer contact.

Degrees of loyalty include: hardcore loyal, loyal, and soft loyal.

A strategy for loyalty-based relationship is put into action by creating superior customer value through personalizing interactions, demonstrating trustworthiness and tightening relations with the customers. To devise a corporate strategy to increase the number of loyal customers, a loyalty approach over and above existing marketing, sales, and service approaches should be identified as part of an overall audit of customer relationship

Strategy for loyalty-based relationship include the creation of superior customer value.

MARKETING ANALYSIS — **LOYALTY PROGRAMME OF AIRLINE COMPANIES**

The air travel industry offers a wide range of bonus or discount programmes under which participants are rewarded free travel, service benefits and other privileges. In the airline industry, loyalty programmes are often referred to as frequent flyer programmes or FFPs. But in fact the term 'loyalty programme' is used to indicate all the measures taken by airlines to enhance the loyalty of customers. The most important are frequent flyer programmes, corporate discount schemes and travel agent commissions. The FFP is the bonus or discount programmes that reward frequent flyers with free travel or benefits of a similar nature. Corporate discount schemes (CDS) are agreements which enable large airline clients to negotiate lower (net) fares on all or on certain parts of an airline's network.

Airline FFPs are mutually beneficial partnerships between banks and airline companies to offer customers some added benefits. Airlines have been consistently attracting banks into partnerships that increase the bottom line for both parties while bolstering consumer loyalty.

The truth is that mileage accruals these days depend less on the frequency of travel and more on how much one spends, both on the ticket and other partner services linked to the programme.

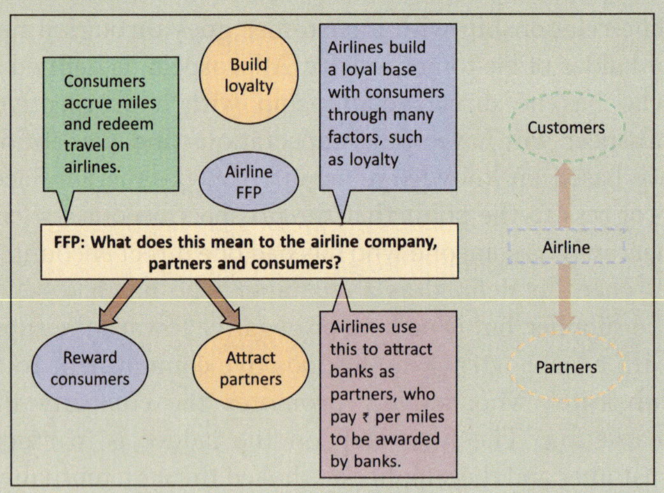

management. These objectives should always contain some financial component. They should then identify the desired aspects of the marketing and service mix which can be deployed most effectively to reinforce and build loyalty. They should also define the qualification levels and segments, then implement the capabilities and finally measure the loyalty earned.

Table 8.2: FFPs of various airline companies

Airline	*FFP*	*Tier 1 miles/sectors*	*Tier 2 miles/sectors*	*Tier 3 miles/sectors*
American Airlines	Advantage	25,000 miles/30 segments	50,000 miles/60 segments	100,000 miles/100 segments
China Airlines	Dynasty Flyer	40,000 miles/10 first class sectors	110,000 miles/40 first class sectors	180,000 miles/60 first class sectors
Delta	Sky Miles	25,000 MQM	50,000 MQM	75,000 MQM
Emirates	Skywards	25,000 miles/20 sectors	50,000 miles/40 sectors	—
Jet Airways	Jet-Privilege	15,000 miles/10 flights over 6 months	30,000 miles/20 flights over 12 months	30,000 miles/20 flights over 6 months
Kingfisher Airlines	King Club	3,000 miles/year	30,000 miles/year	70,000 miles/year
Singapore Airlines	Krisflyer	25,000 miles	50,000 miles	—

Source: www.smarttravelasia.com

To bolster the customer value proposition for their loyal customers, airline companies must create better processes for redemption. Restrictions, fees, blackout dates, fuel surcharges and other 'second bill' items must be considered carefully. A successful and robust frequent flyer programme must offer its customers an accrual and redemption network that has both breadth and depth.

8.4.3 Relationship Equity

Relationship equity is the customer's tendency to stick with the brand, above and beyond objective and subjective assessments of its worth. Relationship equity is especially important where personal relationships count and where customers tend to continue with suppliers out of habit or inertia. Sub-drivers of relationship equity include loyalty programmes, special recognition and treatment programmes, community building programmes, and knowledge-building programmes.

Relationship equity is the customer's tendency to stick with the brand, above and beyond objective and subjective assessments of its worth.

Table 8.3: Benefits offered to loyalty club members

Benefits offered	*Loyal member expectations*	*New customer expectations*
Booking	Preferential pricing, pricing options on miles + cash	Courtesy and welcome
Lounge	Free Wi-Fi, extras	N.A.
Check-in	Upgrade offers, discounted lounge access, priority baggage tagging	Acknowledgement by offers in kind, vouchers, etc.
Gate/Boarding aircraft	Priority boarding, special requests and allowances, personalized greetings onboard	Welcome
Flight experience	Personalized onboard experience, prioritized disruption management	Consistent or superior onboard customers
Arrival & Baggage claim	Priority handling, availability/assistance of complimenting services	Quick and efficient baggage arrivals
Customer retention	Full cycle CRM	Increased number of offers/discounts

8.5 Retailer Relationships

For relationship retailing to work properly, enduring value-driven relationships are needed with other channel members, as well as with customers. The customer base needs to be analysed in terms of population and lifestyle trends, attitudes towards and reasons for shopping, the level of loyalty, and the mix of new versus loyal customers. Gender roles are changing, shoppers are demanding more, market segments are getting more diverse, and time-saving goods and services are increasingly desirable.

A retailer's desired mix of new versus loyal customers depends on the firm's stage in the life cycle, goals and resources, as well as its competitors' actions.

Various factors influence people's shopping behaviour. For example, 70 per cent of women and 40 per cent of men enjoy shopping; and men shop more quickly than women. Core customers are a retailer's best customers—the ones with whom it is worth nurturing relationships. A retailer's desired mix of new versus loyal customers depends on the firm's stage in the life cycle, its goals and resources, as well as competitors' actions. For instance:

(i) A mature firm is more apt to rely on core customers.
(ii) An entrepreneur faces the dual tasks of attracting shoppers and building a loyal following.
(iii) If goals are growth-oriented, the customer base must be expanded by adding stores, greater advertising, etc.
(iv) Attracting new customers is more costly than serving existing ones.
(v) If competitors try to take away a firm's existing customers, the firm may feel it must pursue competitors' customers in the same way.

CASE STUDY — BEST PRACTICES OF INDIAN HOTELS COMPANY LIMITED

Service experience: In its commitment to continually enhance guest experience, Taj Hotels has initiated a series of programmes to upgrade product and service quality. The online customer feedback survey has greatly facilitated the direction and focus of the service enhancement programme and the training efforts as identified through the voice of the customer.

Key guest service touch points like the concierge and butler services, the sommelier and bartender programmes have been further reinforced. Employees who have undergone initial training also receive focused development inputs through dedicated training sessions and onsite interactions with international experts.

There is special focus on energy conservation and the environment. Energy audits are conducted at all luxury hotels and the recommendations are implemented. The use of solar energy is being actively promoted and solar energy panels have been installed in some hotels. As a commitment to the safety and security of hotel guests, the Taj Group has instituted a process of independent external audits to evaluate the preparedness of its hotels from the hygiene and safety perspective.

Maintain high standards: All hotels of the Indian Hotels Company Limited are in the process of enhancing hygiene initiatives and progressively moving from Hazard Analysis and Critical Control Points (HACCP) to ISO 22000 (Food Safety Management) certifications. Hotels have also commenced work on OHSAS certification (ISO 14001 and ISO 18000 covering environment, ergonomics, health and safety).

A **Six Sigma programme** was launched as a pilot project in two Taj hotels. Feedback from guests on their changing needs have been incorporated into the planning of hotel renovations and into the design plans for new buildings. A competency-based training matrix has been introduced to augment knowledge, skill and total quality of service to enhance the guest experience. A 'personal contact' programme has been developed to ensure a consistent guest experience which is unique and personalized to each guest's needs. This helps in building customer loyalty and eventually gaining a competitive edge.

Enriched guest experience: To achieve this it has improved internal performances and streamlined processes which has resulted in an increase in the Customer Satisfaction Index. The number of HACCP-certified hotels increased from nine in 2008 to thirteen in 2009. The increase of certified internal/external Tata Business Excellence Model assessors has helped the Taj Group implement and enforce a process-driven operation. About 80 executives in the SBU have been trained in the usage of quality tools for analysis of their departmental operations. This has been reflected in a positive trend of results in measures pertaining to financials, customer satisfaction, internal processes and human resources.

The phased roll out of the Total Productive Maintenance (TPM) programme has resulted in optimum usage of equipment in the engineering plant rooms, kitchens and laundry rooms as well as reduced incidence of equipment breakdown. The efforts in food and beverage benchmarking to create awareness of global food and beverage trends are continuing. Alternate dining experiences and local cuisine dining experiences are also well-received by hotel guests. A project to cultivate organic vegetables in kitchen gardens and make homemade preserves in all hotels has been initiated. Spa cuisine has also been introduced in all leisure hotels with spas.

Marketing alliances: The Taj Group has entered into several marketing alliances, key amongst them being the one with Okura Hotels & Resorts, one of the largest hotel groups in Japan. The alliance is to develop cross-promotional opportunities for both companies to harness each other's strengths in their respective markets of dominance. During 2008–9, the Indian Hotels Company Limited also tied up with several airlines for their Frequent Flier loyalty programme, including Lufthansa, American Airlines and KLM. The tie-ups are of various kinds. There is the 'Miles & More' frequent flyer programme with Lufthansa, Adria Airways, Air Dolomiti, Air One, Austrian Airlines, Croatia Airlines, LOT Polish Airlines and Luxair; 'Flying Blue' is an innovative frequent flyer programme with a four-tier structure (Platinum, Gold, Silver and Ivory levels) launched jointly by Air France and KLM; and 'Advantage' is the frequent flyer programme of American Airlines.

Indian Hotels Company Limited along with ICICI Bank and American Express has launched the ICICI Bank Ascent American Express Card. The card is six times more rewarding for the consumer than other leading credit cards in India. Consumers earn attractive reward points per ₹100 spent on dining, shopping, travel and overseas expenses. Additionally, there are exciting offers and privileges to help Taj customers save, even as they prepare for that long-awaited getaway.

Source: Investors' Report of Indian Hotels Company Ltd., January 2010.

Customer service has two components: expected services and augmented services. The attributes of the personnel who interact with customers, as well as the number and variety of services offered, have a big impact on the relationship created. Some firms improve customer service by empowering personnel, giving them the leeway to bend some rules. In devising strategy, a retailer must make broad decisions and then enact specific tactics with regard to credit, delivery, etc. Customer satisfaction is achieved when the value and customer service provided in a retail experience meet or exceed expectations. Otherwise, the consumer will be dissatisfied. Loyalty programmes reward the best customers, those with whom a retailer wants long-lasting relationships. To succeed, the loyalty programmes must complement a sound value-driven retail strategy.

Customer service has two components—expected services and augmented services.

Customer satisfaction occurs when the value and customer service provided in a retail experience meet or exceed expectations.

By studying defections, a firm can learn how many customers it is losing and the reasons for the loss.

Is your Loyalty Programme effective?

A check list of characteristics:

(i) The rewards are useful and appealing, and they are attainable in a reasonable timeframe.
(ii) The programme honours shopping behaviour.
(iii) A database tracks behaviour ('keeps score').
(iv) There is a range of rewards to stimulate short- and long-run purchases.
(v) There are features unique to particular retailers.
(vi) Communication with customers are personalized.
(vii) Frequent shoppers are made to feel 'special'.
(viii) Participation rules are publicized and rarely changed.
(ix) The programme is well promoted and membership encouraged.

8.6 Relationship Marketing-Oriented Technological Processes

A customer-oriented process is one which has as its main objective as satisfying customer needs, with a subsidiary requirement being that of checking the 'correctness' of the transaction.

An internally-oriented process reverses these priorities. As processes are the main methods by which management can make the organization move, they are critical in determining the quality of customer relationship. If processes are internally oriented, then the staff will continually have to fight against these processes to meet customer needs.

A customer-oriented process has as its main objective satisfying customer needs.

Irrespective of the degree of centralization of an organization, two forces increase the need for systems support to relationship marketing. They are:

Requirements of CRM includes higher quality offerings and greater operational efficiency/productivity.

(a) *The need for higher quality in relationship marketing:* Systems are increasingly being used to marshal company resources (including information) to meet customer needs.
(b) *The need for greater productivity in relationship marketing:* Information systems carry out the job of automating and monitoring work that is typically done by humans (e.g. record keeping). This means that information about customers should be automated in strict order of priority and measured by the importance of the customers to the organization. There is little point in having plenty of information available about customers with whom the organization is rarely in contact. Where particular customers are attached to particular locations (e.g. if they are managed by a particular sales or service office), it may be better to decentralize the information to these locations. The corporate mainframe keeps updated copies of this information for corporate purposes like invoicing analysis.

The information supplied by the system to policymakers should allow them to identify customer needs and not just be a record of a few aspects of the relationship between the organization and its customers. The integrity and usefulness of systems depends critically on data quality. This has led to a strong emphasis on systems to capture data at the point of contact with

The integrity and usefulness of systems depends critically on data quality. IT and IS (information systems) are most essential to provide the information needed for successful relationships or partnering.

the customer. This applies to everything from sales transactions, through engineer service calls to public utility meter reading, telemarketing and complaint handling. IT and IS (information systems) are most essential to provide the information needed for successful relationships or partnering. Without information partnership (relationship based on information) and information sharing, Tom Peters emphasizes, 'all other aspects of partnership remain stuck at the stage of lip service or less'.

8.6.1 Information Technology Advances and the Market

(a) The Internet

The Internet and the World Wide Web (WWW) have dramatically altered the way companies conduct business and establish business or customer relationships, changing both the market opportunities and the IT and network infrastructure. The Internet affects every facet of the company—with a potential to obliterate current business models, open new market opportunities and redefine customer relationships and interactions.

Marketing on the Internet bring together the needs of consumers with cyber technology. It permits a depth of sale that no other medium can provide. Another benefit of online marketing is that it is interactive. One-to-one marketing is a unique capability on online business.

(b) Intranets, Extranets and EDI

Internet marketing enhances company reach and allows interaction with customers (one-to-one marketing).

Intranets are one of the hottest applications of the internet technology in business. They capitalize on the fact that most organizations distribute far more information internally than they do to the outside world. The intranet serves as an easily accessible repository of corporate information, for everything from strategic targets to health plans.

EDI is an IT-based system that links, for example, channel members to facilitate the flow of a product or service through the channel.

One of the most significant changes in IT in recent years has been the emergence of electronic data interchange (EDI). It is an IT-based system that links, for example, channel members for purposes of facilitating the flow of a product or service through the channel. EDI can also be a 'tie that binds'. Getting customers to invest in sharing information about sales and inventories can provide a powerful disincentive to switching suppliers.

Quick-response (QR) logistics and inventory systems use EDI applications to automatically replenish stock as it is sold.

Information exchange between manufacturers, suppliers and retailers can include sales data, purchase orders, invoices, shipment tracking data, and product return information. Quick-response (QR) logistics and inventory systems use EDI applications to automatically replenish stock as it is sold. QR systems also build customer satisfaction by reducing stock-outs. However, a high level of commitment between channel members must exist throughout the logistics pipeline for QR to operate. The benefits are reduced system costs, efficiency and increased customer and consumer satisfaction.

Technologies that assist and expedite information exchange between channel members are also contributing to a revolution in manufacturing processes. By operating in real time, Just-in-Time (JIT) management eliminates the need for excess inventory. QR takes JIT further and applies the principles in the retail industry.

8.6.2 Pitfalls of Lagging Behind in IT Advances

Using an effective IT structure allows each linked firm to do more with less. It affords new market opportunities for channel members, suppliers, consumers, and so on. Companies that cling to a 'go-it-alone policy without exploring IT opportunities' attitude are in danger of going the way of the dinosaur. Therefore, IT is not only merely a linkage of computer systems. It can represent a change in a company's philosophy towards sharing and building strong and long-term relationships with respective partners or consumers based on IT and information transfer.

Companies that cling to a 'go-it-alone without exploring IT opportunities' attitude are in danger of going the way of the dinosaur.

Overall, the emergence of IT relationships and alliances has encouraged the use of new practices and technologies by organizations to share more real-time information and thus reduce business uncertainty. Technologicalship marketing is a general approach that can be used by the consumer marketing as well as industrial marketing (business to business) concerns. This combined perspective yields comprehensive insight into the impact of technologies on relationship marketing and business.

8.6.3 Technologicalship Marketing

Nowadays, with much work being subcontracted, relationship among partners becomes crucial to better accomplish overall goals. Relationships which are based on IT enable organizations to address and integrate the overall customer and company performance requirements. As such, partnerships should consider the long-term objectives as well as short-term needs of the participant organizations, thereby creating a basis for mutual investments and rewards. The building of a relationship-based technology (RBT) therefore should address the means of providing regular communication and information sharing among participants (organizations or consumers) to enable them to evaluate progress, modify objectives, and accommodate changing conditions.

Organizations are expected to include key suppliers and customers in quality improvement, planning and control activities. This requires sharing of information technology, planning together and systems coordination. The free and smooth flow of information about such factors as consumers, product and service performance, operations, logistics, competitive comparisons, suppliers, cost and finance, is crucial in creating, developing, and enhancing long-term relationships in the IT era.

Organizations are expected to include key suppliers and customers in quality improvement, planning and control activities.

IT is not a separate factor in relationship marketing. The quality of decisions is determined by the quality of shared information upon which those decisions are based. In short, twenty-first century organizations should be managed on the basis of facts rather than on the basis of instincts or feelings. And if information technology is the basis for business relationships, the information systems (IS) group is the catalyst to manage and utilize powerful IT structures needed for information flow and sharing among the aligned partners.

Relationship marketing cannot be established without IT-based relationships using advanced technological tools (e.g. EDI support systems, intranet,

IT is the basis for business relationships, information systems (IS) group is the catalyst to manage and utilize powerful IT structures.

extranet, local area networks (LANs), client server architecture, executive information system (EIS), video/teleconferencing, groupware, multimedia). A study by Spethmann (1993) showed that 77 per cent of marketing executives viewed linking electronically to their customers as being vital to their organization's marketing strategy for the next five years. One reason for the growing number of EDI systems is the need for real-time information to make proactive decisions. Relationship marketing will fall short of success if it is not supported by a good IT base that is easily accessible by partners. Lightning quick reaction to market responses will only be possible by being directly wired to the pulse of the market.

Relationships based on IT could be called technologicalship.

Technologicalship offers a natural linkage between the internal environment and the interaction process. It emphasizes how IT, consumers and organizations are a function of win-win interaction.

New IT-based relationships could be termed technologicalship. The effective use of technologicalship encourages the establishment of long-term relationship marketing with customers, suppliers, competitors, and others in the organization's external environment. Through this, marketers and managers can keep their finger on the customer's pulse and respond to changing needs.

Technologicalship offers a natural linkage between the internal environment and the interaction process because it emphasizes how IT, consumers and organizations are a function of a win-win interaction. IT and other technologies present opportunities to develop new relationships with end-users (of consumer or industrial goods/services) at low costs. Many companies recently did so by allowing customers to track offerings through websites on the Internet. Now customers can locate an offering in transit by connecting online to the company site and entering their bill number. Once the product has been delivered, they can even identify the name of the person who signed for it. To meet customer needs and to create and extract value using IT, IKEA outlets, for instance contact their VIP customers (holders of family cards) and provide them bonus offerings and information about its products/services.

8.6.4 Transaction Marketing, Relationship Marketing and Technologicalship Marketing

Technologicalship marketing allows for different types of solutions for different customers, and different kinds of interactions and relationships with varied customers. Indeed, technologicalship customers expect new kinds of relationships and solutions because technology makes them possible. Technologicalship is a fully integrated marketing system which simultaneously combines the activities of all marketing tools.

The differences between traditional marketing (including relationship marketing) and technologicalship marketing depend upon the nature of the technologies used to substitute for physical proximity.

The differences between traditional marketing (including relationship marketing) and technologicalship marketing depend upon the nature of the technologies used to substitute for physical proximity. For example, the retailer of the future with a multi-media interactive website will be able to become more involved with customers, respond to queries, make suggestions and offer many of the audio-visual sensations of physical retailing. Success in designing and running such technologicalship marketing depends on developing or using technology (in the broadest sense) to manage the relationships between the involved parties. These relationships will have to be managed differently as long as technology provides anything short of a total replication of physical presence.

8.6.5 Online Marketing

Online marketing gives companies the ability to establish an enduring relationship with individual consumers.

One of the most important loyalty-building benefits of IT is online marketing, which permits one-to-one marketing. It gives companies the ability to establish an enduring relationship with individual consumers. McDonald's McFamily on America Online is a good example. This site reinforces the idea of McDonald's being a parent's best friend. Parents can get information on the latest Happy Meal offer or nutritional information about McDonald's products. But even more valuable is the community McDonald's has created. For not only can parents talk directly to McDonald's, they can also dialogue with experts and with each other on a whole range of parenting issues, from how to keep the family healthy and safe to how they can spend more quality time with their kids.

8.6.6 The Changing Nature of Marketing

Computerizing and making relationships electronically viable also provide organizations with a powerful tool to profile its existing customer base and to create and retain stronger relationships within it, as well as to find new potential collaborators, e.g. customers, suppliers and distributors.

However, as the technologicalship approach suggests, using an effective, profitable mix of physical elements, IT, human resources and skills is a vital aspect to develop an organization's competitive position in the marketplace.

8.6.7 Potential Technologicalship Partners

To create value with IT, managers must gather, organize, select, and distribute information about the partners involved.

IT links together an organization's sales agents, factories and warehouses. To create value with IT, managers must gather, organize, select, and distribute information about the partners involved. The data about customer needs and behaviour enables an organization to identify today's key customers, develop relations with tomorrow's customers (e.g. consumers, distributors or suppliers), calculate the revenue that each customer generates, and estimate its own future investment opportunities.

End-user opinions should be involved at every step in the marketing process.

End-user opinions should be involved at every step in the marketing process (e.g. design and delivery). Buyers of products/services should always be encouraged to respond, on a continuing basis, to the experience of purchase and consumption. Feedback from different actors, including end-users, can be obtained by using a feedback loop through customer hotline numbers, customer satisfaction surveys or any other feedback method.

Four primary candidates for technologicalship are: customers, suppliers, distributors and facilitators.

When analysing the relationship strategies, managers should consider, in addition to the internal technologicalship, four primary candidates for such a technologicalship, namely customers, suppliers, distributors and facilitators. Members of a distribution channel jointly represent a value delivery system. Each one is dependent on the other, and every activity must be enumerated and responsibility assigned. Small retailers may have to use suppliers outside the normal channel to get the items they want and gain supplier support.

A delivery system is as good as its weakest link. A relationship-oriented technique that some manufacturers and retailers, especially supermarket chains, are making use of is *category management*. The growing interdependence among these vital business connections provides added incentive for using the technologicalship approach to strengthen these links. Through efficient technologicalship management, management of human resources and skills, and the use of relationship marketing mechanisms of mutual benefit and respect, a company can establish, enhance and sustain ongoing business relationships with different customers.

8.6.8 Customer Technologicalship

Customer technologicalship permits longer time horizons for the participants to plan and grow together.

Recognizing the importance of the customer is the foundation of a successful technologicalship. Looking to possible customer needs for technological advancements and communication tools may provide great opportunities to create long-term and close customer relationships, and thus garner more of a customer's business. Customer technologicalship permits longer time horizons for the participants to plan and grow together. By serving the customer's technological advancement and communication tool needs, a firm extends its own technical frontiers. An example of this type of customer technologicalship is found in the healthcare field, where cost containment is a paramount concern. Another example is Procter & Gamble's website, where consumers can request a handy dispenser for Ariel brand and find solutions to common laundry problems.

Technology is changing the nature of retailer-customer and retailer-supplier interactions. Point-of-sale electronic scanning equipment is widely utilized because they can quickly complete customer transactions, amass sales data, give feedback to suppliers, place and receive orders faster, reduce costs, and adjust inventory figures. The downside of scanning is the error rate, which can be upsetting to customers. Ironically, although consumer perception is that errors cause overcharges, it has been found that undercharges are more likely. A novel experiment now underway involves self-scanning. Self-scanning checkout, also called 'self-checkout' is an automated process that enables shoppers to scan, bag, and pay for their purchases without human assistance. Other technological innovations influencing retail interactions are electronic cards and interactive electronic kiosks.

Mass customization is the ability to efficiently and economically offer goods and services tailored to individual consumers.

Mass customization is the ability to efficiently and economically offer goods and services tailored to individual consumers. This advance, still in its infancy, is catching on among manufacturers, retailers, and consumers. Among its leading practitioners are Dell and Gateway PC firms, Levi Strauss at its company-owned retail stores, and General Nutrition Centres. In India HUL uses technology to understand the mood of the customers and the number of *kirana* stores in any specific locality through the PDA of their sales force.

In general, technology in retail relationships should allow better information flow between retailers and customers, as well as between retailers and suppliers, leading to faster and more dependable transactions. There are two points to keep in mind when studying technology and its impact on relationships in retailing:

(a) The role of technology and humans should be clear and consistent with the objectives and style of business, and

(b) Customers expect certain advances to be in place so they can rapidly complete transactions and get feedback on product availability.

8.7 Internal Marketing

Internal marketing is the first step in relationship marketing. It involves treating employees like external customers through proactive programmes and planning, like setting targets, extending incentives and enhancing skills and motivation. Internal marketing is a definite prerequisite for external marketing. It can play a key role in change management, building a corporate image and capitalizing on strategic internal marketing.

Internal marketing involves treating employees like external customers through proactive programmes and planning, like setting targets, extending incentives, enhancing skills and motivation.

The cornerstone of human resource management is employee value. It is enhanced through policies and practices that build continuity and commitment among employees. Employee satisfaction and productivity may vary in the course of a worker's association with an organization. Over time, employees may reach the peak of job satisfaction and productivity, after which their diligence may wane. When this happens, despite the organization's efforts to provide stimulation through continued training, new assignments, and other incentives, the individual and the organization may best be served by severance of the relationship. Loyalty master Frederick F. Reich (1996) believed that organizations can build their employee relationship strategies on the following elements: finding the right employees, earning their loyalty and gaining cost advantages through superior productivity.

8.8 Learning Organization

Learning organization explores the idea that the human mind is evolving and that the quality of awareness experienced by an individual will be intimately related to his position on this evolutionary trajectory. In particular, the quality of awareness is related to the development of the image the individual has of himself. Based on these foundations, the learning organization concept can be thought of as the lowest of the three-stage conceptual hierarchy of *learning-wisdom-enlightenment.*

Wisdom can be thought of as a special learning culture that is of a higher order than a general learning culture because it provides conditions to know reality rather than the increased sophistication of representational systems that are a characteristic outcome of other learning environments.

The *enlightened organization* can be thought of as an ultimate goal or condition in which reality is known by looking at the time periods ahead (market downturn/recovery/boom and emerging demand pattern) and focusing on the organizations and their methods adopted in the world of business. Delivering relationship marketing is a question of having systems, management procedures and control processes that allow the staff to meet customer needs, and recruit, train and keep the staff members informed so that they have the skills and capability to meet customer needs.

The enlightened organization *can be thought of as condition in which reality is known by looking at the time periods ahead (market downturn/recovery/boom and emerging demand pattern) and various focus of organizations and methods adopted in the world of business.*

8.9 Emerging Trends in Relationship Marketing

Perhaps the most powerful force for change today comes from the integration of computers and telecommunications. Digitization allows text, graphics,

GOOGLE ANALYTICS

While there are lot of free tools available, the one that has created a flutter in the web analytics space is Google Analytics. While other tools provide minimal functionalities, Google Analytics in its free version provides state-of-the-art functionalities and a very user-friendly interface. The software in itself is complete and equivalent to a proprietary software. In January 2010, Google Analytics is believed to be on over 1.20 million sites. Google Analytics code is inserted on 26 per cent of the nearly 8,800 URLs currently tracked, including 8 of the top 100 sites and 81 of the top 1,000 sites for which data is available. In this regard, Google Analytics is second only to Omniture whose code is detected on 36 of the top 100 sites and 163 of the top 1,000 sites for which data is available.

Interestingly, the Vendor Discover Tool reports that 12 of the top 1,000 sites have both the Omniture and Google Analytics code. Once combined successfully with search engine optimization and search engine marketing, Web analytics has the potential to provide customized and personalized marketing solutions.

Source: www.google.com

video and audio to be manipulated, stored, and transmitted in the digital language of computers. Faster and more powerful software enables firms to create relational databases that combine information about customers with details of all their transactions and then mine these databases for insights into new trends, new approaches to segmentation, and new marketing opportunities. Technological change affects many other types of services, too, from airfreight to hotels to retail stores. Express package firms such as Speed Post, DHL, Federal Express, and United Parcel Service (UPS), for instance, recognize that the ability to provide real-time information about customers' packages has become as important for success as the physical movement of those packages.

The use of technology to create more customer-added value and to facilitate the coordinating of networks is of particular importance for a modern organization and its networks. Jeffrey and Sviokla refer to the virtual IT world as the marketspace, to distinguish it from the physical world of the marketplace. Managers have to look to the marketspace to add value. They have to integrate the activities of the physical world with those of the marketspace in order to create and extract value in the most efficient and effective manner.

When Cola cans and chocolate wrappers start carrying email contact information, one should know that email-based customer service is a powerful communication tool. This widespread adoption would seem to suggest that

WEB METRICS

Web analytics is the measurement, collection, analysis and reporting of data from websites for purposes of understanding and optimizing website usage. The data generated by web analytics tools is classified into several user-defined parameters called Web metrics. Web metrics are tools to assess how people interact with the website and what changes need to be incorporated in the strategy of Internet-based relationship marketing as a whole and the website in particular.

Off-site Web analytics refers to Web measurement and analysis irrespective of whether a website is maintained or not. It includes the measurement of a website's potential audience (opportunity), share of voice (visibility), and buzz (comments) that is happening on the internet as a whole. On-site Web analytics measures a visitor's journey on the website. This includes its drivers and conversions, for example, which pages encourage people to make a purchase. On-site web analytics measures the performance of a website in a commercial context. This data is typically compared against key performance indicators and used to improve the website or the marketing campaign's audience response.

No strategic move is complete without a comprehensive measurement and analysis of its outcome. Most advertising campaigns that a company undertakes and the after-effects of the campaign normally have a vague correlation, which makes it difficult to establish a clear picture about its success. Internet, with the use of Web analytics, provides a way to beat conventional marketing tactics in this respect. Web analytics will provide an indication of traffic trends, a better understanding of the target audience (online audience), a means of comparison and analysis of online relationship building campaigns and the data to calculate return on investment of the website and relationship marketing campaigns.

companies have discovered an effective and efficient way of communicating with customers using technology. A well-integrated application of technology and staff and through operations that respond to customer needs, encourages customers to use a whole range of firms' products/services rather than just a few. It also helps to create deeper and fuller customer relationships by building client loyalty.

Technologicalship partnership, by using effective IT structures and tools, enables organizations to achieve the following potential synergies:

Technologicalship partnership, by using effective IT structures and tools, enables organizations to achieve potential synergies.

- Reduces cost of sales (production, distribution, sale).
- Exceed client expectations of quality at a reasonable price.
- Collaborate with other companies on joint development efforts.
- Jointly develop and use training programmes with other companies.
- Exchange large volumes of data using EDI.
- Share news of common interest exclusively with partner companies.
- Redesign current business processes to create new business capabilities sharing expertise in generic cross-business processes: managing financial resources and services, managing human resources, environment, and safety policy, information systems infrastructure provision.

These synergies permit creating, developing and sustaining mutually effective, efficient, and profitable long-term relationships with internal and external actors in the domestic and global markets. Technologicalship marketing, clearly, shows how technology changes the interactions and relationships between parties involved. The boundary between these parties can no longer be managed in the same way as it is through face-to-face encounters or social exchanges. In short, it is a major step forward in the evolution of marketing, from transaction relationship to technologicalship marketing. For relationship retailing to work, enduring value-driven relationships are needed with other channel members as well as with customers.

For relationship retailing to work, enduring value-driven relationships are needed with other channel members and with customers.

8.10 Summary

- This chapter focused on using and managing IT tools to effectively and efficiently create, develop, and sustain mutually profitable business-to-business and business-to-consumer long-term relationships.
- The technologicalship concept was introduced to indicate the almost inseparable partnership between IT and business relationships. This chapter emphasized the fact that technologicalship marketing (relationship marketing based on IT) should incorporate everything from transaction marketing to relationship marketing. Marketers and managers must be aware of new developments in technology and their possible effects on relationships, because technology can and does affect marketing activities in many different ways. We call such a philosophy 'technologicalship marketing'.
- Technological marketing has strong implications for marketing functions and activities. It can in fact be considered as a new paradigm. It is a relationship that offers natural linkages between the internal environment

and the interaction process because it emphasizes how technologies, consumers and organizations are the function of a win-win interaction.

- Most marketing activity should be based on technology and a desire to make a relationship work. By failing to utilize the technologicalship philosophy, organizations risk being isolated, while successful organizations move ahead toward borderless or virtual reality.
- Retail marketers need to map customer needs and wants with their products. If a product does not fulfil customer needs, retail marketing needs to take the initiative to improve the product. Customers should be an integral part of the product development and improvement process. As customer needs and wants do not remain constant, retail marketing organizations need to constantly monitor the trends so that they can modify their products and services to satisfy their customers.

PART II

Applied Case Studies in Marketing

An Overview

Education is not the filling of a pail, but the lighting of a fire. — WILLIAM BUTLER YEATS

Much research exists documenting that real understanding is a case of active restructuring on the part of the learner. Restructuring occurs through an engagement in problem posing as well as problem solving, inference making and investigation, resolving of contradictions, and reflecting. These processes all mandate for more active learners as well as a different model of education . . . students need to be empowered to think and learn for themselves. Thus learning needs to be conceived of as something a learner does, not something that is done to a learner.

— Active Learning: Cooperation in the Classroom
by JOHNSON, JOHNSON, and SMITH, 1991

For the marketing academic, teaching is a process of experimentation, success, failure and revision as one attempts to create optimal learning experiences for a student by following innovative practices. Fortunately, the 'fuel' for faculty who teach courses in basic marketing is particularly abundant. Students bring into the class a wealth of experiences as both product/service consumers and providers, and are eager to inquire into the unique aspects of marketing. The case study method has been universally identified as the best participative learning pedagogy for applied sciences like marketing management.

1. Overview of Case Analysis

A case is a written description of an organization (or any of its parts) covering all or some of its aspects for a certain period of time. It sets forth events and organizational circumstances surrounding a particular managerial situation. The goal of case analysis is not to develop a set of 'correct' facts but to learn to reason well with the available data. Cases mirror the uncertainty of the real world managerial environment in that the information available is often imprecise and ambiguous. You may perhaps be frustrated that there is no one right answer or correct solution to any given case. Instead, there may be a number of feasible strategies that the management might adopt, each with somewhat different implications for the future of the organization, and each involving different trade-offs.

Marketing managers cannot afford to delay making decisions until they are satisfied with the quality and quantity of available information. Such a time may perhaps never arrive. Like a manager in the real world, a student of marketing management must take a decision to make optimum use of available information and make assumptions about the unknown or unavailable.

If you are using this book in a course or seminar, you will be exposed to a wide range of different management situations within a relatively short time. As a result, the cases discussed here will collectively provide a much broader exposure to product and service marketing problems than most managers experience several years on the job. Recognizing that managerial problems are not unique to a particular institution (or even to a specific service industry) forms the basis for developing a professional approach to management.

2. Objectives of Case Analysis

The objectives of the case analysis include:

- Helping the reader acquire the skills of putting textbook knowledge about management into practice. Managers succeed not so much because of what they know but because of what they do.
- Get the reader out of the habit of being a receiver of facts, concepts and techniques and into the habit of diagnosing problems, analysing and evaluating alternatives, and formulating workable plans of action.
- Training the reader to work out answers and solutions, as opposed to relying upon the authoritative crutch of the teacher/counsellor or a textbook.
- Providing exposure to a range of organizations and managerial situations. In the long-term such an effort will seek to offer a basis for comparison when working as a professional manager.

3. Advantages and Disadvantages

It is important to recognize that even though case writers try to build realism into their cases, these cases differ from real world management situations in several important aspects. First, the information is prepackaged in written form. By contrast, marketing managers accumulate their information through meetings, conversations, memoranda, research studies, observations, news reports, and other externally published materials—and of course, by rumour.

Second, case studies tend to be selective in their reporting as most are designed with specific teaching objectives in mind. Each must fit a relatively short class period and focus attention on a defined category of management problems within a given subject area. To provide such a focus—and to keep the length and complexity of the case within reasonable bounds—the writers may need to omit information on problems, data, or personnel that are peripheral to the central issues in the case. In the real world, management problems are usually dynamic in nature. These call for immediate action, with further analysis and major decisions being delayed until later time. Managers are rarely able to wrap up their problems, put them away, and go on to the next 'case'. By contrast, discussing a case in class or writing an analysis of a case is more like examining a snapshot taken at a particular point in time—although sometimes a sequel, the case provides a sense of continuity and poses the need for future decisions within the same organizations.

A third contrast between case analyses and real world marketing management is that participants in case discussions and authors of written case reports are not responsible for implementing their decisions, nor do they have to live with the consequences. However, this does not imply that one can be frivolous when making recommendations. Instructors and researchers are likely to be critical of contributions that are not based on a careful analysis and interpretation of the facts.

The pedagogical objective of the case method is significantly different from the usual teaching in the classroom. Instead of the professor/instructor/counsellor, it is the student who does most of the talking. The counsellor/instructor's role is to solicit student participation and guide discussion.

Since a case assignment emphasizes student participation, it is obvious that the effectiveness of the class discussion depends upon each student having studied the case beforehand. A case assignment therefore requires conscientious preparation. The case analysis and discussion help students develop analytical, communication and interpersonal skills which are vital for success in management.

4. Preparing a Case

In the case study method, issues are discussed and alternatives and approaches evaluated. Usually, a good argument can be made for more than one course of action. Students must understand that in case analysis it is the exercise of identifying, diagnosing and recommending that counts rather than discovering the 'right answer'. One seeks to become skilled in the process of designing workable action plans through an evaluation of the prevailing circumstances. Just as there is no one right solution to a case, there is also no single correct way of preparing a case. However, the broad guidelines outlined in this subsection may help familiarize you with case preparation.

A case may be prepared for:

- Oral analysis for discussion (by individuals)
- Oral analysis for discussion (by groups)
- Written analysis (by individuals)
- Written analysis (by groups)
- Oral/written analysis and presentation (by individuals/groups).

What particular method would be followed in the counselling sessions depends upon the counsellor and other factors, including the nature of the company and the length of the case.

5. Initial Analysis

A marketing case is a technical paper and deserves careful perusal. A good approach is to read the case thrice: once rapidly, quickly scanning any exhibits; a second time thoroughly and slowly, giving careful attention to the exhibits and noting apparent organizational objectives, strategies, symptoms of problems, root causes, unresolved issues and the role of key individuals; and a third time, rapidly again to reinforce the main points.

It is important to gather an understanding of the overall situation in your first read. Ask yourself:

- What sort of organization does the case concern?
- What is the nature of the industry (broadly defined)?

- What is going on in the external environment?
- What problems does the management appear to be facing?

While no standard procedure can be laid down, the following successive steps will be helpful for analysing the case (whether for oral discussion or written presentation):

Know the facts

Understand the environment of the marketing organization (external and internal) and gather relevant information from outside sources, if necessary appraise and evaluate the environment. Consider and keep in mind the mission of the organization while making recommendations. As you proceed, try to chart answers to such questions as:

- What decisions need to be made and who is responsible for making them?
- What are the objectives of the organization and of each of the key players in the case? Are these objectives compatible? If not, can problems be reconciled, or will it be necessary to redefine the objectives?
- What are the resources and constraints that may help or hinder attempts by the organization to meet its objectives?

You should make particular effort to establish the significance of any quantitative data presented in the text of the case or, more often, in the exhibits. Analyse to see if new insights may be gained by combining and manipulating data presented in different parts of the case. However, do not accept the data blindly. In the case studies, as with real life, not all information is equally reliable or relevant.

6. Developing Recommendations

Once you have diagnosed the company's situation and weighed the pros and cons of alternative courses of action in the market, you may decide on what the company should do to tackle problems or improve performance. Draw up a set of recommendations and prepare an 'action agenda'. This is the most crucial part of the analysis. Bear in mind that proposing a realistic, workable solution is not the same as offering a hasty, or ill-conceived possibility. Do not recommend what you would not be prepared to do yourself if placed in the shoes of the decision-maker. Your recommendations will not be complete unless some thought is given to how the proposed strategy should be implemented. Certain questions you will need to ask include:

- What resources—human, financial, or other—will be required?
- Who should be responsible for implementation?
- What time frame should be established for the various actions proposed?
- How should subsequent performance be measured?

In other words, offer a definite agenda for action, stipulate a timetable and sequence to initiate action, indicating priorities and suggesting who should be responsible for doing what.

7. What an Evaluator Looks for in a Case Analysis

The important elements that a counsellor (or evaluator) would generally look for in a case analysis are:

- The care with which facts and background knowledge have been used.
- An ability to state problems and issues clearly.
- The use of appropriate analytical techniques.
- Evidence of sound logic and arguments.
- Consistency between analysis and recommendations.
- An ability to formulate reasonable and feasible recommendations for action.

Thus, both a future marketing manager as well as the present product and services managers can make use of the case study method to developing a sense of responsibility and commitment while making decisions in the modern business environment.

8. Advanced Levels in Case Analysis

It is important that students be exposed to the practical aspects of making tactical and strategic decisions during market turbulence. Hence, I have demonstrated six live cases of Indian origin with a series of analyses like PEST, SWOT, BCG Matrix, GE Matrix, Ansoff's Matrix, STP marketing, product and services marketing mix, financial performance and current strategies with recommendation.

The following cases will be discussed in this section:

- Spreading mobile culture through 3G revolution
- Rivalry off the air: saga of Kingfisher and Jet Airways
- The great Indian retail story under test
- The heat of recession and destocking: can HUL overcome the pressure?
- Building DTH PC segment: portfolio for Creative Solutions Ltd.
- Nokia connects the world

These cases will provide avenues for readers to apply theoretical concepts, explained in Chapters 1 to 8 of this volume, at the core level of product and services marketing mix. While I have attempted this exercise to share the best practices of leading B-schools, further analysis has been provided on the CD accompanying this book.

CHAPTER 9 

SPREADING MOBILE CULTURE THROUGH 3G REVOLUTION

applied case study 1

One cannot underestimate the importance of mobile as a vital communications tool, connecting so many people, often for the first time in their lives. Against that backdrop, the roll out of Mobile Broadband services, offering high-speed internet and rich media access is well underway and available in more than 73 countries today. Mobile Broadband hails the next era for our vast eco-system, one that is delivering remarkable social and economic benefits to people, businesses and economies throughout the world.

— ROB CONWAY, CEO and Board Member, GSMA

9.1 Genesis

Think of telecommunications as the world's biggest machine. Made of complex networks, telephones, mobile phones and Internet-linked PCs, the global system touches nearly all of us. It allows us to speak, share thoughts and do business with nearly any one, regardless of where in the world he/she might be. Telecom operating companies make all this happen. Not long ago the telecommunications industry was a club of big national and regional operators. However, over the past decade the industry has been transformed by rapid deregulation and innovation. In countries around the world, government monopolies have ended, giving way to a plethora of new competitors. Traditional markets have turned upside down as growth in mobile connection outpaces that of fixed line and the Internet starts to replace voice as the staple business. Table 9.1 presents the value proposition of the new mobile market segment (MVNO—mobile virtual network operator) in India.

Even more interesting is the fact that today more than 700 mobile operators across 218 countries and territories of the world are signing 15 new subscribers for a GSM mobile phone connection every second. According to early estimates of the GSMA (2006), China remains the world's biggest GSM market with over 509 million connections and accounts for 14 per cent of the third billion growths in the subscriber base of world GSM. India

Table 9.1: Elements of value proposition

S. No.	*Elements*	*Value proposition at the current segment*	*Value proposition in the emerging MVNO segment*
1.	Products and services	Music downloads, streaming, ringtones, caller tones, MMS, SMS	Integration of company applications to mobile
2.	Handset	New and catchy handset design	State of art technology, Web enabled
3.	Pricing	Discount on purchase of other accessories/ software/music items	Post paid, premium pricing
4.	Marketing	Brand ambassador, music channel, FM	Empowered employees
5.	Distribution	Web, own stores	Tie-up with enterprises, direct sales
6.	Customer care	Easy and high functionality IVRS	Penalty on higher downtime, Dell service model

with 193 million GSM subscribers is second, accounting for 12 per cent of the third billion growths. Russia with 178 million and Brazil with 93 million subscribers contribute 4 per cent of the third billion growths. India in August 2010 crossed a subscriber base of over 468 million. Mahanagar Telephone Nigam Limited (MTNL), one of India's leading telecom service providers, launched the first 3G service in the country in 2008. What will be the fate of 2G? And how long will 3G services have to wait to acquire the critical mass? Let us analyse.

9.2 Evolution of GSM Technologies

Cellular is a type of wireless communication very familiar to mobile users. It is called cellular because the system uses base stations to divide a service area into many cells. Cellular calls are transferred from base one station to another as the customer travels from cell to cell. A walkie-talkie is a simplex device, operating on a single frequency, which means only one person can talk. The cellular on the other hand is a duplex device operating on two frequencies, one for talking and the other for listening. A walkie-talkie has 40 channels while a cellular can communicate up to 1,664 channels. It can switch from cell to cell and also operate within a cell.

Each cell has a base station that consists of a transmission tower and a building which has the radio equipment. Cell phones have low-power transmitters in them. Many cells have two signal strengths—0.60 and 3 watts. Compared to 5 watts of the CB radio, these have the advantage of less power consumption, meaning smaller batteries and hence smaller handheld phones. Each carrier also operates a Mobile Telephone Switching Office (MTSO). This controls all the base stations in the region and also handles all phone connections to land-based phone systems.

If we were to trace the history of the cellular phone, the credit for inventing it will go to Martin Cooper. His first call was in April 1973 to his rival in Bell Labs, that was also engaged in similar research. Though Martin Cooper and his team has the patent for the radio telephone system (US Patent 3906166 dated 16 September 1975), early technological developments in mobile telephony were largely thanks to AT&T and Bell Labs.

Mobile telephony existed as early as 1921, when the US police department used mobile radio units operating at 2 MHz. On 17 June 1946, AT&T and

Southwest Bell for the first time introduced a commercial mobile radio telephone service. They operated on six channels in the 150 MHz band with 60 KHz spacing.

By the early 1980s Europe had as many as nine analog cellular systems, like NMT450, C-Netz, TACS, Radio com 2000, RTMS/RTMI, and so on. This posed a unique problem for the continent as the systems were incompatible with one other. So the countries planned a new technology in a new radio band which could be used all over Europe, a digital mobile service with advanced features. Groupe Speciale Mobile (GSM), meaning Global System for Mobile Communications, was thus born.

GSM preparations were started by 26 European national phone companies in 1982. The equivalent in the USA was the PC1900. Even the UK got a GSM operating in the higher frequency of DCS1800 in the pre-PCS days. The specifications for GSM were published in 1991. The USA also got TDMA, CDMA, and PCS1900 digital mobile systems but the popularity of the GSM soared. Rather, it is still soaring.

The year 1990 gave birth to TDMA, 1994 saw CDMA, and a combination of both, the PCS1900, was born in 1997. This was basically the European GSM with a higher frequency, dubbed as PCS1900 in the USA.

9.3 The Emergence of Hi-Tech GSM

Technology is changing very fast. Almost every day there is news of improvement and changes. However the near future in mobile telephony will be GPRS, EDGE, and UMTS (Universal Mobile Telecommunications System). 3G technologies which will combine voice and data transmission are the vision of the future. With Bluetooth technology one might be able to talk to machines while on the move. There is no end to dreaming, but science is reality. And the pace at which things are changing, dreams are becoming a reality sooner than later.

It was in 1997 that a small company, Unwired Planet (now known as Phone.com) released a technology that allowed cell phones to connect to websites and receive their contents. In June 1997, Phone.com joined hands with cell phone giants Ericsson, Motorola and Nokia to device a common protocol for building applications that would offer more services on the cell phone and other mobile devices through the Internet. Since then the organization, called WAP (Wireless Application Protocol) Forum, has drafted a global wireless protocol specification for all wireless networks, which is being followed by all those involved in developing software for the purpose. Today, not just cell phone manufacturers, but cellular network operators, Internet Service Providers and software developers are all members of the WAP Forum. In fact WAP is a de facto standard for enabling mobile phones to access the internet and other advanced services. Users can access websites which have been converted by the use of WML into stripped-down versions of the original that are more suitable for the limited display capabilities of mobile phones.

The WAP Forum produces open standards so that all the segments, namely the WAP device manufacturers, the cellular operators, the ISPs and the software application developers, all offer compatible solutions. The WAP Forum is also working with Internet monitoring authorities such as W3C

BOX 9.1: GOOGLE'S AND THE ANDROID MARKET

Unlike RIM (BlackBerry), Apple (iPhone), Nokia (Symbian) and other mobile phone companies that develop the mobile operating system (OS) and the hardware, Google is only developing the OS part while the hardware is being manufactured by other companies like HTC, Lenovo and Samsung. So when someone says 'Google Phone', it essentially means that the phone runs on the Google operating system which is known as Android. And since Android internally runs on Linux, some users have even managed to install the Google Android OS on their Nokia phones and Asus notebooks.

Android, a Linux-based mobile phone operating system was introduced in India in June 2009. Android has been developed by the Open Handset Alliance that includes HTC, Intel, Motorola, Google, and Samsung. The HTC Magic Android phone, that will take on the Apple iPhone, is based on the Android platform and is available in India through Airtel at around ₹30,000. The HTC Magic Android has highly sophisticated features, similar to those of the Apple iPhone and RIM's Blackberry. It has a talk time of up to 350 minutes for WCDMA and 406 minutes for GSM. It features a unique bar coding application—if the carrier of the phone is shopping, s/he can quickly scan the bar code of any product on the shelf and get more information about it through his/her Google phone.

Google has participated in the Android market by offering several applications for its services. These applications include Google Voice for the Google Voice service, Scoreboard for following sports, Sky Map for watching stars, Finance for its finance service, Maps Editor for MyMaps service, Places Directory for local search, Secrets for safely storing passwords and My Tracks, a jogging application. Android phones that include the 'Google Experience' also have Google Search, Google Calendar, Google Maps and Gmail integrated.

Let us trace Google's journey into the mobile world. In July 2005 Google acquired Android Inc., a small start-up company based in Palo Alto, California, USA. Android's co-founders who went to work at Google included Andy Rubin (co-founder of Danger), Rich Miner (co-founder of Wildfire Communications Inc.), Nick Sears (once VP at T-Mobile), and Chris White (headed design and interface development at WebTV). At the time, little was known about the functions of Android Inc. other than that they made software for mobile phones.

Research company Canalys estimates that by the second quarter of 2009, Android had 2.8 per cent of the worldwide Smartphone market. By the following quarter (Q3 of 2009), Android's market share had grown to 3.5 per cent. In October 2009, Gartner Inc. predicted that by 2012, Android would become the world's second most popular Smartphone platform, behind only the Symbian OS which powers Nokia phones outside the US. Meanwhile, the BlackBerry would fall from second to fifth place, iPhone would remain in third place, and Microsoft's Windows Mobile would remain in fourth place. Taiwan's Market Intelligence & Consulting Institute (MIC) predicted that in 2013, 31.80 million Android phones and 126 million Android-based portable products would ship. Analytics firm Flurry estimates that 250,000 Motorola Droid phones were sold in the United States during the phone's first week.

After the successful launching of Android-based portable products, rumours began that Google was planning to enter the mobile phone market, although it was unclear what function it might perform in the market. Reports from the BBC and *The Wall Street Journal* noted that Google wanted its search and applications on mobile phones and it was working hard to deliver that. Print and online media outlets soon reported that Google was developing a Google-branded handset. More speculation followed about Google defining technical specifications, showing prototypes to cell phone manufacturers and network operators. In September 2007, *InformationWeek* covered an Evalueserve study reporting that Google had filed several patent applications in the area of mobile telephony.

Table 9.2: GSM technologies

World	*2,881,123,146*	
Africa	265,076,453	9%
America	297,393,161	10%
Asia Pacific	1,162,251,880	40%
Europe: Eastern	397,925,950	14%
Europe: Western	478,833,084	17%
Middle East	173,200,146	6%
USA/Canada	106,442,472	4%

Source: World GSM Association, 2006.

to provide standards that are compatible with the latest Internet protocols such as HTTP-NG (next generation).

The service that is expected to become most successful on WAP mobile phones is live stock quotes. A subscriber can go to a website through his/her WAP-enabled mobile phone and ask for services which will sound her/him off when his/her favourite scrip jumps the cut-off mark, as defined by him/her. The subscriber could even programme it to automatically send a buy/sell order to the broker when the scrip crosses the cut-off mark.

India is gearing up to face the WAP revolution, which is expected in the next few months. Two Indian software firms (Integra Micro Systems and Silicon Automation Systems) have released their WAP server products. Symbian is a company created by Psion, Nokia, Ericsson and Motorola in 1998 with the aim of developing and standardizing an operating system which will enable mobile phones from different manufacturers to exchange information. The operating system is known as EPOC. Matsushita has subsequently joined Symbian.

Tri-Band refers to a mobile phone able to operate on the three internationally designated GSM frequencies—900, 1800 and 1900 MHz. EDGE UWC-136, the next generation of data heading towards third generation and personal multimedia environments, builds on the GPRS and is known as Enhanced Data Rate for GSM Evolution (EDGE). It will allow GSM operators to use existing GSM radio bands to offer wireless multimedia IP-based services and applications at theoretical maximum speeds of 384 kbps with a bit-rate of 48 kbps per timeslot and up to 69.20 kbps per timeslot in good radio conditions. Google Inc. too has forayed into the mobile market (Box 9.2).

BOX 9.2: GOOGLES FORAY INTO MOBILE MARKET

Google Inc. has invested millions of dollars in its cell phone project and is courting US and European mobile operators. According to *The Wall Street Journal*, a Reuters company that tracks industry trends for institutional investors reported that Google has engaged Taiwan's High Tech Computer Corporation to design a Linux software-based phone for launch in the first quarter of 2011.

The report cited industry sources as saying T-Mobile, owned by Deutsche Telekom, would likely be Google's US partner, with France Telecom's Orange selling the phones in other markets.

Google has also approached the two biggest US wireless services, AT&T and Verizon Wireless, to ask them to sell phones with the Google service. Verizon Wireless has decided not to integrate Google's web search into its phones because of the latter's advertising revenue-sharing demands. However talks between Verizon Wireless, owned by Verizon Communications and Vodafone Group Plc., and Google have ended without resulting in an agreement. T-Mobile and Vodafone already incorporate Google search in their mobile web service in Europe, while AT&T offers it as one of several web search options. 'We talk to a lot of different companies and we're not going to comment on our discussions with any of them,' said Mark Siegel, an AT&T spokesman.

Google said in an e-mailed response that it is 'partnering with carriers, manufacturers, and content providers around the world,' without giving further details. It said wireless was an increasingly important market but it had not announced plans to build a phone. It also said that Sprint Nextel Corporation would feature Google services on devices for a new wireless network that the third largest US mobile service was building. Google has also developed prototype phones and talked over technical specifications with manufacturers including LG Electronics.

According to *The Wall Street Journal*, mobile advertising is still a relatively small market but advertisers and wireless experts expect this to change. The Yankee Group has forecast that the mobile ad market will more than quadruple to $275 million in 2007 and eventually grow to $2.2 billion in 2010, up from an estimated $60 million in 2006. Some experts are forecasting an even bigger market.

Source: Sinead Carew and Paritosh Bansal in New York, Nicola Leske in Munich.

Figure 9.1: 3G revolution.

It is estimated by International Telecommunication Union (ITU) that the GSM subscribers will touch 5 billion worldwide in 2010 and by 2012. India will have 893 million mobile users.

9.4 3G Mobile Revolution

3G is the latest addition to the GSM family. 3G enables the provision of mobile multimedia services such as music, TV and video, rich entertainment content and Internet access. The technology on which 3G services are delivered is based on a GSM network enhanced with a Wideband-CDMA (W-CDMA) air interface—the over-the-air transmission element. Global operators, in conjunction with the 3G Partnership Project (3GPP) have developed 3G as an open standard.

3G is the generic term used for the next generation of mobile communications system. These have been created to support the effective delivery of a range of multimedia services. In addition, they provide more efficient systems for over-the-air transmission of existing services, such as voice, text and data than are available today. Developed by the global GSM community as its chosen path for 3G evolution, UMTS is one of the International Telecommunications Union's (ITU's) family of third-generation mobile communications system. UMTS uses a W-CDMA air interface, which leads some to refer to the technology as simply W-CDMA, creating confusion in the marketplace.

To alleviate this confusion and to highlight the backward compatibility of the system with second-generation GSM, the GSM Association now refers to the range of high-speed multimedia services that can be delivered to users via mobile networks using UMTS/W-CDMA systems such as 3GSM as W-CDMA, rather than simply the air interface technology.

The global 3G Partnership Project (3GPP), a collaboration of telecommunications standards bodies, is the organization through which much of the technnical specifications are devised. The GSM Association is a market representation partner of the 3GPP. It provides the 3GPP with market advice and a consensus view of operator community's market requirements.

The use of the W-CDMA air interface significantly increases the data transfer rate of GSM networks, offering average downlink rates of around 3,000 kbit/s. The 3G Evolution describes the seamless, compatible evolutionary path of enhancements to the existing 3GSM technology family. These will offer GSM operators higher data transfer speeds and greater system capacity that, in turn, will enhance their ability to provide mobile broadband multimedia services. Following an evolutionary path within the GSM family of technologies delivers the generic benefits of GSM such as global roaming, seamless billing, network compatibility and huge economies of scale. The 3G evolutionary path has a series of well-defined technology enhancements. The glossary given in Box 9.3 will familiarize you with the terms used in the discussion.

BOX 9.3: GLOSSARY OF TERMS

1G: The first generation of analogue mobile phone technology including AMPS, TACS and NMT.

2G: The second generation of digital mobile phone technologies including GSM, CDMA-IS-95 and D-AMPS IS-136.

2.5G: The enhancement of GSM which includes technologies such as GPRS.

3G: The third generation of mobile phone technologies covered by the ITU IMT-2000 family.

AMPS: Advanced Mobile Phone System, the analogue mobile phone technology used in North and South America and in around 35 other countries. Operates in the 800MHz band using FDMA technology.

Bandwidth: A term meaning both the width of a transmission channel in terms of Hertz and the maximum transmission speed in bits per second that it will support.

Bluetooth: A low-power, short-range wireless technology designed to provide a replacement for the serial cable. Operating in the 2.4GHz ISM band, Bluetooth can connect a wide range of personal, professional and domestic devices such as laptop computers and mobile phones together wirelessly.

EDGE: Enhanced Data Rates for GSM Evolution; effectively the final stage in the evolution of the GSM standard, EDGE uses a new modulation schema to enable theoretical data speeds of up to 384kbit/s within the existing GSM spectrum. An alternative upgrade path towards 3G services for operators such as those in the USA, without access to new spectrum. Also known as Enhanced GPRS (E-GPRS).

FDMA: Frequency Division Multiple Access, a transmission technique where the assigned frequency band for a network is divided into sub-bands which are allocated to subscribers for the duration of their calls.

GPRS: General Packet Radio Service; standardized as part of GSM Phase 2+, GPRS represents the first implementation of packet switching within GSM, which is a circuit switched technology. GPRS offers theoretical data speeds of up to 115kbit/s using multislot techniques. GPRS is an essential precursor for 3G as it introduces the packet switched core required for UMTS.

IMEI: International Mobile Equipment Identity.

PIN: Personal Identity Number; a number, usually of four digits, that must be keyed into a mobile phone to make it work. A security measure to prevent unauthorized usage.

Roaming: A service unique to GSM which enables a subscriber to make and receive calls when outside the service area of his home network, e.g. when travelling abroad.

SIM: Subscriber Identity Module; a smartcard containing the telephone number of the subscriber, encoded network identification details, the PIN and other user data such as the phone book. A user's SIM card can be moved from phone to phone as it contains all the key information required to activate the phone.

Smartphone: A combination of mobile phone and personal digital assistant.

Churn Rate: The rate at which customers leave for a competitor, largely due to fierce competition. The telecom industry suffers the highest customer churn rate. Strong brand name, marketing and service quality tend to mitigate churn.

ARPU: Average Revenue Per User; used most in the context of a telecom operator's subscriber base, ARPU sometimes offers a useful measure of growth performance. ARPU levels get tougher to sustain as competition and increased churn exert a downward pressure. ARPU for data services have been slowly increasing.

9.5 User Benefits

TV and video on demand, high-speed multimedia data services and mobile Internet access are just a few of the offerings available to users. 3G expands the potential for content-rich information and communication services, as well as providing enhanced capacity for traditional voice services. 3G bridges the gap between the wireless world and the computing/internet world, creating the possibility of seamless inter-operation between the two.

One of the most important characteristics of 3G is that it has been developed to be backward compatible with GSM systems, which have been deployed by 680 operators in more than 200 countries and territories. This inter-operability of systems and services will ensure the continuation of the worldwide roaming experience users have enjoyed with GSM.

Figure 9.2: 3G phones

The look and feel of 3G phones are now being dictated by functionality rather than technical constraints. For example, to support new Internet and multimedia services, larger, more convenient viewing screens are offered. As a result, the variation of form factors offered is likely to increase significantly and handsets could vary from wrist-watch style 'simple telephones' to mini PC-type personal digital assistants (PDAs) for web browsing.

Increased data rates provide the opportunity for operators to launch a wide range of new, value-added, media-rich applications and services. Business users can look forward to high-speed internet access and rapid download of emails with attachments as well as access to wireless audio and video services. Consumer services could include rapid downloading of high-resolution digital images, DVD-quality music downloads, full-motion video and advanced multi-player games.

Currently 83 operators worldwide are using 3G networks. High Speed Downlink Packet Access (HSDPA) is the first step along the well-defined evolution path. High Speed Uplink Packet Access (HSUPA) is the next. The combination of HSDPA and HSUPA will enable users to download and share content-rich multimedia services that will stimulate further growth and business opportunities for operators.

9.6 3G in India

Bharti Airtel launched the iPhone 3G in India on 22 August 2009. The iPhone 3G combines all the revolutionary features of iPhone plus 3G networking that is twice as fast, with built-in GPS for expanded location-based mobile services, and iPhone 2.0 software which includes support for Microsoft Exchange ActiveSync and runs hundreds of third-party applications available through the new App Store.

'The iPhone has been the iconic technology revelation of this year,' said Sanjay Kapoor, president of Mobile Services at Bharti Airtel. 'Airtel has been at the forefront of innovation and customer delight in the Indian telecom sector. Introducing the iPhone 3G to India further underscores our commitment to enrich the communication experience of all Airtel users.'

The iPhone 3G uses the technology protocol HSDPA to quickly download data over UMTS networks. Email attachments and web pages load twice as fast on 3G networks as on 2G EDGE networks. And since the iPhone 3G seamlessly switches between EDGE, faster 3G, and even faster Wi-Fi, customers always get the best speeds possible. Since 3G networks enable simultaneous data and voice, one can talk on the phone while surfing the web, checking email, or using maps. And if the user is in an area without a 3G network, the iPhone connects him/her via GSM for calls and EDGE for data. The iPhone 3G delivers UMTS, HSDPA, GSM, Wi-Fi, EDGE, GPS, and Bluetooth 2.0 + EDR in one compact device using only two antennas.

Table 9.3: Major players in the Indian telecom sector

Fixed line	*GSM*	*CDMA/WLL*	*3G*
BSNL	Airtel	BSNL	BSNL
MTNL	Vodafone	MTNL	MTNL
Bharti Touchtel	BSNL MTNL	Reliance	AIRTEL
Tata Telecom	Aircel	Tata Telecom	Vodafone
HFCL	Idea	HFCL	—
Reliance	Reliance	—	—

Table 9.4 shows the top nine 3G phones as of August 2010 and their price in Indian Rupees.*

Table 9.4: Leading 3G phones in India

S.No.	*Models*	*Price (₹)*
1	Nokia E71	18,500
2	Apple iphone 3GS (32GB)	45,000
3	Samsung i900 Omnia	33,000
4	Nokia N96	22,500
5	Blackberry Bold 9000	35,900
6	Blackberry Storm	27,990 (Only available bundled with Vodafone connection)
7	Motorola Q9h	12,000
8	Sony Ericsson C702	12,000
9	Palm Tree 750	22,990
*Note that there are many new models launched after these phones. Prices may vary based on location, retailer, time, etc.		

9.7 Mobile Revolution in India

As on April 2010 the Indian telecommunication industry, with about 612.2 million mobile phone connections, is the third-largest telecommunication network in the world and the second-largest in terms of number of wireless connections. India's mobile phone market is the fastest growing in the world, with companies adding some 10 million new customers a month since 2007. Table 9.5 details a list of the top mobile phone vendors.

Table 9.5: Company-wise subscriber base (August 2010)

S.No.	*Name of company*	*Total subscribers*
1	Bharti Airtel	141,251,288
2	Vodafone Essar	113,774,409
3	Idea	72,735,921
4	BSNL	70,357,652
5	Aircel	44,906,679
6	Reliance Telecom	16,311,206
7	Uninor	9,093,962
8	MTNL	4,989,546
	All India	481,616,880

Source: TRAI, Government of India, August 2010.

In India, GSM technology was first commercially exploited in the year 1995. At that time, the cost of the cheapest handset was as high as ₹40,000 and the call tariffs at ₹17 per minute were out of the reach of the common man. Initially there were only two major private players—Bharti (Airtel) and Essar and both these companies offered only post-paid services. Growth was limited primarily due to the high tariff rates. Indians who were used to paying much lesser amounts (₹1.20 for 3 minutes) for landline telephone calls found these to be very expensive.

One of the reasons for this sky-high pricing was the absence of competition—there were just two players operating in each circle (an outcome of the telecom policy of the Government of India). But the GSM market dynamics started changing drastically after the creation of TRAI (Telecom Regulatory Authority of India) in 1997. Look at the company-wise subscriber base as on August 2010 (Table 9.5).

9.7.1 Outlook for the Indian Mobile Subscriber Base

Between the late 1990s and early 2008, tariff rates declined 75 per cent. Reportedly, Indian cellular players were offering the lowest cellular tariffs in the world (₹1 for 60 seconds). By August 2010, of the 652,420,000 mobile phones and 481.62 million GSM users in the country, 65 per cent belonged to the pre-paid segment. Also, an estimated 88 per cent of the new add-ons were pre-paid card subscribers. Teledensity in India had reached almost 55.14 per cent by the end of August 2010. It is estimated that by mid of 2010 almost half of the country would own a mobile phone reaching a teledensity of more than 51 per cent (Figure 9.3). However a huge opportunity still exists in rural areas; currently rural India contributes just about 30 per cent of the revenues.

The subscriber base of the telecom market in general and of GSM players in particular has shown an exponential increase in the past few years. The Indian telecom market consists of 23 circles (with each circle representing a different geographic region), including the four metro regions, and out of

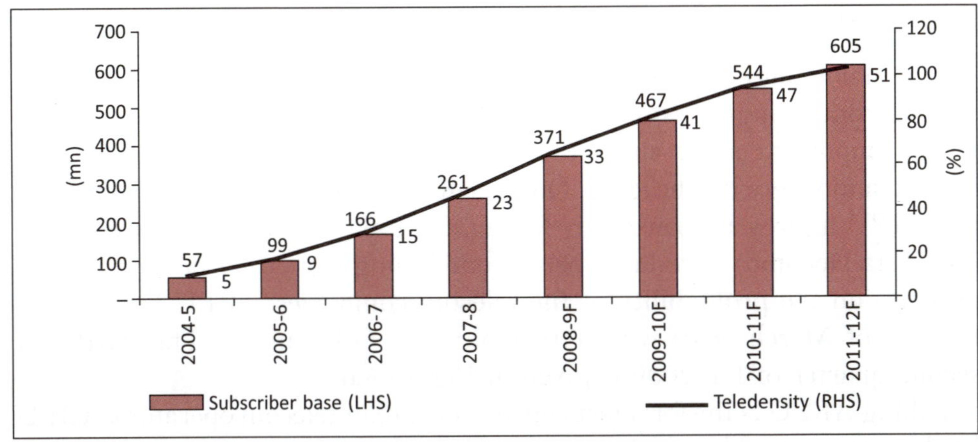

Figure 9.3: Outlook on Indian mobile subscriber base

a total population of 1.10 billion, 481.62 million are already telecom customers (as of August 2010). Figure 9.4 gives the subscriber figure in August 2010.

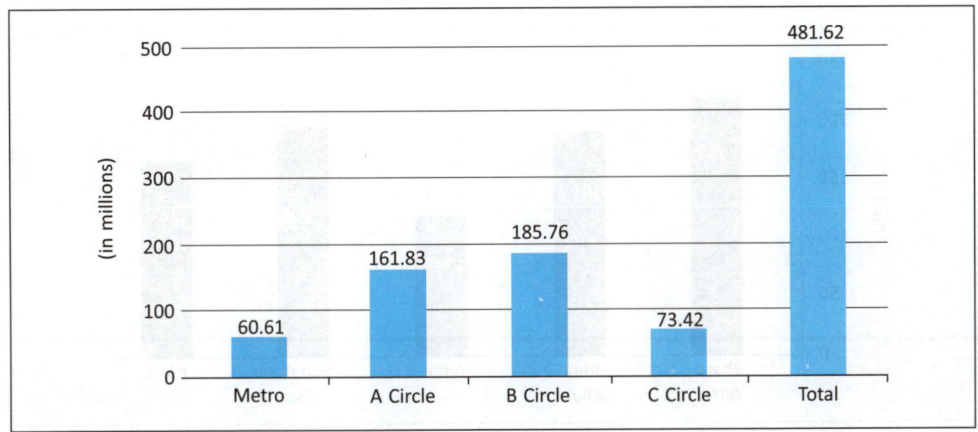

Figure 9.4: Region-wise subscriber base in August 2010

According to the COAI, Bharti Airtel is the market leader with more than 100 million subscribers (as in June 2009). Airtel's net profit figures (₹2,321 crores in the September 2009 quarter) are indicators of its size and strength in the Indian telecom market.

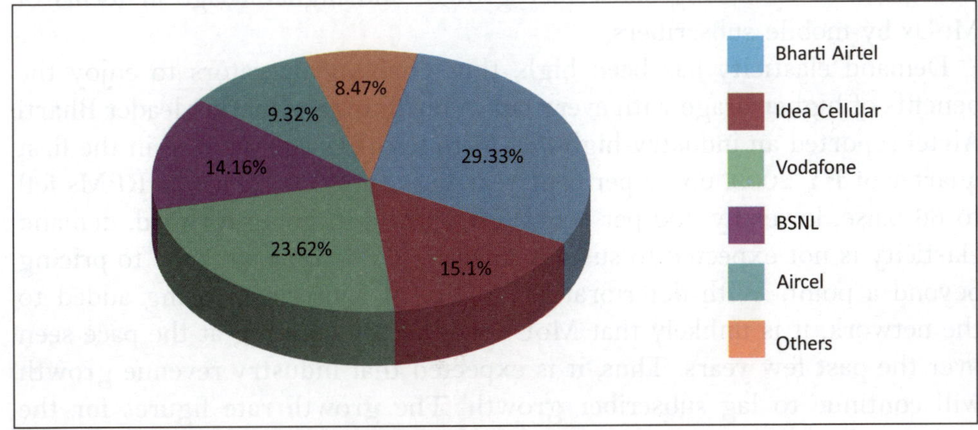

Figure 9.5: Market share of leading telecom players in August 2010

9.7.2 Average Revenue Per User (ARPU)

As the name suggests, ARPU represents the average amount of revenue earned from a single customer. The ARPU figures of all the major players tell an important story about the current scenario of the Indian telecom market, and where it is heading. Due to cut-throat competition in the market the ARPU figures are constantly falling. On top of that, some new entrants (like Tata Docomo) introduced per-second billing plan, thus, putting further pressure on the profitability of the telecom companies. ARPU for GSM is ₹131 as of March 2010 with 410 minutes of GSM usage. The ARPU of second quarter of FY 2009 is given in Figure 9.6.

Falling ARPU is the foremost concern of Indian telecom operators. ARPU levels continue to fall at an increasing rate of 19.7 per cent (industry average ARPU growth in the first quarter of 2009). The ARPU (₹/subscriber/month) has fallen from ₹205 quarter ending March 2009 to ₹144 in December 2009. The blended ARPU of the Indian industry in March 2010 was just ₹131. As a result, operators are focusing more on data and value-added services to meet the revenue deficit caused by fall in revenue of their core business.

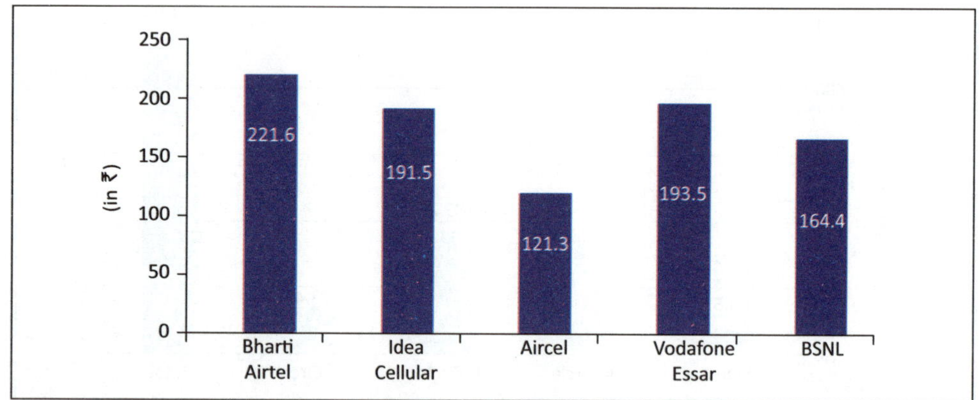

Figure 9.6: ARPU figures of five leading telecom players

Industry ARPUs have fallen at a CAGR of around 10 per cent over FY 2005–8, from ₹378 per user per month to ₹275. Industry ARPUs are expected to fall to ₹238 in FY 2011, a CAGR decline of 4.7 per cent. Even though ARPUs and RPMs have fallen over the past few years, these have been more than justified by strong subscriber growth and higher usage in terms of MoUs by mobile subscribers.

Demand elasticity has been high, thus enabling operators to enjoy the benefits of higher usage with every cut in tariff. In fact, market leader Bharti Airtel reported an industry-high 534 Minutes of Usage (MoUs) in the first quarter of FY 2009, up 12 per cent year-on-year (YOY), even as RPMs fell to 66 paise, lower by 200 per cent YOY. However, going forward, demand elasticity is not expected to sustain, as users do become agnostic to pricing beyond a point. With deteriorating quality of subscribers being added to the network, it is unlikely that MoUs will keep increasing at the pace seen over the past few years. Thus, it is expected that industry revenue growth will continue to lag subscriber growth. The growth rate figures for the period ending March 2009 have been summarized in Figure 9.7.

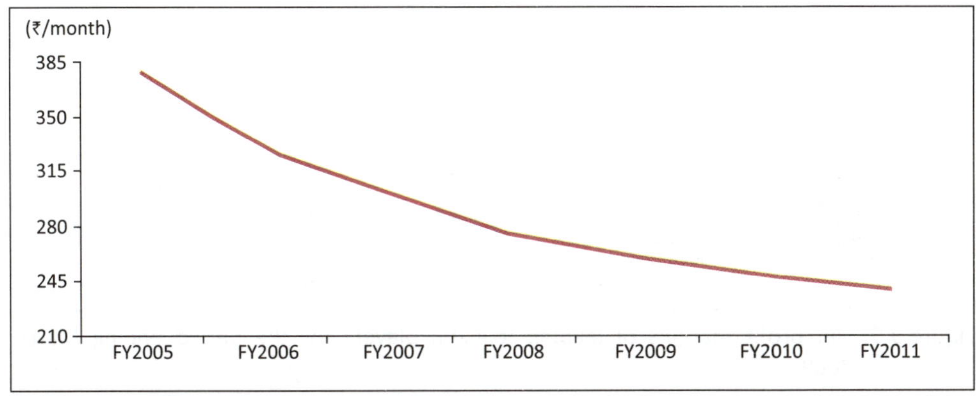

Figure 9.7: Industry ARPU trends (2005–11)

Source: CRIS INNFAC.

The Indian mobile telecom sector has grown at a robust rate over the past few years, clocking an excellent 84 per cent CAGR over FY 2002–8. Going ahead, a good growth in the Indian mobile subscriber base over the next 2-3 years can be expected. However, the business environment, which in any case has never been benign in the telecom sector, is likely to become even more challenging. The key factors that are likely to lead to this include a secular fall in ARPUs and slowing subscriber growth, leading to slowing top-line growth, increasing competition (which could further queer the pitch for tariffs), higher network expansion costs, all leading to margin pressure and regulatory risks. Table 9.6 shows the net sales and PAT of top three private service providers in 2009.

In April 2009, India allowed firms to offer wireless telecom services without owning networks or spectrum. The move, analysts say, is unlikely to bring a flood of new telecom players to the world's fastest growing market.

Table 9.6: Net sales and PAT of leading private service providers in 2009

Service provider	*Net sales (₹ crore)*	*PAT (₹ crore)*	*Profit margin (in %)*
Bharti Airtel	34,014.29	7,743.84	22.8
Reliance Communications	13,610.58	2,352.93	17.3
Idea Cellular	9,916.45	1,008.21	10.2

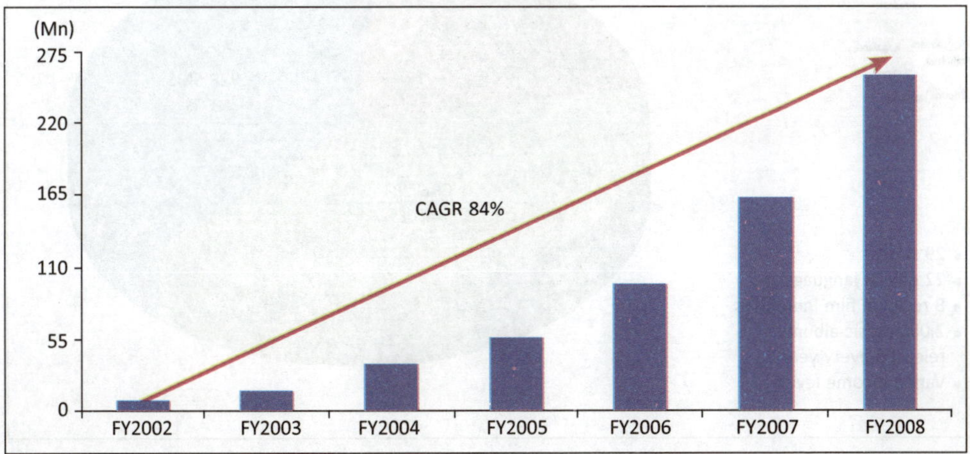

Figure 9.8: Mobile subscriber base (2002–8)

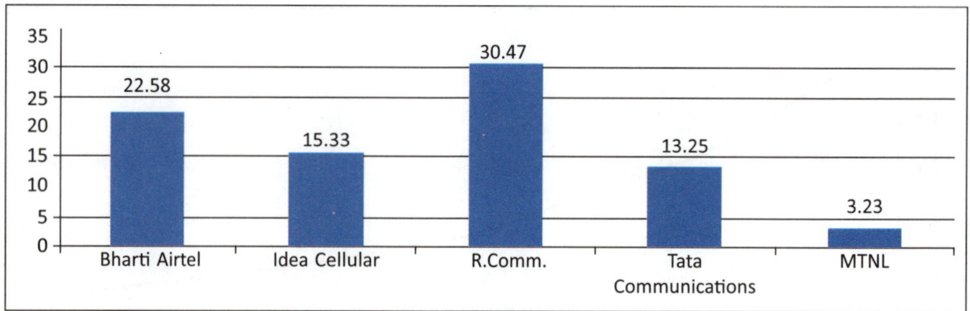

Figure 9.9: Net profit margins of leading telecom players for the period ending March 2009

Mobile virtual network operators (MVNOs) rent radio airwaves and networks from existing telecom firms and sell mobile services to customers, a model popular in mature telecom markets in North America, Europe and East Asia. Virgin Mobile LLC, partly owned by Richard Branson's Virgin Group, operates in the United States as an MVNO, catering to cost-conscious, pre-paid consumers. Branson in 2008 tied up with Indian telecom operator Tata Teleservices to launch youth-focused services in the country. India's diversified Future Group has also said it wants to enter into mobile services as an MVNO.

Recently, the TRAI suggested a foreign holding cap of 74 per cent in MVNOs, in line with other telecom services. Mobile operators would be free to lease spectrum to as many MVNOs as they want. MVNOs would have to pay about ₹1.50 billion ($30.20 million) for a nationwide entry licence, and the annual licence fee would be the same as those paid by mobile operators. This would help operators expand in the highly competitive Indian market. India added a record 15.41 million mobile users to its 12 networks in January 2009, taking the total subscriber base at the end of that month to 362.30 million.

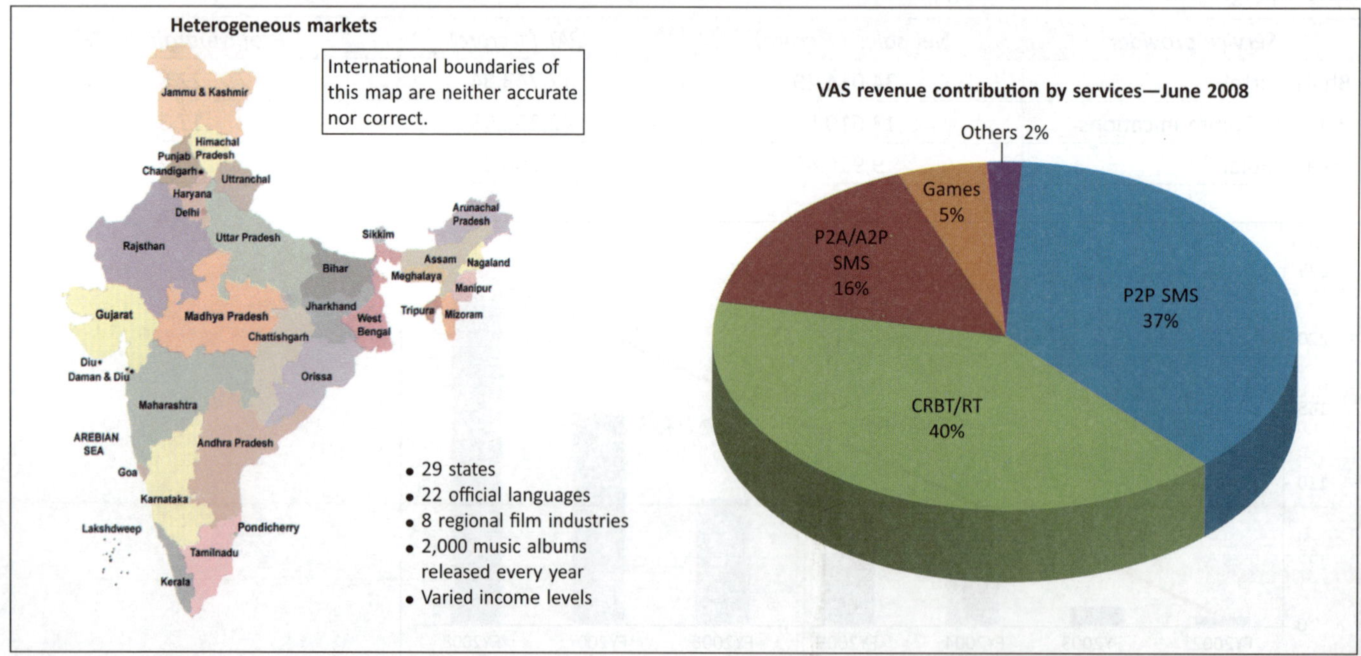

Figure 9.10: MVNO opportunities in India

Source: eTechnology Group@IMRB

9.8 The 'Rural *Chalo*' Programme

Share of prepaid GSM users in the mobile phone market is around 95.78 per cent in March 2010. ARPU (₹ per month) from postpaid subscriber is ₹503 and for prepaid segment is only ₹113 which in turn make the blended ARPU ₹131 in March 2010.

With a teledensity of 5-8 per cent, mobile telephony in rural India is reminiscent of what the industry was like when the first cellular phones made their appearance in urban India some 15 years back—a huge potential. And both operators and handset manufacturers are ensuring that the cost of going mobile is not an obstacle in tapping this opportunity. The way to opening the market is through collaboration—bundled offers that make it easy on the wallet. The challenges in rural areas, though, are manifold: language, the customers' ability to handle technology, the need for face-to-face service, fewer people per tower, discomfort in using automated services and lower ARPUs. In circles like Himachal Pradesh, Airtel has initiated a channel development programme involving *dhabas* across the main highways—the idea is brand visibility as well as an increase in the offtake of recharge coupons.

All the private mobile service providers announced in the early half of 2008 a unique initiative to give a special thrust to rural telephony under the name 'Rural *Chalo*', to reach the benefits of mobile telephony to rural India. The programme had been developed and implemented under the aegis of COAI and AUSPI, the industry associations for GSM and CDMA mobile service providers, respectively. Accordingly all the mobile service providers gave each new rural subscriber an upfront discount of ₹50 on the tariff package and a further ₹75 was passed on as free talk time/usage in two or three instalments spread over six to nine months since May 2008. The Rural *Chalo* programme was another demonstration of the continuing commitment of the mobile operators to give their consumers, especially those in the rural areas, world-class services at the most affordable tariffs. In the first phase, the programme covered 50 million new rural subscriber acquisitions.

It was realized that the benefit of ₹125 offered to new rural subscribers strongly incentivize both the take-up as well as the usage of mobile service in rural areas and thus helped to meet the rural telephony objectives of the government during 2008–11.

9.9 Tune to 3G Mobile Service

India, which had 584 million wireless subscribers as on March 2010, has seen its mobile user base grow 25 times in the last five years making it the second-largest wireless market in the world after China. India joined the elite list of countries to announce a policy for third generation mobile service that will enable customers to enjoy voice, video, data and downloading facilities on their mobile phones. 3G services offer consumers internet access at speeds that are at least 30 times faster than 2G in 2009. Mahanagar Telephone Nigam Limited (MTNL) one of India's leading telecom service providers, launched first 3G services in the country.

State-owned Bharat Sanchar Nigam Ltd launched next generation 3G mobile services in the country even as the private operators are still waiting to get spectrum through auction process. BSNL and another PSU MTNL (for Delhi and Mumbai) were given 3G spectrum in 2008 ahead of auction for private players keeping in mind the cumbersome tendering process involved in the public sector procurement system.

According to BSNL, the subscribers have to pay around 10 paise per minute in a full value plan of ₹1,000 per month. The company put up video calls too at a economic price of ₹1 under unlimited plan of ₹2,500 per month. 3G services customers of BSNL have regular monthly subscription options of ₹350, ₹650 and ₹1,350. Apart from this, customers also get the 3G services through a bundle offer. The subscribers also offered a plethora of services like live TV, high-speed mobile broadband, video on demand and movie download through 3G services. The company had invested ₹27 billion to get its 3G services in India.

3G services also launched in cities like Chennai, Lucknow, Agra, Ambala, Dehradun, Jammu, Shimla, Jaipur, Jalandhar, Patna, Durgapur, Haldia, Ranchi and Bhubaneshwar in April 2009. It is expected that nearly five million subscribers base for BSNL, five per cent would migrate to 3G service in 2009–10.

Spectrum is by far the most important raw material for the mobile telephony sector, the lack of which could lead to growth getting severely hampered. Allotment of spectrum has been one of the most contentious issues, with CDMA operators accusing GSM players of hoarding more spectrum than what they were contractually entitled to (6.2 MHz) and demanding higher spectrum charges for all such spectrum held in excess of entitlement. The GSM lobby, on the other hand, has argued that its members have increased their subscriber base manifold over the past few years, which is now a multiple of what the original subscriber-linked spectrum allocation criteria required, thus justifying higher spectrum allotment and denying any charges of hoarding the scarce resource.

The allotment of spectrum in several circles to operators does give hope that the government will, from time-to-time, be able to allot more spectrum to operators as and when it becomes available. Given the increased demand for the scarce resource from newer operators, it is likely that going forward, incumbent operators will look to buy out some of the new operators as and when consolidation activity kicks in. A 12-13 operator market is not likely to sustain and eventually, 5-6 operators at the most will be able to hold their own. It is most likely that operators like Bharti Airtel, R.Comm., Vodafone Essar and BSNL will survive the consolidation activity in the sector, whereas companies like Idea Cellular, Tata Teleservices and Aircel could witness an interesting battle amongst themselves. The remaining operators, with the exception of MTNL, are likely to get taken over, either by incumbent operators or possibly foreign operators who could not win 3G spectrum and are looking to get a foothold into the Indian market.

After the Indian government gave the green flag to launching 3G services in India, Airtel has launched 3G services in Delhi, Mumbai and Bengaluru and is partnering with SingTel who has experience in offering 3G services. The government is expected to corner ₹400 billion by way of auctioning of spectrum of 3G services to ten service providers. India has 60 MHz of 3G spectrum available. The auction will take place in the 2.1 GHz band. The government has set a base price of ₹2,020 crore (₹20.20 billion) for each bid for a pan-India licence. Initially, there will be three to five operators to sell the 3G services, including State-run BSNL and MTNL. The PSUs have an edge to start the 3G services earlier than others as they do not have to bid for the spectrum; they only have to match the highest bid in their respective circles.

As per the guidelines, any licensed telecom operator can bid for 3G spectrum and the radio waves will be auctioned in 5-10 blocks depending on the availability. Each successful bidder will be allocated only one block in a service area. The spectrum will be auctioned in 450 MHz (for GSM), 800 MHz band for EVDO (CDMA players) and in the 1,900 band (for GSM) when it is available. According to the reserve price for 3G spectrum fixed by the government, a 2×5 MHz block of spectrum for Mumbai, Delhi and Category A cities would cost ₹160 crore (₹1.60 billion), for Kolkata and Category B ₹80 crore (₹800 million) and Category C ₹30 crore (₹300 million).

New players that win bids will, however, have to pay additional cash (₹1,650 crore for an all-India 3G licence) for mandatorily taking a universal access service licence (UASL). 'One can't sustain a business in which ten players are fighting for only 70 million 3G customers. They need a mass consumer base of 2G subscribers to survive, so getting 2G spectrum with 3G is essential,' analysts observes. Also, a new player would need $3 billion to $3.5 billion to roll out a 3G network from scratch. A 2G incumbent can roll out 3G operations for half the cost, giving it a huge competitive advantage. Although new players have to pay more for a UASL, there is no guarantee that they will get the 4.4 MHz start-up 2G spectrum that comes bundled with the licence because such spectrum is in short supply.

9.10 Face the Test

3G Telecom Services—One of the most hyped and most talked term in the field of mobiles and telecommunications using which a mobile phone user can experience seamless data transfer of up to 2-8 MBPS. Initially 3G services were launched by MTNL followed by BSNL in 2008 and the launch was welcome by every mobile phone enthusiast in India. But to the dismay of mobile lovers, immediately security concerns were raised about 3G services as the data transfers and voice calls were encoded and security agencies found that those voice calls cannot be decoded on real time basis and the Indian security agencies were serious about it thinking it (ability not to decode voice calls on real time basis) could be really very serious and harmful keeping Indian security in mind.

Immediately, some security agencies of India asked BSNL and MTNL to temporarily halt such services for general public until some way for decoding voice calls over 3G network can be worked out on real time basis. But it has been reported that the Telcos (BSNL and MTNL) presently providing 3G services denied for halting 3G services and they would continue providing the services to general public. Also, these telcos asked such security agencies that they should work upon decoding such Voice calls as it is security agencies who are concerned about 3G services. So the launch of 3G services in other areas seems to be in dilemma until the problem is sorted out, also any one is not yet sure about what would be the fate of 3G telecom services in India.

Case Discussion Questions

Assume that you are heading the strategic marketing division of an American 3G mobile service provider. You are devising a number of plans for enhancing potential demand and market size for the company's products and services in India.

(a) How do you devise a corporate and communication strategy for the American 3G mobile service provider in the Indian market? Explain the various elements and their significance. What are the new paradigms while marketing 3G handsets and services in India by utilizing the theory explained in this case?
(b) Explain various competitive advantages like pioneering advantage and product differentiation while analysing 2G and 3G GSM market in India by utilizing the theory explained in this case. How do you encash those advantages?
(c) In your opinion, what may be the perceived benefits of consumer learning and brand preferences in 3G mobile phones in the business and home segments in the country?
(d) Comment on the relevance and significance of competitive strategy for the 3G service provider and list all the critical factors like supply-related demand of 3G handsets, key factors for success by exploiting the market strength of competitors like Airtel by utilizing the theory explained in this case.

CASE ANALYSIS

Executive Summary

In 2008, India joined the elite club of countries to announce a policy for the third generation (3G) mobile service that will enable consumers to enjoy voice, video, data and downloading features on their mobile phones. 3G services offer consumers Internet access at speeds that are at least 30 times faster than 2G.

About ten years back, the telecom industry was largely dominated by the big national and regional players. But the last decade has witnessed deregulation and privatization that had made the sector attractive for private players. With 481.6 million GSM customers, India has the second-largest subscriber base after China, and accounts for 12 per cent of the third billion growths.

GSM (or Global System for Mobile) owes its origin to the fact that there were nine incompatible analogue cellular systems which posed a unique problem to the European continent. GSM offers a common platform globally for cellular operators and by far is the most popular service in the world. Rapid technological innovations—GPRS, EDGE, UMTS, and 3G being the latest—enable seamless transmission of data and voice at very high speeds.

As mentioned in the case, 3G offers mobile multimedia services such as music, TV, video, rich entertainment content and Internet access. The technology on which 3G services are delivered is based on the GSM network enhanced with a W-CDMA air interface (the OTA transmission element). The most important feature the 3G offers is backward compatibility with 2G technology, which has been developed by 680 operators in more than 200 countries and regions. 3G technology can be said to bridge the gap between the wireless world and the computer/Internet world, creating a possibility of seamless interoperation between the two.

The look and feel of 3G is largely being dictated by functionality demands rather than technical constraints. Thus, the mobile devices that are used to access the 3G service would play an important role in forwarding the 3G technology. A host of services that can be offered over the 3G network make it essential for a user to have a mobile device with capabilities like a convenient viewing screen, support to internet and multimedia services, and so on. Business users can get high-speed Internet access and rapid download of emails with attachments as well as access to wireless audio and video services. Consumer users could look at rapid downloading of high-resolution digital images, DVD-quality music downloads, full motion videos and advanced multi-player games.

Cellular technology was introduced in India during the early 1990s. Extremely high tariff rates and a huge amount of government regulation initially limited the growth of this sector. Of late, cell phone operators have recognized the potential of the rural market for cellular services and mobile devices, given the fact that the teledensity of mobile phones is only 5-8 per cent in rural India. The operators and cell phone manufactures are ensuring that the cost of buying mobile phone is not a barrier in tapping the rural market. The operators and the cell phone manufactures are increasingly considering collaboration as the way forward in the rural market.

The PSUs would be allotted spectrums (one block for MTNL in Mumbai and Delhi; and one for BSNL in other areas) and they would just have to match the highest bid in their respective circles—thereby giving them an upper hand in the competition. As per the auction guidelines, any licensed telecom operator can bid for a 3G spectrum and it would be auctioned in 5-10 blocks depending on the availability. Each successful bidder will be allocated one block in a service area. The government has fixed ₹160 crore for 2×5 MHz block of spectrum for Mumbai, Delhi and other A-category cities; ₹80 crore for B-category cities (Kolkata, etc.); and ₹30 crore for C-category ones. Industry experts predict that the 3G subscription would stand at 45-70 million customers by 2012, approximately 10 per cent of the mobile customer base.

The issues and challenges that lie ahead of the Indian 3G sector and the players trying to enter this market are:

Upper hand of the PSUs: The government's policy to allocate a block in the 3G spectrum to the PSUs without the need of their bidding for the same puts the private players at a competitive disadvantage. This policy has saved a lot of initial investment for the PSUs and will help them strengthen their position in the long run.

High entry costs: A new player would need $3-3.5 billion to start operations from scratch. A mass consumer base of 2G is essential for survival which forces new players to compulsorily buy the 2G spectrum thereby increasing the costs. Moreover, an existing 2G player can roll out the 3G service at half the above-mentioned cost, putting new entrants into a greater competitive disadvantage.

High service charges: The service charges that would be imposed on the customers would be relatively higher than that for the existing 2G services. This could negatively impact customers and a substantially large number may choose to stay away from 3G services.

High cost of devices: The terminals necessary to access the features offered by 3G are comparatively costly with prices starting from around ₹12,000. Such high costs would again be a major bottleneck in increasing the customer base of 3G.

Penetration into rural markets: Currently, the rural market is largely untapped by the mobile service providers (only about 5-8 per cent penetration). But this market is largely driven by the low-cost model and the penetration of high-end 3G services here is a rare possibility.

The way forward for cell phone manufactures in the 3G market: The most important challenge cell phone operators and manufactures would face is the strategy they should adopt to successfully penetrate the Indian market. Collaboration and co-branding can be the possible options but speculation regarding the same still exists in the industry.

Extreme competition and a limited customer base: Owing to the costly mobile devices and high service charges, the 3G base would contribute to only about 10 per cent of the total customer base of cell phone subscribers by 2012. The operators face a challenge in acquiring and retaining customers given the high churn rate, low ARPU and a very limited customer base to compete for.

Approach to the Case

The case demands the assumption of an American 3G company and strategize its venture into the Indian 3G market. The author assumed that *AT&T, the largest telecom and networking services provider of America,* wants to enter the Indian market mainly to target the new and upcoming 3G market. The entire case analysis is based on this assumption.

Corporate and Communication Strategy

This comprises the long-term plan in which the firm decides which products/services to venture into and how to communicate its existence and offerings to the consumers with the motive of overall growth and development in the market across stakeholders. Following are the major components of such a strategy:

Market Intelligence

It is one of the most important parts of formulating a communication strategy. Every communication strategy is formulated by taking inputs from the market intelligence data. Market intelligence is an integral part of business intelligence; business intelligence is a larger concept covering other aspects of business. Market intelligence processes typically address the following issues:

The legal and regulatory system: The American telecom company (assumed to be AT&T in this case) would require a thorough understanding of the government guidelines. The 3G spectrum guidelines provide for a reserve price for availing radio frequency. The guidelines fix the price for a 2 × 5 MHz block of spectrum for Mumbai and Delhi and Category A locations at ₹160 crore; for Kolkata and Category B locations at ₹80 crore; and for Category C at ₹30 crore. Telecom operators can bid for the 3G spectrum in 450 MHz, 800 MHz and 1,900 MHz bands. Operators will be exempted from paying any annual fee in the first year of operation. They, however, will have to pay 1 per cent of Adjusted Gross Revenue as annual spectrum charge after a period of one year.

Customer intelligence: Customer intelligence is the process of building a deep understanding of the customers of a business. It can be built individually if appropriate and practical, or by grouping customers into segments and clusters, where customers in one segment or cluster share similar attributes and are different from customers that are grouped into other segments or clusters. Customer intelligence is discussed in detail in the following question on Segmentation.

Competitor intelligence: Competitor intelligence is the process of tracking news and information about competitors. The primary objective of competitor intelligence is to reveal the strengths, weaknesses, opportunities and threats of each individual competitor. Knowing your competitor(s) would make it possible to identify AT&T's relative strengths and weaknesses, and to discover its competitive edge. Some basic understanding of competitors' strategies can sometimes be obtained from their mission statements, slogans and the internal values they cherish. A detailed explanation about the process that AT&T should adopt (including Porter's five forces model and SWOT analysis for a leading player in India (Airtel)) is given in the subsequent pages.

Technical intelligence: The company (AT&T) trying to expand in the Indian market should have a sound knowledge of the technology that can be used in the Indian market.

Environment scanning intelligence: Scanning the environment for specific phenomena would help the company become a prime mover (given the fact that AT&T would be a new entrant) and gain an edge in business, or may sometimes identify high risks and emerging competition before it becomes a true threat. Constant monitoring of the surrounding world could be regarded as 'company radar'. The company should continuously scan for the latest market trends so that it can tap its target audience correctly. The latest market trends could be data downloaded per person and sorted according to age, or the number of music websites accessed through the mobile phone device.

Resource market intelligence: Suppose that AT&T plans to enter a new market (India, in this case) by gaining significant ownership of a less developed telecommunications firm based in the country. The company would not face any problem in terms of human or financial resources. The main problem would surface when the technological platform of the acquired company has to be modernized. Certain crucial components of technology were listed under the export licensing order by the American government, i.e. they are not allowed to be exported to the country in question because of security concerns. The new entrant should therefore consider all these factors when formulating a strategy.

Towards a higher intelligence: The various activities that the company should adopt in order to promote its products and services should never be entered into without an understanding of what the customers want, and what the current market situation can allow. Market intelligence should always guide marketing activities. It is, therefore, vital that market intelligence is used and trusted. The market intelligence units must retain impeccable standards of objectivity and deliver facts without taking sides in internal politics or pet projects. In this we are guided by the American President Woodrow Wilson's thought: 'One cool judgement is worth a thousand hasty counsels. This thing to do is to supply light and not heat.'

Market Segmentation

Segmentation is the key to gain market share and sustain long-term profit. Segmentation also is about getting insight of company customers and developing new offerings, and listening to their comments to discover areas for growth innovation. In telecom, segmentation includes process of grouping customers for the purpose of targeted marketing activities such as promotional messages, service development and pricing.

Segmentation Criteria

A customer base can be segmented in numerous ways and no one segmentation is perfect for all situations or for all operators. The size of the customer, the technology of their handsets, and whether the customer is on pre- or post-paid account are all pretty much meaningless as segmentation criteria. A good segmentation model should explain why any given segment would behave differently if faced with some promotion, price or service. Also, the model should help predict behaviour to help target the marketing efforts.

Segmentation by User Behaviour

Telecom operators can go much further than other industries in using the potential power of segmentation, because of the depth of information gathered automatically about every user on the network. In the automobile industry, car manufacturers do not know how many times a given driver opens the boot, or how many times the car is driven over a bump every day. Some information in the car industry can be gathered from user surveys, or from examining data collected at maintenance intervals, but telecom is the only industry where the operator knows every single time that the user presses any key on the keypad of the mobile phone. Various levels of user data can be captured automatically and can be developed for segmentation based on user behaviour.

The actual segmentation based on user behaviour will, by definition, differ for every operator as the behaviour of users differs across countries and within markets. Some very basic early ideas for tracking user behaviour and building powerful segments include tracking:

(a) Which customers initiate calls and which tend to only receive calls.
(b) Some customers show a clear preference for sending text messages while others prefer voice calls.
(c) Some place only a few calls per week but these tend to be long, while other customers make many calls per day but each is of a short duration.
(d) Some customers place calls during office hours but almost none in the evenings or weekends, which suggests that they may have another phone on another network for evening and weekend use.
(e) Some customers make return calls, such as a child calling the mother's phone and the mother returning the call, so that the call is not billed to the child's account but rather to the parent's account.
(f) Some callers have a very tight set people who they communicate with, while others place and receive calls to and from seemingly random sets of numbers.

Such behaviour-based patterns can be identified and then customer segments built. Hence true behaviour-based segmentation is *infinitely* more powerful than any of the traditional methods mentioned earlier. Imagine two 32-year-old women living in the suburb of a city, both housewives and mothers of two kids. Let us also assume both have a WAP phone on a postpaid account. Any of the conventional segmentation methods, whether by age, location, technology, billing system, customer size (residential as opposed to business), will group the two women in the same segment. These two women may seem similar but one might suddenly start to behave differently. If for some reason one woman becomes estranged from her husband and the two take a trial separation, she might start to exhibit mobile phone behaviour very similar to 17-year-old girls with their mobile phones. She could start to send more text messages, perhaps chat on the mobile phone, and possibly even use dating services. This is a typical behaviour pattern of people who have recently become single. They originally did not use the mobile phone in a dating situation, but now will rapidly pick up habits very similar to those associated with older teenagers. The mobile operator needs to observe the *behaviour* of the customer, not blindly place the customer into a demographic category and assume that every married woman will behave in a similar way.

How Many Segments

Mobile telecom segmentation model might have two segments—business and residential customers. There are likely differences in the behaviour of business customers and residential customers, so this model could provide insight, even though it only has two segments.

Nokia has been quoted in the public (such as *The Economist* in January 2009) as having an end-user segmentation comprising 35 defined categories. The company is reportedly addressing about half of those segments, probably for market size and competitive reasons, leaving some of the smaller or less profitable segments to its competitors. Without suggesting that Nokia's model is in any way the 'best' for mobile telecoms, it does provide interesting insights to modern mobile operators.

As Nokia does not sell its handsets directly to the end-users, and uses the mobile operators as its distribution channel, its segmentation model is a good benchmark for considering the customer of the mobile operator. If Nokia already divides all end-user customers into 35 segments, then any model used by a mobile operator which has less segments, has by definition, less precision and is thus actually *weaker than that of its supplier.* A practical segmentation model for a mobile operator today has to have at least one degree of magnitude—at least one dimension—more than that which Nokia reportedly has. In other words an 'adequate' segmentation has at least 20-40 defined segments so that a customer fits only one segment, and no customer is outside the model. The mobile operator does not have to provide services or marketing activities to every defined segment, but each segment must be defined and at least superficially analysed.

One such three-dimensional model could be the segmentation dimensions (i) who pays the phone bill (ii) evolution on the usage of new mobile services and (iii) type of networking activity. An employee who gets free mobile phone services behaves differently from a person who pays the bill, who again behaves differently from a child or spouse whose family member pays the phone bill. The evolution of user means the user doesn't use SMS, or only receives SMS, or sends SMS, or uses e-commerce, or sends MMS. Types of networking activity could be divided, for example, into avoiding contacts (lots of missed calls and voice mails), many more received than initiated contacts, low initiated contacts in general, many but random contacts, or many regular contacts. One segment would consist of persons whose employers pay the phone bill, who send MMS and contact many regular people. Another segment would be users who pay their own phone bill, only receive SMS and have low initiated contacts. This group is likely to be ready for a campaign aimed at increasing SMS usage and could be offered a few months of free SMS to get the user hooked, and so on.

Self-organizing Maps

At some point the utility of employing psychologists and sociologists to work with marketing and segmentation managers to refine and redefine segments will become too costly to justify it. At that stage telecoms have to turn to the science of applied mathematics. Modern tools exist to define micro-segments on patterns that are not intuitively obvious, but which can be identified by mathematical means using neural network technology. Self-organizing maps (SOMs) ignore the labels and sociological 'reasons' for why people behave in a given way; rather they simply identify and isolate groupings of customers who behave in a similar way and group them separate from those with maximally different behaviour. The SOMs analyse massive amounts of data and group them by relevance, producing powerful segments that may at first glance appear random or coincidental. This type of segmentation identifies the correlations between various criteria, often as a combination of several seemingly unrelated items. It is up to marketers to analyse the results, discover the reasons and give labels to emerging micro-segments as needed.

Why Segmentation

When looking at the advanced mobile services arena of 3G and the vast numbers of customers, *segmentation is the only way* to deliver targeted marketing activities. Poorly designed segmentation limits the chances for the company to succeed, while powerful segmentation will deliver competitive benefits throughout the organization.

To conclude, the company should consider the following segmentation:

Two segments: Consumer Users and Business Users

Consumer Users

- Age group: 15–35 years
- Use: Gaming, Internet, multimedia

Business Users

- Age group: 25–60 years
- Use: High-speed email attachments, Internet

Service Development and Management

The service creation environment for 3G will be richer and offer a greater range than any service creation environment ever before. The initial services that will emerge in 2.5G and 3G will tend to be mobile phone variations of services that exist on other media such as fixed Internet, TV, CD-ROMs, etc. First we examine how services can be created for the mobile phone through the theory of the Five Ms.

The Five Ms of mobile service creation are Movement, Moment, Me, Money and Machines.

Movement: Movement includes location information but needs to understand how a moving user and the surrounding environment relate. Movement is the distinguishing aspect of cellular telecoms that other digital service delivery systems cannot easily replicate.

Moment: Moment is more than urgent services. Moment includes managing time, postponing time, catching up on lost time, multitasking, and hence 'creating' time as well as doing things with sudden extra moments of time, or 'killing' time.

Me: Me, extending myself to my communities, is the third attribute of the Five Ms. Me includes personalization, customization and all the ways to interact with our various communities. Me explains why interchangeable covers are so popular with mobile phones, and why so many feel very strongly about the selection of their mobile phone.

Money: The fourth attribute of the Five Ms is Money, expending financial resources. Money relates to how the billing system of the mobile telecom networks can track remarkable volumes of trivial data in its charging engine. Where the internet has no built-in billing system, and the credit card industry imposes a minimum payment of on all transactions, the mobile telecoms' billing system tracks every second of airtime, even if its a local call.

Machines: The fifth of the Five Ms is Machines: empowering gadgets, devices and automation. Machines cover machine-to-machine and man–machine interactions. This group is almost too broad to attempt to cover, as practically all modern machines are automated and most would benefit from being connected.

In Japan the mobile operator KDDI has introduced a totally automated voice-recognition and synthetic-speech-based translation system that understands spoken English, Korean and Japanese and translates it in chunks of 7 seconds at a time. It is by no means perfect, but works in most tourist-oriented situations.

The machine population on 3G networks is estimated to exceed that of the human population generating new types of traffic patterns. The Machines' attribute is a way to bring in cost savings from automation, and is thus the key to profits in mobile services.

The Five Ms is a way to build compelling services. When needs are discovered that can be addressed with the five Ms, then compelling, even addictive mobile services can be built.

Product Management

The product management is the process of utilizing the marketing efforts of an organization to maximize the profits generated by a service product. Product management typically attempts to find an optimal match between customer needs and interests—often expressed by sales and marketing—with those of the technical and engineering side of the organization, while satisfying the profit targets of accounting.

In a high-technology businesses such as 3G it is important to have a structured and well-processed service management function. Not surprisingly, service management (product management) is one of the most central functions of a company maintaining interfaces with all other business areas like marketing, technical department, sales or R&D. Service managers tend to be recent university graduates with engineering and business degrees. They tend to bring modern thinking and new blood to the organization. Where the employer is a mobile operator with an existing 2G network, the organization is likely to be underdeveloped and geared mostly to supplying support for connecting new customers and handling billing concerns, etc.

Where the organization is a former PTT (post-telecom and telegraph) and hence a monopolist, the organization may be very developed, but usually with an overly technical and engineering focus. If the 3G operator is a new player, a so-called greenfield operator, then all structures are new. Each of the above cases presents different issues for service management. In spite of their past history, all 3G operators will approach the mainstream style of business, and will have to evolve to utilize modern marketing methods. The role of service management is central to this.

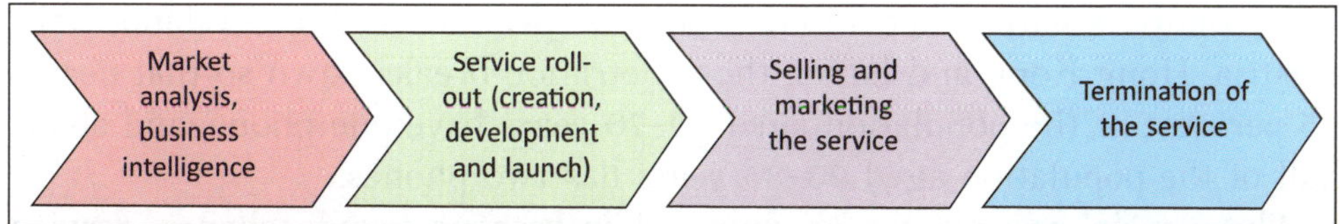

Figure 9.11: Service development cycle

Thus AT&T would have to go through the entire cycle of service development if it ventures into the Indian market.

Combating Churn

A churned customer is one who has stopped using one service provider and moved on to its competitor. In some cases it is very easy to identify a churner, such as in cases of countries with number portability: if the customer, or one of competitor's customer, tells you to port the number of his/her subscription onto competitor's service, it is a definite case of churn.

Figure 9.12: Churn management

Who is a Churner?

Most often, however, it is not that obvious to identify a churner. Often in mobile telecoms a customer simply stops using one service provider. In such cases it is not clear if the customer has moved the traffic and business to a competitor. From the eyes of the mobile operator, this is not distinguishable from a customer who is experiencing a temporary pause in using the service, for example, because he/she is short of money, the phone is broken, or he/she is travelling to a country where the phone does not work. The operator does not know whether someone does not feel like talking on the phone or has left the network altogether.

Prepaid accounts present a particular problem with identifying churning customers. A customer might leave a prepaid subscription to sit unused and start to use another service. As there often exists very limited information on the identity of prepaid customers, it would be difficult to verify whether an unused account is that of a rare user, or that the ending of use is due to natural causes such as illness or death, or the account was set up only for a short-term use such as that of a foreigner living briefly in the country, or it is actually the account of a churner who has moved onto a competitor.

The most difficult to identify are the hidden churners, who get another phone on a competing network and move most, but not all, of their traffic to the new network. Typically such churners still receive some calls on their old number but rarely place calls on that subscription. They keep the old number because many know it and for reasons of convenience occasionally use that SIM (Subscriber Identity Module) card, but for the majority of the calls they use their preferred provider. As second mobile phones are becoming ever more prevalent this will increasingly be the case.

In countries with penetrations of over 90 per cent such as Finland, Italy, Austria, Hong Kong and Israel, the penetration breaks down so that nearly 95 per cent of the population aged 10–70 years have one phone, and about half of the population aged 20–35 years has two phones.

Three main reasons for churning. The reasons people change service providers are varied. Some change for price/tariff reasons, others are unhappy or upset with their current service provider. In countries where mobile handset subsidies are considerable, the prospect of gaining a new phone entices customers to churn. Some customers change to get access to some services that the current provider does not offer while others churn to gain community benefits, such as having the family's phones on one network.

(a) Who is a Joiner, Changer and a Leaver?

A *joiner* is attracted to the offering of a competitor. It is not as if there is something wrong with the current provider, only that something new by a competitor is attractive and that is a reason to switch providers.

A *leaver* does not leave because of something done by the competitor; the leaver is upset with the current choice and wants to get away from it.

A *changer* leaves not because of anything the company did, or what the competition offered, but for his/her own internal reasons.

(b) Selecting Customers to Target

When determining which existing customers to target for churn reduction or customer loyalty programmes, the first criterion must be profitability. For customers who are unprofitable to the company, the only real action can be either to turn them into profitable customers or to get rid of them. AT&T should keep in mind that no churn reduction or loyalty programme helps in turning a currently unprofitable customer into a profitable one; on the contrary, such programmes add further costs to a loss-making customer. If it cannot turn a non-profitable customer into a profitable one by raising tariffs, adding new fees, or getting the customer to use services that bring profits, then the best thing to do with such customers is to give them to your competitors. Customers who are joiners tend to want to change often anyway.

The cost-effectiveness of any loyalty programme must be measured not against the profitability of the average customer over its average lifetime, but rather against the profitability of a joiner-type customer and their much shorter time as company customer. If the loyalty programme or churn reduction plan is cost effective in extending the short-term stay of a joiner, it is worth implementing, but if the programme does not pay itself back by the longer stay of the joiner, then it is not worth undertaking, and the joiner should be allowed to go.

The company shouldn't build loyalty programmes on the premise of locking in joiners, since joiners are only there for a short duration anyway. Regarding the leavers, there is no clear reason within the company why these customers left. It is most likely more cost-effective to deal with the true cause of their leaving rather than trying to entice them to stay with a loyalty programme, while at the same time annoying them with continued action (or lack of action) that they detest. Critical to spotting the company's internal actions that caused leaving is to monitor what the customers truly think, to encourage them to complaint, to reward complainers, and most importantly to deal with any causes that provoke leavers.

The changers are likely to change anyway, irrespective of what the company does, and a loyalty programme will usually not be able to prevent a changer from churning.

Price as a Weapon to Fight Churn

The most common marketing tool in the telecom sector has traditionally been 'let's offer it at a lower price'. At first sight lowering the price might seem like an inexpensive way to acquire a competitor's customer. However, the target groups that are attracted by this are the typical joiners and other bargain hunters. This means that AT&T might get highly volatile and very disloyal customers who keep searching for the cheapest service provider and lowest price.

A low price seems like the simplest argument for a change and like the most important decision criterion for the customer. The important factor is, of course, that all of this requires real work and a good understanding of marketing. It is easy to adjust the price. It takes know-how and hard work to identify what is truly needed to attract (or keep) a customer. When low-price players emerge in the market they are most often likely to be on alternate technologies or as MVNOs or as service providers typically intending to compete only in well-defined niche markets.

The low-price strategy may also be selected by the smallest of the major network players. If your competitor starts to slash prices it is not advisable to compete directly. Small service providers may find innovative business models focused on certain niches and often can live with more meager profit margins than can major network operators with a lot of infrastructure and R&D waiting to be financed.

The problem in using price cuts to answer niche market players is that, invariably, the bigger operator's price cuts affect larger segments of the total customer base, dropping prices for many who would not be attracted to the niche player's arguments. The main question therefore becomes: Why should one eat one's own profitability for disloyal customers who are not very attractive in the end?

Entering a price war is always a bad option. Of course we are not advocating unreasonably high price levels either. If an operator's service prices are clearly too high, sooner or later they will have to lower their price levels to a standard that is more in line with the overall market level. The company should find the optimum point, which should be somewhere lower than the threshold of pain where even a loyal customer would prefer the trouble of changing the operator for the price's sake.

Technical Barriers and Churn

An engineering approach to churn is to consider technical means to 'lock' the customer. Some of the most common such means is non-standard components or systems, such as non-standard SIM cards or non-standard USIMs (UMTS Subscriber Identity Module) in 3G.

The appeal of a technical lock to customers is alluring, especially to such engineers who are not interested in discovering how to attract customers. The term 'lock' is appropriate to describe what is intended: the mobile operator wants to imprison the customers. But, any moderately free market will punish such behaviour in the long run. Some competitors will provide solutions that circumvent or avoid the technical means of binding customers and after that those operators who were seen as abusing the technical means will be punished by the marketplace. Customers will churn if they want. The only way to prevent churn in the long term is to make customers *want* to stay.

Loyalty Programmes

A tool created for the purpose of keeping customers with one service provider rather than switching to a competitor, is the loyalty programme. Loyalty programmes tend to be modelled along the ideas pioneered by the airline industry, collecting airline miles and exchanging them for awards. Many telecoms operators have introduced loyalty programmes and one of the early pioneers was Omnitel Pronto in Italy (and a similar scheme by Virgin in India). Typical of loyalty programmes is that the points collected can be exchanged for telecoms products, such as free messages or free upgrades of the handset, etc., but often include awards with partner companies in non-telecoms services and products as well.

Points can be collected for regular service use, such as minutes called and SMS messages sent. Bonus or campaign points can be given when new services are introduced to promote the early adoption of new services. Anniversary points can be awarded at the anniversary of the contract and in this way to reward long-term loyalty. The variations and complexity of the points programme are only limited by the imagination, but practical limits are brought about by the consumers, they will not want the programme to be too difficult to understand. Usually operators will try to get partners from outside the telecoms industry to join in and give points for purchases. The mobile operator should always include lots of its own services as awards, at very 'competitive' prices when charged by points. It is always less costly to offer own services rather than having to pay for those provided by other partners. This idea of loyalty points in the mobile sector is not prominent in the Indian scenario. So, by using this, AT&T can also get a first mover's advantage in the sector to introduce loyalty points.

Handset Subsidies

This concept was first introduced in India by Reliance CDMA service, which consisted of giving out handsets and a connection for rates as low as ₹500. This, in turn unlocked an entire market segment for Reliance which couldn't afford to invest ₹5,000 as a one-time payment. Currently, given the high costs of 3G capable handsets, AT&T could adopt a similar strategy to address such a market segment, which is willing to switch to 3G, but is constrained due to costly handsets required for 3G. By collaborating with a leading handset provider, the company can offer a 3G connection and a handset (whose cost can be paid off by the customer in instalments). This would surely help in increasing the customer base by adding newer customers as described above.

But, in addition to the above-mentioned benefits of handset subsidiaries, there are also some side-effects of the strategy. With handsets being tied to subscriptions, the following negative effects emerge: (i) handset manufacturers cannot convey quality or worth aspects by price, and (ii) handsets will move to the centre of the discussion. By turning attention away from the actual services, such as the subscription and advanced wireless services, the operators do themselves a massive disservice. The subsidiaries are very difficult to get rid of once they have been introduced into a market.

Branding as a Tool for Customer Retention

Branding plays an important role in the telecom sector and is the key to attracting the youth to using one's services. Compared with the purchase of convenience goods, a mobile subscription is more muted in its market behaviour. Changes in market loyalties are more subdued due to rational choice, coverage and service levels, the linkage of subscriptions to handsets, all meaning longer commitment. In many countries, mobile subscriptions have minimum durations, most commonly 12, 24 or even 36 months. Therefore, increasingly, it matters ever more which company the customer has most faith in.

Again, a company's real value is mirrored best in the people's minds and hearts. An appealing message or image is a good enticement; if not necessarily the only reason, it most certainly enforces change. Given such an importance of branding, AT&T should enter the Indian market with a strong marketing exercise–carefully crafted launch and proper communication of its offerings to various market segments targeted by it. The company should strongly leverage its current brand (present in the US and rest of the world) in order to achieve a strong entry into the Indian 3G market.

Customer Intelligence and Churn

The better the company knows its customers, the more it knows about his/her preferences, and the more it is able to serve the needs, the greater the loyalty. Modern customer intelligence needs powerful customer relationship management (CRM) tools and methods. Ideally, the customer's whole history and relevant data is collected, sorted, analysed, clustered, portrayed, and prioritized in order to make good management decisions about customers and the business. While dealing with similar content, the CRM tool is quite different to the billing (and charging) system. Billing systems should generate data to the CRM but the CRM should also receive input from other sources. A CRM tool should be able to answer the following types of questions:

(a) How was the customer acquired (what was the catch)?
(b) What services does the customer use?
(c) How is the customer classified in the segmentation?
(d) Is the customer profitable?
(e) Is there a typical pattern of customer behaviour?
(f) What is the cross-selling potential?
(g) What activation campaigns have been used?
(h) Are there similarities between other segments?
(i) Have there been complaints, special treatments?

To sum up, the company should formulate ways and means to combat churn and to keep the customers happy. Customer satisfaction and managing churn will be perhaps the biggest competitive challenge in 3G. Success with it will determine to a very large degree the eventual winners of the 3G market. Successful churn management will require professional marketing consistently performed, with lessons learned and applied over time.

Marketing Plan

The most important part of the communications strategy is the marketing plan. A detailed description about the plan given throughout the case. The following paragraph describes a broad framework of all the perspectives to be considered by AT&T for devising a marketing plan while entering the Indian 3G market.

A marketing plan takes intended marketing performance goals such as market share as given from the business plan, and then proceeds to identify the individual marketing activities that need to be accomplished so that the goals can be met. The marketing plan will determine which marketing activities are needed, identify timing, costs, resources, and responsibilities of each. The marketing plan will not go into detail about the production costs of the products or services being delivered, unless the given marketing activities cause incremental costs. The marketing plan is not intended to provide business justification and go into details about profits and losses of any business proposition.

Marketing plans cover all relevant marketing activities that are needed to fulfil the objectives of the marketing side of the business plan. As such, the marketing plan can cover any issues from customer segmentation to product development to brands, promotion, sales, and distribution. The marketing plan will also set specific goals for promotion or advertising plans and, where relevant, goals for sales plans, product development plans, and so on.

The advertising, PR and related promotion activities are often planned together with advertising agencies or PR agencies. They may want to develop what they call a marketing plan for their activities. While it will be important that such a plan covers marketing objectives, it should not supersede the existing marketing plan. The promotion plan should be completed only after the marketing plan has been approved.

AT&T should consider the following points while formulating its communications strategy for the launch of 3G services in India. A detailed description of these is given elsewhere in the case:

- Objectives of the plan;
- Duration of the plan;
- Deliverable targets with exact metrics, dates and responsibilities;
- Target segment(s);
- Service offering and bundle;
- Pricing;
- Promotion;
- Sales and sales support;
- Provisioning of service;
- Customer care and billing;
- Customer satisfaction follow-up;
- Marketing materials;
- Sales support materials;
- Internal marketing;
- Staff to execute the plan;
- Resources to be consumed;
- Responsibilities of plan approval, oversight and review;
- Evaluation of plan execution;
- Budget;
- Schedule of major activities.

Branding, Promotion and Selling of 3G Services

AT&T is a brand that's famous worldwide. But its entry into the 3G market of India requires branding of the product/service it is to offer. At the corporate level, AT&T as a brand is ominous, but at the product level the brand would be new in India and hence would have to establish itself with continuous efforts. It should aim at choosing the right brand ambassador, one who is a youth icon in India and who is also known to the corporates.

As far as the promotional aspect of AT&T is concerned the classic AIDA model can be followed. The pitfall in addressing promotion for any technology is that companies end up promoting technology that is hard for the consumer to understand. The use of acronyms like W-TDMA can turn off consumer interest. The focus should be on showing up the latent benefits and relating them to the consumer. There should be promotional offers that catch and combine the interests of different members of a family and thus result in shared sales.

An important part of the promotions strategy is public relations. The company, being new to India, must work on this aspect as it would have to leverage its partners in every sense to understand and create value for the Indian customer. Sponsorships and product placements are great tools to market a premium product or service. Movies or games can be used to show up products/services, making the customers aware of them. This automatically attaches a brand or fashion statement to the product.

A Tweak in the Tail

BSNL and MTNL, being government aided, have a six-month monopoly in the 3G market as of now. But the market being new is yet to start growing in its full strength. BSNL and MTNL have already invested heavily in their ad campaigns for their product/service offering. 3G is new to Indian customers and so must be promoted first as a service, making the customer aware of its full benefits, and then individually as something offered by some particular brands.

The ad campaigns of BSNL and MTNL would indirectly help AT&T as by the time it enters India, a product/service like 3G would be well known. All AT&T will have to do is promote its value offerings, as the ground work of removing scepticism about 3G would already have been done by BSNL and MTNL.

The Indian Telecom Market

In this section we analyse the 2G/3G GSM market in India and zoom in on the areas where AT&T can make a mark.

The Current Market Status—Flash Points

The global telecommunications market is undergoing a sea-change with respect to diversities in the upcoming technology and market trends. Undoubtedly, the Indian telecom market has a considerable share of the world market (almost ₹19.7 billion). With emerging semiconductor technologies combined with the thrust in the Indian telecom market (which is world's second-largest mobile market, after China), global telecommunications majors are considering India as a potential market for expansion.

(a) *Young India:* Nearly 54 per cent of the population is below age of 24 years.
(b) *Consumer market:* Estimated annual spending of youth is US$10.5 billion, with a growth rate of 12 per cent.
(c) *Internet users in India:* According to I-cube 2008, a survey conducted by IMRB International and IAMAI (Internet and Mobile Association of India), the number of active internet users in India in September 2008 was 45.30 million and total Internet users was 62.50 million.
(d) *Manpower:* About 55 per cent of young Indians are opting for careers in Web-related activities, which guarantees the market demand for Internet access and the manpower required for 3G technology.
(e) *Expert predictions:* The US wireless market would attain near saturation by 2009. Logically, other telecom giants from the West are expected to penetrate India (like Vodafone). Increase in foreign direct investment ceiling clearly implies that the Indian market is opening up.

GSM and CDMA Market Analysis

The GSM and CDMA markets in India are dominated by six major players, namely, Bharti Airtel, BSNL, Vodafone, Idea, Reliance and Tata Indicom. Among these BSNL and Reliance offer both CDMA and GSM services, Tata Indicom offers CDMA services and the others offer GSM services. If we look at the market shares of GSM players in India we see that the market is not fragmented; is mainly dominated by Airtel and Vodafone, the two eating up more than half of the total market share.

3G Market in India

3G service is a completely new and untapped market in India, making it a high-risk and high-return market. The following services are being offered in India by BSNL and MTNL in their current package of 3G services. The ad campaigns for the same are listed below as well:

(a) *Mobile TV:* Using the high-speed bandwidth of 3G networks on-demand TV services shall be provided.

Figure 9.13: Mobile TV promotion ad by BSNL

(b) *Video calling:* Better clarity and video calling can be leveraged over the high-speed 3G networks.

Figure 9.14: Video calling promotional ad by BSNL

(c) *Office solutions:* Applications that were only available on laptops and computers can now be accessed by 3G-enabled phones using high-speed 3G data services which make office work simpler and personal.

Figure 9.15: Office solutions promotion ad by BSNL

(d) *Music on Demand:* The service provider would host songs and videos for download over the 3G network for its customers.

Figure 9.16: Music on demand promotion ad by BSNL

Future Ambitions of Current Players

BSNL covered over 700 cities and net outflow in the launch is expected to be ₹2,700 crore. Mobile value added services are soaring high in revenues and made ₹6,000 crore in 2009 and are expected to reach ₹18,000 crore by 2012.

The Strategy for AT&T Considering the Market Study

Here we have assumed that AT&T is the American 3G company venturing into India. If we go back to the textbooks we'll find a theory given by Igor

Ansoff way back in 1957 in which he devised the widely known Ansoff Matrix. The matrix allows marketers to consider ways to grow the business via existing and/or new products in existing and/or new markets using four possible product/market combinations. This matrix helps companies decide what course of action to take given the current performance.

Applying the Ansoff Matrix to the case at hand, we can see that AT&T shall have to aim at market development. They already have an 'existing' 3G product/service range set up in America. But they are entering a 'new' market, India, and are targeting a new set of customers with different mindsets and buying decisions. Thus their target strategy should aim at market development, an area that involves medium level of risk, lesser than 'diversification', but more than 'market penetration'.

AT&T enjoys high brand value all across the globe. Thus it does not have to take much effort on brand promotion at the company level, considering the fact that the users of 3G would be the premium segment of customers, who would be aware of AT&T as world-class service providers. The company should leverage on all the services it offers and best practices it follows in America and use them in the Indian market. One way in which AT&T can create its market in India would be by offering different and unique products in the 3G segment compared to local players.

Considering the fact that the only foreign competitors for AT&T in India are Vodafone and Virgin Mobile, it definitely would have an advantage of technology and know-how in 3G products and services in India over other players. It should use this to get an edge over other players in the 3G segment. The collaboration strategy is discussed in the next section.

Understanding Consumers

In this section, we analyse the home and business segment of 3G phone customers in the Indian market and try to gain insights into their buying and usage habits. These would be used to give AT&T a direction to create value through collaboration with device manufacturers.

The Target Audience

A survey was carried out by IIM-Shillong interns at Euro RSCG while working on the advertisement strategy for BSNL's 3G launch. The aim of the survey was to get insights into how people in India relate themselves to 3G technology. The target audience was divided into two groups:

Youth focus: The youth showed the tendency to use 3G for the following:

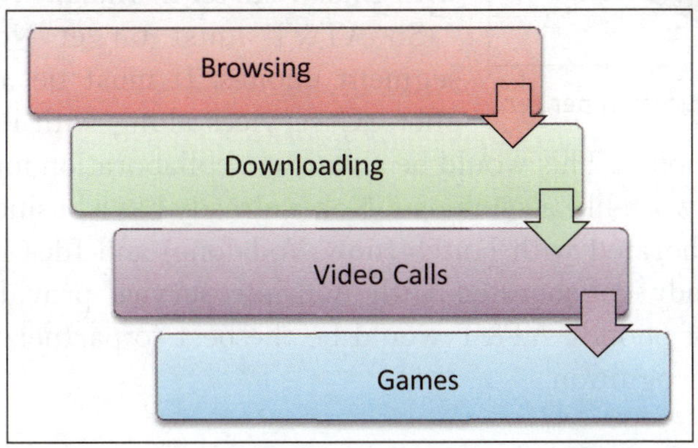

An impressive 59 per cent of the respondents showed their willingness to use 3G services 'Very Often'. The survey clearly indicated that the youth look at 3G as a means of 'communication' and 'entertainment', while 28 per cent regarded it to be a tool of the future and hence to be known and explored. A majority of the youth were however attracted to 3G owing to 'speed' and 'love for new gadgets'.

The corporate on the other side showed interest in 3G services due to 'ease of use' and 'business development'.

Corporate focus: The corporates showed the tendency to use 3G for the following:

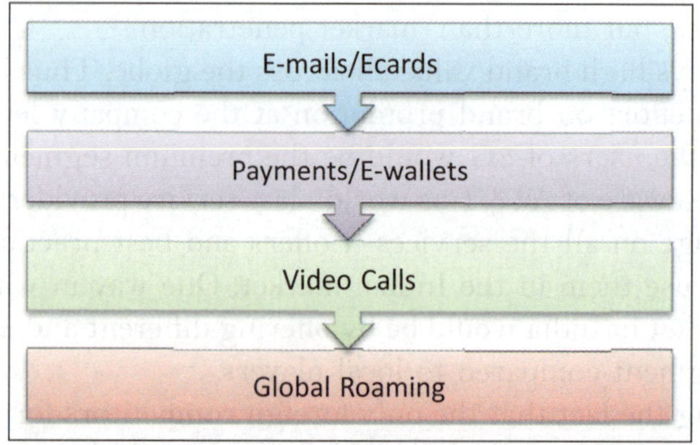

Mobile Handset Market in India

Figure 9.18 shows the market shares of players in the Indian handset market.

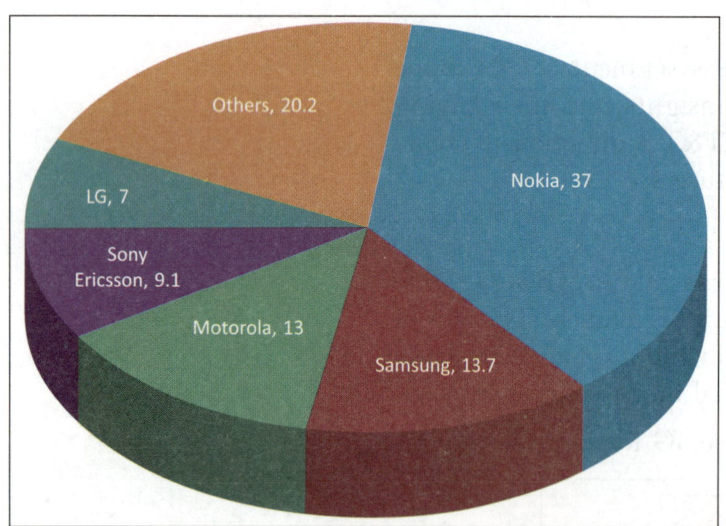

Figure 9.18: Market share of mobile handset producers in per cent

Nokia is a market leader and India is a key region for it. Nokia is by far the most sold brand across segments in the handset market of India. AT&T's success is in its 3G venture in India and for this we suggest it to tie up with Nokia.

We shall further analyse the premium segment of Nokia's mobile devices in circulation in India. According to a survey conducted by the Nielsen Company, a market research firm, Nokia's N95 was at the top of the mind of technology-savvy respondents. AT&T has a tie up with the Apple iphone in the US but Apple has already tied up with Bharti Airtel in India.

So AT&T must target Nokia's premium-segment phones. It must tie up with Nokia to offer 3G services along with its N95 and other high-end phones. This would be a win-win collaboration for both companies as it would work like a symbiosis. Nokia already has a business history where it has collaborated with Hutch (now Vodafone) and Idea in the past. Thus it has already collaborated with multiple service providers for different segments of phones. AT&T would be the best to partner with considering its brand recognition.

Thus AT&T should come up with promotional schemes along with Nokia handsets. It can also take chance by paying some extra costs to influence Nokia to offer its services with all 3G-enabled handsets at a premium shared by the two companies.

The learning from the brand preferences and consumer study can be that India is a young nation; its premium segment targets mobile devices that make a fashion statement. So AT&T must collaborate with Nokia for its premium segment of gadget and smart 3G-enabled phones to gain strategic advantage.

Look at the brands of 3G Handsets available in India in 2009: Apple iPhone 3G, BlackBerry Bold 9000, HPi PAQ 910c, HTC Advantage X7510, HTC S740, HTC Shift, HTC Touch Cruise, HTC Touch Diamond, HTC Touch Pro, HTC TyTN, HTC TyTN II, i-mate 810-F, i-mate Ultimate 7150, i-mate Ultimate 9502, LGCU915 Vu, LGGM 730, LGIncite, LGKC 910 Renoir, LGKF 700, LGKM 900 Arena, LGKT 770, Motorola A3100, Motorola Q9h, Motorola RAZR V3i, Motorola RAZR2 V9, Motorola RAZR2 V9x, Motorola Tundra VA76r, Nokia 3120 classic, Nokia 5320 Xpress Music, Nokia 5610, Nokia 5800 Xpress Music, Nokia 6120 classic, Nokia 6124 classic, Nokia 6210 Navigator, Nokia 6500 classic, Nokia 6500 slide, Nokia 6555, Nokia 6600 fold, Nokia 6600 slide, Nokia 6650, Nokia 6720 classic, Nokia 7900 Crystal Prism, Nokia E51, Nokia E51 camera-free, Nokia E55, Nokia E63, Nokia E66, Nokia E71, Nokia E75, Nokia N75, Nokia N78, Nokia N85, Nokia N95, Nokia N95 8GB, Nokia N96 Palm Treo Pro, Samsung A867 Eternity, Samsung F480, Samsung i8510 INNOV8, Samsung i900 Omnia, Sony Ericsson C510, Sony Ericsson C903, Sony Ericsson C905, Sony Ericsson G705, Sony Ericsson K850, Sony Ericsson W508, Sony Ericsson W760, Sony Ericsson W995, Sony Ericsson XPERIA X1 and Sony Ericsson Z750.

Competitive Strategy

In order to devise a competitive strategy for the American company (assumed to be AT&T), we need to analyse Porter's Five Forces Model. The model analyses the different aspects of attractiveness of the market. These include the bargaining power of customers, the bargaining power of suppliers, the threat of new entrants, the threat of substitute products, and the intensity of competitive rivalry. Since the company is considering expanding its products and services to the Indian 3G market, it should evaluate the attractiveness of the 3G market in India by considering the five factors mentioned above.

Beat the competition. Get more customers.

Further, it should look at the competitors and players in the Indian market, how do these companies market and brand their offerings and how do they manage the various factors associated with the terminals (3G-enabled mobile handsets), and so on. Finally, the company should also consider the CSFs

(Critical Success Factors) necessary for successful entry and sustained growth in volumes and profits.

Porter's Five Forces Model

Following is the Porter's Five Forces Model for the attractiveness of the 3G market in India:

(i) Bargaining Power of Customers: High

The potential customers for 3G services can be broadly classified into two categories—consumer class which mostly comprises youngsters, including students and working individuals in the age group of 15 to 25 years, the business class which includes executives and other working professionals spread over a wider age group of 25 to 60 years. The former class would mostly use the 3G services for downloading music, content-rich multimedia and other entertainment services. The latter would be more interested in emails and high-speed downloading and uploading of attachments.

Customers in the telecom sector have a huge bargaining power owing to the fact that the churn rate is the highest here. If a customer doesn't like the service of any of the network operators—be it voice quality, VAS, GPRS, etc.—he/she can immediately switch over to a different network operator. The customers may also defect for different reasons—difficulty in bill payments, difficulty in recharging, and so on.

Further, the buyers of 3G services are very diverse across demography, age, occupation, and so on, making it very difficult for the players to satisfy each and every customer. Another important factor that increases the bargaining power of the consumers is the lack of very high product differentiation. The major differentiating factor is the quality of voice and service over the network, but overall, the offerings of the players are barely differentiated.

(ii) Bargaining Power of Suppliers: Medium

The operators need to consider the bargaining power of the suppliers in two major aspects—the service part and the handset part.

Since the telecom operators themselves are the service providers, they have a very low threat from service providers. The important consideration is the bargaining power of the handset suppliers. In case the company is collaborating with a particular handset provider (for example, Airtel and Apple iPhone), the bargaining power of the supplier is very high. Further, in case there is no collaboration, the bargaining power of suppliers is low because they are not directly related to the service providers.

Apart from the handsets, other necessary equipment such as transmission gear, cabling, and so on are provided by the suppliers competitively smaller in size than the service provider. They have an overall medium to low bargaining power as they also make profits by dealing with the service providers.

(iii) Threat of New Entrants: Low

Very strict norms concerning the auctioning and allocation of 3G spectrum should be an important point under consideration. A new player would need

$3-3.5 billion to start operations from scratch. A mass consumer base of 2G is essential for survival, which forces new players to compulsorily buy the 2G spectrum thereby increasing the costs. Moreover, an existing 2G player can roll out the 3G service at half the above-mentioned cost, putting new entrants into a greater competitive disadvantage. Further costs would be incurred in launching the service, in promotions and branding campaigns, and so on.

Access to technology is not as issue in the 3G telecom sector since it is available in the public domain and a new entrant would not find it difficult to access that technology. Brand loyalty would be a major deterrent for the new players entering into the Indian market.

Customers are keen to go for well known brands (even though the churn rate is very high), so the prospects of a new entrant in the market are significantly reduced.

(iv) Threat of Substitutes: High

The churning rate is a pointer to the fact that the threat of substitutes is a major factor of concern for a firm considering the attractiveness of the telecom sector. Customers are often ready to switch users and try out different competitors in their search for the best possible deal in terms of tariffs, quality of service, and so on. This is aggravated by the fact that there exists very little or no differentiation among the tariffs of competitors, for example, Vodafone, Airtel and Idea. Finally the threat of substitutes depends on the cost of switching between two service providers. This cost is very low in case of switching between operators in India—the exit cost from a service provider is zero and the cost of a new SIM card is about ₹100. Thus, the threat of substitutes is very high in the telecom sector.

(v) Intensity of Rivalry: High

The structure of competition in the Indian 3G sector would be very tough with 10 players vying for 45-70 million customers, which forms only 10 per cent of the total subscriber base (by 2012). Rivalry is more intense as there are lots of equally-sized competitors. Companies need to bear high fixed costs and this necessitates the need to increase the sales volume to boost sales and recover the cost as soon as possible.

Degrees of product differentiation, based on offerings and tariffs, are very low and as a result there's greater rivalry among the players. Low switching costs further adds to the rivalry among the competitors.

The strategic objectives of companies like Vodafone, Airtel or Idea Cellular are very aggressive in terms of increasing customer base. If competitors pursue aggressive growth strategies, rivalry will be more intense. Since the barriers for leaving the industry are high, owing to the large initial investment, competitors tend to exhibit greater rivalry.

Competition Mapping of the Existing Players

The Apple iPhone 3G was rolled out in India on 22 August 2008 via Airtel and Vodafone. Airtel and Vodafone also launched iPhone 3GS (16GB and 32GB) subsequently in India. As you are aware, Bharti Airtel, formerly known as Bharti Televentures Limited (BTVL) is India's largest cellular service provider with a footprint in all the 23 telecom circles. In 2010, Bharti is the world's third-largest, single-country mobile operator and sixth-largest integrated telecom operator. Globally, Bharti Airtel is the third-largest in-country mobile operator by subscriber base, behind China Mobile and China Unicom. In December 2008, Bharti Airtel rolled out third generation services in Sri Lanka in association with Singapore Telecommunications. SingTel is a major player in the 3G space in Asia. It operates third generation networks in several markets across Asia. Airtel's operation in Sri Lanka, known as Airtel Lanka, commenced operations on 12 January 2009.

Given below is a SWOT analysis for Airtel, a potential competitor in the Indian market. AT&T should compile a similar SWOT for all possible players it sees as competitors in the Indian 3G market.

SWOT Analysis

Strengths

1. Bharti Airtel has more than 141 million customers (August 2010). It is the largest cellular provider in India, and also supplies broadband and telephone services, as well as many other telecommunication services to both domestic and corporate customers.
2. Other stakeholders in Bharti Airtel include Sony Ericsson, Nokia and SingTel (Singapore Telecommunications Ltd) with whom they hold a strategic alliance. This means that the company has access to knowledge and technology from other parts of the telecommunications world.
3. The company has covered the entire nation with its network. This has underpinned its large and rising customer base.

Weaknesses

1. An often cited original weakness is that when the business was started by Sunil Bharti Mittal over 15 years ago, the company had little knowledge and experience of how a cellular telephone system actually works. So the start-up business had to outsource to industry experts in the field.
2. Until recently Airtel did not own its own towers, which was a particular strength of some of its competitors such as Vodafone Essar. Towers are important if any company wishes to provide uninterrupted coverage.
3. The fact that Airtel has not pulled off a deal with South Africa's MTN could signal the lack of any real emerging market investment opportunity for the business once the Indian market matures.

Opportunities

1. The company possesses a customized version of the Google search engine which will enhance broadband services to customers. The tie-up with Google can only enhance the Airtel brand, and provide advertising opportunities in India for Google.
2. Global telecommunications and new technology brands see Airtel as a key strategic player in the Indian market. The new iPhone was launched in India via an Airtel distributorship. Another strategic partnership is held with BlackBerry Wireless Solutions.
3. Though forced to outsource much of its technical operations in the early days, it allowed Airtel to work from a blank sheet of paper, and to question

industry approaches and practices, for example, replacing the Revenue-Per-Customer model with a Revenue-Per-Minute model which is better suited to India, especially as the company moved into small and remote villages and towns.

4. The company is investing in its operation in 1,20,000 to 1,60,000 small villages every year. It sees that less well-off consumers may only be able to afford a few tens of rupees per call. This will bring more benefits to the business which are scalable—using its 'Matchbox' strategy.
5. Bharti Airtel is embarking on another joint venture with Vodafone Essar and Idea Cellular to create a new independent tower company called Indus Towers. This new business will control more than 60 per cent of India's network towers. IPTV is another potential new service that could underpin the company's long-term strategy.

Threats

1. Airtel and Vodafone seem to be having an on/off relationship. Vodafone, which owned a 5.6 per cent stake in the Airtel business sold it back to Airtel. Knowledge and technology previously available to Airtel now moves into the hands of one of its competitors.
2. The quick changing pace of the global telecommunications industry could tempt Airtel to go along the acquisition trail which may make it vulnerable if the world goes into recession.
3. Bharti Airtel could also be a target for the takeover vision of global telecommunications players that wish to move into the Indian market.

The above SWOT analysis reveals the following points about competition:

- The incumbents with 2G technologies surely have an upper hand over new entrants in terms of lower initial costs, branding, and the reach to the public. The competition would be very fierce for the new entrants because of the strong position of the existing players.
- The most sought after 3G device—the iPhone, is already launched by an existing player in the market. So, the competitors should focus on other handset manufactures to collaborate and gain a competitive advantage in the 3G market.

Critical Success Factors

(a) ***Network infrastructure:*** If the auction stretches more than expected, the telcos are likely to bleed as they have a huge CAPEX ahead of them.

(b) ***Availability of handsets:*** Since they are widely available (around ₹20,000 a piece, slightly expensive), the only factor handset manufacturers must focus on is to have better usability using browsers for Internet access.

(c) ***Availability of applications and content:*** Currently most of it is focused on youth and entertainment. Get killer applications to generate higher revenues.

(d) ***Pricing and tariff:*** Voice usage is inversely proportional to tariff. Revenue sharing for VAS should be chalked out to make it affordable to the masses.

(e) ***Strong branding:*** It would be the key to pull customers toward the service provider.
(f) ***Collaboration and partnering:*** The foreign player may enter into a JV with an Indian firm not having enough funds to venture into 3G, but with a sound subscriber base. IT should also tie-up with a handset provider so that it supplies handsets exclusively in the country.
(g) ***Choosing the right infrastructure platform:*** In the transmission section of the network, the 3G upgrade cost will depend on the solution chosen for 2G backhauling. The optimal investment for an operator is to choose infrastructure platforms that support both 2G and 3G requirements, better known in the industry as 'converged packetoptics'. It can deliver significant reduction in an operator's 3G transmission spends.
(h) ***Managing CAPEX and OPEX:*** While deploying 3G networks, operators will need to carefully manage both their OPEX and CAPEX spending. From a CAPEX perspective, networks need to be flexible and scalable, leveraging existing 2G infrastructure as much as possible but making provision to add necessary investments when customer demand justifies it. From an OPEX perspective, many operators are also looking at vendors to provide them with a unified management system that supports both the 2G and 3G networks, various network design and planning tools that help operators optimize their network roll-out and asses future build requirements.
(i) ***Capacity planning:*** One of the main challenges any network operator faces is predicting customer demand and preparing the network to support it ahead of time. Operators should plan for initial, ideal and worst case scenario when it comes to their network capacity.
(j) ***Scalability:*** A key priority for any operator is choosing the optimal 3G migration strategy, partnering with the right infrastructure vendor that will not only provide quality product portfolio, but will also serve as a long-term partner for growth. This includes providing operators with products/solutions that are scalable and flexible, and which will allow them to fully leverage their existing infrastructure investment.

References

1. Tomi T. Ahonen, Timo Kasper and Sara Melkko (2004), '3G Marketing: Communities and Strategic Partnerships', John Wiley & Sons Ltd.
2. *Statistical Outline of India 2007–8.*
3. *CYGNUS*, Quarterly Performance Analysis Of Companies (April–June 2008), Indian Telecom Industry.
4. *Telecom Watch*, Tariff Databank, July 2008.
5. www.marketingteacher.com/SWOT/bharti_airtel_swot.htm
6. http://convergence.in/blog/2008/08/07/comparison-success-of-3g-india-vs-asia-europe/
7. http://en.wikipedia.org/wiki/Competitive_Strategy
8. http://www.stylusinc.com/internet_potential_india.htm
9. http://www.hardwaresecrets.com/article/151
10. http://ojr.org/japan/wireless/1084495929.php
11. http://trai.gov.in

CHAPTER 10  RIVALRY OFF THE AIR: SAGA OF KINGFISHER AND JET AIRWAYS

applied case study 2

Civil aviation scene in general may be looking downcast but private aviation in Asia, India in particular, is poised to soar high.

— Mark Baier, CEO Bjets
Asia's first dedicated fractional ownership and block charter jet operator based in Mumbai and Singapore, with an operations centre in Hyderabad

10.1 Genesis

Through fiscal 2009, a year when oil prices scaled a record of US$147 a barrel, airfares fell by almost 25 per cent on domestic and international routes. The period also dovetailed with the onset of a recession in the US, Europe and Japan and a slowdown in the Indian economy, causing passenger traffic to contract by 10 per cent after expanding at an annual 35 per cent rate in 2007. Indian full-service carriers now recognize the strategic relevance of the low-fare airline model in a market with air travellers turning increasingly thrifty. Airlines industry lose US$9.9 billion in 2009 globally. Passenger traffic fell 2.1 per cent and cargo dropped 9.8 per cent. Average yield tumbled 14 per cent, industry revenue fell 15 per cent (US$85 million) to US$479 billion globally.

The Indian civil aviation market grew at a CAGR of 18 per cent and was worth US$7.80 billion in 2010. India has jumped to the ninth position in world aviation market, up from its twelfth position in 2009. Domestic traffic will increase by 25 to 30 per cent until the close of 2010. The government plans to invest US$9 billion to modernize existing airports by 2011. With a growth rate of 18 per cent per annum, the Indian aviation industry is one of the fastest growing industries in the world. The government's Open Sky policy has allowed overseas players to enter the market and the industry has witnessed growth both in terms of players and number of aircraft.

With the liberalization of the Indian aviation sector, the aviation industry in India has undergone rapid transformation. From being primarily a government-owned industry, it is now dominated by privately owned full-service airlines and low-cost carriers. Private airlines account for around 75 per cent share of the domestic aviation market. The current private players are Jet Airways, JetLite, Jet Konnect, Kingfisher Airlines, Kingfisher Red, SpiceJet, GoAir and IndiGo, along with the government-owned Indian. India has five key players who command 94 per cent of the market share. The leader is Jet Airways (26 per cent) followed by Kingfisher Airlines (21 per cent) Air-India (18 per cent), IndiGo (16 per cent) and SpiceJet (13 per cent) as of May 2010.

Indian carriers have a fleet size of 310 aircraft. Earlier, air travel was a privilege only a few could afford, but today it has become cheaper and the privilege of a large number of people. Furthermore, the price of aviation turbine fuel (ATF) dropped drastically in December 2008, hitting US$0.665–US$0.789—its lowest since 2004. Jet Airways, the country's largest private carrier, slashed domestic fares by 40 per cent and 60 per cent in February 2009 following the drop in ATF prices. While looking at our glorious past, Singapore Airlines, inspired by Air-India, transformed from a small airline to a world-class airline and a trendsetter in the aviation industry. The Indian aviation sector continued to put up an impressive performance of 20 per cent growth in domestic passengers with high load factor (75-80 per cent) and stable crude oil price (US$75/barrel) during April-August 2010.

In terms of infrastructure, India has 1,125 airports but only 15 handle international flights. Explosive growth in passenger and cargo traffic in the last couple of years has made investment in new airstrips and allied infrastructure imperative. The navigational services and systems at most Indian airports are outdated by decades when compared to other airports worldwide. Though only Indira Gandhi International Airport at Delhi has installed CAT III B, most airlines have not bothered to train their pilots or equip their aircrafts to make use of it. The government has outlined several initiatives like privatization in airport development, 100 per cent FDI for greenfield airports and 74 per cent FDI for brownfield projects. The government has initiated modernization of the Delhi, Mumbai, Chennai and Kolkata airports and announced massive greenfield developments in other cities—initiatives expected to bring in an investment of US$10 billion in the next couple of years. Airport Authority of India's ambitious plans to modernize the airports include modernization of communication and navigation systems with the latest satellite-based systems, installing Differential Global Positioning System (DGPS) and, automatic air traffic control services.

At the beginning of the twenty-first century, the Indian aviation industry saw companies offering a powerful combination of low prices and high quality. The once dominant high-priced airlines faced stiff competition from value-based players. The former lost product and service superiority which set them apart from the latter. Rivalry among the service providers was by way of price cuts, dynamic fares, enhanced customer service, loyalty programmes and pre-flight and in-flight customer delights in the form of customized entertainment, varied cuisines, wireless support, personal care and attention. This had far-reaching effects on the industry's domestic and international services.

The low price and service of the low cost airlines had an adverse impact on the full-range service providers. The ultimate effect was a series of takeovers of the low cost airlines by cash-rich companies to expand their business model. Jet Airways and Kingfisher are a case in point. The Indian aviation industry is still at a nascent stage and incurring a loss of US$20 million annually. Look at the industry indicators and how Indian premium service providers rate against global leaders (Table 10.1).

Table 10.1: Comparative analysis of industry parameters

Parameter	*Jet Airways*	*Kingfisher*	*Singapore Airlines*	*Cathay Pacific*	*British Airways*
Available Seat Kilometres (ASKm) (mn)	17,698	16,788	1,12,543	89,118	1,48,321
Revenue per RPKm ($)	12,307	11,567	89,148	71,205	1,13,016
Cost per ASKm (₹)	3.28	5.20	3.00	4.00	4.50
Revenue per ASKm (₹)	4.58	5.30	4.00	5.50	7.00
Load factor %	66	62	79.9	80	75.6
Break-even load factor %	82.1	95.9	70.2	78.9	63.6

Source: *CLSA*-Asia Pacific Markets, 2009.
Note: Assume that US$1 is ₹50.56.

Take a look at the competitive space of the Indian aviation sector (Figure 10.1).

Following the acquisition of Air Deccan, Kingfisher entered the international sector with its strategy of non-stop, hassle-free flights. But stiff competition, low load factor and consistent loss in the three quarters of 2009 quickly became matters of concern for the airline. During 2010, domestic load factor reached an all-time high of 79.2 per cent by strong passenger traffic and capacity nationalization. Full service carriers such as Jet Airways, Kingfisher and Air-India who commands 63 per cent of the market reduced their total fleet size to 373 and started operating 70 per cent of their capacity as low cost carrier due to high demand. Jet Airways, which had dominated the market in the 1990s was losing its market share and service superiority to competitors. Figure 10.2 shows the passenger numbers and load factor for various service providers in 2007–8.

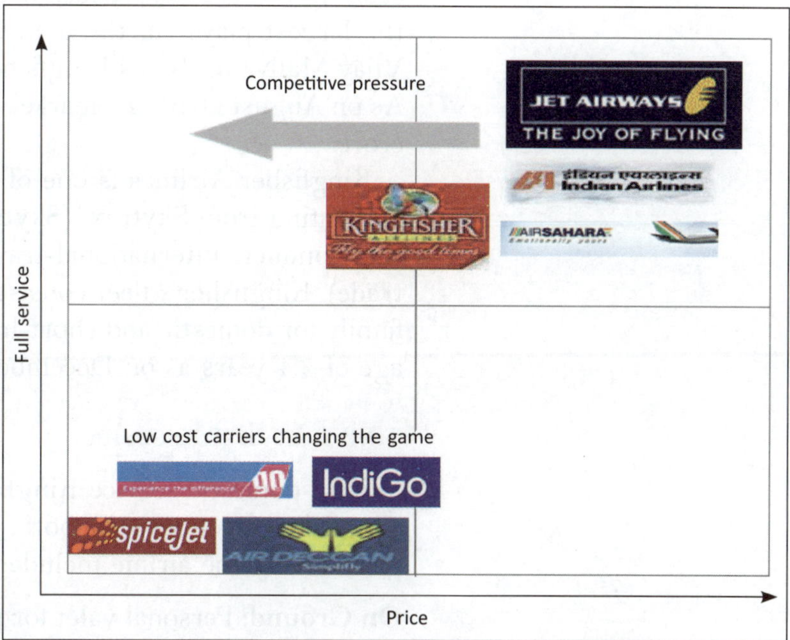

Figure 10.1: Competitive landscape of Indian service providers

The intense competition on the international routes and excess capacity on the domestic routes eroded the yields of Indian carriers during 2009–10. The difference between the fares offered by full-service and low fare carriers narrowed. Jet Airways, Kingfisher Airlines, Paramount Airways Ltd. and National Aviation Co. of India Ltd. (NACIL) run full-service operations, while SpiceJet Ltd., InterGlobe Aviation Pvt. Ltd. (that runs IndiGo), and GoAirlines (India) Pvt. Ltd. (GoAir) are low fare carriers. Indian domestic passenger traffic has grown consistently since 2002 and touched all time high of 45 million in 2007 and all time low of 6 million in 2009. In 2010, it has already touched 26 million mark in August 2010. Let us look at individual players and their performance.

10.2 Kingfisher Airlines

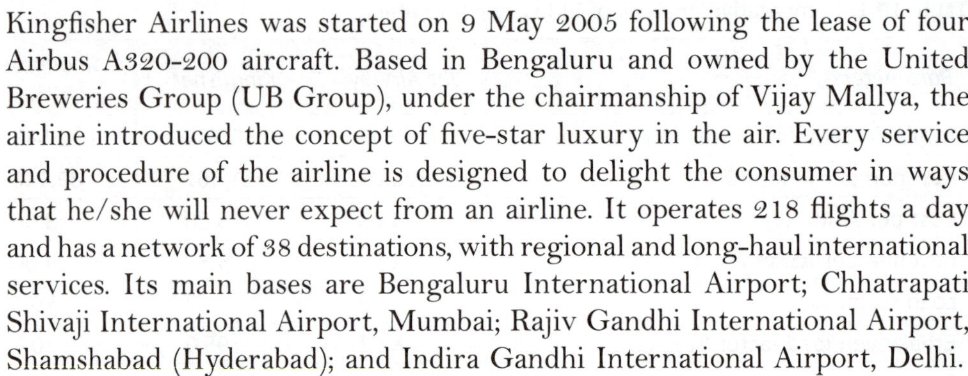

Kingfisher Airlines was started on 9 May 2005 following the lease of four Airbus A320-200 aircraft. Based in Bengaluru and owned by the United Breweries Group (UB Group), under the chairmanship of Vijay Mallya, the airline introduced the concept of five-star luxury in the air. Every service and procedure of the airline is designed to delight the consumer in ways that he/she will never expect from an airline. It operates 218 flights a day and has a network of 38 destinations, with regional and long-haul international services. Its main bases are Bengaluru International Airport; Chhatrapati Shivaji International Airport, Mumbai; Rajiv Gandhi International Airport, Shamshabad (Hyderabad); and Indira Gandhi International Airport, Delhi.

Through its holding company, the UB Group, Kingfisher acquired 26 per cent stake in the budget airline Air Deccan and effectively invested ₹1,000 crore in the ₹419-crore loss making company in 2007. The merger created the largest player in the domestic aviation market and paved the way for Vijay Mallya to fly his Kingfisher Airlines to overseas destinations in 2008. As on August 2010, the market capitalization of the company is Rs. 1,316.25 crore.

Kingfisher Airlines is one of the six airlines in the world to have a five-star rating from Skytrax. (Skytrax is a United Kingdom-based consultancy that conducts international-traveller surveys to find the best in the airline trade). Kingfisher's fleet consists of the ATR 42, ATR 72 and Airbus A320 family for domestic and short-haul services. The airline fleet has an average age of 3.4 years as on December 2009.

10.2.1 In-flight service

Within domestic service Kingfisher has two classes—Kingfisher First and Kingfisher Economy. In both, passengers are called guests and facilities provided by the airline include:

On Ground: Personal valet for passengers to assist them at every step, from baggage to boarding. Exclusive lounges with private space, with facilities for music and refreshment.

In-Flight: Kingfisher has the world's most advanced personal in-flight entertainment system: 8.4 inch LCD swivel, wide-screen with noise cancelling headphones; live TV, Kingfisher radio, news, infotainment and video games. The guests can play virtual tournaments with fellow guests using the multi-player option. The airline provides elegant executive restrooms with premium toiletries. Steam-ironing of guests' jackets and spectacle cleaning are also available.

The hand-picked cabin crew is warm and highly professional, and trained to anticipate every need of their guest on board.

Each member in the King Club of the airline starts as a base member and depending on the number of flights he/she takes, his/her membership will move through Red, Silver and Gold Memberships.

Figure 10.2: In-flight service as a promotion tool

10.2.2 Financial Performance

Kingfisher restructured its operations and continued to maintain stringent cost control. This helped the company show a positive EBITDA of ₹44 crore as against a loss of ₹207 crore in September 2008 for its domestic operations. The performance is noteworthy in the backdrop of intense competition and a lean monsoon traffic season leading to an overall pressure on yields (−32 per cent as compared to 2008). Certain technical issues also led to grounding of aircrafts, in turn causing revenue loss and hence a negative impact on the bottom-line in 2009.

Table 10.2: Financial performance of Kingfisher Airlines

Operational parameters	*June-September 2009*
No. of departures	37,384
ASKm (in ₹crore)	390
RPKm (in ₹crore)	265
Seat factor	68%
Guest flown	28,50,000

Source: www.flykingfisher.com
Note: ASKm: Average seat km, RPKm: Revenue per km; Seat factor: ASKm/RPKm

At the EBITDA level domestic operations showed an operating loss of ₹178 crore in September 2009 as against a loss of ₹464 crore in the corresponding period in 2008. However, on an overall basis, the company incurred an EBITDA loss of ₹336 crore including losses and costs associated with the recent start-up of new international routes. The net loss after tax for 2010 is ₹418.77 crore.

The half-yearly revenue from operations of the airline in 2009 was ₹2,42,568.31 lakh as against ₹2,72,030.41 lakh in the same period in 2008. The revenue from operations of the airline in 2009 was ₹5,068 crore. The company is having a market capitalization of ₹1,729 crore with huge debt of

Figure 10.3: Star power—an effective communication tool

₹7,414 crore in September 2010. The accumulated loss from operations in 2008–9 was ₹2,152 crore. The high cost of aircraft acquisition, depreciation, new routes, training and aviation fuel were the main reasons for the loss.

Table 10.3: An operating loss of Kingfisher Airlines at the EBITDA level

Net Sales	*Key Financials*		
	2008	*2009*	*2010*
(₹crore)	5,239	5,068	6,423
EBITDA	– 1,807	– 899	– 156
Net profit/loss	2,152 (loss)	1,647 (loss)	875 (loss)
Source: Investors' Report of Kingfisher Airlines, June 2010.			

10.2.3 Recent Developments

Kingfisher has introduced seven more sectors, adding five cities to its network which make 238 daily departures to 42 destinations with a fleet of 37 planes. Kingfisher also fly to Singapore, Pakistan, United Arab Emirates, Hong Kong, and other nine European destinations from September 2010. In all, Kingfisher has a total of 13 international destinations it can opted to fly.

Kingfisher's operations were just three years old and under the Indian aviation rule an airline has to operate a minimum of five years in the domestic sector before going international. So Kingfisher opted to fly on the Deccan licence which has completed five years of domestic operation. This was one of the reasons for Kingfisher to acquire Deccan.

10.2.4 International Strategy

Even in challenging times, the company continued to take a pragmatic approach towards its international expansion. The Kolkata-Bangkok sector was added during the September quarter of 2009 using single-aisle aircrafts, thereby increasing the block hour usage of the same metal deployed on domestic routes. Kingfisher suspended its operations on the Bengaluru-London and Bengaluru-Colombo routes and started two new routes from Mumbai to Hong Kong and Singapore in September 2009, thereby offering its world class services on these sectors using its state of the art Airbus A330-200s.

India–US–India non-stop flights presented the most unique opportunity and reduced competition. KFA concentrated on this opportunity and has ordered specific aircraft types to undertake this mission. KFA commenced non-stop flights with the Airbus A340-500 between Bengaluru and San Francisco and Mumbai and New York in the second quarter of 2008. It also commenced non-stop flights with the Airbus A330-200 between Mumbai and London and Mumbai and Hong Kong around the same time.

10.2.5 Face the Task

It is a fact that capacity on the domestic routes is growing faster than demand. This is despite the Kingfisher-Deccan combine rescheduling fresh aircraft induction in 2008. Kingfisher-Deccan together, connect 75 cities and offer over 558 flights daily with a fleet of 80 planes. The company believes that there is a premium that people would pay for non-stop travel, given the fact that there are so many problems and hassles at the airports, especially security-related issues. But aviation analysts observe that the airline's flight path will be difficult because of the recent addition in capacity on the India-US route by rivals like Continental, Delta, Jet and Air-India.

The point is how soon can the airline turn around Air Deccan. Air Deccan has been in the red since its inception, having accumulated losses of around ₹420 crore. Kingfisher Airlines had acquired 46 per cent stake in Deccan Aviation in June 2007. The Union Government has notified 13 international destinations including US, UK, UAE, Singapore, Saudi Arabia, Kuwait, Sri Lanka, Bangladesh, Malaysia, Thailand, Maldives, Pakistan and Hong Kong in 2009 which the Kingfisher-Deccan combo can fly to.

Kingfisher opted to fight against domestic and international carriers and followed an aggressive pricing strategy during the initial days. Internationally, leading carriers such as United Airlines, American Airlines (a unit of AMR Corporation), Delta Airlines Inc., among others, deferred flying new international routes due to high fuel costs in the first half of 2008.

At the same time Kingfisher Airlines saw a series of exits in early 2009 including the head of global sales, head of marketing and head of revenue management. And in 2008 the company lost its executive VP and VP-Operations. The airline which has been functioning without CEO since its inception did, for a while, have a COO. However the post has been vacant since 2005. As is widely known, despite the airline cutting capacity, routes and flights, its losses have been mounting, expected to have crossed ₹2,875 crore in 2010–11. Many analysts believe that 20 aircrafts of the company were on the ground at any point of time in 2009 but the company confirmed the number to be 12. About 12,000 employees are keeping their fingers crossed that Mallya will bring some order into the carrier's operations unlike previous attempts at change management.

10.3 Jet Airways

Jet Airways is the second-largest international airway in India, second to Air-India, and the largest among the domestic airlines. It was started by Naresh Goyal in 1993 and operates 400 flights daily to 62 destinations in 2009. Its primary base is the Mumbai's Chhatrapati Shivaji International Airport. Jet Airways operates a fleet of 85 aircrafts, which includes 10 Boeing 777-300 ER aircrafts, 10 Airbus A330-200 aircrafts, 54 classic and next generation Boeing 737-400/700/800/900 aircrafts and 11 modern ATR 72-500 turboprop aircrafts in 2009. With an average fleet age of 4.45 years, the airline has one of the youngest aircraft fleet in the world. The company has a market capitalization of ₹4,582 crore as of August 2010. On the whole, Jet flies to 66 destinations including 23 international destinations across US, Europe and Asia in 2010.

Figure 10.4: In-flight experience as a promotion tool

10.3.1 Timeline

Jet Airways, together with JetLite, its wholly owned subsidiary, continued to retain its market leadership with a market share of 27 per cent for August 2010. Jet Airways' is also the undisputed market leader for the 11 month period from January to November 2009. The Airline increases routes with existing aircraft, reduces flight weight to cut find costs and launches second low cost carrier in 2009-10

In March 2008, Jet Airways' share of India's domestic aviation market stood at 29.8 per cent, including its low-cost subsidiary JetLite's share of 7.1 per cent, making it the largest airline in India. However, the airline faces competition from other domestic carriers like Kingfisher Airlines, SpiceJet and IndiGo.

The combined loss of aviation industry in the wake of downturn in 2008 and 2009 was estimated as Rs 9,340 crore ($2 billion). Jet Airways' market share fell to 20 per cent from 30 per cent in third quarter of 2008 but it again climbed back to 26.3 per cent in first quarter of 2009 as declared by Directorate General of Civil Aviation (DGCA), though its revenue share remained intact. Jet Airways Konnect, low-fare airline, saw improvement in passengers but yield had come down in first quarter of 2009. About 70 per cent of Jet Airways aircraft were deployed in Jet Konnect as the business and first-class segments. However, it did not have many takers even from the corporate sector though July saw some improvement.

The airline has further strengthened its domestic network by selectively introducing routes and enhancing connectivity on key routes in the domestic market. According to Nikos Kardassis, chief executive officer, Jet Airways (I) Ltd, that the company is continuing market leadership, on the back of recent growth in traffic is testimony to the customer centricity that the airline has brought to bear in its operations. In fact it has been their enhanced customer experience, coupled with a number of marketing and network initiatives that have significantly helped Jet Airways grow their market leadership in a highly competitive and price sensitive market.

Jet Airways have consciously worked towards redesigning their business model, and emerge as an organization responsive to the changing needs of domestic and international passengers. This is now being mirrored in their increasing dominance of the Indian skies, Jet Airways' is now more focused than ever before, to consolidate and build on this leadership position during 2010–11. In 2009, Jet Airways saved $600 million through network restructuring, $170 million with cost cutting programmes and $270 million cash conservation measures like delayed repayment of loans and renegotiating with vendors.

Jet Airways operates daily non-stop flights to Sri Lanka, Nepal, Singapore, Malaysia, the United Kingdom and Thailand, on one of the youngest and best maintained fleets of the country. The airline has also judiciously introduced new routes like a Mumbai–Kathmandu service and increased frequency on the Delhi–Kathmandu sector, while it also introduced Mumbai–Dhaka service in 2009. All of which have been undertaken to offer seamless connectivity to destinations across India, as well as to the Gulf, North America, Europe and the ASEAN region.

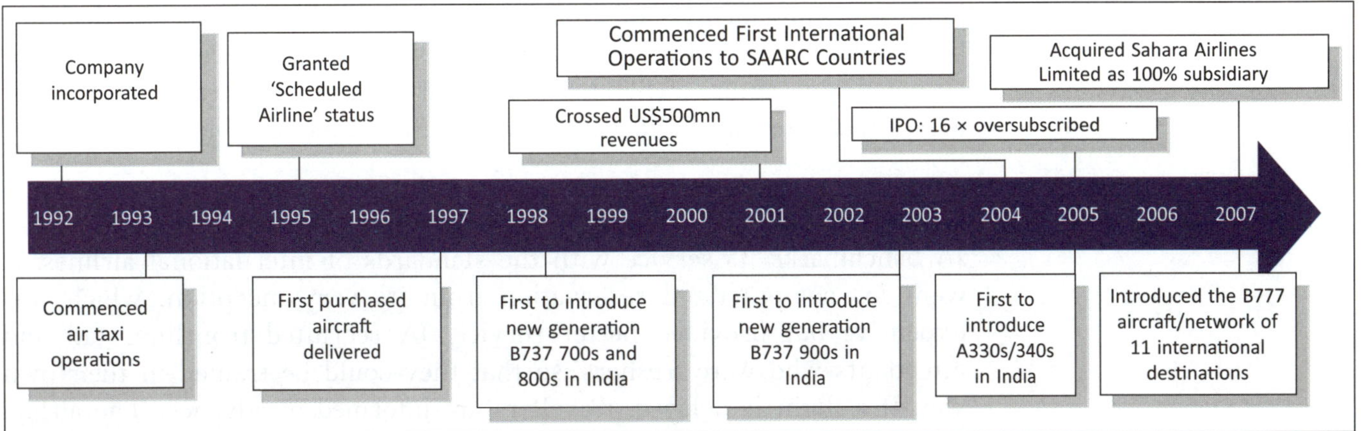

Figure 10.5: Brief timeline of Jet Airways

Table 10.4: Jet Airways' international routes

International routes	*Commenced on*
Mumbai–Newark–Mumbai via Brussels	5 August 2007
Delhi–Toronto–Delhi via Brussels (changed to Delhi-New York (JFK)–Delhi w.e.f. 28 October 2007)	5 September 2007
Chennai–Toronto–Chennai via Brussels	28 October 2007
Delhi–Kathmandu–Delhi (2nd frequency)	10 November 2007
Delhi–Dhaka–Delhi	16 December 2007
Kolkata–Dhaka–Kolkata	16 December 2007
Delhi–Kuwait–Delhi	5 January 2008
Cochin–Kuwait–Cochin	5 January 2008
Cochin–Bahrain–Cochin	5 January 2008
Mumbai–Bahrain–Mumbai	5 January 2008
Cochin–Muscat–Cochin	23 January 2008
Kozhikode–Muscat–Kozhikode	23 January 2008
Mumbai–Doha–Mumbai	23 January 2008
Kozhikode–Doha–Kozhikode	23 January 2008

Jet Airways thus plans to continue enhancing its connectivity by adding more gateway points into its hubs in a planned manner to create a larger customer base and offer enhanced services to its international and domestic travellers during 2010–11. In line with this strategy the airline plans to develop Delhi and Mumbai as major hubs to international destinations.

The airline has entered into codeshare agreements with American Airlines, Air Canada, All Nippon Airways, Brussels Airlines, Etihad Airways, Emirates, JetLite, Malaysia Airlines, Qantas Airways, Virgin Atlantic, thus providing enhanced connectivity for their guests. On 12 April 2007, the Jet agreed to buy-out Air Sahara for ₹14.5 billion ($340 million). Air Sahara was renamed JetLite, and was marketed between a low cost carrier and a full-service airline.

10.3.2 Brand Ownership

Jet Airways (JA) does not own its brand. The brand is owned by Jetair Enterprises Ltd., a separate company substantially owned by Naresh Goyal, which licenses the brand to the airline in return for an annual payment. This kind of arrangement is of vital importance should the concerned airline become the subject of a hostile takeover bid because the bidder(s) will not automatically acquire ownership of their takeover target's brand and without access to the brand the takeover target will be less valuable.

10.3.3 In-flight Service

JA benchmarks its service with the standards of international airlines. It went for computerized reservation from its very inception, which was expensive but provided better service. JA recruited frontline staff and attendants who were freshers, so that they could be trained in their own way. If a flight is delayed, travellers are informed in advance. The airline tries to provide world-class benefits to its customers. It has also brought in new fare schemes, so that passengers get value for money. JA has a three-star rated Business and First Class and is in the top 25 business classes reviewed by Skytrax. It has three classes of services—First Class, Premiere Class and Economy Class.

Figure 10.6: In-flight experience as a symbol of luxury

Jet Privilege is the frequent flyer programme of JA. With five membership levels—Blue, Blue Plus, Silver, Gold and Platinum, it also has promotional schemes under JA Citibank Gold Card and JA Citibank Silver Card. The key features of this programme are ease of enrolment, easy tier upgrades and retention with the help of the Dynamic Tier Review (DTR) system.

10.3.4 Financial Performance

The company's revenue grew by 24.5 per cent year-on-year and 5.1 per cent quarter to quarter to ₹30,232.1 million in the first quarter of 2010. The Airline bagged a market share of 18.7 per cent in first quarter of 2010. The first quarter revenue of the company in 2009 was only ₹24,283.6 million. Now EBITDA is ₹4,604.9 million, PBT ₹35.4 million and PAT ₹35 million in August 2010. The effective change management strategies yield the best results only in the seat factor, which went up by 74 per cent in 2010. The capacity addition was to the tune of 2.5 per cent in domestic sector. The number of guest flown in 2009 were down by 1.2 per cent, ASKms down by 17.9 per cent, RPKms down by 4.6 per cent in 2009 when we compare the performance during the same period in 2008.

Table 10.5: Operational parameters

Operational parameters	*June–September 2009*
Revenue from operations	₹23,810 million
ASKms (in ₹million)	6,914
RPKms (in ₹million)	5,322
Seat factor	77%
Guest flown	2.79 million
Loss before tax	₹4,067 million
Source: www.jetairways.com	

However, in the international sector, Jet Airways scored well. Nearly 62 per cent of the revenue (₹14,676 million) came from that sector in 2009 when compared to 2008, during the same period, it was only 53 per cent. The seat factor improved to 80.6 per cent in 2009 from 66 per cent in 2008 during the same period. 1.03 million passengers flown in 2009.

Although aviation is not the most profitable of businesses to be in globally, Jet Airways did manage to make profits for many years. The domestic market through those years was broadly divided among Jet, Indian Airlines and erstwhile Air Sahara (now JetLite). The year 2005 saw the advent of many low-fare airlines and a dramatic growth in the number of air travellers 30–40 per cent per annum. Airlines jumped in with huge aircraft orders and offered aircraft seats almost of a frenzied pace. In 2007, the $340-million Jet committed what many feel was its first big mistake. It bought loss-making Sahara for ₹1,450 crore.

The buyout of Sahara was expensive and in hindsight not worth it. Many within Jet opine that the deal was not worth the amount of management time and attention it took. The stock market expressed its unhappiness with Jet's share price falling 30 per cent after the buyout was announced. Jet's struggle with the buyout coincided with the domestic environment getting tighter Many new airlines brought in substantial new capacity. Over-optimistic expectations with regard to growth rates led to overcapacity. According to SpiceJet's CEO Sanjay Aggarwal, 'Hundreds of aircraft were ordered and capacity was added like "there was no tomorrow"'. According to ICICIdirect.com equity research (August 2010), Jet Airways is doing well and analysts projected operating income of ₹16,230 crore, EBITDA of ₹2,615 crore and net profit of ₹979 crore in 2011.

Table 10.6: Flagging growth

Year	*Turnover (₹crore)*	*PAT*	*Remarks*
2002–3	2,942	– 244	Loss
2003–4	3,566	163	Profit
2004–5	4,420	392	Profit
2005–6	6,088	452	Profit
2006–7	7,401	28	Profit
2007–8	9,482	– 253	Loss
2008–9	13,153	– 402	Loss
2009–10	12,421	– 420	Loss
2010–11	14,272	525	Profit

Source: Investors' Report of Jet Airways, June 2010.

10.4 Performance Matrix

In India, air travel is still at its nascent stage of growth. Two million passengers travel in train every day. Even a tiny fraction from the burgeoning middle class who opt to migrate from first class train to low cost carrier would mean a huge jump for domestic air travel.

Indian Airlines, which had dominated the Indian air travel industry, began to lose market share to Jet Airways and Sahara. Today, the Indian airlines industry is dominated by private airlines which include low-cost carriers such as Kingfisher Red, GoAir, SpiceJet, and so on, which have made air travel affordable. Let us look at the customer segmentation of premium segments (Figure 10.7).

CUSTOMER SEGMENTATION

The common strategy is to squeeze as much profit as possible from business class passengers and fill the rest of the seats and ensure growth by attracting economy class passengers:

(i) **Business passengers:** Customers attracted by superior services and corresponding high prices. Premium services provided include seats equipped with faxes, and other delights like gambling machines, showers, massage service and suit ironing.

(ii) **Leisure travellers:** Price being their major consideration, will not pay extra for premium services.

The allocation of business and economy class seats on a plane is determined through a process called **yield management.**

Kingfisher Airlines

Target Audience – SEC A, B+; Age: 25–45 years

– Travelled extensively

Modern trendy, upwardly mobile, looking for a great flying experience.

Figure 10.7: Customer segmentation of premium segments

Table 10.7: Financial performance of Jet Airways

Traffic parameters	*April–December 2008*	*April–December 2007*	*Variance %*
Number of departures	1,02,098	92,672	10.2
ASKms (₹ in million)	24,684	16,763	47.3
RPKms (₹ in million)	16,446	11,463	43.5
Passenger load factor (%)	66.6	68.4	–1.8 points
Block hours	2,40,200	1,90,229	26.3
Revenue passengers (₹ in million)	8.54	8.26	3.5
Revenue per RPKm (in ₹)	4.55	4.50	1.2
Cost per ASKm (in ₹)	3.63	3.29	10.5
Break even seat factor (%)	79.8	73.1	6.7 points
Cost per ASKm in ₹ w/o fuel	1.88	1.97	–4.4
Breakeven seat factor (%) w/o fuel	41.3	43.7	–2.4 points
Average gross revenue per passenger in ₹*	9,417	6,708	40.4
Period end fleet size	88	76	15.8
Average fleet size during period	83.8	64.6	29.8
Average head count	—	—	—
Gross	13,518	11,408	18.5
Aircraft utilization	10.4	10.7	–2.9

*ROE used for conversion: 1 US$ = ₹48.71 for third quarter of 2009 and 1 US$ = ₹39.415 for third quarter of 2008

Source: Jet Airways financial results, third quarter of FY 2008–9.

Intense competition and rivalry in luxury and customer services made the players adopt aggressive strategies to take over the weak links in the industry. Accordingly JA identified Air Sahara and Kingfisher opted for strategic partnership with Air Deccan for continuing their dominance. Ultimately JA lost its market share from 31.22 per cent in 2006 to 26 per cent in 2010 (Figure 10.8). Kingfisher gained a lot in the competition. Surprisingly both are now making huge losses and their future looks bleak as does the outlook for the LCAs. Figure 10.8 shows the market share of various domestic airlines.

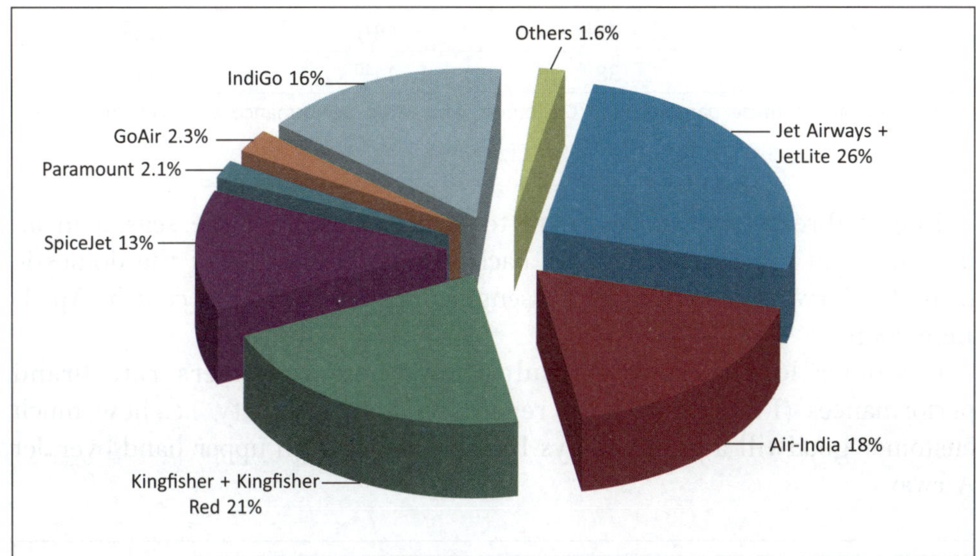

Figure 10.8: Market share of various domestic airlines

As on May 2010 Jet Airways had a market share of 27 per cent in August 2010. The introduction of 'Jet Konnect' has helped the airline to successfully fight competition from LCA (IndiGo, SpiceJet and Paramount) as well as FSC (Kingfisher and Air-India).

Table 10.8: Operating highlights

Traffic parameters	*2007–8*	*2008–9*	*2009–10*
Available seat Km (₹ in million)	24,447	31,652	29,242
Revenue passenger Km (₹ in million)	16,914	21,444	22,640
Passenger load factor (%)	69.2	67.7	77.4
Departure (number)	1,26,676	1,33,736	1,31,108
Revenue passenger (₹ million)	11.43	11.08	12.04
Cargo (tons)	1,65,757	1,81,432	1,87,802
EBITDA (₹ million)	7,508.2	4,061	19,854.7
Operating revenue (₹ million)	88,111	1,14,769.7	1,03,596.9
Average head count	—	13,843	11,328
Average fleet size	—	84.5	85.6

Source: Investors' Report of Jet Airways, June 2010.

Table 10.9: Performance measures of service providers

Performance measures	*Airline industry**	*Jet Airways*	*Kingfisher*	*Air-India*
Ticketing and purchase experience	52	51	59	53
Preboarding experience	44	46	57	41
Boarding experience	47	43	59	43
In-flight experience	50	55	62	44
Call centre/helpline	42[19]	30[30]	48[15]	69[13]
Loyalty programme	71	69	–	–
Advertising and communication	43[12]	41[11]	50	36[15]
Schemes offered	41[16]	43[15]	48[12]	33[20]
Tie-ups offered	44[14]	38[16]	44[10]	41[17]

Superscript: Percentage of people who were unhappy in these parameters; *'Customers who rated performance as 'excellent or very good'.
Source: CSMM-BW loyalty report.

Empty threats and strikes seem to be the flavour of the season in an industry that appears to have its back against the wall. On the domestic front Jet Airways' revenue per passenger declined by 26 per cent in April-June 2009.

Customer loyalty survey result shows how customers rate brand performances (Figure 10.9). As regards customer loyalty, i.e. how much customer goodwill a brand enjoys Kingfisher holds an upper hand over Jet Airways.

Figure 10.9: Ranking of customer experience

KINGFISHER, LOW-COST CARRIERS EAT INTO JET'S MARKET SHARE

In 2007, a year that witnessed three domestic airline mergers in India and saw an easing of a bruising price war among airlines, Jet Airways India Limited, and State-run Air-India yielded share to start-up carriers in a passenger market that expanded about a third, according to reports from the Directorate General of Civil Aviation (DGCA). Jet Airways' share dropped from 31.2 per cent in 2006 to 22.6 per cent in 2007, although the acquisition of Sahara Airlines (now JetLite India Limited) helped it retain the mantle of the largest airline group in India with a 29.9 per cent share of the 43.3 million passengers who flew the Indian skies last year. This customer base grew 32.51 per cent in 2007 over 2006.

Jet Airways' share was eaten into by both Kingfisher Airlines and discount carriers, an aviation expert said. The airline 'finds itself sandwiched between the two,' said Subodh Gupta, an aviation analyst at N.M. Rothschild India Private Limited. 'The business traveller has been taken away by Kingfisher and the bottom layer has been taken away by the low-cost carriers especially on metro routes.' Kingfisher Airlines saw its share increase by 3.5 percentage points in 2007 while Deccan, lost 1 percentage point in the same period. Together, the group reported a 29.3 per cent share. Air-India's share dropped to 19 per cent from 21.5 per cent in 2006.

Wolfgang Prock-Schauer, chief executive of Jet Airways, attributed the decline in market share of his airline to a slow addition of capacity. The airline added just three aircraft compared with the 40 more that all other airlines put together did. 'We will be adding six ATRs and two more (jet) aircraft to our fleet,' he said. But that addition may not be enough given that other airlines plan to do more. Low-fare airline IndiGo added nine planes last year, helping it grow its share to 7.6 per cent from 1.3 per cent in 2006. Another low-fare airline Go Airlines India Limited saw its share climb to 4.2 per cent from 2.8 per cent, while SpiceJet Limited's share moved up from 6.9 to 8.8 per cent. The industry load factor, a measure of the percentage of seats with passengers on a plane, increased from 70.1 to 71.5 per cent.

Source: www.livemint.com

Table 10.10: Loyalty programme of service providers: a comparison

Kingfisher loyalty programme: King Club		*Jet Airways loyalty programme: JetPrivilege*	
Tiers of membership	• King Red • King Silver • King Gold	Tiers of membership	• Blue • Blue Plus • Silver • Gold • Platinum
Benefits	• Earn King Miles and redeem for free flights • Excess baggage allowance • Access to airport lounges • Priority baggage handling • Priority check-in at Kingfisher first counters • Pre-requested meals on-board	Benefits	• Tele check-in • Guaranteed reservation up to 24 hours before departure • Additional baggage allowance • Lounge access • Check-in at premiere counters
Partners	• Hotels • Telecoms • Publishing houses • Investment and insurance	Partners	• Banks • Car Rental • Hotels • Lifestyle

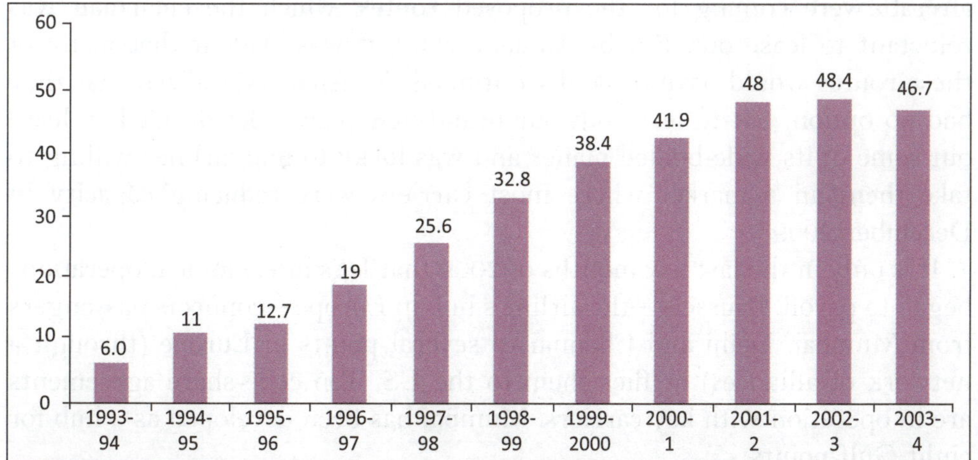

Figure 10.10: Market share (in %) of Jet Airways before the entry of Kingfisher (1993–4 to 2003–4)

Sources: www.livemint.com, economictimes.com and indiainfoline.com

10.5 Strategy Backfires for Jet Airways

In just three months (October–December) in 2007, the total number of international departures of Jet Airways shot up to 3,198 from 1,731 in October-December 2006, a rise of a whopping 85 per cent. Almost all the new offering were done with aggressive introductory fares. In just a few months, flights to 57 destinations spanned the length and breadth of India and beyond, including New York (both JFK and Newark), Toronto, Brussels, London (Heathrow), Singapore, Kuala Lumpur, Colombo, Bangkok, Muscat, Doha, Kuwait and Bahrain. At that time, Jet Airways had plans to extend its international operations to more cities in North America, Europe, Africa and Asia. A large number expat pilots were hired—there were 290 of them at the peak, of down to 140 in October 2009—to command the wide-body aircraft. However, in September 2008, with the global recession hitting hard, the airline's plans began to go awry. Jet Airways had expanded way too fast. Adding 18 wide-bodies in one year was a challenge. Many international routes that had looked attractive began to appear unviable. A much talked-about flight from Mumbai to San Francisco via Shanghai quickly totted up losses of $57 million. It became evident that adding all the proposed routes would be a sure recipe for disaster.

Table 10.11: Loss-making routes of Jet Airways

Routes	*Loss per annum ($ million)*
Amritsar-London (discountinued from 1 December 2008)	26.34
Bengaluru-Brussels (discountinued from 12 January 2009)	12.28
Mumbai-San Francisco (discountinued from 12 January 2009)	57.66
Calicut-Muscat (discountinued from 15 September 2008)	4.73
Delhi-Kuwait (discountinued from 1 September 2008)	4
Delhi-Dubai (downgraded to B737 from 15 December 2008)	3.64
Mumbai-Brussels (downgraded to A330 from 22 January 2009)	19.27

The saying that 'airlines order planes when times are good and receive them when times are bad' proved to be uncomfortably true for Jet. New aircraft were coming for the proposed routes, which the chairman was reluctant to lease out. But by January 2009, it was evident that many of these routes would have to be discontinued. Jet Airways realized that they had no option, but to lease out our brand-new planes. Jet decided to lease out some of its wide-bodied planes and was lucky to find airlines willing to take them, in a market where most carriers were reducing capacity in December 2009.

It is only in the last few months of 2009 that Jet's international operations began to payoff. Brussels—the airline's hub in Europe—connects passengers from Mumbai, Delhi and Chennai to several points in Europe (through a network of alliances) or flies them to the US. Ten code-share agreements are in operation with key carriers. Mumbai has been developed as a hub for eight Gulf points.

Jet Airways is fast evolving as a network carrier instead of a point-to-point carrier. The hub-and-spoke model is being developed to maximize

Table 10.12: Jet Airways' revenue per passenger on the international front

Traffic parameters	*April–June 2008*	*April–June 2009*	*Change (%)*
No. of departures	6,021	6,438	6.9
ASKms (₹ in million)	5,216	4,431	–15
RPKms (₹ in million)	3,374	3,391	0.5
PLF (%)	64.7	76.5	11.8
Revenue per passenger (₹ in million)	0.72	0.81	12.1
Revenue per RPKm (₹)	3.28	2.68	–18.1
Cost per ASKm (₹)	2.78	2.23	–19.9
Breakeven seat factor (%)	84.9	83	–1.9

Note: ASKm—Average Seat Km, RPKm—Revenue Per Km, PLF—Passenger Load Factor (how much of an airline's passenger carrying capacity is used)

Sources: www.jetairways.com and Annual Report 2008.

Table 10.13: The improvement of load factor on international routes in first quarter of 2010

Routes	*Q1FY2009*	*Q1FY2010*
United Kingdom	60.9	70.9
United States	67	79.6
ASEAN	67.7	83
Gulf	61.6	73.2
SAARC	66	71.7

traffic and revenues. A little over half the airline's revenues in 2009 came from international operations. The airline sees the two—domestic and international—as 'two equally strong pillars'. Since fuel for international operations can be uplifted at a lower rate, the average revenue per passenger on international routes has been much higher than domestic. In fact, aviation analysts and senior aviation ministry officials say it was Jet's international foray that helped it withstand the carnage in the domestic market. Jet Airways may have expanded too fast, but the international network provided a buffer against the steep drop in domestic traffic.

Jet left no stone unturned in its drive to cut cost. The airline drew up a $600-million improvement plan on three fronts—wastage reduction, network restructuring and cost saving and cash conservation—implemented with a missionary zeal.

Vendors and lenders can vouch for its fighting spirit. Term loans, maintenance and lease agreements have been renegotiated. Improved credit lines were worked out with fuel providers. It closed down some city offices and gave up space at airports. Catering costs were cut.

The airline cut staff by 2,515 people in 2009–10. A handful of senior people took a 25 per cent salary cut, 400 employees a cut in a graded manner and allowances for pilots and crew reduced. In short, anything that could be cut has been or will be cut. The salary cut wasn't a huge saving but it sent a message that the company was entering this kind of cost-cutting or even turnaround mode. International route rationalization helped save money. Stopping four-five routes that were burning close to $4-$5 million a month would net the airline $60 million on an annual basis.

Jet Konnect is Born

If things stabilized on the international front, Jet's domestic traffic took a big hit on various counts in the past two years. Internet, video-conferencing and other technologies have reduced the 'lap-top' crowd's—Jet's primary clientele—propensity to travel. Also, many less price-sensitive fliers were taken away by Kingfisher's glitz and glamour, wooed by both a better experience at the airport initially (Kingfisher was using Indian Airlines' terminal and the terminals allotted to private airlines were a nightmare) and on-flight pampering (the entertainment system and gourmet cuisine).

But ever since the downturn hit in the second half of 2008, Jet's domestic traffic moved southward at an alarming pace. The airline quickly cut domestic capacity in a phased manner by 20 per cent. Despite that, by January 2009 loads on Jet's economy class were down to 55-60 per cent—new lows as far as the airline was concerned.

Jet's senior management also watched in horror at the rapidity with which the market was moving towards the low-fare segment. 'We noticed two trends. One, morning and evening departures do well and traffic dips during the day. Second, Jet flights were pretty full on weekdays, but on the weekends there was a dip, whereas for the low-fare airlines it was the reverse,' says Anita Goyal, executive vice-president, network planning and revenue management of Jet Airways. Call it two-faced if you like, but Jet wanted to present one face on weekdays, and another on weekends.

That proved easier said than done. That's when the management decided that a new low-fare brand, targeted at leisure travellers and avoiding prime-time departures, could answer their dilemma. In what may well be record time for the launch of any new brand, over a four-hour brainstorming session on 23 April 2009 Jet Konnect (the name retains the 'connect' with the mother brand Jet Airways) was born. It was launched—in panic, it would appear—two weeks later on 8 May 2009. 'Jet Konnect was the fastest and cheapest way to respond to this trend. In a very short time, we created a low-cost carrier of the size of IndiGo or SpiceJet,' says Wolfgang Prock-Schauer, ex-CEO of Jet Airways. The airline pulled out the business class seats from the aircraft and launched Jet Konnect with six ATRs and three Boeing 737s. It operates over 125 flights a day with a fleet of 10 ATRs and 9 Boeing 737s as of November 2009.

By October 2009, Jet Konnect constituted two-third of the airline's total domestic capacity, up from the earlier one-third (revenues from the two will be roughly the same). The airline's chief commercial officer, Sudheer Raghavan, says the changeover is 'flexible'. 'If we feel there is a shift again, we will just put in the business-class seats again and nothing will be lost.' The speed with which it could be done was also highly attractive. 'The time between decision and implementation was very short. We didn't have to market or spend on advertising,' he adds.

Jet Konnect allows Jet to convert its existing capacity to a low-fare option without creating a new airline. Jet Konnect will be positioned between full-service Jet and JetLite. Even the latter has now finally begun to payoff—the airline posted a ₹2 crore net profit in the first quarter of 2009–10. 'For the first time in many months, I can say JetLite is now fixed,' says Prock-Schauer.

A huge question mark remains over Jet's new strategy. Can Jet do what many global giants have failed to do? There has been no case globally where a strategy of the kind employed by Jet—a legacy carrier running a low-cost airline under the same wing—has worked. Aviation experts say the model has inherent problems since the low-fare wing begins to 'cannibalize' the legacy carrier's market. But by setting up Jet Konnect and running JetLite, Jet has done precisely what the experts say should not be done.

But Jet Airways insists that routes of the carriers have been planned so as not to 'cannibalize' each other's market. Jet Airways had to see what worked for them and at that moment it was pushing up seat factors. Prime-time departures were avoided for Jet Konnect services so that it does not touch Jet Airways' share of the pie. Jet, Jetlite and Jet Konnect will have minimum overlap on routes, frequencies and timings, so that each targets a different segment of travellers. Jet Airways have handpicked flights to avoid overlaps.

The airline's gamble appeared to be working. By targeting leisure customers on Jet Konnect, company officials say loads were finally climbing back to mid- to high 70s from the low- to mid-60s at the end of 2009. Despite a fall in yields, revenues increased because more seats were filled. Director General of Civil Aviation's December 2009 statistics showed a drop in Jet and JetLite's market share (to about 26 per cent in 2008 from 20 per cent in 2009). In the best of times, aviation is not the most profitable business to be in. In today's scenario, raising money to fund airline operations is close to impossible.

Many aviation experts say not only does the legacy airline lose passengers to its own lost-cost subsidiary, costs are inherently higher for legacy carriers. Legacy airlines have a higher cost structure built in. Jet's DNA is full service and so higher cost. Unless they can lower that dramatically, no one sees how Jet Konnect can work. Typically, the low cost airlines in India have a cost per ASKm (Available Seat Kilometres) of 2 or 2.25, whereas that of the legacy airlines is almost double.

Jet officials counter this argument by saying that Jet Konnect with more seats per airplane (170-180 versus 144), a low cost (no catering cost and some revenue from selling food) and lesser crew per flight, already has a lower cost per ASKm (3.4-3.5) than Jet Airways (4.5). The goal is to bring it down to 3 per ASKm. Although direct comparisons are unfair (headcount depends on aircraft mix), employee-aircraft ratio needs to be closer to 100 : 1 than 130-odd, which is the case with Jet in 2009.

But a more serious problem that Jet may need to contend with is the hit to its reputation. While passengers swear by Jet's international product offering, some of Jet's sheen has rubbed off with the entry of younger players such as IndiGo and SpiceJet, which have offered people credible, efficient and on-time service, with fair prices. Many travellers felt that there seems to be a reordering of the tiers of quality in the domestic skies. IndiGo has moved way ahead in value-for-money, and probably even ahead on overall quality, though some still put Kingfisher (not Red) there. Jet is one or two notches below. Many company executives have become wary of Jet in the last couple of months as the airline began to cancel flights without sufficient warning. Jet officials say this was an aberration because schedules were hit when they pulled out planes to convert them to Jet Konnect's configuration. Many experts feel Jet's reliability is questionable. That is a pretty serious allegation for an airline that is legendary for its service and reputation.

Then, there could be things well beyond Jet's control. Investors—the world over—are refusing to bite the aviation bait. With a $3-billion debt—although there are assets on Jet's books against this debt, unlike other airlines—the company desperately needs to raise around $400 million in stages (either through equity or through sale and lease back). But, for over two years, Jet made no progress on this front. Jet was listed in 2005 with a price of ₹1,100 per share—a level it has never touched since.

Also, one of Jet's main strengths in the past has been its 'lack of unionisation', as many observes it. They argue that Air-India can never compete with a Jet unless it puts its unions 'in place'. Despite Jet's high staff turnover and an HR disaster when it tried to fire around 1,900 staffers at one go—pilots and crew so far have been no real trouble to the management. But the National Aviators Guild, set up in July 2009 to represent around 650 Jet pilots, threatens to change that. Jet management is refusing to recognize the guild.

The following are the corrective measures including financial and operational steps taken by the Jet Airways as on December 2009 to start making profits again:

- Discharged 150 expat pilots
- Salary cuts effected for managers of grade III and above
- Renegotiation of contracts with vendors
- Released 43 managers on completion of contractual employment
- Released of crew employed in overseas stations
- Reduction in catering costs and meals
- Surrender of excess space at airport, city and corporate offices
- Surrender of lounges (one in domestic and one in international) in Mumbai
- Reduction in staff fuel benefits
- Renegotiation of volume credits with Indian Oil Corporation

Like rival Kingfisher, Jet Airways is a one-man show (without Naresh Goyal or Vijay Mallya, both companies would be rudderless), making it a shared weakness. But unlike Kingfisher, which is yet to build a strong foundation, Jet already has one. It has a phenomenal network and expanded by 20 aircraft from April 2007 to 70 aircraft in 2009 .

According to Wolfgang Prock-Schauer, since 2008, it has been tough for the entire aviation industry in India, not just for his airline, and he doesn't think that the rise of one airline—with India and its gigantic market—has to necessarily coincide with the fall of another. 'While things may look rosy for Kingfisher right now, Jet has been through and survived worse,' says a former Jet Airways board member, his point being that Mallya should not underestimate Goyal's strengths. 'I have never known a man so persistent once he's made up his mind. If Naresh Goyal wants to talk to you, no matter which corner of the world you are in, he will get to you,' says a former Jet board member, adding that after he's got what he wants out of you, it may be a long while before you hear from him again.

Goyal's problems on employee turnover were intensified when four senior executives of the airline resigned together in April 2007, including the highly trusted vice-president for corporate and public affairs, Nandini Verma, who'd spent 20 years with Jet. Jet's attrition rate has been constant and that in any industry with competition and new opportunities, things like this will happen.

Goyal has a phenomenal network across the world, knows his business like Mallya knows liquor, and never forgets a face, name or number. A hard taskmaster, he expects a lot from his staff. The Sahara acquisition in retrospect looked better than one would imagine: the airline had ordered 10 B737-800s, which in today's market would fetch a premium; it gained two hangars in the process (which Jet was finding difficult to get) and entered the lower-end market segment where growth is concentrated today. Twenty-one of its 24 aircraft are up and running and a turnaround looks within reach, Jet officials believe.

The other factor in Jet's favour is a recognition of Kingfisher's strengths, especially in terms of quality. CEO Prock-Schauer says: 'We have to take the product and the quality of its service very seriously,' but he maintains that none of this is reflecting on Jet's loads. 'Our business class loads have not gone down and our Jet Privilege membership is expanding rapidly. Yes, instead of people saying "I fly only one airline," they now choose. But that hasn't made any material difference to us,' he says, arguing that his airline's strong brand and obsession with quality and consistency will stand the test of time.

The airline business the world over is cyclical, primarily about keeping costs in check to ensure survival. And here is where Jet Airways officials feel it has a distinct edge over rival Kingfisher. In the end, they feel, this one factor alone will separate the wheat from the chaff.

10.6 Foul Game or Not

With rising incomes and a large population of young people eager to travel, the airlines industry is likely to generate higher revenue. The emerging economy along with a travel-minded youth has made India the world's fastest-growing and most competitive aviation market.

Domestic passenger traffic is expected to touch 60 million by 2012 and reach 200 million by 2025. Among India's passenger carriers, however, the outlook is challenging as long as the fare wars continue. Discounted tickets represent 20 per cent of total fares in India versus a global average about 10 to 15 per cent. The price war in the industry to preserve market share, even if it meant selling at below the cost of doing business, has seen all the participants bleed profusely. Budget airlines can't make tickets any cheaper, and price wars are likely to end.

Although the demand for air travel is increasing in India, as of now supply exceeds demand. Further consolidation has started in the sector, and is expected to intensify over the next five years. The three main airlines—Air-India, Jet Airways and Kingfisher—with an 65 per cent market share are therefore expected to strengthen their position further.

The Competition Commission of India (CCI) is studying whether a particular airline has a dominant market share on various routes or city pairs which might lead to anti-competitive practices. According to Amitabha

Kumar, director general, CCI, they have commissioned a study on the various competition issues in the civil aviation sector in India. Among other things, the study will look at the performance of airlines in various city pairs as well as the time slots allotted to various airlines.

Industry experts believe that sector and slot-specific domination would be a better way to look at market domination of a particular airline which could lead to anti-competitive practices rather than total market share of passengers carried across the country. While market share of an airline shows its share of the total number of passengers carried in the country, looking at a sector-wise market might be very different. For instance, while low-cost carrier GoAir has an overall market share of 3.1 per cent as of September 2009, it has a disproportionately larger share of around 13 per cent in the Mumbai-Delhi sector. Similarly, although the Kingfisher-Deccan combine has a market share of 29.3 per cent as of September 2009, its share of flights in most Bengaluru-connected sectors such as Bengaluru-Mumbai, Bengaluru-Hyderabad is 40-50 per cent. The combine also has a huge advantage in terms of key flight slots out of Bengaluru. For instance, in the Bengaluru-Chennai sector, the combine operates six out of nine flights in the key business class time slots of 6-9 a.m. and 6-9 p.m. Similarly, the combine operates around 7 out of around 13 flights in the key morning and evening slots in the Bengaluru-Hyderabad sector.

In the Delhi-Mumbai sector, the Jet Airways-JetLite combine has a market share of around 25 per cent, which is close to its overall market share of 29.9 per cent. However, the carrier operates almost 35-40 per cent of the business schedule slots in this sector, which is the single largest revenue contributor for an airline in the country. On the other hand, GoAir has most of the flights in the daytime and afternoon slots. Also, the Jet-JetLite combine has a share of almost 50 per cent in western Indian markets such as Mumbai-Ahmedabad and Mumbai-Indore.

10.7 Slow Down

The world's airlines are collectively lost $9.9 billion in 2009. The International Air Transport Association raised its forecast for 2010 industry losses as the deteriorating global economic conditions further hit demand for air travel and cargo. By March 2010, cargo and passenger traffic were within 1 per cent of prerecession highs. But yields were 13 per cent down. Risks such as the Greek debt crisis and the ice/andic volcano eruption remain large unknown. Globally premium travel fell 25 per cent, economy travel fell 9 per cent, the decline softened by a shift to cheaper seats. Overall passenger demand dropped 2.1 per cent in 2009. By the end of 2009, passenger capacity in international market had shrunken by 5 per cent and freight capacity by 10 per cent.

India's two largest private carriers, Jet Airways (India) Ltd and Kingfisher Airlines Ltd, took another hit at the low-fare, no-frills segments in a clear and renewed attempt to break into that market during the slowdown. Jet Airways launched Jet Konnect that is 15 per cent cheaper than the full-service option, despite already running low-fare service airline JetLite. Again,

Kingfisher converted 25 full-service flights to its low-fare segment Kingfisher Red on 15 May 2009. Full-service carriers have been pulling back flights in an attempt to trim seat capacity in the air, while their low-cost peers are increasing frequency of flights and are on course to take delivery of planes ordered. Airlines are also offering lower fares through imaginative promotions, both their own as well as through online booking sites.

The website www.makemytrip.com offered 50 per cent cash back on a ticket's base fare were when passengers booked using an HDFC Bank credit card in October 2009. The offer was for up to ₹2,500. Air ticket fares in India comprise a base fare, fuel surcharge and levies such as airport fee. Online travel firm Yatra Online Pvt. Ltd (Yatra.com) offered up to 60 per cent discounts on domestic flights if booked 30 days in advance in 2009.

To celebrate its 16th anniversary, Jet Airways introduced a special 'scratch and win' promotion wherein fliers were guaranteed a 6-16 per cent discount on the base fare (taxes and charges are extra) in 2009. It has also introduced special return fares for economy, business and first class to London from several Indian cities between 11 May and 30 June 2009. Kingfisher allows its boarding pass to be used for discounts at partner firms such as Taj Hotels, car rental firm Hertz, electronics retail chain Croma, and purchases from stores of designers Satya Paul and Rohit Bal. Whether such incentives drew passengers back, however, is an entirely different issue. Domestic carriers have seen passenger traffic decline by almost 10 per cent for fiscal 2009, from 43.97 million to 39.40 million, according to the DGCA. International traffic for the same fiscal was almost unchanged.

Further, average airfares for fiscal 2009 fell by 10-20 per cent to Europe, 10-40 per cent to Malaysia, Singapore and Thailand and at least 10 per cent to countries such as Australia and New Zealand. Indian carriers, whose expectations of a surge in passenger growth were dashed by the global

SLASHING JOBS, RETRENCHING EMPLOYEES AND PAY CUTS

The Indian aviation industry carried 39 million passengers in 2008–9 as against 44 million in 2007–8. The combined losses of the industry are estimated to rise from ₹4,000 crore in 2007–8 to ₹10,000 crore in December 2009.

In 2007–8, Jet Airways' salary bill had shot up to ₹1,205 crore from ₹938 crore in 2006–7. From a market share of 45 per cent in January 2006, the airlines' share had dropped to 16.7 per cent in May 2009. By that time, Kingfisher had consolidated its market leadership position to 25 per cent in May 2009. Battling the clawing downturn enveloping the aviation industry, Jet Airways laid off 1,900 employees in December 2008. This move was expected to save US$ 1 million a month.

However, within 48 hours, owing to high political pressure, Jet Airways Chairman Naresh Goyal made a dramatic announcement revoking the termination of employees who were retrenched. However in May 2009, Jet Airways imposed a pay cut of 25 per cent for the employees who draw salaries above ₹75,000 and axed 50 top executives as a part of its restructuring. Jet staff strength across the country was 13,200 in 2009.

Vijay Mallya-promoted Kingfisher Airlines also slashed salaries of its trainee pilots 'significantly' as part of the cost-cutting initiatives of the company. Kingfisher had laid off nearly 300 workers in December 2008. Chief Vijay Mallya gave enough hints of these measures, saying the company would do whatever it took to cut costs. Line pilots and commanders of flights, were, however, exempted. However, in early 2009, Kingfisher slashed the salary of its pilots by ₹1 lakh and trainee pilots were sanctioned an allowance of ₹25,000 per month and asked not to join immediately. Further, Kingfisher, cut its fleet size, pushed 25 Kingfisher flights into Kingfisher Red (low cost) and reduced flights in the domestic circuits in May 2009.

Source: Business Standard, January 2010.

economic downturn, high fuel prices and excess seat capacity, were now staring at a collective $2 billion in losses for the fiscal 2009. Part of the reason for the airlines' declining fortunes, was their over-reliance on a narrow, but premium, segment of fliers. The primary reason behind erosion of yields on international routes was due to weak seat occupancy in the front end. On domestic routes, passengers are sliding towards low fare side. Seating on commercial planes are designed such that premium (first and business class) seats are placed in the front section of the aircraft. Business class sections typically cost six-eight times more than economy fares, while first class fliers pay at least 10 times the price of an economy class ticket. Most painfully for network carriers in the Asia Pacific region, the unimaginable slump in premium travel—a larger market segment than for other parts of the world—seriously undermined a bloated over-reliance on high yielding traffic. The suddenness of the reversal, along with a large backlog of aircraft orders in this region, caught managements unaware and unprepared.

Summary

Faced with stiffening competition, increasingly demanding customers, high labour costs, and, in some markets, slowing growth, airline businesses around the world are trying to boost productivity. But whereas manufacturing businesses can raise it by monitoring and reducing waste and variance in their relatively homogeneous production and distribution processes, airline service businesses find that improving performance is trickier. Their classes of customers (Economy, Business and First Class) and deals vary too widely. Moreover, customer services are highly customizable, and people—the basic unit of productivity in services—bring unpredictability due to differences in experience, skills, and motivation to the job. Such seemingly uncontrollable factors cause many airline executives to accept a high level of variance in pre-flight and in-flight experiences and a great deal of waste and inefficiency in service costs.

Look at the demand and supply differentiators for premium service providers in the Indian aviation space. It has to be seen how airline companies are going to cross the breakeven mark after wiping off their accumulated losses in an era where airline companies are grounding their flights and gasping for survival. How are Goyal and Mallya, faced with losses of ₹880 and ₹2,000 crore respective, going to drive business in the aftermath of the downturn? It has to be seen in the days to come.

Case Discussion Questions

Assume that you are heading the research activities for a UK-based aviation organization to ascertain the demand of luxury seats in the US and UK circuits from Mumbai, New Delhi and Bengaluru airports.

(a) How do you undertake competitor analysis in the Indian civil aviation market for inbound and outbound flights? Explain the anticipated competitor response profile with current strategies, future goals and their capabilities with working assumptions.

(b) Explain the nature of the rivalry between full-range service carriers and LCAs. Also narrate the comparative assessment of competitors in terms of price, products, customer class, and in-flight and pre-flight customer service, within a category and across categories.

(c) In your opinion what may be the perceived benefits of a competitive information system and global intelligence system for international and domestic carriers? Also explain the competitive advantage on the business performance of JA and Kingfisher.

(d) Comment on the relevance and significance of differentiation, focus and low cost strategy for domestic carriers by utilizing the theory explained in this case.

CASE ANALYSIS

We have to first look at the major and minor problems followed by aviation industry and environmental analysis of the same.

Major Problems

1. Kingfisher Airlines

(a) Should it go ahead with its plan of non-stop flights to the US and increase its operating cost?

(b) Whether to buy the 113 aircrafts that it has ordered?

(c) How to turn the company into a profitable organization?

2. Jet Airways

(a) Whether to go for non-stop flights to the US or operate from its base at Brussels?

(b) Whether to buy the already ordered aircrafts and in case they take delivery how to use them profitably?

(c) How to improve its service to match Kingfisher, which is a benchmark in passenger services?

(d) In case Jet Airways also goes for increased services, then how can it contain the cost?

(e) How can it make the company profitable?

Minor Problems

1. Kingfisher Airlines

(a) Kingfisher, which has established itself as a full-service airlines and differentiated itself from other airlines by offering world-class services to its passengers, fears brand dilution following the acquisition of low cost carrier Air Deccan.

(b) Price war with Jet Airways is eating into margins and creating problems for the already loss-making company.

2. Jet Airways

(a) Jet Airways has also acquired Sahara Airlines which it is sub-branding as JetLite. The airline fears brand dilution that may happen due to the sub-branding.

(b) Price war with Kingfisher Airlines is eating into margins.

3. Problems for Both

Both the airlines are not sure whether they should suspend services on the unprofitable routes and discontinue with those aircrafts to reduce leasing expense.

Environmental Analysis of Both Companies

The factors contributing to the air traffic growth can be broadly classified into economic and policy factors. Business cycles have a wide reaching impact on the airline industry. During recession, air travel is considered a luxury and therefore spending on it is reduced, which leads to reduced prices. During times of prosperity people indulge in travel and prices increase. In view of the recessionary phase prevalent in the United States and slowdown experienced by most countries around the world, airline revenues have been impacted severely. The loss of income for airlines has led to higher operational costs not only due to low demand but also due to higher insurance costs, which increased after the WTC bombing. This has prompted the industry to lay off employees, which has further fuelled the recession as spending has decreased due to the rise in unemployment.

Effects of the liberalization and economic reforms undertaken by the government include:

Fast expansion of industries in consonance with economic reforms
Emergence of service sector
Average GDP growth of around 8.9 per cent during the last 5 years
Increase in inbound and outbound tourists and medical tourism
Over 300-million strong middle class
Disposable incomes expected to increase at an average of 8.5 per cent per annum till 2015
Emergence of low cost airlines
The organized retail boom that would require the need for timely delivery thus contributing to the growth in the air cargo segment
Corporate showing increasing preference for private jets and air charter services
Modernization and setting up new airports across country
City-side development of non-metro airports
Providing international airport status to major tier I and tier II cities
Open sky policy
Policy of licence to new scheduled operators
Permission to acquire new aircrafts
Permission to private operators to operate on international sectors
Encouraging private investments in airlines and airport infrastructure
Facilitative foreign direct investment norms
Liberal bilateral service agreements
Emphasis on development through PPP mode

The airline industry is susceptible to changes in the political environment as it has a great bearing on the travel habits of its customers. An unstable political environment causes uncertainty in the minds of the air travellers regarding travelling to a particular country.

Another aspect is that in countries with high corruption levels like India, bribes have to be paid for every permit and licence. The State-owned airlines suffer the most due to this problem. These airlines have to make several special considerations with respect to selection of routes, free seats to ministers, and so on, which privately owned airlines need not do. Some positive measures taken by the government in favour of the aviation industry are:

Open sky policy: International airlines are greatly affected by trade relations that their country has with others. Unless governments of two countries trade with each other, there could be restrictions on flying to particular area, leading to a loss of potential air traffic (e.g. Pakistan and India). India has this agreement with 40 countries and has lately signed the policy with the UK, USA and the European Union.

Modernization of airports: The Indian Cabinet has approved a proposal mandating the State-run airport operator to modernize 35 airports in second-tier cities within the next two years.

Reduction on excise duty: The excise duty on ATF was reduced thus leading to lower fares and giving a boost to air travel.

Landing charges abolished: There is no landing tax for aircrafts with less than 80 seats. The changing travel habits of people have very wide implications for the airline industry. In a country like India, there are people from varied income groups. The airlines have to recognize these groups and serve them accordingly. For instance, low cost airlines need to focus on their clientele which is mostly low income groups. The destination, kind of food, etc., have to be chosen carefully in accordance with the tastes of the major clientele.

PEST is an acronym for the Political, Economic, Social, and Technological factors of the external macro-environment. Such external factors usually are beyond a firm's control and sometimes present themselves as threats. Let us look at the gaps found in the Indian aviation sector:

Gaps Found

- Attracting customers
  - Advertisement is lacking
  - Community service is a form of persuasive communication
- Airport service
  - Infrastructure seems to be a bottleneck
- Lounge
  - Huge gap
- Onboard activity
  - Nothing innovative
- ATF
  - Hedging went wrong!

The average annual income of middle class households is expected to rise to ₹1,94,000 by 2011, while the number of households is projected to be 43.60 million. This will cause passengers to shift from railways' first air-

Table 10.14: Fleet size of scheduled operators as of August 2008

Airlines	*Fleet size*
NACIL (Air-India)	41
NACIL (Indian Airlines)	76
Air-India Express	20
Alliance Air	20
Jet Airways	87
Deccan Aviation	43
Kingfisher Airlines	43
JetLite	24
SpiceJet	18
IndiGo Airlines	19
GoAir	7
Paramount Airways Ltd.	5
MDLR	2
Jagson	2
Indus Airways	2

conditioned class to low cost airlines. There will be a rise in leisure travel with the growth in the tourism industry.

SWOT Analysis of the Indian Airline Industry

Strengths

1. Low entry barrier
2. Attraction of foreign shores
3. Foreign equity allowed
4. Rising income levels and demographic profile: The disposable income of people has increased due to increase in the income level, and this factor is supposed to increase the number of flyers.
5. Growing tourism: Growth in tourism has given a rise to both domestic and international passengers. The estimated growth of the domestic passenger segment is 50 per cent per annum and growth for the international passenger segment is 25 per cent.

Weaknesses

1. Under-penetrated market: The total passenger traffic was only 50 million in 2005, amounting to only 0.05 trips per annum in contrast to developed nations like United States that have 2.02 trips per annum.
2. Untapped air cargo market: The air cargo market has not yet been fully tapped in India. It is expected in the coming years to attract a large number of players with dedicated fleets.
3. Infrastructural constraints: Though the industry is growing fast, the infrastructure of the industry is not keeping pace.
4. Huge investments are required in the physical infrastructure of airports. Currently the location of airports is also unplanned.
5. There is an absence of institutionalized funding.
6. Acute shortage of trained pilots severely limits growth prospects.

Opportunities

1. Expected investments: Investments of about US$30 billion will be made by 2013.
2. Expected market size: Average growth of the aviation sector is about 25-30 per cent and the expected market size is projected to grow up to 100 million by 2013.
3. Huge investments are expected to take place in the aviation sector in the near future.
4. *Airlines liquidating assets*: Any airline going in for liquidation will help reduce the excess capacity that has been created.

Threats

1. High fuel cost is a major hindrance for growth.
2. Though a large number of LCAs have come into existence, the majority of the population is still unable afford to air travel and go for cheaper modes of transport.
3. There is shortage of airports. Many cities are still not connected by air, reducing the number of passengers.

4. Crippling 'Oil Shock'.
5. The large-scale use of technologies like videoconferencing and conference calls is limiting physical air travel.
6. All airlines in India are running at a loss (especially due to LCAs, which continue to offer dirt-cheap fares, much to the discomfort for full-service carriers). Full-service airlines have seen a dip in their market shares and yields.

Overview of the Aviation Industry

1. Pre-2004

(a) Domestic Market

Limited carriers (9W, S2, IC)
Stable 8-10 per cent growth per annum
Supply in line with demand
Yield stable at relatively high levels

(b) International Market

Restricted bilaterals–limited access to foreign carriers, Air-India/Indian Airlines the only designated Indian carriers. Both have limited fleet/networks. As a result, limited capacity to/from India.

2. Post-2004

(a) Domestic Market

Sudden inflow of new carriers and spurt in capacity.
High market growth stimulated by huge fare reductions.

(b) International Market

Opening up international markets commenced in 2003–4 with private carriers being allowed to fly international routes.

(c) Key Bilaterals Expanded

UK bilateral (56 + Open skies on all routes except Delhi/Mumbai-Lahore), USA (open skies), European countries (enhanced rights), ASEAN countries (enhanced rights).

3. Impact of Changes Post-2004

(a) Domestic Industry

Low yields/high fuel costs led to huge losses (estimated at $500 million for 2007).
Airport and air traffic infrastructure are under increasing pressure due to added capacity. Delays at major metros, lack of slot availability, high costs due to holding times (approximately $25 million in additional fuel burn for Jet Airways alone).
Ongoing airport privatization and modernization programmes at Mumbai, Delhi, Hyderabad and Bengaluru will relax capacity constraints to some extent by 2008–9.

(b) International Market

(i) Private carriers allowed to fly SAARC routes from 2003–4; international routes from 2005 onwards.

(ii) Key bilateral also liberalized and access increased substantially. BA increased from 18 to 43 frequencies, LH increased from 23 to 45 frequencies, SQ increased from 24 to 49 frequencies, EK increased form 42 to 71 frequenciees.
AA, DL, CCO started daily frequencies.

(c) Evolving Business Model

Air travel has now increasingly become a way of life rather than a luxury. The growth in passenger traffic figures so far has been driven by greater air connectivity, affordable air travel due to the emergence of low cost carriers and increased air capacity. However the industry has seen a few dark clouds looming over its growth story in recent times. Both full-service and budget carriers have seen a dip in passenger growth. Airport development has achieved considerable progress since the sector was first liberalized and private players allowed. Several PPP models have been developed for different airports, each catering to the requirements within the purview of the regulatory framework.

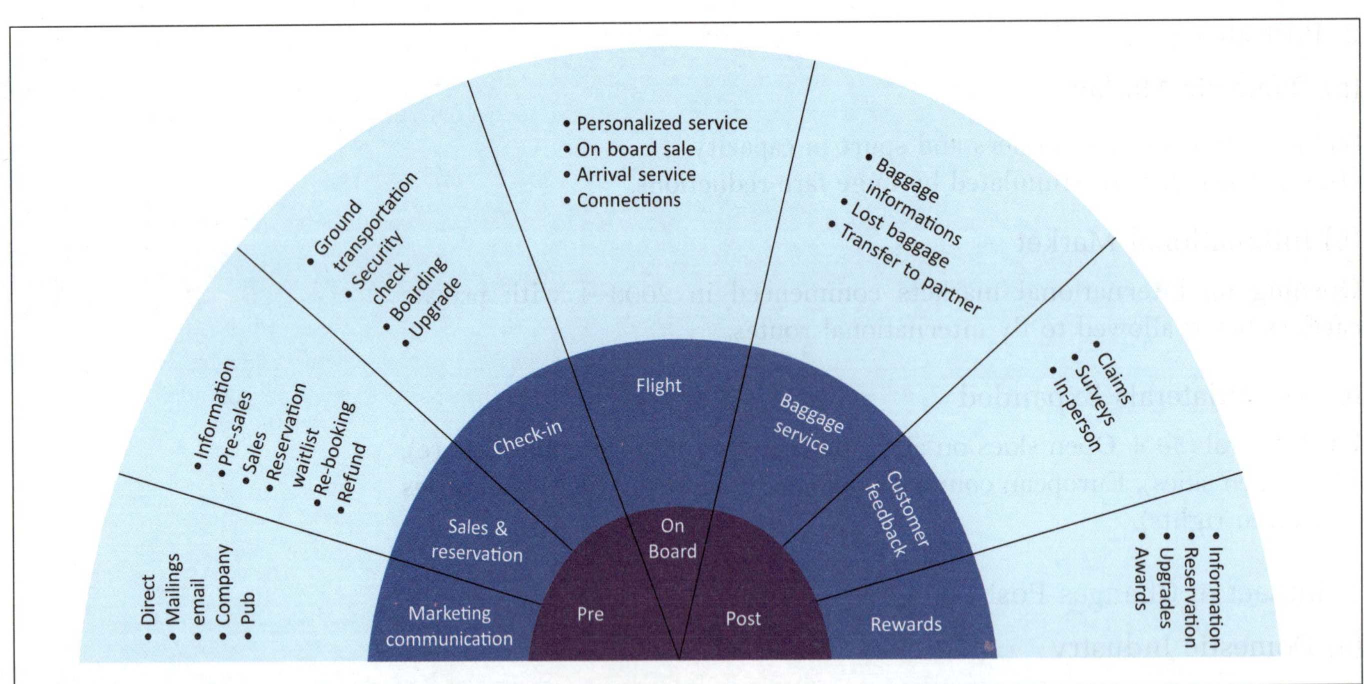

Figure 10.11: Market share of service providers

(d) Performance

From 2008 onwards, the market is anticipated to accelerate and post a higher compound annual growth rate (CAGR) for 2006–11 compared to that of 2002–6. The compound annual growth rate of the industry in the period 2006–11 is predicted to be 14.4 per cent. In 2011, the Asia-Pacific airlines industry is forecast to have a volume of 829.90 million passengers, an increase of 87.6 per cent since 2006. The compound annual growth rate of the industry volume in the period 2006–11 is predicted to be 13.4 per cent.

India is today one of the fastest expanding aerospace markets in the world, as a growing number of airlines and corporates are expected to acquire about a thousand planes over the next five years. Porter's Five Forces when analysed for the aviation industry can be summarized as hereunder:

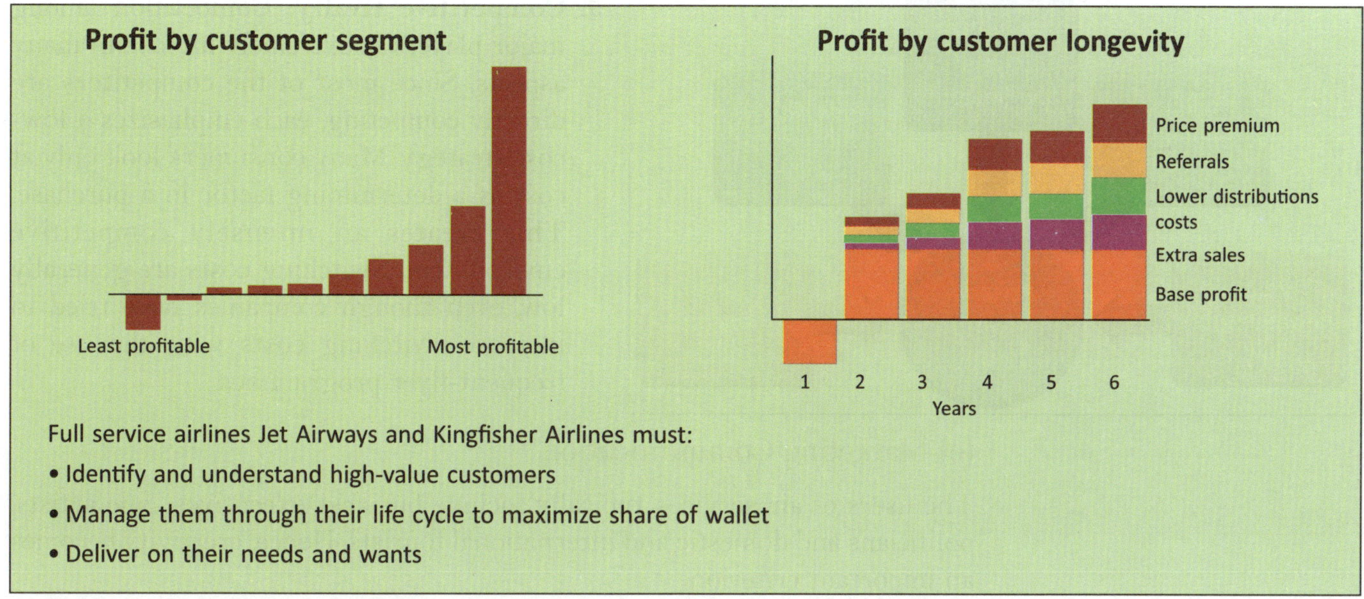

Figure 10.12: Understand and act upon customer value

1. **Threat of new entrants:** Entry into the airline industry is very hard due to several factors. These include government regulations and licensing, brand loyalty, contracts between airlines and airports for use of runways and terminals and the substantial cost associated with forming an airline (aeroplanes purchased, labour costs, fuel costs, maintenance, etc.). The three consolidated groups, Air-India, Jet Airways, and Kingfisher, dominate the Indian skies with 65 per cent market share.
2. **Power of suppliers:** In case of the airlines industry the suppliers have tremendous bargaining power. The aircraft supply business is mainly dominated by Boeing and Airbus. For this reason, there isn't a lot of cut-throat competition among aircraft suppliers. There exist limited fuel providers and no reliable alternative to fuel. Short supply of pilots and mechanics in the job market enables premium pricing. Moreover, flight attendants provide services that cannot be easily replicated. Lastly airports are in limited supply.
3. **Power of buyers:** Generally speaking consumers, business or regular travellers, have little bargaining power with the airlines. One traveller does not hurt the airlines. Either he/she buys the ticket or not. Also there are only select airlines to choose from and even less at some individual airports.
4. **Availability of substitutes:** Substitute products are of little threat to the airline industry, especially in long-distance travel. No other product

domestically competes directly with airlines in terms of speed of travel. The First AC fares of train are comparable with to those of the airlines. The lower class fares are less but travel is much slower and less comfortable. Bus services may cost less but travel speed is extremely slow and tedious. Besides there are many stops before the destination. Taxis are extremely expensive for long distances and are subject to speed limits and road layouts.

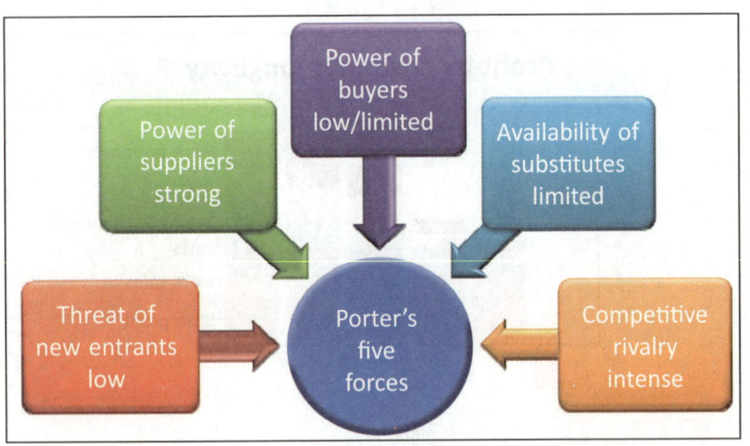

5. **Competitive rivalry:** Competition among major players is extremely intense in many aspects. Since most of the competitors are directly competing, each emphasizes a low-cost strategy. Many consumers look only at cost as a determining factor in a purchase. This creates an intensely competitive environment. Switching costs are generally low, even though companies have tried to increase switching costs with the use of frequent-flyer programmes.

(e) Marketing Communication

The users of air services typically include business executives, cine artists, politicians and domestic and international tourists. Hence, creativity becomes an important criterion.

Advertising should be done keeping in mind the quality and nature of the target audience as well as the level of expectations. Advertisement slogans, messages and campaigns need to be proactive. Conventionally, the airline sector advertising has been skewed towards news channels. Air-India faces an image problem but advertising may be efficacious in transmitting facts and removing the image problem.

The top five domestic airline advertisers together contributed to a 98 per cent share of the overall domestic airline advertising on TV during 2010.

In-flight advertising has recently been identified as an effective promotion medium in which the audience is 100 per cent captive. This is achieved by airing advertisements during entertainment programmes on television sets installed on the aircraft. Other than advertising via television screens, advertisers hop on-board and communicate through ad films inside and outside the aircraft. Kingfisher Red, formerly Air Deccan, had partnered with Cutting Age Media to effectively communicate through this non-traditional niche media.

Figure 10.13: Competitive advertising between airlines

Source: AdEx India (A division of TAM Media Research)

(f) Customer Segmentation

Most airlines use a very traditional segmentation strategy, dividing passengers into business travellers and economy travellers (mostly leisure travellers). The common strategy is to maximize profit from businesses-class passengers, and at the same time, fill the rest of the seats and ensure growth by attracting economy class passengers with lower fares.

(g) Business Passengers

They are crucial for airlines' profitability. With less spare time and more cash in their pockets, they agree to pay premium price for premium service. Today business passengers account for approximately 48 per cent of passengers, and these 48 per cent contribute 66 per cent of airlines' revenues. The premium price they pay provides them wider and more comfortable seats, better choice of meals, luxurious lounges.

Business passengers believe it is worth the extra money if they can save time and arrive looking fresh for a meeting. They will avoid transit flights even if a longer flight could save them money. But amongst other perks, flexible reservation services are probably the most important to them.

Reservations for business trips are often made just a couple of days in advance. A no-penalty cancellation policy is also very important to business passengers.

The best way to reach business travellers is through print advertising. Business news media, such as *The Economist* or *The Wall Street Journal* are some of the best publications through which airlines can reach business travellers. Many airlines design special promotional programmes that target corporate bookers and meeting planners who are responsible for business trips reservations. Frequent flyer programmes are an added bonus for business passengers.

(h) Leisure Travellers

They represent an entirely different market. The lower the airfare, the more people will fly the airline from the middle class. By and large, with the exception of some wealthy travellers, this segment will not pay extra for premium services.

Despite lower margins provided by this segment, leisure travellers are important to an airline's bottom line. Part of the reason is that technological progress in the area of tele-conferencing and increased use of the Internet for business communications is expected to reduce the number of business travellers. Thus, airlines are counting on the leisure segment to provide further growth.

An airline needs to maintain a fine balance between the growth opportunities in the leisure segment without losing immediate profit opportunities in the business segment. By improving services and reducing prices for economy class passengers, airlines risk that some business passengers will switch to economy class. On the other hand, if an airline focuses on business class passengers, it risks losing its economy class passengers to another airline.

The allocation of business and economy class seats on a plane is determined through a process called *yield management.* A good yield manager knows the approximate proportion of business and leisure travellers for each flight in advance, based on sophisticated statistical models. Thus he/she tries to sell the economy seats early at a cheaper price, while keeping enough seats reserved for business travellers, who usually book at the last minute. Keeping just the right amount of business seats reserved is important: selling too few economy seats in advance may result in a less-than-full plane while selling too many economy seats may result in a full plane, but with insufficient revenue to gain a profit. This kind of segmentation serves airlines well when implemented within one company. It would be very difficult for an airline to target just one of these two segments—business or leisure—successfully.

There are of course exceptions. Small regions that serve destinations where the major airlines do not fly, for example, are in a better position to implement a low price policy. They can even get business travellers to fly them despite the lack of premium services because no other airline would get them there. Premium airlines must focus on information, convenience and quality.

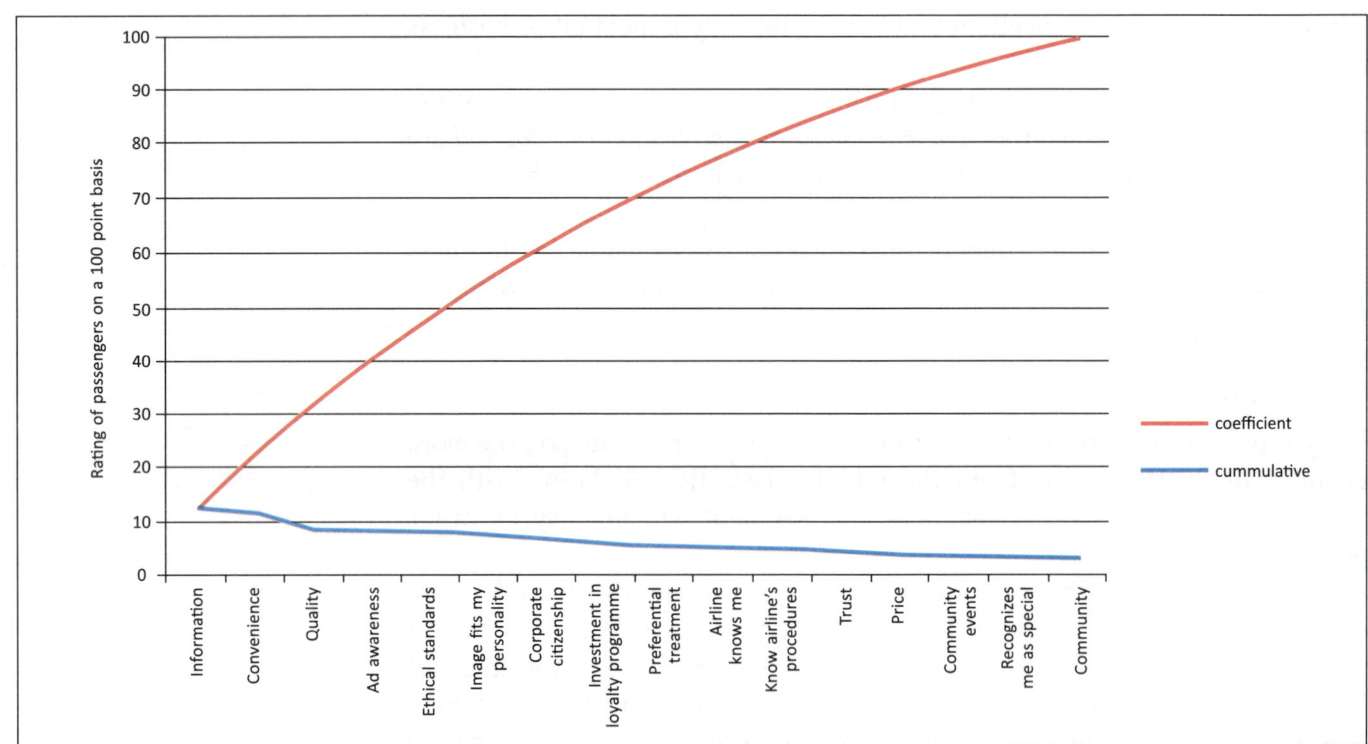

Figure 10.14: Rating of passengers

Source: Field data.

Table 10.15: How Kingfisher and Jet will respond to the current economic climate market share or profitability

S.No.	*Airline business model*	*Impact on reaction to current economic climate*
1	Age of current fleet	Older aircraft are less fuel efficient and more expensive to maintain. Operators with older fleets are at an increasing disadvantage as fuel prices increase
		Average age of Kingfisher Airlines: 1.7 years (March 2008). Average age of Jet Airways Aircrafts: 4.2 years
2	Intensity of routes	Focus on the more profitable routes. Kingfisher Airlines: Bengaluru-Mumbai, Bengaluru-Hyderabad (40–50%), Bengaluru-Chennai (66%)

S.No.	*Airline business model*	*Impact on reaction to current economic climate*
		Jet Airways: Delhi-Mumbai (35–40% in Business Class). Discontinue loss making routes (Jet)
		International Route: London, New York, San Francisco. Kingfisher flying to Dubai
3	Airline size	Larger airlines are better able to move capacity between routes, but tend to have a larger fixed cost base due to in-house capabilities. Kingfisher: 45 aircrafts. Jet Airways: 85 aircrafts.
		As airlines grow, they can stay flexible by outsourcing a majority of services. Jet to reduce by 25%. Lease out 15 from its fleet (4 to Gulf Air, 3 to Turkish), Kingfisher to lease 6 (2 to Arik, 4 to Air-India)
4	Financial backing	Large debt for Aircrafts. But payable over 12 years. Present value of aircrafts much higher than the loans outstanding against them Jet Airways: principal lenders being Citibank and Barclays. Raised, ₹1,000 crore from south banks.
		Kingfisher: Backing of United Breweries. ₹2,000 crore from SBI
5	Market experience	Kingfisher started in May 2005 and Jet Airways is operating from 1993

Overall, airlines seem to achieve best results when they subscribe to the segmentation theory, supported by yield management techniques and a careful monitoring of the economic changes in their geographical markets.

Look at the perceived value of both service providers in line with global best service provider.

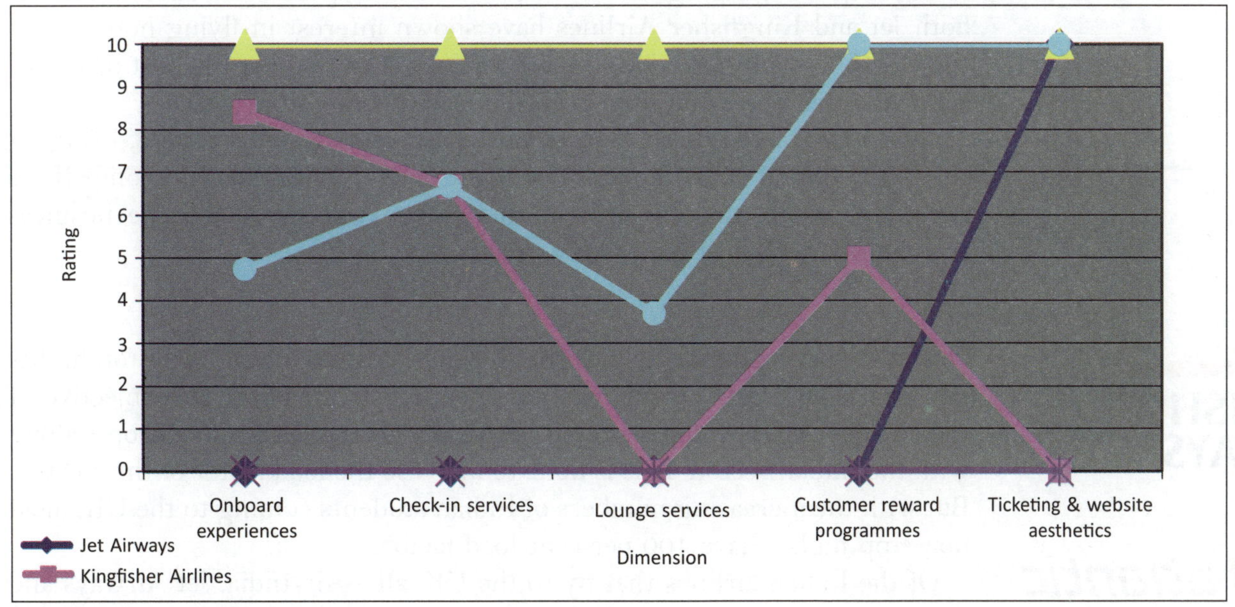

Figure 10.15 : Perceived use value

Recommendation for Jet Airways

- Advertisement
- Tie-up with events
- Charity and humanitarian activity
- More emphasis on membership programmes
- Lounge services need to be revamped
  – Kingfisher got a rating of 3/5!

Recommendation for Kingfisher Airlines

- Concentrate on premium segment
- Kingfisher is in a better position than Jet Airways
  - Intangibility (employee)
  - Younger and dynamic crew
  - Younger fleet
  - Better perceived value (customer matrix)
  - Force India (Formula One)

Questions

Assume that you are heading the research for a UK-based aviation organization for finding the demands of luxury seats in the US and UK circuit from Mumbai, New Delhi and Bengaluru airports.

Look at the various segments in the light of the case study facts.

None of the 27 international airlines that the US has operates a non-stop flight between India and any of the US cities. All these flights stop over in Europe to pick up passengers. This increases the flight timing. The main objective of every airline on this sector is to give superior service and experience and cater to both the European and the Indian markets using the same flights.

Of the Indian airlines that fly to the US, only Air-India has direct flights. Jet Airways also has flights that stop-over in Europe. But in the recent times both Jet and Kingfisher Airlines have shown interest in flying non-stop to the US. The main objective of these airlines is to provide the best on-board service and at the same time keep the prices competitive.

Air-India started direct flights to the US on 8 February 2008, bringing the flight timing to 15 hours. The main objective was to gain competitive advantage as it was the first in this category. It attracted the business travellers for whom time is very precious.

India-UK Segment

Of the 17 international airlines that UK has, only two have non-stop flights to India. These are Virgin Atlantic and British Airways. The objective of the airlines in UK-India segment is to cater to the Gulf and Europe, along with the Indian sector. This is done to increase the load factor of the airlines. But with the increasing numbers of Indian students coming to the UK, most non-stop flights have 100 per cent load factor.

Of the Indian airlines that fly to the UK, all—Air-India, Jet Airways and Kingfisher—have non-stop flights. The main objective of these airlines is to provide the best on-board service and at the same time keep the prices competitive.

Both Jet and Kingfisher enjoy high on-board rating from Skytrax.

Competitors' Strategy

India-US Segment

Of the international airlines, Delta is the market leader followed by American Airlines. The strategy followed by these airlines is to maintain a high load factor by catering to both the European and the Indian markets simultaneously.

But in February 2008, Air-India started its first non-stop flight to New York, which got a good response and helped it maintain a favourable load factor. This prompted some US airlines like Continental and Delta to operate non-stop flights to India. Most aircrafts in the US are 50 per cent leased and 50 per cent owned.

The US airlines comprise both luxury airlines, with five-star on-board service, and budget airlines like South-West which provide basic facilities. Most of these airlines have three classes with some having suite facilities.

Of the Indian airlines flying to the US, Air-India is the oldest. Jet started its operation in 1999 and Kingfisher is a new player in the segment. Air-India has the only non-stop service to the US, which gives it a competitive advantage over other players. Kingfisher is about to acquire long-haul flights and will soon start its non-stop flights to the US. Its strategy is to avoid establishing a base in the US and to operate non-stop flights. Jet Airways is also considering operating direct flights. Both these airlines have five-star on-board rating and in many cases offer better services than many of the American airlines.

The Indian airlines mostly lease aircrafts, from other airlines or firms, and as a result have high operating expenses. During times of downturn, companies may consider returning the aircrafts if the same loss prevails.

India-UK Segment

Of the international airlines, British Airways is the market leader followed by Easy Jet. The strategy until now has been to cater to the Indian

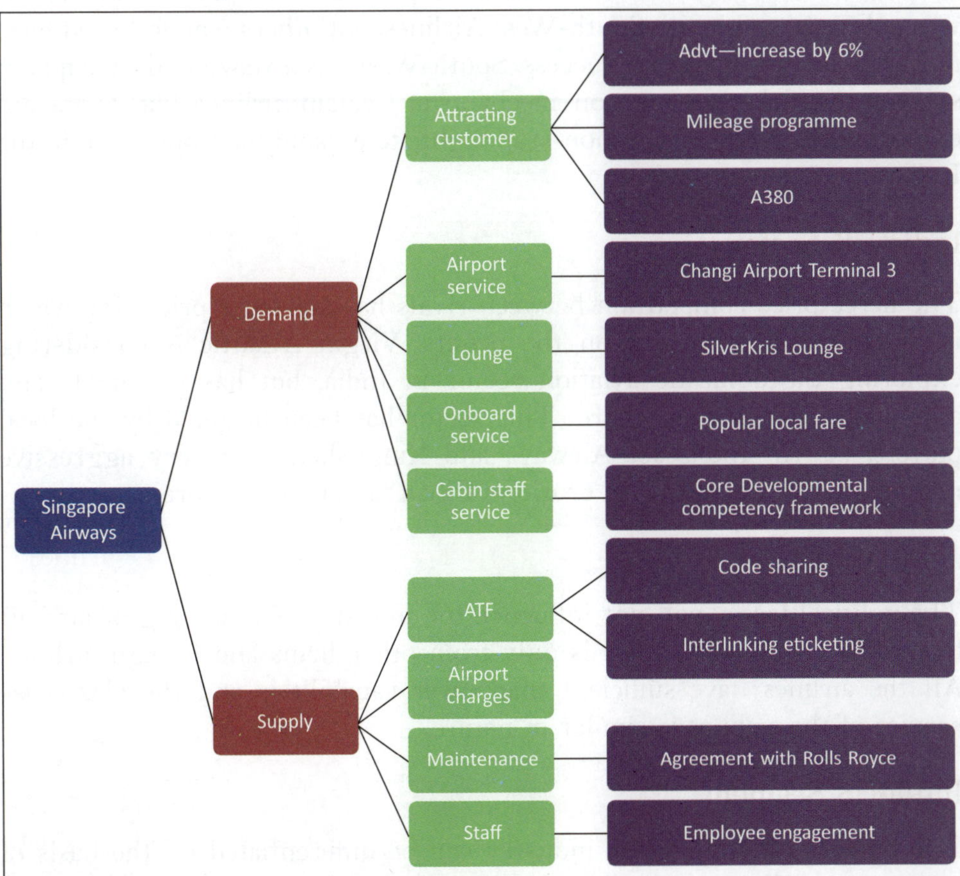

Figure 10.16 : Singapore Airways offerings

subcontinent via the Gulf and other European countries. This leads to high load factor in the India-UK segment. But most airlines that operate between India and the UK are Gulf-based airlines. About 60 per cent of their passengers get off in the Gulf countries on these connecting flights.

Virgin was the first international airline to introduce non-stop flights on this sector. It grew rapidly in the Indian market and now has around 20 per cent market share of the India-UK segment. British Airways was the next to introduce this facility. The load factor of all these flights is 100 per cent, showing very profitable operation. But there is an intense price war to gain market share.

Of the Indian airlines flying to US, Air-India is the oldest. Jet started its operation in 1999 and Kingfisher is a new player in the segment. Both Air-India and Jet have non-stop flights to the UK. Kingfisher under the licence of Air Deccan started its non-stop flight in August 2008.

Superior service and competitive prices are the main strategy of these airlines. The increased competition among these local players has started a price war which is taking its toll on the profitability and load factor of the airlines.

Competitors' Capabilities

India-US Sector

The Indian US aviation sector has displayed growth despite the global economic slowdown. Almost all the US airlines posted heavy losses and adopted cost cutting measures. The concept of low cost airlines in the US was only successful with South-West Airlines, but others who followed have not been able to repeat the success. South-West has a very good IT support system and ticket reservation mechanism. Certain airlines like Delta are exploring the possibility of non-stop flights to expand their operation in the Indian market.

India-UK Sector

The fierce price competition between rivals has started a price war which is in turn taking its toll on the profits. Virgin Atlantic is considering exploring the domestic aviation sector in India, but has not made any announcements in this regard. This sector has been targeted by the local players, i.e. Air-India, Jet Airways and Kingfisher, in a very aggressive manner. This has lead to an erosion of load factor for the foreign airlines.

Assumptions

The political factor will not influence the industry. The leasing of aircraft by Indian airline companies is only from other firms and foreign airlines. All the airlines have sufficient manpower capabilities and the class-wise service of the airlines is similar in nature.

India-US Segment

The offerings in the airline industry can be differentiated on the basis of products as well as service dimensions: performance, reliability, comfort, ease of ordering and delivery, customer consulting and hospitality and caretaking. Another major positioning of the brand or the product comes from the 'best quality' products as well as services. The major research studies conducted in this area showed a positive correlation between product quality and return on investment. A high-quality business unit earned more because premium quality allowed it to charge more and it benefitted from repeat purchases, consumer loyalty and positive word of mouth.

In the case of full-range airlines, this becomes more important as price is not the only driving factor for consumers. A consumer, if he/she is satisfied with the services of an airline, prefers to use the same one the next time. For the airline industry the cost of retaining those customers is less than acquiring a new customer.

It is important to recognize that what the consumers are demanding are not products, or features of products but the benefits they offer. Producing added benefits thus helps the marketer to distinguish one product from another. Good design or style of service can form the basis of differentiation. This enables the company to create a personality for its service. The design and decor of the aircraft provides opportunities to personalize the product as well as periodically update it. Eagle Airlines created an entirely new market between New York and Bermuda by developing the image of a friendly airline distinctive from other airlines serving that route. 'Welcome on board Kingfisher Airlines. I have instructed my staff to *treat each one of you as my personal guest*.' This is a part of the welcome message delivered by Vijay Mallya, chairman of Kingfisher Airlines, to passengers aboard his flights. This simply emphasizes the role customer service plays in the aviation industry.

Airlines are trying hard to differentiate themselves from others using the best possible range of customer services. The core service of an airline is the service of transport. The supplementary services are classified into different clusters and each one is analysed with respect to the airline industry.

Information

In the airline industry, up-to-date information about flight schedules, fares and promotional schemes are services which customers expect from the airlines. Customers can avail of this information through airline websites, which give the required details to the customers and also entertain queries through toll-free numbers. The websites also provide information to employees regarding new policies affecting the airline and equipping them with information that customers might demand.

Extensive training is provided to in-flight attendants regarding handling customer queries, knowledge about the airplane itself, knowledge about the cuisine, and so on.

Consultation

Airlines are moving more actively into the role of consultants today. They are doing away with travel agents and designing and selling packaged tours to consumers directly. In this aspect they often act as consultants to the customer, giving them advice and suggestions regarding the type of plan they can choose, the benefits they will get and, the various modes of travel to choose from.

When a customer approaches an airline regarding travelling to particular destination, the airline gives him a variety of routes that he can take. Kingfisher, for instance, introduced non-stop flights to the US to attract business-class consumers who want to avoid unnecessary check-in delays.

In some cases airlines may even design special menus and benefits in consultation with its frequent fliers and asking them for suggestions as to what they want in their airline which will make their experience more comfortable.

Booking

Reservation of airline tickets is now easy and reliable since it is fully computerized. There is 24-hour reservation facility. Passengers can specify their seat preferences at the time of reservation. Most airlines use the telephone, fax, and email methods of booking. The emphasis here is on speed as well as getting the required information from the customer. This is done by establishing a standard reservation procedure and format, thus reducing the risk of inconsistent service delivery. The online booking system also facilitates better order taking and processing.

The scheduling aspect assumes importance as reservations on the wrong flight to the wrong destination are likely to be unpopular.

Hospitality

With increasing competition and increasing similarity of services offered by each airline, hospitality has emerged as a key differentiating factor between competitors. This aspect of an airline is tested right from the time of the reservation to check-out at the destination airport.

Handling Complaints/Suggestions/Special Requests

Suggestions and complaints: Every airline today has a customer service centre which entertains customer suggestions and complaints. Jet Airways receives 16,500 service-monitor questionnaires (SMQs) every month which are analysed at various levels to plug loopholes in service. On the flight, customers are often asked for their opinion regarding service quality. Frequent corporate travellers are often consulted before making service changes.

Special requests: Airlines very often receive special requests from customers with regard to meal preferences, special amenities for elderly people or children, medical needs, and so on. These needs have to considered and acceded to wherever possible.

Billing and Payment

The billing procedure should be made simple. The customer should have the option of paying through credit card or travellers' cheque. Airlines use the open account system with corporate clients. Frequent fliers are also given special payment privileges.

With the introduction of information technology, airlines offer online reservation facility. This gives flexibility to consumers who can book their tickets online. It also helps airlines as they don't need to pay commission to travel agents for those bookings.

With the advent of LCA, it has become much more important for the full-service carriers to differentiate themselves from others. Full-service carriers attract consumers in the India-US and India-UK route by providing a bouquet of services which consumers desire as it gives them value for money. To identify what services the full-service carriers can provide to consumers and create differentiation in the minds of consumers, we have divided the benefits as perceived by the consumers into five stages. These are core benefits, basic benefits, expected benefits, augmented benefits and potential benefits.

Potential benefits are what consumers get from the products or services offered by an airline that makes it different from its competitors. From full-service carriers, the private suite offered by Jet Airways is a potential benefit that consumers get from the airline. This service or offering differentiates the Jet from other airlines in the eyes of potential consumers. Jet Airways the second airline in the world to offer private suites.

On international routes, airlines focus on business- and executive-class fliers. Such fliers prefer to access their emails on-board. Jet Airways came with a solution for those wishing to work while flying. Laptop power and in-flight telephones were made available with the unique ability to send SMS and email. Clearly Jet's focus was on retaining first-class passengers as well as attracting passengers who prefer to work on-board. The services offered by airlines can be further classified as:

The core service: The core service of the airline industry is to transport goods and services to various destinations. As the needs of the people increase the system becomes more organized and formal. After this stage comes the stage of various supplementary services.

Supplementary service: All airlines in the India-US and India-UK route, like Air-India, Jet Airways, British Airways had some common services to offer like connecting flights, through check-in, food on board, and complementary gifts for children. Singapore Airlines was the first to introduce individual 8″ television screens for passengers. But with time, almost all airlines started offering the same service. So having a television screen is no more differentiating to a passenger. More important, with time those services become basic and come to be expected by consumers. Offering those services doesn't make much of a difference, but compromising on them may leave a negative impression on the minds of consumers. As competition increases and customers want more, the next phase evolves, which is that of augmented service.

Augmented service: This phase is where the customer's expectations are met; the service providers keep working on new methods to meet the ever-changing customer demands. The players introduced online booking, which was very convenient for the service users. British Airways business class has showers; the seats are more spacious and comfortable. Virgin Atlantic has gambling on board. It also offers massage services to offer to its passengers. Air Emirates has customized pick up and drop cab service.

Among the potential services which can be offered to create differentiation in the minds of consumers are VIP lounges with private spaces for first-class fliers. This service provided by Jet Airways is unique and makes it different from other airlines.

This aspect is the most crucial; with increased competition service will become the final factor of differentiation.

Future Service

Since customer needs keep changing, the future is unknown. The customers may be looking for more frequent, inexpensive air travel, something like supersonic air taxis. These decrease travel time and thus cost. The LCAs offer tickets at unbelievable prices and differentiate themselves from full-service airlines by limiting the kind of services to be offered on- and off-board. Clearly airport charges, fuel and maintenance are the major cost components for LCAs. They however control the prices by giving less services to consumers, including narrower seating, higher plane utilization, lower staff costs, lower airport fee costs, no sales commissions due to Web sales and low cabin crew to passenger ratio. The LCAs apply differential fare strategy, whereby they charge different fares at different times of booking. So, during peak travel time when there are more consumers for a particular route, they charge a higher fare. They try to take advantage of the demand-supply gap during periods of high demand. Further, the lowest fares are highly publicized to attract more consumers.

Pricing Strategy

The pricing of tickets is the most crucial aspect for LCAs. This is the feature with which they differentiate themselves from full-service airlines and attract consumers. The strategy applied by the LCAs in pricing are: seats are sold on first-come first-served basis, so passengers get cheaper fares by booking earlier. Price thus automatically respond to variations in demand. The airline can also adjust the price bands if demand is greater or less than expected. All fares are one way and there is no difference in fare conditions. There's also no attempt to buck the market by imposing ticket conditions (return trip required or Saturday night stay) to get the best fare. For example, Air-India Express is an international LCA operating from India with fares 25-40 per cent cheaper than legacy carriers like Lufthansa. AI Express was launched in response to the demand from the Gulf and South-East Asia for lower prices. LCAs can operate at 20 per cent lower fares than full-service airlines. An airline' differentiation factor is the value addition it creates by providing free standardized meals and limited entertainment aboard its international flights. In the case of AI Express, rising fuel prices remain a concern along with the poor perception consumers have about the services of its sister airline, Air-India. The airline's strategy and services place it as the intermediary of low-cost airlines.

The reason why those LCAs don't impose ticketing conditions is because most of their consumers are first-time fliers. So imposing conditions adds to their confusion about fare schemes. Moreover they are attracted to the low fares more than the bundle pricing offers.

The number of passengers carried by LCAs is continuously on the rise. The LCAs are exploiting a powerful, previously-untapped market opportunity to leverage low unit costs to stimulate demand among more price-sensitive travellers using low fares and seizing market share from less agile competitors saddled with legacy, labour and infrastructure costs.

LCAs deliver superior margins primarily through cost advantages. More flexible work models, better aircraft utilization, reengineered processes, fewer amenities, direct distribution and simplified fleets all contribute to a significant gap between the unit costs of traditional full-service airlines and that of low-cost carriers.

The LCA model has demonstrated its ability to change the market permanently–lowering fares, increasing share and stimulating volume. Low-cost carriers are capitalizing on what appears to be a global trend—an ever-increasing number of travellers willing to forgo amenities for lower costs. The entry of LCAs is eroding the market share of traditional carriers and forcing them to reassess their business models. New entrants and spin-offs alike need to compete based on marketing factors known to guarantee success, such as innovative customer experience, balanced growth, simplicity and efficiency in route structure and fare structure, effective marketing and differentiation in the eyes of consumers.

References

1. Data Monitor, Industry Market Research, 5 December 2009.
2. http://www.iht.com/articles/ap/2009/03/19/business/AS-Malaysia-Airlines-Industry.php
3. http://indiaaviation.aero/news/airline/20326/59/IATA-reports-Jan-09-traffic
4. http://www.esri.com/industries/transport/business/delta_usesav.html
5. http://www.atwonline.com/channels/informationTechnology/article.html?articleID=2618
6. http://www.atwonline.com/channels/informationTechnology/article.html?articleID=2632
7. www.ficci.com/media-room/speeches-presentations/2007/feb/air-con/session3
8. www.thehindubusinessline.com/2007/06/01/stories/2007060106400100.htm
9. www.prenhall.com/scarbzim/html/smallbus.html
10. www.coolavenues.com/know/gm/manasi_6.php3
11. www.coolavenues.com/know/gm/manasi_8.php3
12. www.marketingteacher.com/Lessons/lesson_bowman.htm
13. www.flykingfisher.com

14. Jet Airways (India) Limited—16th Annual Report 2007–8, 2008-9 and 2009-10.
15. Continental Airlines, Inc.—Annual Report 2007–8.
16. Delta Airlines, Inc.—Annual Report 2007–8.
17. *Economist*; 7/10/2004, vol. 372, issue 8383, pp. 59-61.
18. http://www.etravelblackboardasia.com/article.asp?id=60268&nav=2
19. *Asia Africa Intelligence Wire*, 21 September 2004.
20. *Aviation Industry*, Issue 1Q, 2010, ISI Analytics.
21. 'Contemporary Issues in Asian Aviation', National Aviation Company of India Ltd.
22. 'Indian Aviation Scaling New Heights', 16 October 2009, Federation of Indian Chambers of Commerce and Industry.
23. 'Airports, Wings of Growth', 20 August 2010, Edelweiss.
24. E-Newsletter, 'Civil Aviation Sector in India: Period 1', 7 November 2008–10 January 2009, Research Department, Exhibitions India Group 2008.
25. Directorate General of Civil Aviation, www.dgca.nic.in
26. Ministry of Civil Aviation, www.civilaviation.nic.in
27. Airports Authority of India, www.airportsindia.org.in
28. International Air Transport Association, www.iata.org
29. Delhi International Airport Limited, www.newdelhiairport.in
30. Mumbai International Airport Limited, www.csia.in
31. GMR Hyderabad International Airport Limited, ww.newhyderabadairport.com
32. Bengaluru International Airport Limited, www.bengaluruairport.com
33. Cochin International Airport Limited, www.cochin-airport.com
34. Website of Kingfisher Airlines, www.flykingfisher.com
35. Website of Jet Airways, www.jetairways.com
36. Website of JetLite Airlines, www.jetairways.com
37. Website of IndiGo Airlines, www.goindigo.in
38. Website of GoAir, www.goair.in
39. Website of Indian, www.indian-airlines.nic.in
40. Website of SpiceJet, www.spicejet.com

CHAPTER 11  THE GREAT INDIAN RETAIL STORY UNDER TEST

applied case study 3

11.1 Genesis

The great Indian retail story that made India the second-largest retail destination globally now seems to be taking a U-turn. The estimated ₹2,500 crore Indian retail sector that experts thought would be the only one to weather the economic slowdown is also showing signs of shrinking sales and flat growth rates. With 12 lakh retail outlets, India has among the highest per capita outlets in the world. These retail outlets contribute over ₹14,000 crore to the country's GDP. India is considered as fifth-largest retail destination globally in 2010. It is projected to grow from US$350 billion in 2009 to US$637 billion by 2015.

In the first half of 2009, retailers like Reliance Fresh shut down around 25 non-performing stores, Radhakrishna Group's Foodland Fresh discontinued 39 of its 42 outlets and Vishal Retail discontinued all its daily and express format stores besides shutting down two Vishal Mega Marts, one in Mumbai and the other in Delhi. Wadhawan Group's Spinach and Aditya Birla Retail too have downsized their operations considerably. When quarter three of 2008 growth figures of the retail industry fell to around 12 per cent as compared to 35 per cent of third quarter of financial year 2007, happy grins fast turned into nervous smiles.

Over the last few years, modern retail has emerged as one of the fastest growing sectors in the Indian economy. After agriculture, retailing provides the highest employment in India. This trend is poised to grow further, with customers ready to spend more on products if the retailers can provide high service quality with increased efficiency, convenience, and a wide product range.

The modern retail sector in India is around 4.6 per cent of the wider retail market, compared to 20 and 38 per cent in China and Brazil, respectively. This provides enormous opportunity for modern retailers to benefit from rising consumption expenditure as well as capture a larger pie of the wider retail market. The modern retail sector is expected to enjoy 30-35 per cent compound annual growth rate (CAGR) and gain 11 per cent share of the retail market within 2008–11.

Retail was still in a nascent stage when market turbulence hit. Subhiksha, for instance, expanded rapidly to open 1,500 stores in two years. The company's turnover went up seven times from ₹330 crore in 2006 to ₹2,305 crore in 2007. However in 2008 due to rapid unplanned expansion and soaring rentals profits slowly began to diminish and the company was pushed into debt. The unavailability of sufficient cash prevented the retailer from buying fresh stock, which led to the collapse of its trade cycle in October 2008. According to R. Subramanian, MD, Subhiksha, the opportunity to shut

BOX 11.1: MALL CULTURE IN INDIA ON THE RISE

While the mall culture in India is surely rising, the moot question is how many of the malls will succeed. As organized retailing in India grows, tier II and tier III cities witness hectic activity in the mall space. The Indian retail market, which is the fifth-largest retail destination globally, is the most attractive emerging market for investment in the retail sector, according to AT Kearney's Eighth Annual Global Retail Development Index (GRDI, published 2009). The share of retail trade in the country's GDP was between 8 and 10 per cent in 2007. At around 12 per cent in 2009, it is likely to reach 22 per cent by 2012.

The organized retail sector, which at present accounts for around 5 per cent of the Indian retail market in 2009, is all set to witness a surge in large-format malls and branded retail stores in south India, followed by the north, west and the east, by 2011. According to the 'Mall Realities: India 2010', a report by leading property consultants Jones Lang LaSalle Meghraj and Cushman & Wakefield India, in association with Shopping Centres Association of India, over 100 malls with over 30 million sq. ft. of new shopping space, are projected to open in India between 2010 and the end of 2012.

'Mall management isn't just about controlling the crowds and security, but it starts right from the time when the mall is being designed. Before building a mall, it is very important to understand the demographics of the area. You cannot plan a super-luxury mall in an area where the spending power is not much,' says T. Anupam, associate vice-president, Korum Mall, Thane. The location of the mall is one of the main factors that decides its success. Good visibility and access via roads are some of the main prerequisites for a mall.

Zoning of the mall comes next. This essentially means deciding which tenants would occupy what space and where. It is very important to have the right mix of tenants at the right place, so as to ensure a smooth flow of customers.

'When we were conceptualizing Nirmal Lifestyle, we studied other world-famous shopping destinations, like Oxford Street, etc., and came up with the idea of having an open space mall. People can hang around and also window shop, at the same time,' says Dharmesh Jain, managing director, Nirmal Lifestyle. The anchor tenant also plays an important role, as it is the one that would attract the crowds. For example, anchor tenants like Shopper's Stop and Lifestyle stores at Inorbit, Malad have been placed in such a way that they both have individual entrances. For the rest of the stores, there is a common entrance to the mall, which avoids crowding at the foyer.

It is necessary to create visibility in the market to get the desired footfalls. Timely events and promotional activities will make sure the mall remains in the news. Food festivals, exhibitions and film promotions are some promotional activities that malls often undertake. According to Jain, the challenge today is to constantly keep the interest of the people high. 'We talk to our retailers on a regular basis, to know the consumer trends,' he explains.

Facility management refers to the integration of people, place, process and technology in a building. It means optimal utilization of resources while ensuring the well-being of the tenants, providing good ambience and traffic management. 'You have to see to it that all things promised to the retailer are being delivered, that the ambience of the mall is maintained and there is a smooth flow of traffic, along with enough security,' says Anuradha Gandhi, business head, Property Solutions.

T. Anupam says that a well-managed mall will always attract retailers, as well as consumers. 'The design of a mall also makes a lot of difference. There are two famous designs which have proven to be most attractive: "Racetrack" (circular in shape) and "Dumble design" (shops along the corridor),' he elaborates. Even simple things, like clean toilets can make people come back to the mall, points out Gandhi.

'During the upswing, many jumped on to the bandwagon to grab a share of the profits. However, they totally misunderstood the common man's psyche. Just building a mall will not get you the footfalls; you need to have the right mix of everything—from tenants to design to hospitality,' insists Jain.

Source: www.indianrealtynews.com

comes from two factors, one is that in a matter of two years the company opened 1,500 stores. Retail is a probable business, so when anyone opens 1,500 stores there could be 5-10 per cent of things going awry. The second issue is high rent. During a recession no one can afford to pay such high rent. Let us therefore take a fresh look.

11.2 Retail Intensity and Potential Under Check

Even though India has well over 5 million retail outlets of all sizes and styles (or non-styles), the country sorely lacks anything that resembles a retailing industry in the modern sense of the term. This presents international retailing specialists with a great opportunity.

According to a survey by AT Kearney, an overwhelming proportion of the ₹4,00,000 crore retail market is unorganized. In fact, only a narrow ₹20,000 crore segment of the market is organized. As much as 96 per cent of the 5 million-plus outlets are smaller than 500 sq. ft. in area. This means that India's per capita retailing space is about 2 sq. ft. (compared to 16 sq. ft. in the United States). India's per capita retailing space is thus the lowest in the world. (*Source:* KSA Technopak (India) Private Limited; India operation of the US-based Kurt Salmon Associates).

Just over 8 per cent of India's population is engaged in retailing (compared to 20 per cent in the US). There is no data on this sector's contribution to the GDP. From a size of only ₹38,000 crore, the organized retail industry will grow to ₹1,60,000 crore by 2012. Given the size and the geographical, cultural and socio-economic diversity of India, there is no role model for Indian suppliers and retailers to adapt or expand in the Indian context. Look at the international partners of leading retail chains in India (Table 11.1).

The great Indian retail story appears to have fallen victim to the slowdown. Indicators such as footfalls, conversion and same-store sales, once used to justify ambitious store rollouts, show that the growth story is now in the 'pause' mode. It is widely felt that modern retail is based on the liquidity model of business that requires upfront cash in the first few years. As liquidity has dried up in the marketing place retailers need to find more sources of funds or slow down their growth. Retail experts also say that weak supply chains lacking good infrastructure like warehouses, store space and transport facilities are equally responsible for the mess. And while some

Table 11.1: International partners of leading retail chains

Retail chain	*International partner*
Reliance Retail	M&S, Pearle Optical, Vornado, Office Depot, Hamley's, Diesel and others
Future Group	Staples, Axiom, Etam, Celio, Converse, Speedo, Wilson and others
K. Raheja	Mothercare, MAC, Argos and others
RPG	Cellucom, BHPC, Au Bon Pain, Ladybird, Chad Valley Toys and others
Trent + Tata	Tesco, Woolworth, Sisley and others
Deviyani International	Pizza Hut, Cream Bell, Costa Coffee
Landmark	Kappa, Bossini, VNC, Gloria Jeans

are struggling to balance growth and profitability there are others who are managing the act quite well.

To compound problems, the expansion frenzy has left players grappling with a significant funds crunch. While modern retailers across all segments of the industry are closing or relocating unviable stores to stem losses and tackle operational costs, retailers such as Reliance Fresh, More, India Bulls, Spencer's and Subhiksha, which concentrated on replacing neighbourhood *kirana* stores, are among the worst hit. Many of them are renegotiating rentals with developers. Privately-held Lifestyle International, which runs Lifestyle departmental stores, Home Centre stores and value format Max stores, posted a pre-tax loss of ₹46.50 crore for the first nine months of 2008–9, further to its losses of ₹18.90 crore in 2007–8.

Stocks of Indian retail players—once the darlings of the bourses and enjoying premium valuations—have been among the worst performers over the past year, with valuations of leading players whittling down to half their earlier levels. Nor have these stocks participated actively in the recent market 'recovery'. Persisting hiccups in the retail sector have affected value and premium retailers alike. Smaller players like Gitanjali Gems Ltd. and Vishal Retail have seen their valuations cut down to low single digits. Lifestyle retailers such as Lifestyle International, Shopper's Stop, Trent and Pantaloon had face liquidity pressure for at least for a year due to slower sales coupled with growing debt, high rentals and slow expansion, which brought down profitability. Analysts have observed that retailers were borrowing more debt to fund their expansion and operations. Shopper's Stop's gearing (debt to equity) has increased about 3 times as on 30 September 2008, from around 2.5 times as on 31 March 2008, while that of Lifestyle International has improved, despite losses, because of heavy promoter-fund infusion. Its adjusted gearing is expected to be 2 times as on 31 March 2009, as against 2.5 times as on 31 March 2008. Rating agency Fitch has downgraded the credit rating assigned to Pantaloon Retail's short-term debt instruments from F1 to F2+, reflecting the pressure on operating cash flow due to

BOX 11.2: SPECIALTY MALL MAY ANCHOR FUTURE RETAIL GROWTH IN INDIA

Specialty mall was the retail buzzword in 2007 and is likely to dominate the Indian retail market again from 2011 onwards. With a huge influx of sparkling malls with finely tuned marketing strategies mushrooming in cyber cities like Gurgaon and Noida, the mall mania has certainly gripped every shopping enthusiast. With the competition growing fiercer in the Indian retail sector, specialty malls are resetting the trends and transforming the fundamental activity of shopping into a lifestyle statement.

Also known as theme malls, specialty malls are believed to be more popular than simple shopping malls. People in India have a craze for theme malls. Lack of large space has encouraged property developers to create niche markets or specialty markets for different segments of customers. However, the country needs to grow much faster to support the emergence of these shopping malls.

The first specialty mall was the Gold Souk in Gurgaon. Dedicated entirely to jewellery collections, the mall houses some of the biggest brands in the jewellery business in India as well as abroad.

At present, there are only a few specialty malls in India but the Retailers Association of India (RAI) expects to push specialty malls to constitute nearly 10 per cent of the total malls in India, thereby taking the Indian retail sector to a new high during 2012.

Source: www.indianrealtynews.com

slowing sales. In a rating action note, Fitch said that Pantaloon Retail was witnessing pressures in its operating cash flow and losses were continuing at some of its key subsidiaries. The revised rating denotes a good capacity for timely payment of financial commitments, whereas an F1 rating indicates the strongest capacity for on-time payment.

Adding worries due to the drop in sales and footfall put many retailers in a spot since September 2008. As the economic slowdown began to bite organized retail, Mumbai-based retail food and grocery player Wadhawan Food Retail deferred plans to launch ten hypermarkets in the country. The hypermarket was to be spread over 1,50,000 sq. ft. and would have come up at a cost of ₹100 crore. The company had planned to open nine more hypermarkets of at least 1,00,000 sq. ft. each over the next three years. Since January 2009, Wadhawan Food Retail has also shuttered 18 of its 200 food and grocery retail outlets across 15 cities. The group runs retail chains Spinach in Maharashtra, Sabka Bazaar in Delhi and Uttar Pradesh, and S-Mart in Bengaluru. However in 2010, the fortune of retailers are slowly reversing. Shopper's Stop reported a total sale of ₹145.843 crore in 2009-10 as against ₹130.723 crore in 2008-9. Eventually the company made a net profit of ₹3.745 crore in 2009-10 as against the loss of ₹8.199 crore in 2008-9. At this point, it is imperative to understand the Indian middle class which supports the retail revolution in India.

11.3 Indian Middle Class ... still an Enigma for Retailers

India has registered an impressive growth of its middle class—a class which was virtually non-existent in 1947 when India became a politically sovereign nation. At the start of 1999, the size of the middle class was unofficially estimated at 300 million people. The middle class comprises three sub-classes: the upper middle, the middle middle and the lower middle. The upper middle class comprises an estimated 40 million people. They have annual incomes of US$6,00,000 each in terms of Purchasing Power Parity (PPP). The middle middle class comprises an estimated 150 million people, each with PPP incomes of US$20,000 per year. The lower middle class comprises an estimated 110 million people. An estimate of their annual income is not available, but they are mostly the relatively affluent people in

Table 11.2: India's consuming class

Estimated households by annual income		*Structure of the Indian consumer market (1995–6)*				
Annual income (in ₹) at 1994–5 prices	*No. of households (in million)*	*Annual income (in ₹) at 1994–5 prices*	*Classification*	*Number of households (in million)*		
				Urban	*Rural*	*Total*
<25,000	80.7	<16,000	Destitutes	5.3	27.7	33.0
25,001–50,000	50.4	16,001–22,000	Aspirants	7.1	36.9	44.0
50,001–77,000	19.7	22,001–45,000	Climbers	16.8	37.3	54.1
77,001–1,06,000	8.2	45,001–2,15,000	Consumers	16.6	15.9	32.5
>1,06,000	5.8	>2,15,000	The rich	0.8	0.4	1.2
Total number of households: 164.9 million		Total number of households		46.6	118.2	164.8

Sources: National Council of Applied Economic Research (NCAER) and IndiaOneStop.Com

the rural areas of India. The middle classes *on the whole* (i.e. upper middle + middle middle + lower middle classes) is expected to grow by 5 to 10 per cent annually.

Data on income distribution of households is insufficient in determining market size for different consumer products in India. This is because of the lack of homogeneity of the consuming class and the varying prices of a single product in different parts of India. For example, vegetables generally cost more in Mumbai than in Kolkata, hence vegetable purchasing power for identical income groups would be different in the two cities even though they are the two biggest cities in India with comparable populations. In other words, purchasing power is location-specific, not income-specific. Consumption habits of households are therefore better determinants of consumer market size than income distribution. Of course, other factors are also to be considered as detailed below.

While determining market size for a consumer product, the structure of the consuming class as seen in Table 11.2 can be both revealing as well as misleading, depending on the kind of product. For example, any consuming class would be a market for consumer products like tea or soap, but a product such as a vacuum cleaner would find a market largely in the 'consumers' and 'rich' segments of the market as defined in Table 11.2. Furthermore, even this may be incorrect, because the need for a vacuum cleaner is not necessarily a function of purchasing power but of culture and/or taste as well. Identifying a plausible market size for a consumer product is therefore a hazardous task in a heterogeneous country like India.

Yet, marketers need some data to come as close to the real picture as possible. For this purpose, it can be cautiously assumed that purchasing power is proportional to income despite variables such as location, taste, and so on. Companies are therefore advised to plan their consumer product marketing strategies on an area-by-area basis, rather than on an all-India basis.

Income data is insufficient. Therefore, it must be supplemented by product-specific information regarding its existing stock in the marketplace (in the case of consumer durables) and existing rate of purchases. It is also advisable to further refine the plausible market size by taking into account details based on social, cultural and demographic factors. Marketing a super-premium product such as a Rolex watch is relatively easy. Marketers can easily target the income class above ₹1,06,000 per annum (in 1995-96) as per Table 11.2. This class, the exhibit shows, comprises 5.8 million households. But the problem lies in the fact that the 5.8 million households are spread all over India. The prime market for consumer products in India is aware of the cost-benefit or value for money aspect. Their concept of value incorporates socio-cultural benefits in addition to product utility. For example, many households in the 'consumers' class and the 'rich' class (as defined in Table 11.2) may have two television sets, but both the sets may not be top-of-the-line. Thus, while there may be demand for an additional TV set in many households in the two mentioned classes, it must not be mistaken as demand for higher-priced TV models. The prime consumer market in India therefore is not a market for absolute premium products, but for something between the 'high-end popular brands' and the 'premium brands'.

The 'consumers' class as defined in Table 11.2 comprises 33.5 million households as in 1995-96 and owned and 'consumed' expensive consumer products such as refrigerators and washing machines as well as premium expendables. At 1994-95 prices, their annual household incomes ranged between ₹45,000 and ₹2,15,000 (to calculate the latest income statistics, use an annual inflator of 5 per cent). In addition to this class, the 'climbers' and 'aspirants' (defined in Table 11.2) totalling 23.9 million households in urban India, also have the socio-cultural traits of the 'consumers' class and, with time, will join them.

A medium-to-long-term marketing strategy must therefore aim at the aspirants and the climbers as well. This is based on the safe assumption that, with the exception of the destitute class as defined in Table 11.2, the other classes are on the way to the next higher class. For companies with long-term marketing plans in India, the 'consumers' (urban + rural), 'climbers' (urban only) and 'aspirants' (urban only) classes can be clubbed together to give a market size of around 57 million households which can be considered the 'prime segment' of the Indian consumer market. This becomes even more true as consumer financing and the credit card culture picks up.

In general, India's consumption growth is at the margin that always drives powerful macro and micro market trends. It is accelerating growth off a low base. The potential comes from the structure of the Indian economy: private consumption currently accounts for 64 per cent of the GDP. This is higher than shares in Europe (58 per cent), Japan (55 per cent), and especially China (42 per cent). India's transition to an 8 per cent growth path in recent years is very much an outgrowth of the emerging consumerism of one of the world's youngest populations. The increased vigour of private consumption provides a powerful leverage to the Indian growth dynamic rarely found in the externally-dependent developing world.

The global customer, on the other hand, is a shopper who demands honesty and respect from retailers and brand manufacturers, more than the highest-quality merchandise or the lowest prices. The new consumers are fair weather friends, less likely to remain loyal to any one particular brand. Modern consumers are educated and experienced, and familiar with a growing choice of products and services. They take for granted the competitive trading environment that operates in most markets and expect high-quality service and value for money, as well as good marketing and information provision.

The flitting from one brand to another does not arise out of lack of choices, but confusion due to the tremendous amount of choices available. When people are overwhelmed by choices, they are left watching things spin past them. As a result, decisions are deferred or even discarded. As customer expectations change, so does a retailer's approach to service. Several retailers who have kept pace with the evolving customer say the one thing that has remained constant is the belief that personal attention to customers is the key to repeat business and ultimate success. It seems like people's expectations increase as the amount of money they are going to spend or the cost of the item increases.

Another development in retail space is polarization. This is the process of eliminating the in-between stores. Consumers are either willing to spend extra money to get service from a high-end retailer or are satisfied with rock-bottom prices and little service. As the aspects that hold value vary with different customers, retailers have to determine where they want to position themselves in the market.

11.4 Evolution of Modern Retailing

The face of the retailing industry has undergone significant global changes over the last two decades. Understanding these changes will help us assess the future of the industry. Retailing has evolved from a small-time local merchandising business to its present global state involving e-tailing (retailing on the internet).

The effectiveness of e-commerce and its influence on the retail industry has been a subject of constant debate among marketers. Retailing has always focused on offering the best quality products to customers. Every retailer wants to offer customers the right products at the right time at the right place and at the right price. However, the way in which retailers try to fulfil this mission changes continuously because of certain disruptions. These technologies help retailers innovate new business models that change the economics of the industry.

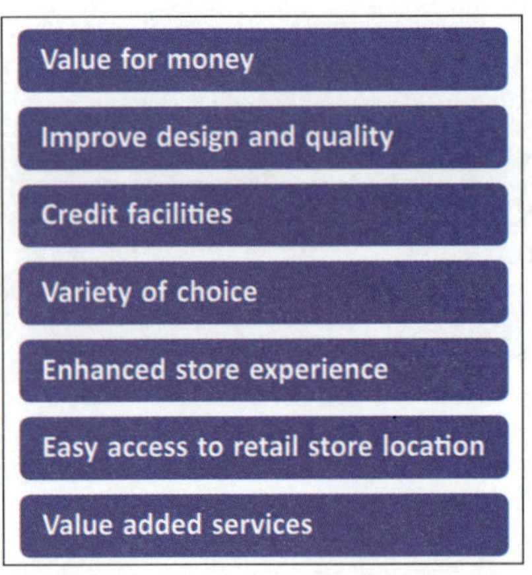

Figure 11.1: Customer expectations

The primary disruption in retailing took place with the setting up of departmental stores. Local merchandisers, who initially ruled the retailing business, offered high-quality service to customers by giving them tailor-made solutions. They maintained huge inventories and offered extended credit periods. These benefits, however, reduced their growth rate and left them with no choice but to charge high prices for their products. With the mushrooming of departmental stores, retail witnessed a transformation in the 1980s. Departmental stores stocked more items when compared to local retailers. This was convenient for customers as they could find many products at one place. Moreover, the superior customer service offered by these stores was instrumental in creating tough competition for the conventional retailers.

This disruption in the retailing industry was followed by others such as the origin of catalogue retailing, discount department stores, and Internet retailing. Although catalogue retailing was initially targeted at rural customers, it eventually became a successful business model for the entire retailing industry. The subsequent disruption in the retailing industry was seen in the form of discounted departmental stores. These stores offered significant discounts on products throughout the year. Retailers were able to afford these discounts by establishing their retail outlets at places where real estate prices were low. As people became increasingly mobile, access to such stores was no longer difficult.

BOX 11.3: ORGANIZED RETAIL EXPECTED TO GROW 60 PER CENT IN NON-METROS

It is time for players in the organized retail sector to focus on rural India, including small towns. According to the Associated Chambers of Commerce and Industry of India (Assocham), the industry is set to grow at a whopping rate of 60 per cent in small towns against around 35 per cent in the metros. The study also reveals that by 2012, the rural market is expected to contribute to almost 50 per cent business of the retailers. Supporting these projections, another study, conducted by the NCAER reported that 8 per cent households are living in mega-cities, while 22 per cent have their bases in boom towns and niche cities. The remaining 70 per cent households belong to rural areas.

Considering these facts, over 1,000 malls are set to come up in the smaller towns and once open, they are expected to maintain a CAGR of 20 per cent. Sufficient availability of land and increased purchasing power of the buyers living in those areas, thanks to increased economic activities, offers enormous growth potential to the industry. In 2008, the metros contributed to more than 60 per cent of the sales of the industry, even though the growth rate was low because of less availability of space.

The market size of the organized retail sector in India is expected to cross the figure of $22 billion by 2011 with its space requirement exceeding 220 million sq. ft. Currently, the organized retail sector generates business of about $4 billion with usage of 40 million sq. ft. of space in 2010. This size of business is less than even 5 per cent of the total market size of the retail sector in India. Organized retail is growing faster in towns only because of the fact that in metros, there is a scarcity of space, which is not the case in towns. The cost of space too is reasonable. Therefore, large players tend to set up their shops in towns and rural areas.

The potential in towns for the value format is huge, given its good performance in tier II-III cities. More than 60 per cent of Future Group's revenue is generated from value format stores in the small cities. Each value format store in towns posts growth rates of around 20 per cent. Modern retail is new for people in these areas. Moreover, fed up with traditional buying from the 'mom-and-pop' stores, they are bound to respond well to malls, at least in the initial stage.

Source: Ankur Parikh, Ahmedabad.

The fourth and the final disruption took place in the form of online retailing. Online retailing offers a wide variety of products, spanning from hair pins to heavy industrial goods. The products can be offered at substantially lower prices due to the absence of the middleman's margin and negligible stock holding costs. Customers can also email of the convenience of shopping from anywhere and at any time.

However, online retailing has its drawbacks. It does not facilitate immediate delivery of the product to the customer. Products, which customers want to feel and touch, are not suitable for online business. Even during market turbulence, we have many success stories. On the one hand, Reliance Fresh is finding it tough to make ends meet while on the other hand, Reliance Retail's other wing Sahakari Bhandar, under the same circumstances, is celebrating a turnover of ₹100 crore, a 25 per cent growth over 2008. A heritage of over 50 years with a strong brand name, well-trained staff and reasonable rent is what gives it an edge over the newer retailers—a strategy that has helped it to survive the downturn. Unlike other retailers who pay over ₹100 per sq. ft. as rent, Sahakari Bhandar spends only ₹35 for the same. Good service, good products and value for money have worked very well for them, not requiring them to depend on any marketing gimmicks to woo customers. In 2006, net sales growth of the organized retailers was 66.06 per cent which ultimately dropped to 31.97 per cent in 2009 but recovered slightly in 2010 (44.89 per cent). The net profit margin of the retailers was dropped from 3.57 per cent in 2006 to 2.02 per cent in 2009 and improved to 1.57 per cent in 2010.

11.5 Malls Induce Growth

Since the setting up of India's first mall in 1999, there has been a steady proliferation of malls, a trend specially pronounced in the urban areas. The total number of malls was estimated at 200 for 2005–6, projected to increase to 600 by 2012. With the increasing number of malls, there is more retailing space availability for players, with malls providing further incentives like lower rentals for anchor tenants and greater consumer exposure. Activity in the retail sector has gained further support by the allowance of FDI in real estate by the government.

The total mall space across seven cities (NCR, Mumbai, Bengaluru, Kolkata, Hyderabad, Pune and Chennai) was over 40 million sq. ft. in 2006–7.

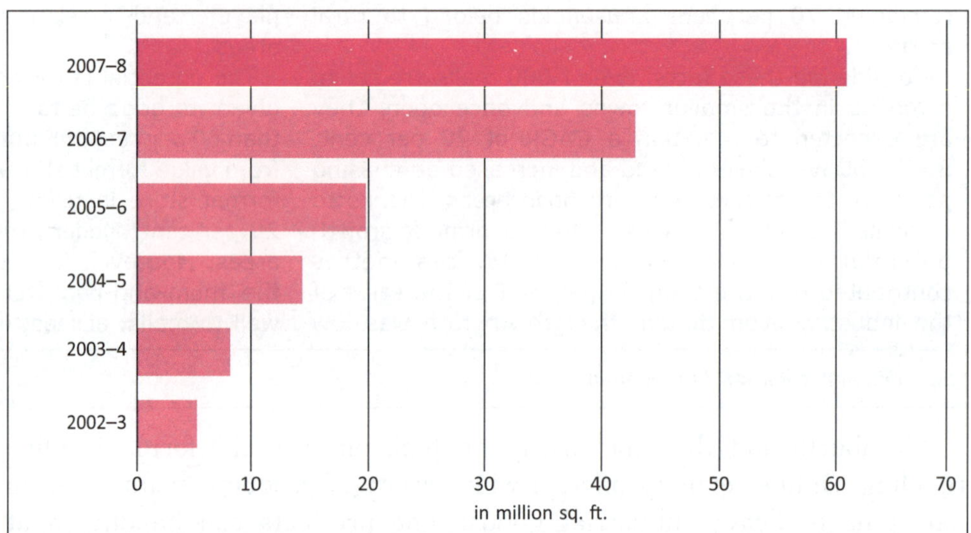

Figure 11.2: Total mall space availability
Source: Jones Lang LaSalle Meghraj Retail Report.

BOX 11.4: JEWELLERY MALL INDUCES RETAIL GROWTH

Jewellery malls are the hot news in the $12 billion Indian retail industry. With the burgeoning disposable income of shoppers and easy availability of loans, retailers and real estate developers see a huge market for large jewellery formats in the country.

Vardhaman Developers, in association with Bherumal Shamandas, an old-time jeweller, has launched the Jewel World mall at Zaveri Bazaar in Mumbai at an investment of ₹35 crore. The developers have converted the eight-floor Cotton Exchange Building in Mumbai into Jewel World. Of the ₹2 lakh crore gold and diamond jewellery market, 70 per cent is contributed by Zaveri Bazaar. The mall has 70 national and international branded jewellers as anchor tenants. It is targeting jewellers from Dubai, Singapore, Hong Kong, Malaysia and Italy. The high-security mall comprises a basement with locker system, apart from eight floors of retail shopping zone. The target audience of Jewel World are high-end customers, including the young generation, apart from semi wholesalers-cum-retailers.

Meanwhile, Gitanjali Gems Limited too is evaluating plans to launch jewellery malls. According to Sadanand Pawar, president, Gitanjali Gems, plans are afoot to launch 18 Gitanjali Lifestyle malls in metros with an area size of over 70,000 sq. ft. each in 2010–12. They may eye areas such as Shivaji Park in Mumbai to set up a mall. The Gitanjali Lifestyle mall will have national as well as international branded jewellers and also sell cosmetics, watches, apparels and accessories.

DLF's retail sales division is also contemplating the jewellery mall concept in India. According to them, the concept is expected to pick up in India within two years providing the company a good opportunity to tap. Aerens Gold Souk International too is in the process of opening a number of Gold Souks (mega malls) across the country by 2010–11.

Source: www.indianrealtynews.com

With impressive transactions-to-customer footfalls ratio (conversion ratio), the market trend promises a positive future for malls.

Mall development activity is being pursued aggressively across metros and high-growth cities, with significant investments in the pipeline. A pan India evolving cosmopolitan population with rising aspirations and growing incomes is the driving force behind increasing domestic and international

BOX 11.5: MALL MANAGEMENT: A REAL CHALLENGE

Mall mania that has gripped the Indian real estate poses several challenges for mall owners. A study by ICICI Property Services-Technopak on the Indian retail sector in 2009 reported that mall management is going to be a major challenge for the retail industry in 2010–11. So far, the trend has been that some property developer develops a mall, sells it to an investor who then leases it out to retailers. This process creates an ownership issue, which creates problems in maintaining the malls.

The ICICI-Technopak study projected that such malls are owned neither by developers nor by retailers but by individual financial investors, which creates unplanned and haphazard development and eventually depreciates the rental value of the malls. The report suggests that mall owners and developers need to keep in mind the importance of controlling and managing their malls in order to capitalize on their investments. The lack of differentiated offerings was termed as one of the major shortages in the Indian retail industry.

As of 2009 most developers offer the same kind of malls with spaces for shopping, food and films. But as the number of malls increase people will look for more locations. This will become a major factor in raising or lowering its asset value. According to the report, the mix of retail planning and tenant selection will be one of the key factors for the success of malls and real estate developers in India. It will be required to renegotiate the lease that comes up for renewal on specific transparent performance measures. Last but not the least, before going for mall development, issues such as facilities management, utilities management, market and promotions, event management, and hospitality should be taken into account.

Growth plans during 2010–12

Some 330 new malls are expected to come up in metros and tiers II and III smaller cities by 2012, which will force developers to find innovative ways to attract stores and maintain foot traffic. A report titled 'Upcoming Malls: 2008 and Beyond', compiled by the real estate consultancy firm Jones Lang LaSalle Meghraj, says north India will lead the retail boom, with 136 new malls by 2012.

While Delhi is expected to get 15 malls, its suburbs Faridabad and Ghaziabad will get seven new malls each. Mumbai will lead the pack among individual cities with 30 malls planned during 2010–12. Real estate firms such as DLF, Akruti City Limited, Nirmal Lifestyle and Oberoi Constructions all have retail plans in the western and central suburbs of the country's financial centre. Kolkata, probably one of the last metros to be hit by the retail boom, has 18 malls lined up during 2010–12. The landmark Statesman House in central Kolkata, which is to be turned into a 2 million sq. ft. shopping destination by Emaar MGF Land Limited, is slated to be one of the biggest malls coming up in India.

This new breed of malls is expected to have facilities that were lacking in earlier malls. Developers will now give more importance to determining factors like parking, design and soft strategies like customer relationship to make these malls work.

Some experts are skeptical about the numbers. Retail consultants note only 22 new malls became operational in 2007 nationally. For example, just 3 of the slated 15 malls opened in Mumbai in 2008. Still, the Jones report points out a large number of emerging hot spots—smaller cities and towns that will get their first malls by 2011. For instance, with 15 new shopping malls being set up by film director Prakash Jha, who has ventured into mall development, several areas in Bihar and Jharkhand, such as Patliputra, Sitamarhi, Hazipur and Bettiah would soon feature for the first time on the Indian organized retail map.

In southern India, Cochin in Kerala is expected to have 13 malls by 2012, just one less than a shopping hub such as Bengaluru. With huge townships and residential ventures, such as Sobha Developers' largest township in Maradu, Cochin developers are upbeat about prospects for the city.

The study forecast both local and national developers setting up malls in previously unlikely places. The business strategy of EWDPL India Private Limited, a three-year-old developer, revolves around setting up first-time malls in small towns.

Organized retail in India constitutes only 2 per cent of the global retail industry. So new mall developers here are still going through the learning curve, trying not to repeat past mistakes.

Source: www.indianrealtynews.com

investments. However EBIT margin for the organized retailers dropped from 7.58 per cent in 2005 to 2.48 per cent in 2009 thus bounced back to 4.2 per cent in 2010 with slow recovery of Indian economy.

Growth Drivers

Favourable demographics combined with increasing disposable incomes is progressively changing the face of Indian consumerism. With new vistas of employment and employers offering attractive compensation packages and perks, Indian skilled professionals are boasting of higher disposable incomes. The various growth drivers of the mall phenomena in India are as follows:

High disposable income: Disposable incomes are on the rise with the economy providing new avenues of employment in IT/ITeS. The increase in per capita income has been more pronounced in metros and emerging cities, with progressive growth in the standard of living.

Increasing urbanization: India's urban population is estimated at 286 million, constituting 27.8 per cent of the total population of 1,029 million as in 2001. The urban population is projected to increase to 468 million, constituting 33.4 per cent of the total projected population of 1,400 million by 2010.

Young working population: An increase in the number of young employed executives and the increasing population of working women is stimulating the growth of modern retail in urban areas.

Easy availability of credit: Higher penetration and availability of credit facilities and increasing credit card and debit card subscriptions have further fuelled the growth of the retail sector. Most banks and financial institutions have increased their range and amount of retail credit and loan service offerings. The average exposure of banks to retail loans was at 25.5 per cent of total loans in 2005–6.

11.6 Indian *v.* Global Customer

For many retailers moving forward into this new century will mean taking a step back. It is becoming increasingly apparent that in order to survive and prosper, retailers are going to have to change the way they do business—they are actually going to have to go back to the future. Back to the days when the customer really was number one, when stores were filled with salespeople ready to go out of their way to help, and when retailers could count on their customers' loyalty. The findings of a recent study given in Box 11.6 appear significant.

There are distinct types of Indian customers; classified according to the analytical partitioning of a product's target consumer group, either according to their socio-demo type or according to psychological typing. They can be labelled as: the pleasure-seekers, the value-seekers, the novelty-seekers and the bargain-hunters. Whichever label a customer falls under, he/she is likely to be sophisticated and demanding.

BOX 11.6: NIELSEN SURVEY FINDINGS ON INDIAN CUSTOMERS

With over a third (34 per cent) of Indian consumers buying Calvin Klein at some point of time, the brand has emerged as the number one foreign luxury brand on their buying list, though in their opinion Gucci was the most coveted foreign brand, if money was not a constraint.

Besides Calvin Klein, Indian consumers have also bought other luxury brands like Gucci, Diesel, Christian Dior and DKNY. These are the findings of a survey of 26,312 persons, spread across 48 markets, conducted 'online' by well known global market research firm The Nielsen Company. The survey conducted in November 2007, included Indian shoppers.

'The number of outlets that brands (like Gucci, Calvin Klein, Diesel, Christian Dior, Fendi, and DKNY) have opened up in the country in recent times is a testimony in itself of the increasing fashion consciousness amongst Indians.' — Vatsala Pant, Associate Director, Client Solutions, The Nielsen Company

Respondents in the survey included shoppers from Europe, Asia Pacific, North America and the Middle East.

The fruits of the rapid increase in the economic growth of the country have begun reflecting not only in terms of increased consumer spending, but also on the quality of such spending, an increasing number of them preferring to buy branded luxury goods. According to experts the Indian luxury goods market is expected to grow exponentially from $1 billion now to $30 billion by 2015. Interestingly, according to the survey results, India is the third most brand-conscious country in the world, Greece and Hong Kong topping the list. Over one-third (35 per cent) of the Indians in the survey said they spent money on luxury brands.

India has also emerged as among the top ten markets for certain luxury brands. According to the survey, India ranks as the third most important market globally for Gucci, the sixth most for Calvin Klein, number nine for Diesel, and the tenth most for Fendi.

According to The Nielsen Company, the overall awareness about designer brands has been aided by people travelling overseas. Although three-fourths (or 73 per cent) of Indians consider designer brands to be overpriced, India is among the top countries where customers believe that branded designer goods are of better quality than unbranded ones.

Interestingly, Indian consumers are equally conscious of Indian luxury brands, as over 40 per cent of them said that they also purchased Indian designer brands. This puts India among the top six countries that buy local brands.

Source: www.indiaretailing.com

At the store management level, managers need to go back to placing more emphasis on individual customers. In the past a manager would want to know what happened with every customer. There needs to be an increased emphasis on sales techniques and satisfying individual customers. Today's managers seem to be more concerned with making sure their staff knows how to open and close the store and make certain that no one is stealing, than with making certain their customers are being taken care of.

11.7 Service Mix and Retailing Environment

(a) **Price:** Pricing is a vital aspect of any retail strategy. Customers are gained or lost based on this major attribute of retail strategy. Pricing should be value driven, especially in countries like India where consumers want to derive the maximum value for the price they are paying. Before implementing the pricing strategy, a retailer should consider macro-environmental factors such as the pricing strategies of competitors, government regulation and technological advancements. Generally, price adjustments helps the retailer adapt to the pricing patterns by reducing or increasing the prices owing to changes in the market dynamics like competitive price changes, demand fluctuations, seasonal changes, and so on.

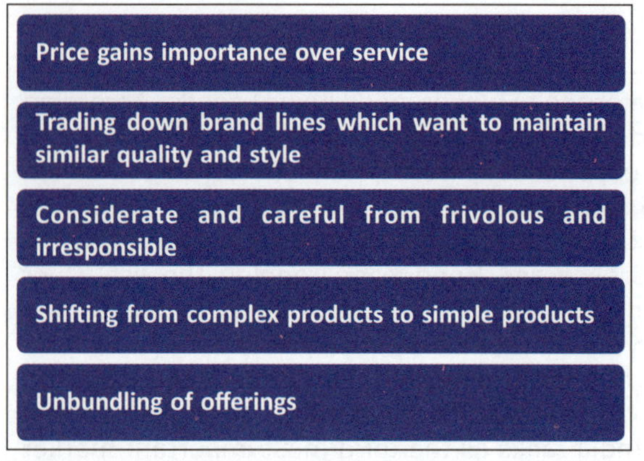

Figure 11.3: Changing customer expectations due to market turbulence

(b) **Place:** Stores located at a corner site of a shopping area have the advantage of offering more space for window display and thus have higher visibility and capacity to attract customers. Such locations are therefore best suited for products that have to be prominently displayed to catch the sight of the customer, such as garments and jewellery.

(c) **Promotion:** The promotional strategies adopted by a retailer include different forms of communication to attract customers to the retail outlet. This may be through advertising, sales promotions, public relations, or personal selling. To begin with, the objectives of the promotional strategy have to be developed. For instance, the objective of a promotional strategy may be to increase short-term sales, generate greater customer attraction, enhance store image, create awareness among customers, or promote private brands. After developing the objectives, the retailer can use various methods of budgeting to allocate financial resources for the implementation of the strategy. The budget can be determined on the basis of affordability of the retailer, and it can be increased as and when required in the future.

(d) **Product and service innovation:** Box 11.7 describes retail innovation in the Indian context.

BOX 11.7: RETAIL INNOVATION

The considerable movement in the industry is a result of frequently changing consumer demands, purchasing trends, and a focus on time management in merchandising to enhance value for existing buyers. Thus, certain factors need to be considered during the conception of strategies for innovation.

(a) Price gains importance over service: However, it is imperative to have consistent and professional service. When dealing with buyers, one should convey a consistently professional image. Give the buyer confidence that services are reliable. Communicate clearly and honestly. Make eye contact. Put time and energy into establishing and maintaining a long-term relationship with retail. Most people approach retail sales by thinking about their own need to sell their products at a certain price within a specified time frame. But a retailer may meet with better success if he tries to solve a buyer's problems or point out a new opportunity his product offers.

(b) Technology brings transformation: Technology has been a great facilitator of retail enterprise. We are now wireless, seamless and cashless, and can get any information we want and require. Retail technology has gone beyond being an enabler. For many organizations, intelligent application of technology like RFID, Retail PR and Retail CRM packages takes mind-boggling amounts of data, translates and transforms it into information, then synthesizes and transmogrifies it into intelligence. And after all the investment and effort, it is converted to superior performance and competitive advantage.

(c) Enhanced store experience: Today, with the emergence of malls, supermarkets and hypermarkets, there is immense competition to retain customers. There are greater choices available to consumers than ever before. It is inevitable for retailers to develop business strategies that focus on creating and maintaining customers. A differentiated shopping experience is an important step in this direction. Visual merchandising and store layout are key functions that need serious attention in enhancing the customer shopping experience. Merchandising is much more than simply the arrangement of products on the shelf; it is also about understanding the way customers shop.

(d) Price and value relationship: Price is important, but value is more important. While value is in the eye of the beholder, there are things a retailer can do to increase the value of his products. There are several marketable characteristics that demand a premium. Is the product organic? Is it produced on a farm? Does it have production characteristics or nutritional advantages to document? Can one tell a story about the product or business that makes it unique? These characteristics can increase the perceived value of a product. When the perceived value is greater, one can expect to receive a better price for it in a retail outlet. In the case of a discount supermarket, however, one will need to have rock-bottom prices.

(e) Product marketing and communication: It is important to approach product marketing with the right blend of strategic thinking and creative execution to help influence consumer purchase behaviour and build long-term loyalty to products. In addition, creating content that persuades is the single-most important function of any business. Intelligent customers make buying decisions worth millions on the basis of information offered to them about products that are becoming increasingly similar. Right communication makes an impact that not only captures attention, but also ensures recall and builds brands.

The conquest of customer satisfaction lies in quick and efficient customer service. Retailers have to invest in a quick response system. Instead of predicting months before a season starts, retailers have to closely observe what's selling and what's not, and continuously adjust what they produce and merchandise. In a move to fulfil consumer demands, the product assortments need to be continuously modified or even created. Thus, convenience and innovation are constant elements that retailers need to take into account in order to remain at a competitive edge in today's global marketplace.

Source: www.indiaretailing.com

11.8 Key Players

The retail sector has played a phenomenal role the worldover in increasing the productivity of consumer goods and services. It is also the second-largest industry in the US in terms of number of employees and establishments. There is no denying the fact that most developed economies rely heavily on their retail sector as a locomotive of growth.

The Indian retail industry is the largest among all the industries, accounting for over 10 per cent of the country's GDP and around 8 per cent of the employment. It has emerged as one of the most dynamic and fast paced industries with several players entering the market. But not all have tasted success because of the heavy initial investments required to compete in the market. There's no doubt that the Indian retail sector is inching its way towards becoming the next boom industry. Let us look at some of the key players in this sector.

Pantaloon Retail (India) Limited

Pantaloon Retail (India) Limited (PRIL) is undoubtedly the leader in the Indian retail segment with a presence across most sectors of organized retail. The company entered modern retail in 1997 with the opening of its department store format Pantaloons. In 2001, PRIL launched Big Bazaar, a hypermarket chain, followed by Food Bazaar, a supermarket chain. A five-format company two years back, it now operates over twenty formats which include Central (seamless malls located in city centres), Collection I (home improvement products), E-Zone (consumer electronics), Depot (books, music, gifts and stationery), aLL (fashion apparel for plus-size individuals), Shoe Factory (footwear), and Blue Sky (fashion accessories). It has recently launched its e-tailing venture, futurebazaar.com.

The company currently operates over 8.6 million sq. ft. of retail space and plans to take this up to over 30 million sq. ft. of retail space spread over 450 stores across 40 cities in India. The consolidated turnover increased by 27.6 per cent to ₹97, 865 crore in 2009-10 with a massive growth of EPS from ₹0.56 in 2008-9 to ₹3.18 the company announced a record dividend of 40 per cent.

Table 11.3: Projections for PRIL

Head	*2007*	*2008*	*2009*	*2010*	*2011+*
Sales (₹million)	48,853	50,489	64,507	97,865	1,12,800
Profit (₹million)	1,262	1,260	1,384	2,251	2,820
*Cost of goods sold	68.3	69.6	70	70.3	70.3
*Operating expenses	92.2	90.2	90.2	90.3	90.5
Profit margin	2.1	2.5	2.1	2.3	2.5

Source: Edelweiss Equity Research, May 2009.
Notes: *as a percentage of net profit, + estimates

PRIL's lifestyle retail segment consists of luxury apparels, footwear and leather accessories and jewelllery. Since these segments form a smaller portion of the total retail pie in India, the penetration of organized retail was easier in these segments. Through its value retailing format, Pantaloon caters to the segments least to catered by organized retailers in lifestyle formats. While the other retailers initially focused only on the lifestyle segment, targeting the upper middle class and above, Pantaloon was the first to identify opportunity in the value retail segment and introduced its flagship value retail brand 'Big Bazaar', targeting the average middle class population. In a country like India, the growth potential of this segment is enormous as the middle class is vast and willing to spend on value retail goods.

With new positioning under the name 'fresh fashion', the brand image and offerings have been tailored to suit the modern day consumer. In the second quarter of 2009 the company registered a net sales from the operations of ₹1,777.02 crore as against ₹1,511.21 crore during the same period in 2008. Accordingly, the profit before tax (PBT) shot up to ₹64.11 crore in second quarter of 2009 with respect to the corresponding figure of ₹55.75 crore during the same period in 2008. The year ended June 2009 showed a total turnover of ₹6,341.70 crore with a PBT of ₹216.23 crore. Core retail turn over increased by 49.98 per cent to ₹2,493.72 crore, core retail PAT increased by 170.91 per cent to ₹94.89 crore, same store growth in value retailing was 11.46 per cent, lifestyle retailing stood at 19.43 per cent and home retailing at 57 per cent in fourth quarter of 2009-10.

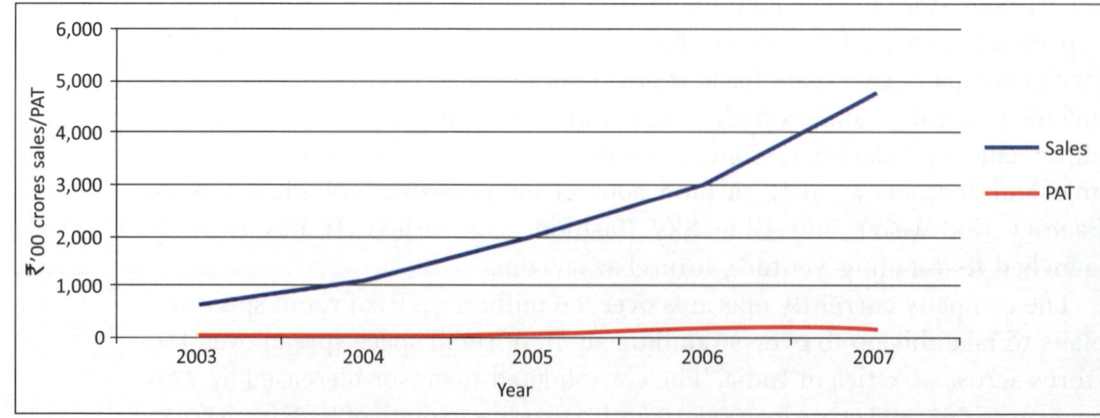

Figure 11.4: Sales and Profit After Tax (PAT) of Pantaloon Retail (India) Limited during 2003–7

Shopper's Stop Limited

Established in 1991 by K. Raheja Group with its flagship store Shopper's Stop, the chain has now expanded to over 100 retail outlets spread across 1.10 million sq. ft. of built-up area, spanning a spectrum of retailing verticals and formats. The group offers formats in the lifestyle and luxury segment, with the growing affluent middle class population as its target consumer base.

Shopper's Stop began by operating a chain of department stores. In 2009 it had 27 stores across the country and three stores under the name HomeStop. It has also begun operating a number of speciality stores, namely Crossword Bookstores, Mothercare, Brio, Desi Café and Arcelia. Shopper's Stop retails a range of branded goods and private labels under the categories of apparel, footwear, fashion jewellery, leather products, accessories and home products. These are complemented by cafe, food, entertainment, personal care and various beauty-related services.

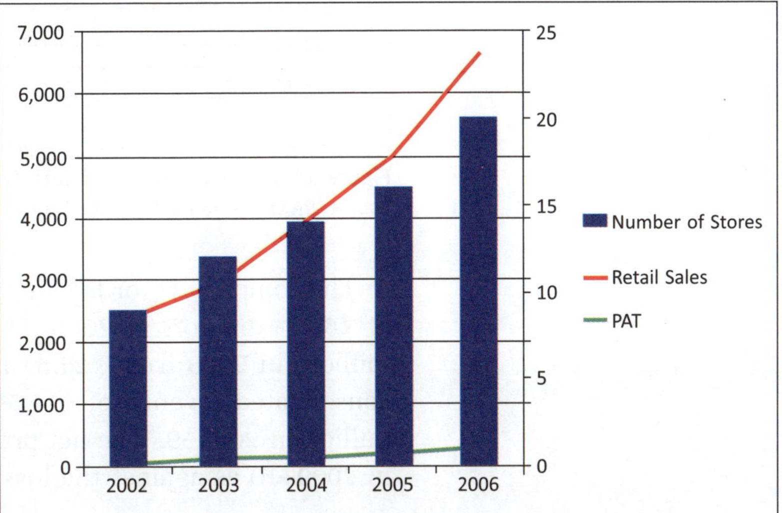

Figure 11.5: Sales and PAT of Shopper's Stop Limited during 2002–6

Source: Investors' Report of Shopper's Stop, December 2009.

In 2008 Shopper's Stop launched its e-store with delivery across major cities in India. The website retails all the products available at Shopper's Stop stores, including apparel, cosmetics and accessories. In April 2008, the store changed its logo and adopted the mantra 'start Something New'. The shop retails products of domestic and international brands such as Louis Philippe, Pepe, Arrow, BIBA, Gini & Jony, Carbon, Corelle, Magppie, Nike, Reebok, LEGO, and Mattel. It also retails merchandise under its own labels, such as STOP, Kashish, LIFE and Vettorio Fratini, Elliza Donatein and Acropolis. The company is a licensee for Austin Reed (London), an international brand whose men's and women's outerwear are retailed in India exclusively through the chain. In October 2009, Shopper's Stop bought the licence for merchandising Zoozoo the brand mascot for Vodafone India.

Shopper's Stop has a loyalty programme called First Citizen with a customer base of 14.5 lakh in 2009. They also offer a co-branded credit card with Citibank for its members.

In the second quarter of FY 2009, the company registered a net sales from the operations of ₹41,329 lakh as against ₹37,248 lakh during the same period in 2008. Accordingly, the net profit shot up to ₹1,458 lakh in second quater of 2009, an increase of 155 per cent. The half-yearly results ended June 2009 showed a total turnover of ₹72,148 lakh as against ₹67,693 lakh with a profit of ₹1,458 lakh against a whopping loss of ₹2,633 lakh during the same period in 2008. This is a remarkable achievement given the high market turbulence, demand shrinkage and lower footfalls across malls in the country.

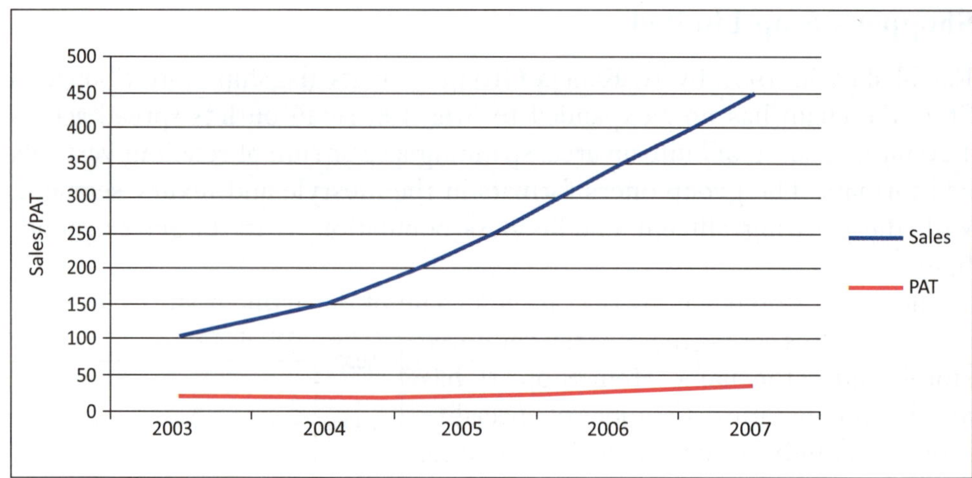

Figure 11.6: Sales and PAT of Tata Trent during 2003–7
Source: Investors' Report of Tata Trent.

The company recorded a turnover of ₹1,104.19 million, operating a profit of ₹63.84 million in 2008. However, PAT came down to negative (₹0.07 million) in 2008 from ₹24.34 million in 2007. However the company had a consolidated revenue of ₹14,548.3 million in 2009-10 as against ₹13,072.3 million in 2008–9. The net profit of the company shot up to ₹347.5 million in 2009–10 as against the loss of ₹819.9 million in 2008–9.

Tata Trent

In 1998 Tata sold its 50 per cent stake in the cosmetic products company Lakmé to HLL for ₹200 crore and created Trent. All shareholders of Lakmé were given shares in Trent. Simone Tata, the chairperson of Lakmé, went on to head Trent. The reason behind the sale was that Simone Tata saw greater growth potential in retail, and believed it would be more difficult for an Indian company to release new cosmetic products in a market that had opened up to global companies which could afford to invest more in research.

Trent's flagship store is Westside. Its retail sector activities are apparel and specialty books and music. The current store formats of Tata Trent are hypermarkets and supermarkets. It operates 36 stores in the major metros and mini-metros of India. Providing an international shopping experience, giving a perception of values, and offering the latest styles has created a loyal following for Westside's own brand of merchandise.

Westside was named the 'Most Admired Large Format Retail Chain of the Year' by the Lycra Images Fashion Awards 2005. In August 2005 Trent acquired a 76 per cent controlling stake in Landmark, a Chennai-based privately owned books and music retailer and completed 100 per cent acquisition in April 2008. Landmark had 10 stores in 2009. Trent also operates the hypermarket Star Bazaar in Ahmedabad, Bengaluru and Mumbai.

For the year ended 31 March 2009 the company reported a total revenue increase of 18.51 per cent to reach ₹9,170 million, net profit slump to ₹2.2 million, EPS down 17.87 per cent to ₹13.7 million and a negative cash flow.

Given the downturn faced across the industry, the company posted flat sales for the financial year 2009 over 2008. A comparative increase in expenditure, though slight, brought operating profits down 18 per cent in 2009. On a consolidated basis, therefore, a sales growth of 18 per cent was wiped out with a 24 per cent increase in expenditure driven by higher employee and selling expenses. However in 2009–10 the company made a record profit of ₹40.22 crore as against ₹26.75 crore in 2008–9.

11.9 Combating Slowdown

Kishore Biyani-owned Pantaloon Retail recorded a 30 per cent growth rate in 2007. However, the 70 per cent growth it recorded in 2008 meant the slowdown had not spared it either. The group froze its expansion plans and reworked its strategy to effectively beat the slowdown. Private labels like Tasty Treats, Fresh and Pure, Clean matter and Dream Line helped it weather the economic slowdown and earn reasonably higher margins as compared to branded products.

Also, functioning in large formats like hypermarkets has given the group more scope to enjoy larger gross margins. The first six months of 2009 have been difficult for the retail industry. The sector has entered into a mode of correction and getting rid of the flab it had accumulated over the past five years of rapid expansion. Experts say the restructuring exercise may continue for the next 12-18 months before retailers begin another serious round of expansion.

As investors turn more defensive, stocks of retailers with less ambitious expansion plans and stronger cash coffers are being preferred to their more aggressive counterparts. This may partly explain the high double-digit multiples enjoyed by Titan (low debt, diversified and branded presence), Pantaloon (restructuring moves, operation across retail lines, wide footprint), Trent (low debt, steady performance, gradual expansion), Koutons (value retail concept holding up, large store network) and Bata India (brand equity, low debt). The demographic push towards a younger India and a newfound buzz in the real estate sector were key factors that drove investor interest in the retail sector for much of 2005 to 2007.

Over eight retailers went in for initial public offers during this time, collectively raising more than ₹666 crore for expansion and technology investment. For PRIL, sales per sq. ft. were down 5.7 per cent, continuing the decline of the past eight quarters y-o-y during 2007–9.

In a bid to maximize sales per sq. ft., India's frontline retailers are increasingly looking at ways to restructure their stores. Leading players like Future Group, Spencer's Retail, Shopper's Stop and Vishal Retail planned to right-size their stores and replace slow-moving categories with speciality formats under the shop-in-shop model. Retailers feel such an approach will help them improve gross margin returns per sq. ft. in the present environment when same-store sales growth is weak. According to the Future Group, the shop-in-shop approach helps increase revenue per sq. ft. It enables best utilization of space and is a good way to do away with excess space while also reducing space for categories which are not doing well. The Future Group offers wider choice in large-format stores like Big Bazaar by setting up speciality zones under the shop-in-shop model. This approach provides consumers with a wider choice.

Shopper's Stop has tied up with Café Coffee Day to manage cafes within its stores. It is part of an ongoing process to maximize returns and the most common categories where retailers are looking for shop-in-shop outlets include food and beverage, Indian apparel and areas which have more customer-connect requirement like cosmetics, personal care products, fine jewellery and salons.

Spencer's Retail, which is right-sizing by cutting down on 20 per cent of its retail space, is also focusing on shop-in-shops. In a slowdown, shop-in-shops are the best way to leverage domain knowledge of speciality players and maximize returns. Such outlets will be set up through the group's speciality formats like Books & Beyond, Mera World, Music World as well as in collaboration with other players.

Vishal Retail group is restructuring its 171 stores nationally. In fact, small and regional brands are lapping up the opportunity to follow the shop-in-shop model since it reduces their capital expenditure and ensures assured footfall.

Retailers are also analysing items outside their portfolio. For these products, they either set up new departments or give out space as concessions, to create more reasons for customers to come back. Let us look at the factors that kickstarted the retail boom and eventual began to drag the industry down.

Factors Affecting Indian Retail Business

Indian consumer not so resilient: India's indigenous consumption was thought to be the key factor that would keep retailers in good health even as export-reliant sectors fell prey to the slowdown. As it turned out, the urban population, the main target for leading retailers, was not entirely insulated from global events, and potential job losses, deferring of pay hikes, and a cautious consumer sentiment sent footfalls sliding for most retailers. These trends became apparent in the December 2008 quarter, with the sales of retailers increasing by a modest 15 per cent, down from the 40 per cent-plus growth rates seen in earlier quarters, even with the festival sales slotted in these months. Cutbacks in spending persisted in 2009, affecting lifestyle players such as Shopper's Stop and the home solutions division of Pantaloon.

Expansion sprees: Driven by the economic boom, real estate activity had picked up across residential and commercial sectors. With the choice of locations for malls driven more by availability of land than by proximity to consumers, the mall-based model for retail has not delivered as expected. Hectic real estate activity sent land prices and thus rentals zooming, building a high cost structure into retail expansion. Players currently fork out about 4 per cent of sales on rentals alone—too high in a sector where operating profit margins are at 8 per cent.

Rental rates were fast becoming too high for retailers to find viable and, as the realty sector faced a funds crunch, retailers whose store roll-outs hinged on malls saw their capital locked up in these stores.

Organized retail penetration: With only about 5 per cent of India's retail organized, the vast untapped potential drew retailers. But leading players such as Shopper's Stop are concentrated in the metros and tier I cities, with only a few, for instance, Vishal Retail, penetrating further into tier III cities, where the bulk of the demand is located. Organized retailers are also still unable to match the convenience offered by traditional corner shop retailers.

Credit flows: Rosy demand projections and easy availability of funds (driven partly by a buoyant stock market) led to the charting of aggressive expansion plans. For example, Koutons Retail went from 999 outlets at the time of its IPO in September 2007 to more than 1,400 stores in 2008. Besides IPO funding, retailers took on debt to bankroll expansion. The average debt to equity ratio for retailers was 2.57 for 2008, against the 0.85 times in 2006. Working capital, the lifeblood for any retailer, also relied on debt. With faltering growth, servicing this debt became a difficult proposition for most retailers.

Margin squeeze: High rentals, high inventory levels and interest payouts together imposed a squeeze on net profit margins of retailers, which shrank from 6 to 2 per cent in the quarters between December 2006 and December 2008. Quarterly interest payments for eleven leading listed retailers shot up 80 per cent in just one year—from December 2007 to December 2008.

11.10 Coping with Recession

Organized retail players tried every trick in the book, which includes closing unviable stores, focusing more on private labels and expanding with great care. At the same time, they took advantage of softening rentals. The Aditya Birla Group which runs the *More* chain of food and grocery stores also took a number of steps once the downturn cast its dark spell. Footfalls for most retailers come down, as per a KPMG report titled 'Indian Retail-Time to Change Lanes'. The report also pointed out that many retailers borrowed a lot. For instance, Vishal Retail's interest expenditure was ₹7 crore per month.

Retailers such as Kishore Biyani's Future Group, Mukesh Ambani's Reliance Retail, Videocon and the Wadhawan Group placed their cash and carry plans (bulk buying and sale to wholesale trade) on the backburner. The aim was to conserve cash given the slowdown.

Meanwhile, international players like Walmart and Carrefour, cautious until now, may show more pace in beginning their cash and carry operations here. Expecting a growth rate of 35-40 per cent a year, a host of Indian and international retailers had announced plans to enter the space. Analysts tracking the retail sector felt the longer gestation period of cash and carry operations, coupled with lower margins made Indian retailers do a rethink. While the retail business takes three-four years to break even, cash and carry turns profitable in seven to eight years. While retailers have gross margins of 18-20 per cent, cash and carry operators have a much lower margin of 10-12 per cent.

Figure 11.7: Strategies to help cope with the recession

Though value retailers may stand a better chance of weathering the slowdown, in the long-term, both value and lifestyle players should see growth. In the short-term, however, indicators to look out for are same-store sales growth figures and footfalls—in a climate of scaled back expansion, sales growth will have to come from existing stores. Reach of the retail network plays a key role as well. Also important is short-term liquidity and working capital as retailers require quick short-term funding to keep merchandise on shelves. Interest cover is another important measure, as a fair number of retailers have a cover of less than five times interest obligations at presant.

Propping flagging sales: Same-store sales growth was on a decline for most retailers, going negative in some cases such as Shopper's Stop and the home solutions division of Pantaloon. Retailers are now turning to smaller cities which are less competitive, going in for discount sales to eliminate old stock, launching more offers to attract footfalls, banking on customer loyalty, and so on. For example, Koutons had an offer giving out five items free for every one item purchased. Westside temporarily lowered bill-size cutoff for its ClubWest membership from ₹2,000 to ₹1000, though how far such schemes spur sales may be seen only in the coming quarter.

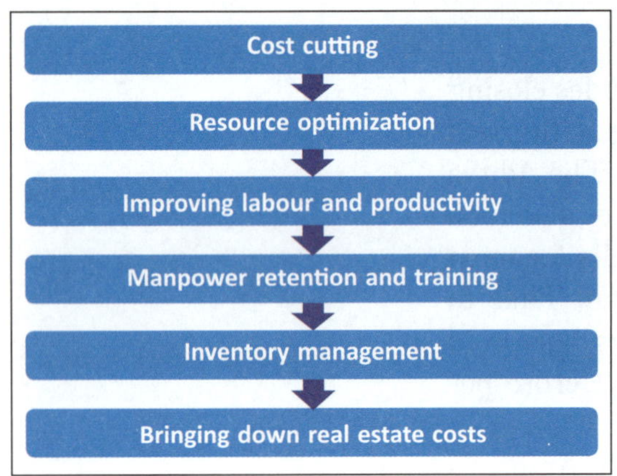

Figure 11.8: Managing costs

Cost controls: Retailers are now looking to optimize costs by going in for a supply chain revamp, focusing on private labels (they offer better margins), closing unviable stores, lowering inventory, and expanding through franchisees. Vishal Retail, for instance, remodelled its distribution system to a centralized version. The rental front is also looking up. Developers are now open to negotiation on rentals as well as new models such as revenue share, an option with which Pantaloon is experimenting.

Expansion cutbacks: Retailers, who only in 2008 were busy painting rosy pictures, are now struggling to put their houses in order. Neighbourhood discount chain Subhiksha could be going bust, though large-format chain Vishal Retail managed not to slip into a financial distress through substantial reduction in lease rentals, which form a good 30 per cent of operational costs. Shopper's Stop registered a sluggish 4 per cent growth in same-store sales in the nine months ended 31 December 2008.

A combination of lack of funding, sluggish sales and store delivery delays has forced retailers, such as Pantaloon, to scale back expansion plans, while others, such as Vishal Retail, are not likely to expand at all. But a few remain optimistic; Bata India plans to open 240 stores in the space of three years. Pantaloon Retail has taken advantage of its presence in multiple retail lines and plans to restructure, transferring its retail and fashion operations into wholly-owned subsidiaries, while retaining the consumer goods section. The idea is to allow the raising of funds, especially from private equity players, in segments that are money-spinners, without being bogged down by poor performances in other segments.

The retailers' ability to fund expansion is another aspect, as credit lines are freezing and the equity route may not be very well-received in the present circumstance. On most, if not all counts, players such as Titan, Pantaloon and Trent may fare better than their counterparts. In the long-term, both value and lifestyle players will see growth. During a downturn, people do not stop consuming. As a retailer, it is important to look beyond recession and find ways to bring customers to the stores.

The group has undertaken several strategic initiatives to ensure robust growth despite the slowdown in consumer demand. For starters, it has decided that the price of products sold through the Pantaloons chain will be reduced to the level of 2007. It expects such a strategy will provide a compelling entry-level price point to consumers vis-à-vis competing retail chains. Also on the cards are plans to expand the Pantaloons private-label portfolio. This will build a value-for-money proposition for consumers and will also help increase sales. New private labels will also have a similar pricing strategy. The Future Group currently operates 44 Pantaloons outlets across India over a total of 1.2 million sq. ft. On an average, each of the Pantaloons outlet has an operating space of around 25,000 sq. ft. As per recent reports, the Future Group CEO Kishore Biyani has stated that the group has downsized its retail space expansion plans by almost half as the market continues to reel under a slump. Earlier, they were planning to add 4 million sq. ft. of space but that has now been scaled down to 2.5 million sq. ft. in 2009–10.

Same-store sales, a common metric in the retail industry, compares sales of stores that have been in the business for a year or more. The measure allows investors to determine what portion of new sales has come from growth and from opening new stores. Pantaloon Retail's same-store sales in April 2009 grew the most in six months because of strong consumer demand. Same-store sales in the value retailing segment grew 7.02 per cent, the most since Novemeber 2008, to ₹308.19 crore. Sales in the lifestyle segment grew 6.03 per cent to ₹119.53 crore, while sales in the home retailing segment fell 28.21 per cent to ₹34.57 crore. The total sales for April rose 20.03 per cent to ₹595.81 crore. In absolute terms, value retailing rose 23.44 per cent to ₹367.20 crore, while lifestyle retailing grew 18.1 per cent to ₹135.81 crore. Home retailing grew 10.61 per cent to ₹92.80 crore.

In November 2008, the same-store sales for value, lifestyle and home retail fell 13.78, 10.32 and 36.01 per cent, respectively. A key reason for faster growth in lifestyle retailing could be steeper discounts. In January and February 2008, Pantaloon's discount offers removed the difference between lifestyle products and value products—the reason behind the constant increase in the sales figures of the company since then. Analysts felt the overall market has also revived and without discounts, Pantaloon should be able to post similar growth in the future. However, the home retail segment will take two-three months to revive.

BOX 11.8: EMERGING RENTAL MODEL FOR ORGANIZED RETAILERS

While retailers worked with the option of cutting costs and negotiating rentals to gear up for expansion, mall owners, who are vital for the organized retail sector, are experimenting with a new method—rent on a daily basis. Atul Ruia-owned Phoenix Market City mall has implemented the system at a few of its locations, while others such as Inorbit and Nirmal Lifestyle are actively considering it as an innovative option for their forthcoming malls. Currently, the fixed rental or revenue share scheme is widely practised with minimum guarantee money, depending on the brand, product and location of the space. Fixed rental was preferred till the liquidity crisis spread and the global demand slump hit both retailers and mall owners.

'We are receiving quite a positive response and have planned to implement it (the daily rental model) across the country,' says Phoenix Market City managing director Atul Ruia. 'It is a viable option in an industry that is just recovering from a period of uncertainty.'

India's organized retail market, roughly estimated at ₹40,000 crore, and which is closely connected with malls, was among the first sectors in India to be affected by the crisis as consumers dithered about purchases. As a result, many retailers and mall owners started looking at various options including revenue sharing and a minimum guarantee amount during 2010–11.

Under the new process, the retailer will have a joint account with the mall owner and at the end of each day the share of the mall owner is debited to his account. In the previous method—the revenue sharing model—percentage rents were payable annually, quarterly, monthly, or upon achieving breakpoint sales. 'We believe any innovative method that could streamline the system and synergy between the owner and the retailer is welcome,' says Inorbit CEO Kishore Bhatija. 'We are looking at implementing it first at our Hyderabad mall.'

Like Phoenix, Inorbit too has been in favour of the new model for its malls at Hyderabad, Pune and Bengaluru. Inorbit's mall at Hyderabad has seen 66 per cent occupancy on the revenue sharing model, while the remaining would be on daily basis. Phoenix was the first to implement it at its new malls in cities such as Mumbai, Pune, Bengaluru and Chennai. Phoenix has three malls operational and plans to open seven in the next three years, where this method will be applicable. Phoenix also plans to open malls in smaller cities like Lucknow, Agra and Indore.

Nirmal Lifestyle, which is all set to launch its second phase of expansion during 2010–11, has planned for 30 per cent remaining space at its new mall in Mulund, a Mumbai suburb. Chairman Dharmesh Jain says this model will evolve as a realistic method of revenue collection. 'It would be beneficial with much transparent transaction between the two,' Dharmesh Jain added.

However, the industry sees this practice at a very early stage. Jones Lang LaSalle Meghraj managing director (retail) Shubhranshu Pani says, 'Though this method would de-risk the retailer from the pain of high rentals, it will take another two-three years to be widely used. Retailers are pressing for better options before signing revenue sharing agreements rather than going for pure rental arrangements with mall owners.'

Low rentals boost commercial real estate sales

Following the correction in commercial realty rates in metros by 20 to 40 per cent in October 2009, top builders expected sales to improve considerably. In the first two quarters of 2010, sales of office space rentals grew 10 to 15 per cent. To tap the growing opportunity, large builders in various metros are offering ready-to-possess offices, shops and commercial plots, and under-construction offices at 15 to 20 per cent discount. According to Harinder Dhillion, vice-president (marketing) of Delhi-based Raheja Builders, 'New Delhi followed by Gurgaon and Noida have witnessed 15 per cent increase in sales of commercial space since the second quarter of 2010. As a result, the company offered price discounts of up to 10 to 15 per cent on office space rentals through their commercial properties based in Gurgaon.' Mumbai-based Royal Palms India has launched ready-to-possess offices, shops and commercial plots as well as under-construction offices for corporates at 3,999 per sq. ft. at Goregaon East, Mumbai. Royal Palms has a total of 4 lakh sq. ft. of office space/plots. Depending on the need of the buyer, the company can offer offices or buildings ranging from 400 sq. ft. to 80,000 sq.ft.

Says Dilawar Nensey, joint MD, Royal Palms India, 'The land on which these properties are located was acquired over 26 years ago at negligible cost and hence, even at these rates the company will make reasonably good profit.' Royal Palms has sold over 1,600 offices so far with top names like Topsgroup and Monarch having their business HQ there.

There are industry experts who believe that rentals do vary according to specific occupier profiles. Office space rentals in the metros have corrected by up to 40 per cent, which would mean that they are now back to the 2005–6 levels, which is when the economic up-cycle began.

Source: www.indianrealtynews.com

The group is also enforcing operational efficiency by tightening the supply chain and maintaining an optimized product replenishment system. The Pantaloons chain contributes around 14 per cent to the group's turnover. Incidentally, the Pantaloons format is slightly different in the east, where it is positioned more as a department store selling apparel, accessories, consumer electronics, food, grocery and a host of other items. Nationally Pantaloons focuses only on apparel and accessories.

Summary

Retailing involves the selling of products/services to customers for their non-commercial individual or family use. Normally, retailing is the last stage of the distribution process. The Indian retail market has seen immense transformation in the post-liberalization era. The vast increase in the availability of product varieties and the purchasing power of consumers, companies achieving economies of scale with superior supply chain management and a world-class customer service are responsible for tremendous growth witnessed by the Indian retail market.

However, the government is still protecting the retail sector and foreign direct investment is not allowed. However, once this sector opens up entirely to foreign competition like other sectors, it will witness substantial changes and the Indian consumer will benefit the most. The ability to overcome the recession is an acid test for many of the retail chains during 2009–12.

Case Discussion Questions

Assume that you head the strategic marketing division of a UK-based food and grocery (F&G) retailer. You are devising a number of plans to improve the retail penetration, footfall, retail promotions and average spent per visit of in-store customers in Mumbai, Delhi, Chennai, Bengaluru, Kolkata, Pune, Lucknow, Visakhapatnam and Ahmedabad.

How do you devise a positioning strategy and service mix for the company in the Indian market? Explain the various elements and their significance. How do you analyse the profitability of various customer groups by utilizing the theory explained in this case?

Explain various comprehensive models like Nicosia, EKB, Howard and Sheath to analyse Indian F&G retail customers' behaviour by utilizing the theory explained in this case study. What are the factors influencing their behaviour?

In your opinion, what may be the perceived benefits of customer analysis and LTV of F&G retail customers for a high-end retailer?

Comment on the relevance and significance of VALS segmentation for organic fruits and vegetables (F&V) segment customers. List the strategic factors of performance like market attractiveness, competitive strength, value added structures, people and organization by utilizing the theory explained in this case .

Sources: Kala Vijay Raghavan and Rajiv Banerjee of Brand Equity, *The Economic Times; Business Standard* and *Financial Express* (April to August 2010), India retailing.com, Pantaloon Retail Group and walmart.com

CASE ANALYSIS

The Indian Retail Environment

The Indian retail industry remained a largely unorganized industry until the 1980s. It started changing with the entry of Titan, Bombay Dyeing and Raymond's. Owing to tremendous growth over the past few years, the retail industry in India was predicted to grow at 28 per cent in the period of 2003–8. With 12 lakh retail outlets in the country, the industry contributes ₹14,000 crore to the GDP and provides maximum employment, after agriculture as can be seen in Figure 11.9.

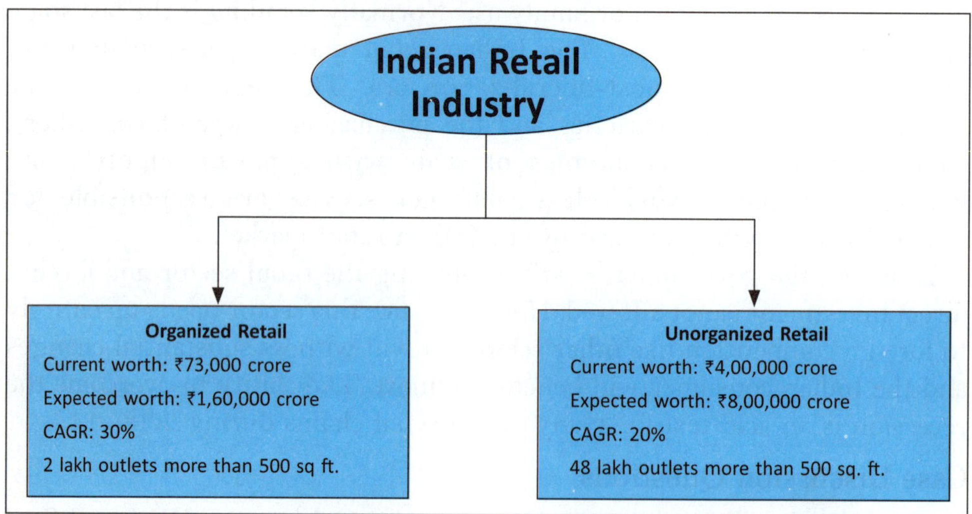

Figure 11.9: Indian retail industry provides maximum employment (2003–8)

Another data point available is that the number of luxury households in India is 1.6 million currently, which has crossed 3 million in 2010.

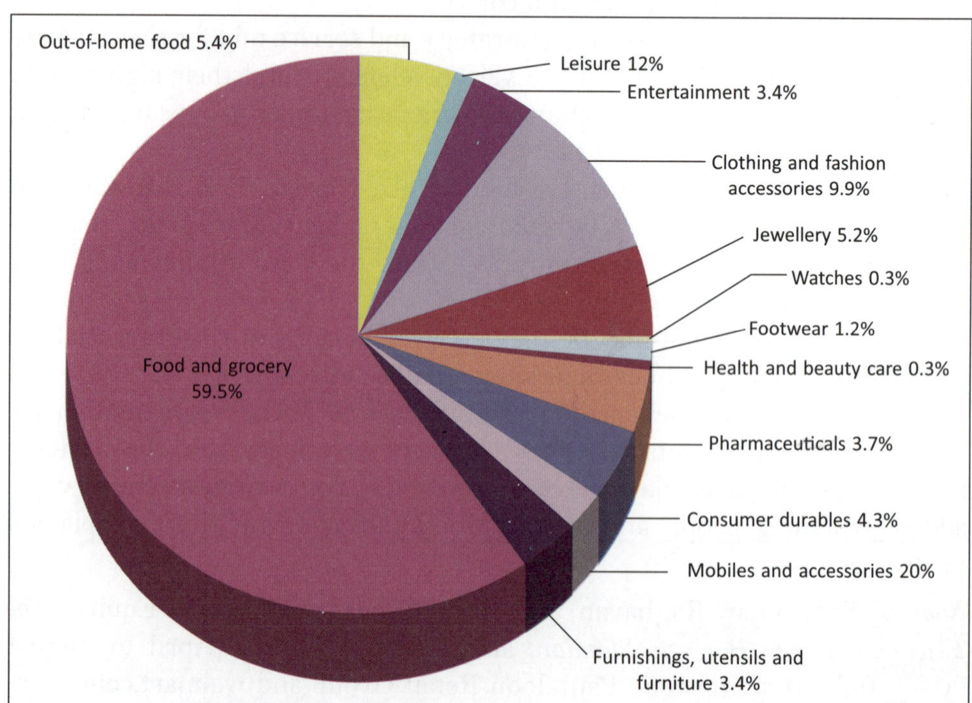

Figure 11.10: The Indian retail pie

Control Over Prime Retailing Space

Increasing real estate prices and thus increasing rentals hamper the profitability of retailers. In order to have better control on retail space, many enter into long-term leases (ranging from 10 to 25 years). Retail players are now tying up with developers to ensure access to the best retailing locations at reasonable rentals.

Emergence of Multiple Modern Retailing Formats

Multiple modern retailing formats have emerged to provide different value propositions and capture the maximum share of the consumer wallet. Nowadays, consumers prefer value for money, convenience and a wide variety of offerings, coupled with a pleasant shopping experience, which the traditional retailing format has failed to meet. This has created an opportunity for modern retailing formats to emerge and plug the existing gaps. A number of these have sprung up, each offering a distinct value proposition to the consumer.

The history of the development of the global retail industry indicates that in the opening and peaking stage of retail development, the retail space is dominated by supermarkets and hypermarkets. These typically account for 75-80 per cent of all formats, in line with the rush to set up hypermarkets witnessed in the Indian scenario. The leading Indian retailers have extended their businesses into the hypermarket space to capture the retail opportunity from the swelling middle class.

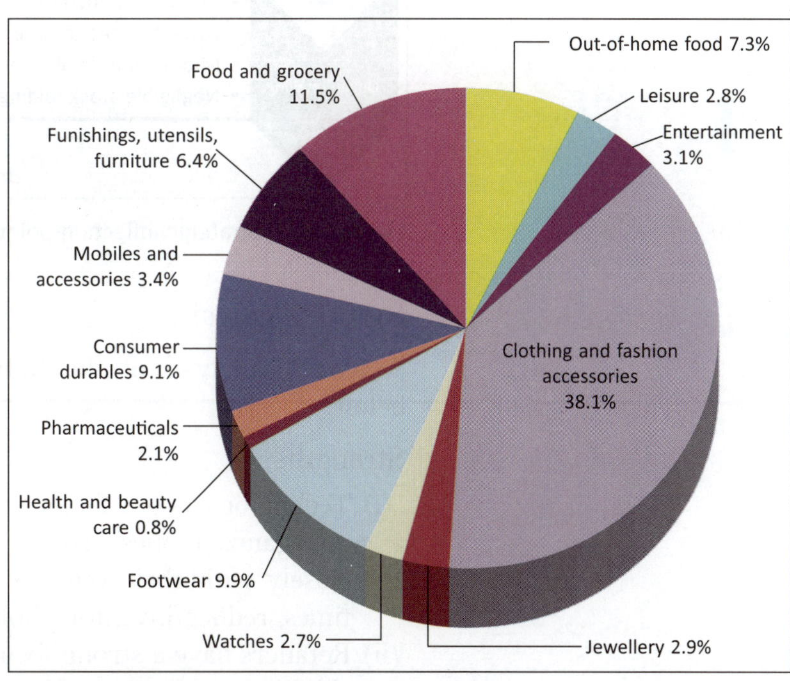

Figure 11.11: Organized retail pie

Modern retailing began in India through players catering to the lifestyle segment via various department stores that largely focused on branded apparel merchandise. Moving forward, one notices several of these departmental stores (at present mainly restricted to the metros) increasingly trickling down to the smaller cities.

Speciality stores are fast catching the fancy of Indian retailers. Such a format concentrates on specific merchandise and focuses on a single category, offering a large range of selection within that. These stores enjoy strong customer loyalty with interesting loyalty programmes. A recent trend in the segment is the development of specialty malls like Gurgaon's Gold Souk and Bengaluru's EVA mall.

Most leading retailers are however aiming at a well-diversified presence across the consumption basket. The recent addition by leading players is in the form of catalogue retailing. This strategy gives the retailers the flexibility to cater to a broad-based buying basket of the consumer and also manage competition better in the near term.

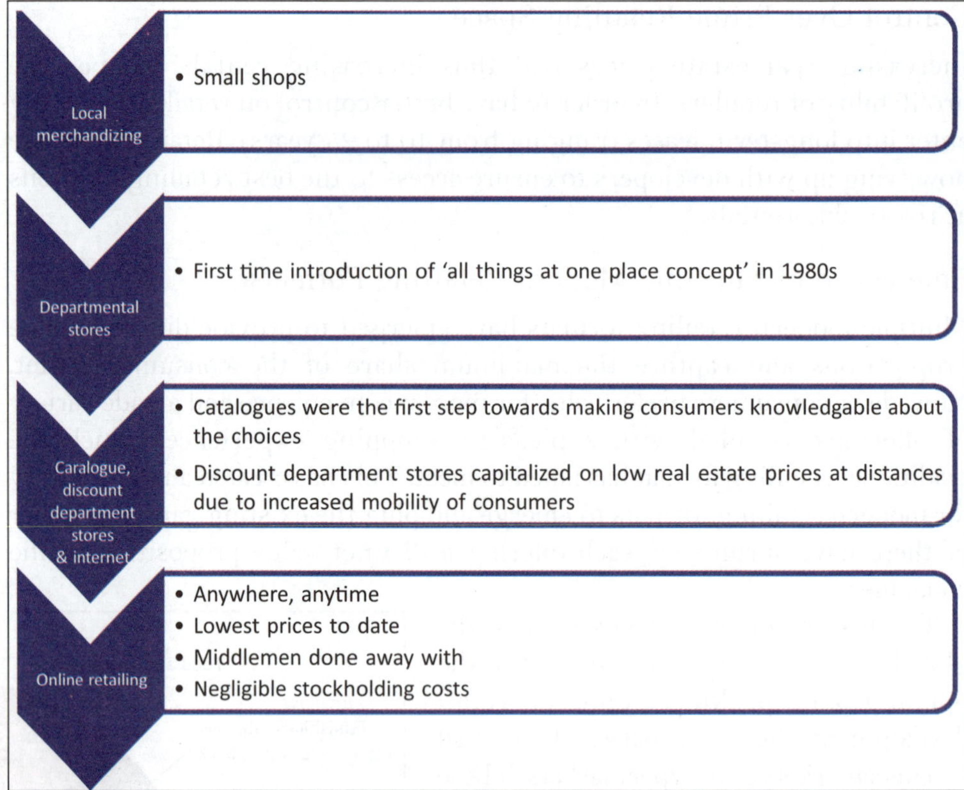

Figure 11.12: Strategic inflection points in global retailing

SWOT Analysis

A SWOT analysis of the Indian organized retail industry is presented below:

Strengths

(i) Technology is one factor which helps organized retailers score over the unorganized ones. Today, successful organized retailers today work closely with their vendors to predict consumer demand, shorten lead times, reduce inventory holding and ultimately save cost.

(ii) Retailers have a strong focus on systems and processes. They have been able to capture years of learning and use it to create Standard Operating Procedures (SOPs) for every activity, from planning and setting up of new stores to their day-to-day operations.

(iii) Growth of the Indian service sector such as IT/ITES, BPOs and an increasing population of working women has led to an increase in the household disposable income. Increase in per capita income increases household consumption, which in turn influences the brand consciousness of Indian youth.

(iv) A rising number of nuclear families has changed consumption habits of the Indian family.

Weaknesses

(i) Low conversion level: Despite high footfalls, the conversion ratio has been very low in retail outlets in malls as compared to their standalone counterparts. It is seen that actual conversion of footfall into sales in mall outlets is approximately 20-25 per cent. On the other hand, a high-street store of a retail chain has an average conversion of about 50-60 per cent.

(ii) Customer loyalty: Retail chains are yet to stock their outlets in malls with the right merchandise mix. Since standalone outlets were established a lot earlier, they have stabilized in terms of footfalls and merchandise mix and thus have a higher customer loyalty base.

(iii) Lack of expertise in supply chain management: Supply chain is a major concern in the growth of the modern retail industry in India. Indian retail players are far behind world leaders such as Walmart regarding supply chain integration into their business process.

Opportunities: Inadequate Infrastructure

(i) Format diversification: Indian retail players can have different retailing formats such as speciality stores, supermarkets and hypermarkets.

(ii) Rural retailing: The huge rural population of India has caught the attention of retailers. ITC launched India's first rural mall 'Chaupal Sagar', offering a diverse range of products from FMCG to electronic goods to automobiles, attempting to provide farmers a one-stop destination for all their needs. 'Hariyali Bazar', started by the DCM Sriram Group, provides farm related inputs and services. Godrej has launched 'agristores' named 'Adhaar' which offer agricultural products such as fertilizers and animal feed along with the required knowledge for effective use of the same to the farmers. Pepsi, on the other hand, is experimenting with farmers of Punjab to grow the right quality tomatoes for its tomato purees and pastes.

(iii) Growing middle class: The Indian middle class is projected to grow from the present 30 crore to over 60 crore by 2010, making the country one of the largest consumer markets of the world. According to IMAGES-KSA, India will have over 55 crore people under the age of 20 years by 2015, which provides enormous opportunities in the children and teens' retailing segment.

(iv) Change in consumer behaviour pattern and increase in disposable income: Organized retail is only 4 per cent of the total retailing market in India. It is estimated to grow at the rate of 25-30 per cent per annum and reach ₹1,00,000 crore by 2012. The top six cities contribute 66 per cent of the total organized retailing in India. While the metros have already been exploited, the focus has now shifted towards the tier II cities. The contribution of these cities to total organized retailing sales is expected to grow to 20-25 per cent.

Threats

If the unorganized retailers are put together, they are parallel to a large supermarket with no or little overheads, high degree of flexibility in merchandise, display, prices and turnover.

(i) Shopping culture: The shopping culture as it is understood in the west has not developed in India as yet. Even now malls are more a place to hang around with family and friends and do some window shopping.

(ii) Threat of new entrants: With India becoming an attractive retail market and the gradual increase in foreign participation in the sector, many new entrants are expected, thus sharpening competition.
(iii) Competitive rivalry in the industry: There is intense rivalry among leading national retailers for new locations and quality real estate.
(iv) Economic slowdown: Retail is the 'last mile' and the impact of the economic slowdown would have seen a direct manifestation in lowered consumer spend.

Unorganized Sector: Key Challenges for Retail in India

Table 11.4: Organized and unorganized retail compared

Factors	*Organized retail*	*Unorganized retail*
Operation cost	High due to involvement of labour	Owner-operated, so low cost
Land cost	Expensive and prime land locations	Traditional business, so land is owned or cheap
Consumer psychology	Bigger and brighter is more expensive	Known for their lacklustre shops
Taxes	High	Negligible
Overall cost	High	Low
Overall pressure on margin	High	Low

Segmentation, Targeting and Positioning (STP) Challenge

The organized retail industry faces a much more difficult challenge from the perspective of creating a strategic marketing mix for consumers owing to India's atypical demography. Consumer segmentation is the most difficult task owing to the variability of preferences for various products. The following are the problems faced during segmentation and targeting:

(a) Value to the consumer implies not just product utility but also socio-cultural benefits.
(b) The purchasing power varies a lot even in similar locations across the country.
(c) The attitude of consumers towards spending is very product specific.
(d) Demography is not uniform.
(e) Shift in income-based classes due to changing earning patterns.
(f) Butterfly existence due to choices in the market.

The issues faced above are related. Figure 11.13 illustrates the relationship.

Segmentation leads to customization: If the retail industry is able to get the segmentation right then it clearly follows that the parameters used to segment will help them customize the product or service according to those parameters.

Targeting aims at higher sales: Understanding the target group would help to create a product or buying experience which is coherent with the target group. This would automatically generate higher sales.

Promotion aims at low cost: Right segmentation and right targeting would help create the right promotion strategy. This would get converted into lower cost as the conversion rate (amount of sales per rupees spent in promotion) would be high.

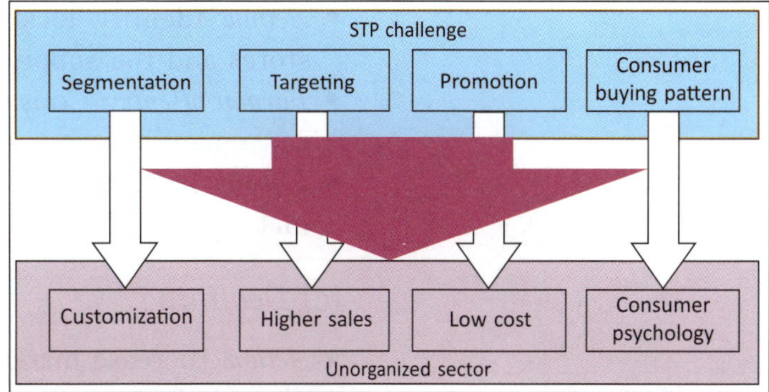

Figure 11.13: STP challenge

Consumer buying pattern based on consumer psychology: This is one area where the unorganized retail scores over the organized sector. Once a company understands the consumer buying pattern, it would have understood the consumer mindset which would help them in every stage, i.e. knowing the touch points for the right promotion strategy.

Hence getting the right STP is imperative to formulating the right marketing mix and to sustain the growth that has been projected. If the industry gets the STP right the threat from the unorganized sector would be minimized.

Positioning Strategy

A positioning strategy is created keeping in mind the following essential elements:

- Profile of the market
- Segmentation of the market
- Competition
- Position with respect to the competitors
- Value proposition

With respect to the information given in this case, the following is the analysis of the various elements of the positioning strategy.

Profile of the Market

The profile of the market can be ascertained by keeping in view the following:

1. **Size of the market:** According to AT Kearney estimates, organized retail, which accounts for lesser than 6 per cent of the market, is expected to grow at 40 per cent CAGR from $8 billion to $22 billion by 2012. Overall, India's retail sector is expected to grow from $315 billion to $427 billion by 2012 and $635 billion by 2020.
2. **Life cycle of retailing industry:** There are basically four stages in the life cycle:

(a) *Opening*

- *Action*: Monitor markets and conduct consumer research
- *Format of entry*: Consider minority investment in a local retailer
- *Labour market*: Identify skilled labour pool from the market

(b) *Peaking*

- *Action*: Identify local partners and real estate locations; establish pilot stores and the supply chain
- *Format of entry*: Consider supermarkets, hypermarkets, cash and carry and convenience stores
- *Labour market*: Hire and train local talent and balance the expatriate mix

(c) *Declining*

- *Action*: Increase market entries to capture market share
- *Format of entry*: Consider discount, warehouse stores and apparel
- *Labour market*: Change balance from expatriate to local staff

(d) *Closing*

- *Action*: Determine leadership status (profitability) in the segment
- *Format of entry*: Move to wave-two formats, including EEO, DIY and specialized apparel
- *Labour market*: No pattern identified

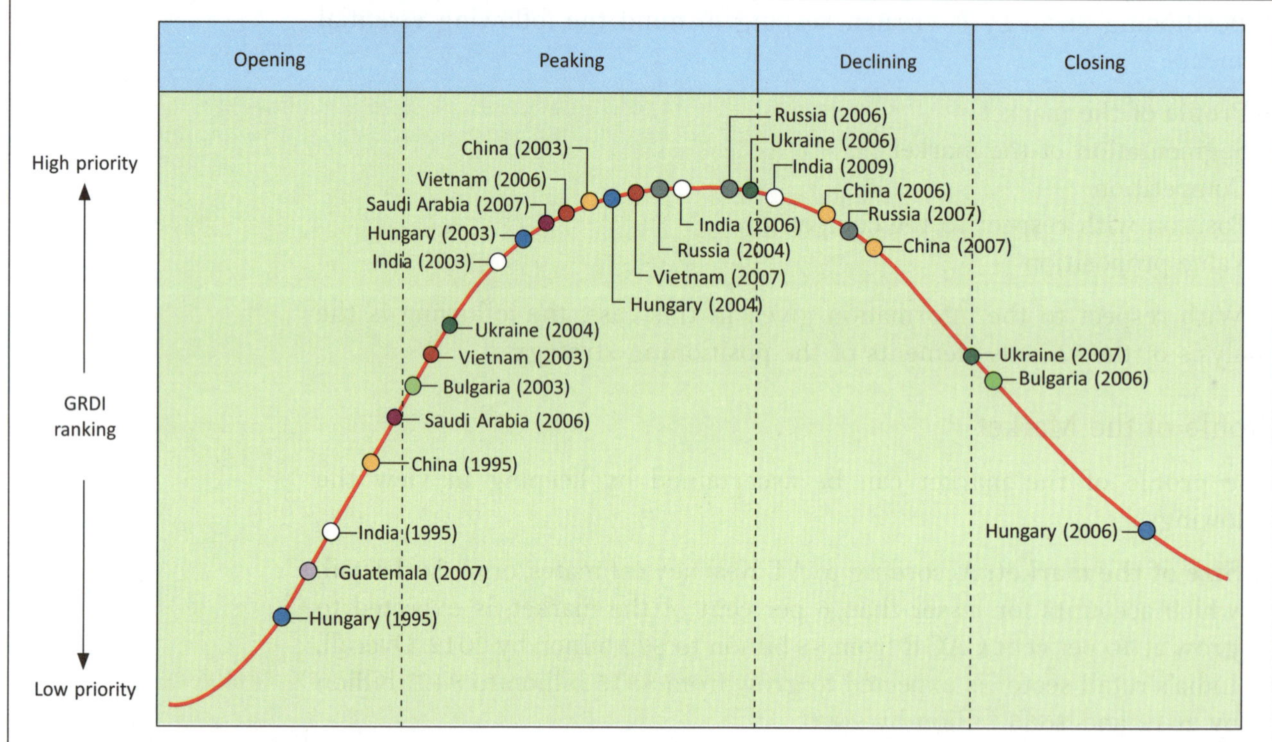

Figure 11.14: Life cycle of organized retailing across the years in various countries
Source: AT Kearney

Segmentation of the Market

There are two steps to be followed in order to segment the market:

Problems of the market: First, one needs to understand the emerging needs of the middle class consumers in this market. Consumer needs for the food and grocery retail industry are as follows:

- Low price
- Convenience
- Reliability of product
- Buying experience
- Offers
- Time saving
- Credit
- Proactive care of consumer needs

Grouping on the basis of similar needs: Once the needs have been identified, the target group can be divided into groups with similar needs. First we will examine the needs of various groups given in this case:

- **Destitutes:** Low price, value offers.
- **Aspirants:** Low price, reliable product, buying experience, offers, time saving (not at the cost of money, i.e. they would avail a service which saves time if it is free).
- **Climbers:** Low price, convenience, reliable product, buying experience, offers, time saving.
- **Consumers:** Convenience, reliable product, buying experience, time saving.
- **Rich:** Convenience, reliable product, buying experience, time saving.

Competition

The company would face competition from the following two quarters:

Unorganized retail industry: The generic features of the unorganized retail industry are given as under:

- Cost Price is low as they are self-maintained and do not pay taxes or have high cost of land.
- Selling Price is low but still has higher margin due to low Cost Price.
- Products are same if not inferior to organized retail stores products. The most important part of product offering is giving credit to the consumer.
- High intimacy with customers.

Organized retail industry: The generic features of the unorganized retail industry are given as under:

- Cost Price is high due to expensive land, employee salaries and taxes.
- Selling Price is still low with discounts but gets revenue due to economy of scale.
- Products are same if not better than the unorganized sector products.
- Offers include discounts, buying experience, usage of plastic money, reliability of goods.
- Almost negligible level of intimacy and no provision of credit.

In order to make a strategy we need to understand what the competition is doing to fulfil the needs of customers and what are the needs that it is not fulfilling. The following were identified with respect to the different kinds of retail store formats:

Unorganized Retailing

The fulfilled needs

Convenience: In most cases the *kirana* storekeeper knows consumer buying patterns and is able to give a personal touch to the buying experience. In fact it is not very uncommon to find that the storekeeper would know exactly when the consumer bought sugar and when it would be running low.

Credit: Many *kirana* stores offer monthly credit which is settled at the start of the next month when working class consumers get their salary. Sometimes this leads to over-spending on the part of the consumer.

Home delivery: Most *kirana* stores provide home delivery in their vicinity so as to differentiate their service against that of organized retailers. The consumer merely has to call the storekeeper and tell him what he/she needs. The storekeeper makes sure that the person who delivers the goods, services several consumers in a single trip.

Consumer psychology: The storekeeper knows his consumers, sometimes from their childhood. Overtime, he knows the consumer's spending power and is therefore able to give relevant suggestions.

The unfulfilled needs

Lack of reliability: The reliability of a product is less in unorganized food stores as compared to organized food stores.

MRP selling: Almost all unorganized stores sell the products at the Maximum Retail Price. This is to keep up the margin as they do not have the advantage of economy of scale.

Lack of offers: In order to protect their margin *kirana* stores are unable to give offers which would make products more attractive. Moreover since they do not have sales volume, they are not in a position to negotiate with the product manufacturers over prices, discounts and value-add offers.

Buying experience: The biggest lack in the unorganized sector is the ambience that the organized sector provides. Neither do they have airconditioned shops in prime locations to please the consumer nor do they create the pull to increase footfall.

Organized Retailing

The fulfilled needs

Low price: Organized retail stores are able to negotiate deals with product manufacturers to reduce prices. Some also buy from local food manufacturers and sell it under their brand name. This helps them achieve lower costs which translates into higher margins.

Offers: They are able to give offers owing to their negotiating power with manufacturers and the economy of scale. With sales volume on their side they can afford to reduce their margin.

Reliability: Consumers are aware that a product sold at an organized retail store is reliable because of the risk of being sued in consumer court. Therefore consumers can repose higher faith in them.

Convenience: Organized retailers do their level best to provide the consumer with all the conveniences possible. An example is the use of plastic money which allows the consumer to buy products even if he does not have ready cash. Another example is the availability of staff who are supposed to respond at every beck and call of in-store customers.

Buying experience: Airconditioning, attractive displays and larger scale of operations are the characteristics of most retailers. The service they provide in the form of friendly staff and special treatment also make the experience memorable.

Time saving: Since consumers get all items under one roof, it saves on time and therefore becomes a preferred choice for working people.

The unfulfilled needs

No home delivery: Most F&G retailers for instance Reliance Fresh and More refrain from providing home delivery. As a result *kirana* stores gain an upper hand in this regard.

High land cost: Organized retailers have to buy land in premium locations, thereby increasing the investment, which consequently reduces their margin.

No intimacy: The buying experience does not have any element of the personal touch. This is because the organized retailer caters to a large number of consumers and it is difficult for staff to remember each individual customer.

Food and Grocery Sector: SWOT Analysis

Strengths

India's populations holds the key to the growth prospects of the F&G sector. The Indian F&G sector is characterized by some large multi-state players like Procter & Gamble, Hindustan Unilever, Marico, Imperial Tobacco Company, and so on, and a huge list of small players who operate in comparatively small geographic spreads. Together, they make available products across a broad spectrum at competitive prices.

Weaknesses

The foremost setback in expanding the food processing sector, in terms of both investment and exports, is lack of adequate infrastructure. There is an absence of a strong and dependable cold chain system, without which a vital sector like food processing, which is based mostly on perishable products, cannot survive and grow.

Cold chain facilities are miserably inadequate to meet the increasing production of various perishable products like milk, fruits, vegetables, poultry, fisheries, and so on. About 30 per cent of farm produce is wasted every year only because there is inadequate storage, transportation, cold chain facilities and other infrastructure supports.

Prevention of Food Adulteration laws are not only stringent but also time consuming. There are more than 15 laws enforced by multiple ministries. Food standards overlap; they are contradictory and highly prescriptive. There is an urgent need to simplify them and make them industry-friendly.

The high cost of raw materials and packing materials puts pressure on margins. Some commodities in one segment are used as inputs in another segment of the food processing industry, e.g. skimmed milk powder (SMP) is used as raw material for chocolates and ice creams; sugar and edible oil are used as raw materials for a number of items; molasses is an input for making alcohol, and so on.

There has been a rise in the prices of all such commodities, which has impacted the overall cost of production in the food processing industry. There is a need for review of all such cases involving the users and the producers.

Opportunities

The purchasing habits of Indian customers are changing fast. This has in many ways led to an increase in consumerism. As the Indian economy flourished during the last few years, consumers found themselves with more disposable income. As a result the spending habits of the Indian middle class took a giant leap. For instance, a service sector employee is young, savvy and has high disposable income.

Indian food and beverage companies are making a beeline for regional overseas markets like Bangladesh, Pakistan, Nepal, Middle East and CIS countries because of similar lifestyles and consumption habits. Godrej consumer products, Marico, and Dabur are among the companies to make a foray abroad.

The government is giving priority to the development of the food processing industry to encourage commercialization and value addition to agricultural produce. Liberal reform measures and various tax benefits are being extended to the sector. Policy initiatives taken by the government in the food processing sector include:

- Food processing industry declared a priority area.
- Entire sector is de-licensed.
- Automatic approvals for foreign investment up to 100 per cent, except for some products like alcoholic beverages and also technology transfer.
- Zero import duty on capital goods and raw material for 100 per cent export-oriented units.
- Agro-based, 100 per cent export-oriented units allowed sale up to 50 per cent in domestic tariff area.
- Export earnings are exempted from corporate tax.
- All processed fruit and vegetable products exempted from Central Excise Duty.

- Government grant given for setting up common facilities in agro-food parks.
- Full duty exemption on all imports for units in Export Processing Zones.
- Use of foreign brand name is freely permitted.

Threats

There is multiplicity of taxes; local taxes and levies are charged on different commodities belonging to the F&B industry. Different states have different sales tax rates; *mandi* taxes charged by local market committees in different states are different; inter-state charges and levies like *Chungi* Tax and procedural complexities add pressure on margins and put hurdles in the growth and development of the food processing sector.

Higher railway freight has pushed up the cost of raw materials which has added to the cost of production. Different commodities are subject to different laws and licensing rules, e.g. dual taxation system for tea, dual licensing for sugar, different labelling rules for some alcoholic beverages. These are mentioned in detail in the section on segmentation.

Global F&G giants like Walmart, Tesco and Carrefour are foraying into India in a big way. Given the notoriety of Walmart in mauling government norms in any country it enters, the Indian F&G sector may be soon taken for a ride.

Counterfeit products or low quality variants of most packaged branded grocery items are available in the market without any restriction.

PEST Analysis of the Indian F&G Retail Sector

Political

- A package of fiscal incentives provided by state governments like Himachal Pradesh and Uttaranchal has encouraged companies to set up manufacturing facilities in these regions.
- The excise exemption for 10 years and income tax exemption for 5 years for units located in backward regions under section 80-IA has encouraged many companies to set up new units.
- The food processing industry has been declared a priority area and the entire sector is delicensed. There's automatic approvals for foreign investment up to 100 per cent, except for some products like alcoholic beverages and technology transfer.
- Zero duty import on capital goods and raw material for 100 per cent export-oriented units.

Agro-based export-oriented units allowed sale up to 50 per cent in domestic tariff areas.

- Export earnings are exempt from corporate tax.
- All processed fruit and vegetable products are exempt from Central Excise Duty.
- Government grant given for setting up common facilities in agro-food parks.

- Full duty exemption on all imports for units in Export Processing Zones.
- Use of foreign brand name is freely permitted.

Economical

- Growth in the processed food segment has been achieved by reaching lower price points to make products more affordable to a bigger consumer class.
- The foremost setback in expanding the food processing sector, in terms of both investment and exports, is lack of adequate infrastructure. Farm produce of about 30 per cent is being wasted every year only because there is no adequate storage, transportation, cold chain facilities and other infrastructural support.
- Unorganized, small players account for more than 70 per cent of the industry output in volume terms and 50 per cent in value terms. Big companies have started sourcing their products from local manufacturers as part of their cost saving measures and also to enter the mass consumer segment.
- Semi-processed food/Cooked/Ready-to-eat food sector is growing by 20 per cent due to rising demand.

Social

With changing lifestyle and rising disposable income of the growing middle-income group, branded food, health food and convenience food segments are gaining vast popularity. The market for branded foods is growing at a healthy 10-15 per cent. The middle class segment will continue to hold the key to the success of the processed food market in India.

The profile of the middle class is changing steadily as hired domestic help is becoming costlier. This is conducive to an expansion in demand for ready-to-eat Indian-style foods. Indian F&B companies are making a beeline for regional overseas markets like Bangladesh, Pakistan, Nepal, Middle East and CIS countries because of similar lifestyles and consumption habits. Godrej consumer products, Marico and Dabur are among the companies eyeing export markets.

Technological

There are huge opportunities for investments in food and food processing industries in different fields including upgradation of technologies and improvement of skills, with installation of modern machinery and equipment, especially in areas of canning, dairy plants and specialty processing.

The opportunities for investment lie in various stages like packaging, preservation of food with suitable refrigeration and thermo-processing, quality control and also in creating a good marketing and distribution infrastructure and an efficient network of cold chain management system. As about 10 per cent of the output is processed and consumed in packaged form, there is huge potential for expansion of the food processing industry which will require technological upgradation.

Legal

- Harmonization of multiple food laws is an urgent necessity. It has been observed that there are thirteen laws enforced by nine ministries. There is a need to integrate these into one common food law.
- The Prevention of Food Adulteration law is not only stringent but also time consuming and needs review.
- The Food Safety and Standard Bill, 2005 with penal provisions requires a review as it gives huge powers to the inspecting officers to seize food articles without authorization. This can create unwanted confusion to the detriment of the industry.
- There is a need for a review of the Agricultural Produce and Marketing Act to ensure freedom to farmers to sell agricultural produce to sellers of his choice at remunerative prices rather than selling them through regulated market committees or authorized agents.
- The Essential Commodities Act (ECA) puts a lot of hindrances including to easy inter-state movement of foodgrains and essential food items.

Value Proposition

One of the key elements of the positioning strategy is value proposition. There are three types of value: operational excellence, product leadership and customer intimacy. These have been described in detail below:

Operational excellence: The reason of having operational excellence is to provide a good product to the consumer at the lowest possible price. Here

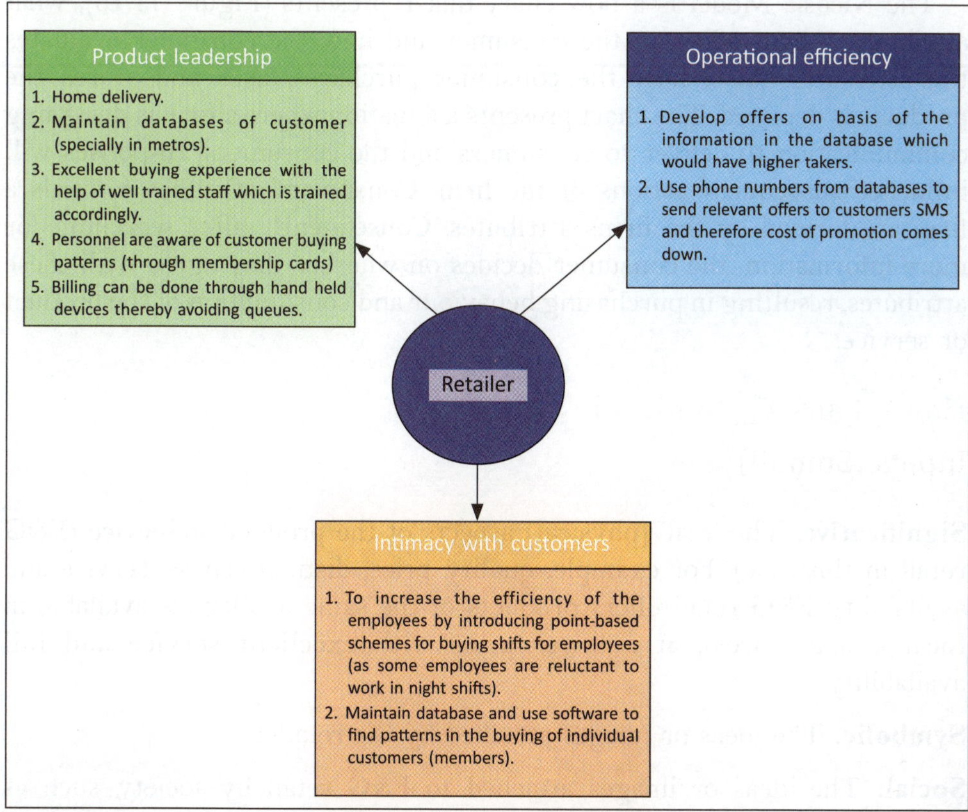

Figure 11.15: The value proposition

the consumer focus is not on the frills and service quality over a threshold level, but on the quality of the product and the price that has to be paid.

Product leadership: Here the core is always innovation and quality with respect to the product or the service. The retailer has to continually work on service/product improvement and new ideas so that he can bring them to the market. He has to know what his customers are doing and has to be one step ahead in order to increase sales.

Customer intimacy: Retailers have to customize their product/service according to the needs of their consumers. They should strive to know as much as they possibly can about the consumer so that they can deliver the correct solutions at the correct time. This part of the proposition should come across to the consumer at every point of interaction or touch point.

On the basis of the analysis above we have suggested a value proposition for the UK-based F&G retailer. Figure 11.15 depicts the proposition which combines the three pillars of value proposition.

Indian F&G Retail Customers

Nicosia Model

The Nicosia Model explains the consumers' buying behaviour from the marketers' perspective. However, it fails to explain in detail the firm's and consumer's attributes and doesn't take into account that a consumer might already be having a predisposition with respect to a particular product/ brand.

The Nicosia Model is a flow chart that represents (Figure 11.16), what attributes a firm offers to the consumer and how the consumer evaluates the attributes. Also, how the consumer purchases, uses and stores the products is depicted. The chart presents a situation where a firm is designing communication to deliver to consumers and the consumers' responses will influence subsequent actions of the firm. Consumers' attitudes towards a firm are formed by the firms attributes. Consequently after searching for more information, the consumer decides on whether they agree with these attributes, resulting in purchasing behaviour and consumption of the product or service.

Howard and Sheth Model

Inputs (Stimuli)

Significative: The 'real' (physical) aspects of the product or service (F&G retail in this case). For example, quality, price, distinctiveness, service and availability. F&G retail offers products of the same quality (as available in local *kirana* stores), at a lower price with excellent service and full availability.

Symbolic: The ideas or images attached by the retailer.

Social: The ideas or images attached to F&G retail by society, such as reference groups, family and social class. More people have started visiting

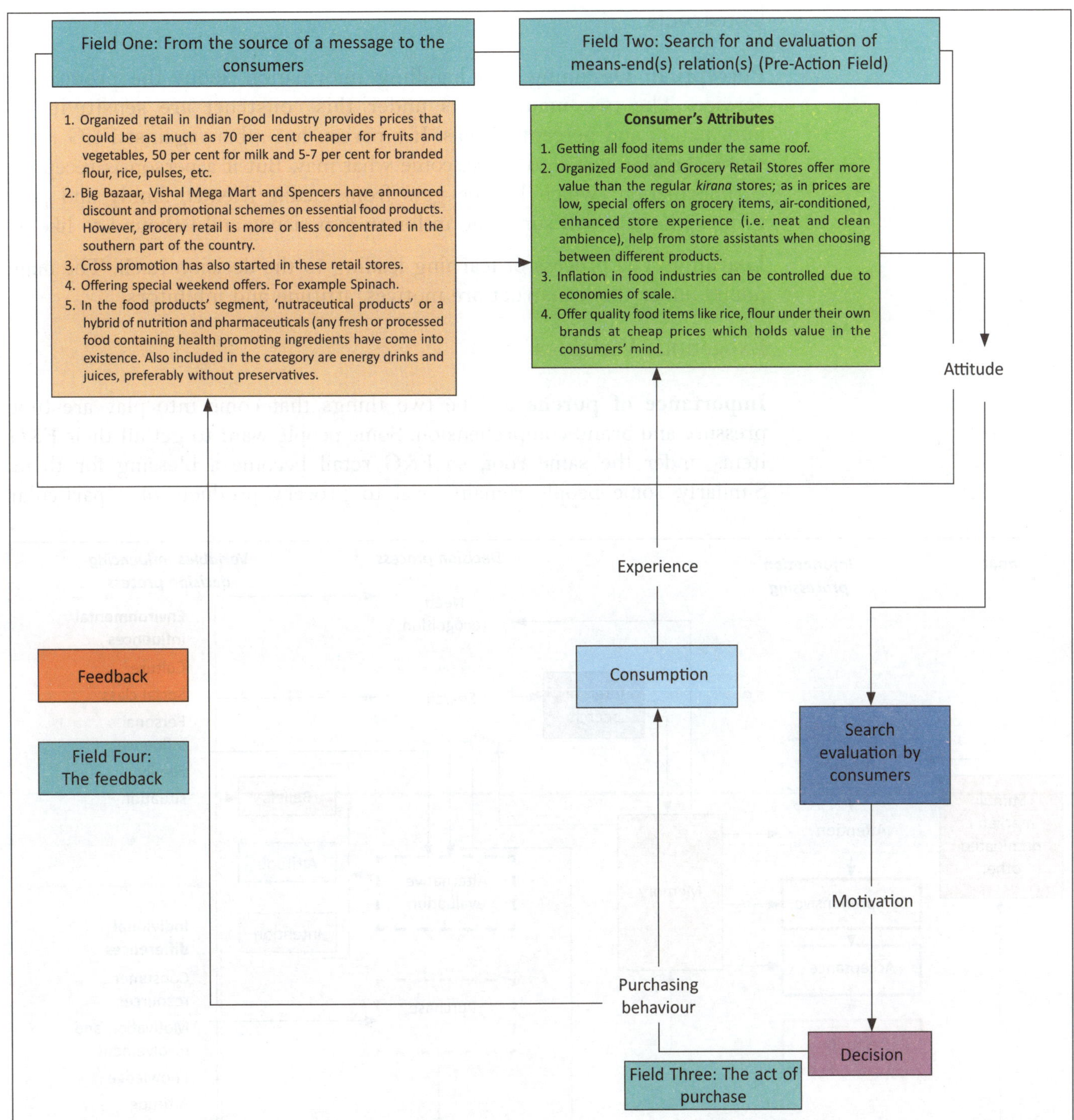

Figure 11.16: The Nicosia Model

the F&G retail stores and therefore others who thought that products in such big stores were costly are getting aware of the affordability and constant availability of F&G retail stores through their peers, friends and family.

Outputs

The consumer's actions, i.e. attention, brand comprehension, attitude, intention and purchase.

Constructs

Perceptual: Obtaining and handling information about the product or service. The two main points under this construct are sensitivity to information and perceptual bias. If a person has a bias against F&G retail stores, he/she won't go there, come what may. But if a person is receptive to information (which he/she gets from media, friends, family and peer groups), he/she will surely go in for an experience and is bound to like it.

Learning: The process of learning leading to the decision itself. The main points under this construct are motives, attitude and inhibitors.

Exogenous Variables

Importance of purchase: The two things that come into play are time pressure and brand comprehension. Some people want to get all their F&G items under the same roof, so F&G retail become a blessing for them. Similarly, some people remain loyal to grocery products of a particular

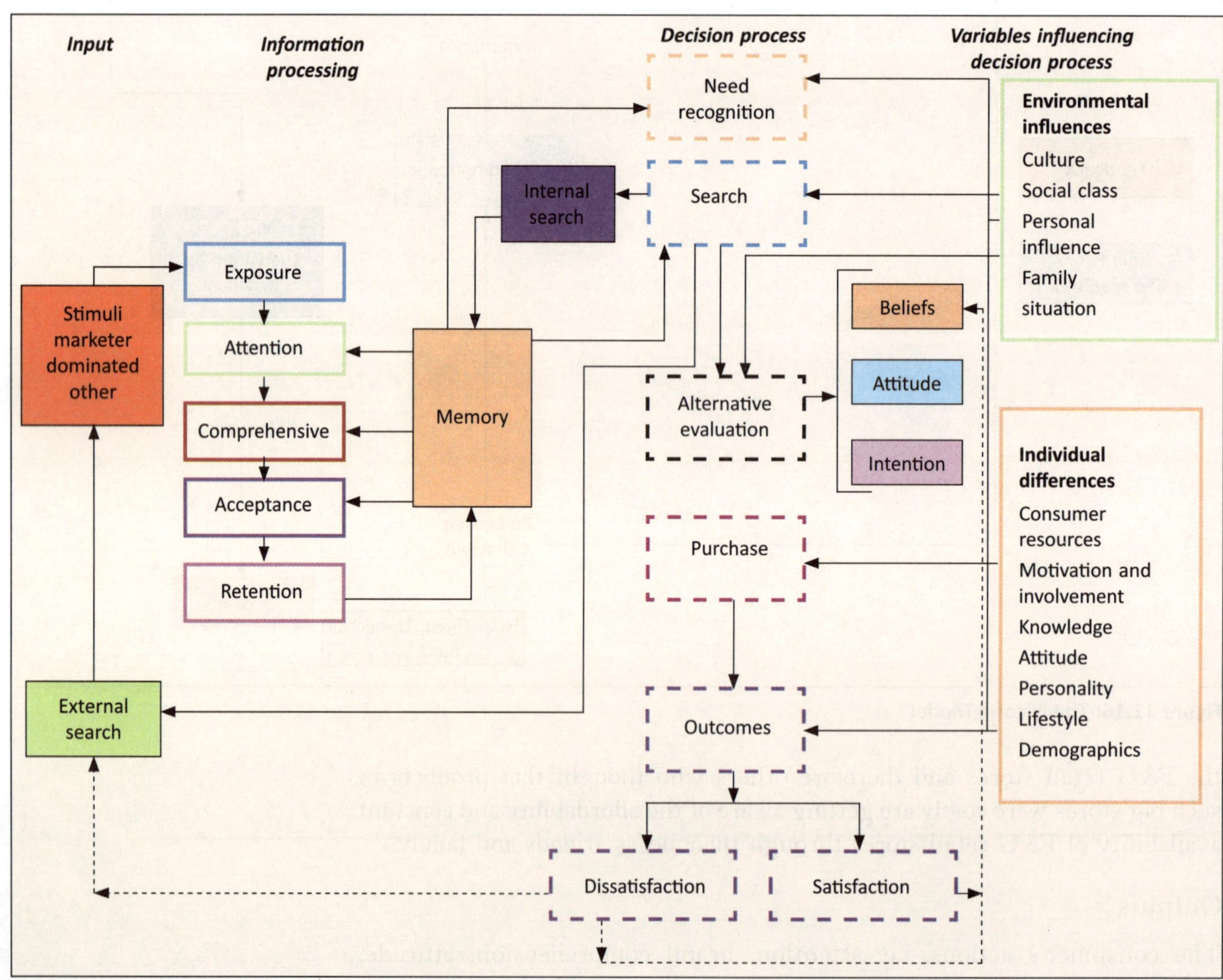

Figure 11.17: The Engel-Blackwell-Kollat Model

FMCG company. Since F&G retail stores have depth and width of product lines, the shopper will get the product or brand that he/she desires.

Personality variables: It affects the non-specific or specific motive of the purchase.

Social class, culture, and organization: It has an effect on motive, choice criteria and brand comprehension.

Time pressure and financial status: These two along with Social Class, Culture and Organization are called inhibitors and have a direct impact on the final purchase decision of the consumer. For some people shopping at a F&G retail store is a reflection of their financial status. Some are really busy and want everything under the same roof. Others give a lot of importance to the overall shopping experience.

Factors Influencing Consumer Behaviour

Looking in more detail, the major factors that influence consumer behaviour or decision process in F&G retail industry are as follows:

Core offering: The F&G retail industry needs to give a dependable core offering that appeals to customers. Companies that have focused intently on what they know appeals to the type of customers they want to attract, and have determinedly concentrated on delivering what is expected every time. Also the retailer needs to improve this core offering by tailoring and molding it more closely to the customers' needs and desires. Elements of the core offering that have a large role in affecting consumer behaviour include:

Location and premises: Location and premises clearly play a part in influencing people. The three Ls of retail—'location, location and location'—are undoubtedly important. So, F&G retail stores constructed within residential areas or in places where there is a large amount of footfall helps. The ambience and a differentiated store experience are also important. Visual merchandising and store layout are key functions that need serious attention for enhancing customer shopping experience.

Service: Whether selling services or products, the level of service perceived by the customer is the key to generating loyalty. It can be argued that some customers buy only on price, so all that is necessary to retain their loyalty is consistently low prices. This is true to a certain extent. But in most cases, any loyalty shown will be only to the price instead of the business. The service and amount of indulgence shown to the consumer by the assistant or member of the staff is very important.

The product or service: The products or services offered must be what customers want. The days when businesses could decide what they want to sell or supply, and customers would buy it, are long past. Customers' needs and wants are now paramount. If you don't meet them, someone else will.

1. Environmental Influences
    - Culture
    - Social class

- Personal influence
- Family
- Situation

2. Individual Differences
   - Consumer resources
   - Motivation and involvement
   - Knowledge
   - Attitude
   - Personality
   - Lifestyle
   - Demographics
3. Financial Status (Due to demographics and variation in income distribution across India).

Food and Grocery Retailing

Situation in 2010

1. F&G market in India has a total turnover of $330 billion.
2. It has become the sixth-largest grocery market in the world.
3. It is expected to reach $482 billion by the year 2018.
4. It contributes approximately 70 per cent of the total retail sales.
5. 99 per cent of the total F&G market is still unorganized and it comprises mostly the 'mom and pop' *kirana* stores.
6. The modern high-end formats account for just 1 per cent of the total F&G market.

Modern Trade: The Organized High-end Retailers

The Indian organized food retail market is characterized by several coexisting formats. In modern trade, the classifications are:

1. The discount supermarkets (Apna Bazaar, Margin Free)
2. The value for money stores (Nilgiris)
3. The experience shop (FoodWorld, Trinethra)
4. Convenience stores (Fabmart)
5. Hypermarkets (Giant, Metro, Big Bazaar)

Organized Retail

The organized retail is just making its presence felt in different parts of the country. The retail revolution in the grocery sector was started by the RPG Group which started the FoodWorld chain of retail outlets with a focus on the south Indian markets. Then in 1905 came the traditionally owned retail chain known as Nilgiris.

Looking at their success, several new models such as Trinethra, Subhiksha, MarginFree and others came into the market. Today, the food retail sector has a value of about ₹10,00,000 crore.

Currently the retail landscape is filled with supermarket chains with over 1,000 outlets all over the country. This is expected to increase to around 5,000 by 2012. The success of a couple of hypermarkets indicates the evolution of this format in the country, prominent among them being Giant, Metro and Big Bazaar models. While the average bill value at a supermarket is in the range of ₹300 per customer, the average bill amount at a hypermarket is in the range of ₹750-₹1,000, indicating that the model is in tune with global models where the average spend is increasing with the shopping experience.

Categories of Indian Consumers

1. Loiterers

(a) Roam around at high speed
(b) Cover a lot of the store
(c) Spend short amount of time
(d) Waiting for a friend or a partner
(e) Less interacting with products
(f) Probability of buying: 0 per cent

2. Planned Buyers

(a) Move through the store to get their specific product
(b) Already have plans regarding what to buy
(c) Interact with products meeting their needs
(d) Probability of buying: 82 per cent

3. Category Focused

(a) Directly move into the specific department or category
(b) Look at the products in that category
(c) Have focus on the target product group
(d) Probability of buying: 37 per cent

4. Conventional Buyers

(a) Cover a large part of the store
(b) More focused than Loiterers
(c) Interact with the products but in an unplanned way
(d) Probability of buying: 2 per cent

5. Just for Fun Buyers

(a) Spend lot of time in the store
(b) Move through their interested departments
(c) Influenced by staff service
(d) Mostly visit after pay-day
(e) Probability of buying: 79 per cent

Customer Life Time Value

Customer Life Time Value (CLTV), in marketing terms, may be defined as the present value of the future cash flows attributed to the relationship with customers. Using CLTV as a measurement of marketing would help in focusing on customer service and long-term customer relationship, rather than on maximizing profit.

Issues, Benefits and Challenges for High-end Retailers

1. To become successful, consumers have to be drawn away from *kirana* stores and hawkers. This can be possible by focusing on the pricing strategy. Low prices can be offered by understanding and optimizing the supply chain.
2. The high-end retailers provide convenience to the shoppers as they have a wider variety of products. In general, a supermarket keeps 5,000 to 20,000 SKUs in comparison to a few hundred in *kirana* stores.
3. The demographic characteristics vary widely from region to region in India. Hence, the high-end retailers have to cater different lifestyles with different identities. Thus, a majority of the players are region focused rather than expanding in the whole country.
4. The industry is undergoing tough times with little support from the government. But once the ban on FDI is lifted, the industry is hopeful of getting large investments.
5. F&G retailing is a tough business as it has very low margins. Moreover, the good customer service delivered by the next-door grocer is making the situation more difficult for high-end retailers as the consumers are not dissatisfied with their present retailer.
6. The topography of the industry makes it difficult to have a presence across the country. FoodWorld and Nilgiris in the southern region, Sabka Bazaar in Delhi, Haiko and Radhakrishna in Mumbai are some of the regionally focused high-end retailers in the F&G segment. Due to supply chain and logistics issues, it takes a lot of investment to have a presence across the country.
7. Organized retail has been registering growth rates of approximately 40 per cent over the last three years and it is expected to grow to ₹70,000 crore in 2010. If projections were to be made considering the current trends in food retailing in India, some years down the line, F&G stores will become dominating trade partners in the food industry, which, in turn, will be forced to offer special discounts and trade terms to get the shelf space in such stores.
8. As for the spread geographically, strong chances stand that the major chains would spread to the tier II grade by 2012 cities in the country so and then progressively start covering every corner of the country. Most chains have already started developing their own unique supply chains, one that would suit their needs precisely. Replicating the success stories of big names in the West may still be a distant dream for Indian F&G retailers, but at least the winds are blowing in the direction of growth.

VALS Segmentation for Organic F&V Segment Customers

Psychographic variables can be used individually in segment markets or can be combined with other variables to provide a more detailed description of market segments. One well known combination approach offered by SRI International is called VALS (Values and Lifestyles Programme). VALS categorizes consumers by their values, beliefs, and lifestyles rather than by traditional demographic segmentation variables (like income, age, gender and ethnic background). Many advertising agencies have used VALS segmentation to create effective promotion campaigns.

Figure 11.18 shows that the segments in VALS are classified on two dimensions: vertically by their resources and horizontally by their self-orientation. Resources include education, income, self-confidence, health, eagerness to buy, intelligence, and energy level. The resources dimension is a continuum ranging from minimal to abundant. It generally increases from adolescence through middle age and decreases with extreme age, depression, financial reverses, and physical or psychological impairment.

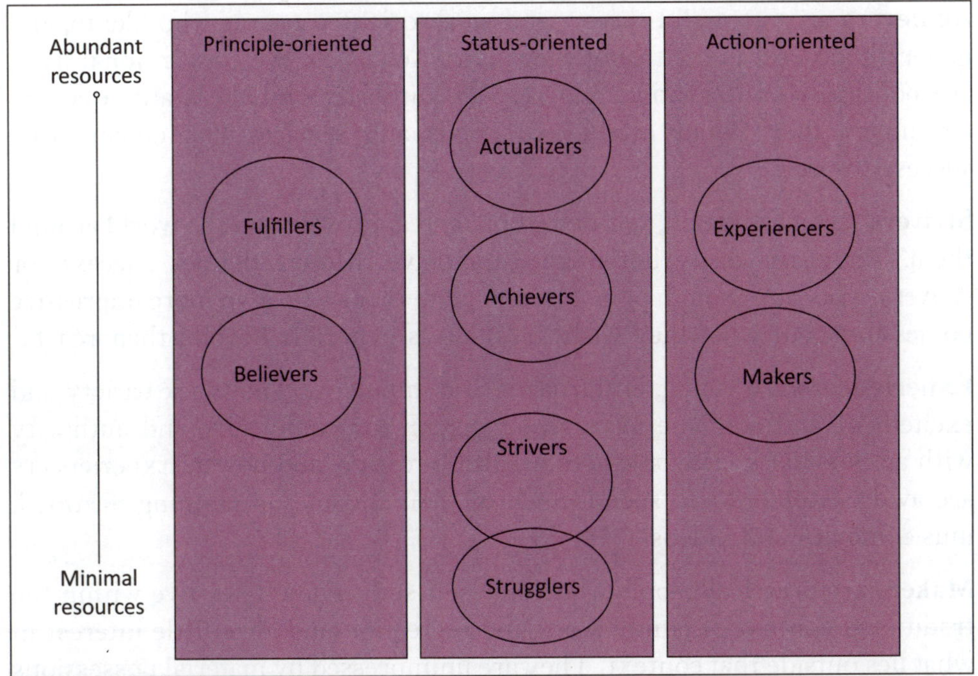

Figure 11.18: VALS dimensions

- Beliefs or principles rather than feelings, events, or desire for approval guide principle-oriented consumers in their choices.
- Other people's actions, approvals, and opinions strongly influence status-oriented consumers.
- Action-oriented consumers are prompted by a desire for social or physical activity, variety and risk.

There are eight VALS psychographic segments. Using only two key dimensions—resources and self-orientation—VALS defines groups of adult consumers who have distinctive attitudes, behaviour patterns, and decision-making styles.

VALS Psychographic Segments

Actualizers are successful, sophisticated, active, 'take-charge' people with high self-esteem and abundant resources. They are interested in growth and seek to develop, explore, and express themselves in a variety of ways. Their possessions and recreation choices reflect a cultivated taste for the finer things in life.

Fulfillers are mature, satisfied, comfortable, reflective people who value order, knowledge, and responsibility. Most are well educated, well informed about world events, and professionally employed. Fulfillers are conservative, practical consumers; they are concerned about value and durability of the products they buy.

Believers are conservative, conventional people with concrete beliefs and strong attachments to traditional institutions—family, church, community, and nation. As consumers they are conservative and predictable, favouring US products and established brands.

Achievers are successful career- and work-oriented people who like to, and generally do, feel in control of their lives. Achievers live conventional lives, are politically conservative, and respect authority and the status quo. As consumers they favour established goods and services that demonstrate success to peer.

Strivers seek motivation, self-definition, and approval from the world around them. They are easily bored and impulsive. Money defines success for strivers, who lack enough of it. They emulate those who own more impressive possessions, but what they wish to obtain is generally beyond their reach.

Experiencers are young, enthusiastic and impulsive. They seek variety and excitement and combine an abstract distain for conformity and authority with an outsider's view of others' wealth, prestige, and power. Experiencers are avid customers and spend much of their income on clothing, fastfood, music, movies and videos.

Makers are practical people who value self-sufficiency. They live within the traditional context of family, work and recreation and have little interest in what lies outside that context. They are unimpressed by material possessions other than those with a practical or functional purpose (for example, tools, pick-up trucks or fishing equipment).

Strugglers have lives that are constricted—chronically poor, ill educated, and low skilled. They lack strong social bonds; they are focused on meeting the urgent needs of the present moment. Ageing strugglers are concerned about their health. Strugglers are cautious consumers who represent a very modest demand for most goods and services but are loyal to favourite brands.

Importance of Retailing Organic Produce in India

Organic farming is being practised in about 100 countries. The ill-effects of chemicals used in agriculture changed the mindset of some consumers who are now buying organic products with a high premium on health. Policy makers are also promoting organic farming for restoration of soil health and regeneration of rural economy apart from making efforts for creating a better environment.

Organic farming has a place where there is a market to accept the produce at a higher price. This is because the growing interest in organic farming practice is due to an expectation of higher premium for organically produced farm commodities. The basic focus of organic farming should be first to produce farm products for the home (domestic) market and second for the export market.

As more and more people in India want to purchase organic F&V (fruits and vegetables), VALS segmentation is both relevant and significant. This is because there are still some amount of people who are either unaware of the advantages and health benefits of organic foods or are indifferent to it. There is obviously a premium charged for purchasing organic foods and not all people would be interested in the same. So VALS segmentation is mandatory.

For this we actually need to know the regions in India where the concept of organic F&V is welcomed. Also it needs to be decided whether there'll be altogether different stores for selling organic F&Vs or will they be sold along with the conventional products. So it would be better to have two store types and also segmenting according to state and region (health conscious people).

Market Attractiveness and Competitive Advantage

AC Nielsen, a leading market research firm, surveyed about 21,000 regular Internet users in 38 countries to find their preference for functional foods—foods that have additional health benefits. The survey revealed that India was among the top ten countries where health food, including organic food, was demanded by the consumers (also, Indian people are getting ever more health conscious and this adds to the market attractiveness of organic foods). So, there is a huge market for organic foods in India.

The increase in organic food consumption evident from the fact that several organic food stores are coming up in India. Today almost every supermarket has an organic food store and every large city has numerous organic food outlets and restaurants. This is a huge leap from 1997 when the first organic food store, '24 Lettered Mantra' opened in Mumbai.

The organic food market is currently growing and segments lie untapped. It would take a while for it to enter the maturity phase. So, if one enters this market right now, the returns will be high. According to the VALS psychographic segmentation, there are various segments of people who would like to get associated with the concept of consuming organic foods. The competitive strength of the organic food market lies in providing customers with healthy food. But this competitive strength can only be transferred into reality if the people are made aware about the advantages of organic food. Awareness is the key to success in this case. The future may look good once the retailers think along the following lines:

Retail life cycle: Organized retail in growth phase

Location change: More focus on tier II and tier III cities

Consumer demand: Indian private consumption to quadruple by 2025

Buying Patterns

- India's burgeoning middle class armed with more disposable income
- More focus on building customer loyalty and store image

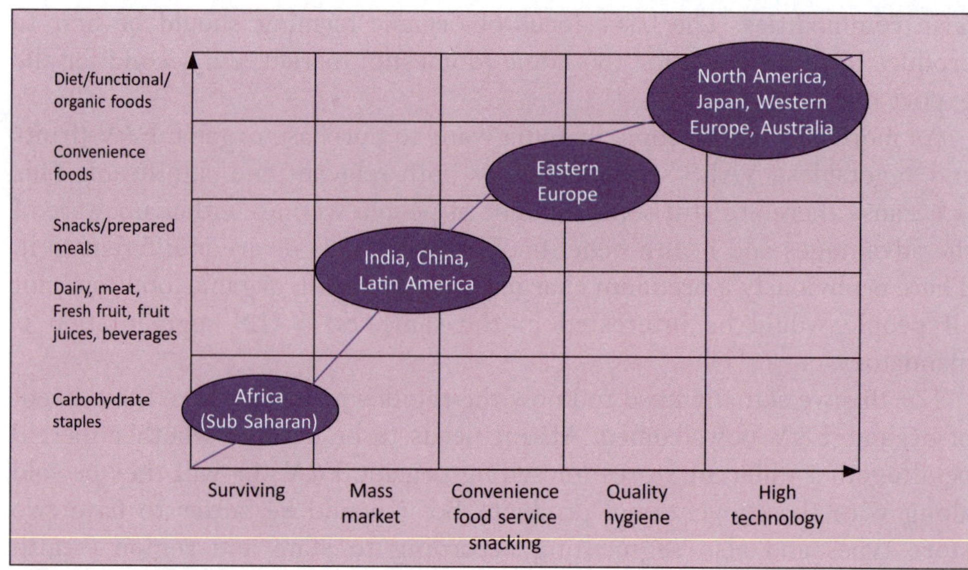

Figure 11.19: India rising high on food demand curve

- Loyalty cards for the customers
- Special discount to frequent visitors.

More IT integration in future for catering to consumers' individual buying needs at low cost.

- Inventory control to cater to customer needs
- Cost optimization to deliver more value

Right positioning, effective visual communication, strong supply chain and changing price perception are the key success factors.

Limitations

However, the consumer in India needs to be educated more since there are many consumers who are unaware of the difference between natural and organic food. They purchase products labelled as 'natural' thinking that they are organic. Further, consumers are not aware of the certification system. Since certification is not compulsory for domestic retailers in India, many fake organic products are available in the market.

According to a survey by Yes Bank, India is on the path to becoming a nation where more and more importance would be given to the organic fruits and vegetables.

References

1. www.cinemax.com
2. www.imax.com
3. www.inoxleisures.com
4. www.pvrcinemas.com
5. www.bigcinemas.com
6. www.funcinemas.com

7. www.shringar.com
8. 2007–8, 2008-9, 2009-10 Annual Reports of all the multiplex companies listed under 1 to 7
9. www.forum.org
10. www.pantaloon.org
11. www.shoppersstop.com
12. www.mapsofindia.com
13. www.en.wikipedia.com
14. www.theindianexpress.com
15. www.thetelegraph.com
16. Annual report, Shopper's Stop 2008-9, 2009-10
17. Annual report, Pantaloon Retail
18. Annual report, Tata Trent 2008-9, 2009-10
19. www.ibef.org

CHAPTER 12 

THE HEAT OF RECESSION AND DESTOCKING: CAN HUL OVERCOME THE PRESSURE?

applied case study 4

12.1 Genesis

Hindustan Unilever Limited (HUL) played a vital role in combating recession and inducing private consumption-led growth in the Indian economy. The company displayed an ability to effect price hikes and avoid impact of inflation on vegetable oils, which, combined with improved outlook for fabric wash and strong growth in processed foods and beverages, lent a positive outlook for the stock during 2010–13. The consolidated profit made by HUL in financial year 2010 is ₹2,063.27 crore. The net sales has come down to ₹175,238 million in financial year 2010 from ₹202,393 million in financial year 2009; registering negative growth of 13.4 per cent. But projected to grow up 6.8 per cent in financial year 2011 with a net sales of ₹187,100 million and ₹203,018 million in financial year 2012.

Powerful brands and an envious distribution network are HUL's primary strengths. The company operates in five segments—soaps and detergents, personal products, beverages, foods and ice creams, exports, and other operations. While soaps and detergents contribute 45 per cent of net sales, the high-margin personal products segment contributes the most to operating profits at 45 per cent in 2009. Together, personal products and soaps and detergents, which constitute the home and personal care (HPC) division, contribute 71 per cent of net sales and 82 per cent of operating profits in 2009. In 2009, the company's move to dispose of its non-core assets including some properties gave it a near-term upside. Analysts believe the price war in the detergent segment with rival P&G has ended and is likely to add to the profitability from the segment going forward.

HUL's portfolio of products covers a wide spectrum including soaps, detergents, skin creams, shampoos, toothpastes, tea, coffee, and branded wheat flour (*atta*). In 2008, it generated net sales of ₹163.50 billion and a profit of ₹21 billion. However the market performance of the leader was quite disappointing. HUL posted a marginal growth of 5 per cent in net sales of ₹3,988.30 crore in March 2009. Operating profits grew by 35 per cent y-o-y to ₹5,449.30 crore and operating margins expanded by 3,302 basis points. Net profits grew by 4 per cent y-o-y to ₹394.90 crore.

Though HUL is a market leader, it has been losing market share in key categories. In order to regain this, HUL can either opt for further price cuts, promotional offers or invest more in brand building, but these are likely to affect profitability. They may result in marginal growth (de-growth in a few categories like oral care) in the top-line as well as profitability in the financial year 2010 (estimated earnings). Table 12.1 shows the market capitalization of HUL along with other top FMCG companies in the Indian stock market.

Table 12.1: Market capitalization of HUL and other FMCG majors

Company	*Market capitalization (₹ billion)*	*Earnings per share (EPS) FY 2008 (₹)*	*EPS FY 2009 (₹)*	*EPS FY 2010 (₹)*
HUL	686.604	7.8	11.5	9.7
ITC	1,370.585	8.3	4.4	5.4
Nestlé India	317.275	43	55.4	66.2
Dabur India	89.8	3.9	4.5	5.6
Colgate-Palmolive	57	17.4	20.6	25.5
Marico	41.4	2.7	3.1	4
Britannia	37.1	74.3	90	107
Godrej Consumer Products	36.9	7.1	6.7	9.2
GSK Consumer Co.	35	38.7	44.8	56.5

Sources: Respective companies; Edelweiss Research.

It seems HUL is losing its relevance in the Indian FMCG space. Let us evaluate the company's strategies.

12.2 HUL: A History

In 1888, Lever Brothers started exporting Sunlight laundry soap to India. Meanwhile, Margarine Unie also exported *vanaspati*, or hydrogenated edible fat to the same country. Therefore, when Margarine Unie and Lever Brothers merged in 1930, the products already had considerable presence in India. In 1931, Unilever established the Hindustan Vanaspati Manufacturing Company, its first subsidiary in India, followed by two more subsidiaries—Lever Brothers India Limited and United Traders Limited. In 1956, these three companies, which marketed soaps, *vanaspati* and personal products, merged to form Hindustan Lever, in which Unilever now has a 51 per cent stake. (See Appendix 1 for more details.)

The company has pursued growth through acquisitions and joint ventures. In April 1993, Hindustan Vanaspati merged with Tata Oil Mills Company in an amalgamation that brought in a soaps and detergents brand portfolio to compliment that of Hindustan. In a related move, in 1995, Hindustan and yet another Tata company, Lakme, formed a 50 : 50 joint venture, Lakme Lever, to market Lakme's market-leading cosmetics and other appropriate products of both the companies.

Subsequently, in 1998, Lakme Limited sold its brands to Hindustan and divested its 50 per cent stake in the joint venture to the company. Growth continued in 1994 when the company formed 50 : 50 joint ventures with two US-based companies, Kimberly-Clark Corporation and S.C. Johnson & Son, and the Netherlands-based Gist Brocades. Kimberly-Clark Lever Ltd. markets Huggies diapers and Kotex sanitary pads. The portfolio of Lever Johnson (Consumer Products), formed in 1995, includes the Raid range of mosquito repellent mats, coils and cockroach killing aerosols and Glade air fresheners. Furthermore, the company established a subsidiary in Nepal, called Nepal Lever Ltd. (NLL). Its factory is the largest manufacturing investment in the Himalayan kingdom. The NLL factory manufactures Hindustan products like soaps, detergents and personal products both for the domestic market and exports to India. The 1990s also witnessed a string of crucial mergers, acquisitions and alliances on the foods and beverages front. In 1992, Brooke Bond acquired Kothari General Foods, with significant interests in instant coffee. In 1993, it acquired the Kissan business from the UB Group and the Dollops ice cream business from Cadbury India.

As a measure of backward integration, Tea Estates and Doom Dooma, two plantation companies of Unilever, were merged with Brooke Bond. Then in July 1993, Brooke Bond India and Lipton India merged to form Brooke Bond Lipton India Ltd. (BBLIL), enabling greater focus and ensuring synergy in the traditional beverages business. Further expansion occurred in 1994 when BBLIL launched the Wall's range of frozen desserts. By the end of the year, the company entered into a strategic alliance with the Kwality ice cream group families and in 1995 the Milkfood 100 per cent ice cream marketing and distribution rights too were acquired. The same year, the company also bought from Pepsi Foods its tomato processing assets at Zahura (Punjab). Finally, BBLIL merged with Hindustan in January 1996. Meanwhile, in 1995, Hindustan restructured its businesses, selling its fertilizer and industrial chemicals business to the group company, Hind Lever Chemicals (erstwhile Stepan Chemicals), and acquiring from Stepan its popular detergents business. This was done to allow the fertilizer and industrial chemicals business to grow rapidly through fresh investments in expansion.

The internal restructuring culminated in the merger of Pond's India Ltd. (PIL) with Hindustan in 1998. The two companies had significant overlaps in personal products, specialty chemicals and exports businesses, besides a common distribution system since 1993 for personal products.

Table 12.2: Corporate performance of HUL (₹million)

Head	*FY 2009**	*FY 2010*	*FY 2011*	*FY 2012E*
Net sales	202,393	175,238	187,100	203,018
Operating expenses	175,428	149,695	161,918	175,648
Net profit	25,026	21,099	22,754	24,712
PAT (%)	44.3	– 15.9	7.8	8.6

*This includes 15 months as the accounting year has changed from December to March.
Sources: Company, Edelweiss Research and Emkay Research, 27 August 2010.

In January 2000, in a historic step, the government decided to award 74 per cent equity in the State-owned Modern Foods Industries Ltd. (MFIL) to Hindustan Lever, thereby kick-starting the first major strategic sale of government equity in a public sector undertaking (PSU) to a private partner.

Meanwhile, in 2001 HLL decided to focus on power brands, entered the confectioneries category and also launched supporting services like Lakme beauty salons. The Lever Gist Brocades, a 50 : 50 joint venture of HLL and DSM of The Netherlands, was sold to Burns Philip India in 2002. The year 2003 saw the company merge its key food brands Knorr and Annapurna under one brand name, Knorr Annapurna. Let us now look at the bottom line of the company, shown in Table 12.2, as the end result of the company's business plan.

HUL reported a like-to-like growth of over 15 per cent in financial year 2009; however, while the first half growth was a healthy volume and value mix, the growth in the last two quarters of 2008 were predominantly value led price hikes in the soaps and detergents category at over 25 per cent. However, analysts see substantial slowdown in HUL's growth as price-led growth disappears (in fact there are price cuts in soaps and detergents category) and volume growth subsides. Volume growth has declined sharply from 10 per cent in the quarter ended March 2008 to 6.8 per cent in the quarter ended September 2008 to 2.3 per cent in the December 2008 quarter to – 4 per cent in the first quarter of 2009. HUL's volume growth is expected to remain at best in low single digit. This could pose a risk to the company's growth estimates of 10-11 per cent in 2009–10.

The financial year 2011 poses huge challenges to the company as its power brands are losing market share to local and regional players. HUL had a tough time with fluctuating sales in 2007, and then picked up well after corporate restructuring and innovative campaigns. A 33 per cent spurt in advertisement and promotion in the first quarter ended 30 June 2010 dragged down HUL's net profit by 1.8 per cent to ₹533.21 crore, despite a 60 basis point reduction in supply chain cost. HUL's volume grew by 11 per cent and net sales grew 7 per cent at ₹4,794 crore as compared to ₹4,476 crore in June 2009. HUL's current operating margin of 14 per cent is lower than its peak operating margin registered in 2002.

12.3 Product Lines

HUL's journey began in 1933, when the company was incorporated and it celebrated its platinum jubilee in 2008. The company claims to have by touched the lives of 700 million Indians, looking after their nutrition, hygiene and personal care and making them feel good, look good and get more out of life. In 2007 Hindustan Lever Limited became HUL, showing its alignment with the parent company. Its corporate mission was also redefined ('Adding vitality to life'). Today, HUL is a pre-eminent corporation and its brands are household names across the country. HUL is undoubtedly the company that has virtually shaped India's FMCG market over the decades. The company has built some of the most successful brands in India and many of its advertising campaigns have become part of the country's advertising folklore.

The company operates through two major divisions: food and beverages (F&B), and home and personal care (HPC) products.

12.3.1 Food and Beverages Division

Within the F&B division, the company markets ice creams. As the Indian branch of Unilever, the largest ice cream manufacturer in the world, a number of its brands are available in more than 90 countries. International brands include Carted'Or, Cornetto, Magnum, Solero and Vienetta. Other brands are more regional, such as Kwality-Walls in India; Algida, Langnese, Ola and Wall's in Europe; and Ben & Jerry's, Good Humor and Breyers in the US.

The division also sells tea, of which it markets under seven brands: Red Label, Taaza, A1, 3 Roses, Super Dust, Top Star and Ruby Dust. The company also markets Yellow Label and Green Label teas and has also launched New Lipton Taaza and FX Tazgi Dust Tea. The division's coffee business, comprising Bru Instant Coffee and Deluxe Green Label Roast & Ground Coffee, is the market leader in India. Bru Expresso is an innovative coffee pre-mix that delivers creamy, frothy coffee. In order to strengthen its share of the premium-segment roast and ground coffee market, a new product, Brooke Bond Green Label Classic, was also launched.

The F&B division also includes the Kissan range of culinary products, which comprises jams, squashes, tomato ketchups, pureees, and cooking pastes. The company has also launched sachet packs for jams and squashes to target new users. The business is backed by contract farming in Punjab and Karnataka.

Overall, beverages and ice creams continued to grow in double digits in 2008–9; the former driven by sharp price hikes and the latter by healthy volume offtake. However, processed foods slowed down to single digits for the first time since the September 2005 quarter. The company's conscious strategy to exit non-core, low profit margin commodity export business led to a 45 per cent decline in export revenues.

12.3.2 Home and Personal Care Division

In the HPC Division, HUL's hair care brands include Clinic, Sunsilk, Lux and Organics shampoos and Clinic Plus, Clinic All Clear, Cococare and Nihar hair oils. In the oral care sector of the division, its portfolio comprises Close-up and Pepsodent toothpastes, toothbrushes and toothpowders. Close-up Oxy Fresh was launched in 1999.

Another sector of the division is skincare. Hindustan Lever markets Fair & Lovely skin cream and lotion, the largest selling skincare product in India. The other major skincare franchises are Pond's, Vaseline, Lakme and Pears. Additional ranges in the division include colour cosmetics, for which the company markets the Lakme, Orchids and Elle-18 ranges; and deodorants and fragrances, including brands such as Rexona, Ivana, Shie, Elle-18 and Axe.

HUL's brands and people have its unparalleled strengths and they delivered very good results in 2007–8. For the year 2007, the company achieved an overall turnover growth of 13.3 per cent; both HPC and the foods businesses grew by 12.3 and 20.2 per cent, respectively. Profit After Tax (PAT) registered a growth of 14.9 per cent. While analysing the company's performance in March 2009, personal care offsets soaps and detergents' growth in HPC which increased by 11.5 per cent. Foods went up by 13.2 per cent and exports were down by 45 per cent, restricting the overall revenue growth to 6 per cent.

Lower input costs aided by cost reduction measures and lower taxes improved profitability from core operations. Exceptional items in the form of incremental provision for retirement benefits, restructuring costs and provision for remediation of a site affected bottom line. Overall volumes declined by 4 per cent on account of destocking at trade level in anticipation of further price action by the company, consolidation in modern trade and lacklustre performance by the oral care segment.

Within the HPC segment, the almost stagnant sales of personal care products (up by 1.9 per cent y-o-y) affected the price-led growth of 15.8 per cent in the soaps and detergents segment. Personal care was mainly affected due to the dismal performance of oral care proucts (Pepsodent in particular) and lower offtake in the modern trade outlets due to consolidation.

HUL has witnessed downtrading in its personal and fabric wash categories, losing share to the regional and other national competitors in these price-sensitive categories. The company has taken corrective actions in terms of reduction in MRP of soaps and increase in grammage of detergents, along with increased advertising of the same. Going forward, market analysts expect the competitive pricing in the mass consumption segments to improve volume offtake and hence improve performance in this segment in the quarters to come.

HUL initiated price hike in August 2010 on soap portfolio Lifebuoy (+ 6.7 per cent), Liril (+ 5.2 per cent), Dove (+ 3 per cent), Pears (+ 4 per cent) and Lux (+ 10 per cent). Price increase initiated to mitigate rise in palm oil price (+ 20 per cent). Typically raw material costs above 50 per cent (53 per cent in 2009 and 50.7 per cent in 2010). In September 2010, a single process change by introducing plough share mixer (psm) technology, HUL earned 15,000 tons carbon emission reduction in an year. This is a typical example of economic advantage of going green strategy.

Table 12.3: Market share performance of HUL product line (in %)

Products	*Quarter ending*				
	March 2009 (%)	*March 2008 (%)*	*Change (bps)*	*December 2008 (%)*	*Change (bps)*
Laundry	37	37.8	(80)	38.2	(120)
Personal wash	48.2	54.3	(610)	49.6	(140)
Hair	44.9	46.3	(140)	46	(110)
Skincare*	52	55.4	(340)	53.1	(110)
Toothpaste	28	29.5	(150)	29.1	(110)
Tea	23.4	22.9	50	22.7	70
Instant coffee	41.3	42.7	(140)	43.1	(180)

Source: Company, Edelweiss Research.
Note: *12 month MAT.

BOX 12.1: WHEEL SALES CROSS RS.2,000 CRORE

It's turned out literally to be HUL's Wheel of fortune. Detergent brand Wheel has become FMCG giant Hindustan Unilever's (HUL) first brand to cross the ₹2,000 crore mark in India. It also makes Wheel the first ever non-tobacco consumer goods brand to reach that milestone. What makes this achievement unique is the fact that Wheel is not an international brand, but one that was conceptualized specifically for the Indian market.

In the calendar year 2008, the brand single-handedly made up nearly 13 per cent of HUL's turnover. Given that it was launched a mere 22 years ago, it is a relatively young brand in the stable. Wheel came into existence in 1987, as a low-cost detergent to combat local rival Nirma, which had been rapidly gaining market share at HUL's expense. Back then the dominant detergent brand was Lever's Surf, but the brand had come under severe pressure from Nirma. Lever executives decided that downgrading Surf was not an option and they decided to launch a new detergent. The launch was a success almost instantly. Not only did it manage to stem Nirma's assault, but soon overtook Surf, the dominant Lever brand of the time.

Wheel's march to the top is no mean feat if you consider that Unilever first introduced a detergent brand, Sunlight in 1988 that still sells in certain states. Surf, too, has been around for almost 50 years.

Based on sales charts for the calendar year 2008, Wheel has moved into a league of its own. So big is the brand that its net sales are greater than the turnover of 273 of India's largest companies that feature in the *ET 500*. On its own strength, Wheel also sold more than the standalone sales of FMCG companies like Gillette, Colgate-Palmolive, Marico, Godrej Consumer Care, GlaxoSmithKline Consumer Products and Procter & Gamble Hygiene and Healthcare in India (standalone sales in 2007–8).

Source: Hindustan Unilever Ltd.

12.3.3 Other Businesses

However, the 'Other' business, mainly comprising bottled water, increased by 27.6 per cent with Pureit becoming a ₹2 billion brand (1 million units) in financial year of 2009 (15 months). Despite healthy operating profits and lower tax provision during the quarter, the net profit increased by a meager 3.7 per cent due to exceptional items, namely incremental provision for retirement benefits, restructuring costs and provision for remediation of a site.

HUL has acknowledged downtrading as being one of the factors responsible for slower volume growth and eroding market share in a few categories in first quarter of financial year of 2009. The management, however, remained confident of being able to drive profitability and recoup its lost market share by increasing grammage and effecting pricing cuts in mass brands. Advertising expenses dropped by 37 bps as a percentage of

Table 12.4: Segment-wise revenue of HUL product line

Segment-wise revenues	*(₹million)*		*% change*
	Fourth quarter of financial year 2009	*First quarter of financial year 2009*	
Soaps and detergents	20,122	17,382	15.8
Personal products	10,386	10,189	1.9
Beverages	4,893	4,310	13.5
Processed foods	1,634	1,520	7.5
Ice creams	453	370	22.4
Exports	2,186	3,973	(45)
Others	540	423	27.6

Source: Company, Edelweiss Research.

sales, growing by only 3 per cent y-o-y. HUL's management, however, pointed out that media spends had increased by 27 per cent, while below-the-line promotional activities were scaled down. Media rates for the company have come down, and this will help contain any increases in ad spends going forward. Other expenses came down by 70 bps, as the company put in place a number of cost-cutting measures on fixed costs and overheads.

Revenue from personal products rose by only 2 per cent y-o-y. Oral care declined the most, mainly due to the sharp fall in sales of lower-priced SKUs of the Pepsodent brand. Top end skincare and shampoo segments were negatively affected by the slowdown in organized retail. A mild winter also hurt sales of winter-care creams. Personal products' Earnings Before Interest and Tax (EBIT) margin was also down despite lower raw material prices, as sales mix turned adverse as high-margin oral care and skin and hair products had lower sales contributions.

12.4 Core Competency and Business Strategy

Core competence is clearly an important concept, and HUL seems to have been able to make it work for itself in the past. But for most of its counterparts in India, it is like a mirage: something that from a distance appears to offer hope in a hostile environment, but that turns to sand when approached. HUL's strength was tested in the Indian market between 2002 and 2004. Rising to the challenge, the company realigned its operations and strategy and regained its top slot with more than 30 per cent growth in 2008.

There are three distinct paths to developing a competence, each with its own benefits and drawbacks; and sustaining a core competence requires just as much rigour as developing one in the first place. To mount a winning competence-based strategy, it is not enough to rely on broad generalizations like 'marketing', 'product development', or 'service'. That means a consumer goods company like HUL with a reputation for marketing excellence assumed during 2002–4 that it was superior in all aspects of marketing. In reality, the company is not particularly skilled at pricing, is only average at channel management, and has made some serious errors resulting in a string of new product failures. Its true competence is much narrower: demand stimulation through image-based advertising.

Companies must define their core competences with precision if they are to use them to their full advantage. Basically, a core competence is a combination of complementary skills and knowledge bases embedded in a group or team that results in the ability to execute one or more critical processes to world-class standard. In principle, a world-class competence must steer the power structure in a company. The keeper of the skill drives all the company's major decisions, even in unrelated functions. At Procter & Gamble, for instance, the core consumer marketing skill resides in the advertising department (the company's name for brand management). Brand managers exert a dominant influence on all decisions throughout the company.

In confronting the challenges of the past ten years since 2000, HUL began by reshaping its product portfolios through mergers and acquisitions, with the aim of becoming a global leader in a few core categories. Then HUL focused on its core brands, where it concentrated marketing and other resources, and eliminated weaker brands. Eventually, strengthened brands made it more difficult for retailers to insist on price cuts.

In the coming years, success will require ever sharper capabilities in the four main areas that sustain consumer goods companies: brand marketing, sales, innovation, and supply chain. Average performance and best practices have improved spectacularly in each area compared with a decade ago. Tomorrow's winners will be companies that not only adopt and roll out best practices quicker than others, but also introduce new approaches, often borrowed from other industries.

Although HUL views innovation as vital, few are happy with what they have accomplished in this respect, especially compared with pharmaceutical and consumer electronics companies.

Pharmaceutical and consumer electronics companies concentrate on the small percentage of the population that can afford expensive, Western-style goods, leaving local competitors to target the overwhelming majority of consumers with modest means. The locals have the edge in supplying neighbourhood stores, which global companies find harder to reach. The former have held off the big players by selling some products at very low prices while nonetheless generating profits. In this respect, however, HUL scripted several success stories in the rural market. The latest in 2010 is the going green strategy of reducing CO_2 footprint by introducing psm technology.

In modern marketing, consumers opt for experience, not products and services, and brands continue to rule. So the management can concentrate entirely on dealing with customers—the main engines of growth—by outsourcing production and logistics. Indeed, companies like HUL find that they can think more creatively about developing new products and stretching their brands into new categories when they no longer have to worry about keeping factories occupied. This approach would also promote a great leap in a company's return on capital employed.

12.5 Innovative Campaigns

In 2005–7, the employees of HUL was undertaking a promotional exercise in the rural areas—Madhya Pradesh, Bihar and Orissa, for its utensil-cleansing detergent bar Vim under the campaign, 'Vim Khar Khar Challenge', visiting rural towns and demonstrating how vessels are cleaned with Vim.

'For the purpose, HUL is educating the rural masses on the . . . "Vim Khar Khar Challenge" TV commercial by conducting live demonstrations about vessel cleaning. Company's aim was to tap the growth rate of the ₹4 billion scouring bar market.

The HUL had, in fact, earned the distinction of becoming one of the few Indian companies to tap the country's vast rural population so extensively and now around 50 per cent of its turnover came from the rural markets.

12.5.1 Product Launches: A Regular Affair

The 1960s and 1970s witnessed a series of new product launches—Anik (clarified butter, in the early 1960s), Sunsilk (shampoo, in 1964), Rin (detergent bar, in 1969), Clinic (shampoo, in 1971), and Liril (bathing soap, in 1974). In 1975, HUL entered the oral care market with a gel toothpaste called Close-Up. In the late-1970s, it set up 70 medium- and small-scale factories in the rural areas for manufacturing soaps and detergents.

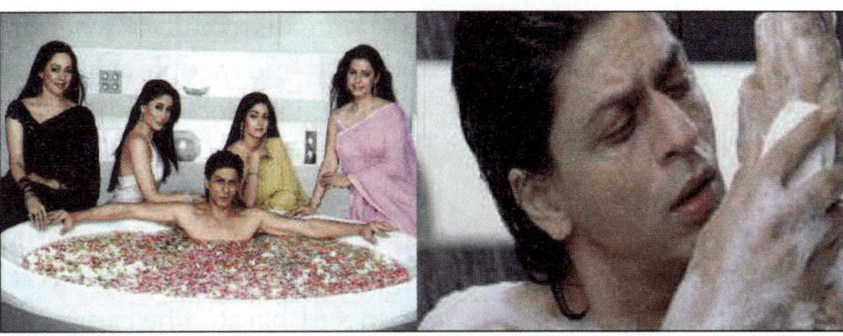

Figure 12.1: Lux campaign featuring Shahrukh

Amongst the over 110 brands that it owns, HUL terms the 30 best selling ones as 'Power Brands'—a title well deserved. This is because brands such as Fair & Lovely, Pond's, Pepsodent, Close-Up, Sunsilk, Clinic, Lakme, Surf, Rin, Wheel, Lifebuoy, Lux, Breeze, Vim, Kwality, Brooke Bond, Lipton, Annapurna, Kissan, and Dalda have become an integral part of almost every Indian household. Interestingly, many of these products, and especially those in categories like fabric wash, personal wash and beverages, derive over 50 per cent of their sales from rural areas. HUL's efforts to build a market for its products in these areas had started way back in the days it began operations in the country. By 2010, the rural markets had become a destination for FMCG marketers like never before.

12.6 Spreading to Villages

12.6.1 Project Streamline

HUL adopted a phased approach in order to meet its 16 million village household target. It decided to address the key issues related to availability, awareness and overcoming prevalent attitudes and habits of rural consumers. Penetrative pricing was also an important factor that was addressed.

This project was to be carried out with the help of a rural distributor who had 15-20 rural sub-stockists connected to him in the villages. The sub-stockists would drive distribution in the neighbouring villages using unconventional means like bullock-carts and tractors. As part of Project Streamline, HUL aimed at providing higher quality services to consumers in terms of 'frequency', 'full-line availability' and 'credit'. As a result, the number of HUL brands and the Stock Keeping Units (SKUs) stocked by village retailers increased.

12.6.2 Project Bharat

HUL carried out its direct marketing operations in the high potential districts of the country to attract first-time users. Under Project Bharat, HUL vans visited villages and sold low unit-price packs each of its detergents, toothpastes, face creams and talcum powders for ₹5 and ₹15. During the sale, company representatives took the help of a video show to explain to the people how to use these products. The villagers were also educated about the superior benefits of using the company's products as compared to their current habits. This was very helpful for HUL as it created awareness about its product categories and the availability of the affordable packs.

Under this, the company provided self-employment opportunities to villagers through Self-Help Groups (SHG). The SHGs operated like direct-to-home distributors wherein groups of 15-20 villagers who were below the poverty line (people whose monthly incomes was less than ₹750 per month) could take micro-credit from banks. Using this money, villagers could buy HUL's products and sell them to consumers, thereby generating income as well as employment for themselves. This activity also helped the company increase the reach of its products.

By the end of 2009, HUL had covered 2.3 million households through Project Bharat. The campaign was successful in increasing penetration levels, usership and the awareness about the company's products in the districts targeted. This also helped HUL grow at a better pace than the industry. In the shampoo market, while the urban growth rate was only 4-5 per cent, HUL's rural growth was at 15-16 per cent. Similarly, in the skincare market the urban growth was only at 7-8 per cent whereas it was 14 per cent in the rural markets.

12.6.3 Community Dental Health Campaign

HUL launched a nationwide Community Dental Health Campaign in association with the Indian Medical Association (IMA), to promote its toothpaste Pepsodent.

The Community Dental Health Campaign's vision was 'to make every person in urban and rural India adopt a good oral care regime'. Company sources placed the total investment in the programme at between ₹100-₹200 million.

The Community Dental Health Campaign was carried out for a period of three years and targeted 100 million people across rural India. The IMA-Pepsodent project increased the overall dental care penetration in the country to 65 per cent from the prevailing 48 per cent in 2010.

12.6.4 Project Millennium

HUL planned ways to tap the *chai ki dukan* (tea vendors). It provided affordable tea packets that were suitably blended to appeal to the rural taste of *kadak chai* (strong tea). The company test-marketed a specially designed product, *chai ki goli* (fully soluble tea balls) that was dropped in a boiling milk-water combination. These were priced very attractively at four for a rupee.

12.6.5 Rural Communication Programme

Inspired by the success of its earlier ventures, HUL went on to participate in a rural communication programme called *Grameenon ke Beech* (Amidst Villagers) in August 2001. It involved setting up company stalls, conducting product briefings and demonstrations, organizing interactive games, lucky draws, magic shows and screening hit movies interspersed with product commercials.

12.6.6 Project Shakti

In late 2001, HUL launched a six-month project called Project Shakti in Andhra Pradesh. The project sought to create a sustainable partnership between HUL and its low-income rural consumers by providing them access to micro-credit; an opportunity to direct that credit into investment opportunities as company distributors; and reward them for growth and enterprise through shared profits. During 2001, the 'rural cell' within HUL worked closely with SHGs, NGOs and governmental bodies in Andhra Pradesh to put in place a comprehensive experiment in training the SHGs.

12.6.7 Tapping the Village Market

HUL decided to highlight concepts of health and hygiene in rural areas to support the relaunch. The Lifebuoy soap was given a completely new look (size and shape), formulation, fragrance, lather profile and was repositioned as a family soap rather than a male soap. The company introduced several variations of the product including Lifebuoy Active Red, Lifebuoy Active Orange, Lifebuoy International Plus and Lifebuoy International Gold.

12.7 Combating Recession

HUL's volume disappoints, reporting a 4 per cent decline during the March 2009 quarter, while profit growth is ahead of estimates on account of sharper margin expansion. While the FMCG business has grown by 11.8 per cent to reach ₹37.2 billion, export revenues have declined by 45 per cent to stand at ₹2.2 billion. Within FMCG, the soaps and detergents business has grown by 15.8 per cent and the foods business by 12.6 per cent. The personal products category has disappointed with a revenue growth of just 1.9 per cent. Oral care in particular has seen a decline, while the skincare category has got impacted by high base effect and mild winter.

While part of HUL's volume decline can be attributed to 4-6 days of destocking (in soaps and detergents in particular), part of the volume decline is also on account of HUL's strategy of portfolio premiumization and thereby vacating certain mass segments. This was reflected in the improved margin profile too.

Most analysts believe that HUL's strong and professional management will take the necessary steps and strategize to continue its growth path. HUL has one of the highest return ratios in the industry. The company has limited capex plans going ahead.

The sales growth for both Marico and GSK Consumer Healthcare remained robust in the March 2009 quarter. Volume growth for Marico remained steady (8 per cent growth in the oil brand Parachute, 5 per cent in Saffola cooking oil and 3 per cent y-o-y growth in the December quarter). For GSK, volume growth was very high at ~20 per cent (out of this ~6 per cent came from growth in international business and pipeline inventory of new products). Both Marico and GSK benefitted from new product launches. In the past few quarters, Marico launched Saffola Cholesterol Management, Saffola Diabetic, Parachute Advansed (revitalizing hot hair oil), Saffola Zest and Saffola Rice. GSK too introduced three new products in the past few quarters (Horlicks Nutribar, Dood, Activ Grow). These new product launches are likely to propel incremental sales growth for the company. In fact, GCPL's soap volumes are likely to grow faster than HUL's, owing to downtrading in favour of GCPL's value-for-money (VFM) platform and the successful launch of Godrej No.1–Strawberry and Walnut.

Table 12.5: Quarterly and annual performance of HUL

Head	*Fourth quarter 2009*	*First quarter 2009*	*% change*	*Fourth quarter 2009*	*% change*	*Financial year 2009*	*Financial year 2010*
Net rev. (₹million)	39,883	37,626	6	43,077	(7.4)	202,393	175,238
EBITDA (₹million)	5,493	4,078	34.7	6,931	(20.7)	29,779	27,964
Net profit (₹million)	3,950	3,810	3.7	6,157	(35.9)	25,076	21,099
Diluted EPS (₹)	1.8	1.7	3.7	2.9	(37.5)	11.5	9.7

Source: Company, Edelweiss Research.

Case Discussion Questions

1. Discuss the importance of building a strong distribution system to effectively market a personal care product during recession, especially in the rural areas. What were the reasons behind HUL deciding to focus its efforts and resources on building the rural consumer base?
2. Discuss the various measures taken by HUL to increase the awareness and penetration levels of its products in the Indian rural market. What do you think are the crucial differences between marketing FMCG products in rural areas and urban areas?
3. Comment on the relevance and significance of social and economic imperatives of HUL's strategies and campaigns.
4. Comment on the marketing structure adopted by HUL to ensure the availability of its products in the rural areas. How far has the distribution strategy contributed to HUL's growth in rural India?
5. Devise a recession-proof marketing strategy for the home and personal care products division of HUL by analysing its target customers and their felt needs, competitor and market analyses, environment analysis and SBU (own) analysis, core competency and business strategy analyses utilizing the theory explained in this case.
6. 'Growth potential for FMCG brands was more in the downtown suburbs rather than the urban metros and rural areas.' Comment on the emerging market scenario in India for FMCG products and discuss whether FMCG companies need to shift their focus to the suburbs in the future. Justify your answer.

Sources: The Economic Times, January to August 2010; indiatimes.com; rediffmail.com; *Business Standard*, April to August 2010.

CASE ANALYSIS

Case Summary

HUL's journey began in 1933, when the company, was first incorporated, and celeberated its platinum jubilee in 2008, touching the lives of 700 million Indians, looking after their nutrition, hygiene and personal care. In 2007 the company Hindustan Lever Limited (HLL) became Hindustan Unilever Limited (HUL), showing its alignment with the parent company and redefining its corporate mission as giving vitality to life.

Today, HUL is a pre-eminent corporation and its brands are household names across the country. HUL is undoubtedly the company that has virtually shaped India's FMCG market over the decades. The company has built some of the most successful brands in India and many of its advertising campaigns have become part of the country's advertising folklore.

History

In 1888, less than four years after William-Hesketh Lever launched Sunlight soap in England, his newly-found company, Lever Brothers, started exporting the revolutionary laundry soap to India. By the time the company merged with The Netherlands-based Margarine Unie in 1930 to form Unilever, it had already carved a niche for itself in the Indian market. In 1931, Unilever set up its first Indian subsidiary, Hindustan Vanaspati Manufacturing Company, followed by Lever Brothers India Limited (1933) and United Traders Limited (1935). These three companies merged to form HUL in November 1956. Unilever now holds 51.55 per cent equity in the company. The company has since expanded its operations through organic growth, mergers and acquisitions to become the largest FMCG company in India.

Timeline of HUL

- 1888 Sunlight introduced in India.
- 1931 Hindustan Vanaspati Manufacturing Company registered by Unilever.
- 1933 Lever Brothers India Limited incorporated to manufacture soaps.
- 1935 United Traders Limited incorporated in India to market personal care products.
- 1956 HVM, BBLIL, UTL merge to form HLL.
- 1958 HLRC established.
- 1962 Exports operation begins.
- 1979 Chemicals complex commissioned in Haldia.
- 1986 HLL launches an agri-foods unit.

The 1990s witnessed a string of crucial mergers, acquisitions and alliances.

- 1993 The erstwhile Tata Oil Mills Company (TOMCO) merged with HUL.
- 1994 HUL forms a 50 : 50 joint venture with the US-based Kimberly-Clark Corporation to form Kimberly-Clark Lever Limited.
- 1995 HUL and Lakme Limited form a 50 : 50 joint venture, Lakme Lever Limited.
- 1998 Internal restructuring culminates in the merger of Pond's (India) Limited (PIL) with HUL.
- 2000 The government awards 74 per cent equity in Modern Foods to HUL.

- 2001 Joint venture with ICI for disposal of the perfumery and flavours business.
- 2003 HUL acquires the cooked shrimp and pasteurized crabmeat business of Amalgam Group of Companies, a leader in value-added marine products.

The company also established a subsidiary in Nepal, called Nepal Lever Ltd. (NLL). The NLL factory manufactures products like soaps, detergents and personal care products for both the domestic market and for exports to India. The 1990s also witnessed a string of crucial mergers, acquisitions and alliances on the food and beverages front. In 1992, Brooke Bond acquired Kothari General Foods, with significant interest in instant coffee. In 1993, it acquired the Kissan business and the Dollops ice cream business from Cadbury India.

In 1993 Brooke Bond India and Lipton India merged to form Brooke Bond Lipton India Limited (BBLIL). In 1994 BBLIL launched the Wall's range of frozen desserts. By the end of the year, the company entered into a strategic alliance with the Kwality Ice Cream Group and in 1995 with the Milkfood ice cream brand, acquiring 100 per cent marketing and distribution rights. Finally BBLIL merged with Hindustan in January 1996.

In January 2000, in a historic step, the government decided to award 74 per cent equity in State-owned Modern Foods Industries to Hindustan Lever, thereby kick-starting the first major strategic sale of government equity in public sector undertakings (PSU) to a private partner.

Product Lines

The company operates through two major divisions:

- Home and personal care products (HPC)
- Food and beverages.

Home and Personal Care Products (HPC)

The HPC business is made of fabric wash, household care, personal wash and personal care categories, which include products like toothpastes, shampoos, skincare, deodorants and colour cosmetics. The major products and services under the HPC divisions are:

- **Personal wash:** Under this category, HUL has various soaps, each with its unique target segment and marketing strategy. These include Lifebuoy, Lux, Liril, Hamam, Pears, Rexona, Dove and Breeze.
- **Fabric wash:** HUL has a very good hold in this segment on the strength of an excellent brand portfolio; Surf, Rin, Wheel and Sunlight address the needs of consumers at different income levels.
- **Household care**: Vim in the dishwash segment and Domex in floor and toilet cleaning segment offer a powerful proposition.
- **Oral care:** Its portfolio consists of Close-Up and Pepsodent toothpastes, toothbrushes and toothpowders.
- **Haircare:** Positioned as the 'Hair Expert', Sunsilk is the largest beauty shampoo brand in the country. Clinic Plus is India's largest selling shampoo. Also included in the group is the anti-dandruff shampoo Clinic

All Clear. The shampoos portfolio also consists of Organics and Lux brands. HUL is also into the hair oil segment, selling brands like Clinic Plus, Clinic All Clear, Cococare and Nihar hair oils.

- **Skincare:** HUL markets Fair & Lovely skin cream and lotion, the largest selling skincare product in India. The major skincare franchisees are Pond's, Vaseline, Lakme and Pears. Additional ranges in the division include colour cosmetics, for which the company markets the Lakme, Orchids and Elle 18 ranges.
- **Perfumery:** The key brands in this division are Rexona, Ivana, Shie, Elle 18 and Axe.

Food and Beverages

The Foods Division of HUL comprises beverages, processed foods, ice creams and Modern Foods businesses. The major products and services are:

- **Tea:** This division markets evergreen brands Brooke Bond, Lipton, Red Label, A1, 3 Roses, Super Dust, Top Star and Ruby Dust. The company also markets Yellow Label and Green Label Teas and the New Lipton Taaza and FX Tazgi dust tea.
- **Coffee:** This division comprises Bru Instant Coffee and Deluxe Green Label Roast and Ground coffee.
- **Kissan sauces and ketchups:** The Kissan range of culinary products includes jams, squashes, tomato ketchups, purees and cooking pastes.
- **Frozen desserts and ice creams:** The Indian branch of Unilever is the largest ice cream manufacturer in the world; a number of its brands are available in more than 90 countries. Kwality-Walls has been a big name in the ice cream category along with the Cornetto brand.

Core Competency and Business Strategy

Core competence is a combination of complementary skills and knowledge bases embedded in a group or team that results in the ability to execute one or more critical processes to world-class standards. Core competence is clearly an importance concept and HUL seems to be able to make it work for itself. HUL's strength was tested in the Indian market between 2002 and 2004. Slowly the company realigned it operations and strategy and the net outcome was HUL regaining the top slot in 2008 with more than 30 per cent growth and again it is undergoing another test. In confronting the challenges of the past ten years, HUL began by reshaping its product portfolio through mergers and acquisitions, with the aim of becoming the global leader in a few categories. Then, HUL focused on its core brands, concentrating its marketing and other resources on these and eliminating the weaker ones.

In this competitive world, success requires sound capabilities in the four main areas that sustain consumer goods companies: brand marketing, sales, innovation, and supply chain. HUL views innovation as vital and is at par or even better than the pharmaceutical and consumer electronics companies.

HUL has scripted many success stories in the rural market by understanding the fact that the local entities have an edge in supplying neighbourhood stores, which global companies find hard to reach.

Innovative Campaigns

During 2005–7, employees of HUL literally took to the streets with its promotional exercise in the rural markets, for its utensil-cleaning bar Vim. As part of the 'Vim Khar Khar Challenge', company officials visited rural towns for live demonstrations.

In 1961, HUL introduced the Lux soap in a range of colours. To begin with it picked the reigning queens of Bollywood to figure in its ad campaign—a tradition it faithfully held on to. Later, its Shahrukh ads proved to create a similar buzz.

The 1960s and 1970s witness a series of new brand launches—Anik, Sunsilk, Rin, Clinic and Liril. In late 1970s HUL set up 70 medium- and small-scale factories in the rural areas for manufacturing soaps and detergents.

The early 1990s was a period of global recession and 'value-for-money' became the buzzword for many FMCG companies all around the world including India. Growth in the urban markets had slowed down and even the rural market showed signs of sluggishness in terms of both value and volume.

Apart from launching new products on a regular basis HUL categorized its 30 best-selling brands as 'Power Brands'—brands which have become an integral part of almost every Indian household.

HUL's effort to build a market for its products in these areas had started way back in the days it began operations in the country. It was one of the first companies to recognize the rural market as a significant destination.

HUL goes to the Villages and Stays On

The period from the 1970s to the 1990s can be considered as the 'rural sensitization stage' for the FMCG sector. It was during this time that two of the major FMCG firms namely, Nirma and CavinKare, started out their operations aimed at the lower income groups and focused on the rural market. HUL executives were dismissive of the products and never considered the potential and opportunity of this sector.

But very soon, Nirma's success in the detergent market and CK's success in the shampoo market convinced HUL that it needed to take a closer look at the lower-income market. But post-liberalization not only saw a higher number of homegrown products, but also imported ones. The lowering of trade barriers encouraged MNCs to invest in India to cater to the needs of 1 billion Indians. As an outcome of increased competition it was not until the late 1990s that HUL had achieved any significant growth in the rural sector.

HUL launched a series of projects in the late 1990s to capture the largely untapped rural market. It started off with Project Streamline, which targeted setting up of new distribution networks in the rural market and address the problems of rural supply chain management. This project helped HUL increase its reach in the rural markets from 25 per cent in 1995 to 37 per cent in 1998.

Project Bharat was launched by HUL in mid-1998. It aimed at increasing HUL's penetration and brand awareness in the rural market. It was a direct marketing project which helped HUL understand the attitudes and habits of rural consumers and reach almost 13 million villages by 1999.

HUL also carried out various activities with SHGs. It started the 'Integrated Rural Promotion Van' to help widen the reach of its products. It also launched a nation-wide Community Dental Health Campaign in August 1999. The campaign went on for nearly three years while HUL also organized around 200 health fairs in the rural areas.

In order to increase its share in the tea market, HUL came up with Project Millennium. Some of the other initiatives of HUL include Project Shakti, which offered micro-credit options to rural consumers. Through this project 45,000 people got self employed and HUL penetrated in 1 lakh villages spread across 15 states in India in 2010. In February 2002, the company relaunched Lifebuoy with a focus on the rural market. It brought out various variants of the soap like Lifebuoy Active Red, Lifebuoy Active Orange, Lifebuoy International Plus and Lifebuoy International Gold.

The rural marketing campaigns helped HUL achieve double-digit growth and proved the effectiveness of HUL's campaigns.

Competitor Profiles

Colgate-Palmolive Limited

Colgate is promoted by Colgate-Palmolive USA, which has a 51 per cent stake in the Indian subsidiary. The company's flagship product, Colgate Dental Cream, is the largest selling toothpaste in India with an estimated market share of over 30 per cent in 2010. The company has over 45 per cent share in the ₹21 billion oral care market.

Colgate-Palmolive also has a presence in the personal products category with brands such as Palmolive (soaps, shaving products) and Charmis (face cream). The company has discontinued the production of toilet bar soaps (Palmolive) from third quarter of financial year 2006, which it now imports through one of the subsidiaries of its parent company.

P&G Hygiene

P&G Hygiene and Healthcare (PGHH) is a 69 per cent subsidiary of the FMCG major P&G, USA. The company dominates both hygiene and healthcare segments backed by strong brands, Vicks in the anti-cold segment and Whisper in the feminine care segment (40 per cent market share). The company's parent has two other 100 per cent subsidiaries in India which have well known brands in the shampoos (Head & Shoulders, Pantene, Rejoice) and detergents space (Ariel, Tide).

Earlier PGHH used to undertake contract manufacturing for its parent's detergent portfolio in India, which it has discontinued. P&G, USA recently acquired the shaving products major, Gillette, and has dethroned Unilever to take the top slot in the global FMCG space.

Marico Industries

Marico is a leading Indian group in consumer products and services in the beauty and wellness space. It has products and services in haircare, skincare

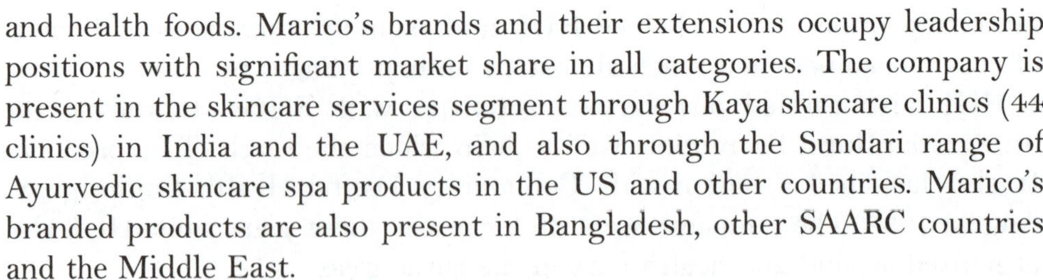

and health foods. Marico's brands and their extensions occupy leadership positions with significant market share in all categories. The company is present in the skincare services segment through Kaya skincare clinics (44 clinics) in India and the UAE, and also through the Sundari range of Ayurvedic skincare spa products in the US and other countries. Marico's branded products are also present in Bangladesh, other SAARC countries and the Middle East.

Marico has been growing both organically and inorganically. It acquired Nihar, Oil of Malabar and Manjal herbal soap brand in India. It also acquired a clutch of brands namely, Camelia, Aromatic and Magnolia in Bangladesh.

Nirma Limited

Nirma sells over 8,00,000 tons of detergent products every year and commands a 35 per cent share of the Indian detergent market, making it one of the world's biggest detergent brands. The brand promotion efforts are complemented by Nirma's distribution reach and market penetration through a country-wide network of 400 distributors and over 2 million retail outlets, making Nirma products available from the smallest rural village to the largest metro.

The operating division of Nirma Industries Limited (NIL) owns inter alia the trademark 'Nirma', 'Nima' and others, as well as limestone mining rights and a unit to manufacture soapstone.

Gillette India

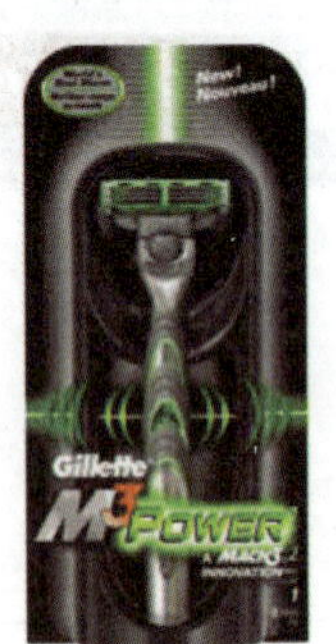

Gillette India is the 52 per cent subsidiary of the US shaving major Gillette USA. The company came back into the black in 2003 after a spate of restructuring in 2001 and 2002. Gillette hived off its battery manufacturing plant (Duracell) at Manesar and also saw cash infusion from the parent, which helped it restructure and pay of all its debt. It is now a focused shaving products major, which also markets the Duracell range of batteries.

ITC

ITC is not a pure-play FMCG company, since cigarettes are its primary business. It is diversifying into non-tobacco FMCG segments like food, personal care, paper products, hotels and agribusiness to reduce its exposure to cigarettes.

ITC has over the last 100 years established a very close business relationship with the farming community in India and is currently in the process of enhancing the Indian farmer's ability to link to global markets through the e-Choupal initiative, and produce the quality demanded by its customers. This long-standing relationship is being leveraged in sourcing best-quality agricultural produce for ITC's foods business.

The foods business extends to four categories in the market: ready-to-eat, staples, confectionery and snack foods. In order to assure consumers of the highest standards of food safety and hygiene, ITC is engaged in assisting outsourced manufacturers in implementing world-class hygiene standards through HACCP certification.

The unwavering commitment to internationally benchmarked quality standards has enabled ITC to rapidly gain market standing in all its six brands: Kitchens of India, Aashirvaad, Sunfeast, Mint-o, Candyman and Bingo!

ITC launched an exclusive line of fine fragrances under the Essenza Di Wills brand in mid-2005. In September 2007, it launched Fiama Di Wills, a premium range of personal care products comprising shampoos, conditioners, shower gels and soaps. Between February and June 2008, it expanded its personal care portfolio with the launch of Vivel Di Wills and Vivel brands. Vivel Di Wills, a range of soaps, and Vivel, a range of soaps and shampoos, cater to the specific needs of a wide range of consumers. In the popular segment, ITC launched a range of soaps and shampoos under the brand name Superia.

Britannia Industries Limited

Britannia Industries Limited is an Indian company based in Kolkata and famous for its Britannia and Tiger brands of biscuits, which are highly recognized throughout the country. Britannia is India's largest biscuit firm, with an estimated 38 per cent market share. The company's principal activity is the manufacture and sale of biscuits, breads, rusks, cakes and dairy products. Some of the popular biscuit brands include MarieGold, Treat, Maska Chaska, Good Day, Milk Bikis, Little Hearts and Pure Magic.

Between 1998 and 2001, the company's sales grew at a compound annual rate of 16 per cent and operating profits reached 18 per cent. More recently, the company has been growing at 27 per cent a year, compared to the industry's growth rate of 20 per cent. At present, 90 per cent of Britannia's annual revenue of ₹2,200 crore comes from biscuits.

Nestlé India

Nestlé's relationship with India dates back to 1912, when it began trading as The Nestlé Anglo-Swiss Condensed Milk Company (Export) Limited, importing and selling finished products in the Indian market.

The company continuously focuses its efforts to better understand the changing lifestyles of Indians and anticipate consumer needs in order to provide taste, nutrition, health and wellness through its product offerings. The culture of innovation and renovation within the company and access to the Nestlé Group's proprietary technology/brands expertise and the extensive centralized R&D facilities give it a distinct advantage in these efforts. It helps the company create value that can be sustained over the long term by offering consumers a wide variety of high-quality, safe food products at affordable prices.

Nestlé India manufactures products of international quality under internationally famous brand names such as Nescafé, Maggi, Milkybar, Milo, KitKat, Bar One, Milkmaid and Nestea. In recent years the company has also introduced products of daily consumption and use such as Nestlé Milk, Nestlé Slim Milk, Nestlé Fresh 'n' Natural Dahi and Nestlé Jeera Raita.

Godrej Consumer Products Limited

Godrej Consumer Products Limited (GCPL) is amongst the well known mid-cap companies in the Indian FMCG space with a presence in the

personal care, haircare and fabric care categories and top-of-the-mind brands such as Cinthol, Fairglow, Godrej No.1 (soaps), and Ezee liquid detergent, to name a few. The company bought over the Snuggies brand in the child nappy segment in 2003. It acquired 100 per cent ownership of the UK-based Keyline Brands, which owns several international brands and trademarks in Europe, Jordan, Australia and Canada. In July 2006, GCPL entered into an agreement to acquire the South African hair colour business of Rapidol, UK, as well as its subsidiary Rapidol International, which had a combined turnover of ₹330 million in 2005.

K.S. Oils Limited

K.S. Oils (KSO), established in 1985 with a crushing capacity of 1,475 metric tons per day of mustard seeds is one of the largest manufacturers of mustard oil in India. It enjoys a 4.5 per cent share of the total mustard oil market with a dominant 25 per cent market share of branded mustard oil market. The company accounts for 40 per cent market share in north-east India.

KSO's product portfolio also comprises refined oils, *vanaspati* and non-edible solvent oil. KSO is one of the largest and regular supplier of edible oils to the Indian defence organization and a leading exporter of soyabean/ rapeseed (mustard) meal to foreign buyers.

Dabur India Limited

Dabur India Limited has marked its presence with some very significant achievements and today commands market leadership. Its story of success is based on dedication to nature, corporate and process hygiene, dynamic leadership and commitment to partners and stakeholders. The results of its policies and initiatives speak for themselves.

- Leading consumer goods company in India with a turnover of ₹2,233.72 crore (financial year 2007).
- Two major strategic business units (SBU)—Consumer Care Division (CCD) and Consumer Health Division (CHD).
- Three subsidiary group companies—Dabur Foods, Dabur Nepal and Dabur International, and three step-down subsidiaries of Dabur International (Asian Consumer Care in Bangladesh, African Consumer Care in Nigeria and Dabur Egypt).
- 13 ultra-modern manufacturing units spread around the globe.
- Products marketed in over 50 countries.
- Wide and deep market penetration with 47 C&F agents, more than 5,000 distributors and over 1.5 million retail outlets all over India.
- CCD deals with FMCG products relating to personal care and health care. Leading brands include:
  Dabur: Healthcare brand
  Vatika: Personal care brand
  Anmol: Value-for-money brand
  Hajmola: Digestive products brand
- **Dabur Amla**, Chyawanprash and Lal Dant Manjan—₹100 crore turnover each.
- **Vatika** hair oil and shampoo—High growth brand.

- Strategic positioning of honey as a food product, leading to market leadership (over 40 per cent) in the branded honey market.
- Dabur Chyawanprash, the largest selling Ayurvedic medicine with over 65 per cent market share.
- Leader in herbal digestives with 90 per cent market share.
- Hajmola tablets command over 75 per cent market share of the digestive tablets category.
- Dabur Lal Tail tops the baby massage oil market with 35 per cent of total share.

CavinKare

CavinKare Private Limited offers beauty products, including hair, skin and personal care products; food products; and home essentials. The company also offers packaging solutions to confectionery, cosmetics, detergent, soap, pharma, pest control/insecticide, food, and beverage industries. In addition, it operates salons offering personal styling and beauty solutions and spa treatments to men, women and children.

CavinKare offers its products in India and internationally. The company was founded in 1983 and is based in Chennai. Started as a single product company, CavinKare's products are born out of a keen understanding of consumer needs. They have built in India a consciousness to use branded cosmetics made from natural herbs. Products like Nyle, Fairever and Spinz are established brands in the Indian cosmetic market.

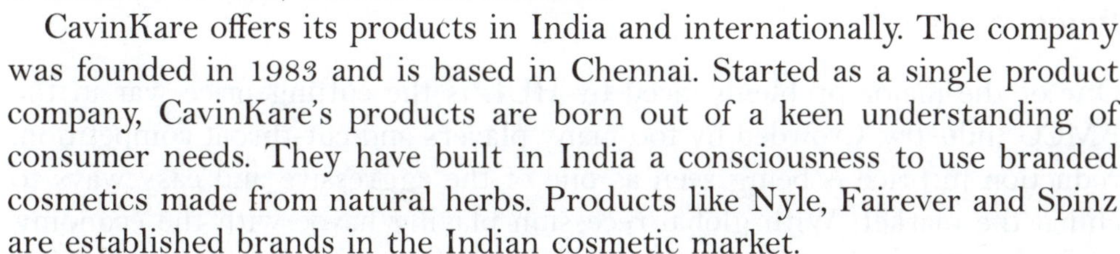

CavinKare popularized the concept of shampoo sachets with its Chik brand, which restructured the packaging trend in 1983. The company had a turnover of over ₹5,000 million in 2007–8. It has an employee strength of 976, an all-India network of 1,300 stockists catering to about 25 lakh outlets. CavinKare's astute professionalism, innovative products and consistent quality are results of its significant corporate practices.

Johnson & Johnson

Johnson & Johnson Consumer Products Division is one of the leading FMCG manufacturers in India. It is also among the most consistent and successful enterprises not just in the J&J worldwide group of companies, but also in India. Johnson & Johnson Consumer Products Division has been growing steadily over the last few years, and is one of the few companies in the Indian market to grow at extremely healthy levels.

The consumer products division owes its success to the strength of its brands, and the loyalty they enjoy from consumers, a strong sense of values driven from the credo, and an environment which sets the toughest standards of leadership. It currently has brands Clean and Clear, Stayfree, Carefree, Shower to Shower powder, and a range of baby products..

Problems Faced by HUL

Recession and Inflation

The biggest problem to hit the FMCG industry was the current recession and decreasing inflation. As per the data on 19 March 2009,[1] inflation hit its lowest levels and the markets started tumbling with the FMCG sector taking the lead. The BSE Sectoral Index fell by close to 1 per cent to 1,906.24. HUL, which surged by close to 8 per cent in the previous week, plunged by close to 3 per cent to hit ₹226 soon after the inflation data was released by the government. FMCG major Marico Limited witnessed a fall of 3.39 per cent to ₹59.80, while ITC fell by 0.56 per cent to ₹168.50 on the BSE. Dabur India too witnessed a fall of over 1 per cent to ₹93.20.

However, during his visit to India Paul Polman, group chief executive officer of Unilever Plc., commented that 'recession could help firms such as Unilever. Consumers postpone buying cars, televisions and that frees up a lot of money to spend on everyday needs. HUL don't see personal care or food markets go down substantially.'[2] Hence, in fact, beneath the surface problem of recession lies an untapped opportunity for HUL. Everything depends on how it taps the opportunity. This is further worsen by the escalation of input costs in 2010.

Price Wars

One of the major problems faced by HUL is the cutting price war in the FMCG industry. Crowded by too many players and cut-throat competition, reduction in price is being seen as one of the aggressive and easy ways to churn the market. With global recession playing havoc with the economy, every sector is going through a rough patch, including the once promising retail sector.

Retailers like Big Bazaar and More started renegotiating deals with FMCG companies like HUL and P&G to keep the cash registers ringing by selling cheaper products in an otherwise slowing retail environment.[3] This means that FMCG players will have to give higher margins to retailers as compared to previous years. Newer packaging techniques will be introduced to help retailers, which could minimize operational cost in terms of logistics and shelf management.

HUL, ITC and P&G have already started a price war to grab a larger chunk of the consumer's wallet and obviously market share. HUL has undergone a strategy change by abandoning premium positioning strategy to take up cost cutting to compete with P&G. These price cuts are causing profit margins to shrink, making difficult to sustain the previous profit margins without affecting product quality.

Increased Competition

Given its bigger portfolio HUL faces challenges from all fronts. For instance, in the shampoo market Dabur India has upped the ante by introducing new variants of Vatika with specific benefits. The move will propel the company into the same league as other big-ticket multinational players HUL and P&G, which already offer different variants of anti-dandruff shampoo brands.[4] HUL faces stiff competition in the detergents segment too from local players like Ghadi of Kanpur Trading Corporation and CavinKare.[5]

Changing Customer Preferences

Over time there has been paradigm shift in consumer taste and preferences. There is dire need for constant innovation to address changing customer needs such as health consciousness and increased utility of products.

Capacity Over-utilization

Another problem that HUL faces is that of capacity over-utilization which plagues the industry today. The FMCG industry is extremely competitive and consumers have high demands on price and quality. They are increasingly disloyal to brands, quickly choosing a different brand or product if it appears better. The recent rise of private-label goods has led to increased competition within the FMCG industry. A focus on bringing high volume products at low prices to the market has placed greater demands on all actors. Producers must differentiate their products and quickly bring them to the market.

This has spurred the rise of numerous product variants and a frequent replacement of products in order to achieve best positioning in the current market scenario. Manufacturers must adapt and be able to produce products in smaller batch sizes to win the battle on the shelf. It is necessary to have the freshest product. Additionally, demand for FMCG can be very seasonal. Therefore manufacturers must be very flexible to produce different goods. Quick installation of a production line is necessary to achieve this.

Employee Surplus

HUL's employee surplus led it to cut managerial jobs. In February 2008, it cut about 50 managerial jobs and its parent company announced a reduction of 20,000 jobs worldwide over the next four years.[6]

Purchase-on-Impulse Products

Impulse-purchase products like chocolates, toffees, colas, and ice creams follow the Say's Law which states that 'supply creates demand'. This implies that availability is the most critical factor for these products to be sold and consumed. Therefore transport and logistics for these products becomes very important.

HUL has only one product in this impulse-purchase category—Kwality-Walls (ice cream). It is next to Amul in this FMCG segment. To increase the brand's sale and market share, availability, visibility and consumer mindshare have to be increased and improved.

Competitor Analysis

Approaches to Competitor Analysis include:

- Identify competitor's objectives
- Identify their strategy
- Identify their strengths and weaknesses
- Predict their future actions

Once the environmental survey is complete, the information thus gathered is integrated in a meaningful pattern. The Opportunities–Threats Profile

(OTP) is constructed to understand where the company stands with respect to the environment and competitors. The summary of the environmental survey is of core importance to the strategic planning process. The fact that industry structure, competition and customer are constantly in flux compels a company to be vigilant towards the environment and have a dynamic analysis of the environmental factors. The main purpose of the constant vigil towards environmental factors is to facilitate an appropriate strategic response at the right time.

Once the opportunities present in the environment are identified, the next step is to understand one's own strengths and weaknesses through internal appraisal. The firm should get rid of untested assumptions which it might have developed over time. Only properly assessed facts can be of use. Internal appraisal helps in:

- Assessing the firm's position in terms of capabilities, strengths and weaknesses.
- Selecting opportunities to be tapped in line with its capabilities.
- Assessing capability gap and taking steps to elevate the same in line with growth opportunities.

Assessment of strengths and weaknesses should cover all functional areas in the company. This includes:

- Marketing
- Product-wise positioning
- Finance
- Manufacturing
- R&D
- Human resources
- Corporate factors (corporate image, organizational culture, organizational structure, use of IT, adequacy of policy deployment, assessment and review mechanism).

An analysis of strengths and weaknesses reveals the core competencies of a company and the competitive advantage it has over its competitors.

Competitive Advantage

Competitive advantage is a position of superiority on the part of the company in some function/factor/activity in relation to its competitors. It is through this superiority that the company attempts to carve out a comfortable position for itself in the industry. For example, some companies may be strong in production and others may be in marketing. The strength in production may infer that a particular company is an efficient producer when compared to its competitor, or it may have more a flexible production system, or strength of variety. As a general rule, big firms have strength of size and smaller ones have the strength of flexibility.

The phenomenal winners in any industry usually possess a competitive advantage in several functions/areas. It serves as a backup for strategy as a company without a competitive advantage may struggle to find a worthwhile strategy. It is not strategy alone but the acquisition of competitive advantage and its utilization through strategy that takes a company to its objectives. Scoring over competition and defending against competition require a solid and sustainable base of competitive advantage. In short, competitive advantage is the heart of strategy and for strategy to succeed the firm should have the relevant competitive advantage.

All strengths identified in internal assessments do not amount to competitive advantage. Strength is a necessity but not a sufficient condition for competitive advantage. For a strength to become competitive advantage, whether from production factors or marketing factors, it must lead to a cost or differential advantage to the company. A cost or differential advantage may accrue through lower cost of capital, unique production facilities, efficient distribution, latest technology or innovative raw material handling. The general rule is that a factor could be counted as competitive advantage if it can influence in company's favour one or more of the forces shaping competition.

HUL has distribution as its distinctive competitive advantage with a network to reach the remotest rural areas of the country. Well-managed firms are aware of the competitive advantage they enjoy and factors that contributed to it, but with innumerable changes taking place in the environment and new forces of competition, a firm can maintain the competitive edge it enjoys only through a process of continuous monitoring.

Companies should correctly spot their competitive advantage factors and draw up their competitive advantage profile (CAP). Competitive advantages are spotted only after internal appraisal as well as industry and competition analysis since competitive advantage is always relative to the competition.

Corporates create a built-in mechanism in their corporate strategy to take care of competitive advantage building. In fact corporate-level decisions on acquisitions, mergers, alliances and fresh investments are steps that would result in competitive advantage building. Corporates may use benchmarking as a practice to ensure excellence instead of mere improvement, and in the process build some competitive advantages.

Auto major Ford used this tool effectively in its 'Taurus' project and built up competitive advantage in that segment of cars.

Michael Porter's Five Forces Analysis

The 'value chain' concept proposed by Michael Porter can also be applied to competitor analysis. Value chain is a tool to identify ways in which value can be created/enhanced by a company. This can be used for making a comparison with the value chain of the competitor.

Value creation depends not only on how well each department of the company performs its activities but also how the various departmental activities work in coordination with each other. The business process is a value-creating and value-delivering process. Customers patronize the company that offers the highest delivered value. Hence, the name of the game is to locate activities in which value can be created and provide maximum possible value for each. In analysing the value chain of the competitor, the company actually identifies the strengths and weaknesses of the competitor; it also gets insights into the strategy followed by the competitor. These revelations help the company improve its assumptions about the competitors while formulating its own strategy.

Value Chain Approach

Value chain approach is also used to develop a competitive advantage through customer value created by crafting/enhancing value in each activity. Developing and nurturing durable competitive advantages involves a conscious choice and medium/long-term efforts. The right share of resources should always go to factors that constitute the source of competitive advantage.

A durable and higher-order competitive advantage rests on some fundamental and enduring strengths that are unique to the firm. This unique strength of the company cannot be easily imitated by competitors. Also, newer and stronger competitive advantages can keep emerging from it. Companies which enjoy such unique and fundamental strengths win consistently. Such strength is referred to as the core competency of the firm. In other words, companies can acquire lasting and higher competitive advantages only by building core competencies. Competency can be in technology, process or any other field of expertise but it should be an exclusive preserve of the company or the company should possess it in substantially large measure when compared to the competitors. Such a preserve of competency is core competency.

Buyer Power

Consumers face weak buying power because customers are fragmented and have little influence on price or product.

- Retailers are in a position of power as they are able to negotiate price with the companies.

Verdict: Strong buyer power from retailers.

Supplier Power

- Consumer products face some amount of supplier power simply because of the cost they incur when switching suppliers.
- Suppliers that do a large amount of business with these companies are also beholden to their customers.

Verdict: Limited supply power.

Threat of New Entrants

- Given the amount of capital investment needed to enter certain segments of household consumer products, the threat of new entrants is fairly low.
- Whether the new entrant can get his products on the shelves of the same retailers as his much larger rivals is a question to be answered.

Verdict: Low threat of new entrants.

Threat of Substitutes

- Within the consumer products industry, a brand may succeed in building a competitive advantage but the pricing power of the brand can be eroded.

Verdict: High threat of substitutes.

Degree of Rivalry

- Consumers in this category enjoy a multitude of choices.
- It does not cost anything for a consumer to buy one brand of shampoo instead of another, making the industry quite competitive.

Verdict: Intense competition and rivalry.

SWOT Analysis of HUL

Strengths

- Strong and well-differentiated brands with leading share positions. Brand portfolio includes both global Unilever brands and local brands of specific relevance to India.
- Consumer understanding and systems for building consumer insight.
- Strong R&D capability well linked with business.
- Financial resources.
- Integrated supply chain and well-spread manufacturing units.
- Distribution structure with wide reach, high quality coverage and ability to leverage scale.
- Access to Unilever global technology capability and sharing of best practices from other Unilever companies.
- Productive and professionally trained the manpower resources.
- Distinctly placed products providing reach to every segment of society.
- Consumer understanding and systems for building consumer insight.
- Project Shakti helped HUL create brand awareness and reach extensively into rural India.
- Well placed to take advantage of growth in rural India and lower strata of the society through 'shakti'.
- It could look at introducing products (like margarine) from its parent company in order to cater to changing consumer tastes and opportunities in the food sector.
- It can be a leader in exports by positioning itself as a sourcing hub for Unilever companies in various countries.

Weaknesses

- Increased consumer spends on education, consumer durables, entertainment, and travel resulting in lower share of wallet for FMCG.
- Limited success in changing eating habits of people.
- Complex supply chain configuration, unwieldy number of SKUs with dispersed manufacturing locations. HUL already has taken steps to minimize the same.

- Price positioning in some categories allows for low price competition, like Amul captured Kwality's market.
- High social costs (subsidised housing, foodgrains and firewood, health and other welfare measures) in the plantation business.
- Competitors focusing on a particular product and eating up HUL's share, like Nirma focusing on soaps and detergents.

Opportunities

- Market and brand growth through increased penetration, especially in rural areas.
- Brand growth through increased consumption depth and frequency of usage across all categories.
- Potential outsourcing business in India.
- Upgrading consumers through innovation to new levels of quality and performance.
- Emerging modern trade can be effectively used for introduction of more upscale personal care products.
- Growing consumption in out-of-home categories.
- Position HUL as a sourcing hub for Unilever companies in various countries.
- Leveraging the latest IT technology.
- Growing consumer base due to increasing income levels and new consumers from lower strata of the society.
- Untapped market in branded Ayurvedic medicines and other such consumer products.
- Opportunity in the food sector: changing consumer tastes.
- Expand horizon to more countries.

Threats

- Low priced competition now present in all categories.
- Grey imports.
- Spurious/counterfeit products in rural areas and small towns.
- Changes in fiscal benefits.
- Unfavourable raw material prices in oils, tea, and so on.
- Unfavourable raw material prices due to inflation reducing profitability.
- Heavy onslaught of competition in the core categories from emerging players like ITC will result in higher advertising expenditure.
- Reduction in real income of consumers due to high inflation.
- FMCG dealing with overcapacity utilization.
- Health conscious environment friendly customers.
- Scarce water problem affecting demand for detergents and related goods.

Strategies Ahead

- Develop brand recognition in smaller cities through campaigns.
- Promote power brands through ads and campaigns.
- Outsourcing to achieve economies of scale.

- Use financial resources to innovate high-utility products with short PLC.
- Price weaker brands competitively with local brands.
- Deploy resources for brand extension.
- Diversify existing product line for health-conscious consumers.
- Use power brands to differentiate from low-cost product.
- Take measures to stop counterfeiting of products effectively.
- Pursue true value, cost-leadership strategy for power brands.
- Introduce innovative products which can be used with minimum water.
- Launch educational and mass awareness health and hygiene programmes jointly with industry leaders.

PEST Analysis

PEST analysis is used to identify the external forces affecting HUL. This is an analysis of HUL's political, economic, social and technological environment.

Political

The first element of a PEST analysis is the study of political factors. Political factors influence organizations in many ways. They can create advantages and opportunities, and also place obligations and duties on businesses. Political factors include the following types of instruments:

- Legislation such as minimum wage laws or anti-discrimination laws
- Voluntary codes and practices, market regulations
- Trade agreements, tariffs or restrictions
- Tax levies and tax breaks
- Type of government regime, e.g. communist, democratic, dictatorship

Non-conformance with legislative obligations can lead to sanctions such as fines, adverse publicity and imprisonment. Ineffective voluntary codes and practices will often lead to governments introducing legislation to regulate the activities covered by the codes and practices. Various political factors that have affected HUL are:

- Stimulus package for the FMCG sector implemented in March 2009.
- Various taxes and levies imposed on commodities that have a cascading effect on prices.
- Very limited international trade regulations and restrictions; Indian economy deregulated since 1991.
- Market committee legislation in various states restricts free movement of agricultural produce and restricts the firm from directly buying from farmers.
- India's food law restricts innovation and needs to be brought in line with international Codex.
- Fully acquired the government-owned Modern Foods in 2002.

Economic

The second element of PEST analysis involves a study of economic factors. All businesses are affected by national and global economic factors. National and global interest rates and fiscal policies will determine the economic conditions. The climate of the economy dictates how consumers, suppliers and other organizational stakeholders such as suppliers and creditors behave within society.

An economy undergoing recession will have high unemployment, low spending power and low stakeholder confidence. Conversely a 'booming' or growing economy will have low unemployment, high spending power and high stakeholder confidence.

A successful organization will respond to economic conditions and stakeholder behaviour. Further, organizations will need to review the impact economic conditions have on their competitors and respond accordingly.

In this globalized world, organizations are affected by regional/national economies throughout the world and not just in the countries in which they are based or operate from. For example, a global credit crunch originating in the USA contributed towards the credit crunch in the UK in 2007–8. Cheaper labour in developing countries affects the competitiveness of products from developed countries. An increase in visa fee draught in the USA will affect the share price of IT stocks, or draught weather conditions in India may affect the price of tea bought in an English café.

A truly global player has to be aware of the economic conditions across all borders and needs to ensure that it employs strategies that protect and promote its business through unfavourable economic conditions.

Taking account of the current scenario looming over the world, the various economic factors affecting HUL are:

- Economic slowdown might affect HUL sales.
- Positive growth prospects in developing and emerging economies.
- 4 per cent reduction in Cenvat tax in the recent stimulus package by Government of India.
- Exchange rates stable; depend on the global economic condition.
- In the present scenario, the Indian economy is on a bullish run.
- Unfavourable raw material prices of oils, tea, commodities reducing profitability.

Social

The third aspect of PEST focuses on forces within society such as family, friends, colleagues, neighbours and the media. Social forces affect our attitudes, interests and opinions. They shape who we are as people, the way we behave and ultimately what we purchase. For example in the UK, people's attitudes towards their diet and health are changing. As a result the country is seeing an increase in the number of people joining fitness clubs and a massive growth in the demand for organic food. Products such as Wi Fit attempt to deal with society's concern about children's lack of exercise. In India, there are growing awareness for sustainable development and conserve our natural resources. HUL thus implemented 'Go Green' strategy in 2010 and reduced CO_2 footprint by 15,000 tons per year in the detergent manufacturing unit.

Population changes also have a direct impact on organizations. Changes in the structure of a population will affect the supply and demand of goods and services within an economy. Falling birth rates will result in decreased demand and greater competition as the number of consumers fall. Conversely an increase in the global population and world food shortage predictions are currently leading to calls for greater investment in food production. Due to food shortages African countries such as Uganda are now reconsidering their rejection of genetically modified foods.

In summary, organizations must be able to offer products and services that aim to complement and benefit people's lifestyle and behaviour. If organizations do not respond to changes in society they will lose market share and demand for their product or service.

Hence the social factors that affect HUL are:

- With more than a billion consumer base, India offers good growth prospects.
- Growing awareness in rural India and higher disposable income.
- Good growth prospects in tier I and tier II cities for FMCG industry.
- Growing consumption in out-of-home categories.
- Spurious/counterfeit products in rural areas and small towns.
- Change of eating habits of people; consumers have become more health conscious. Increased consumer spends on education, consumer durables, entertainment, travel, resulting in lower share of consumer's budget for FMCG products.
- Fashion and hypes.

Technological

Unsurprisingly the fourth element of PEST is technology. Technological advances have greatly changed the manner in which businesses operate. Organizations use technology in many ways. They have:

1. Technology infrastructure such as the internet, intranet and other information exchange systems including telephone.
2. Technology systems incorporating a multitude of CRM and ERP software to help manage the business.
3. Technology hardware such as mobile phones, laptops, desktops, Bluetooth devices, photocopiers and fax machines which transmit and record information.

Technology has created a society which expects instant results. The technological revolution has increased the rate at which information is exchanged between stakeholders. A faster exchange of information can benefit businesses as they are able to react quickly to changes within their operating environment. However the ability to react quickly also creates extra pressure as businesses are expected to deliver on their promises within ever-decreasing time scales. For example, the internet is having a profound impact on the marketing mix strategy of organizations. Consumers can now shop 24 hours a day from their homes, workplaces, and internet café's and via 3G phones and cards.

The pace of technological change is so fast that the average life of a computer chip is approximately six months. Technology is utilized by all age groups. Children are exposed to technology from birth and a new generation of technology-savvy pensioners, known as 'silver surfers' has emerged. Technology will continue to evolve and impact consumer habits and expectations, organizations that ignore this fact face extinction.

The technological factors affecting HUL are:

- Leveraging the latest IT technology; industry focus on technological effort.
- SAP implementation started in 2006 across HUL.
- New inventions and development; upgrading consumers through innovations to new levels of quality and performance.
- Rate of technology transfer.
- Access to Unilever global technology, capability and sharing of best practices.
- Life cycle and speed of technological obsolescence.
- Energy use and costs: need to use renewable sources of energy to protect the environment and natural resources.

Financial Positions of HUL

For the year 2007, HUL achieved an overall turnover growth of 13.3 per cent; both HPC and foods businesses grew by 12.3 per cent and 20.2 per cent, respectively. Profit After Tax registered a growth of 14.9 per cent. Earnings per share for the year 2007 at ₹8.73 reflects a 3.8 per cent growth in net profit (after exceptional items). The Board of Directors recommended a final dividend of ₹3 per share. The total dividend to the shareholders for the year 2007 stood at ₹9 per share, including an interim dividend of ₹3 per share paid in August 2007 and ₹3 per share paid in November 2007 as Special Platinum Jubilee Dividend to commemorate the company's 75 years of operations in the country.

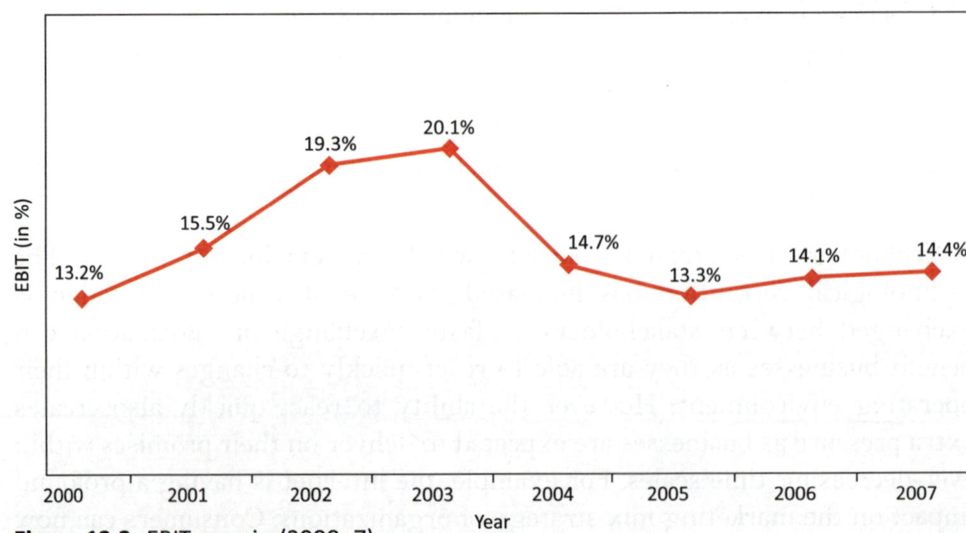

Figure 12.2: EBIT margin (2000–7)

Source: HUL investors presentation, February 2008.

Table 12.6: Ten-year financials of HUL (just before the slowdown)

₹ lakh	*1998*	*1999*	*2000*	*2001*	*2002*	*2003*	*2004*	*2005*	*2006*	*2007*
Profit & Loss Account										
Sales*	10215.24	10917.69	11392.14	11781.30	10951.61	11096.02	10888.38	11975.53	13035.06	14757.42
Other income	244.74	318.98	345.07	381.79	384.54	459.83	318.83	304.79	354.51	462.68
Interest	(29.28)	(22.39)	(13.15)	(7.74)	(9.18)	(66.76)	(129.98)	(19.19)	(10.73)	(25.50)
Profit before taxation @	1130.44	1387.94	1665.09	1943.37	2197.12	2244.95	1505.32	1604.47	1861.68	2184.53
Profit after taxation @	837.44	1069.94	1310.09	1540.95	1731.32	1804.34	1199.28	1354.51	1539.67	1769.06
EPS of ₹1 (adjusted for bonus)	3.67	4.86	5.95	7.46	8.04	8.05	5.44	6.40	8.41	8.73
DPS of ₹1 (adjusted for bonus)	2.20	2.90	3.50	5.00	5.16	5.50	5.00	5.00	6.00	9.00
Balance Sheet										
Fixed assets	1053.77	1087.17	1203.47	1320.06	1322.34	1369.47	1517.56	1483.53	1511.01	1708.14
Investments	697.51	1006.11	1769.74	1635.93	2364.74	2574.93	2229.56	2014.20	2413.93	1440.80
Net deferred tax	—	—	—	246.48	269.92	267.44	226.00	220.14	224.55	212.39
Net current assets	226.06	187.25	(373.38)	(75.04)	(239.83)	(368.81)	(409.30)	(1355.31)	(1353.40)	(1833.57)
	1977.34	2280.53	2599.83	3127.43	3717.17	3843.03	3563.82	2362.56	2796.09	1527.76
Share capital	219.57	220.06	220.06	220.12	220.12	220.12	220.12	220.12	220.68	217.74
Reserves & surplus	1493.46	1883.20	2268.16	2823.57	3438.75	1918.60	1872.59	2085.50	2502.81	1221.49
Loan funds	264.31	177.27	111.61	83.74	58.30	1704.30	1471.11	56.94	72.50	88.53
	1977.34	2280.53	2599.83	3127.43	3717.17	3843.03	3563.82	2362.56	2796.09	1527.76

Source: HUL Annual Report 2007.
Notes: *Before exceptional items, @Before exempted items.

Table 12.7: Segment-wise sales breakup

Year	*1998*	*1999*	*2000*	*2001*	*2002*	*2003*	*2004*	*2005*	*2006*	*2007*
Gross sales (₹ crore)	10,215	10,918	11,392	11,781	10,952	11,096	10,888	11,976	13,035	14,757
By segment % of sales										
Soaps, detergents and household care	39	41	40	40	45	44	45	45	47	47
Personal products	16	17	17	21	22	24	26	28	29	29
Foods	35	34	37	33	30	29	27	25	22	22
Chemicals, agri, fertilisers and animal feeds	6	6	4	3	2	2	1	1	1	1
Others	4	2	2	3	1	1	1	1	1	1
EBIT as % of sales	9.5	10.7	12.3	14.0	17.6	18.4	13.4	12.3	13.1	13.4
Fixed assets turnover (times)	9.7	10.0	9.5	8.9	8.3	8.1	7.2	8.1	8.6	8.6
Working capital turnover (times)	45.2	58.3	—*	—	—	—	—	—	—	—
Economic value added (EVA) (₹ crore)	548	694	858	1,080	1,236	1,429	887	1,014	1,125	1,340
EPS of ₹1@	3.67	4.86	5.95	7.46	8.04	8.05	5.44	6.40	8.41	8.73
OPS of ₹1@	2.20	2.90	3.50	5.00	5.16	5.50	5.00	5.00	6.00	9.00
PAT/Sales (%)	8.2	9.8	11.5	13.1	15.8	16.3	11.0	11.3	11.8	12.0
ROCE (%)	58.7	61.8	64.6	62.4	59.4	60.2	45.8	68.7	67.0	79.4
RONW (%)	48.9	50.9	52.7	53.9	48.4	82.8	57.2	61.1	68.1	80.1

Source: HUL Annual Report 2007.
Note: *Denotes working capital is negative, @Adjusted for bonus issue.

Turnover, net of excise, in respect of continuing businesses increased by ₹1,614 crore and was 13.3 per cent higher than the previous year. This increase was from more volumes sold, better mix of products, and selective price increases effected during 2008.

Now the company is struggling to maintain its leadership and sales has recorded negative growth in 2010.

Table 12.8: Profit and EPS (just before the slow down)

Heads	2008**	2007	2006
Continuing sales growth*	19.2%	13.5%	10.0%
EBIT/Sales %	14.0%	14.1%	14.1%
EBIT Growth	18.4%	15.4%	16.2%
EPS (cents)	22	20	19
Operating cash flow*	N.A.	$420 Mn	$365 Mn

Note: **Before restructuring, disposal; *Unaudited results of financial year 2008. Year ending will be 15 months ending March 2008

Table 12.9: HUL: Market leader in the FMCG sector in 2008

Particulars	*Laundry (%)*	*Soaps (%)*	*Shampoo (%)*	*Skin (%)*	*Tooth-paste (%)*	*Tea (%)*	*Coffee (%)*
HUL share	38.1	51.6	46.3	51.7	29.6	23.0	45.2
Nearest competitor	12.2	9.4	23.7	7.5	48.5	21.1	39.2

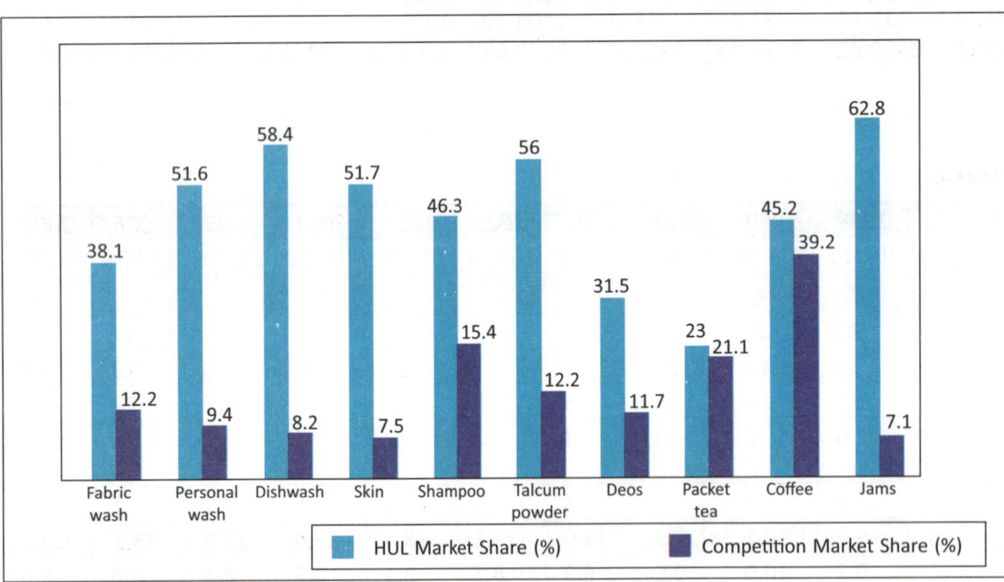

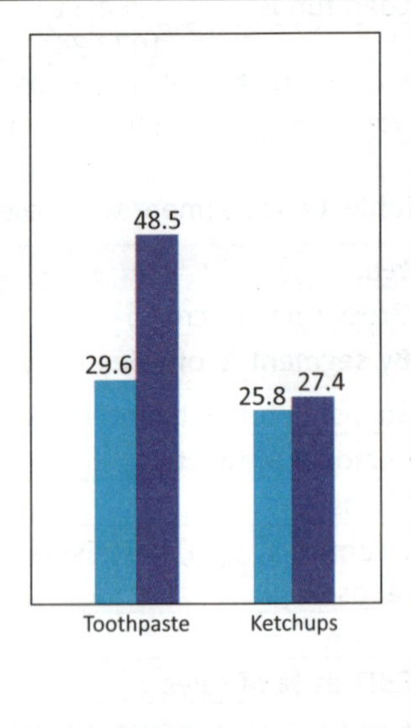

Figure 12.3: Tracking HUL's growth
Source: A.C. Nielsen-2008 value shares.

Insight into Case Questions

Answer 1

HUL has revamped its sales organization in the rural markets to fully meet the emerging needs and increased purchasing power of the rural population. The company has brought markets with a population below 50,000 under one rural sales organization. The team comprises an exclusive sales force and exclusive redistribution stockists, under the charge of dedicated managers. The team focuses on building superior availability, while enabling brand building in the deepest interiors.

The principal issue in rural development is creating income-generating opportunities for the rural population. Such initiatives are successful and sustainable when linked with the company's core business and mutually beneficial to both, the population for whom the programme is intended and for the company.

Based on these insights, HUL launched Project Shakti in 2001, in keeping with the purpose of integrating business interests with national interests. HUL's strategy of targeting rural and urban consumers separately has paid rich dividends for the company. Consider the case of Vim bar and HUL's strategy for it. Although the urban consumers were responsible for the high sales of Vim bar, the management at HUL realized that it is the rural market that has more potential for future growth. It faced its biggest challenge from the popularity of flying/firewood ash and powder as a cleaning agent for dishwash. Entry was not easy, especially because of the easy availability of ash in villages. HUL decided to adopt the strategy of lowering input costs to arrive at a low-cost Vim bar for the rural consumers.

Answer 2

HUL's strategy revolves around brand marketing. The company has a large portfolio consisting of nearly 110 bands. In 2008, HUL undertook the exercise of limiting it to 44. In every product line, it has built a number of brands over a period of time. Quite a few of them have come to its fold from the parent company. It has also acquired several ongoing brands from the market. HUL also vigorously pursues the brand extension strategy. And concurrently, it undertakes line pruning and brand restructuring and consolidation, based on marketing compulsions. HUL is also playing the rejuvenation and relaunch game very successfully. Business expansion and diversification are also throwing new challenges on the brand strategy front. HUL lends itself for a study into the complexity of the brand management task. We shall examine how the company handles the complex demands of brand management.

HUL's impressive array of brands is the outcome of a conscious corporate strategy. As a corporate, HUL wants to be a leader in every one of its businesses and the strategy is to fight on the strength of the competitive advantage arising from the possession of strong brands. It is this strategy that is reflected in the development of a multitude of strong brands. If we take the business of bathing soaps, as an example, HUL has the objective of being a national player (not a niche or a regional marketer) and the leader therein. It also wants about 30 per cent of the corporate income to come from this line. So, HUL developed a few strong brands in this line, which among them would cover different market segments and price points. Dove, Lux, Liril, Rexona, Pears and Lifebuoy are the outcome of such a well-planned brand strategy implemented over time. Lifebuoy is 110 years old and Liril 25 years old. In fact, HUL has about 10 brands of toilet soaps,

each with a good volume of sales to its credit. Decisions on brand portfolio are an expression of a company's objectives and the strategy governing a given business.

Creating New Opportunities by Hiring Brand Names

Towards the close of the 1990s, HUL found that the germicide segment of the soap market was growing fast, with RCI's Dettol antiseptic soap leading. HUL did not have a suitable product in its stable to capture a share of this segment. Lifebuoy was not strictly meeting the particular benefit.

HUL knew that launching and developing a new brand would take time and resources, and the company would miss the market if it chose this route. It did not have the product formula either to enter this segment. It was against this background that HUL decided to hire the Savlon brand from J&J. Savlon was a successful antiseptic lotion, a competitor to Dettol lotion. Just as the Dettol soap owed its origin to the success of the Dettol lotion, HUL assessed that a Savlon antiseptic soap could be successfully extended from the Savlon lotion.

It entered into an agreement with J&J for the use of the Savlon brand name and the product formula, and launched the Savlon antiseptic soap. HUL very deftly managed the brand launch and Savlon is today a challenger to Dettol soap. J&J in turn has got a good royalty from HUL for lending the brand name. It turned out to be a potentially win-win arrangement for both companies.

Measures Taken by HUL for Rural Markets Penetration

Traditionally HUL used both wholesalers and retailers to penetrate the rural market. A fleet of motor vans covered small towns and villages. These vans induced retailers to stock HUL products and display advertising material in their shops. In many towns, there were redistribution stockists who carried bulk stocks and serviced retailers. There were some 7,000 redistribution stockists who served over a million retail outlets. In the late-1990s, HUL realized that despite its pioneering efforts to expand its rural consumer base, a large part of the market remained untapped. Thus, the company set itself a target of contacting 16 million new village households. This was to be achieved by strongly focusing on the sales, marketing, and production of the 'Power Brands' in the rural markets.

HUL adopted a phased approach in order to meet its target and decided to address key issues related to the availability, awareness and overcoming of prevalent attitudes and habits of rural consumers.

Project Streamline

Project Streamline was conceptualized to significantly enhance HUL's control on the rural supply chain through a network of rural sub-stockists, based in these very villages. As part of the project, higher quality servicing, in terms of frequency, credit and full-line availability would be provided to rural trade, thereby giving the company a substantial competitive edge over the next decade.

The principle of Project Streamline is to leverage HUL's scale and organizational synergy to increase reach in rural markets. The pivot of Streamline is the Rural Distributor (RD) who has 15-20 rural sub-stockists attached to him. Each of these sub-stockists is located in a rural market and performs the role of driving distribution in neighbouring villages using unconventional means of transport such as tractors, bullock carts, and so on.

From 1998, the project has been rolled out in select states of the country where the terrain or poor stage of market development typically makes any distribution system unviable. The Streamline system has extended HUL's reach in these markets to about 37 per cent of India's rural population. Most important, the number of HUL brands and SKUs stocked by village retailers has gone up significantly.

Project Bharat

Project Bharat, the first and the largest rural home-to-home operation ever mounted by any company to engage the unemployed youth and unutilized talents from the villages. The operation was conducted in high-potential districts of the country. The exercise was started by the Personal Products Division in 1998 and covered 13 million households by the close of 1999. Company vans visited villages across the country and distributed sample packs comprising a low-unit-price pack each of shampoo, talcum powder, toothpaste and skin cream. The distribution was supported by explanation of product usage and a video show, which was interspersed with product communication. Thus HUL generated awareness about its product categories and the availability of affordable packs. Consumers were also made aware of the superior benefits of using products vis-à-vis their current habits, and the affordability of the pack sizes on offer. The project, successfully addressed issues of awareness, attitudes and habits.

The project saw a 100 per cent increase in penetration, usership and top-of-the-mind awareness in the districts targeted.

Project Shakti

The objective of Project Shakti was to create income-generating capabilities for underprivileged rural women by providing a sustainable micro-enterprise opportunity, and to improve rural living standards through health and hygiene awareness.

Under the project, HUL offers a range of mass-market products to the SHGs (Self-Help Groups) which are relevant to rural customers. The company is investing significantly in human resources who work with women on the field and provide them with on-the-job training and support. This is a key factor in ensuring the stabilization of their fledgling businesses.

HUL imparts the necessary training to these groups on the basics of enterprise management, which women need to manage their enterprises. For the SHG women, this translates into much-needed, sustainable income, contributing towards better living and prosperity. Armed with micro-credit, women from SHGs become direct-to-home distributors in the rural markets.

Self-Help Groups

HUL's rural growth engine raises the incomes of rural families by channel intervention through rural SHGs, which operate like direct-to-home distributors. The model consists of groups of (15-20) villagers below the poverty line (₹750 per month) taking micro-credit from banks, and using that to buy HUL products, which they will then directly sell to consumers. In the process, they will generate employment and incomes for themselves and increase the reach of HUL's products.

Marketing in Rural and Urban Markets

Traditionally HUL's distribution network consisted of wholesalers and retailers. HUL had a presence in 80 lakh retail outlets and there was a 'one size fits for all' distribution strategy to serve all those outlets. But due to a change in consumer demography, consumer behaviour and market structure, the traditional distribution system failed to deliver the results. Urban customers wanted products with unique, value-added and customized offerings with convenient shopping.

Apart from this, the emergence of the rural market also forced HUL to change its distribution system. HUL dealt with these two issues differently. For the urban market it developed a distribution system to cater to different types of customers. Along with this, it provided value-added services, convenience and customized offerings. On the other hand, in the rural markets it increase brand awareness and product availability, it introduced alternative distribution systems. Through these changes, HUL brought its brands closer to customers. HUL's approach to distribution was holistic and developed a three-way convergence of product availability, brand communication and brand experience.

Answer 3

HUL has been proactively engaged in rural development since 1976, beginning with the Integrated Rural Development Programme in the Etah district of Uttar Pradesh, in tandem with the company's dairy operations. This programme now covers 500 villages in the district. Subsequently, the factories that HUL continued establishing in less-developed regions of the country have been engaged in similar programmes in adjacent villages.

Social Impact

Lifebuoy Swasthya Chetna (LBSC) is HUL's rural health and hygiene initiative which was started in 2002. LBSC has been initiated in media-dark villages of UP, MP, Bihar, West Bengal, Maharashtra, Orissa, Andhra Pradesh, Karnataka and Rajasthan with the objective of spreading awareness about the importance of washing hands with soap. According to a study done by the London School of Hygiene and Tropical Medicine, the simple practice of washing hands with soap and water can reduce diarrhoea by as much as 47 per cent. However, ignorance of such basic hygiene practices leads to high mortality rates in rural India. Being India's leading personal wash brand, Lifebuoy saw a role for itself in propagating the message of hygiene and health in villages.

LBSC targets children as they are seen as the harbingers of change in society, and mothers since they are the custodians of health. The campaign has been divided into various phases and uses a number of tools such as a pictorial story in a flip chart format, a 'glo-germ' demonstration and a quiz with attractive prizes to reinforce the message.

Eight years since 2002, the project has touched 100,000 villages and 12 crore people. In 2010 alone the programme contacted 13,000 villages in MP, AP, Maharashtra and Rajasthan.

The Indian postal department released a special postal cover on Lifebuoy Swasthya Chetna with a special 'Lifebuoy' collection on the occasion of World Health Day (7 April) in 2006. Lifebuoy is the first and the only brand to receive this honour and recognition in India.

In the same year, LBSC was recognized by the Rural Marketing Agencies Association of India as the 'Best Long-term Rural Marketing Initiative'. Over the years, LBSC has won many such accolades, the latest being the Emvies award for 'Best Innovation of Event' and the 'Best Integrated and Best Effective Long-Term Marketing Campaign' award by the Promotion and Marketing Awards of Asia in 2008.

To ensure that there is continuous improvement in the programme, in 2007 the Global Health and Hygiene Programme, a research wing of Unilever, developed a scientific method of tracking soap usage time and frequency of usage. The study was conducted in LBSC-intervened villages of Andhra Pradesh. This study revealed a 15 per cent increase in average consumption of soap for bathing purposes in rural households. The level of awareness of hygiene and disease-causing germs had also increased significantly.

Project Shakti's Social Benefits

A Shakti entrepreneur earns around ₹700-₹1,000 a month. The earnings are around 7 per cent, after 3 per cent goes towards principal and interest payments. The per capita income of entrepreneurs increased by 50 to 100 per cent. HUL estimates around 10,00,000 entrepreneurs by 2012. The social benefits equal to $20 to $30 million.

Economic Impact

The market sizes of urban and rural areas are approximately equal. With these rural initiatives HUL had a sales turnover of $250 million. The net margins are around $25 million.

Answer 4

HUL shifted its approach to marketing to the rural poor. Because of widely varying levels of literacy and access to television, HUL had to minimize its reliance on traditional media channels and find ways to get its message to consumers in a more personal, more direct way. Their solution involved hiring actors, dancers, and magicians to perform travelling shows which entertained villagers, educated them on health and hygiene and increased their awareness about HUL brands. These events would often generate excitement in the villages several days before the show arrived.

The company also took advantage of festivals that would draw thousands of people to the same location to set up demonstrations. Such demonstrations educated potential customers about the dangers of dirt and germs, and used ultraviolet light to show where on the hands germs tended to reside.

Finally, HUL found new ways to sell. Much in the style of Avon and Amway, it encouraged villagers by the dozens to go into the business themselves, selling HUL products. While the company also distributed its products to local stores, this more personal approach augmented the marketing effort to educate customers on the benefits of using HUL products. The initiative required tremendous training, as many of the people anxious to sell products to neighbours were illiterate and had no relevant work experience.

HUL's rural marketing initiatives were paying off well and in some cases more than it had expected. The company had left competitors Colgate-

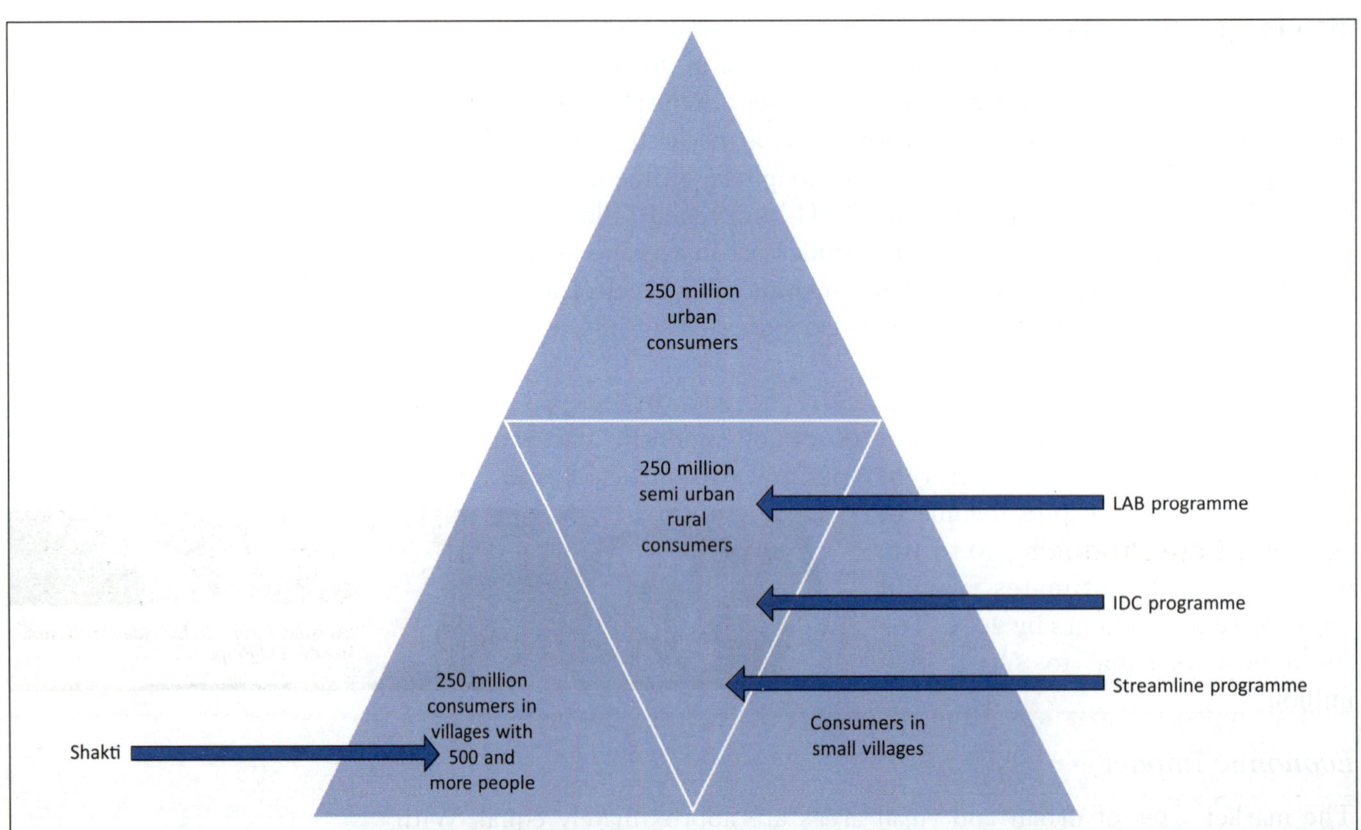

Figure 12.4: Structure of HUL's market reach in India

Palmolive and Nirma way behind in terms of overall market penetration in rural areas.

Distribution Strategy

Project Streamline was targeted at places that had a poor market development base, thus making any kind of distribution unavailable. This project was to be carried out with the help of a rural distributor who had 15-20 rural sub-stockists connected to him in the villages. The sub-stockists performed the role of driving distribution in the neighbouring villages using unconventional means like bullock carts and tractors. As a part of the project, HUL aimed at providing higher quality services to consumers in terms of frequency, full-line availability and credit. As a result, the number of HUL brands and SKUs stocked by the village retailers increased. This initiative helped HUL increase its reach in the rural market to 37 per cent.

Answer 5

Corporate Purpose

Unilever's mission is to add vitality to life. HUL meets everyday needs of nutrition, hygiene and personal care with brands that help people feel good, look good and get more out of life.

HUL has deep roots in local cultures and markets in India. This gives it a strong relationship with consumers and could be the foundation for its future growth.

Being the subsidiary of the world's largest FMCG company, it can bring the knowledge and international expertise of Unilever to the service of local consumers—a truly multi-local multinational. For the long-term success HUL requires:

- Total commitment to exceptional standards of performance and productivity.
- A willingness to embrace new ideas and learn continuously for understanding Indian rural and urban customers.

The highest standards of corporate behaviour towards everyone it works with, the communities it touches, and the environment on which it has an impact.

Personal Care Products

The personal products business of HUL addresses oral, hair and skincare needs. Oral care includes Pepsodent and Close-Up toothpastes, toothbrushes and toothpowders. In haircare the company has a host of products, ranging from shampoos to hair oils. Clinic, Sunsilk and Lux are the main haircare brands. In skincare, the company markets Fair & Lovely, Pond's, Lakme, and Pears. In colour cosmetics the company markets the Lakme range of beauty products. In deodorants and fragrances, the main household names are Rexona, Axe and Denim.

Consumer Analysis

In the current scenario, there may be some hit to the premium FMCG brands, because of two reasons:

- Products which are not differentiated and have low perceived value will be impacted.
- Consumers may reconsider buying expensive skincare products and high-end food items.
- Some consumers who were ready to upgrade from popular to premium brands may put their plans on hold, as they may find more value in popular brands.

External Environment Analysis

According to Assocham, despite the global economic slowdown, the FMCG sector in India will grow at 25 per cent.

The FMCG industry will grow at a compounded annual growth rate of 9 per cent to reach a size of ₹1,43,000 crore by 2010, from the previous level of ₹93,000 crore, under favourable conditions says a CII-AT Kearney Report. In short, the consumption forecasts for developing and emerging economies is positive.

Although, these economies are not completely insulated from the meltdown effect, they have become far more resilient than in the past. The macro-economic management is more transparent and foreign exchange reserves better. But that doesn't mean that the present global economic downturn will not affect HUL's business in India.

By combining the two dimensions of brand equity at the onset of recession and brand investments during recession, we get four categories:

Category 1: **Brand equity (High), Reduction in brand investments:** High loss potential.

Category 2: **Brand equity (High), No reduction/increase in brand investments:** Recession is opportunity.

Category 3: **Brand equity (Low), Reduction in brand investments:** Survival game.

Category 4: **Brand equity (Low), No reduction/increase in brand investments:** Double or nothing.

Brands in category (1) run the distinct danger of their equity being significantly eroded in the current recession. They start from a favourable position, but their behaviour will lead to a significant weakening of their position vis-à-vis private labels and the brands in category (2). Managerial decision-making for these brands is overly cautious and focused on the short term. These brands should emphasize activities that keep their customers satisfied (and, hence, retain them), rather than focus on cost-saving activities. Indeed, customers lost during the recession may never come back, even when the economy's outlook improves.

For brands in category (2), the recession is an opportunity to pull ahead of their short-sighted competitors in category (1). Their proactive behaviour will strengthen their (relative) position, not only in the recession period, but also in subsequent years.

Brands in category (3) are in the worst possible situation: they start weak, and their management makes wrong decisions. They are prime candidates to be delisted by retailers who tend to push their private labels during recession. Their brand equity will decline, and many will not even survive the recession.

The brands in category (4) have the opportunity of a lifetime to fight back. They start from an unfavourable position—their equity is low and, in normal times, it would take tremendous marketing investments to break through the competitive clutter. However, given that most brands cut back during recession [and, hence, belong to categories (1) and (3)], brands in categories (4) are able to increase their share of the total market communication by maintaining or—even better—increasing their marketing investments. But it is a risky strategy. If poorly executed, the anticipated increase in sales and profits will not materialize and the brand may be discontinued.

HUL should try to maintain the position of its brands in category (2), although it might be better prepared because in the past three years it has strengthened its brands and improved its cost structure. But HUL should do its best to realign its plans continuously and dynamically to fight the economic downturn.

Competitor and Market Analysis

Past Scenario

Apart from the global meltdown, competitors like P&G and ITC might have an adverse effect on HUL's business. Unilever may see global revenue growth slow down in 2010 as P&G and ITC boost marketing in India. Unilever, which has relied heavily on accelerating the sale of its Surf Excel detergent in India to make up for sluggish sales throughout Europe, has been challenged to compete with P&G since the latter has nearly halved the prices of its Ariel and Tide detergents in the Indian market. Now, P&G is stepping up the competition by offering Olay skincare products in Asia's third-largest economy, and is expected to gain share in India in the next five years.

Soaps Business

According to AC Nielsen, HUL's soaps business, which accounts for more than a quarter of its total revenues, grew by 7 per cent. While the industry grew at 8 per cent, HUL's closest rival Godrej Consumer Products Limited (GCPL) saw its soaps business grow by a whopping 24.3 per cent. Though HUL still dominates the ₹5,500-crore soap market with a 53 per cent market share, its share went down by 2.6 per cent in terms of units sold and 2.4 per cent in terms of value over the 15-month period from April 2006 to June 2007.

GCPL is emerging as a strong player in the value-for-money products category (products that are not priced too steeply) and it is constantly eating into HUL's market share, especially its mass brand Lifebuoy.

Oralcare Business

In the oralcare category, HUL is feeling the heat from competitors both at the top and lower end of the market. The company's oralcare portfolio that includes brands such as Pepsodent and Close-Up, grew 11 per cent, with Pepsodent growing by only 4.5 per cent, according to AC Nielsen.

Against this, Colgate-Palmolive (India) Limited's Colgate brand grew at 14 per cent and the toothpaste business of Dabur India, which owns brands such as Babool and Meswak, grew at an impressive 32 per cent.

Detergents Business

HUL's market share in the detergents category was 35 per cent of the total in the quarter June 2007 compared to June 2006. 'HUL's low-priced brand Wheel dominates the laundry segment, but with rising incomes, consumers are now shifting to mid-level brands from rivals such as P&G and Nirma,' said Sameer Deshmukh, analyst, IL&FS Investsmart Securities Limited.

Skincare Business

The company's skincare business also registered a marginal decline, with brands such as Fair & Lovely and Pond's losing 0.4 per cent market share, as of 2007. The segment had been impacted by planned reduction of inventory in the distribution pipeline in preparation for a re-launch of Fair & Lovely in July 2007.

The primary reason for HUL losing market share is that while the company has a varied brand portfolio, its rivals, big and small, have focused on niches and are pushing growth aggressively in those categories. While the top-end players such as Procter & Gamble or Colgate-Palmolive are getting aggressive in premium categories, mid-rung players such as Dabur, Marico and Godrej are muscling in with their value-for-money strategy.

Emerging Scenario at HUL

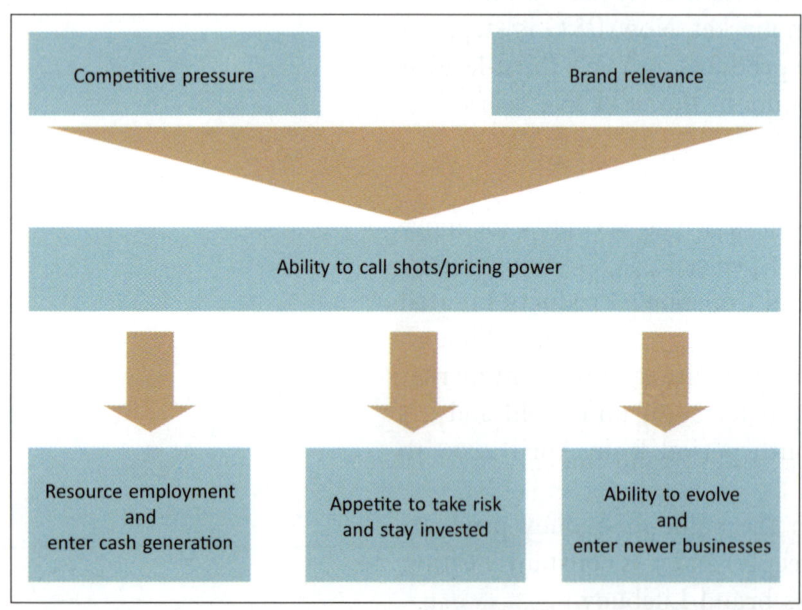

The key differentiators for an FMCG player are the ability to call the shots and pricing power, and HLL has shown weakness in both these areas. HUL's weakness was its inability to transform its strategies at the right time. It continued with the same old strategy which no doubt helped it gain profits but was inadequate in this changed environment. HLL's risk aversion and market myopia led to stagnation of business, and the ferocity of competition forced it into a defensive mode. Lack of pricing power in the core business and absence of growth drivers have put HLL on a deflationary mode.

In order to survive the recession, HUL took necessary measures such as:

- reduced travel budgets and manpower
- readjusted the fixed component of salary and variable payments

- accelerating cost savings through the appointment a global procurement officer to procure raw materials
- scrapping previous sales margin targets
- simultaneous launch of products in different regions in India

Some Future Predictions

- **Increased competition:** In the last few years, we have seen a large number of companies expanding their portfolio into other categories, which is leading to fragmentation of the market. This will lead to cut-throat competition from regional/national companies, giving ultimate benefit to the consumers. In this environment, only the innovators will survive. Focus will be the key to profitability.
- **Micro-segmentation:** The new trend is for companies to develop products targeting niche segments by addressing specific needs. For example, marketers are segmenting Horlicks into Horlicks for Women, Junior Horlicks and Horlicks Lite. There are separate fairness creams for men and women. Pepsodent and Colgate both makes special toothpastes for children.
- **Growth of under-penetrated categories:** There is huge scope in a lot of under-penetrated categories like household cleaners, deodorants, skin creams, shampoos, and so on.
- **Organized retail:** The modern retail format will slowly occupy a bigger share. This will lead to change in shopping behaviour and growth of the FMCG sector.

Way Ahead—New Marketing Strategy

Rural, semi-urban and urban areas contributed 57, 21 and 22 per cent, respectively in 2007–8 to the FMCG sector. The rural market with the highest base is growing the fastest. So even if there is a marginal drop in premium and value-added products, the overall sales can be improved by focusing on the rural market. Thus, HUL should continue to promote its personal care products in the rural areas.

During recession, shoppers have a natural tendency to switch to private labels in order to save money. The logical thing for HUL would be to counter this tendency by either lowering its own price, or by offering sufficient non-price reasons for consumers to buy its brand in the personal care category. Since consumers are more price-sensitive during recession, so offering more price promotions makes sense.

HUL can counter the price advantage of private labels by investing more in advertising, especially for personal care products. This will provide non-price competitive advantage for HUL, like a better brand image, improved functional qualities and performance. Instead of creating new brands, the company should aim at consolidating and strengthening its current brands in the personal care segment.

To prevent downtrading, HUL should introduce packs with lower SKUs so that per unit purchase does not pinch the consumer's wallet. With this strategy HUL will be able to sharpen its focus on the existing smaller packs and increase their availability.

It should strengthen its distribution and logistics by bringing in more efficiency and innovation in the supply chain. It should also closely monitor the stock levels and loading patterns.

Answer 6

Traditionally, India has always lived in the villages and a large portion of its retail sales still emerges from the unorganized sector. Before we begin answering the given question, it would be appropriate to plot the overall retail growth trend in the Indian context and map the numbers pertaining to the segments of sales based on their contribution—rural, urban and downtown suburbs.

As discussed through the case, the overall growth in the Indian retail sector has followed a healthy trend over the past decade and India does rank as a major player in the emerging markets as far as retail is concerned.

Interestingly, as the graph illustrates above, a major chunk of the great Indian growth story comes from food, beverages and tobacco, which primarily represent the FMCG sector. In fact, India is ranked second in the Global Retail Development Index of 30 developing countries drawn up by AT Kearney.

As per a report by KPMG, the annual growth of department stores is estimated to be 24 per cent. In the context of analysing the foray of Indian retail into the suburban domain, it would be beneficial to consider the point that retailing in India is still evolving and the sector is witnessing a series of experiments across the country with new formats being tested out. Some of these include quasi-malls, suburban discount stores, and cash and carry.

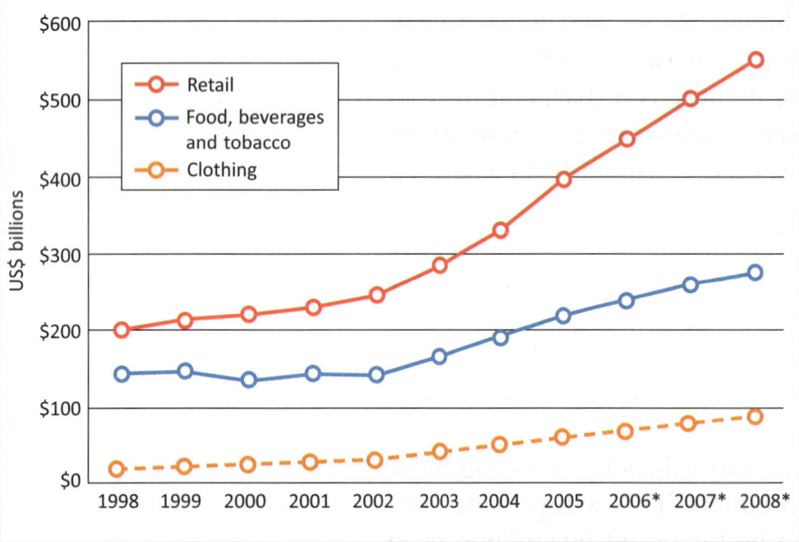

Figure 12.5: Real growth of Indian retail, food & beverage and clothing segments during 1998–2008

Source: Economist Intelligence Unit and AT Kearney analysis.

*Data for 2006–8 is based on estimates.

Let's consider the example of Metro Cash and Carry, the German giant which had faced significant opposition when it entered the Indian market. Metro positioned itself in the suburban locales, which was indeed a strategic decision.

Customers, primarily wholesalers, are cognizant of the fact that stores such as Metro Cash and Carry, though located in suburban areas, offer value for money and therefore don't mind covering the extra mile to reach the optimally located suburban warehouses-cum-stores.

This is also supported by trends in certain segments of retailing where unorganized retailing is getting semi-organized, thus adding to the pie of suburban markets. For example, 25 stores in Delhi under the banner of Provision Mart are joining hands to combine monthly buying. Bombay Bazaar and Efoodmart are aggregations of *kiranas.*

The consumption in suburban segments will primarily be driven by the following major factors:

- Favourable demographics
- Growth in income
- Increasing population of women
- Rising aspirations: Value-added goods at lower price

The case provided also cites several instances which support the theme of 'encashing rural India' as an emerging market. As with any business cycle, there are several entry barriers in the rural market, erected by companies such as HUL. From the HUL perspective, the suburban market can well be a good arena to explore. This is supported by the following analysis:

With increased infrastructural development in roads, highways and transportation connectivity, the villages are getting nearer to the cities. This brings with it a void between the 'true' rural and the all-expansive 'urban' markets. The best example would be the Bangalore-Mysore Express Highway that has effectively transformed the villages along the corridor into bustling satellite townships of suburban activity, which are duly connected by two major hubs of economic activity.

What's more, for an already established group like HUL, the foray into suburban markets would act as risk hedging and would also provide new opportunities to boost top-lines with a fair focus on bottom lines as well.

In conclusion, it would serve well for FMCG companies to explore the suburban markets, of course considering the fact that this option well integrates into the overall growth strategy of the companies with due cognizance of risk and rewards in the medium- and long-term growth plan.

Appendix

The Power of Simple and Consistent Purpose

Industrial growth draws its strength from a number of roots, which are economic, social, or even personal. Unilever's business history offers at least two lasting lessons to managers. First, the evolution of HUL over many decades demonstrates the power of a simply stated and consistent purpose. Even in its 76th year in India, Unilever states its purpose as simply 'meeting everyday needs for nutrition, hygiene and personal care'. Different words but similar to what William-Hesketh Lever stated in the 1880s—'to satisfy the washing needs of the teeming millions of India'.

Second, like people, a company too has a *sanskar*. This *sanskar* shapes the corporation over a long period. Born in September 1851, William-Hesketh Lever started the Lancashire business that became Lever Brothers in 1877. The export of Sunlight and Lifebuoy soaps into India began in the 1880s, facilitated no doubt by the Empire. By the time Lever died in May 1925, he had built a global soap empire with great brands like Lifebuoy and Lux. In the 1920s, advertising agency J. Walter Thompson cannily associated Lux with Hollywood stars like Ginger Rogers and Rita Hayworth. In 1940, the first non-Western actor, an Indian, was signed to model for Lux. The actor was Leela Chitnis. It was a huge risk but smart to associate an unknown and upcoming actor with an international brand.

Lever amassed a great fortune. During his lifetime, Lever gave away large sums of money for local purposes with very little publicity. Just prior to his death in 1925, he wrote a remarkably brief will. The Lever Hulme Trust was thus able to continue his works of philanthropy. At his centenary in 1951, it was said of him 'that the ruling passion of his life was not money or even power, but the desire to increase human well-being by substituting the profitable for the valueless'. In fact, Lever likened himself to 'the road maker who is the best anonymous servant of humanity. He drives great broad thoroughfares from town to town and for generations men travel over the road, with all their hopes and fears, with all their cares and joys, never once asking who it was that made their way easier for them.'

On 1 January 1930, Unilever was created through the biggest corporate merger until then—between Lever Brothers of England and Margarine Unie of The Netherlands. It was governed by 32 directors. History records that it did not take long to realize that 'this travelling circus was too big to be effective and that its perambulations wasted an unnecessary amount of everyone's time. . . . There were committees on everything and everybody was looking over somebody else's shoulder, while too many people were minding everybody's business but their own!'

Until 76 years ago, India's needs were met by export from England. The peculiar problems of the primitive, illiterate market were covered by ingenious methods of salesmanship. A 1920s report reads, 'An essential plan of our selling organization is the lorry crew . . . which consists of a chauffeur, a propagandist, a coolie . . . . We are able to popularize our goods and show their use anywhere the lorry can go, which in India is practically anywhere.'

William Lever was a creator, but his son was a coadjutor who did not desire dynastic succession in the firm or the trust. Lever's son engineered a managerial revolution in 1929 by transiting from 'owner-manager' to 'management without ownership'. Professional chairmen were appointed to The Netherlands and British subsidiaries. Unilever was a shrewd marriage of business convenience and also a great experiment in international relations.

With regard to India, chairman D'Arcy Cooper observed 1933 that 'India was too large a gap in the world's surface . . . to leave uncovered'. It was the same purpose expressed by Lever, but in a more contemporary language. Lever Brothers India was thus incorporated in 1933 to expand and actively promote local manufacture and selling. By the end of the Second World War, Unilever worked as a 'commonwealth' rather than as an 'Empire' centred in London or Rotterdam. This meant continuous efforts to build a mood of tolerance and understanding by consultation and communication as illustrated by the following anecdote.

India was the first among overseas countries to promote local nationals into managerial positions usually occupied by Europeans. Prakash Tandon joined HUL in 1937 and became chairman in 1961 when Lord George Cole was the chairman of Unilever. Despite his colonial background, George Cole was not autocratic and brought to Unilever a risk-taking and trading mentality born out of intuition. Cole was born in Malaysia, educated in Singapore and joined Unilever's subsidiary in Africa at 17 years. He had said of Unilever, 'Firms are compared to ships. Unilever is not a ship, it is a fleet—several different fleets, several hundred subsidiary companies and the ships are many sizes, doing all kinds of different things, all over the place.'

In 1965, when India was caught up in the Licence Permit Raj, Lord Cole lectured Prakash Tandon to exert his influence with government to free the business from excessive controls. Years later, Tandon would chuckle about the cheeky response he got away with, 'George, my influence in Delhi is not very different from yours in Whitehall. I have the same problems in Delhi as you had with the Harold Macmillan government.'

When Unilever started its Unilever CMDS (Company Management Development Scheme) in 1950, India too did so with the recruitment of Vasant Rajadhyaksha (later chairman), Ranjan Banerjee (later vice-chairman), and Jagdish Chopra (later marketing director). Independent India was charting its own economic agenda and desired the Indianization of capital. Then the finance minister T.T. Krishnamachari arm-twisted Tandon and Unilever to dilute the 100 per cent foreign holding. Thus it was that in 1956, when Lever Brothers became Hindustan Lever with Indian shareholders.

With the enactment of the 1972 Foreign Exchange Regulation Act (FERA), an obvious option was for Lever to dilute foreign holding to 40 per cent. Chairman T. Thomas realized that the long-standing Unilever vision and commitment to India would get substantially eroded if this were to happen. He was convinced that it would also not be good for India. To ensure that Unilever retains 51 per cent and management control, Thomas mounted an intensive and exacting communication exercise in 1974. This was continued later by Ashok Ganguly and both were ably assisted by the redoubtable 'Pepsi' Suman Sinha.

At that time, it was considered to be an exercise in futility. But it turned out to be a professional act, completely consistent with the long-standing purpose of 'washing the teeming millions of India'. Thus thousands of employees over the years have been the road makers, whom Lord Leverhulme called the anonymous servants of humanity. Inevitably future travellers will not remember those who made their journey possible. In this 76th year, it is appropriate to remember those 'anonymous servants of humanity'.

Sources: Gopala Krishnan, CEO, Tata Sons.

Notes

1. http://www.commodityonline.com/commodity-stocks/HUL-Marico-dip-as-markets-turn-negative-2009–03-19-16148-3-1.html
2. http://www.livemint.com/2009/03/14003203/Recession-helps-consumer-goods.html
3. http://profit.ndtv.com/2009/03/20223944/Retailers-push-FMCG-cos-for-mo.html
4. http://www.business-standard.com/india/storypage.php?autono=349967

5. http://profit.ndtv.com/2008/10/03112040/HUL-faces-growing-threat-in-ru.html
6. http://world.rediff.com/news/article/www/money/2008/feb/04hul.htm

References

1. http://www.hul.co.in
2. http://www.jnjindia.com/consumer_marketing.asp
3. http://en.wikipedia.org/wiki/Britannia_Industries
4. http://www.britannia.co.in
5. http://www.nestle.in/nestle_india_landing.aspx
6. http://in.rediff.com/money/2004/jun/09hll.htm
7. http://www.dabur.com/
8. http://www.pg.com/
9. http://www.cavinkare.com/
10. http://www.colgate.co.in/
11. http://timesofindia.indiatimes.com
12. http://www.livemint.com
13. http://profit.ndtv.com
14. http://www.brandchannel.com
15. http://www.sap.com/india/company/successes/pdfs/HUL.pdf
16. http://economictimes.indiatimes.com/Features/Brand-Equity/India-critical-over-nextfive-years-PG/rssarticleshow/3916700.cms
17. http://search.ebscohost.com/login.aspx?direct=true&db=bsh&AN=35047927&site=ehost-live
18. http://www.chillibreeze.com/articles_various/fmcg-in-india.asp
19. www.moneycontrol.com/
20. http://en.wikipedia.org/wiki/PEST_analysis
21. http://en.wikipedia.org/wiki/Growth-share_matrix
22. http://www.hllshakti.com/
23. http://in.biz.yahoo.com
24. www.ibef.org
25. *Marketing Management—A South Asian Perspective*, 12th edition, Philip Kotler, Kevin Lane Keller, Abraham Koshy and Mithileshwar Jha (2007).
26. Marketing as Strategy: Understanding the CEO's Agenda for Driving Growth and Innovation, Harvard Business School Press, 2004.

CHAPTER 13 

BUILDING DTH PC SEGMENT: PORTFOLIO FOR CREATIVE SOLUTIONS LIMITED

applied case study 5

13.1 Genesis

The global computers and peripheral industry generated total revenue of $540.1 billion in 2008 representing CAGR of 5 per cent during 2004–8. Personal computer segment provide the most lucrative, which generated a total sales of $236.9 billion, equivalent to 43.9 per cent of the industry's overall values. The industry is projected to grow a CAGR of 5.9 per cent during 2008–13.

Home computers have come a long way in a span of three decades. The home computer, a class of personal computers, entered the market in the late 1970s and early 1980s. Its introduction led to predictions of automation of day-to-day activities and the emergence of the 'Intelligent Home'. However most of these predictions went unrealized as the computers of that time were simply not intelligent enough to multitask and the storage memory was too small (for example, the floppy).

As technology matured and the internet entered lives and homes, home-browsing PCs made their presence felt once again. As technology improved and microprocessors came to be mass produced, the home computer became more affordable. These days people purchase multiple computers for the family depending on the needs and requirements of each family member. Initially portability was an issue, but now, with the advent of the Notebook, even that has been resolved. Some of the early personal computers to be introduced were the TRS-80 (1977), various models of the Apple (first introduced in 1977), the Atari 400/800 (1979) along with its follow-up models the 800XL and the 130XE, and the Commodore VIC-20 (1980) and Commodore 64 (1982). The VIC was the first computer of any type to sell large-scale.

The world is becoming increasingly network-oriented every day. Not only are the number of interconnections amongst individuals, businesses, and governments increasing, but there is also the increased recognition of connectivity being a key component of public infrastructure. Next generation technologies such as Wi-Fi and WiMAX being adopted rapidly and enhancing connectivity. Wi-Fi has quickly evolved from only a WLAN application, providing indoor, short-range wireless internet access for mobile computers, home/office PCs to a broadband wireless service with numerous opportunities on a global scale. Therefore, cutting edge technology is a must for every enterprise to serve its customers profitably and for a country to sustain its competitive advantage in the global arena. Computer hardware and software industries are becoming the lifelines for both corporates and individuals.

Even though India lacks connectivity, her citizens are actively buying computer and internet connectivity for home use. Most see it as an investment for the future/forward planning and for their children's education. But we have to examine these potentials against the backdrop of the world economic situation in general and Indian economic growth in particular.

According to International Monetary Fund's (IMF) World Economic Outlook (WEO), global real GDP growth on a purchasing power parity basis was decelerated from 5 per cent in 2007 to 4.1 per cent in 2008 (3.7 per cent in WEO, April 2008) and further to 3.9 per cent in 2009 (3.8 per cent in WEO, April 2008).

13.2 The PC Industry

The technology industry is characterized by a high degree of global competition, cyclical revenues, earning volatility and moderate-to-high capital intensive.

Modern IT systems rely upon a number of aspects, namely people, networks and hardware. With computers becoming an integral part of our lives and involved in the most quotidian (online banking) to the most miraculous breakthroughs (DNA decoding), the quality of human life has improved significantly. IT has changed the way we approach problems and deal with them.

This change in the environment can also be felt in the PC industry which has picked up in a big way with the advent of the internet and related technologies. The global shipments of PCs, which include desktops, laptops and low-cost Netbooks, was 301.5 million units in 2009, up from 299.4 million units in 2008 (based on iSuppli figures).

Table 13.1: PC shipment by region and form factor (in millions)

Region	*Form factor*	*2007*	*2008*	*2009*	*2010*	*2011**	*2012**
USA	Desktop & X86 Server	37	34.4	30.1	27.7	26	24.3
	Portables	30	34.7	37	41	45.7	50.8
	TOTAL	67	69.1	67.1	68.7	71.7	75
International	Desktop & X86 Server	124.1	122	115.8	119.4	125.3	132.3
	Portables	78	111.2	131	159.8	194.8	235
	TOTAL	202	233.2	236.8	279.3	320.1	367.3
Worldwide	Desktop & X86 Server	161.1	156.4	145.8	147.2	151.3	156.6
	Portables	108	145.9	168	200.8	240.5	285.7
	TOTAL	269.1	302.3	313.9	348	391.9	442.3

Source: IDC Worldwide Quarterly PC Tracker, December 2008.
Note: *Estimate.

Table 13.2: PC shipment by region and form factor (%)

Region	*Form factor*	*2007*	*2008*	*2009*	*2010*	*2011**	*2012**
USA	Desktop & X86 Server	−2.8	−7	−12.6	−7.8	−6.2	−6.8
	Portables	23.6	15.6	6.7	10.7	11.5	11.1
	TOTAL	7.5	3.1	−2.9	2.4	4.4	4.6
International	Desktop & X86 Server	7.7	−1.7	−5.1	3.2	4.9	5.6
	Portables	38.5	42.6	17.8	22	21.9	20.6
	TOTAL	17.8	15.4	5.8	13.2	14.6	14.7
Worldwide	Desktop & X86 Server	5.1	−2.9	−6.7	0.9	2.8	3.5
	Portables	34	35.1	15.2	19.5	19.8	18.8
	TOTAL	15.1	12.4	3.8	10.9	12.6	12.9

Source: IDC Worldwide Quarterly PC Tracker, December 2008.
Note: *Estimate.

Acer (2353.TW), the world's third-largest PC brand, was the best performer, its shipments up 57.9 per cent in 2008, fuelled by the success of its low-cost netebooks.

According to IDC estimates in September 2010, the worldwide PC microprocessor shipment and revenue in second quarter of financial year 2010 increased 3.6 per cent and 6.2 per cent respectively compared to first quarter of financial year 2010.

The Indian PC market however, was also severely affected, with notebook sales going completely flat. PC shipments in India in 2008 have shown a disturbing trend. Vendors such as HP, Acer, HCL and Lenovo, 67 per cent of whose business comes from the domestic consumer, saw sales take a nosedive in Q4 of 2008 to almost half. For example, HP Notebook sales came down 50 per cent, from 2,20,000 units in Q3 2008 to 1,25,000 in Q4 2008. Acer Notebook shipments came down from 1,09,000 in Q3 2008 to 55,000 in Q4 2008. Lenovo saw a drop from 78,000 in Q3 2008 to 51,000 in Q4 2008. Overall, 2.6 million notebooks were shipped in the calendar year 2008, reflecting a 51.6 per cent y-o-y growth.

In the past, notebook sales have grown by almost 100 per cent. The Indian desktop market saw a negative 3.8 per cent y-o-y growth in 2008, shipping 6.7 million desktop PCs. In Q3 2008, it reflected a 5 per cent growth but towards the closure of Q4 2008 it turned out to be a negative 14 per cent growth on a y-o-y basis.

Spending on technology was expected to halve in most corporate organizations and little money will be available for the people to spend on computer purchases for the home segment during 2009–11. This is worrying the semiconductor and PC industry at large. FMCG companies in the latter half of 2008 decided to cut the freebies during festival seasons and concentrate on customer services and product innovation, owing to high customer demands. That meant the recession has put an end to their aggressive price cut and discount strategies in 2009. Then how did the PC industry fare?

What's really interesting to note is that the whiteboxes, i.e. unbranded PCs, are dominating the computer market. As per IDC estimates, assembled PCs or whiteboxes form nearly 40 per cent of the market with the branded category bringing up the balance 60 per cent. However, some industry estimates peg the share of branded desktops to be as low as 49 per cent. Individuals were among the biggest buyers of whiteboxes. On the commercial side, buyers were increasingly choosing major local and multinational brands. Flexible configurations were noticed to be a key selling point.

Table 13.3: Sale of notebook and PC desktop during 2005–10

Year	*2005*	*2006*	*2007*	*2008*	*2009*	*2010*
PC Notebook						
Sales (₹million)	9,780	20,220	38,300	72,890	58,860	95,770
Units	177,105	431,834	850,860	1,822,139	1,516,459	2,508,564
PC Desktop						
Sales (₹million)	75,200	86,840	104,310	102,160	130,250	112,670
Units	3,632,619	4,614,724	5,490,591	5,522,167	5,279,648	5,525,992

Source: Department of IT, Govt. of India as on 5 August 2010.

PC sales in India have jumped 20 per cent since 2005. The figure stood at 6.5 million in 2007 up from 5.4 million in 2006. Notebook PC sales surged to 1.8 million from 9,80,000, as prices fell below ₹20,000 ($500) and since 2007 made laptops the favoured choice of young, first-time buyers. Sales of Notebook PCs grew the most, by 81 per cent as compared to 7 per cent growth in the desktop segment during that period. Consumer PC sales grew by 23 per cent in 2007, outpacing commercial client PC sales which expanded by 19 per cent. HP was the market leader (23 per cent), while HCL (13 per cent) and Lenovo (10 per cent) followed. Servers registered a growth of 50 per cent over the first half of 2008. The growth of whitebox

BOX 13.1: TOP PERFORMERS IN THE INDUSTRY

The sunrise Indian IT industry recorded a growth of 32 per cent in rupee terms, in fiscal 2006–7, to cross the $50 billion mark, according to a survey by *Dataquest* magazine. The industry growth in dollar terms was at 30 per cent. Export earnings of ₹1,53,744 crore and a domestic market of ₹73,135 crore contributed to the revenue of ₹2,26,879 crore. Export revenues grew at 35 per cent and the domestic market at a consistent 27.2 per cent, roughly the same for three years now.

According to *Dataquest*'s 20th DQ Top 20 Annual Survey of the Indian IT Industry, the IT services exports crossed the trillion rupees mark to reach ₹1,03,647 crore, representing a growth of 37 per cent. BPO services grew 33.5 per cent to touch ₹37,800 crore. Engineering services (₹4,146 crore) and entertainment and gaming (₹1,810 crore) too emerged as strong export areas.

Discussing the Indian IT industry crossing the $50 billion mark, Praveen Gupta, publisher of *Dataquest*, said, 'After a consistent 30 per cent-plus growth for over three years, this achievement marks a truly proud moment for Indian IT's entrepreneurs, as well as the 1.6 million technology professionals who contributed directly to it.' The top 20 players accounted for as much as 77 per cent of the software services exports by growing at 44.2 per cent, the highest in the first seven years of the millennium. The top three players, Tata Consultancy Services (TCS), Infosys and Wipro got into the big league having bagged several large deals and expanding their consultancy business in the face of competition from established players in North America and of late, Europe. British Telecom awarded a billion dollar contract to Tech Mahindra, a company that recorded a growth of 134 per cent to jump into the top 10 list.

The next 20 players comprised companies like Hexaware, L&T Infotech and NIIT Technologies who contributed nearly 11.4 per cent of the total revenues. Several hundred smaller players contributed to the remaining 12 per cent. The top eight software firms—TCS, Infosys, Wipro, Satyam, HCL, Cognizant, Tech Mahindra and Patni—earned nearly 63 per cent of their export earnings from North America, 29 per cent from Europe and 5 per cent from the Asia-Pacific region.

The *Dataquest* study noted that Application Development and Maintenance still contributed to nearly two-thirds of the total software export revenues, despite efforts to bring this down. Infrastructure and engineering services contributed to 5 per cent and 4 per cent of the revenues.

Source: Dataquest, March 2007.

sales was almost stagnant, growing at 1-2 per cent y-o-y in 2008 and in 2009. The customized PC market is growing and consumers are shifting from CRT to TFT or LCD monitors. Incidentally, the market for printers actually shrank, with an 82 per cent decline for line printers, 24 per cent for dot matrix, 9 per cent for lasers and 2 per cent for inkjets in 2008.

Falling laptop prices were a major catalyst in the soaring sales. Notebook/ laptop sales are expected to grow further and corner 40 per cent of the overall client PC sales in India by 2011. What's interesting to note is the dent that laptops have caused in the peripheral market. This will directly impact third-party sales, which pushes bundled products, while Original Equipment Manufactures (OEMs) will still rake in the moolah. The Indian Institute of Technology Chennai and the Indian Institute of Science Bengaluru, have partnered to build the world's cheapest laptop to be priced at $100. The laptop, when produced, will prove to be a breakthrough device that could solve the problems of low computer literacy and e-learning not only in India, but also the worldover.

Finally, the IDC study presents an updated look at the worldwide PC marketplace as going forward. It provides forecast and growth figures for PC shipments at the global level and for key regional markets. 'In September 2010, forecast update, the outlook for worldwide PC shipments calls for a 11.1 per cent growth, equalling 252.9 million units. These figures represent a slight dip due to the lull in the desktop market, specifically in mature markets, in the commercial segment,' says Doug Bell, analyst, US Quarterly PC Tracker Program.

Look at the top performers according to a recent *Dataquest* survey (Box 13.1).

BOX 13.2: PC SOFTWARE PIRACY STILL HIGH, DROPS MERE 1 PER CENT IN INDIA IN 2008

Software piracy levels in the personal computer segment in India showed just 1 per cent drop for the year 2008, standing at 68 per cent as against 69 per cent in 2007, according to a global software piracy study conducted by Business Software Alliance (BSA) and IDC. However, the software piracy in value terms rose to $2.7 billion in 2008 as against $2 billion in 2007, the study said. 'The bad news is that software piracy remains so prevalent all over the world, undermining local IT service firms, giving illegal software users an unfair advantage in business, and spreading security risks,' said BSA president and CEO Roben Holleyman.

'We are hopeful that the new government, together with the state governments, will take positive steps in driving anti-piracy initiatives, such as the formation of a national anti-piracy taskforce, the setting up of special IP courts, the promotion of IP rights and the training of enforcement officials,' said Keshav Dhakad, who chairs the BSA India Committee.

The average PC software piracy rate in Asia-Pacific increased to 61 per cent in 2008 up from 59 per cent in 2007, with losses reaching over $15 billion, said Jeffrey J. Hardee, BSA's vice-president and regional director, Asia-Pacific. The worldwide PC software piracy rate rose for the second year in a row, from 38 to 41 per cent as PC shipments grew faster in high piracy countries such as China and India, the study maintained.

The loss to the software industry from PC software piracy broke the $50 billion level for the first time. The worldwide losses grew by 11 per cent to $53 billion, but half of that growth was due to the falling US dollar; excluding the effect of exchange rates, losses grew to $50.2 billion. The lowest-piracy countries are the US, Japan, New Zealand, and Luxembourg, all near 20 per cent. The highest-piracy countries are Armenia, Bangladesh, Georgia, and Zimbabwe, all over 90 per cent.

According to an economic impact study of software piracy conducted and published by IDC in 2007, in India, reducing software piracy by 10 percentage points over a four-year period could generate an additional 43,000 new jobs, $3.1 billion in economic growth, and $200 million in tax revenue.

Source: IDC, August 2008.

13.3 The Company

Ramji, General Manger Marketing, Creative Solutions Limited (CSL), a mid-sized PC Manufacturer, grimaced at the headlines in the morning's *Financial Express*: 'PC sales in India go on Dipping'. Reports showed that the decline in computer shipments was the worst since the mid-1980s. According to NASSCOM, PC sales in India during the first half of fiscal 2009–10 showed a decline of 4 per cent over the corresponding period in fiscal 2008–9.

What was worse was that NASSCOM projected a decline of 12.5 per cent in PC sales this fiscal! After all the whiteboxes took away 40 per cent of the total market share and the times were tough for companies to roll out new plans. The PC notebook sales has declined from 18.22 lakh units in 2008 to 15.16 lakh units in 2009. PC Desktop also suffered from 55.22 lakh units in 2008 to 52.79 lakh units in 2009.

Ramji scanned the Reserve Bank of India guidelines published in the newspaper, and got further worried. All commercial, home, personal, computer purchase and car loans were going to cost more with the RBI's announcement of checking the personal loan segment and creditworthiness of individuals and firms on the eve of a global financial meltdown.

This was going to upset the company's consumer finance schemes and sales in the coming quarter. 'It's terrible,' Ramji remarked to his CFO, Reji Raman, and Marketing Manager (MM) Ashuthosh. Reji Raman jumped on the opportunity to score a point, declaring assertively, 'The recessionary pressure in the Indian economy is one of the most important causes.'

'There is definitely more to it than that,' shot back Ashuthosh, annoyed that the CFO hardly ever thought from the customers' angle. 'Even though economic factors cannot be ruled out, an important issue that has to be mooted is whether PC manufacturers are delivering value to their customers.' Further, he stressed the segments and purpose of buying computers and the power of the internet in reaching across to the global community across all sections. For instance, see Figure 13.1.

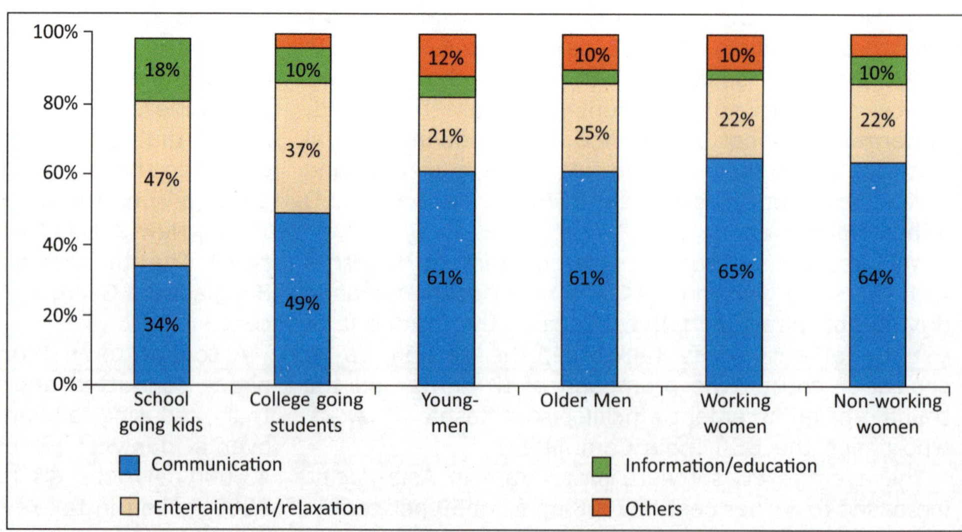

Figure 13.1: Segments and their purposes of buying computers (%)

'One important aspect of value lies in the way a product is delivered to the customer. I doubt whether the distribution channel for PCs in India is tuned to the needs of the customers, especially the home PC browsing segment. I strongly feel that the performance would have been much better if the home PC browsing segment had lapped up more PCs,' explained the Marketing Manager.

The after-sale and service package holds key importance. He quoted Whirlpool India's recent campaign of customer care and engineering support for its products and highlighted the business model of training service engineers for attending to customers' problems and boosting their confidence in company products. The company engaged service engineers under the stockist or distributor who tracked customers from product purchase, installation, initial run and after-care service through a five-year warranty system, offering additional products and ancillary parts befitting customer need. Ashuthosh argued for implementing such packages to tap new segments and overcome the recession without affecting the bottomline of the company.

13.4 Logistics: The Key Demand Driver

The business channels that dominate the PC industry are the direct sales force and the dealer channels. Certain computer vendors have also taken the lead in establishing themselves as retailers by selling their computers through retail stores. '"The home PC browsing segment neglected!" That is interesting,' the GM cut in. 'What is the potential of this segment?'

It was a month ago that Ashuthosh had approached his boss with his idea of 'the importance of the home PC browsing segment' and hence the meeting this morning. 'Sir,' explained Ashuthosh, 'According to IDC/NASSCOM estimates, around 18 lakh PCs were sold during 2007–8 and of these approximately one-third found their way into internet parlours. However, a reason why the home PC browsing segment is not growing in India as because there is no channel which will specifically cater to the needs of this segment. In fact, all the attention of the vendors is on the corporate sector with its huge IT budgets, and the end result is that the home PC browsing segment is being neglected.'

'I do appreciate your initiative,' remarked Reji Raman, 'but surely since it's your idea that we target this home PC browsing segment, isn't it important that you point a finger on its needs?'

For his part, Ashuthosh had done an impressive amount of work developing his idea, conducting surveys and focus groups. Now he began to unveil his thoughts.

13.5 New Horizons

'Sir,' began Ashuthosh, 'most owners of home PCs complain that in spite of purchasing the Annual Maintenance Contract (AMC), the service engineers don't respond promptly. Again, even though all computers come with a warranty period, some resellers say that they do not by themselves give free service during this period and that customers would have to contact the company (which is a big hassle) if anything goes wrong.'

Reliable after-sale service is the most important thing a potential home PC browsing customer (with usually a single computer at his disposal) has in mind. Even when vendors promise prompt and reliable service, so poor is their track record that customers wonder whether they will get prompt service despite paying extra for it. Ashuthosh again quoted the experience of the Whirlpool Magic campaign and its customer service. He also pointed to Dell Computers' home delivery strategy and customer care packages in detail.

'This may be one of the reasons why home PC browsing segments trust the local manufacturers and opt for whiteboxes because they always attend to the customer's problem and give them confidence that their investment and machine, despite spurious products and false fabrications, are safe!'

Ashuthosh summarized his plans and briefed the huge potential for the company's products and services in this segment. He also put up a slide highlighting the product line-up of Dell (Figure 13.2).

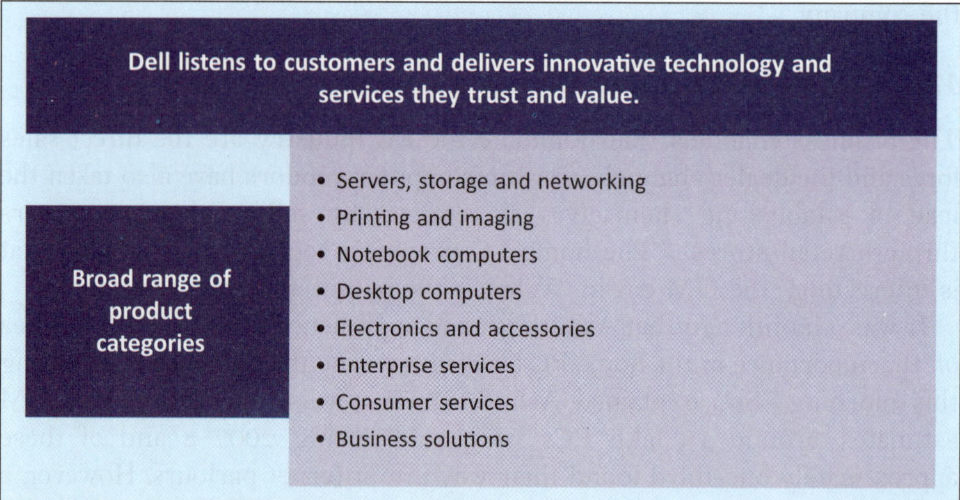

Figure 13.2: Dell's product line-up

Again, another unique characteristic of the Indian home PC browsing segment is the fear of obsolescence. Unlike users in the West who welcome short life cycle chips. Indian users want durable chips that will not be underpowered for the software five years from now. Uncertainty avoidance is so great in the Indian psyche that customers want the vendor to guarantee that he will inform them about the latest advances in processing power and help them upgrade their machines at a reasonable cost. In fact, in India, the home PC browsing segment needs a high degree of handholding and even the very basic knowledge about operating systems and software has to be imparted.

'Most vendors give only a very preliminary demonstration of the various parts of the PC and few are willing to take the effort to constantly inform customers regarding upgradation possibilities,' Ashuthosh explained. He further emphasized on the value definition and value proposition of Dell's direct-to-home (DTH) strategy (Figure 13.3).

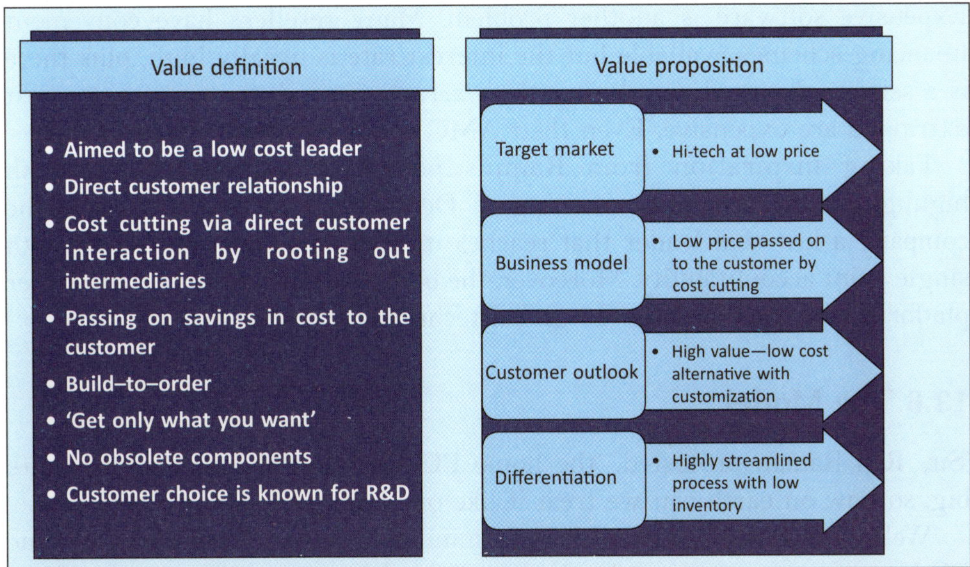

Figure 13.3: Value definition and value proposition of Dell

'What about price?' quipped the CFO Reji Raman.

This time it was Ramji, the GM who replied. 'Price is one of the most important factors hindering the growth of PCs in the home PC browsing segment. An average branded PC with multimedia costs around ₹35,000 (minimum) which means for the majority of people, saving up for months.

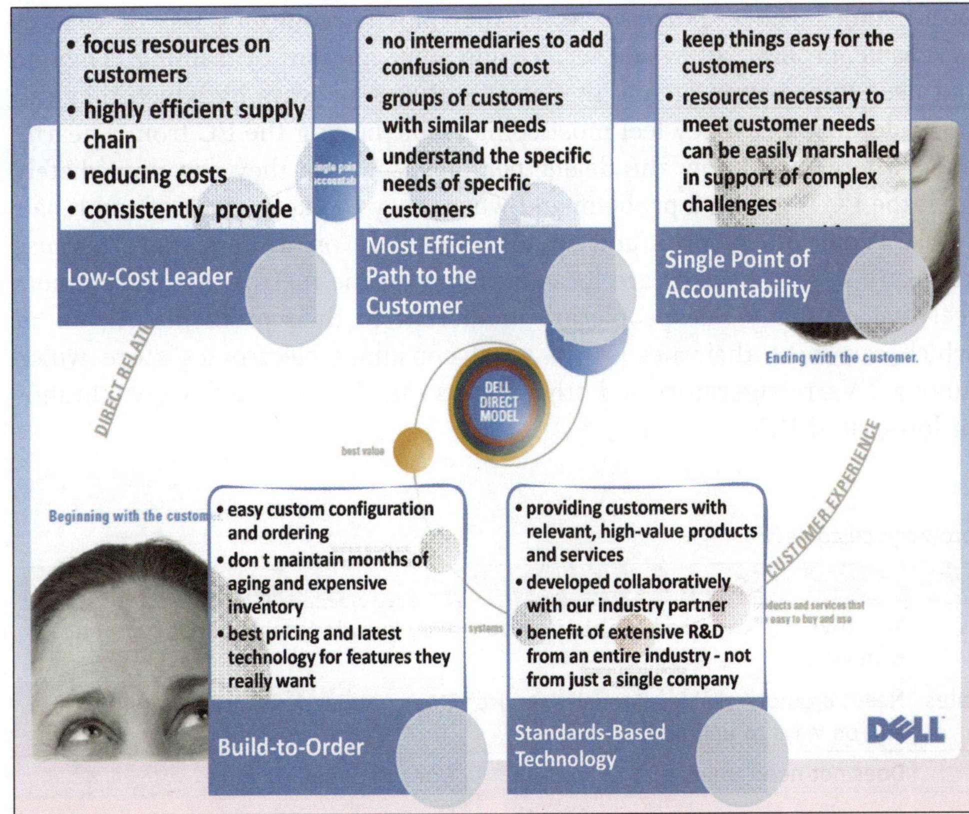

Figure 13.4: Dell's USP

Expensive software is another problem. Many resellers have convenient financing schemes available but the interest rate is usually high, plus there is a service charge. Even during the warranty period, the spare parts cost extra and are expensive. Even their AMC is quite pricey.'

Taking inspiration from Ramji's positive comments, Ashuthosh highlighted the unique positioning of Dell's DTH strategy. It made the company a low-cost leader that reaches its customer most efficiently with single point accountability. Moreover, the business is based on built-to-order platform with standards-based global technology.

13.6 The Model

'Sir,' Reji Raman protested, 'the home PC browsing segment seems quite big, so how on earth can we treat it like one homogeneous group?'

'Well,' smiled Ashuthosh. 'I have in mind certain segments that the home PC browsing segment can be further divided into, according to the needs of the customers.' These are shown in Table 13.4. At present, these three segments, even though different in their requirements from the distribution channel, are being catered to by the same distribution channel, that is by the authorized resellers.

'The first segment,' explained Ashuthosh, 'consists of people who are not very knowledgeable about computers and for whom affordability and price are the most important factors. These people need the computer perhaps for their children who are learning computers in school, for home accounting or for some business purpose.' What they mostly require by way of services is reliable, prompt, after-sale service and some amount of training. They do not need information on say the latest software or ways by which they can upgrade their PC. They feel most comfortable buying the PC from a nearby shop where they know the dealer personally, where they can immediately go if the PC is giving a problem and where they can keep track of any repair work. People in suburbs and small towns rely on dealers more because company service centres are located mainly in the metros. Also, customers feel that company salespeople are indifferent to their problems. An outlet which can meet their needs is a local consumer electronics store which among TVs, refrigerators and other things can also stock a few good brands of low-priced PCs.

Table 13.4: Segmenting of home PC browsing customers

Segment 1	Segment 2	Segment 3
Not knowledgeable about computers	Somewhat knowledgeable about computers	Very knowledgeable about computers
Needs reliable, prompt, after-sales service	Needs prompt, reliable after-sales service and on ways to upgrade	Does not need after-sales service
Needs training	Does not need training	Does not need training
Are willing to pay little	Are willing to pay a premium for these services	Very price sensitive

Many resellers have convenient financing schemes available but the interest rate is usually high, plus there is a service charge. Prices can be kept reasonable because the dealer does not have to stack too many fancy software or multiple configurations of PCs. Besides there is also the economy of scope. What the dealer needs is only a small staff well-versed in repairing computers and who can offer a limited amount of training to the customers.

The second segment constitutes those who are somewhat knowledgeable about computers and who may want to buy a PC for some amount of professional work. In this segment, customers primarily want availability, broad assortments, multiple brands and prompt and reliable after-sales service. They are willing to sacrifice some price benefits to avail of these facilities. Computer specialty stores should be ideal to provide services to this segment; the stores can have various brands and all accessories and software under one umbrella. Imparting training to customers is not essential in this case, because often customers learn how to operate the software from their workplace itself. However, the seller should be able to provide the latest information regarding the various possibilities of an upgrade, latest software, as well as after-sales service.

The third category of the Home PC browsing segment consists of those well-versed in computers and self-reliant, but who are price sensitive and therefore buy from the grey market. However, there is always a fear in the customers' minds about spurious parts, lack of accountability on the part of the vendor and no resale value.

They know enough about computers to service small faults on their own, or are willing to get repairs done by a third party. A mail order or telephone order system, by doing away with distributor margins, should provide them with branded, reliable PCs and accessories at reasonable prices. Ashuthosh went on to explain his STP strategy on how to reach his target group most effectively (Figure 13.5).

'In fact, the manufacturing company can also set up a centralized telephone support system for all these segments,' suggested the CFO, adding, 'To be honest, I don't think we have the resources to target all the three sub-segments at the same time. Again, how do we estimate the demand potential for each of these three segments?'

Before coming to the demand, Ashuthosh presented the strategy-portfolio analysis of various players in the PC industry to highlight the problem of liquidity faced by numerous MNCs. This problem was mainly due to unplanned product/market extension by several firms in the recent past when demand began to diminish due to the economic slowdown.

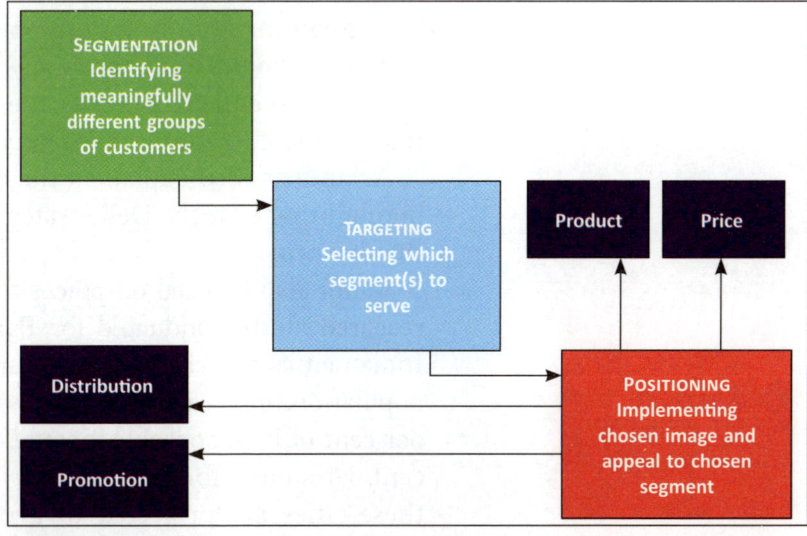

Figure 13.5: STP strategy for the Home PC market

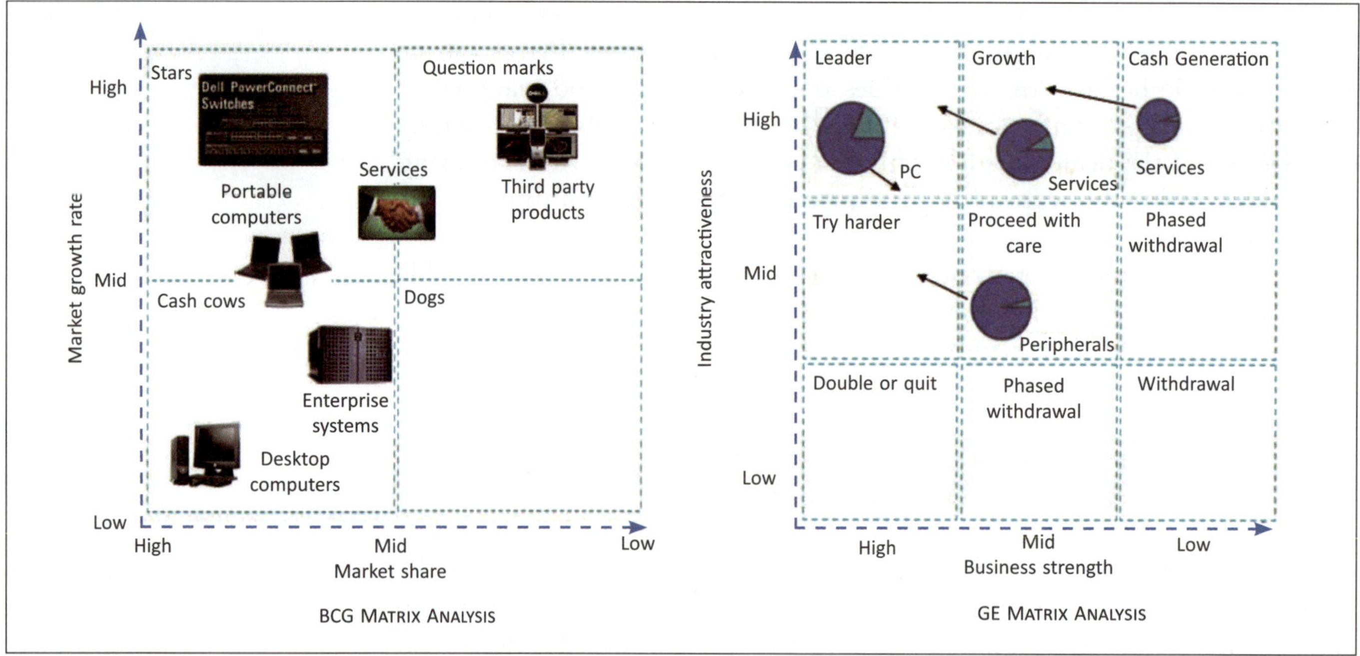

Figure 13.6: Strategy-Portfolio analysis

13.7 The Road Ahead

'Regarding the estimation of demand,' Ashuthosh pondered, 'can't we, as a starter, assume that all the three segments have equal potential?'

'No!' Reji Raman snapped back. 'I suggest we prepare a macro-economic forecast projecting inflation, interest rates, consumer spending and other variables. This can be used along with other environmental indicators to forecast sales for each Home PC browsing sub-segment.'

'A survey of buyers' intentions may help too; or perhaps we could advertise, clearly outlining our position for each of the three segments and ask prospective customers to respond to us? Or perhaps take demand estimates from our sales representatives, dealers or trade associations? They ought to have good insights into developing trends,' suggested Ramji, the GM. 'In fact, how should we determine which of the three Home PC browsing sub-segments to enter? Is it only the size of the segment, or the ease of serving that segment, or any other factor? We need to research these further.'

Ashuthosh also explained the customer loyalty matrix of DTH segments highlighting how the Dell strategy worked well for the company even during the downturn.

Ramji also focused on places they could begin from. He recalled a recent research study conducted for Pantaloon. The reports said that the 20 top Indian cities, which though accounting for only 10 per cent of the country's population, generate as much as 60 per cent of its surplus income and 31 per cent of its disposable income. They have registered a growth of 11.2 per cent per annum for the last three years since 2006. The report also said that these cities are projected to grow at a healthy rate of 10.1 per cent per annum until 2016. And the demand for durables, including PCs, may go up by a substantial 84 per cent (Appendix 1).

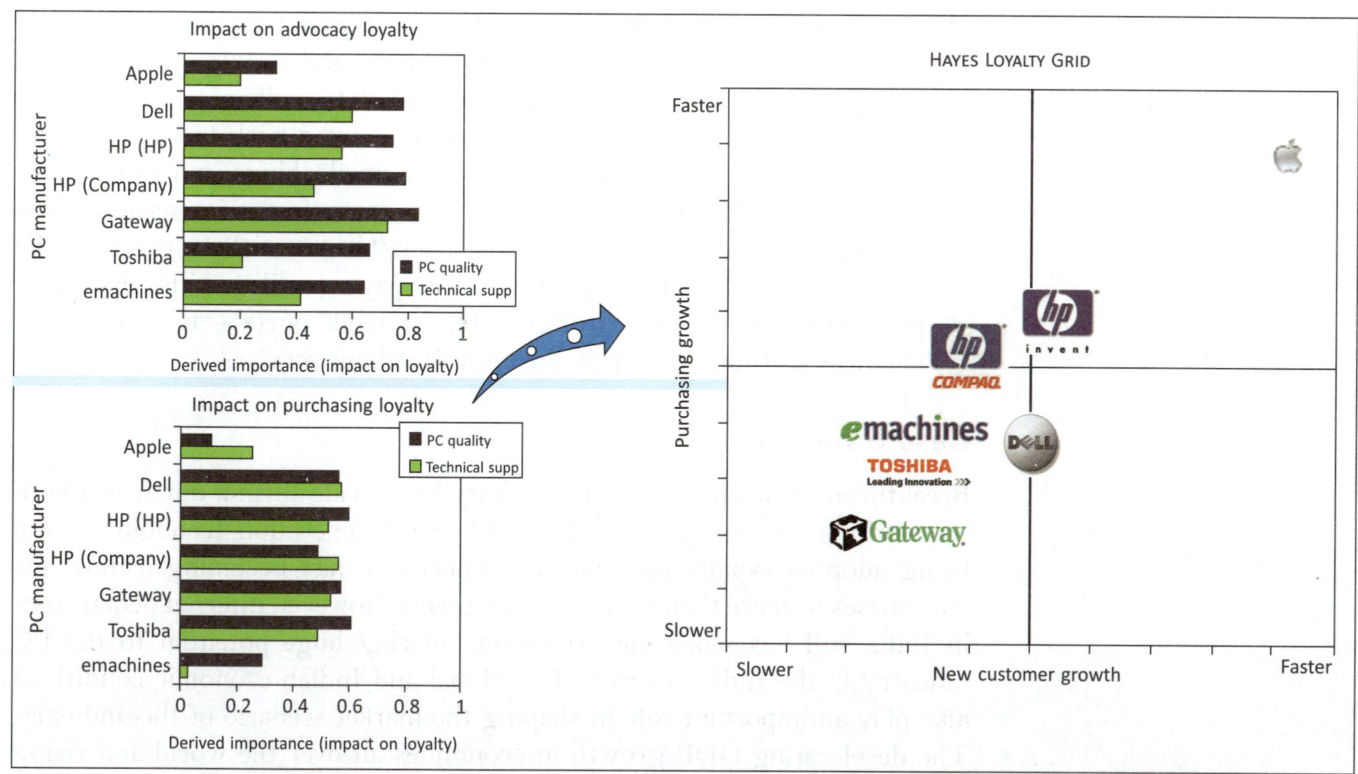

Figure 13.7: Customer Loyalty Matrix Analysis
Source: Customer loyalty (by Hayes)

'That is encouraging . . . the company has to grow or maintain its current cash flow in order to survive in the market during turbulence and here was the Home PC browsing segment that had been neglected and that ought to explode in the years to come, thanks to increasing awareness about PCs, increasing buying power and the advent of the internet. We need to think fast and present the business plan in the next meeting,' Ramji said as he concluded the meeting with a big thank you to Ashuthosh for his exploratory study, well-documented findings and business ideas.

Case Discussion Questions

(a) How did Ramji, GM of Creative Solutions Limited, decide on which home browsing segment to enter, taking into account the potential and capabilities available or to be made available within the firm? Also evaluate the company's ability to compete on factors like price, software support, training support, home visits by service engineers, market share by segment and product and customer loyalty by utilizing the theory explained in this case.

(b) Explain the various dimensions of the PC industry analysis like actual and potential industry size, growth opportunities available for Small Technology-Based Firms (STBF), strategic options available to them by analysing industry and market potentials and usage gaps among home browsing segments.

(c) Comment on the relevance and significance of the Five Forces Model for CSL for understanding the PC industry competition by utilizing the theory explained in this case.

(d) Devise a new competitive e-positioning strategy for the Home browsing segment of CSL so it can place its products and services to the target groups (like schoolchildren below the age of 15, college goers aged 15-22 years), office goers, educated housewives who wish to communicate with the world through social networks, emails, blogs, and researching information through global networks, executing class assignments through search engines, reserving train/bus/air tickets through the internet, seeking career guidance and paying utility bills, insurance premiums, and so on through internet bank portals, tracking bank balances and fund transfers through i-banking services.

Case Summary

Breakthroughs in the field of technology have made shrunk our world with 'networking' becoming the buzz word. Next generation technologies are being adopted rapidly to enhance connectivity, fast becoming a must for enterprises to serve their customers profitably. However, internet penetration in India still has scope for expansion, offering huge potential to the PC industry in the Indian market. The global and Indian economic conditions also play an important role in shaping the market scenario of this industry. The decelerating GDP growth in economies all over the world and rising inflation have raised serious concerns in emerging market economies, mainly on account of supply and demand imbalances in food, fuel and commodity markets.

The Indian PC Market

The Indian PC market is dominated by unbranded assembled PCs, with individuals as the biggest buyers and flexible configurations being their key selling point. On the commercial side, the trends favour major local and multinational brands. PC sales in India have jumped up significantly in the last few years with a massive shift from the desktop segment towards the mobile PC sector that includes laptops and other on-the-move PCs. The sharp fall in prices has made laptops the favoured choice of young, first-time buyers. This market is clearly witnessing a period of boom in comparison to a stagnating desktop PC market, with HP, HCL and Lenovo being the market leaders. While the growth of assembled PCs has remained stagnant, the customized PC and servers market has been growing. The falling laptop prices is a major catalyst in the soaring sales of Notebooks. Studies suggest that Notebook sales will corner around 40 per cent of the overall client PC sales in India by 2012. Future achievements in the field of technology could further promote the same, and could solve the problem of low computer literacy and e-learning.

The Indian IT industry has witnessed a period of boom over the past few years with the export market as well as domestic earnings contributing significantly towards revenues. BPO services have shown tremendous growth along with engineering services and entertainment emerging as strong export areas. The top three players—Tata Consulting Services (TCS), Infosys and Wipro—have bagged several large deals and gained international recognition. Other players like Hexaware, L&T Infotech and NIIT Technologies have also earned good profits and established themselves in markets worldwide.

Creative Solutions Limited (CSL)

CSL is a mid-sized PC manufacturer that experienced a decline in sales under the market turbulence. Besides economic factors, other important issues to be addressed were whether the company was delivering value to its customers and whether the distribution channel was well-tuned to the needs of the customers. The after-sales and service package was also a crucial aspect. It was proposed that the company aim at following a business model focussing on good service to customers at all times, right from the product purchase. This strategy was directed at tapping new segments to overcome the recession without affecting the bottom line of the company.

A major customer concern was that in spite of purchasing the annual maintenance contract (AMC), service engineers did not respond promptly. Moreover, the retailers did not by themselves give free service during the warranty period; customers had to contact the company if anything went wrong. In addition, customers expected their vendors to constantly inform them about upgradation possibilities, something few vendors were willing to do. Price is another important factor hindering the growth of the Home browsing PC segment.

Major Issues

1. Prompt and reliable after-sales service
2. Fear of obsolescence
3. Falling price

The Way Forward

Going forward, the company plans to follow a business model focusing on service to the customer and targeting a particular customer segment. To identify this segment it is proposed that a macroeconomic forecast be prepared projecting inflation, interest rates, consumer spending and other variables. Based on this model, the demand for each sub-segment of Home PC browsing can be estimated. The company also plans to focus more on advertising and clearly outlined its position for each of the three segments and observed the responses. These inputs along with insights into developing trends would help determine which segment to enter. The decision would thus be mainly based on factors like the size of the segment, ease of serving that segment and other similar factors. The company also needs to decide on its marketing strategy to position its product. With the growing awareness about PCs, increasing buying power and the penetration of the internet, the prospects for the company look promising, provided they are tapped with an effective marketing strategy.

Answer 1

The company plans to choose the target segment based on factors like the size of the segment and, ease of serving that segment. It does not have the resources to serve all the three segments described in Table 13.4. Taking into account the potential and capabilities available or to be made available within the firm, it is recommended that the company focus on Segment 2 of the Home browsing PC market.

A segment comprising individuals who have same knowledge about PCs and may wish to purchase one for professional purposes, to each them it is necessary to offer:

- Availability of computer and its peripherals
- Broad assortments of products and services
- Multiple brands
- Prompt and reliable after-sales service

It is advisable to target this segment because of the following reasons:

(a) It offers huge potential during the downturn, being in the mid-price range and thereby catering to a segment which is large and is willing to sacrifice on some price benefits to avail of the desired product and service.

(b) The company's profit margins are unaffected as this segment is emerging as a strong market with increased buying power that is willing to pay higher prices for desired features.

(c) The segment offers bright growth prospects with an increasing number of consumers from the current Segment 1 gradually shifting to Segment 2.

(d) The requirements of this segment are in sync with the proposed business model of the company of aiming at after-sales services and catering efficiently to the needs of customers.

(e) Being a mid-sized PC manufacturer, the company should get its target and positioning right to gain recognition. It is advisable to cater to one large segment with a huge potential that would in turn ensure a good market share—something which the company at present does not enjoy.

(f) The company aims at following a business model with after-sales and service package as its core strength. Training service engineers to attend to customers' problems and building customer confidence in the company's products are already on its agenda. Thus, the company is on its way to building the competency required for serving this segment, which expects strong service support since it is relatively less knowledgeable.

(g) The company currently does not enjoy strong customer loyalty but with increased penetration in this segment with the help of good service, it can expect to build a strong customer base in a short time.

(h) Software support is at present not one of the strengths of the company. It needs to improve in this area to reach the target segment.

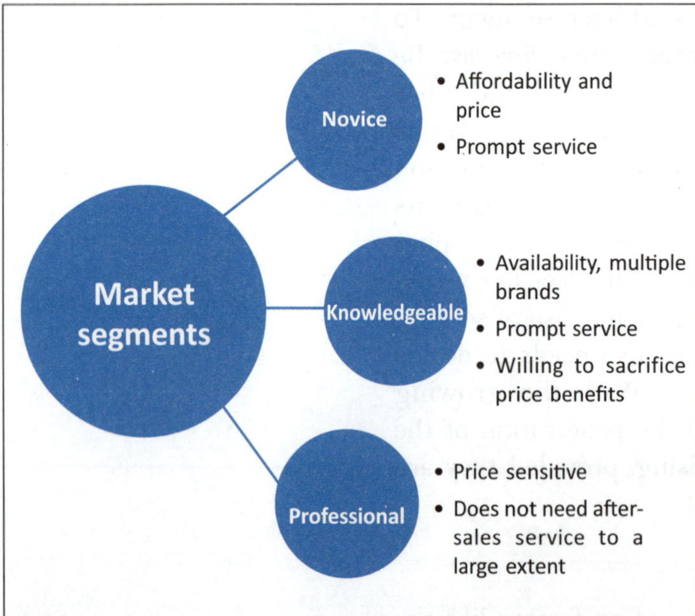

Figure 13.8: Market segments for the Home browsing PC industry

Answer 2

The PC industry has various dimensions on which it can be analysed. Over the year the industry has indicated a strong trend of growth. The industry has grown steadily from October 2005 until September 2008, as shown in Figure 13.9. Until the third quarter of 2008 the industry as a whole showed strong signs of growth, but the last quarter of 2009 saw a decline in PC sales on a worldwide scale. Researchers have changed their forecast for 2009 due to the economic recession.

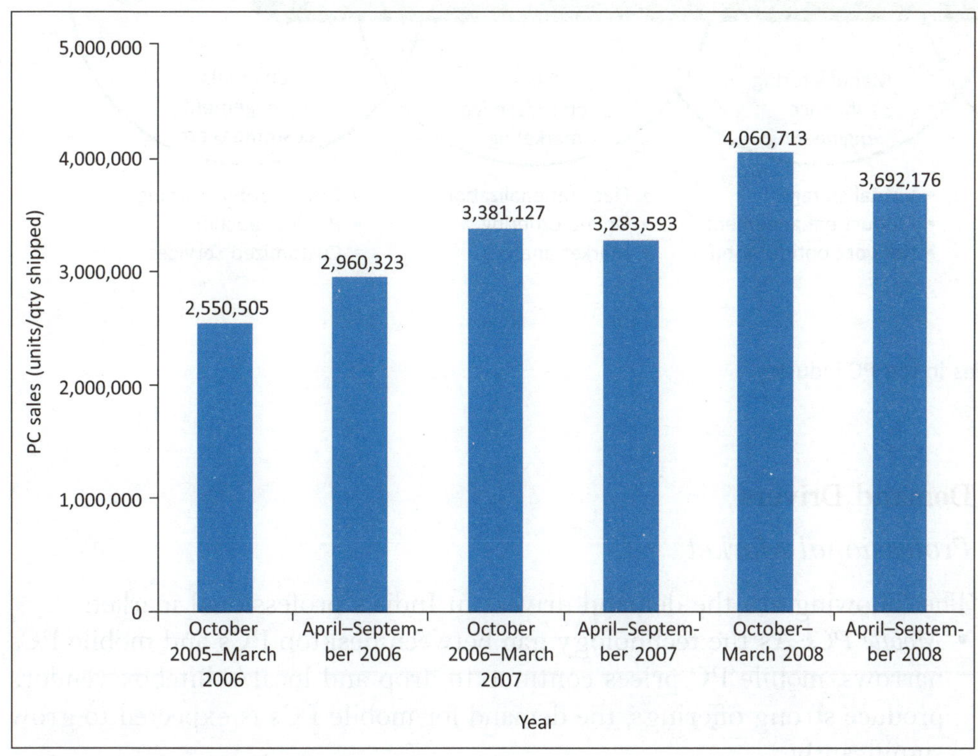

Figure 13.9: PC industry growth trends

In India, the majority of the PC sales take place in the metropolitan cities where the population of the technology-savvy working class is high. Going forward, small technology firms have to target these cities to form a strong base and slowly move towards capturing the tier II and other cities.

The Indian PC market has been the most important performer for many years. In 2002, the market grew by 12 per cent, putting India in fourth place in the Asia-Pacific market (excluding Japan) with a 9.5 per cent share, up from 5.2 per cent in 1998. Based on 2002 sales figures, 66 per cent of all PCs sold in India came from local vendors. This drops to 61 per cent in the professional market, but jumps to 79 per cent in the private market. In 2002, almost 98 per cent of all PCs shipped in India were desktops.

If we analyse growth, profit margins are tight and local competition is strong but India still appears to be a strong growth market. The true challenge for the company lies in making the business profitable. The professional market includes the government, educational institutions, large enterprises and the small and medium business (SMB) market. The private market includes the home and small office/home office (SOHO) markets.

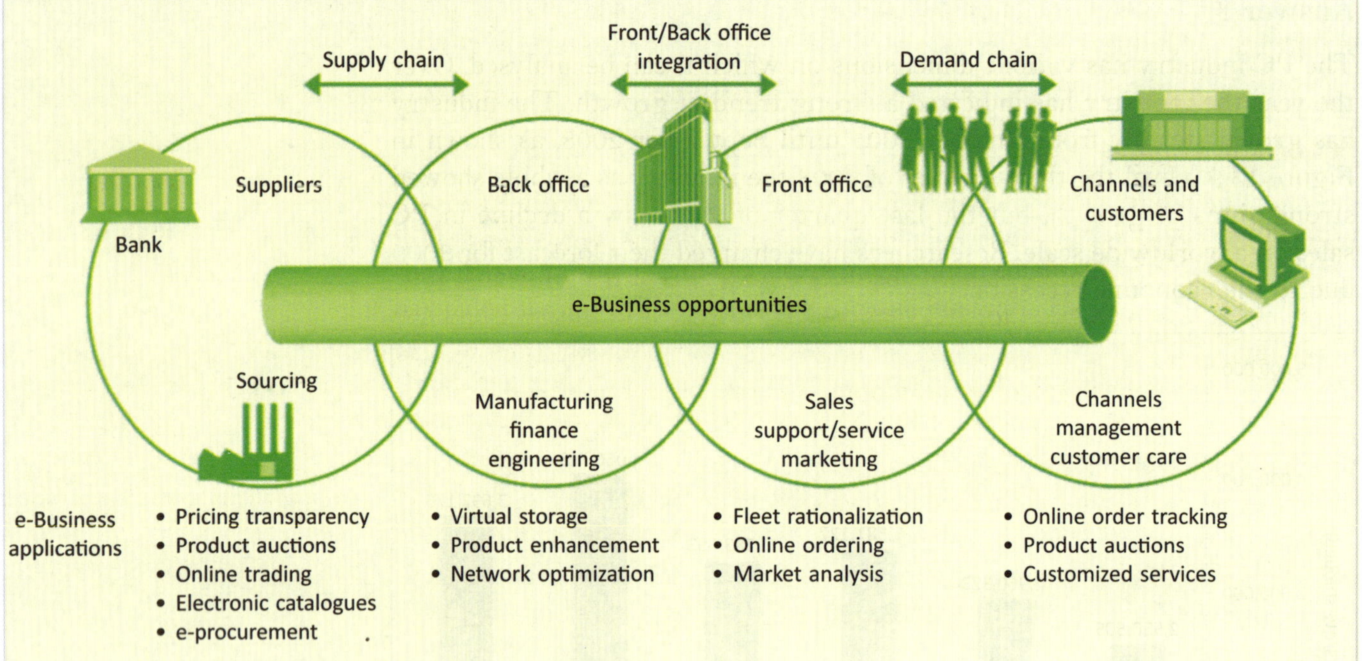

Figure 13.10: E-business opportunities in the PC industry

Sources: The Yankee Group; BA&H Analysis.

Demand Drivers

Professional Market

The following are the demand drivers in India's professional market:

- *Mobile PCs:* As the technology gap between desktop PCs and mobile PCs narrows, mobile PC prices continue to drop and local/whitebox vendors produce strong offerings, the demand for mobile PCs is expected to grow significantly.
- *Economic recovery:* Although not impacted as severely as other countries, India had its share of worries because of the global economic slowdown. Recent positive trends indicate that there is a potential for growth in the PC industry.
- *SMB growth:* As a significant number of Indians are employed in SMBs, any growth in this sector is likely to have a major effect on PC sales.

Private Market

The following are the demand drivers in India's private market:

- *Economic strength:* A fast growing middle-class and downward trend in prices are making it affordable for home users to buy PCs.
- *Education:* Students increasingly need to access a PC for their studies. Many middle-class families purchase desktops for their children to fulfil academic requirements; most of which will be first-time users.
- *Competition from local vendors:* The middle-class is drawn to these vendors because of the price and personalized services from the local vendors compared with the bigger branded players—trend that seems to continue. With service capabilities getting better, it will become more difficult

for branded vendors to compete with locals unless they augment their service capabilities to significantly differentiate themselves from the competition.

Economic Growth

Though India has a huge potential for the PC industry, it has to go a long way before becoming an economic powerhouse. Although its per capita GDP is low, India's large middle class in absolute numbers is still significant. This is a very important market for PC vendors because most in this section have never owned a PC. This middle class is growing very quickly. The Global Retail Development Index of 30 developing nations produced by AT Kearney placed India at no. 1 in growth rate. That, combined with the already impressive size of the middle class, suggests that this is a significant group of end users for vendors (particularly MNCs) to market to.

Profit margins are tight in India, and prices are low. Yet, this low margin can be adjusted by economies of scale production. Local vendors may have some cost advantages over the MNCs. Most MNCs are cash-rich and have financial support to fall back on—something local manufacturers lack. Therefore, they need to recognize these advantages and disadvantages and attribute budgets accordingly.

Target Markets

Vendors need to target SMBs strategically, because this segment will be the main business contributor in the near future. A look at the different market segments reveals that there is vast potential among the lower segment of small and medium business enterprises. This segment is fairly price-conscious, but also expects professional services from vendors. At this stage, vendors have been able to cater only to the top strata of the SMB segment. Lower down, it has been dominated by local assemblers. Vendors must target this layer with an apt price-service combination, keeping in mind the features that the end users actually require.

The education sector, i.e. secondary and higher education institutions, is slowly gaining momentum, with the government moving to computerize schools in the country. Vendors have an opportunity to drive this initiative through schools and make special offers. The offers could be easy financial terms, packaged educational software and higher-level courses. Local and multinational vendors may compete with the same offerings. Therefore, it is important to understand what extras one gives for the extra cost.

End users should work closely with their resellers to understand what they are offering and what they themselves need. Vendors should be flexible with their product offerings and those with the most flexible product development process should have an advantage. For many multinationals, this may mean creating a range of PCs specifically for the Indian market.

Market Maturity

As the Indian economy grows, FDI will increase, mobile PC prices will come down and local PC manufacturers and vendors will begin to produce good alternatives to the global vendors' laptops. Mobile PCs are forecast to grow at a rapid rate in India during 2010–11. Vendors must penetrate the professional market with strong branding messages, as well as very aggressive price points, because they are competing with other mobile PC vendors as well as with desktop vendors.

Unlike desktops, component-level repairs for mobile PCs are as yet unavailable in India. As more vendors start eyeing this market, service capabilities will also increase, thereby bringing the overall costs down. The improved offerings from local vendors will play a vital role in this growth.

Mature markets are moving toward a situation in which many homes will have two or more home PCs—a segment with huge potential in India. The Indian PC market is still immature and dominated by first-time PC buyers. Local and multinational vendors and resellers must respond to this growth and treat these new customers with respect and offer good value.

Word-of-mouth is very significant and will help vendors build brand image. It is typical for developing markets to tend toward the less-expensive local PCs, while mature markets are better aligned with large brands. Cost reduction and reducing redundancies will play a major role—meaning different strategies for different markets.

End users must make sure they get all they need from their vendor (not just from the chosen product) before signing a purchase order. A local vendor may actually be the best option for a small firm with only one location; however, a local vendor cannot meet the needs of a firm with multiple offices across the country. Overall, the future prospect for India is very positive indeed.

Answer 3

Porter's Five Forces Model

1. *Threat of New Entrants*

Leaders in the PC industry largely dominate the world market share, thereby constructing a barrier to the entry of smaller computer manufacturers. Every firm has strong brand names and the right mix of resources and capabilities. Small firms lack resources and the capability of acquiring enough capital to compete with the larger firms. The top five firms own 50.9 per cent of market share while the other 49.1 per cent is shared by smaller firms around the world. Any small firm with the right resources and capability may be able to achieve economies of scale given the openings of a foreign market.

- *Capital cost requirements of entry:* High cost of investment in technology makes it difficult for new, smaller players to enter this market.
- *Access to distribution channels:* The distribution channel for PCs in India is not well tuned to the needs of customers, especially the Home browsing PC segment. This poses another threat for new entrants.
- *Product differentiation:* The brand loyalty of established market leaders is a major barrier for new entrants who find it hard to overcome competition and gain recognition.

2. *Factors Influencing the Bargaining Power of Buyers*

Buyers can exert a certain level of influence in this industry. This is because:

- The penetration of PCs in the Home browsing segment has not been very significant.
- The concentration of buyers is still high.
- A majority of the customer segments in DTH is price sensitive.
- Switching to another product is not costly.

3. *Factors Influencing the Bargaining Power of Suppliers*

The bargaining power of suppliers such as Intel and Microsoft holds a significant amount of power in the industry. Dislocations with these suppliers would lead to an industry-wide disadvantage. Due to cut-throat competition leading to price wars, the price for computing power has decreased while the demand for computer hardware has increased. However, the pace of growth is expected to vary by segment. Product life cycles are short and to remain competitive, vendors must develop new products and services. Lower prices should continue to limit revenue growth for vendors. To become profitable, vendors must request lower costs from suppliers with a combination of efficient distribution channels.

4. *The Threat of Substitutes*

Substitutes can either entirely replace an existing product or introduce new technology to enhance or reduce product cost. In the case of the PC industry, the threat of substitutes is high due to the following reasons:

- *Threat of product obsolescence:* Being a dynamic product segment, the fast pace of technology advancement poses a threat of product obsolescence, thereby making it attractive for customers to switch to substitute products offered at a similar price range.
- *Ability of customers to switch:* With a vast availability of closely priced competitors, customers can easily switch, posing a high threat of substitutes.

5. *The Extent of Competitive Rivalry*

The high competitive rivalry for the PC industry can be attributed to the following factors:

- *Degree of concentration:* The number of competitors is large with almost similar offers. Though the market is dominated by established players, there is high competition amongst the leaders as well. Many of these competitors have deployed similar strategies.
- *The rate of industry growth:* The slow growth of the PC industry, especially in the Home browsing segment, under the present economic conditions leads to an intensification of competition.
- *The degree of differentiation:* Low differentiation can result in customers switching frequently.

- *High exit barriers:* Organizations find it costly to leave this industry due to which the excess capacity further increases competition as an increasing number of players fight just to stay on.

Answer 4

Political Factors

Policies of political parties: In the run-up to the 2009 elections, political parties focussed on the 'IT enabling the poor' agenda. An 'IT Vision Document' released by a mainstream political party just before general elections in 2008 proposed a Multipurpose National Identity Card (MNIC) with a unique Citizen Identification Number for every Indian citizen in three years.

Tariff policy: The 20-45 per cent tariffs on PC purchases in India are too high to support the sector's growth. If the import tariffs are not reviewed, major global manufacturers will be reluctant to devote their marketing and sales resources to the Indian market as there is already precious little money to be made on PCs.

Economic Factors

GDP growth rates and inflation: With the deceleration in GDP growth rate, i.e. after a three-year 9 per cent-plus growth rate, the Indian economy was estimated to grow at 7.1 per cent in 2008–9 and even an slower 7.5 per cent in 2009. This, along with inflation, hiked up PC prices. This ultimately led to a decrease in technology spending in both consumer and business segments. The demand for PCs by the home segment is primarily driven by the price factor.

Income distribution levels and bands: Figure 13.11 shows the segmentation of household PC users as per a study by MAIT. The study claims that the overall household market declined by 11 per cent but at the same time sales

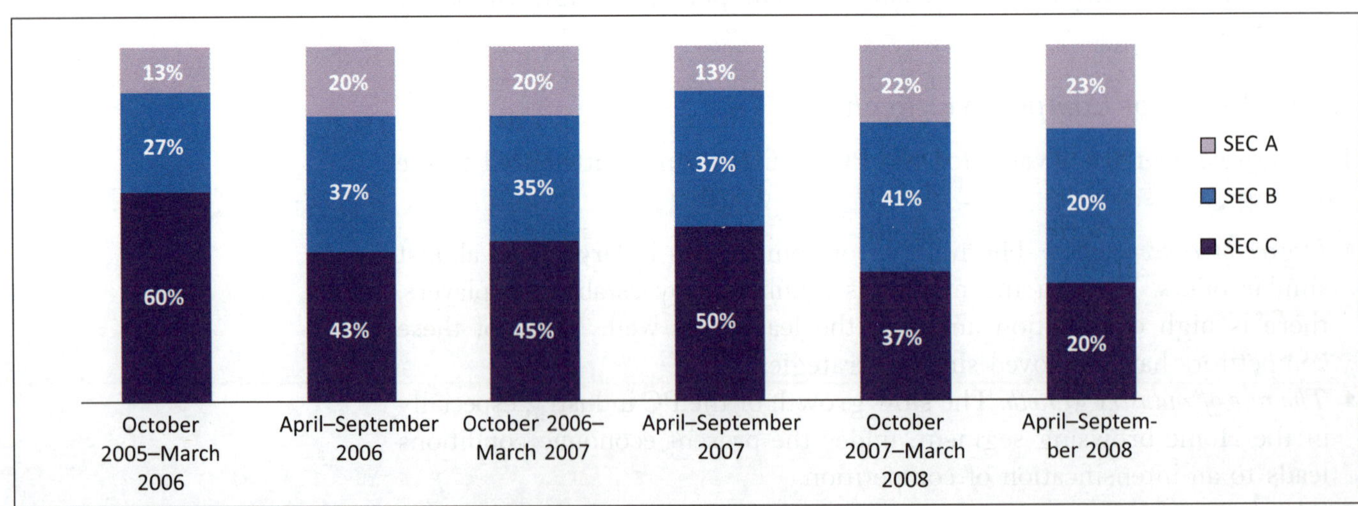

Figure 13.11: SEC profile of household desktop buyers

Source: MAIT IT industry performance, Mid-Year Review, 2008–9.

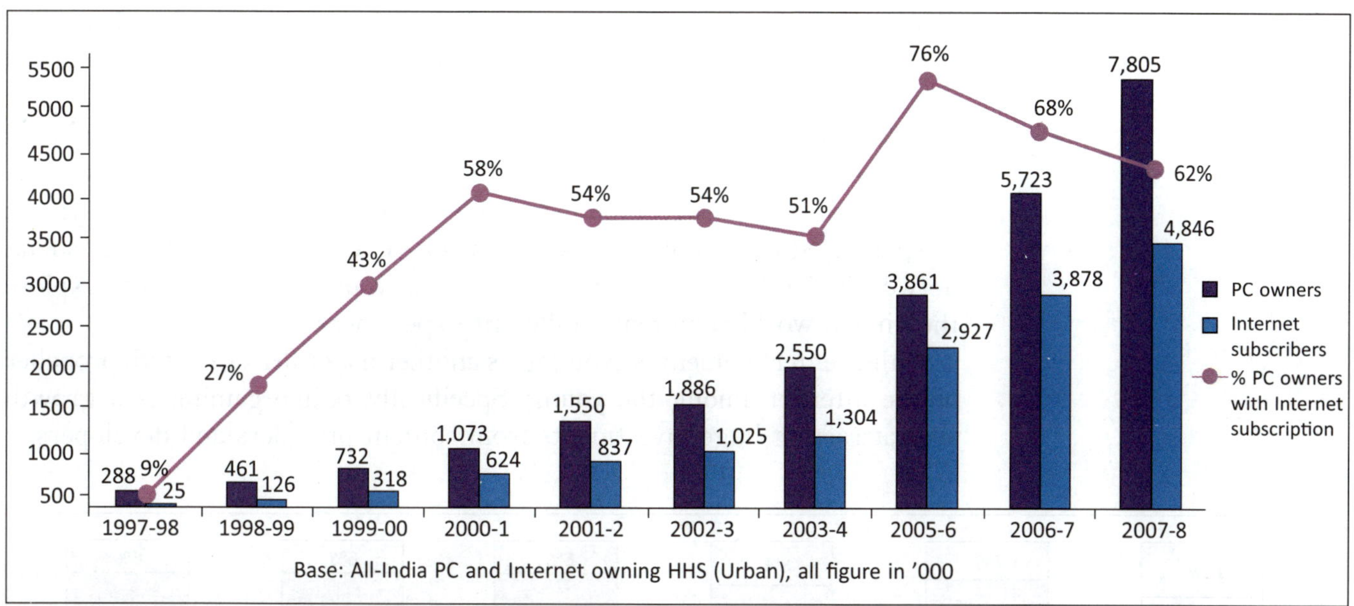

Figure 13.12: PC owners and internet subscription data

Source: eTech and IMRB study on internet usage growth in India.

to SEC B and SEC C of the household increased by 6 and 56 per cent, respectively. The SEC A sales however decreased by 42 per cent over household income/2007–8.

Interest rates and lending levels: In 2008, there was a 36 per cent growth in the number of PC owners. This is attributed to the fall in PC prices and the ease with which loans were sanctioned for the same. The fall in interest rate to 8.5 per cent also has a role to play in the growth of PC owners.

A 25 per cent increase in the number of internet subscribers was also been observed. This increase is in part due to the penetration of the internet into the less affluent classes of society and smaller towns.

Social Factors

Table 13.5 shows internet penetration by town, class and socio-economic classification. It indicates a clear market potential across the economic strata. Also, the metros have a high market share of internet users, giving ease for operation for existing players.

Table 13.5: Socio-economic distribution

Particulars	*Business segment (in %)*	*Home (in %)*
Overall	44	22
Top 4 metros	49	27
Next 4 metros	39	18
Other 8 metros	45	18
Remaining 6 metros	29	13
SEC A	–	46
SEC B	–	17
SEC C	–	6

Age demographics and usage: The adoption of new technologies and services is very high among the young; most of the content over the internet is focused on the 18-35 year-olds. A significant increase in the percentage of college-going students is seen in the Active Internet User base compared to the other demographic segments. Such an increase could be due to various information searches required for academic, entertainment or employment purposes. Sticky applications like user-generated content and social networking websites are attractions for the youth and helps them explore the virtual world comprising different experiences.

Online entertainment is evolving as another major driver growth propeller of the internet among the young. Specifically, online gaming is a growth area attracting huge investments from content providers and developers.

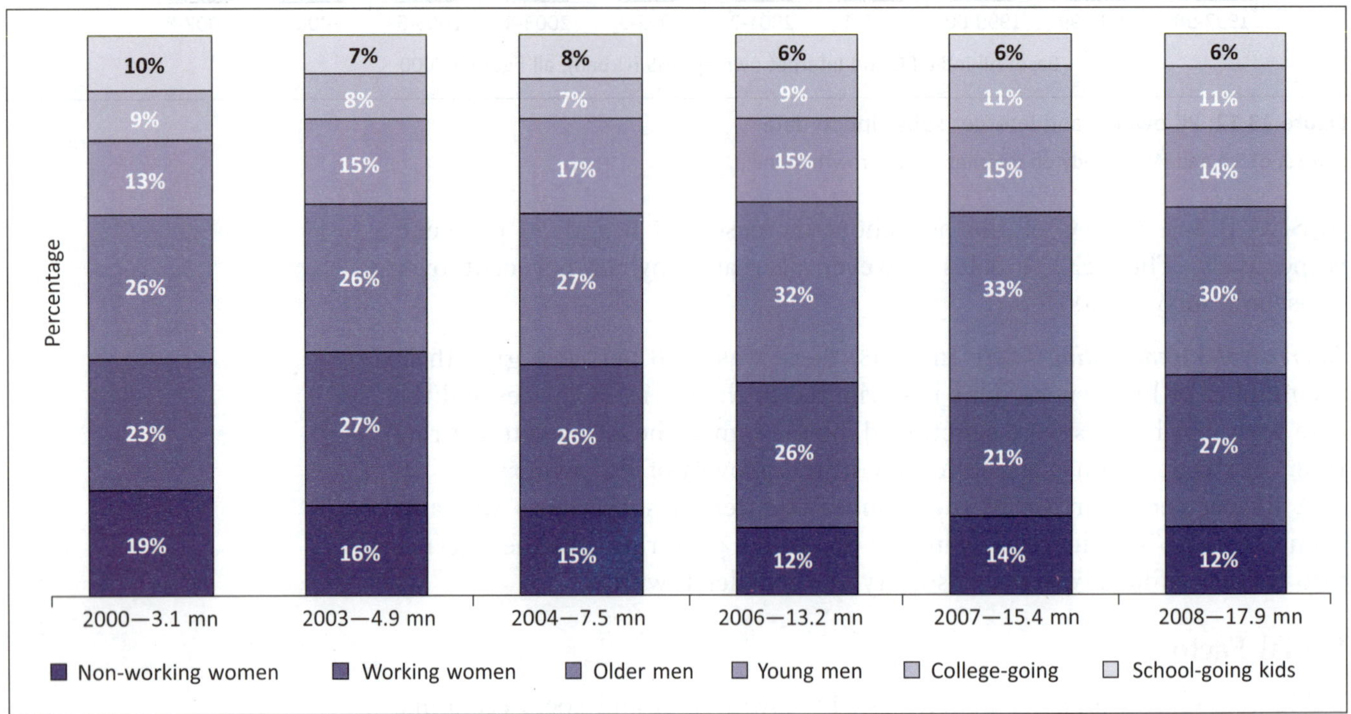

Figure 13.13: Demographic distribution

Source: eTech and IMRB study on internet usage growth in India and age distribution.

Base: Active Internet Users (Urban) (30 cities in 2007–8, 26 cities in 2006, 22 cities in 2004, 16 cities in 2000–3).

Technological Factors

Emerging technologies: Emerging technologies like WiMAX and 3G-enabled BWA (Broadband Wireless Access) at much higher speed, anywhere and anytime, with the main agenda of increasing internet penetration. These technologies also act as a platform for introducing high-end applications such as IPTV. BSNL has already chartered the introduction IPTV and in February 2009 launched the first Indian 3G service in Chennai. These technologies act as pivot factors in increasing the utility of the computer.

Preferences and offering improvements: Communication applications like email and online chat are the main purposes of accessing the internet for the young generation, followed by information search. Increase in the usage of internet also supports e-commerce applications like online bill payment, online ticket booking, and so on. These are gaining more popularity. As mentioned earlier, online entertainment (gaming, music and video downloads) is another key driver for the growth of the Internet in India. The 'India Gaming Summit', organized in 2008, witnessed the launch of the 'gaming revolution' in India and laid the foundation for developing a gaming ecosystem in the country.

BCG's Growth Share Matrix

This technique is particularly useful for multi-divisional or multi-product companies. The divisions or products compromise the organization's 'business portfolio'. The composition of the portfolio can be critical to the growth and success of the company.

The BCG Growth Share Matrix is divided into four cells or quadrants, each of which represents a particular type of business. As per the data on the average market share for a company dealing in the household PC segment, in the overall client PC (notebooks and desktops combined) market, HP retained the top spot with a market share of 19.7 per cent, followed by HCL at 9.8 per cent and Dell at 9.6 per cent in terms of unit shipments. Given the situation, the product line for a home PC seems to be set at the border of the cash cow quadrant. This is a critical stage and has the possibility of losing its present market share.

Cash Cows

These are characterized by high relative market share in low growth industries. As the market matures, the need for investment reduces. Cash cows are the most profitable products in the portfolio. The situation is frequently boosted by economies of scale that may be present with market leaders. Cash cows may be used to fund the businesses in the other three quadrants. It is desirable to maintain a strong position as long as possible and the strategic options include:

- Product development
- Concentric diversification

If the position weakens as a result of loss of market share or market contraction, then the options would include retrenchment (or even divestment).

Dogs

These describe businesses that have low market shares in slow growth markets. They may well have been cash cows. Often they enjoy misguided loyalty from the management, although some dogs can be revitalized. Profitability is, at best, marginal.

Strategic options would include:

- Retrenchment (if it is believed that it could be revitalized)
- Liquidation
- Divestment (if you can find someone to buy)

Successful products may well move from question mark though star to cash cow and finally to dog. Less successful products that never gain market position will move straight from question mark to dog. Companies looking to enter the market should focus on product development to suit the changing needs of the consumers.

Competitive Strategies

There is an increased awareness in India about the growing need of PCs in every sphere of life. India has become a global IT giant over the years and IT has touched millions of lives across the country. India has got a vast pool of human resources and consumer base for IT. There are people who are somewhat knowledgeable about computers and who may want to buy PCs for their personal or professional work. They are looking for a machine which is low on price, reliable and a little trendy, as keeping computers has become a sort of fashion. They require machines which can be easily operated (less complex) and are low on maintenance. The Indian middle class looks at buying a PC as a potential one-time investment, so the lesser the hassle of buying and operating the PC, better the machine.

Table 13.6: Segment-wise analysis

Segment	*Need*	*Requirement*
Children below 15 years	To get familiarized with computers, status, entertainment, information search, social networking	Low cost, trendy, potable, easy to operate, latest technology for gaming, etc.
Office-goers	Professional work, report generation, analysis, social networking, running heavy application	Reliability, quality, high end machines
Educated housewives	Social networking, bill payment, tracking bank balances, shopping through internet, i-Banking, information search	Low cost, trendy, easy to operate, don't require high technology
10+2/graduates	Career/job information, knowledge sharing, content building, social networking	Low cost, up-to-date machine, trendy, good service and maintenance

Woking on these lines, the company should position its product as a low-cost, reliable trendy machine for the Home browsing PC segment. It should also build good service centres to solve customers' servicing problems. The product should be positioned in such a way that the people are attracted to the looks of the machine and also don't see much complexity or hassle in operating and maintaining the machine in the long run.

Customers in the Home browsing segment are very price conscious, so it is important that the company projects itself as a low-cost leader for the quality of goods delivered. Also, as the middle class in India becomes richer, the machine has to keep up with the changing designs and trends in the industry. Therefore, the e-position strategy of the company should to position its PCs as fashionable, low-cost, reliable, intelligent machines which understand the needs of the contemporary middle class.

PC Market Growth during Economic Turbulence

Understanding how to make profit during market turbulence is the key for vendors and resellers, while end users need to make sure they are getting what they actually need. The business scenario has changed after the financial turmoil and this, in turn—directly or indirectly—has affected the PC market in India. Following roughly six years of growth, with the last five averaging 15 per cent increases, the worldwide PC shipments were down 0.4 per cent y-o-y in the fourth quarter of 2008 (IDC's Worldwide Quarterly PC Tracker). The dramatic slowdown was enough for a sequential decline of 2.5 per cent from the third quarter, in place of an expected increase during the holiday season.

According to Gartner Inc., the worldwide PC industry experienced its sharpest shipment decline in history in 2009 as the global economy continued to deteriorate. PC shipments declined 11.9 per cent to 257 million units in 2009. Until now, the worst decline in PC shipments was in 2001, the height of the tech-bust-fuelled recession. That year, unit shipments contracted 3.2 per cent, according to Gartner. Mobile PC sales grew to 155.6 million units in 2009 (up 9 per cent y-o-y), while desktop PC shipments fell 31.9 per cent in 2009 from 2008 figures. Emerging markets contracted 10.4 per cent in 2009, while mature markets were down by 13 per cent. Growth in both emerging and mature markets was driven by similar dynamics even if the precise impacts vary somewhat during 2010–11. HP, the world's biggest PC maker, cut its 2010 profit outlook, with the economic turmoil hurting nearly all of its businesses. It also reported a 13 per cent drop in its fiscal first-quarter profit in 2009. Dell, the No. 2 PC maker, posted a 48 per cent decline in its fourth-quarter earnings of 2008. Gartner anticipated both emerging and mature markets to suffer 'unprecedented' slowdowns in 2009. The impact of reduced replacements will be especially acute in mature markets, where

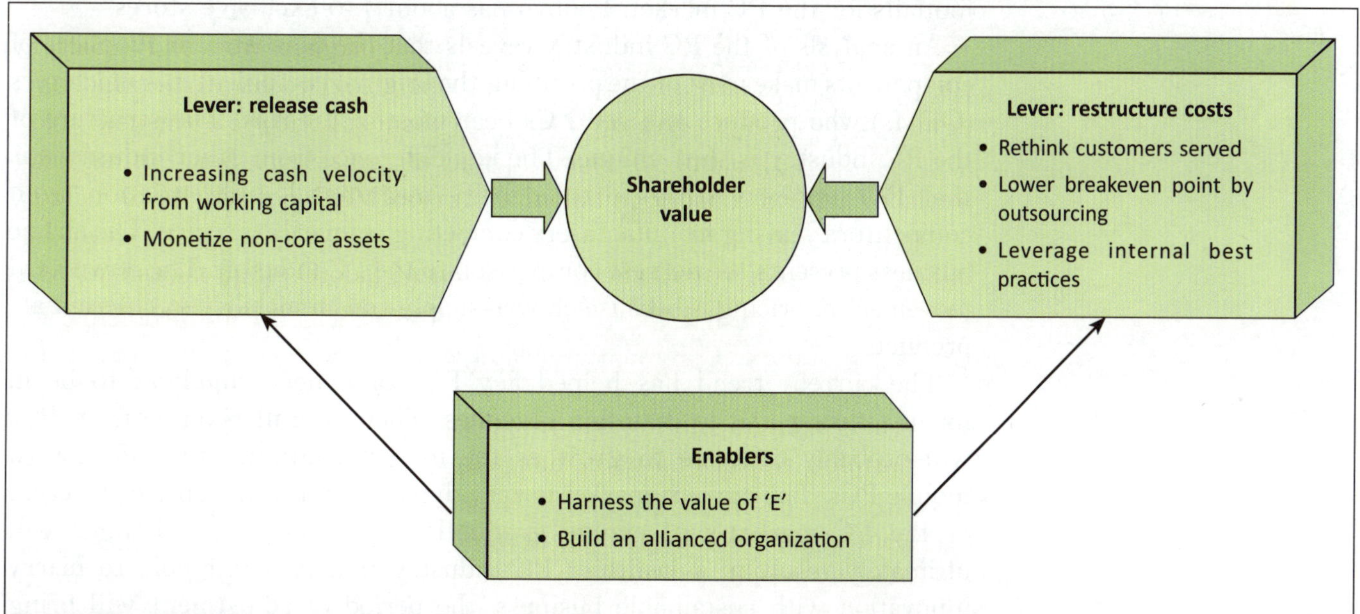

Figure 13.15: Profiting from a recession in the PC industry

Source: Booz-Allen & Hamilton.

replacements are estimated to account for around 80 per cent of shipments. Mobile PC shipments are expected to grow, boosted by growing demand for Mini-Notebooks—low-cost, low-power computers.

The Indian PC market is growing because of its increasingly affluent middle class. The industry has witnessed significant growth in recent years due to several factors, such as retail boom, growing disposable income and availability of easy finance schemes. But the penetration level of the PC market is still very low compared to other developed countries; this represents a huge potential base for PC. We need an insight into the future trend in all the categories and the key strategies that need to be worked upon to succeed in this highly competitive industry.

Some key research findings on the Indian consumer electronic industry are as follows:

(a) Propelled by a growing middle class population, changing lifestyle and rapid urbanization, the Indian consumer electronics industry is forecasted to grow at a rapid rate 10 to 12 per cent in the coming few years.
(b) The low penetration of consumer electronics goods coupled with increasing preference for luxurious goods is widely attracting foreign as well as domestic players to the industry.

The Way Forward for Indian PC Makers

The consumer PC market grew 23 per cent y-o-y in 2007, compared with 19 per cent for the commercial PC market (IDC India report). PC notebook has registered a higher sales of ₹95,770 million and desktop PC clicked ₹112,670 million from ₹58,860 million and ₹103,250 million respectively in 2009 and 2010. In 2010, 55.25 lakh desktop PCs and 25.08 lakh notebook PCs sold in India. Large electronics retail stores such as Croma, Next, and E-Zone are gradually becoming the preferred destination and driving large footfalls for the PC market. Lenovo has about 140 exclusive stores.

An analysis of the PC industry reveals that the downstream suppliers of components make most of the profit but the original equipment manufacturers (OEMs) who produce and sell PCs bear most of the risk. The structure of the PC industry is thus unique. The key difference from other industries is that PC suppliers struggle to identify meaningful differentiation from competitors, leaving manufacturers competing primarily on price. The airline business presents the nearest comparison to the PC industry. The downward movement of pricing is because of over-supply and an inability to differentiate products.

The current trend has helped key PC component suppliers to be in manufacturing and to maintain revenues. Their overall revenue from PCs will probably continue to grow as the market continues to shift toward mobile PCs. The current market is very dynamic and so the entire structure of the PC market will evolve gradually. Although these changes will ultimately result in a healthier PC industry that is better able to marry innovation with sustainable business, the period of adjustment will bring additional challenges to both the buyers and users. Choice of supplier and continuity of supply will be less certain, while the adoption of emerging PC technologies will present additional risk.

Appendix

India's Top 20 Cities Account for One-third of Disposable Income

Roopa Purushothaman and Rajesh Shukla, the celebrated co-authors of Goldman Sachs' famous BRIC report, which in 2003 had predicted that by 2050 Brazil, Russia, India, and China put together will have larger economies in US$ terms than the G6, consisting of the US, Germany, Japan, the UK, France and Italy, have collaborated again to come out with a joint study entitled 'The Next Urban Frontier: Twenty Cities To Watch'. The study has identified 20 top Indian cities, which though accounting for only 10 per cent of the country's population, generate as much as 60 per cent of its surplus income and 31 per cent of its disposable income. The authors have classified these 20 large cities, which accounted for nearly $100-billion of consumption expenditure in 2007–8, into three groups: Mega Cities (8), Boom Towns (7), and Niche Cities (5).

The eight Mega Cities that apart from a large population also have large consumer markets are Mumbai, Delhi, Kolkata, Chennai, Bengaluru, Hyderabad, Ahmedabad and Pune. The seven Boom Towns that have big population and high expenditure per household are Surat, Kanpur, Jaipur, Lucknow, Nagpur, Bhopal and Coimbatore. The five Niche Cities that are relatively smaller in population but have above national-average household spend are Faridabad, Amritsar, Ludhiana, Chandigarh and Jalandhar.

According to the report, these 20 cities will grow at a healthy rate of 10.1 per cent per annum for the next eight years (2008–16) compared to other cities growing at 7.9 per cent per annum, the impending economic slowdown notwithstanding. In the past during 2005–8, the top 20 cities had registered a growth of 11.2 per cent per annum.

The increase in income levels will also have a direct impact on the income profiles of households. In the next eight years since 2008 (by 2016), while the share of the middle-income households ($6,000 to $30,000 per annum) in these 20 cities will increase from the current 39 to 55 per cent, the share of high-income households (more than $30,000 per annum) will increase threefold to 13 per cent. The share of very low-income households (below $3,000 per annum), not surprisingly, would come down by half from the present 16 per cent to 7 per cent by 2016.

The changing household demographics will no doubt bring about a major shift in the demand pattern of different classes of goods. According to the study, there is a 52 per cent increase in spending as households graduate from the low-income to the middle-class segment. The demand for durables, for example, may go up by a substantial 84 per cent, says the study. The report has also predicted that even on a conservative basis, in the next 40-odd years, by 2050, the share of the urban population in India will almost become equal (45 per cent) to that of the rural population (55 per cent). Currently, the ratio is 30 : 70 in favour of the rural population. This rapid urbanization will mean an additional 379 million people in urban India. Interestingly, this would mean adding more than the entire current population of the US to urban India.

Sources: The Economic Times, January to August 2008; indiatimes.com; rediffmail.com; *Business Standard*, April to August 2008.

Recommendations

- The PC industry should concentrate on mobile PC growth along with gaming which is not completely developed to its potential.
- The industry must realize that although India offers strong volume growth rates, the individual players must hit aggressive price points, while also considering what is included in the price and what end users actually want.
- Global companies should consider creating India-specific product lines to take the large local companies head-on. They should concentrate on achieving better service capabilities as that will be a differentiating factor.
- India's vast geography makes it difficult and time consuming for new entrants to establish an identity. Therefore, coming in at the last minute will not work.

References

1. IDC 2008, 2009, 2010 (Performance Report).
2. Gartner Inc. report, 2009, 2010.
3. e-data global: Forrester research report, 2010.
4. IDC Worldwide Quarterly PC Tracker, December 2008, 2009, 2010.
5. The Yankee Group; BA&H Analysis, 2010
6. MAIT IT Industry Performance Mid-Year Review 2008–9, 2009–10.
7. eTech and IMRB study on internet usage growth in India, 2009.
8. CGSStrategines.com

CHAPTER 14  NOKIA CONNECTS THE WORLD

applied case study 6

We must adjust our resources to reflect reduced market demand in order to also maintain our competitiveness in the future. — PETER ROEPKE, senior vice-president Devices Research and Development, Nokia, Helsinki

14.1 Background

Nokia has lost over 20 per cent in the handset market in India since 2007. It is now betting big on new applications and services, on new models and personalized services to stay in the top place. The first GSM handset manufacturing company to make a move to thrill customers with latest applications and contents.

Nokia has selected 300 pilot stores as Nokia Solution Providers (NSP). Nokia has provided each NSP with a laptop, Bose Companion 2 speakers, a high-end noise-cancelling JBt headphone, three of the latest Nokia smartphones, a modern counter, complete with hi-speed broadband connection, Wi-Fi router and a trained executive. NSPs are crucial links in the experiment of the world's largest handset maker and the €50-billion Nokia Corporation, to generate new revenue streams and fend off half a dozen rivals, who are nibbling market share from practically every segment. Nokia hopes the NSPs will eventually sell customers music downloads, latest games and new applications (apps), besides hooking the customer with freebies such as email, calendar and contacts sync. Its NSPs are its first brush with an offline, physical infrastructure to build a brand new monetizable services ecosystem around its handsets.

Nokia's rival Apple Inc. has paved the way, clocking $4.05 billion in 2008 through online content and services. But Nokia is trying to leverage its distribution with physical touchpoints. NSPs' success or failure will reverberate at Nokia's Helsinki headquarters and will determine whether these can be rolled out in other parts of the world such as China, the Middle East and Africa, where handsets sell independent of mobile connections. 'We need to sell a lot more apps and solutions from our retail points so that consumers can experience and sideload it. We will have to move from a physical business model to a combination of physical and virtual business model,' says D. Shivakumar, Nokia India's vice-president and managing director.

Nokia's market share in India has been sliding since 2007; 72 per cent in 2007, it was 53 per cent in 2008 and 49 per cent in 2009. Its rival Samsung has made inroads into Nokia's dominance; touching 7.6 per cent in 2009 from 6.4 per cent in 2007. Further, LG has made a substantial comeback in the Indian market by cornering a market share of 6.9 per cent in 2009 from 2.3 per cent in 2007. Is Nokia's dominance over?

Few companies can match Nokia's ingenuity. It was founded in 1865 as a wood pulp and paper making unit; made a successful transition to electric cables, footwear, tyres, industrial rubber and raincoats in the 1920s; it entered computers and the electronics business in the 1960s; by the 1970s it was manufacturing digital telecom switches; by the 1980s it was into mobile car phones and televisions; and by early 1990s, it had shed all its earlier businesses to concentrate on cellphone and telecom equipment. Now, Nokia has to leverage every bit of its gene pool to make that next transition to services, tools and apps.

14.1.1 Nokia's India Story

When mobile phones were first introduced in India in the mid-1990s, US-based Motorola, Sweden's Ericsson and Finland's Nokia dominated the handset market. Over the years, Asian players like Samsung and LG and European players Philips and Siemens entered the highly lucrative Indian mobile market. However, Nokia managed to surge ahead of all other players to become the dominant mobile handset brand in India with 65 per cent market share.

India's mobile market is growing at lightning fast pace at the rate of over two million mobiles a month. In an intensely competitive market Nokia has to constantly revise its strategy and face stiff competition from cheaper handset makers like Samsung and LG. Also, while Nokia has concentrated on generic designs and models, competitors like Ericsson, Motorola and Samsung have posed a threat to Nokia's dominance because of their innovative designs and technologically advanced phones. Nokia, in an attempt to take over its competitors, has, after extensive market research, segmented the Indian mobile consumers into distinct consumer groups. Based on this segmentation, Nokia has introduced phones at all price points, from cheap entry-level handsets to the mid-market camera phones to high-end exclusive phones like the N- and the E-series. Nokia today has a substantial share of both ends of the market. It has 77 per cent of the ₹2,000–₹4,000 phone market and about 55 per cent of the over ₹15,000 phone market in early 2008.

The N-series from Nokia offered stylish 'multimedia phones' targeted at the young, affluent and the techno-savvy. These phones come

BOX 14.1: NOKIA'S ACHIEVEMENTS

- Ranked fourth in the Most Trusted Brand Survey by *Brand Equity* in 2007.
- Ranked the leading MNC in India by *Business World*, India's leading business weekly, in 2007.
- Ranked No. 1 in the durables segment for the second consecutive year by *Business World* in its annual survey of Most Respected Companies in India, 2006.
- Ranked Asia's most trusted brand in 2006 by the Media-Synovate survey. The survey was aimed at gauging Asia's top 1,000 brands across 15 product and service categories.
- Nokia India has been ranked as the overall No. 1 telecommunications equipment vendor (including wireless infrastructure) in the country by *Voice & Data* for four consecutive years (2004–7).
- Named 'Brand of the Year' at the Confederation of Indian Industry (CII) Brand Summit held in Chennai in 2005.
- Won the Golden Peacock Award 2004 for the Nokia 1100, which was selected as the most innovative product in the telecom segment.
- In October 2004 and again in 2006, Nokia India was recognized as the Most Respected Company in the Indian consumer durables sector in an *Economic Times-Brand Equity* annual survey.

with some of the best features that ensure a world of information, entertainment and connectivity. All the models in this series boast of high megapixel cameras digital music players, Bluetooth, and 3G support with streaming video. Nokia aggressively promoted the N-series phones through advertising, celebrity (Shahrukh Khan) endorsements, sales promotion schemes such as 'Soul of the Night' contest and 'World Press Photo' contests. It also opened concept stores which feature the full range of Nokia products including handsets, accessories, ring tones, graphics, games and software.

Figure 14.1: Nokia store

Nokia's distribution strategy ensured that it made a presence in 2,000 cities and towns that have cellular coverage. Its network of over 35,000 outlets is roughly double that of its competitors. The result? The company registered a spectacular turnover/net sales of €50.70 million and held a global share of 39 per cent in the GSM handset market (as in 2008).

However, projections for 2009–11 worried the company. Nokia found it difficult to maintain leadership even though one out of three GSM handsets used in the world is that of Nokia!

14.2 Managing Market Turbulence

In 2008, Nokia's global handset sales fell 14.2 per cent while the recession-hit market shrank 6.5 per cent. As a result, its profits fell 40 per cent to €4.97 billion. In the first quarter of 2009, Nokia saw a 90 per cent profit erosion, citing an 'exceptionally tough environment'. Earlier, it had predicted that the industry's handset volumes in 2009 might fall for the first time in two decades by 10 per cent from the 2008 level of 1.22 billion. Goldman Sachs projected that Nokia's share of the top-end smartphones costing $350 and more could shrink to 13 per cent in 2011 as against 33 per cent in 2007, largely because its average product price witnessed a steeper fall (from €79 in first quarter of 2008 to €65 in first quarter of 2009) than its rivals'.

According to Gartner, Nokia still has a dominant 45.2 per cent share in the global smartphone market in the first quarter of 2008. But in the US, where 50 per cent of the world's smartphones are sold, Nokia lags behind BlackBerry and Apple. Clearly, there is a lot at stake for Nokia in the NSPs, which will define its strategy in China and India which together account for nearly one-third of its handset revenues.

Nokia's traditional markets abound with bad news. In November 2008, it withdrew all its products (except Vertu) from Japan, the world's fourth-largest market, after years of struggle to penetrate the country. Its last reported share was less than 1 per cent in that market.

However, India has been an unexpected success story for Nokia. The Finnish vendor registered a huge 140 per cent growth in its business in

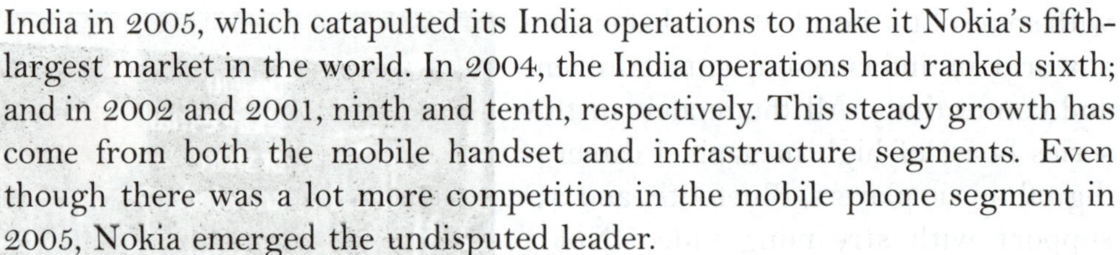

India in 2005, which catapulted its India operations to make it Nokia's fifth-largest market in the world. In 2004, the India operations had ranked sixth; and in 2002 and 2001, ninth and tenth, respectively. This steady growth has come from both the mobile handset and infrastructure segments. Even though there was a lot more competition in the mobile phone segment in 2005, Nokia emerged the undisputed leader.

Besides its wide range of phones and the widespread business infrastructure that it has in India, Nokia's deepening commitment to the Indian market has aided its growth in the mobile phone business. Its growing faith in and commitment to India is reflected not just in its India-centric product strategies and marketing campaigns but also in its plans to invest in the manufacturing of handsets as well as infrastructure space.

In many ways, Nokia's success in India is a manifestation of the success of the telecom sector in the country. The vendor has been a key beneficiary of the tremendous growth that the mobile subscriber base has witnessed in the past few years and the huge investments that operators have made in expanding their networks. Nokia India's revenue in financial year 2007–8 was ₹1,56,609.380 million as against ₹57,521.765 million in 2005–6. However the company has often been clueless when faced with a global recession and the parent company showed a dip in sales of €0.348 billion in 2008.

Table 14.1: Nokia losing its grip

Brand	*Indian market (%)*			*Global market (%)*		
	2007	*2008*	*2009(Q1)*	*2007*	*2008*	*2009(Q1)*
Nokia	72.2	53.9	49.7	37.8	38.6	36.5
Samsung	6.4	6.7	7.6	13.4	16.3	19.2
LG	2.3	7.6	6.9	6.8	8.4	10.3
Motorola	7.3	3.1	0.9	14.3	8.7	5.9
Sony Ericsson	8.1	2.3	1.6	8.8	7.6	5.05

An apps and solutions ecosystem is vital for parent Nokia Corporation to morph into a 360-degree mobile company. According to Olli-Pekka Kallasvuo, CEO, Nokia Corporation, 'Wow (factor) more and more will come from tight integration of service. Hardware alone won't be enough.' Incidentally, this is the view that Apple also champions, and other smartphone makers are following.

Nokia's network equipment business Nokia Siemens Networks is incurring losses and the handset business is also under intense pressure. Its global market share has shrunk from 38.6 per cent in 2008 to 36.5 per cent in the first half of 2009, according to research firm Gartner. But Kallasvuo insists Nokia's share has fluctuated in the range of 34-40 per cent since 2004. 'This has been our normal level,' he says.

14.2.1 Slash Workforce

Faced with a slump in business due to the global financial turmoil, Nokia made 3,500 job cuts in early 2009, as part of its cost saving efforts. In a statement it affirmed its reorganizing efforts would globally affect nearly

170 employees working in logistics, production management and production support in India. The plans were not affect production employees at Nokia's mobile device manufacturing facilities. The company has about 10,000 employees, including nearly 8,000 workers at its manufacturing plant in Chennai. Meanwhile, the company would offer a voluntary resignation package for 320 employees at its mobile device manufacturing facility in Salo, Finland. In February 2009, Nokia had given the package to 1,000 employees. These measures are part of previously announced plans to adjust business operations and cost base in accordance with market demand to safeguard future competitiveness.

In order to make the organization more meaningful, Nokia slashed its global workforce again by another 490 jobs in mid-2009, with as many as 170 positions being axed in logistics, production management and production support areas in India. It is estimated that 31 per cent of the workforce is in Research & Development.

Domestic demand for goods and services in the country is likely to increase in financial year 2011 on account of a possible decline in commodity prices globally and reduction in the prices of branded goods following excise cuts in India. This will help augment demand in 2009–10.

14.2.2 Competence Over Innovation

For a while analysts have been attributing the erosion in Nokia's market share to its inability to produce a 'Wow' product any more. From a highly innovative company that beat cellphone inventor Motorola, Nokia grew to an enormous size, making four out of every 10 cellphones on the planet. But that size became as much its weakness as it was its strength. Like a charging elephant that takes time to turn around, Nokia in 2010 is a competent manufacturer, a dexterous marketer and a nimble distributor, but it isn't the most innovative. All through the 2000s, it has been playing catch-up with

BOX 14.2: HI-TECH HANDSETS RING IN CHEER FOR NOKIA AMIDST BLUES

When Nokia launched its touch screen gizmo, 5800 XpressMusic in January 2009, the Indian cell phone industry was all ears. The industry was in a daze since Nokia had dared to launch the phone at just a shade below ₹20,000, when the industry was experiencing flat sales growth in the aftermath of the meltdown. But believe it or not, Nokia's channel partners claim the handset has created a new sales record in India with over 58,000 units being sold within three weeks of its launch. 'This testifies Indian consumers value innovation even when the economy slows down,' said a Nokia India spokeswoman.

At a time when consumer demand is at an all-time low, handset makers are witnessing a new category of phones coming up trumps, be it Nokia's 5800 or the N96, Samsung's Omnia or Innov8, HTC's Touch HD or Sony Ericsson's Xperia. These hybrid devices, with the best of business and multimedia capabilities, are typically priced upwards of ₹20,000.

Spurred by the success, the vendors are fondly referring to this category as super-phones, high-definition handsets or converged devices. Business and multimedia phones are truly converging into these super-phones. These handsets started hitting the Indian market in October 2008 and estimates suggest some 50,000 such units were sold until December 2008, a growth rate upwards of 100 per cent.

The converged devices are positioned as lifestyle products rather than as smart phones. Nokia is finding a niche segment of consumers making up this market. They are mostly technology enthusiasts or high-net-worth individuals (HNIs). These handsets also have much higher margins and push up the average selling price.

Nokia successfully pre-marketed the N97 before its launch in June 2009. According to company sources, the mobile phone has truly emerged as a utility device, and more so for these convergence handsets.

rivals on new technologies, software and form factors. Take, for instance, touch screens. The world's first touch screen phone Simon was launched by IBM in 1993, Nokia launched it only in 2003. Nokia is also among the last to offer online content. Its own music, games and apps store Ovi.com was launched in 2007, much later than Apple, which introduced the Apple Store in 2003. Even the tilting slider form factor that defines Nokia's N97 is similar to T-Mobile-HTC's G1 (the world's first phone with Google's Android OS) and AT&T and HTC's Pro.

All this is in stark contrast with the 1990s when Nokia 2100 was the first phone ever to feature a tune. In 1997, the Nokia 6110 was the first phone to feature a game, Snake. In 1999, the Nokia 7110 was the first WAP phone, bringing the internet to the cellphone. These innovations rocketed Nokia to the No. 1 status in 1998 from where nobody has been able to unsettle it yet. But now its market share, revenues and profits are all under tremendous pressure (Table 14.2).

Table 14.2: Rivals beat Nokia on innovations

Features/Type	*Pioneers*	*Nokia's move*
Touch screen	IBM Simon (1993)	Nokia 6108 (2003)
Clam Shell	Motorola Star Tac (1996)	Nokia 282 (1998)
Enterprise phone	Nokia 9000 (1997)	N.A.
3G phone	Panasonic Foma (2001)	Nokia 6650 (2002)
Flat keypad	Nokia 6200 (2002)	N.A.
Camera phone	Nokia 7650 (2002)	N.A.
Music phone	Sony Ericsson W800 (2004)	Nokia 7710 (2005)
Android phone	T-Mobile G1 (2008)	Does not have

14.2.3 Tapping Rural Customers

Rural India has seen four consecutive years of agricultural growth and hike in minimum support prices of many agro-commodities. In addition, sale of farmlands for industrial purposes has put more disposable income in the hands of farmers. Nokia India is hoping for a better outcome during financial year 2011.

14.2.4 Better Product and Service

Gearing up to meet the challenges of 3G, Nokia, announced a slew of new services like online music and location-based services to be made available on its new phones. 3G mobile services began in the middle of 2009 and the company projected that revenue from non-voice services would increase significantly. In fact, Nokia called upon Indian mobile and web application developers to create innovative consumer applications exclusively for the N97. This new way of establishing business partnerships with the world's best developers during the global economic meltdown was a welcome sign. However, a genuine doubt is cast on Nokia's supremacy. Is it losing business or market share globally?

14.3 Story Board

Nokia is the world leader in mobility, driving the transformation and growth of the converging Internet and communications industries. It makes a wide range of mobile devices and provides people with experiences in music, navigation, video, television, imaging, games and business mobility through its devices. It also provides equipment, solutions and services for communications networks.

Nokia India is a registered private limited company with a line of business including mobile phones, multimedia, enterprise solutions and networks and MIRA rating of AA which means the company possesses adequate working capital. No caution is needed for credit transaction and the company has above-average (strong) capability for payment of interest and principal sums.

14.3.1 Subsidiaries

Nokia's holding company is Nokia Corporation, Finland with subsidiary companies Nokia Network, Brazil; Nokia (Hong Kong) Limited; Nokia (Thailand) Limited; Nokia Inc. USA; Nokia TMC Limited, Korea; Nokia UK Limited; Nokia Australia Pty. Limited; Nokia Gmbh, Germany; Israel Communication Limited, Israel; Nokia Italia S.P.A. Italy; Nokia Japan Company Limited, Japan; Nokia Pte. Limited, Singapore; Nokia Kounikasyon Limited; Nokia Taiwan Company Limited, Taiwan; Nokia Devenezuela C.A. Nokia Mobil Phone, Australia; Nokia (Philippines) Inc., Philippines; Nokia Indonesia; Nokia Denmark A/s; Nokia Poland Ps Zoo; Nokia (China) Investment Company Limited; and Nokia Spain S.A.U.

Nokia's telecom factory is based at Sipcot Industrial Park in Chennai, Tamil Nadu. Its registered office is in New Delhi with branches in Hyderabad, Ahmedabad, Mumbai and Bengaluru.

14.3.2 Transforming Nokia into a World Leader

Nokia Corporation was established as a corporation under the laws of the Republic of Finland. This was the result of the merger of three Finnish companies: Nokia, a wood-pulp mill founded in 1865; Finnish Rubber Works, a manufacturer of rubber boots, tyres and other rubber products founded in 1898; and Finnish Cable Works, a manufacturer of telephone and power cables founded in 1912. Nokia entered the telecommunications equipment market in 1960, when an electronics department was established at Finnish Cable Works to concentrate on the production of radio transmission equipment. Deregulation of the European telecommunications industry in the late 1980s stimulated competition and boosted customer demand.

The group introduced the first fully digital local telephone exchange in Europe in 1982. The same year, Nokia introduced the world's first car phone for the Nordic Mobile Telephone analogue standard. Nokia was soon listed on the major stock exchanges like London in 1987 and Frankfurt in 1988.

According to Nokia, the first GSM call was made with a Nokia phone over the Nokia-built network of a Finnish operator called Radiolinja in 1991.

In the same year, Nokia won contracts to supply GSM networks in other European countries. During the early 1990s, the group made a strategic decision to make telecommunications as core business and divested basic businesses from 1989 to 1996 to form two main business groups: Nokia mobile phones and Nokia networks. Nokia was listed on New York Stock Exchange in 1994. During the same year, it launched mobile phones for all major digital systems: GSM, GSM 1800 (PCN), TDMA and Japan Digital. The company added CDMA and GSM 1900 mobile phones in 1997. Two years later, it launched the first WAP handset to the global mass market with the Nokia 7110. It acquired DiscoveryCom, a provider of broadband digital subscriber line (DSL) services in 2000. In the following year, the company acquired Ramp Networks, a US-based provider of purpose-built internet security appliances specifically designed for small office applications. Later in the year, it acquired Amber Networks, a US-based networking infrastructure company that developed fault tolerant routing platforms. Also in 2001, Nokia and Sony collaborated to develop an open middleware platform.

During 2002, Nokia acquired a stake in Redback Networks, a US-based provider of subscriber management and optical platforms that enable carriers and service providers to construct next-generation broadband networks. Nokia unveiled the world's first TDMA handset with a full-colour display in 2003. The company also reached an agreement with IBM to collaborate on the delivery of enterprise wireless e-business solutions. In the same year, Nokia was de-listed from the London Stock Exchange.

In 2004, Nokia took control of Symbian, a developer of operating systems for smart-phones. Nokia increased its shareholding in Symbian to 63 per cent after paying Psion approximately £130 million for its stake. During the same year, Nokia's shares were de-listed from the Paris Stock Exchange. Also in 2004, Nokia reorganized into four business groups: mobile phones, multimedia, enterprise solutions and networks, to further align the company's overall structure with its strategy. Nokia sold its professional mobile radio business including TETRA infrastructure and terminals to EADS, a defence and space company, in 2005.

In February 2006, Nokia acquired Intellisync Corporation, a leader in platform-independent wireless messaging and applications for mobile devices, for a cash consideration of approximately €368 million. The company also entered into an agreement with Sanyo Electric to form a new global company comprising their respective CDMA mobile phone businesses.

Nokia inaugurated its manufacturing facility in Sriperumbudur, Chennai, India, in March 2006. This made it the only company in India whose facility manufactured both mobile devices and network infrastructure equipment. Nokia reinforced its commitment to the Middle East and Africa by opening an office in Beirut in May 2006. Nokia and Siemens announced plans to combine Nokia's networks business and Siemens' carrier-related operations for fixed and mobile networks in June 2006 to form a new company called Nokia Siemens Networks, owned by Nokia and Siemens and consolidated by Nokia. During the same month, Nokia acquired LCC International's US deployment business.

In September 2006, Nokia signed agreements with its Chinese customers: China Mobile and PTAC valued at over €2 billion for the year 2006. During the same month, Motorola and Nokia announced cooperation for interoperability among their DVB-H (Digital Video Broadcast-Handheld)-enabled mobile devices and network services. Also in September 2006, Nokia entered into an agreement with Microsoft to integrate Live Search capabilities into its Mobile Search platform for the Nokia N-series multimedia computers and other compatible Nokia S60 devices.

Nokia made two key acquisitions in October 2006 including Loudeye, a leader in digital music platforms and digital media distribution services; and gate5, a leading supplier of mapping, routing and navigation software and services. Citigroup, MasterCard Worldwide, Cingular Wireless and Nokia started a consumer technology trial of Near Field Communication (NFC)-enabled mobile phones in December 2006 with MasterCard PayPass contactless payment capability in New York City. During the same month, Giesecke & Devrient (G&D) and Nokia formed a global joint venture company called Venyon, 57 per cent owned by G&D and 43 per cent by Nokia.

Sprint Nextel selected Nokia as a key infrastructure and consumer electronic device provider in January 2007 for Sprint Nextel's 4G WiMAX next generation mobility network along with Intel, Samsung and Motorola to create the advanced network infrastructure and access devices. During the same month, Nokia decided to apply for the de-listing of Nokia's Swedish Depository Receipts (SDRs) from the Stockholm Stock Exchange, due to their decreased trading volumes. The final trading day of Nokia SDRs on the Stockholm Stock Exchange was in June 2007.

Nokia received a contract from Sprint Nextel in March 2007 for four Texas markets of Dallas, Fort Worth, San Antonio and Austin for the initial build-out of Sprint Nextel's mobile WiMAX network. During the same month, the company announced its plans to set up its eleventh mobile device production facility globally in the county of Cluj in Romania.

Nokia Siemens Networks started operating in April 2007, as a communications infrastructure services provider. Nokia entered into a strategic partnership with China Postel Mobile Communication Equipment of China P&T Appliances in May 2007. China Postel is expected to purchase mobile devices from Nokia to the value of approximately $2.5 billion in 2007. Nokia also acquired substantially all assets of Twango (www.Twango.com), a provider of media sharing solution for organizing and sharing photos, videos and other personal media in July 2007.

In August 2007, Nokia opened its first design studio in India through a two-year partnership with the Srishti School of Art, Design and Technology in Bengaluru. During the same month, Nokia issued a product advisory related to the overheating of Nokia-branded BL-5C batteries manufactured by Matsushita Battery Industrial of Japan between December 2005 and November 2006. There were approximately 100 incidents of overheating reported globally. The company recalled 46 million batteries manufactured by Matsushita. It has filed a complaint with the United States International Trade Commission (ITC) in August 2007 alleging that Qualcomm has engaged in unfair trade practices by infringing on five Nokia patents in its CDMA and WCDMA/GSM chipsets.

The applications for the Nokia N97 phone are made available in India through the Ovi store 9a platform created by Nokia for offering value added services. The N97, launched in India in June 2009 was the first device from the Finnish handset maker to feature the Ovi store.

India has the largest and most vibrant pool of qualified developers in the world. As the Internet is entering into the core of mobile experiences, the company sees unprecedented opportunities for Indian developers in shaping the future of mobile experiences.

Targeting the youth, Nokia also announced the availability of its gaming services 'N-gage' in India with additional games and expanded online offering. Nokia N-gage is a part of Nokia's internet service brand Ovi and brings alive a made-for-mobile gaming service to provide consumers the power to personalize the Internet experience.

14.4 Portfolios

Nokia India has played a pioneering role in the growth of cellular technology in India, starting with the first-ever cellular call a decade ago, made on a Nokia mobile phone over a Nokia-deployed network. Nokia started its India operations in 1995, and presently operates out of offices in New Delhi, Mumbai, Kolkata, Bengaluru, Hyderabad and Ahmedabad. The Indian operations comprise the company's handset and network infrastructure businesses, R&D facilities in Bengaluru, Hyderabad and Mumbai and manufacturing plant in Chennai.

The handset business is supported by a team of professionals across three business groups, namely mobile phones, multimedia and enterprise solutions. The company has grown manifold over the years with its manpower strength increasing from 450 people in 2004 to close to 6,000 people in 2009.

It has established itself as the market and brand leader in the mobile devices market in India. It has built a diverse product portfolio to meet the needs of different consumer segments, ranging from entry-level phones for first-time subscribers to advanced business devices and high-performance multimedia devices for imaging, music and gaming. India is a very important country for Nokia and is amongst the top three markets for it globally. Nokia has been working closely with operators in India to increase geographical coverage and lower the total cost of ownership for consumers. The company has also launched seven Nokia 'concept stores' in Bengaluru, Delhi, Jaipur, Hyderabad, Chandigarh, Ludhiana and Chennai to provide customers a complete experiential mobile experience.

While tracing its position globally, Nokia is a leading manufacturer of mobile devices and network equipment. It also provides equipment, solutions and services for network operators, service providers and corporations. In the fiscal year 2006, the company had production facilities in 9 countries and marketed its products in more than 150 countries.

Nokia operates through four business segments: mobile phones, multimedia, enterprise solutions and networks. During April 2007, Nokia's networks segment became part of a 50 : 50 joint venture company, Nokia Siemens Networks.

14.4.1 Mobile Phones Segment

The mobile phones segment of Nokia offers a wide range of mobile phone devices with voice and data capabilities. The company primarily targets high-volume sales of mainstream mobile devices, where design, brand, ease of use and price are customers' most important considerations.

The company's global product folio includes new features with mass market appeal, such as mega-pixel cameras and music players. The company offers mobile phones and devices based on all major technologies including GSM/EDGE (Global System for Mobile Communications/Enhanced Data GSM Environment), 3G/WCDMA (third generation/(Wideband Code Division Multiple Access) and CDMA (Code Division Multiple Access).

Nokia offers mobile phones in five categories: broad appeal, lifestyle products, entry, CDMA and Vertu. The company's phones with a broad appeal are mid-range products with a balance between price, functionality and style. Most of the company's mobile device models fall into this category, including the Nokia 6000 family.

The broad appeal phones are featured with mega-pixel cameras, music players and advanced messaging capabilities. Nokia's lifestyle products include top-end devices with better material inputs, design and features. These include Nokia 8000, 7000, 5000 and 3000 product families.

The entry-level mobile phones of Nokia are offered in cooperation with local mobile operators at a low cost of ownership. The company offers these mobiles primarily in markets with a potential for growth and where mobile penetration levels are relatively low. The entry devices include Nokia 1000 and 2000 product families with voice capability, basic messaging, calendar features, colour displays and radios.

It offers CDMA mobile phones to operators in the US, Venezuela, Brazil, India, Indonesia and China. The company currently works with partners for co-development in selected CDMA markets, with a special focus on North America, China and India. Vertu mobile devices of Nokia are luxury mobile phones. They are sold at approximately 350 points in 40 countries. The company's new products in this category include: Constellation, a phone available in 18-carat yellow gold or stainless steel; Ascent Collection; and the 2006 Signature Diamond Collection, a limited edition handset in collaboration with French jeweller Boucheron.

14.4.2 Multimedia Segment

The multimedia segment offers mobiles with multimedia capabilities in the form of advanced mobile multimedia computers and applications with connectivity over multiple technology standards. The company's strategy in this segment is to make multimedia computers the device of choice for people participating in the Web 3.0 phenomenon, where people can create and share online communities.

The company continues to build the Nokia N-series sub-brand and multimedia computer category. The N-series multimedia computers can record video and still pictures, print-quality images, TV, music, web access and email, and phone. In addition to supporting 3G/WCDMA connectivity, certain Nokia N-series multimedia computers also feature non-cellular connectivity, including WLAN, FM radio, Digital Video Broadcasting Handheld (DVBH), and Bluetooth. Multimedia also includes pre-Nokia N-series multipurpose mobile devices, such as the Nokia 7610 and Nokia 6600.

The company's two main entities responsible for the development of multimedia products include multimedia computers and multimedia experiences. Multimedia also offers a business programme, Convergence Products. Multimedia computers focus on managing, delivering and expanding the Nokia N-series multimedia computer portfolio, as well as developing accessory products and car communications solutions. Multimedia experiences develops multimedia applications and solutions in the following areas: imaging, music, internet and computing, TV and video, games and navigation and search. Convergence products develop and drive technologies and products based on Internet Protocol (IP) applications and multi-radio connectivity. The company's first device in this programme is the Nokia 770 Internet Tablet. Based on the open source Linux operating system, the Nokia 770 is a non-cellular device optimized for internet communications, with key applications include internet browsing and email. In January 2007, Nokia launched the second product from this programme, the Nokia N800 Internet Tablet.

14.4.3 Enterprise Solutions Segment

The enterprise solutions segment offers a range of products and solutions including enterprise-grade mobile devices, underlying security infrastructure, software and services for businesses and institutions. The segment collaborates with a range of companies to provide fixed IP network security, mobilize corporate email and other IT systems, and extend corporate telephone systems to Nokia's mobile devices. The enterprise solutions segment has four business units: mobile devices, mobility solutions, security and mobile connectivity, and sales, marketing and services.

The mobile devices business unit offers mobile devices specifically for businesses to address security, manageability, cost and ease-of-use concerns. The product portfolio includes devices with both cellular connectivity, such as GSM and 3G/WCDMA, and non-cellular connectivity such as WLAN.

These mobile devices support network connectivity, personal information management and email access, connectivity to IT infrastructures, device management, and security solutions. The company's products in this business unit include the Nokia E50, E60, E61, E62, E65, E70, 9300, 9300i, and the 9500 Communicator.

The mobility solutions business unit develops software solutions for mobile email, business telephony, device management and other mobile data services. The company offers wireless email and other applications over an array of devices and application platforms across carrier networks under the Intellisync brand name. The company also collaborates with external vendors such as IBM, Microsoft, Research in Motion, Seven and Visto to make its mobile devices compatible with vendor solutions. In addition, the company maintains relationships with leading vendors like Avaya, Alcatel and Cisco to connect its mobile devices to corporate fixed line telephone networks and PBXs over cellular and WLAN technologies.

The security and mobile connectivity business unit offers a broad range of applications and secure connectivity offerings to companies. These applications and secure connectivity products provide authenticated employees access to corporate information, and establish secure remote connections between corporate network, offices and employees' mobile devices and computers. The company's offerings consist primarily of firewall gateways and software-based tools that operate with both Nokia and non-Nokia devices, as well as with other existing IT infrastructures. The company's security appliances run software including Checkpoint Corporation and SourceFire. Nokia and Checkpoint have common distributors, integrators and Value Added Resellers (VARs) that integrate Nokia gateways with Checkpoint. Nokia also provides end user and reseller support for these security products.

14.4.4 Networks Unit

The Nokia Siemens Networks is a joint venture company established by Nokia and Siemens, which started operations in April 2007. The company combined Nokia's networks business and Siemens' carrier-related operations for fixed and mobile networks into a new company owned approximately 50 per cent each by Nokia and Siemens, and consolidated by Nokia. It operates in six business units: radio access, broadband access, service core and applications, IP networking and transport, operating support systems, and services.

Nokia Siemens Networks has an alliance with Nokia's mobile device business with respect to product and service offerings as well as customer interface. The new company also includes certain intellectual property contributions owned by Nokia and Siemens. In the infrastructure business, Nokia Siemens Network has made significant progress in realizing business opportunities and increasing its market share in India. It is now a key supplier to all the top GSM operators including Bharti, BSNL, Vodafone and Idea.

Nokia has set up its Global Networks Solutions Centre in Chennai, India. The centre performs network operation tasks for selected operator customers in the Asia-Pacific region as well as Europe, the Middle East and Africa. Nokia has three R&D centres in India, based in Hyderabad, Bengaluru and Mumbai. These are staffed by engineers who are working on next-generation packet switched mobile technologies and communications solutions to enhance corporate productivity.

Nokia has set up its tenth manufacturing facility in Chennai to meet the burgeoning demand for mobile devices in the country. The manufacturing facility is operational with an investment of US$150 million announced in March 2006 and employed over 4,100 people in 2008.

14.5 Revenue Analysis

Nokia India's revenues in 2008 grew just €35 million to €3.72 billion (Brazil grew the highest, €645 million to €1.9 billion). Its share in the domestic market shrank from 72.2 per cent in 2007 to 49.7 per cent in the first quarter of 2009 (Gartner and GFK). Among its biggest rivals, Samsung gained market share from 6.7 per cent in 2008 to 7.67 per cent in 2009. Samsung has doubled from what they were in 2007. Nokia declined to share any sales numbers, and insisted its market share in India was 64 per cent.

Nokia has traditionally been a strong player in the below-₹4,000 segment that accounts for 77 per cent of the market. But in the past couple of years over 20 China-made local brands such as Fly, Spice and Micromax and Samsung's Guru have cornered about 15 per cent of the market due to their low price points. People (in this segment) are looking at low-value, high-feature handsets.

At the top end, the ₹10,000-plus segments constitute barely 6 per cent of the market where rivals such as BlackBerry, iPhone and HTC are gaining ground. In Croma, the sale share of Nokia is coming down. They used to have a large share of Nokia products, but of late HTC, iPhone and Samsung are doing well. Among the high-end phones, Croma sells an equal number of Nokia, BlackBerry and HTCs. In modern trade, HTC has a higher presence than most of the big players in high-end phones. HTC in 2008 sold 3,00,000 units. Nokia does not disclose its smartphone numbers separately.

In the middle segment, Nokia is no more the customer's only choice. Customers now want to see Samsung, LG and Sony Ericsson as well. In such a market situation, Nokia is relying heavily on what is inarguably its most potent weapon—the industry's largest distribution network set up painstakingly over its 15-year presence in India. Its unmatched FMCG-like sprawl covers 1,90,000 retailers. Its biggest rival Samsung reaches barely 50,000 outlets. Nokia is pumping its distribution bandwidth with 50 new handsets this year, up from an average of 28-30 in the previous two-three years. Currently, of the 350-400 models in the market at any point in time, Nokia has 60-75. Rivals Samsung and LG too are introducing 40 and 45 models annually.

While looking at the recent past, Nokia recorded revenues of €50.710 billion in 2007, with a dip in sales of €0.348 billion. This warranted the company to be cautious about safeguarding its market viability and securing operational cash flow during 2009–11. China, the company's largest geographic market, accounted for 11.9 per cent of the total revenues.

Table 14.3: Financial growth of Nokia globally (figures in € million)

Particulars	*2008*	*2007*	*2006*	*2005*	*2004*	*2003*	*2002*
Net sales	50,710	51,058	41,121	34,191	29,371	29,533	30,016
PBT	4,970	8,268	5,723	4,971	4,705	5,294	4,917
PAT	3,988	7,205	4,306	3,616	3,192	3,543	3,381
Dividends	2,048	1,760	1,761	1,641	1,539	1,433	1,340
Return on equity (%)	24.04	41.50	35.5	27.1	21.5	23.8	25.4
Change in sales (%)	– 0.68	24.16	20.26	16.41	– 0.55	– 1.6	2.2

Nokia generates revenues through four business divisions: mobile phones (60.2 per cent of the total revenues), multimedia (19.2 per cent), networks (18.1 per cent) and enterprise solutions (2.5 per cent) in 2007. In India Nokia sales shot up to ₹15,66,609.30 million in 2007 from ₹57,521.765 million in 2005. However the change in sales in 2008 was – 0.68 per cent, which in turn affected the return on equity from 41.5 per cent in 2007 to 24.04 per cent—a matter of great concern.

Nokia is facing severe competition in all segments of the communications market. In the mobile devices segment, the company has been facing competition from other mobile device companies such as LG, Motorola, Samsung and Sony Ericsson. Additionally, it is also facing competition from mobile network operators offering mobile phones under their own brand. In the multimedia and enterprise solutions segment, the company is facing intense competition from Internet-based products and services, consumer electronics manufacturers and business device and solution providers. The launch of the iphone by Apple and Microsoft's entry into this segment have further intensified competition.

The network infrastructure business of the company, now part of Nokia Siemens Networks, is also facing intense competition. The merger of Alcatel and Lucent to form LucentAlcatel is a major threat and Ericsson is another major competitor in this segment. Increasing competition would put pressure on the company's revenue growth and margins.

14.6 Innovative Campaigns

14.6.1 Environmental Concerns and Recycling

Nokia and Emirates Environmental Group (EEG) rolled out the Take-Back Programme to raise awareness about the opportunities to recycle old mobile devices and accessories. Only 3 per cent of people recycle their mobile phones, despite the fact that most have old devices lying around at home that they no longer want, according to a global consumer survey released by Nokia. Three out of every four people added that they don't even think about recycling their devices and nearly half were unaware that it is even possible to do so. In the UAE, around 65 per cent of people said that when thinking of recycling, they do not think about recycling their old and unwanted mobile phones. Fifty-nine per cent admit that they did not know that it is even possible to do so.

Nokia is strengthening its take-back capability in the UAE to cover all its service centres in the country. Consumers can also drop off phones at the EEG office and Nokia branded stores across the UAE.

14.6.2 'Indianizing' Services

Nokia India's focus on the Indian consumer has made the subsidiary a billion-dollar organization global corporation, particularly when world leaders are rarely open to localization of their products and strategies. For most of them, the term 'glocal' is more a smart management term than a pointer to act local. For Nokia India, however, glocal is becoming more of a habit. In its first experiment with localization in 1998, Nokia believes it created a bond

BOX 14.3: SOME FIRSTS FOR NOKIA IN INDIA

1995	- First mobile phone call made in India on a Nokia phone on a Nokia network.
1998	- *Saare jahaan se achcha*, the first Indian ring tone, in a Nokia 5110.
2000	- First phone with Hindi menu (Nokia 3210).
2002	- First camera phone (Nokia 7650).
2003	- First 'Made for India phone', the Nokia 1100.
2004	- Saral Mobile Sandesh, Hindi SMS on a wide range of Nokia phones.
	- First Wi-Fi phone, the Nokia Communicator (N 9500).
2005	- Local User Interphase (UI) in additional local language.
2006	- Nokia manufacturing plant in Chennai.
2007	- First vernacular news portal.

with the Indian consumer with tunes like *Saare jahaan se achcha* in its 5110 model. In 2000, its first Hindi user interface in the 3210 model gave Nokia the confidence to target its product development efforts at the Hindi-speaking population. The next year, Nokia introduced the Hindi text messsaging facility in the 3610. But in 2006, Nokia India became more Indian than ever before. It launched two models—1100 and 1108 that had been developed specifically for India, after intensive research on the Indian customer's specific needs. The phone gave an integrated torch, a sheath-covered keypad for dust protection and a slip-free grip. The models were creations of Nokia's Mobile Entry Business Unit, a team created to focus exclusively on developing products for markets with high population and low penetration. India, apart from China, Indonesia and Africa, was one of the top-priority markets.

The strategy worked. Nokia's first 'Made for India' model, the 1100, is the largest selling model in the Indian GSM handsets market. Some of its features, like the torchlight, have become standard in models like the 3112 CDMA handset. Nokia's market share has gone up from 58.2 per cent in July 2003 to 59.6 per cent in July 2004. The five largest selling handset models in the market are all Nokia's. Besides, the company in 2008 has a substantial share of both ends of the market.

14.6.3 Cashing in on Music

The Finnish mobile handset maker has MoU with leading music content providers and music companies for rolling out its virtual music stores in India. The company has tied up with around 150 music companies, including Universal Music, Warner Brothers, Sony BMG and other national players. Nokia offered the service in India with a free one-year subscription on purchase of select Nokia handsets. Similar services launched in the UK on 5310Xpress music device is evincing good response from music lovers in 2010.

The Nokia N-series, the premium multimedia sub-brand of Nokia has joined hands with India's leading fusion artist Rabbi Shergill to premiere his new music album in digital format on its N-series devices. This marked the first-ever launch of a complete music album on a mobile handset prior to its physical launch. Titled *Avengi Ja Nahi*, made exclusively available across the country for a month on the iconic Nokia N-series multimedia devices: the N95, the N70 Music Edition and the N73 Music Edition since June 2009.

Nokia India's format may be different from the one in the UK as people's preferences in the two countries are different. Also, unlike the UK, in India the service has to be made compatible on low-end handsets for a better click with customers. The service helped in boosting the handset sales as the service allowed users to download and store unlimited songs on their mobiles and computers even after the subscription expires during 2009–11.

14.6.4 A Dash of Entertainment

Shahrukh Khan endorses Nokia hand phones. Nokia India is planning to bundle exclusive content featuring him for handsets sold in India. It bundled the full-length film *Om Shanti Om* in the Nokia N96. It will also look at bundling video clips and music of Shahrukh Khan's movies in the handsets. Khan, on his part, would extend collaboration with Nokia for such possibilities through his production house, Red Chillies Entertainment.

This new offering takes forward the N-series' promise of offering the Next Episode in entertainment on mobile devices. According to Devinder Kishore, director of marketing at Nokia India, the company believes that the mobile device is emerging as the Fourth Screen for entertainment after the big screen, the television and the personal computer. 'Nokia's endeavour has been to offer the best of entertainment on the go on the best of devices. This announcement breaks new ground for mobile music and entertainment in India, bringing people closer to their passion of music and performers closer in ways they would never have imagined.'

As part of this unique music experience, Nokia N-series also rolled out a first of its kind contest, titled *Nokia N-series My Music My Muse*, targeted at young music enthusiasts in the country. The contest invited aspiring participants above 18 years of age to shoot a video using their mobile phones for Rabbi's lead track from the album *Bilqis*. The theme was 'sharing inspirations' and each film had to be at most 20 seconds long. Thirty shortlisted entries were to be judged by Rabbi himself and footage from five best entries would be edited to create a three-minute online music video for the song. This was the first user-generated online Indian music video and perhaps the only initiative of its kind to bring to the forefront the unique and passionate mix of technology and music. This contest opened up another chapter in the Web 3.0 story with consumers becoming broadcasters and carrying forward the N-series strategy of enabling people to explore, capture and share their experiences using mobile devices.

14.6.5 Nokia Life Tools

This is a range of innovative agriculture information and education services targeted at non-urban consumers. Designed specifically for emerging markets, Nokia Life Tools helps overcome information constraints and provides services to this next generation of mobile users. Nokia launched the service in the first half of 2009 with the Nokia 2323 Classic and the Nokia 2330 Classic as the lead devices in India and to expand across select countries in Asia and Africa later in 2009.

According to Jawahar Kanjilal, global head, Emerging Market Services, 'Filling in the information gaps in agriculture and education with Nokia Life Tools, Nokia strives to contribute towards empowering people with the right tools to help them make informed decisions in their daily lives. Nokia Life Tools was developed to help bridge the digital divide in the emerging markets.'

According to Shivakumar, Vice-President, Nokia India, 'Nokia is a global innovator with a strong pulse of local markets. Agriculture employs more than 60 per cent of all workforce in India. This sector of the economy needs fresh inputs via technology for the sector to get to a 3 per cent growth. Nokia, through services in Agriculture and Education, will fulfil these opportunities for the Indian population.'

Before the national launch of such services, Nokia had conducted a limited scale pilot project in India in 2008. Reuters Market Light (RML) was the content service provider collaborating with Nokia for agriculture services in the pilot project, where accurate and regular information on weather, prices and availability of seeds, fertilizers, pesticides, and prevailing market prices for produce were provided to farmers. The information was customized to the farmer's location and selection of crops, and delivered directly to their Nokia mobile phones. By getting the latest information directly on their mobile phones, farmers overcame uncertainty and received advice just in time to grow and sell their crops.

The education service of Nokia Life Tools aims to give students a decisive advantage by boosting their English language and knowledge about local, national and international events. Language lessons, quizzes on English words and phrases, and general information were designed—together with EnableM for the pilot—to give students an edge. In future, the education service will also come with information on higher education, career guidance and tips, exam preparation quizzes and access to exam results.

Astrology services and ringtone downloads, with content from OnMobile during the pilot phase, bring the fun element to Nokia Life Tools. Nokia Life Tools services use an icon-based, graphically-rich user interface that comes complete with tables and which can even display information simultaneously in two languages. SMS is used to deliver the information to ensure that the service works wherever a mobile phone works, without the hassles of additional settings or the need for GPRS coverage.

Idea Cellular Limited is the first GSM operator in India to collaborate on Nokia Life Tools. The Nokia Life Tools is available in local languages for the target audience. The pilot will be enabled on the Nokia 2600 classic and the Nokia 1680, and available in Marathi, Hindi and English.

Nokia Life Tools has been developed in collaboration with the target users and the industry. The success of this initiative can be assured through regular consumer feedback to ensure that their needs are best met. More importantly, it requires a collaborative effort between Nokia, industry participants and information providers across the agriculture and education sectors as Nokia connects the next billion mobile phone subscribers—many of whom will indeed hail from these developing regions.

Summary

In 2009, Nokia launched nine phones, including the N97, N95 and 5230. Nokia does not disclose product-specific numbers, but said the N97 flew off the shelves. Its dealers, however, say the product is encountering many problems, including hung software. Bloggers across the world have hailed the device and its features but have unanimously thumbed down its touch screen and the operating system (OS). Ginny Miles' blog on pcworld.com says: 'It has more memory than the Palm Pre, iPhone and T-Mobile G1. . . . But the N97 falls short of its potential, largely because . . . it lacks the refinement. . . . Still, the N97 impresses in . . . audio and video.' According to Damian Koh on cnet.com, 'the touch interface is still very inconsistent and bears traces of a stylus-centric design. This should have been avoided for a touch screen device . . . . Clearly, the S60 platform is still playing catch-up.'

Nokia's retailers say one of the key reasons why Nokia's market share has fallen is the firm's intransigence in offering price protection for not more than a week when its rivals offer up to 30 days.

Shivakumar says Nokia does not intend to change the price protection policy. 'Nokia policy hasn't changed since 2006. At 30 days there's no way Nokia will make money.' Nokia believes its dominant market share, fast-moving products and high volumes justify a lower price protection. 'The No. 2 in India has changed every year for the past five years. That's the inherent resilience of the Nokia brand,' says Shivakumar.

But retailers are also clamouring for margins over 1.5-3 per cent that Nokia offers; rivals offer up to 4-5 per cent. But the company claims that competition is so intense that it has to sell phones at nearly the purchase price.

Even though Nokia followed the path shown by Apple Store with its own Ovi.com in 2008, poor penetration of Internet in India called for physical touch points such as NSPs. The NSP executive is paid ₹150 for each activation of customer ID and the shop gets another ₹75. As for monetization, the greatest emphasis is on music for which Nokia set up its first India-specific apps site. So far every phone comes with a complimentary voucher of 10-100 songs that can be downloaded at the NSPs or over the Internet. Its NSP retailers say they are benefiting from higher footfalls. Novelty's monthly sales have shot up from ₹14-₹15 lakh to around ₹20-₹25 lakh, while its average sale price of a phone has nearly doubled from ₹4,000-₹5,000 to ₹7,000-₹8,000 since it set up NSPs.

Globally, Nokia has opened another front in its quest for more revenue streams by entering the laptop business with the Booklet 3G, a two-inch netbook powered by Intel's Atom processor. Though Nokia has not yet projected revenues from its sales, the netbook is answer to PC maker Apple's entry into cellphones. Earlier, in 2005, Nokia's 'Internet tablets' failed as spectacularly as tablet PCs from all manufacturers did, but the Booklet 3G is getting rave reviews. It may never bring huge revenues to Nokia, but it completes the portfolio of the world's largest cell phone company.

Nokia's biggest challenge in India and abroad, however, continues to be the transition from a purebred hardware maker to a hardware and services provider. Apple has shown this is possible. So while Nokia has strengthened its offerings at Ovi.com, it has also forged new relationships to safeguard its interests. It has a tie-up with Microsoft to load MS Office applications on its proprietory mobile as Symbian in 2009. The company believes an open source Symbian will remain its biggest guard against Google's Android and Microsoft's MS.

Nokia expects industry mobile device volumes in the second quarter 2010 to reflect normal industry recovery. The company expects its device market share in the first quarter 2011 to be at approximately the same level sequentially. It expect the segment to experience value growth in 2011, but expects some decline in industry ASPs, primarily reflecting the increasing impact of the emerging markets and competitive factors in general. Nokia continues to target an increase in its market share in mobile devices in 2010-11.

Case Discussion Questions

1. Analyse the micro and macro marketing environment of Nokia India (P) Limited.
2. Apply SWOT and Porter's Five Forces Model to the GSM handset market in India.
3. Comment on the marketing mix of Nokia India.
4. Analyse the industry structure and competition in the GSM handset market in India.
5. How do you test the financial health of Nokia India and the parent company Nokia? Can the company retain its leadership position in 2014?

CASE ANALYSIS

Company Overview

Nokia is the world leader in mobility. It drives the transformation and growth of the converging Internet and communications industries. Involved in a wide range of mobile devices with services and software, it enabled

BOX 14.4: COMPANY OVERVIEW HEAD OFFICE—FINLAND

- R&D, production, sales, marketing activities around the world.
- Strong R&D presence in 10 countries with over €5.60 billion investment.
- Ten manufacturing facilities in nine countries. Each of the plants employs state-of-the-art technology and is highly automated.
- World's leading manufacturer of mobile devices (over 437 million units), with over 38 per cent share of global device market in 2008.
- Net sales (2008): €50.70 billion (US$70.60 billion)
- Net profit (2008): €4 billion (US$5.60 billion).
- Number of employees (2008): 1,25,829
- Sales in more than 150 countries
- Nokia devices available at approximately 3,50,000 points of sale
- Website: www.nokia.com
- World's fifth most valued brand (*Interbrand, 2008 and 2007*); #1 brand in Asia (*Synovate, 2006 and 2007*); and #1 brand in Europe (*European Brand Institute, September 2007*).
- World's number one supply chain (*AMR Research, 2007*)

Company	*Country of incorporation*	*Nokia ownership (%)*	*Nokia voting (%)*
		Interest	*Interest*
Nokia Inc	United States	100	100
Nokia GmbH	Germany	100	100
Nokia UK Limited	England & Wales	100	100
Nokia TMC Limited	South Korea	100	100
Nokia Telecommunications Ltd	China	83.9	83.9
Nokia Finance International B.V.	The Netherlands	100	100
Nokia Komarom Kft	Hungary	100	100

Nokia India Pvt. Ltd.	India	100	100
Nokia Spain S.A.U.	Spain	100	100
Nokia Italia S.P.A.	Italy	100	100
Nokia Romania S.R.L.	Romania	100	100
Nokia do Brasil Tecnologia Ltd.	Brazil	100	100
NAVTEQ Corporation	United States	100	100
Nokia Siemens Networks B.V.	The Netherlands	50 (1)	50 (1)
Nokia Siemens Networks Oy	Finland	50	50
Nokia Siemens Networks GmbH & Co KG	Germany	50	50
Nokia Siemens Networks Pvt. Ltd.	India	50	50

The Nokia Organization

Devices Unit is responsible for developing the best device portfolio for the marketplace, including sourcing of components.

Services & Software Unit reflects the strategic emphasis on the developing and growing of offered consumer Internet services and enterprise solutions and software.

Markets Unit is responsible for management of supply chains, sales channels, and brand and marketing activities.

The *Corporate Development Office* focuses on strategy and future growth, and provides operational support for integration across all the units.

The infrastructure and related services business is conducted through *Nokia Siemens Networks*, a separate company jointly owned by Nokia and Siemens and consolidated by Nokia.

NAVTEQ is a leading provider of comprehensive digital map data for automotive navigation systems, mobile navigation devices, internet-based mapping applications, and government and business solutions. NAVTEQ's map data is an important part of the Nokia Maps service that brings downloadable maps, voice-guided navigation and other Context-aware web services to people's pockets.

Nokia Siemens Networks is one of the world's largest network communications companies, with a leading position in key markets across the world. The company was formed in April 2007. It is jointly owned by Nokia and Siemens, bringing together the networks business of Nokia and the carrier-related businesses of Siemens. It continues the legacy of these two industry champions, based on their shared commitment to benefitting society through their operations.

Manufacturing facilities: Production at the plant in Salo, Finland, the plant in Beijing, China, and in Masan, South Korea, is geared towards high-value, low- to medium-volume mobile devices. The Vertu business is served by the manufacturing plant in the United Kingdom.

The six other production facilities—Komárom in Hungary, Cluj in Romania, Dongguan in China, Chennai in India, Manaus in Brazil and Reynosa in Mexico—concentrate on the production of high-volume, cost-sensitive mobile devices.

people across the globe to experience music, navigation, video, television, imaging, games, business mobility and much more. The company has constantly been involved in both the development and growth of consumer Internet services, as well as enterprise solutions and software. Nokia also provides equipment, solutions and services for communications networks through Nokia Siemens Networks.

A Brief History

Nokia was established in 1865 as a wood-pulp mill by Knut Fredrik Idestam on the banks of the Tammerkoski rapids in the town of Tampere, in south-western Finland. The company was later relocated to the town of Nokia by the Nokianvirta river, which had better resources for hydropower production. That's also where the company got its name that it still uses today.

Finnish Rubber Works established its factories in the beginning of the twentieth century near the wood-pulp mill and began using Nokia as its brand name. Shortly after World War I the Finnish Rubber Works acquired Nokia Wood Mills as well as Finnish Cable Works, a producer of telephone and telegraph cables. These three companies were merged into the Nokia Corporation in 1967.

The Corporation was involved in many sectors, producing at one time or another paper products, bicycle and car tyres, footwear (including Wellington boots), personal computers, communication cables, televisions, electricity generation machinery, capacitors and aluminium.

Telecommunications Era

The current incarnation of Nokia the result of the founding of the electronics section of the cable division in the 1960s. In the 1967 fusion, that section was made an independent division, and began manufacturing telecommunications equipment.

Nokia had been producing commercial and military mobile radio communications technology since the 1960s. In 1964 it had developed VHF-radio simultaneously with Salora Oy, which later in 1971 also developed the ARP-phone. In 1979 the merger of these two companies resulted in the establishment of Mobira Oy. Mobira began developing mobile phones for the Nordic Mobile Telephony (NMT) network standard that went online in the 1980s and in 1982 introduced its first car phone, the Mobira Senator for NMT 450 networks.

Nokia bought Salora Oy in 1984 and now owns the company entirely. It has changed the company's telecommunication branch name to Nokia-Mobira Oy. The Mobira Talkman, launched in 1984, was one of the world's first transportable phones. In 1987, Nokia introduced one of the world's first handheld phones, the Mobira Cityman 900. While the Mobira Senator of 1982 had weighed 9.8 kg. and the Talkman just under 5 kg., the Mobira Cityman weighed only 800 gm. with the battery and had a price tag of 24,000 Finnish marks (approximately €4,560). Despite the high price, the first phones sold like hot cakes.

In 1988, Jorma Nieminen, resigned as the CEO of the mobile phone unit, and along with two other colleagues, started a mobile phone company of their own called Benefon Oy. A year later, Nokia Mobira Oy became Nokia Mobile Phones and in 1991 launched the first GSM phone.

Nokia and GSM

The Nordic Mobile Telephony was the world's first mobile telephony standard that enabled international roaming and provided valuable experience for Nokia to later participate in developing the Global System for Mobile Communications (GSM). It is a digital standard which came to dominate the world of mobile telephony in the 1990s. In mid-2006 it accounted for about two billion mobile telephone subscribers in the world, or about 80 per cent of the total, in more than 200 countries. The world's first commercial GSM call was made in 1991 in Helsinki over a Nokia-supplied network, by the then prime minister of Finland Harri Holkeri, using a Nokia phone.

Networking Equipment

In the 1970s, Nokia became more involved in the telecommunications industry by developing the Nokia DX200, a digital switch for telephone exchanges. In 1982, the DX200 switch became the world's first digital telephone switch to be put into operational use. It became the work horse of the network equipment division. Its modular and flexible architecture enabled it to be developed into various switching products.

For a while in the 1970s, Nokia's network equipment production was separated into Telefenno, a company jointly owned by the parent corporation and by the Finnish government. In 1987 the government sold its shares to Nokia and in 1992 the name was changed to Nokia Telecommunications. In the 1970s and 1980s Nokia developed the Sanomalaitejärjestelmä ('message device system') for the Finnish Defence Forces.

Personal Computers

In the 1980s, Nokia produced a series of personal computers called MikroMikko. However, the PC division was sold to ICL, which later became part of Fujitsu. That company later transferred its personal computer operations to Fujitsu Siemens Computers, which shut down its only factory in Finland (in the town of Espoo, where computers had been produced since the 1960s) at the end of March 2000, thus ending large-scale PC manufacturing in the country. Nokia is also known for producing high-quality CRT displays for PCs and larger systems application.

Challenges of Growth

In the 1980s, during the era of CEO Kari Kairamo, Nokia expanded into new fields, mostly by acquisitions. In the late 1980s and early 1990s, the corporation ran into serious financial problems, a major reason being the heavy losses incurred by the television manufacturing division.

Nokia responded by streamlining its telecommunications division and by divesting out of the television and PC divisions. Jorma Ollila, who became the CEO in 1992, made a strategic decision to concentrate solely on telecommunications. Thus, during the rest of the 1990s, Nokia continued to divest itself of all of its non-telecommunications divisions.

The exploding worldwide popularity of mobile telephones, beyond even Nokia's most optimistic predictions, caused a logistics crisis in the mid-1990s. This prompted the company to overhaul its entire logistics operation. Today logistics continues to be one of Nokia's major advantages over its rivals, along with greater economies of scale.

The New Millennium

April 2003: Troubles in the networks equipment division caused the corporation to resort to similar streamlining practices on that side, with layoffs and organizational restructuring. This, however, stained Nokia's public image in Finland and led to a number of court cases and the screening of a TV documentary critical of the company. Despite these occasional crises, Nokia has been phenomenally successful in its chosen field. This growth has come mostly during the era of Jorma Ollila and his team of about half a dozen close colleagues.

January 2006: Ollila resigned the CEO position to become the chairman of Shell, being replaced by Olli-Pekka Kallasvuo.

February 2006: Nokia and Sanyo announce an MOU to create a joint venture addressing the CDMA handset business. A few months later, in June, both companies end negotiations without an agreement. Nokia also states its decision to pull out of CDMA R&D, but with the intention of continuing in the CDMA business in select markets.

February 2006: Nokia acquires Intellisync Corporation, a provider of data and PIM synchronization software.

19 June 2006: Nokia and Siemens AG announced the companies are to merge their mobile and fixed line phone network equipment businesses to create one of the world's largest network firms. Both companies will have a 50 per cent stake in the infrastructure company, to be headquartered in the Helsinki area and to be called Nokia Siemens Networks. The companies predict annual sales of €16 billion and cost savings of €1.50 billion a year by 2010. About 20,000 Nokia employees will be transferred to this new company.

March 2007: Nokia signs a memorandum with Cluj-Napoca City Council, Romania, to open a new plant near the city in the Jucu commune.

May 2007: Nokia announces its Nokia 1100; with over 200 million units shipped, it is the best-selling mobile phone of all time and the world's top-selling consumer electronics product.

July 2007: Nokia acquires all assets of Twango, the comprehensive media sharing solution for organizing and sharing photos, videos and other personal media.

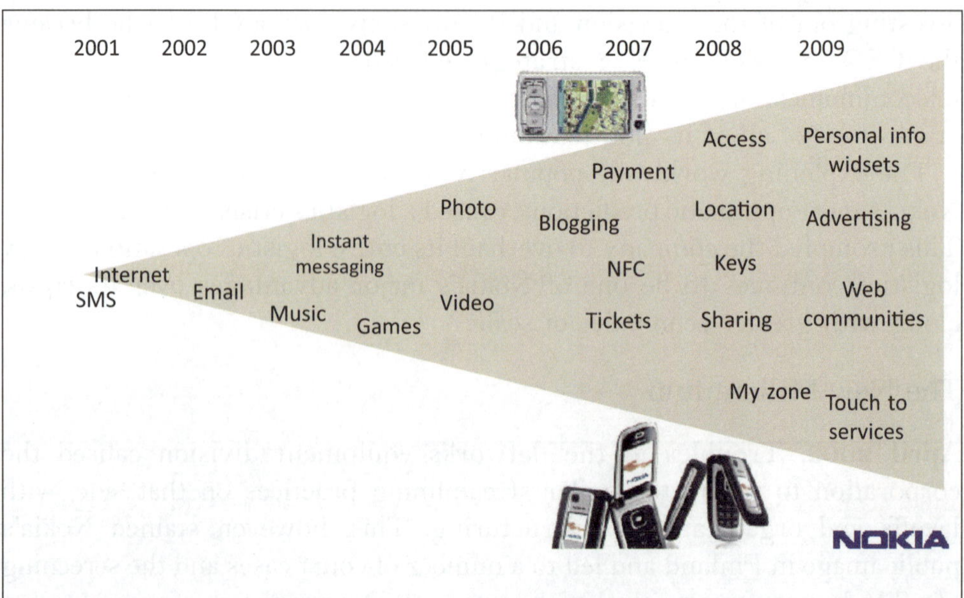

Figure 14.2: Nokia—a time line

August 2007: Nokia launches a series of web services under the brand name Ovi that allows users to download games, maps and music directly to their phones.

September 2007: Nokia announces its intention to acquire Enpocket, a supplier of mobile advertising technology and services.

October 2007: Pending shareholder and regulatory approval, Nokia acquires Navteq, a US-based supplier of digital mapping data, for a price of $8.10 billion.

December 2007: At the Nokia World Conference, the company announced its 'Comes With Music' programme. Nokia device buyers are to receive a year of complimentary access to music downloads.

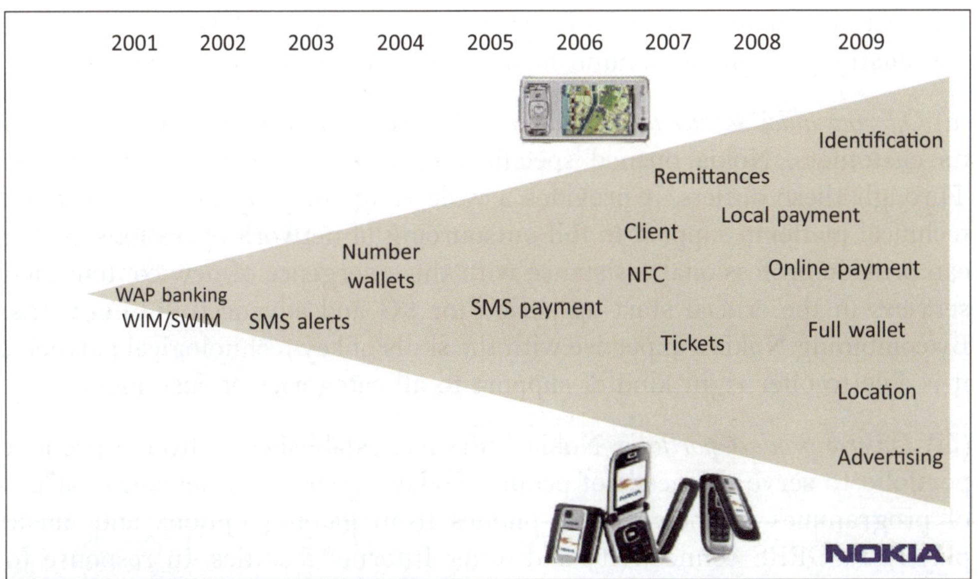

Figure 14.3: Nokia's financial service offers

Nokia in India

Nokia has played a pioneering role in the growth of cellular technology in India. It started its Indian operations in 1995. The Indian operations comprise the company's handsets and network infrastructure businesses, R&D facilities and manufacturing plant. The handset business is supported by a team of professionals across three business groups, namely mobile phones, multimedia, and enterprise solutions. The company has grown manifold over the years with its manpower strength increasing from 450 people in 2004 to close to 6,000 people in 2008.

BOX 14.5: NOKIA'S VISION

- Be a customer-focused products company.
- Be at the forefront of bringing mobile multimedia to consumers.
- Focus for Nokia is to bring increased mobility to enterprises.
- Expand its networks business division.
- Be a leader in product innovation and R&D.

SWOT Analysis

Strengths

(i) *Strong brand name:* Nokia enjoys the advantage of having a strong brand name in the Indian as well as the worldwide market. Consumers acknowledge the innovative features offered by the company by asking specifically for Nokia phones from dealers. The company therefore enjoys a strong market share of 65 per cent. It has also won a number of awards and has been ranked high in several brand surveys. Some of these awards are mentioned below:

- Nokia India the 'Most Respected Company' in the Indian Consumer Durables industry in 2007 as per an annual survey conducted by *Business World.* It held the same position in 2004 and 2006 as well.
- It was ranked 'Asia's Most Trusted' brand in 2006 by the Media-Synovate survey.
- Nokia India ranked fourth in the Most Trusted Brand Survey by *Brand Equity* for the year 2007 and was ranked by *Business World* as the No. 1 multinational corporation set up in India.
- Nokia was named Brand of the Year at the Confederation of Indian Industry (CII) brand summit held in Chennai in February 2005.

(ii) *Offering quick service to its consumers:* In order to provide quick service to its customers, Nokia opened specific outlets by the name 'Nokia Care'. Through these outlets, it provides a wide range of support services, from technical platform support to full outsourcing of network operations. Nokia can provide professional assistance with the emergence of new content-rich services in the crucial start-up period for 3G and advanced 2G networks. By combining Nokia's expertise with the skills of key technological partners, it is able to offer right kind of support to all categories of customers.

(iii) *Diverse product portfolio:* Nokia India has established a diverse product portfolio to serve the needs of people. Today's generation demands variety of programmes in their mobile phones from gaming options and music players to GPRS connectivity and other Internet facilities. In response to that, Nokia India invented a new series of mobile devices with high-performance multimedia devices for imaging, music, gaming, and Internet options.

(iv) *Sound infrastructure and high-tech products:* Nokia won the Golden Peacock Award in 2004 for its N1100 model, which was selected as the most innovative product in the telecom segment. It is a major player in the infrastructure business where the Nokia Siemens Network is now a key supplier to all the top five GSM operators including Bharti, BSNL, Vodafone, Idea and BPL. It was ranked as the leading telecommunications equipment vendor (including wireless infrastructure) in the country by *Voice and Data* for three consecutive years from 2004 to 2006.

Nokia offers its customers a host of mobile technologies some of which are given in Figure 14.4.

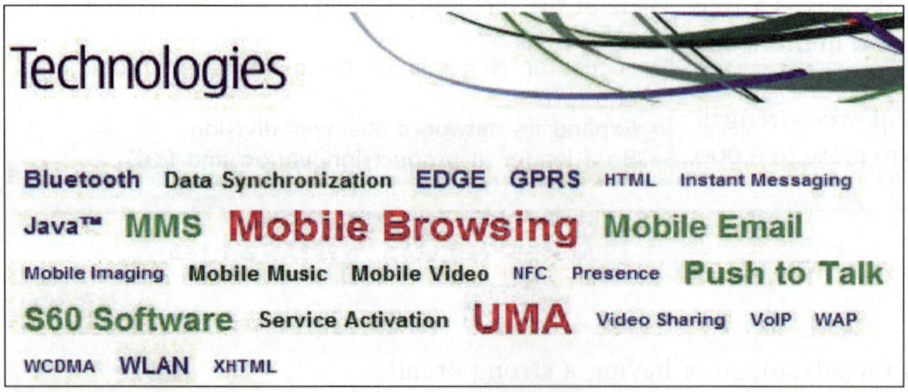

Figure 14.4: Mobile technologies on offer from Nokia

Weaknesses

(i) *Lapse has opened up space for smaller competitors:* Nokia allowed itself to be complacent and did not anticipate changes in the market scenario, leading to a rise in the number of players in the industry. As a result Nokia's market share dropped to 65 per cent. Complacency still remains one of the major internal threats to the company.

(ii) *Design to market takes more time:* Nokia has been slow in responding to the changes in the market demand and the needs of the customers. This has resulted in an increase in the market share of companies like Motorola and Samsung that launched models with designs more in sync with the market demand.

Opportunities

(i) *Consumer Internet services and business solutions:* The model N6233, will be part of seventh 3G-enabled model from Nokia in India. 'Customers are buying these models (with 3G services) because of better camera, imaging and music facilities,' said Mauro Montanaro, Nokia's vice-president for customer market operations, South-East Asia Pacific. He disclosed that by December 2010, the Finnish company would have in total 15 to 20 3G models in India.

(ii) *Untapped demand in rural sector:* There exists a huge demand for mobile handsets in the rural sector as well as tier II and tier III cities. The company, by launching models customized to the needs of the rural people can generate tremendous volume. The growth strategy in these markets would have to be different since the customers there demand robust, dust-resistant handsets at affordable prices. The company should chalk out a strategy to enter these markets in a big way. Service operators play a very crucial role in this case. Unlike the current situation, the operators will have to roll out their services in these markets in a much larger way. Only then can mobile handsets companies devise a growth strategy for these markets. Nokia must follow a low-cost, high-volume strategy. With over 60 million handsets manufactured from its Chennai plant, Nokia must definitely take the Indian low-cost handset market seriously.

(iii) *Entering the CDMA services market:* Between December 2002 and 2004, the CDMA subscriber base in India increased over 500 per cent to reach 14 million users, and the CDMA market share grew from 2 to 25 per cent of the total market. There are six CDMA carriers operating in India today, i.e. BSNL, HFCL Infotel, MTNL, Reliance, Shyam Telelink and Tata Teleservices. Of these Reliance is the biggest player with a 20 per cent market share.

(iv) *Making use of nanotechnology:* Explored by Nokia Research Centre (NRC) in collaboration with the Cambridge Nanoscience Centre (United Kingdom), nanoscale technologies will potentially create a world of radically different devices that can open up an entirely new spectrum of possibilities. One of the areas of research in this field is Morph Concept Technology which can create the following fantastic opportunities for mobile devices:

- Devices become self-cleaning and self-preserving.
- Transparent electronics offering an entirely new aesthetic dimension.
- Built-in solar absorption can charge a device, whilst batteries become smaller, longer lasting and faster to charge.
- Integrated sensors can allow people to learn more about the surrounding environment, empowering them to make better choices.

In addition to the advances above, the integrated electronics shown in the Morph Concept could cost less and include more functionality in a much smaller space, even as interfaces are simplified and usability is enhanced.

Threats

(i) *Entry of new competitors in the current market space:* Certain newer players are trying to enter the mobile telephone market. As billions of dollars are at stake, many companies are watching the action closely and devising ways of entering the market. Korean and Chinese players like Ezze Mobile, Amoi Electronics are planning to flood the Indian market with cheap handsets. Since these players have their manufacturing and sourcing in relatively inexpensive South-East Asian regions their only major cost driver is export cost and duties. Korea Telecom has signed MOUs with BSNL. Singapore Technology and other companies are looking at JVs with Indian companies for entering the Indian market. Equipment manufacturers like ZTE and Huawei are looking at leveraging their Chinese experience in India, considering that the two markets have a lot of commonalities.

(ii) *Wireless Internet:* As laptops and palmtops become cheaper, more people would have access to mobile computing devices. As wireless Internet facilities become commonly available, people would prefer to use Internet tools such as Skype, VoIP-based tools, Chat and email to communicate, due to lower costs. Already players such as Reliance Communications are offering wireless Internet cards that can be used all over India to access the Internet.

(iii) *WLL:* Wireless in Local Loop is a technology that allows cheap access to communication within a short range of around 30 km. It is very popular among businessmen and local traders. This could emerge as a significant threat to Nokia in the future.

(iv) *Public telephones:* Although the Indian public telephone network isn't technologically very advanced, it has a very wide reach and is thus a potential substitute if developed better. As enterprises like Tata Communications invest further in developing modern PCOs and STD outlets, the threat from these would increase.

Let us look at the balance sheet and income statement of Nokia for the years 2002 to 2006 by focusing on the various critical financial ratios in Table 14.4. We will also compare the financial status of Nokia with that of Motorola, the other major mobile handset maker in the industry.

Financial Analysis

Analysing the liquidity position of the company using the common ratio, current ratio and quick ratio (that show the ability of a company to fulfil its

Table 14.4: Financials of Nokia and Motorola: a comparison

Particulars	*Nokia*					*Motorola*				
	2006	*2005*	*2004*	*2003*	*2002*	*2006*	*2005*	*2004*	*2003*	*2002*
Liquidity ratios										
Current ratio	1.83	1.96	2.45	2.43	2.09	2.01	2.23	1.99	1.90	1.75
Quick ratio	1.42	1.58	2.00	2.00	1.75	0.90	0.98	1.61	1.53	1.21
Operating cash flow ratio	0.44	0.43	0.54	0.63	0.69	0.23	0.34	0.29	0.21	0.14
Asset turnover ratios										
Asset turnover	1.82	1.52	1.30	1.23	1.29	1.11	0.98	1.01	0.72	0.86
Receivables turnover	6.98	6.40	6.70	5.65	5.57	5.71	6.24	6.92	6.06	6.01
Average collection										
Period (in days)	52.26	57.07	54.46	64.65	65.48	63.92	58.50	52.73	60.25	60.70
Inventory turnover	17.85	13.31	13.93	14.82	14.31	9.54	9.84	8.24	7.43	6.25
Days	20.45	27.41	26.20	24.63	25.50	38.28	37.09	44.32	49.15	58.38
Inventory (in days)										
Accounts payable turnover	7.43	6.36	6.81	5.94	6.19	5.96	5.55	6.30	6.34	7.91
Days in accounts payable	49.10	57.42	53.59	61.50	58.99	61.20	65.78	57.96	57.56	46.15
Financial leverage ratios										
Debt ratio	0.02	0.02	0.01	0.02	0.03	0.114	0.119	0.171	0.235	0.283
Debt to equity ratio	0.04	0.04	0.02	0.04	0.04	0.257	0.255	0.397	0.594	0.785
Equity multiplier	1.88	1.79	1.57	1.56	1.61	2.25	2.15	2.32	2.53	2.77
Profitability ratios										
Net profit margin (%)	10.5	10.6	10.9	12.0	11.3	8.5	13.0	5.2	3.9	10.6
Gross profit margin (%)	32.5	35.0	38.1	41.3	39.1	29.7	32.4	33.6	32.7	32.8
Net return on assets (%)	19.0	16.1	14.1	14.8	14.5	9.5	12.8	5.0	2.8	8.0
Gross return on assets (%)	59.2	53.4	49.4	51.0	50.3	33.0	31.9	33.5	23.6	28.1
Return on equity (%)	35.7	28.9	22.2	23.1	23.4	21.4	27.5	11.5	7.0	22.1

short-term liabilities and avoid bankruptcy), it has been observed that Nokia's current ratio is above 1.8 and the quick ratio is also well above 1 during 2002–6.

Financial Implications

1. *Liquidity position:* Nokia has a stable liquidity position and a better one than Motorola. A better measure of liquidity position is the operating cash flow ratio that shows the proportion of current liabilities covered by the operating cash flow generated by the operations of a company. Nokia has a better coverage of its short-term liabilities than Motorola.

2. *Turnover ratios:* Looking at the various turnover ratios it has been observed that the average collection period of Account Receivables is approximately 2 months for Nokia, which is on the higher side, but when we look at the same for Motorola we see that Nokia has a better collection period. The inventory turnover ratio that shows how fast the inventory is converted into

sales is high for Nokia with the 2006 figure being the highest (17.85 times).

On the other hand, Motorola has an inventory turnover ratio of 10 which adds to the cost of inventory. We see that on an average the inventory moves out every 24 days for Nokia, whereas the same figure for Motorola is 45 days which is almost double that of Nokia.

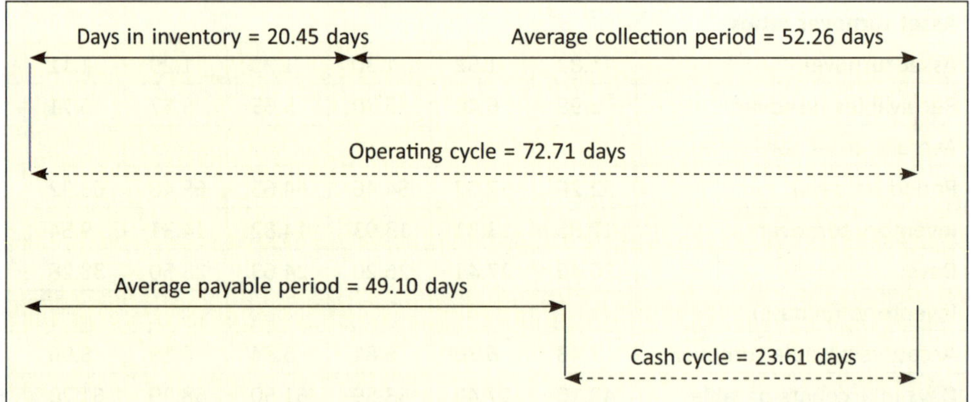

Figure 14.5: Turnover ratio of Nokia

3. *Asset turnover ratio:* The asset turnover ratio shows how much sales is generated using the assets that a company has. This ratio is more than 1 for Nokia in all the years, implying that the company is able to use its assets efficiently to generate sales. The same figure for Motorola has been less than 1 on an average which implies inefficient use of assets.

4. *Financial leverage ratio:* Looking at all the ratios in this category it has been observed that Nokia has very low leverage in its capital structure. Due to a lesser amount of debt it has a better credit rating which allows it to generate funds easily from the debt market for future operations, if required. Nokia should use more debt in its future because the lower level of debt in the capital structure makes the cost of capital higher for the company. If Nokia borrows funds for its future operations it can achieve optimal debt structure and optimal cost of capital.

If we look at same ratios for Motorola we can find that Motorola has a higher amount of debt in its capital structure than Nokia.

5. *Profitability ratios:* Profitability ratios for Nokia show that the Return on Equity has been consistently above 20 per cent. The net profit margin and gross profit margin are also healthy and stable. The profitability ratios for Motorola on the other hand, are less than for Nokia.

Overall, Nokia has been a financially stable company during 2002–6 with all the ratios being equal to or better than its competitor. The collection period should be shortened if possible by putting in place better credit management policies. The debt level in the capital structure should also be increased to bring the cost of capital to the optimal level.

PEST Analysis

Political

The political scenario in India holds promise for the future. The government is stable with no absurd laws or regulations specific to the mobile equipment manufacturing industry. The relationship with neighbouring countries is by and large peaceful and the government is making necessary efforts to build a harmonious relationship with its neighbours, especially Pakistan and China. The problem of unlawful activities and security threats are not widespread but limited to specific areas in the country.

Economic

India is fast emerging as one of the strongest and fastest growing economies in the world. It has consistently achieved a growth rate of 8-9 per cent over the past five years and is set to grow at the same rate for another 5-6 years. The personal disposable income of consumers has increased substantially over the years and this provides a good opportunity for the company to tap the ever-increasing consumption demand of the Indian masses.

Employment levels have dropped compared to 2007 level but slowly picking up and inflation rate is around 9 per cent. The Indian currency (rupee) has appreciated tremendously vis-à-vis the US dollar, making exports a little expensive and imports cheaper. All these are signs of a healthy economy.

Social

There has been a significant change in the lifestyle of an average Indian consumer as a result of an increase in his/her personal disposable income. Competition amongst the mobile network service providers in India has resulted in lower margins for these companies. Low tariff rates translate into increase in the number of customers and hence increase in sales for mobile equipment manufacturing companies like Nokia. Today's generation demands a variety of programmes in its mobile phones starting from gaming options and music players to GPRS connectivity and other Internet facilities. Features like Bluetooth, camera, MP3, radio, and so on are a must for school/college students, whereas GPRS and other Internet-related services are mainly required by business and corporate people.

The Indian middle class with its high disposable income forms the major chunk of the population in the country. There is a huge potential for growth in the rural markets as well as in the tier II and tier III cities. The Indian workforce is a relatively young one with more than half of India's population below the age of 25 years. In fact, India will account for one-quarter of the increase in the world's workforce over the next five years. This provides valuable information to companies to develop their products according to the needs of the young people.

There has also been a shift in the societal image of carrying a cellphone. From being a status symbol owned by only by the wealthy, mobile phones are now being purchased by people belonging to almost every strata of the society. From being perceived as a status symbol, mobile phones are now seen as utility with added features.

Technological

The rate of obsolescence in the Indian mobile market is very high. This is primarily due to the changing needs of the consumers as well as new models with better features being launched by the mobile equipment manufacturing companies like Blackberry's Research in Motion (RIM) operating system. Reasonable prices and a need for change drive consumers to discard their older model and go for a new one. This pushes the companies to invest large sums in R&D activities and come up with new and innovative models with better technology and features.

The Internet provides a major threat to the industry at large. With laptops and palmtops getting cheaper by the day, companies are looking for similar features at affordable prices to stop customers from shifting. The challenge of providing unmatched quality of Internet surfing on mobile phones is proving tough for these companies as 3G services are yet to be launched in the country.

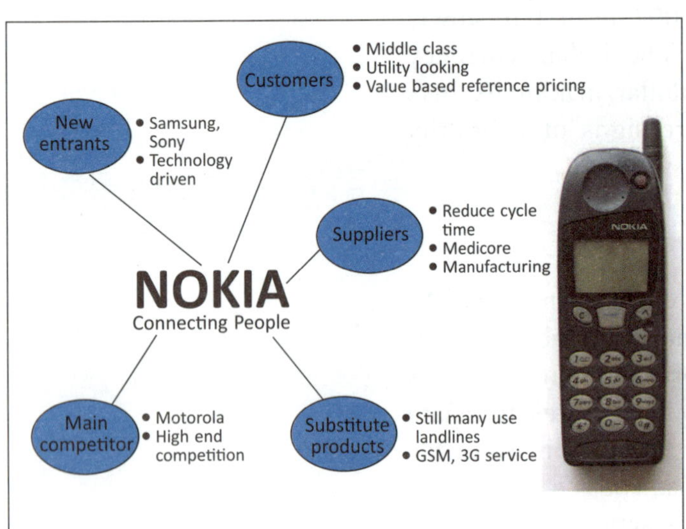

Figure 14.6: Porter's five force theory for Nokia

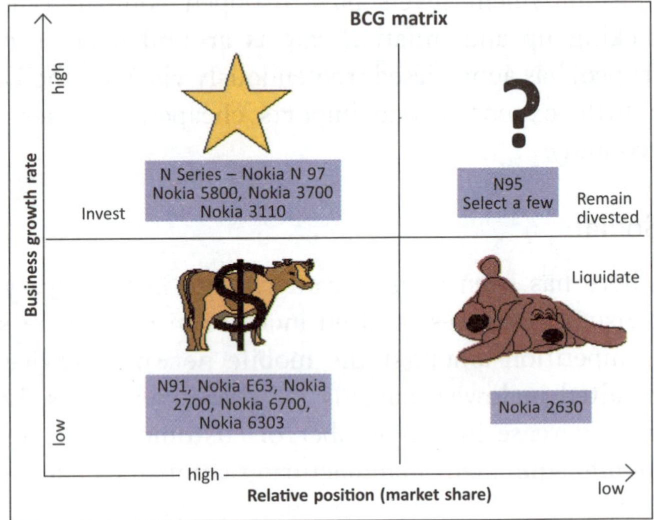

Figure 14.7: Portfolio analysis for Nokia

Corporate Social Responsibility

Addressing Environmental Concerns for Sustainability

Nokia's vision is a world where everyone being connected can contribute to sustainable development. Nokia want to shape global industry and drive best practices.

This vision is substantiated by a number of initiatives for environmental sustenance by Nokia. A few prominent ones are given below:

1. Manufacturing complaint with the European legislation (RoHS restricting the use of certain substances).
2. Since 2006, devices, chargers and headsets are free of PVC.
3. Phasing out the use of Brominated and Chlorinated compounds and Antimony Trioxide.

4. AC-8, Nokia's most energy-efficient charger till date consumes only 0.03W in no-load Mode, saving power equivalent to 1,25,000 energy-saving 15W light bulbs for a year.
5. Largest voluntary mobile phone recycling scheme in the world.
6. Uses 25 per cent renewable electricity in its premises, leading to a reduction in carbon dioxide emissions.
7. Encouraging employees to use video- and teleconferencing as much as possible to replace travel.

Nokia joined several other major mobile manufacturers in 2007 to sign a voluntary agreement based on the results of the European Commission's Integrated Product Policy pilot project on mobile phones. The project focused on finding how the mobile phone industry can reduce the environmental impact of its products throughout their life cycle.

The agreement includes three key commitments:

- Produce an index of environmental facts for each mobile product to enable consumers to compare products easily.
- Increase consumer communications about unplugging the chargers and safe disposal of phones.
- Include a default on-screen message on all new products to unplug chargers once the phone is fully charged.

Lending a Hand in Social Development

Together with INdT (a non-profit research organization in the Amazon), Nokia is developing mobile technology solutions to aid social development. These are aimed to provide benefits across a wide range of issues, from education and health to disaster relief, environmental conservation and the creation of livelihoods. For example, in South Africa, Nokia, the government's department of education and a not-for-profit organization called Mindset Network announced the launch of 'M4Girls', an innovative pilot project using Nokia 6300 mobile phones loaded with educational material to help improve the mathematics performance of Grade 10 girl learners.

In 2007, Nokia launched a new wiki website—www.ShareIdeas.org in partnership with Vodafone. It encourages people to share ideas on how to use mobile communications to address social and environmental challenges.

Employees give their time to community projects they care about through the Nokia Helping Hands programme. In 2007, Nokia employees in some 30 countries volunteered a total of over 32,000 hours. Activities included building schools, cleaning beaches, collecting toys, clothes and other supplies for people in need, and arranging activities for children and the elderly.

Youth Development

Nokia supports youth development programmes that develop confidence, teamwork, leadership and conflict management among disadvantaged young people in around 40 countries. Plan International and the International Youth Foundation are two of Nokia's main partners and their collaboration spans a variety of different causes, based on local needs.

A Responsible Organization

In 2008 after the discovery of a defect in the BL-5C series of batteries, Nokia immediately recalled the defective lot and ensured users' defective batteries were replaced at no additional cost. Nokia also provided awareness regarding the same through the audio-visual as well as print media. Their website even today has a facility to check whether a user's Nokia mobile battery is from the defective lot or not. This has created a sense of faith in consumers that Nokia is a responsible organization.

Competition

Nokia by virtue of the fact that it operates in one of the world's fastest growing mobile phone markets faces intense competition. Some of the prominent competitors are listed below.

Samsung India

Samsung entered India in December 1995, initially to develop it as a hub for the parent company's West Asia regional operations which included apart from India, Nepal, Sri Lanka, Bangladesh, Maldives and Bhutan. Samsung, being a large consumer electronics group, is also into manufacturing TVs, washing machines and refrigerators. It has a manufacturing facility at Noida, from where it manufactures GSM handsets. It controls a total market share of 7.5-8 per cent. For 2008, Samsung has achieved 15 per cent market share, thus achieving sales of 15 million handsets.

Products: Currently Samsung Mobiles has a product line of 11517 GSM handsets and 7-8 CDMA handsets. Samsung has positioned its mobile phones across three design categories: sliders, flip phones and bar-type phones.

Samsung devoted its human resources and technology to create superior products and services, thereby contributing to a better global society . . . . Their aim is to gain technological leadership in the Indian marketplace even as the company's goal is to earn the love and respect of more and more Indian consumers.

Samsung has positioned its products in a wide range of categories. It has targeted the lower end of users with simple basic models such as C1401, C160 and C170—equipped with speakerphones. At the higher end Samsung has introduced E490, J600, U600 and X520: phones that come with Bluetooth, 1-2 mega-pixel cameras and sleek design features.

Samsung has also introduced some premium models like Serenata, a model developed along with

Bang and Olufsen and positioned as a high-end music player cum mobile phone.

Strategic alliances: With Nokia (April 2007), co-develop technology for handsets and DVB-H standardization solutions (January 2007), establish a joint venture for developing a Linux platform (Samsung Electronics, Vodafone, DoCoMo, Motorola and NEC).

Promotion: Samsung has appointed Amir Khan as the brand ambassador for its mobile phones in India. Also, in the past it had appointed the Indian cricket team as brand ambassadors.

Sony Ericsson

Sony Ericsson India was established in October 2001 as a 50 : 50 joint venture between Sony Corporation and Telefonaktiebolaget LM Ericsson. The company has a market share of around 8 per cent of the Indian mobile handset market.

Product: The Walkman series of Sony Ericsson has helped it carve out a strong position for itself in the highly competitive Indian market. They have a huge range of handsets (approximately 90) with each handset having variants. At the lower end they have phones with basic features like colour display and limited memory size. In the higher segment, they have phones like larger memory capacity (up to 4GB), better camera quality (2-3 megapixels) and better quality earphones. They also have premium products with excellent cameras and memory capacities. The styling of these models is such that it appeals to the young, fashion-conscious consumers.

Promotion: Sony Ericsson has positioned itself as a cool, trendy and young brand. This is reflected in its promotional strategy revolving around Bollywood heartthrob Hrithik Roshan. The company has leveraged its superior technology in terms of sound quality. The entire 'I Love the thump' campaign revolves around this. 'Cybershot' and 'Walkman' are some of the technology-related features that SE has used extensively in its promotion campaigns. Cybershot provides high-quality cameras with facilities to organize and transfer pictures. The Walkman series of phones provides high-quality MP3 music and noise cancellation-enabled headphones. Sony Ericsson, with its superb sound quality, high decibel promotion campaigns and trendy young image, is a formidable competitor for Nokia.

INDUSTRY ANALYSIS

Suppliers

Nokia's supplier arrangements are driven by a clearly defined code of conduct. All Nokia suppliers are expected to meet certain performance standards based upon Human Rights practices, workforce practices, and so on. In the US, Nokia has tried to develop supplier relations with women and minority-owned suppliers as an image building exercise.

As per the company document, Nokia considers environmental, ethical, and health and safety issues, as well as labour practices, are not separate add-on features, but are embedded within all sourcing processes, including supplier selection and relationship development.

The suppliers are divided into two categories:

(1) Direct: Components, parts, packaging, software, R&D.
(2) Indirect: Marketing material, IT supports.

Supplier Assessment

Nokia regularly assesses its supplier's practices and performance through experts and NGOs (for environmental practices) regularly. If certain weaknesses are seen, Nokia suggests corrective action to be implemented with the support of Nokia. If suppliers refuse to take concrete steps for improvement, Nokia reconsiders its business relationship.

One major challenge faced by Nokia is that with expanding manufacturing locations, the distance and transportation costs for suppliers are increasing. To overcome this, Nokia has tried to locate its plants closer to supplier bases. In Chennai, where Nokia has set up a plant near Sriperumbudur, ten Nokia suppliers have already set up their own plants.

Nokia is also a part of GeSI, or Global e-Sustainability Initiative for Supply Chain. This is an alliance with members such as Cisco, Bell, and Motorola. As a part of this alliance, industry-wide tools for risk assessment and feedback have been developed.

Substitutes

Nokia's main functional utility is communication. Any device which can ease communication is a potential substitute. Following are the devices that could be formidable substitutes in the near future:

Wireless Internet: As laptops and palmtops become cheaper, more people would have access to mobile computing devices. As wireless Internet facilities become commonly available, people would prefer to use Internet tools such as Skype, VoIP-based tools, Web chat and email to communicate, due to lower costs. Already players such as Reliance Communications are offering wireless Internet cards that can be used all over India for access to Internet.

WLL: Wireless in Local Loop is a technology that allows cheap access to communication within a specific short range of around 30 km. It is very popular among businessmen and local traders and could emerge as a significant threat to Nokia in the future.

Public telephones: Although, the Indian public telephone network isn't technologically advanced, it has a very wide reach and is thus a potential substitute if developed better. As enterprises like Tata Communications invest further in developing modern PCOs and STD outlets, the threat from these would increase.

New Entrants

The Indian mobile handset market has some very strong players like Nokia and Motorola who are firmly entrenched. But certain newer players are trying to enter this market. As billions of dollars are at stake, a lot of companies are watching the action closely and are devising ways of entering the market.

Korean and Chinese players like Ezze Mobile and Amoi Electronics are planning to flood the Indian market with cheap handsets. Since these players have their manufacturing and sourcing in relatively inexpensive South-East Asian regions, their only major cost driver is export cost and duties. Korea Telecom has signed MOUs with BSNL. Singapore Technology and other companies are looking at JVs with Indian companies for entering the Indian market. Equipment manufacturers like ZTE and Huawei are also looking at leveraging their Chinese experience in India, considering that the two markets have a lot of commonalities.

Huawei C228s

Huawei C208s

Newer entrants face the challenges of building a brand image and developing a service network in India, controlled largely by the bigger players. As per industry experts, generating sales of around 20,000 handsets or more on a sustained basis would be the benchmark for newer entrants. For this, the newer players have two options:

(1) Low-cost phones with good features.
(2) Entering newer markets like villages and tier II cities.

Both options come with challenges from the established players. Clearly, the hot and happening Indian mobile industry will see a lot of new players coming in and it would also see a lot of counteractions by established players like Nokia.

Consumers

The Indian mobile phone market has a diverse range of consumers, each with a unique set of requirements. Indian mobile users change mobile phones

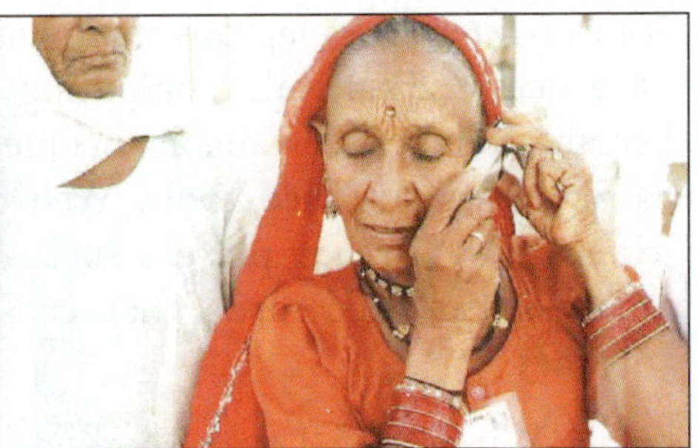

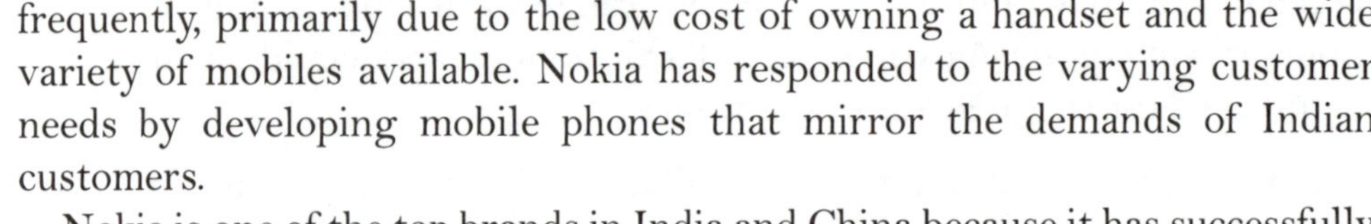

frequently, primarily due to the low cost of owning a handset and the wide variety of mobiles available. Nokia has responded to the varying customer needs by developing mobile phones that mirror the demands of Indian customers.

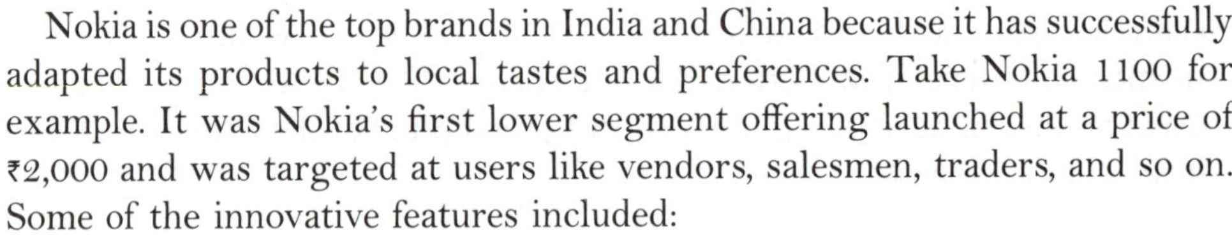

Nokia is one of the top brands in India and China because it has successfully adapted its products to local tastes and preferences. Take Nokia 1100 for example. It was Nokia's first lower segment offering launched at a price of ₹2,000 and was targeted at users like vendors, salesmen, traders, and so on. Some of the innovative features included:

(1) Sturdy design, especially the touchpad which was designed to withstand dust and humidity.
(2) Torch light to be used in case of power failures.
(3) Dust cover and slip-free grip suited to Indian conditions.

Nokia reaped the benefits of customization by establishing itself as the most popular Indian brand in the handset market. It also developed products aimed at specific segments such as Nokia Ngage, targeted at gaming freaks. It had features such as good speakers, graphics support for games and an array of games to be played. Similarly, the Nokia Communicator was aimed at business users looking for feature-rich phones. It supported Windows Live, allowed easy access to the Internet, and quick office tools for document management. It was at targeted users looking for a lot more than making calls and messaging from their phones. The Communicator was positioned as a complete handheld device, a more portable substitute for a palmtop or a laptop.

Considering the rapidly increasing Indian mobile phone market and the specific requirements of different Indian customer segments, Nokia clearly has to keep a tab on consumer demands and adapt its product offerings accordingly. The mobile handset market shall be dominated by the player who is the first to understand consumer preferences and bring out a product that meets the needs of the market, before anyone else and at an appropriate price point. Nokia has done this successfully so far, whether it can continue to do so remains to be seen.

Marketing Mix for the N-Series

Product

'This next step in digital convergence brings together mobile devices, Internet content, still and video cameras, music, email and much more. Nokia N-series devices share similar design traits as mobile phones, but they are actually powerful pocketable computers with a comprehensive set of multimedia features.

Nokia was named 'Brand of the Year' by the CII in 2005, for being 'most preferred' by consumers. Over the last few years Nokia has become more of a pull brand as customers demonstrate strong brand loyalty and brand recall and ask specifically for Nokia while buying.

Nokia is a world leader in mobile communications, driving the growth of the mobile industry. It is adapting to a rapidly changing, highly competitive and innovation-driven market by providing equipment, solutions and services customized to segments.

Nokia has segmented consumers into 12 distinct geographical, psychographic and demographic segments with distinct preferences. Understanding these preferences gives Nokia the ability to respond to consumers in various markets by providing the right combination of design, style, functionality, and price and marketing.

The N-series, Nokia's new offering in 2009, provides stylish handsets positioned as 'multimedia phones'. Mobile phones are becoming more innovative with time. The latest handsets are 3G-enabled and quite a few of them come with advanced multimedia and imaging capabilities. The N-series comes with some of the best features that ensure a whole world of information, entertainment and connectivity on the move. All the models in this series boast of at least megapixel cameras, digital music players, Bluetooth, and 3G support with streaming video.

The edge that Nokia has over its competitors is the large range of phones it offers to consumers. The N-series is no different. For example, the N96 targets the young, on-the-go, technologically-savvy consumer with the tag line, 'Designed for great TV and video entertainment', while the red version of the N76 targets urban women with the tag line 'The computer done beautifully'.

As the N-series mobile phones are based on Series 60, users can choose from more than 3,000 add-on applications to customize their handsets to best suit their needs. Therefore, the N-series range is the preferred choice of customers who want mobility with the latest technology and great design, for both work and leisure.

The target segment for the N-series is the young, urban, fashion-conscious and financially well-off consumer. The N-series phone sales since 2006 show that they are very popular among affluent young adults. These phones provide value to the users and at the same time are a status symbol. The new offerings in the N-series will help Nokia make inroads into the top-end of the market where it is weak, losing out to competitors like Apple and Sony Ericsson that have come out with chic models. Also, this segment is predicted to grow phenomenally in the next few years.

Price

Skimming Price Strategy

As explained earlier, the Nokia N-series targets the younger generation as well as the technology-savvy consumer. This target market is more product-centric and less price-sensitive. The consumers are interested in the integrated features of the phone and the quality of the applications provided.

The mobile market in India is highly competitive and the mobile models become obsolete in a short span of less than a year. To cater to such a market Nokia has followed the skimming pricing strategy for the N-series. It has focused on maximizing profits in the initial stage of the product and then lowering the margin once the product starts losing market attractiveness. Nokia has introduced N-series phones at regular intervals and every time it has launched them with advanced features and better technology. This is the main reason for the loss of attractiveness of existing N-series phones, causing a fall in their prices. This results in self-cannibalization. But the new models brought in the market have a high profit potential because of premium prices charged for the features provided.

N70: Nokia introduced the N-series in the Indian market with the N70. The price at the time of launch was ₹26,000 to ₹28,000. This was a very high price for a mobile phone then but features such as 2 megapixel camera, bigger screen, and advanced applications made this phone a unique one in the market. But within a short span of time, Nokia came up with higher-end phones in the N-series because of which the N70's price was slashed by more than 60 per cent. This is a perfect example of the skimming pricing strategy followed by Nokia.

Differential Pricing Strategy

Nokia follows the differential pricing strategy for certain products in the N-series:.

- N70 and N70 Music Edition
- N73 and N73 Music Edition
- N80 and N80 Internet Edition
- N81 and N81 8GB
- N91 and N91 8GB
- N95 and N95 8GB
- N93, N93i and N93 Golf Edition

The slogan 'connecting people' means that the target of Nokia focuses on building relationships rather than only produce new cellular phones. The N-series products have differential prices for additional features provided. For example, the N70 Music Edition has a dedicated button for music along with extra memory for storing songs. The N93 Golf Edition has an integrated golf playing software for professional golf players. The N80 Internet Edition has an advanced navigation system and better connectivity software. This differential pricing strategy has helped Nokia charge a premium for certain unique features provided.

N73: The N73 was introduced in India in February 2007 at a price of ₹21,000 while the price of N73 Music Edition cost around ₹23,000. The marginal price difference was for better music features along with a 2GB memory card. These features, if purchased separately, would cost around ₹7,000. Thus the differential pricing strategy used by Nokia was to attract the customer towards the higher-end variant which provided more benefits at a lesser price.

Promotion

In the recent past, Nokia's 'pull' promotional strategy by investing heavily in marketing campaigns to build brand awareness and brand loyalty has worked well. The corporate slogan, 'Nokia—Connecting People' runs through most of the company's campaigns as the demand for more innovations and connectivity dominates consumer buying decision.

The Nokia N-series is directed towards the 'Explore' segment, as per its segmentation study in India. This segment is made up of young, technology-savvy customers and the promotional campaigns are directed towards creating an impact on this target segment and influencing their buying behaviour.

Nokia's promotional strategy is directed at promoting platforms. For instance, rather than heavily promoting individual mobile phones which have short product life cycles, Nokia promotes music. By using this strategy, one model can replace another while the branding remains the same.

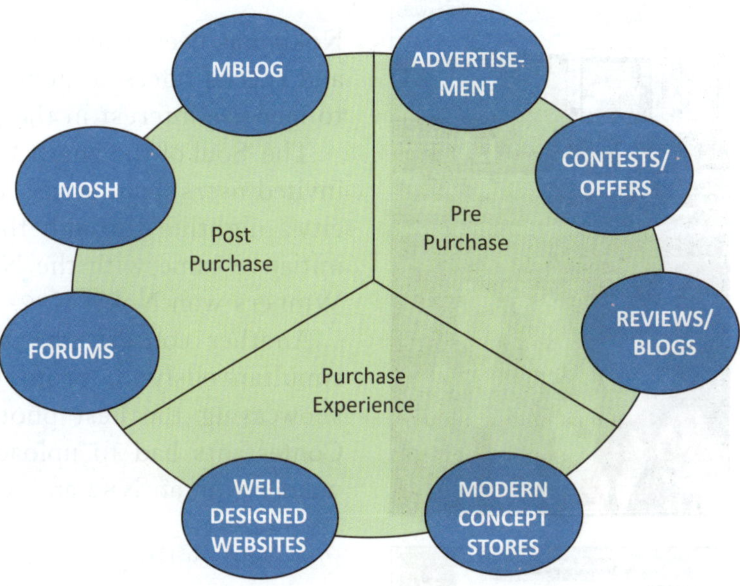

Figure 14.8: Nokia's promotional strategy

Nokia has successfully employed various promotional campaigns such as:

- Advertising (television, print, Internet)
- Sales promotion
- Personal selling

Other promotional types include public relation exercises and free publicity.

Advertising

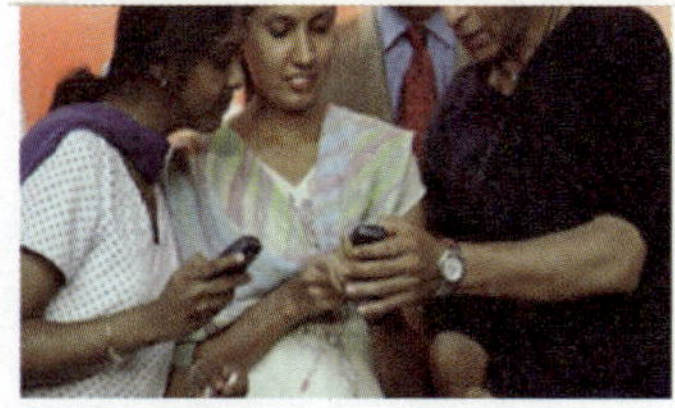

Nokia has come up with innovative advertising campaigns for the print media as well as television to promote the N-series. For the N-series in general, the advertising campaigns focus on superior functionalities and technological features. The advertisements are different for different mobile phones in the range. For example, the N91 which has superior music playback capabilities is being promoted with the slogan 'I am my music' with a picture of a young music lover around a music theme. All the advertisements feature young and dynamic models to convey the essence of the product.

Nokia which worldwide has generally refrained from using any brand ambassador has adapted to the Indian market by getting film star Shahrukh Khan for its latest brand campaign. He was chosen as the brand ambassador because of his pan-India appeal, his tech-savviness and because he has been patronizing Nokia for almost a decade. The TV commercial features

Shahrukh Khan using various Nokia phones in different circumstances and highlighting their functionality.

The Internet has also been used in a big way to promote the buying and use of N-series phones. Websites and blogs (which are generally visited by young Internet-using population) have also been integrated into the promotional campaigns. Blogs like NseriesMBlog and websites such as MOSH.com are designed to generate user interest by providing unique incentives to Nokia users.

Sales Promotion

Nokia has been a master at using sales promotion techniques like contests and special offers to generate awareness when a new model is released or to increase interest in the products.

The 'Soul of the Night Contest' was a unique new-age tech challenge that invited users from across India to discover and capture stories about their city's nightlife through their mobile devices and share with others. This initiative came with the Nokia N82, which redefined mobile photography. Winners won Nokia N82.

Another contest, the World Press Photo (WPP) Contest, was used simultaneously to promote the N82. This was an international event showcasing the best photo-journalism pictures from over 70 countries. Contestants had to upload pictures onto the website to participate. The winner won an N82 and a chance to participate in the WPP exhibition.

Personal Selling

Nokia has taken personal selling to a new level by opening Nokia concept stores in India. The stores guarantee an easy and informative shopping experience. With easy-to-navigate set-ups and aesthetic ambience, the stores provide a relaxed and satisfying customer experience.

According to the Nokia management, the stores reflect the company's leadership in the industry by providing a unique and exciting space to explore a variety of features provided in Nokia's broad range of mobile phones. These stores have skilled sales personnel who demonstrate the latest mobile phones, wireless phone capabilities and also offer expert customer service to new and returning customers looking to buy, maintain or enhance their phones. Customers can also find the latest Nokia enhancements, branded clothing and bags, ringtones, graphics, games and software.

Public Relation Exercises and Publicity

Mobile phone reviews/press releases: Nokia generally releases phone-based kits for journalists to file news reports and multimedia stories, like it did during the release of the N95. This mobile journalist kit contains the newly released phone, a microphone for recording interviews, keyboard for typing text-based stories, and a tripod. Regular press releases are also done by the company.

Nokia has also introduced MOSH, a cross-platform mobile and desktop social networking site created to help developers publicize and distribute their applications. MOSH is a dedicated mobile devices' social networking community where software developers can create, upload, collect and share applications.

Environmental campaigns: Nokia has partnered with WWF through the One Planet Business concept.

Place

Nokia started its distribution in India with a long-term partnership with HCL (formerly Hindustan Computers Limited), which had already built an extensive network for its own products. Nokia and HCL have served the Indian markets for more than ten years. The two companies have also decided to develop a go-to-market strategy to jointly address the coverage needs of the urban and widely dispersed rural areas. HCL was the sole seller of Nokia phones before the latter got into the retail business. But recently, Nokia has decided to supplement HCL distributorship with its own efforts. Both companies realized that there was tremendous growth opportunity and that this was the best way to utilize the resources of both organizations in an optimum manner.

Nokia has also built its first Indian handset manufacturing plant at Sriperumbudur near Chennai. This has helped the distribution channels and the logistics personnel involved in transporting the handsets to the respective regional hubs. From the regional hubs the mobile handsets are delivered to wholesalers who have been allocated specific regions and outlets. Generally there is one wholesaler for a district place in each state.

The wholesaler then satisfies the demand of individual outlets. Maturity and changes in the customers' expectations have been the criteria used by Nokia to determine its distribution strategy.

The distribution channels used by Nokia for selling mobile handsets to end consumers are:

- Nokia priority dealers
- Nokia care centres
- Nokia professionals
- Mobile retail outlets
- E-Retail
- Grey markets

Nokia priority dealers: Nokia-dedicated stores are used to get more visibility in urban areas, metros and tier I towns where mobility has been around for a few years, customer expectations are more evolved, and are continuously evolving. Nokia has been successful in satisfying the customers by providing distribution outlets with relevant competency and skills sets. These outlets try to bring to life all the experiences that Nokia experiential zones across the world offer to customers.

Retail outlets: The mobile retail stores which offer customers all brands of mobile handsets push products based on commissions paid to them and customer demand. The customer who is not biased towards a particular brand or does not have knowledge about mobile handsets is totally dependent on the retail salesman. Nokia has been successful in maintaining cordial relations with retail outlet owners. It is also encouraging dealers to accept exclusive Nokia dealership. People who have been selling consumer electronics, STD booth owners and even cloth merchants are now getting into this business. People who operate existing businesses decide to set up a separate shop only for mobile phones due to customer engagement which requires a completely different approach.

E-Retail: E-commerce in India is accelerating at a fast rate. The Internet is penetrating every corner of India and the security provided by the networking companies is also improving. Thus e-retailing has a good potential but is yet to be tapped in developing countries like India.

Grey markets: Grey markets are widely spread across different cities in India. The main reasons for high selling of mobile handsets in grey markets are:

- Exclusion of taxes, offering customers phones at cheaper rates
- Credit periods offered by dealers

The mobile handsets sold in grey market are generally smuggled from the South-East Asian nations or the Middle East. They generally do not give an invoice to the customer due to which the customer cannot avail warranty. But the mobile market is so dynamic that customers give less preference to warranty and high preference to price. Grey markets are unauthorized in India, but the penetration of these dealers is so high that they have become one of the major distribution channels.

Business-to-Business Strategy

Nokia also deals with business customers like Reliance and Tata Indicom which provide CDMA services in India. The distribution strategy used for these business clients is given in Figure 14.9.

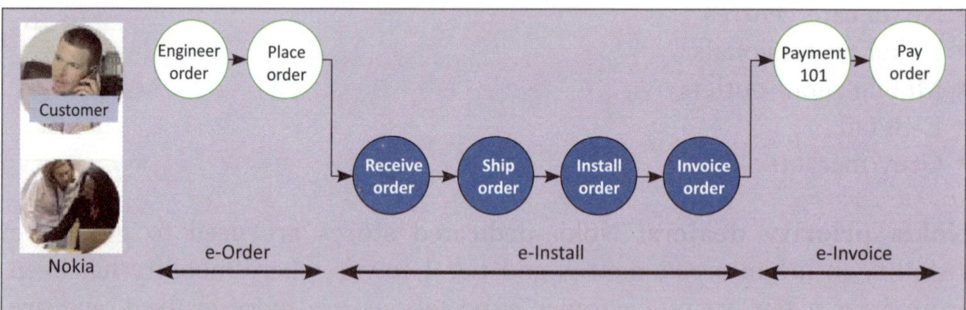

Figure 14.9: Nokia's B2B strategy

This distribution strategy has helped Nokia in the following ways:

- Speed, visibility and collaboration in an extended value chain.
- Efficiency in business transactions.
- Efficiency and speed in implementing new business processes with trading partners.
- Standard-based automated processes.

Emerging Distribution Strategy

The next phase of distribution strategy devised by Nokia and HCL is:

- Penetrate deeper into smaller and rural markets which have high potential growth.
- Maintain current market share while undergoing expansion.
- Align to Nokia's global policy of balanced channel mix.

Consumer Behaviour Analysis

Fishbein Analysis

The results of the Fishbein analysis for the data by AC Nielsen in 2009 are as follows:

Table 14.5: Results of the Fishbein analysis

Attribute	*Nokia*	*Sony Ericsson*	*Samsung*	*Motorola*	*Others*
Price	851	772	657	667	473
Style and design	921	887	763	822	549
Technology	975	892	745	772	547
Ease of use	1129	874	798	731	594
Ergonomics	726	641	559	567	410
Accessories	659	621	518	542	412
Reliability and ruggedness	1045	807	711	698	554
Camera	865	840	646	606	435
Sound quality	844	888	639	693	482
Dimensions and memory	929	831	724	733	529
Battery life	1167	911	808	788	589
Display	960	887	718	742	506
Internet and connectivity	882	765	686	634	509

The analysis provides a comparative understanding of consumer attitude towards each attribute for every brand. As we can see in Table 14.5, Nokia is the leader in all attributes except 'sound quality' where it loses out to Sony Ericsson.

In order to improve further, they used factor analysis on the 13 attributes which one can consider important.

Factor Analysis

By using factor analysis we reduce the number of variables to be considered for the given data set. All 13 attribute variables are rated by the survey respondents on a scale of 1 to 5. The variables are as follows:

(a) Price
(b) Style and design
(c) Technology
(d) Ease of use

(e) Ergonomics
(f) Accessories
(g) Reliability and ruggedness
(h) Camera
(i) Sound quality
(j) Dimensions and memory
(k) Battery life
(l) Display
(m) Internet and connectivity

The factor analysis identifies six important variables for Nokia: (i) Technology; (ii) Battery life; (iii) Dimensions and memory; (iv) Sound quality; (iv) Ergonomics; and (vi) Display.

Nokia's performance vis-à-vis its competitors for each of these attributes is as follows:

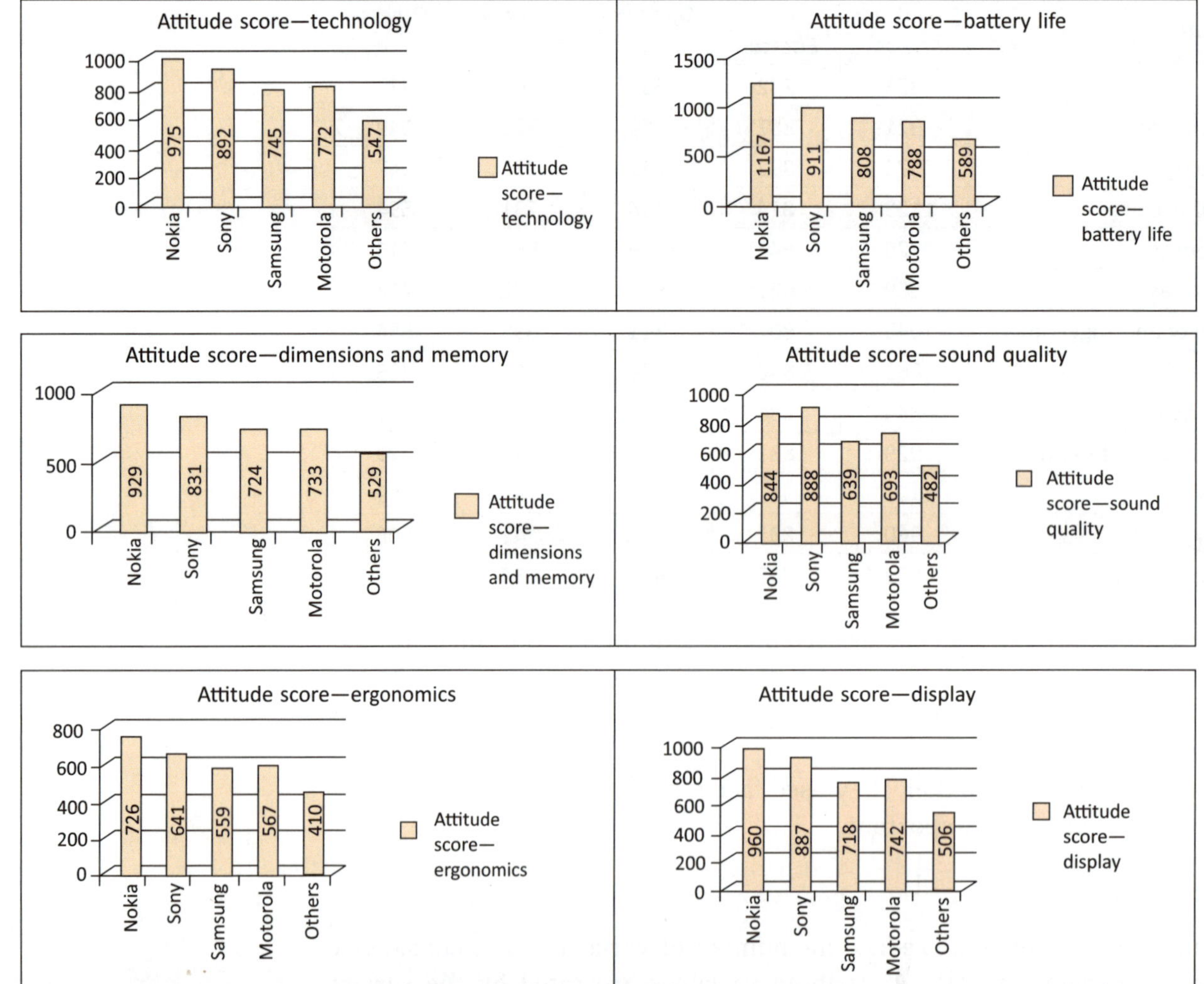

Figure 14.10: Nokia's performance on key variables against that of competitors

Nokia is clearly a leader in technology as compared to its competitors. It needs to maintain this position, by regularly coming up with new models with cutting-edge technology. In fact, using newer technologies like EDGE and WLAN will give Nokia the ability to maintain this position in the market.

Battery life is very critical for all mobile devices and Nokia is again a clear winner in this category. As more feature-rich phones are added, Nokia shall need to address the issue of battery life.

The dimensions and memory capacity of the phone are critical driving factors in determining the popularity of mobile phones. Dimensions relate to the ease of carrying the mobile phone. Memory capacity is a necessary factor as photos, music and graphics-heavy games need higher memory capacity. Nokia needs to ensure that it provides adequate memory capacity in its phones in order to ensure that users are able to utilize features such as games and music to a higher extent.

On sound quality, Sony Ericsson is seen as superior to Nokia. As a lot of mobile users see their mobile devices as portable music players, Nokia should try and improve the sound quality by not just introducing more music edition phones but also by ensuring good quality headphones for all its mobiles across price ranges.

Ergonomics, or the layout and design of the phone is vital in influencing purchase decisions. Nokia isn't really known for stylish phones, but is perceived as having a well-designed, systematically arranged phone. It must ensure that in its pursuit for style, it does not compromise on ergonomics.

Nokia has a good score on display quality. Since this score is driven by screen size and brightness, Nokia must ensure that it increases the screen sizes of some of the lower-end models to drive up this score.

References

1. Rajeev Dubey and Sunny Sen, 'Numeros: A Cover Story on Nokia', *BusinessWorld*, 21 September 2009.
2. HCL (n.d.), 'HCL and Nokia—Long-Term Distribution Strategy', retrieved 20 March 2008, from HCL Infosystems: www.hclinfosystems.com/hcl-nokia.pdf
3. Nokia B2B Marketing (n.d.), retrieved 20 March 2008, from Nokia website.
4. Nokia, 'HCL Infosystems Extend Distribution Pact', retrieved 21 March 2008, from channeltimes.com: http://www.channeltimes.com/India/News/Nokia_HCL_Infosystems_Extend_Distribution_Pact/551-71446-741.html
5. 'Mobiles will Revolutionise Seven Sectors in Rural India', Nokia, CKS, Michael Schwartz, 30 January 2007.
6. 'Nokia Takes Four-lane Road to Consumers', *The Economic Times*, 20 January 2007.
7. 'Nokia: N-series Leads Nokia Brand Revival', Brandrepublic.com, 25 January 2007.
8. 'How Nokia India is Transforming Itself', rediffnews.com, 28 November 2007.
9. http://www.nokia.com/environment
10. http://www.filesaveas.com/nseries.html, N-series handsets
11. Nokia Concept Store in Chandigarh, Mobile Phones India, 3 February 2007.
12. http://www.nokia.com/A4136002?newsid=802540
13. http://www.nokia.com/A4126368
14. http://business.mapsofindia.com/communications-industry/equipment/nokia.html
15. http://www.rediff.com/money/2006/feb/15nokia.htm
16. http://newsinfo.inquirer.net/breakingnews/infotech/view_article.php?article_id=73036
17. www.mobiletechnews.com/info/2005/03/01/004003.html
18. www.indiantelevision.com/mam/headlines/y2k4/apr/aprmam106.htm

ANNEXURE  MODEL COURSE HANDOUT FOR APPLIED MARKETING

annexure

1. Genesis

Higher education is witnessing a general trend toward the use of more active, participatory and collaborative techniques in the classroom. These approaches share mutual goals, including the promotion of active learning, bridging the distance between students and educators, creating a sense of community, and ensuring that knowledge is created rather than transferred. The integration of active learning methods into the classroom also signals a paradigm shift in graduate and postgraduate instruction. Preparing students for the increasingly complex workplace environment takes more than minor modifications in current teaching practices. It requires a break with the traditional ways of thinking about education (the 'passive learning' paradigm) and a willingness to explore a novel approach to instruction. For long, knowledge creation through the development and empirical testing of theory was viewed as the primary driver of human progress in the Lockean system of knowledge and learning.

However, with the world growing increasingly complex, it has become apparent that B-Schools have not adapted adequately to the new environment. They have been criticized for failing to prepare MBA graduates for the rapid changes or equipping them with new skills necessary to cope with today's diverse and global business environments. In response to these criticisms, certain business schools have begun to focus on both teaching quality and instructional methods. With increasing frequency, business instructors are using cases, simulations, and team assignments to improve the communication skills of students and structure course material that is more closely related to organizational reality.

The underlying assumption of active and experiential learning is that the student is the worker, while the teacher is the coach. 'Teacher talk' is replaced or supplemented by student research, oral presentations, team projects, and class debates or discussions. Instructors give up absolute control over the flow of information (in the form of pre-designed lectures) and guide students who are engaged in actively creating and presenting knowledge. The rationale behind such an approach is two fold: first, students are actively involved in constructing their own learning experiences; and second, they are exposed to the exploratory, collegiate patterns of adult learning (particularly in work situations).

Moreover, in my opinion, while expanding the basic marketing course content (under Active and Experiential Learning methodologies), a business school faculty must also impart new skills in the classroom. There is increasing evidence to indicate that business leaders and employees must develop abilities in key areas, such as:

(a) **Cross-functional integration**: Employees must be able to communicate across functional boundaries to solve problems. Effective employees are those who can integrate information across the various business segments. As industry has urged business schools: It's not just skills. It's the interrelationship of skills that matter.

(b) **Teamwork and team building:** Employees need to work together to reach decisions by consensus, to allocate tasks across a group, and to pool the talent of diverse workers. Employees must foster teamwork and partnership not just within their own organizations but also with suppliers and customers. Team building--a skill acquired by practice, is also being added to B-School curricula in the form of Outward Bound Survival trips and experiential exercises into MBA programmes.

(c) **Listening skills:** Business employees must learn to listen as never before because organizational and individual success depends upon understanding other employees, customers, partners, suppliers and outsourcers and regulators. Listening includes the ability to hear and comprehend disparate views that arise out of diversity in the workplace, cross-functional integration, globalization and other forces.

(d) **Critical thinking and problem solving:** Employees must be able to digest information, explore it for relevance to their work, and then translate it into useful knowledge for themselves and others in the organization. They especially need the skills to detect and articulate problems when they are unstructured. Employees must also be able to assemble and synthesize information from unrelated sources to solve problems.

Though a seemingly overwhelming proposition, these skills can be integrated into the traditional business school environment, specially through the use of 'active and experiential learning'—an educational paradigm that involves students in constructing their own learning experiences and exposes them to the collegiate patterns of work situations. When used in the context of an Applied Marketing course (which provides new content), active learning offers an educational underpinning for the pivotal work force skills required in business.

2. Session Plan with Coverage, References and Activities Under Active and Experiential Learning Methodology

This section provides a selection of active and experiential learning applications as well as exercises that address the four content areas for marketing discussed in *Applied Case Studies in Marketing.*

Module I: Principles and Drivers of the Value-Driven New Age Marketing

Coverage includes: The paradigm shift in marketing, positioning marketing as a primary driver in the digital economy, customer value, core competencies and collaborative networks which includes mastering value in the digital economy, a shift in operational marketing, reverse product designs, reverse pricing, reverse advertising, reverse promotions, reverse segmentation, capturing the customer's cognitive space and capturing the collaborator's resource, space-building enabling environment, moving towards relationship marketing during market turbulence, e-drivers, the Internet and mobile phone marketing, and the ten Cs for Internet marketers.

Recommended reading

Philip Kotler, Dipak C. Jain and Suvit Maesincee, *Marketing Moves: A New Approach to Profits, Growth and Renewal*, Harvard Business School Press, Chapters 1 and 2, pp. 3–55.

S. Shajahan, *Relationship Marketing: Text and Cases,* McGraw-Hill, New Delhi, Chapter 1, pp. 1–17.

Richard Gay, Alan Charlesworth and Rita Esen, *Online Marketing: A Customer-Led Approach,* New Delhi: Oxford University Press, Chapter 1, pp. 1–32.

Extended learning/activity

Marketing Model: Issues Raised by the Marketing Model and in Search of Good Marketing, Peter Cheverton, *Key Marketing Skills,* 2nd edn, Kogan Page Ltd., London, pp. 3–34.

Case Study: 'Nokia ... Connecting People', Group presentation/report.

Market/Sector Focus: 'Telecom/3G mobile revolution' Group Term Paper.

Corporate Insight: Bharati Airtel Ltd., Group Research activity/report.

Module II: Shaping the Market Offerings

Product characteristics include: Classification, product-focused organization, changes affecting product management, product differentiation, product form, design, features, product quality, durability, service differentiation, personnel differentiation, channel differentiation, image differentiation, product line analysis, line stretching, filling and pruning, product life cycle, developing product strategy, positioning new product development, ethical issues concerning the product, packaging and its importance in marketing, designer tools which include shape, size, colour, graphics, materials and fragrance-packaging.

Branding and packaging include: Brand as a concept, value and asset, types of brands, the new rules of brand management, key principles of competitive branding, six facets of brand identity, the changing nature of retail brands, managing global brands, brand architecture, managing brand and product relationship, tracking brand equity, brand strategy decision and, recent advances in brand management.

Strategy mix and models for the virtual world: This includes Internet relationships, dot.com flashbacks, business models for the modern economy, online product attributes and web marketing implications, augmented product concept (APC) and its application to the Web, customizing the product offering and new product development online.

Value drivers include: Operational excellence, product leadership, customer intimacy, delivering value, total business experience, identifying a customers' TBE and adding value by removing features.

Recommended reading

Philip Kotler, Kevin Keller, Abraham Koshy and Mithileswar Jha, *Marketing Management: A South Asian Perspective*, 13th edn, New Delhi: Pearson Education, Chapter 12 , pp. 316–35.

David Jobber and John Fahy, *Foundations of Marketing,* 2nd edn, McGraw-Hill Education, UK, Chapter 6, pp. 137–70.

Peter Cheverton, *Key Marketing Skills,* 2nd edn, London: Kogan Page Ltd., Chapters 14 and 18, pp. 118–25, 186–97.

Donald R. Lehmann and Russell S. Winer, *Product Management*, McGraw-Hill, USA, Chapters 1, 8 and 9, pp. 1–25, 237–300.

P.R. Smith and Jonathan Taylor, *Marketing Communications: An Integrated Approach*, 4th edn, London: Kogan Page Ltd., Chapter 17, pp. 542–65.

Jean Noel Kapferer, *The New Strategic Brand Management,* London: Kogan Page Ltd., Chapters 1, 4–6, 12, pp. 9–29, 75–121, 293–328, 395–438.

Richard Gay, Alan Charlesworth and Rita Esen, *Online Marketing: A Customer-Led Approach,* New Delhi: Oxford University Press, Chapter 2, pp. 37–72.

Extended learning/activity

Lateral Marketing at the Product Level: Philip Kotler and Fernando Trias De Bes, *Lateral Marketing: New Technique for Finding Breakthrough Ideas,* John Wiley & Sons Inc., USA, pp. 155–73.

Products and Brands: Jonathan Groucutt, Peter Leadley and Patrick Forsyth, *Marketing: Essential Principles and New Realities*, London: Kogan Page Ltd., pp. 253–74.

Where brands came from and why that matters? The brand as an emotional charge, as a mark of loyalty and the B2B and service brands: Peter Cheverton, 'Understanding Brands', *The Sunday Times*, New York, pp. 1–50.

Case Study: (1) 'Kingfisher *v.* Jet Airways', Group presentation/report, (2) 'P&G's Brand management system', Group presentation/report, (3) 'Nivea: Managing an Umbrella Brand'.

Market/Sector Focus: (1) Indian full-line aviation sector, (2) FMCG, Group Term Paper

Corporate Insight: (1) Jet Airways Ltd., (2) Proctor & Gamble (P&G) and, (3) Beiersdorf (Nivea), Germany, Group research activity/report.

Module III: Pricing and Marketing

Coverage includes: Understanding pricing, significance and importance, consumer psychology and pricing, pricing decision framework, systemic pricing model, pricing methods, competitive pricing strategy matrix, pricing strategy *v.* tactics, approaches to price adjustments, experience curve pricing, Lopez factor, effects of price change and the competitor's reactions.

Pricing issues on the web: Online pricing strategies and tactics, online pricing methods, online pricing and marketing sophistication, online price and customer value, pricing and segmentation, Internet pricing influences and, outlook during market turbulence.

Recommended reading

Philip Kotler, Kevin Keller, Abraham Koshy and Mithileswar Jha, *Marketing Management: A South Asian Perspective*, 13th edn, New Delhi: Pearson Education, Chapter 14, pp. 363–93.

Rajan Saxena, *Marketing Management,* 4th edn, New Delhi: Tata McGraw-Hill, Chapter 14, pp. 320–40.

Peter Cheverton, *Key Marketing Skills,* 2nd edn, London: Kogan Page Ltd., Chapter 28, pp. 186–97, 332–55.

Richard Gay, Alan Charlesworth and Rita Esen, *Online Marketing: A Customer-Led Approach*, New Delhi: Oxford University Press, Chapter 10, pp. 349–83.

Extended learning/activity

Pricing: Els Gijsbrechts and Katia Campo, *Text Book of Marketing*, Keith Blois, ed., London: Oxford University Press, pp. 212–40.

Price and pricing strategies: Jonathan Groucutt, Peter Leadley and Patrick Forsyth, *Marketing: Essential Principles and New Realities*, London: Kogan Page Ltd., pp. 301–18.

Case Study: (1) Hype With Low Cost Airlines, (2) Coca-Cola: India's thirst for the rural market

Market/Sector Focus: Indian LCA Services and Soft Drinks & Beverages (Group Term Paper)

Corporate Insight: (1) SpiceJet, (2) Coca-Cola India, Group Term Paper

Module IV: Communication Mix in Marketing

Coverage includes: Marketing and the integrated communication mix, intensive marketing communications, media mix, media jargon, media characteristics, media buying, global misses, marketing communication tools, advertising, creative briefs, media strategy, sales promotion, creative promotions, PR mix, measuring media relations, running a sponsorship programme, personal selling and, hybrid marketing systems.

Online communication tools include: Internet and the communication process, promotional communication mix, online advertising, email marketing, viral marketing, public comment sites, affiliate marketing, public relations, commercial newsletters, blogging, online sales promotions, automation for online sales and integrating multi-channel strategies.

Recommended reading

Philip Kotler, Kevin Keller, Abraham Koshy and Mithileswar Jha, *Marketing Management: A South Asian Perspective*, 13th edn, New Delhi: Pearson Education, Chapters 17, 18 and 19, pp. 443–529.

P.R. Smith and Jonathan Taylor, *Marketing Communications: An Integrated Approach*, 4th edn, London: Kogan Page Ltd., Chapters 1, 7, 11–15, pp. 3–30, 189–214, 249.

Monle Lee and Carla Johnson, *Principles of Advertising: A Global Perspective,* 2nd edn, Haworth Press Inc., Chapters 8–10 and 14, pp. 143–211, 269–81.

Richard Gay, Alan Charlesworth and Rita Esen, *Online Marketing: A Customer-Led Approach,* New Delhi: Oxford University Press, Chapter 11, pp. 388–436.

Extended learning/activity

Marketing Communications: Gustav Puth, *Text Book of Marketing*, Keith Blois, ed., London: Oxford University Press, pp. 271–90.

Three graces of direct marketing: Drayton Bird, *Common Sense Direct and Digital Marketing,* 5th edn, London: Kogan Page Ltd., pp. 14–35.

Case Study: (1) Convergence of Global and Domestic Strategies: HUL Shows the Way, (2) Magic Campaign of Airtel: Express Yourself, (3) Maggie: Nestle's problem child?, Group presentation/report.

Market/Sector Focus: Developing an integrated communication programme through the IPL tournaments/Sony Max Channel: Event Management/Media, group term paper.

Corporate Insight: (1) Hindustan Unilever and Unilever, (2) Nestle SA and Nestle India Ltd, (3) NDTV and Bloomberg UTVi, group research activity/report.

Module V: Marketing of Services

Coverage includes: Growing importance of services in marketing, building SCA, focus strategies, developing marketing strategies for services, service differentiation, offer, delivery, image, managing service quality, new service development, hierarchy of new service categories, pricing strategies and techniques, customer complaints, tactical audit, customer satisfaction surveys and tracking of promotion.

Marketing of BFSI products: Major characteristics include technological innovations, profile of consumer, financial marketing strategy, bank product, e-banking, pricing, new product development regulatory mechanism, financial product mix, quality standards, products of LIC of India and insurance promotion mix.

Recommended reading

Philip Kotler, Kevin Keller, Abraham Koshy and Mithileswar Jha, *Marketing Management: A South Asian Perspective*, 13th edn, New Delhi: Pearson Education, Chapter 13, pp. 339–58.

S. Shajahan, *Services Marketing: Concepts, Practices and Cases from the Indian Environment*, 3rd edn, Mumbai: Himalaya Publishing House, Chapters 1, 4 and 5.

Valarie A. Zeithaml, Dwayne D. Gremler, Mary Jo Bitner and Ajay Pandit, *Services Marketing: Integrated Customer Focus Across the Firm*, 5th edn, McGraw-Hill, USA, Chapters 1 and 2, pp. 2–48.

S. Shajahan, *Marketing Research: Concepts and Practices*, New Delhi: Macmillan, Chapter 11, pp. 312–34.

Extended learning/activity

Credit card business of Standard Chartered Bank, Thomas Cook—to be or not to be? and Namdhari Fresh: R. Srinivasan, *Case Studies in Marketing: The Indian Context*, New Delhi: Prentice-Hall, pp. 229–42, 276–86, 287–95.

Blueprint for marketing success, persuasion in writing and presentations: Patrick Forsyth, *Marketing and Selling Professional Service*, 3rd edn, London: Kogan Page Ltd., Chapters 1 and 7, pp. 3–17, 179–210.

The tactical audit: Peter Cheverton, *Key Marketing Skills*, 2nd edn, London: Kogan Page Ltd., pp. 265–8.

Case Study: Riding Banking Reforms Under Your Palm, group presentation/report.

Market/Sector Focus: Marketing of value added services in telecom, airlines, health care, higher education, BFSI, event management and professional services, group term paper.

Corporate Insight: CITI Bank/Apollo Hospitals/PWC, group research activity/report

Module VI: Retailing

Coverage includes: Retail industry format, structure and composition, private labels, positioning and promotion, value gaps, demand drivers, shopping malls, multiplexes, success factors, impact of IT, e-tailing strategic issues in retailing, location, store image decisions, market decisions, product assortment and procurement, service mix and retailing environment and global trends in retailing.

Recommended reading

Philip Kotler, Kevin Keller, Abraham Koshy and Mithileswar Jha, *Marketing Management: A South Asian Perspective*, 13th edn, New Delhi: Pearson Education, Chapter 13, pp. 339–58.

S. Shajahan, *Services Marketing: Concepts, Practices and Cases from the Indian Environment*, 3rd edn, Mumbai: Himalaya Publishing House, Chapters 1, 4 and 5.

Valarie A. Zeithaml, Dwayne D. Gremler, Mary Jo Bitner and Ajay Pandit, *Services Marketing: Integrated Customer Focus Across the Firm*, 5th edn, McGraw-Hill, USA, Chapters 1 and 2, pp. 2–48.

S. Shajahan, *Marketing Research: Concepts and Practices*, New Delhi: Macmillan, Chapter 11, pp. 312–34.

Extended learning/activity

Credit card business of Standard Chartered Bank, Thomas Cook—to be or not to be? and Namdhari Fresh: R. Srinivasan, *Case Studies in Marketing: The Indian Context*, New Delhi: Prentice-Hall, pp. 229–42, 276–86, 287–95.

Blueprint for marketing success, persuasion in writing and presentations: Patrick Forsyth, *Marketing and Selling Professional Service*, 3rd edn, London: Kogan Page Ltd., Chapters 1 and 7, pp. 3–17, 179–210.

The tactical audit: Peter Cheverton, *Key Marketing Skills*, 2nd edn, London: Kogan Page Ltd., pp. 265–8.
Case Study: Riding Banking Reforms Under Your Palm, group presentation/report.
Market/Sector Focus: Marketing of value added services in telecom, airlines, health care, higher education, BFSI, event management and professional services, group term paper
Corporate Insight: CITI Bank/Apollo Hospitals/PWC, group research activity/report

Module VII: Customer Relationship Marketing & IT Enabled Marketing (ITEM)

Coverage includes: An overview of relationship marketing, relationship marketing programmes, striving for interactivity, life-time value, frequency, monetary value (REM) model, customer acquisition strategies, customer retention strategies and add-on selling strategies.

Recommended reading

S. Shajahan, *Relationship Marketing: Text and Cases*, New Delhi: McGraw-Hill, Chapters 2–4, 5, 9–10 and 11.
Richard Gay, Alan Charlesworth and Rita Esen, *Online Marketing: A Customer-Led Approach*, New Delhi: Oxford University Press, Chapter 13, pp. 483–515.
Jonathan Reuvid, ed., *The Secure Online Business Handbook*, 3rd edn.

Extended learning/activity

Drayton Bird, *Common Sense Direct and Digital Marketing*, London: Kogan Page Ltd.
Case Study: Building Home Browsing PC Segment, group presentation/report.
Market/Sector Focus: (1) Automobile: passenger car (2) Technology, group term paper.
Corporate Insight: (1) Maruti Udyog Ltd. (2) Infosys, group research activity/report.

3. Indicative Reading (General) Source*:* EBSCO/HBR Digital Library Networks

CHANGE AND GROWTH
ADVANCES IN THE USE OF CASES IN MARKETING

Charles T. Crespy, David W. Rosenthal and Fames M. Stearns, Special Issue Editors

The story goes like this. As a young woman, her father told her there were three secrets to success in life: (1) find something you like, (2) stick with it and, (3) get better at it. She became a successful entrepreneur on her fourth try and in doing so became an inspiration to all.

(a) **Case learning:** How does it work? Why is it effective? Please refer to article prepared by Harvard case study group based on Questions and Answers About Case Learning, adapted by Thomas Angelo and John Boehrer at the Kennedy School of Government from and article of the same title by Professor Thomas V. Bonoma of the Harvard Business School.

(b) J. Boehrer and M. Linsky. 'Teaching with Cases: Learning to Question', in M.D. Svinicki, ed. *The Changing Face of College Teaching: New Directions for Teaching and Learning*, no. 42, San Francisco: Jossey-Bass, 1990.

(c) Jeffrey S. Lantis, Lynn M. Kuzma and John Boehrer, eds., *The New International Studies Classroom: Active Teaching, Active Learning*, Boulder: Lynn Rienner, 2000.
(d) Selma Wassermann, *Introduction to Case Method Teaching: A Guide to the Galaxy*, New York: Teachers College, Columbia University, 1994.
(e) Clyde Freeman Herreid, What Makes a Good Case? Some Basic Rules of Good Storytelling Help Teachers Generate Student Excitement in the Classroom.

4. Course Pedagogy and Justification

The teaching methods employed for the course include voice-over PowerPoint packed lectures, video cases, simulated corporate exercises, sector seminar/cases, assignments, term papers and action-oriented research and project work. Candidates are expected research books, periodicals, national and international journals (those available online as well) and working papers and dissertations in the area of marketing. Apart from these, they are expected to index search services from major databases like EBSCO, Emerald, to enhance classroom discussion.

Group projects, a major component of this course, help participants develop and refine their marketing skills in the diverse environment. Groups are formed from pools of varied disciplines, backgrounds, corporate/government experience, and career orientations with a mentor to leverage on and improve the enormous diversity in perspectives.

5. Evaluation Mechanism

- Group presentation (15 per cent), group term paper (25 per cent); group corporate/sectoral research activity/report (25 per cent)
- Class Tests (best of three): 15 per cent and end-term examination is 20 per cent (individual level)

Such evaluation components lend themselves well to a business school set-up because corporations demand students who can work well in teams without 'bosses', who are good communicators, and who can listen to and understand the perspectives of others.

6. Learning Outcomes

The active and experiential learning principles employed in the course allow students to 'create knowledge' as they collaboratively workout marketing concepts. Peer discussion enables them to develop a better understanding of the scope and complexity of the material. This may be especially important in an MBA marketing class where concepts can seem simplistic and irrelevant to students if they are allowed to simply skim the surface of the content through the traditional course lecture format.

Students are expected to achieve the following skills on the completion of seven modules of Applied Marketing: Achieve an ability to understand the forces at work and gain mental strength to operate within a dynamic, economic, technological, social, legal and political environment when they assume the role of a global corporate manager. They should also have acquired a theoretically sound, yet operationally useful understanding of the various components of the marketing management from an integrated system perspective. And finally, they should have acquired competency for effective decision-making and problem-solving skills through the use of analytical tools, sectoral focus, corporate insight, market watch and case studies in marketing.

7. Summary

The objective of this model handout is to describe both content (a course) and process (active learning) that could be incorporated into the marketing management curriculum to improve the viability of marketing education. I have provided an overview of marketing course content and its ability to address existing gaps in applied business content, contrasted the traditional educational paradigm with the new educational paradigm, described the basic pedagogy of active and experiential learning, and illustrated active and experiential learning cases/exercises designed to address key content areas in marketing in the form of a course handout.

In using the active learning paradigm, faculty must help create a culture that allows collaborative activities to be effective--just as leaders in corporations must establish a culture that supports employees through the uncertainty and change the face at work. Marketing educators need to revisit material throughout the course--create, revisit, reconstruct with additional information--just as employees need to continue building upon learning to improve their work products. By integrating both the new content and process described in the model handout, one can prepare students of marketing management to be effective global managers and leaders in the increasingly challenging workplace of the future.

Bibliography

Aaker, D.A. and G.S. Day, 'Corporate Response to Consumerism Pressure', *Harvard Business Review*, vol. 50, no. 6, 1972.

———, eds., *Consumerism*, New York: Free Press, 2nd edn, 1974.

Abbott, L., *Quality and Competition*, New York: Columbia University Press, 1955.

Abell, D.F., *Defining the Business: The Starting Point of Strategic Planning*, Englewood Cliffs, and NJ: Prentice-Hall, 1980.

Abratt, R., 'Industrial Buying in High-Tech Markets', *Industrial Marketing Management*, vol. 15, 1986.

Adler L., 'Phasing Research into the Marketing Plan', *Harvard Business Review*, vol. 38, no. 3, 1960.

———, 'Systems Approach to Marketing', *Harvard Business Review*, vol. 45, no. 3, 1967.

Alexander, R.S., J.S. Croos and R.M. Cunningham, *Industrial Marketing*, Homewood, Illinois: Irwin, 1961.

American Accounting Association, 'Report of Committee on Cost and Profitability Analyses for Marketing', Supplement to the *Accounting Review*, vol. 47, 1972.

American Management Association, 'The Marketing Audit: Its Nature, Purpose and Problems', in *Analysing and Improving Marketing Performance*, AMA Management Report no. 32, New York: AMA, 1959.

American Marketing Association, *The Marketing Audit: Its Nature, Purposes and Problems*, vol. 21, no. 2, 1957.

Ames, B.C., 'Marketing Planning for Industrial Products', *Harvard Business Review*, vol. 46, no. 5, 1968.

Amit, R., 'Cost Leadership Strategy and Experience Curves', *Strategic Management Journal*, vol. 3, 1986.

Anandarajan, A. and M.G. Christopher, 'A Mission Approach to Customer Profitability Analysis', *International Journal of Physical Distribution and Material Management*, vol. 17, no. 17, 1987.

Ansoff, H.I., 'Strategies for Diversification', *Harvard Business Review*, vol. 25, no. 5, 1957.

———, H.I., *Corporate Strategy*, Harmondsworth, Penguin Books, 1968.

———, *Implementing Strategic Management*, Englewood Cliffs, NJ: Prentice-Hall, 1984.

Armstrong, J.S., 'The Value of Formal Planning for Strategic Decision: Review of Empirical Research', *Strategic Management Journal*, vol. 3, 1982.

Baker, K., quoted in E. Clark, 'Acorn Finds New Friends', *Marketing*, 16 December, vol. 13, 1982.

Baker, M.J., *Marketing Strategy and Management*, London: Macmillan, 1985.

Barclay, I. and M. Benson, 'Success in New Product Development: Lesson from the Past', *Leadership and Organization Development Journal*, vol. 11, no. 6, 1990.

Barrett, T.F., 'When the Market Says "Beware!" . . . .', *Management Decision*, vol. 24, 1986.

Bass, R.M.V., *Credit Management*, Cheltenham: Thornes, 3rd edn, 1991.

Baumol, W.J. and C.H. Sevin, 'Marketing Costs and Mathematical Programming', *Harvard Business Review*, vol. 35, no. 5, 1957.

Bellis-Jones, R., 'Customer Profitability Analysis', *Management Accounting*, CIMA, vol. 57, 1989.

Berman, Bary and Joel R. Evans, *Retail Management: A Strategic Approach*, 7th edn, Prentice-Hall, 2008.

Bhaskar, K.N. and R.J.W. Housden, *Accounting Information Systems and Data Processing*, Oxford: Heinemann, 1985.

Biggaidike, R., *Entering New Markets: Strategies and Performance*, Cambridge, Massachusetts: Marketing Science Institute, 1977.

Boag, D.A, 'Marketing Control and Performance in Early-Growth Companies', *Journal of Business Venturing*, vol. 2, no. 4, 1987.

Bonini, C.P., R.K. Jaedicke, and H.M. Wagner, eds., *Management Controls: New Directions in Basic Research*, New York: McGraw-Hill, 1964.

Bonoma, T.V. and B.H. Clarke, 'Managing Performance Assessment', Boston, Massachusetts: Harvard Business School Press, 1988.

Bonoma, T.V. and B.P. Shapiro, 'Evaluating Market Segmentation Approaches', *Industrial Marketing Management*, vol. 13, 1984.

Boston Consulting Group, *Perspectives on Experience*, Boston, Massachusetts: Boston Consulting Group, 1971.

Boyd, S.H. and J.S. Britt, 'Making Marketing Research More Effective by using the Administrative Process', *Journal of Marketing Research*, vol. 23, no. 4, 1965.

Brion, J., *Corporate Marketing Planning*, New York: Wiley, 1967.

Brown, S., *Postmodern Marketing*, London: Routledge, 1995.

Brownlie, D.T., 'Analytical Frameworks for Strategic Market Planning', in *Marketing: Theory and Practice*, ed. M.J. Blake, London: Macmillan, 1983.

Brownlie, D.T. and M.A. Saren, 'A Review of Technological Forecasting Techniques and Their Application', *Management Bibliographies and Reviews*, vol. 9, no. 4, 1983.

Bureau, J.R., *Brand Management*, London: Macmillan, 1981.

Buzzell, R.D., D.F. Cox, and R.V. Brown, *Marketing Research and Information Systems*, New York: McGraw-Hill, 1969.

Buzzell, R.D., B.T. Gale and R.G.M. Sullivan, 'Market Share: A Key to Profitability', *Harvard Business Review*, vol. 53, no. 1, 1975.

Calingo, L.M.R., 'Achieving Excellence in Strategic Planning Systems', *SAM Advanced Management Journal*, vol. 54, no. 2, 1989.

Cardozo, R.N. and D.K. Smith, 'Applying Financial Portfolio Theory to Product Portfolio Decisions: An Empirical Study', *Journal of Marketing*, vol. 47, 1983.

Carter, C.F. and B.R. Williams, *Investment in Innovation*, London: Oxford University Press, 1958.

Challagalla, G.N. and T.A. Shervani, 'Dimensions and Types of Supervisory Control: Effects on Salesperson Performance and Satisfaction', *Journal of Marketing*, vol. 60, 1996.

Chandler, A.D., *Strategy and Structure*, Cambridge, Massachusetts: MIT Press, 1962.

Child, J., *Organization*, London: Harper & Row, 1st edn, 1977.

Christopher, M.G., J. Jeffries, J. Kirkland, and R.M.S. Wilson, 'Status Report on Marketing Theory', *British Journal of Marketing*, vol. 2, no. 5, 1968.

Churchman, C.W., *The System Approach*, New York: Dealcorte Press, 1968.

Coates, D., P. Finlay, and J. Wilson, 'Validation in Marketing Models', *Journal of the Market Research Society*, vol. 33, no. 2, 1991.

Cohen, W.A., *The Practice of Marketing Management: Analysis, Planning and Implementation*, New York: Macmillan, 1988.

Cook, R., 'Aspects of Customer Service', *ITC Magazine*, March–April 1992.

Cook, V.J. Jr., 'The Net Present Value of Market Share', *Journal of Marketing*, vol. 49, 1985.

Cox, K.K. and B.M. Enis, *Experimentation for Marketing Decisions*, Scranton, Pa: Intertext, 1969.

Cravens, D.W., 'How to Match Marketing Strategies with Overall Corporate Planning', *Management Review*, vol. 70, no. 12, 1981.

Cunningham, M.I. and D.A. Roberts, 'The Role of Customer Services in Industrial Marketing', *European Journal of Marketing*, vol. 8, no. 1, 1974.

Dace, R.W., 'Exporting to Japan: Key Factors for Success', *Quarterly Review of Marketing*, vol. 16, no. 1, 1990.

Davidson, J.J., 'Going on the Offensive', *Marketing Polytechnic*, 1987.

Davis, J., *Experimental Marketing*, London: Nelson, 1970.

Day, G.S., *Analysis for Strategic Marketing Decisions*, St. Paul, Minnesota: West Publishing, 1986.

Donald R. Lehmann and Russell S. Winer, *Product Management*, McGraw-Hill, USA, 2007.

Driver, J.C., 'Marketing Planning in Style', *Quarterly Review of Marketing*, vol. 15, no. 4, 1990.

Drucker, P.F., *The Practice of Management*, London: Heinemann, 1955.

———, 'Long Range Planning: Challenge to Management Science', *Management Science*, vol. 5, no. 3, 1959.

———, 'Managing for Business Effectiveness', *Harvard Business Review*, vol. 41, no. 3, 1963.

———, *The Age of Discontinuity*, New York: Harper & Row, 1969.

———, *Management: Tasks, Responsibilities and Practice*, New York: Harper & Row, 1973.

Feder, R.A., 'How to Measure Marketing Performance', *Harvard Business Review*, vol. 43, no. 3, 1965.

Festinger, L., *A Theory of Cognitive Dissonance*, Stanford, California: Stanford University Press, 1957.

Foxall, G.R., 'Marketing's Domain', *European Journal of Marketing*, vol. 18, no. 1, 1984.

Frey, J.B., 'Pricing Over the Competitive Life Cycle', speech presented at the 1982 Marketing Conference, New York, 1982.

Fuld, L.M., *Monitoring the Competition: Finding Our What's Really Going on Out There*, New York: Wiley, 1988.

Gay, Richard, Alan Charlesworth and Rita Esen, *Online Marketing: A Customer-Led Approach*: New Delhi: Oxford University Press, 2007.

Goldman, S.R., *Techniques of Profitability Analysis*, New York: Wiley, 1970.

Goold, M.C and J.J. Quinn, *Strategic Control: Milestones for Long-Term Performance*, London, Hutchinson, 1990.

Hussey, D.E., 'Management in the 1990s', *Management Training Update*, 1989.

Jefkins, F., *Modern Marketing Communications*, Glasgow: Blackie, 1990.

Jean Noel Kapferer, *The New Strategic Brand Management*, London: Kogan Page Ltd., 2007.

Jobber, David and John Fahy, *Foundations of Marketing*, 2nd edn, McGraw-Hill Education, UK, 2008.

Johnson, G. and K. Scholes, *Exploring Corporate Strategy*, London: Prentice-Hall, 2nd edn, 1988.

Kahaner, L., *Competitive Intelligence*, New York: Simon and Schuster, 1996.

Kaplan, R.S. and D.P. Norton, 'The Balance Scorecard—Measures that Drive Performance', *Harvard Business Review*, vol. 70, no. 1, 1992.

———, 'Putting the Balanced Scorecard to Work', *Harvard Business Review*, vol. 71, no. 5, 1993.

Kay, J., *Foundations of Corporate Success: How Business Strategies Add Value*, Oxford: Oxford University Press, 1993.

Keiser, B.E., 'Practical Competitor Intelligence', *Planning Review*, vol. 15, no. 5, 1987.

Kelly, J.M., *How to Check Out Your Competition*, New York: Wiley, 1987.

Kohli, A.K. and B.J. Jaworski, 'Market Orientation: the construct, research propositions and managerial implications', *Journal of Marketing*, vol. 54, 1990.

Kotler, P., Dipak C. Jain and Suvit Maesincee, *Marketing Moves: A New Approach to Profits, Growth and Renewal*, Harvard Business School Press, 2008.

Kotler, P., *Marketing Decision: Marketing, A Model Building Approach*, New York: Holt, Rinehart & Winston, 1971.

———, 'What Consumerism Means for Marketers', *Harvard Business Review*, vol. 50, no. 3, 1972.

———, 'From Sales Obsession to Marketing Effectiveness', *Harvard Business Review*, vol. 55, no. 6, 1977.

———, ed., *Marketing Management and Strategy: A Reader*, Englewood Cliffs, NJ: Prentice-Hall, 5th edn, 1984.

———, *Marketing: An Introduction*, Englewood Cliffs, NJ: Prentice-Hall, 1987.

Kotler, P., Fahey and S. Jatusripitak, *The New Competition*, Englewood Cliffs, NJ: Prentice-Hall, 1985.

Lalonde, B.J. and P.H. Zinszer, *Customer Service Meaning and Measurement*, Chicago: NCPDM, 1976.

Lamb, R. and P. Shrivastava, eds., *Advances in Strategic Management*, Greenwich, Conn.: JAI Press, vol. 4, 1986.

Lee, Monle and Carla Johnson, *Principles of Advertising: A Global Perspective*, 2nd edn, Haworth Press Inc., 2008.

Levitt, T., 'Innovative Imitation', *Harvard Business Review*, vol. 44, no. 5, 1966.

———, 'The Augmented Product Concept', in *Corporate Strategy and Product Innovation*, ed. R.R. Ruthberg, New York: Free Press, 1976.

McCarthy, M.J. and W.D. Perreault Jr., *Essentials of Marketing: A Global Managerial Approach*, Homewood, Ill.: Irwin, 1990.

McDonald, M.H.B., *Marketing Plans: How to Prepare Them, How to Use Them*, London: Heinemann, 1984.

———, 'Ten Barrier to Marketing Planning', *Journal of Marketing Management*, vol. 5, no. 1, 1989.

Milton, F. and T. Reiss, 'Competitive Strategy', *Accountancy Ireland*, vol. 17, no. 5, 1985.

———, 'Developing a Competitive Strategy', *Accountancy Ireland*, vol. 17, no. 5, 1985.

Mulvaney, J., *The Use of Network Analysis in Marketing*, Cookham: Chartered Institute of Marketing, 1969.

Nilson,T.H., *Chaos Marketing: How to Win in a Turbulent World*, Maidenhead: McGraw-Hill, 1995.

Ohmae, K., *The Mind of the Strategist*, London: Penguin, 1983.

Peattie, K.J. and D.S. Notley, 'The Marketing and Strategic Planning Interface', *Journal of Marketing Management*, vol. 4, no. 3, 1989.

Peters, T.J., *Liberation Management*, New York: Knopf, 1992.

Peters, T.J. and R.H. Waterman, *In Search of Excellence: Lessons from America's Best Run Companies*, New York: Harper & Row, 1982.

Piercy, N.F., *Marketing Budgeting*, London: Croom Helm, 1986.

Porter, L.M. and K.H. Roberts, eds., *Communication in Organizations*, Harmondsworth: Penguin, 1977.

Porter, M.E., 'How Competitive Forces Shape Strategy', *Harvard Business Review*, vol. 57, no. 2, 1979.

———, *Competitive Strategy*, New York: Free Press, 1980.

———, 'How to Attract the Industry Leader', *Fortune*, vol. 111, no. 29, 1985.

———, *Competitive Advantage: Creating and Sustaining Superior Performance*, New York: Free Press, 1985.

Posner, M., *The Competitive Advantage of Nations*, New York: Free Press, 1986.

Rapp, S. and T.L. Collins, *The Great Marketing Turnaround: The Age of the Individual and How to Profit from It*, Englewood Cliffs, NJ: Prentice-Hall, 1990.

Ries, A. and J. Trout, *Positioning: The Battle for Your Mind*, New York: Warner Books, 1982.

Ries. A. and J. Trout, *Marketing Warfare*, New York: McGraw-Hill, 1986.

Rothschild, W.E., *How to Gain (and Maintain) the Competitive Advantage*, New York: McGraw-Hill, 1984.

Saunders, J.A., 'Marketing and Competitive Success', in *The Marketing Book*, ed. M.J. Baker, London: Macmillan, 1987.

Schiffman, L.G. and L.L. Kanuk, *Consumer Behaviour*, Englewood Cliffs, NJ: Prentice-Hall, 2nd edn, 1983.

Schoffler, S., 'Market Position: Build, Hold or Harvest?', *The Pimsletter on Business Strategy*, no. 3, Cambridge, Massachusetts: Strategic Planning Institute, 1977.

Sevin, C.H., *Marketing Productivity Analysis*, New York: McGraw-Hill, 1965.

Shajahan, S., *New Products Strategy and Management: Text & Cases*, Mumbai: Himalaya Publishing House (P) Ltd., 2001.

———, *Relationship Marketing: Text and Cases*, New Delhi: McGraw-Hill India Ltd., 2004.

———, *Marketing Research: Concepts and Cases*, New Delhi: Macmillan India Ltd., 2006.

———, *International Business: Text and Cases*, New Delhi: Macmillan India Ltd., 2007.

———, *Business Research Methods*, Mumbai: Jaico Publishing House (P) Ltd., 2009.

———, *Research Methods for Management*, 4th edn, Mumbai: Jaico Publishing House (P) Ltd., 2010.

———, *Strategic Marketing: Text and Cases*, New Delhi: Viva Books (P) Ltd., 2010.

———, *Applied Multivariate Analysis*, New Delhi: Oxford University Press, 2010.

———, *Services Marketing Concepts: Practices and Cases*, 3rd edn, Mumbai: Himalaya Publishing House (P) Ltd., 2010.

Shapiro, B.P. et al., 'Manage Customers for Profits (Not Just Sales)', *Harvard Business Review*, vol. 65, no. 5, 1987.

Sheth, J.N., *The Theory of Buyer Behavior*, New York: Wiley, 1969.

Smith, D.C. and J.E. Precott, 'Demystifying Competitive Analysis', *Planning Review*, vol. 15, no. 5, 1987.

Smith, P.R. and Jonathan Taylor, *Marketing Communications: An Integrated Approach*, 4th edn, London: Kogan Page Ltd., 2007.

Thomas, M.J., 'Does Your Marketing Pay?', *Management Decision*, vol. 25, no. 4, 1987.

Thomas, P.S., 'Environmental Scanning—the State of the Art', *Long Range Planning*, vol. 13, no. 1, 1980.

Toffer, A., *Future Shock*, New York: Bantam Books, 1970.

Toffler, K., *The Third Wave*, New York: Bantam Books, 1980.

Ulrich, D. and D. Lake, 'Organizational Capability: Creating Competitive Advantage', *The Executive*, vol. 5, 1991.

Vella, C.M. and J.J. McGonagle, 'Shadowing Markets: A New Competitive Intelligence Technique', *Planning Review,* vol. 15, no. 5, 1987.

Wall, S.L., 'What the Competition is Doing: You need to know', *Harvard Business Review,* vol. 52, no. 6, 1974.

Ward, A.J., *Measuring, Directing and Controlling New Product Development,* London: In Com Tec, 1968.

Weihrich, H., 'The TOWS Matrix: a tool for situational analysis', *Long Range Planning,* vol. 15, no. 2, 1982.

Wensley, J.R.C., '*Marketing Strategy*', in *The Marketing Book,* ed. M.J. Baker, London, 1987.

Wernerfelt, B., 'The Relation Between Market Share and Profitability', *Journal of Business Strategy,* vol. 6, no. 4, 1986.

Zeithaml, Valarie, Dwayne D. Gremler, Mary Jo Bitner and Ajay Pandit, *Services Marketing: Integrated Customer Focus Across the Firm,* 4th edn, USA: McGraw-Hill 2007.

Subject Index

Note: *b* is used for box, *f* is used for figure and *t* is used for table

Brand, Company, Organizations Index

Index of Names